JEWISH MAGIC
before the Rise of Kabbalah

Raphael Patai Series in Jewish Folklore and Anthropology

JEWISH MAGIC

before the Rise of Kabbalah

———

YUVAL HARARI

Translated by Batya Stein

Wayne State University Press | Detroit

Original Hebrew edition, *Early Jewish Magic: Research, Method, Sources* by Yuval Harari, was published in 2010 by the Bialik Institute and Ben-Zvi Institute.

ISBN 978-0-8143-4881-9 (paperback)
ISBN 0-978-8143-3630-4 (hardcover)
ISBN 978-0-8143-3631-1 (ebook)

Library of Congress Cataloging Number: 2016957099

Typeset by Westchester
Composed in Adobe Caslon Pro

On cover: Magic bowl. Collection of Shlomo Moussaieff; photographed by Matthew Morgenstern.

The translation of this book was supported by Publication Grant 1841/11 from the Israel Science Foundation.

Published with support from the fund for the Raphael Patai Series in Jewish Folklore and Anthropology.

Wayne State University Press
Leonard N. Simons Building
4809 Woodward Avenue
Detroit, Michigan 48201-1309

Visit us online at wsupresswayne.edu

Wayne State University Press rests on Waawiyaataanong, also referred to as Detroit, the ancestral and contemporary homeland of the Three Fires Confederacy. These sovereign lands were granted by the Ojibwe, Odawa, Potawatomi, and Wyandot nations, in 1807, through the Treaty of Detroit. Wayne State University Press affirms Indigenous sovereignty and honors all tribes with a connection to Detroit. With our Native neighbors, the press works to advance educational equity and promote a better future for the earth and all people.

Contents

CONTENTS

Plates

Preface

Magic is a rather boring matter: practical action, supernatural technology. In its simple version, a few words are uttered, some of them meaningless. In more developed versions, some acts are performed and then the words are uttered. That is all. Nevertheless, something in it captures the imagination. And so, quite a few years ago, when seeking a subject for study and research and drawn from one topic to the next, I became acquainted with magic and started dealing with it. Academically, of course. I knew what it was, or at least I had an inkling of what it was, and I knew it existed (in texts, of course). One only had to turn around to find it, and I did. My teachers opened up to me a rich world of Jewish magical texts that captured my imagination. Angels were ordered about and sent to perform their tasks under threat, evil spirits were enchained and expelled, devils assembled in their kings' heads, evil spells knocked on the door, enemies were exiled, foes were tortured and killed, thieves were caught, escaped slaves were returned to their masters, prisoners were released, buyers gathered in stores, fish were caught in the net, worms were removed from fruit, crickets were sent away from the house, wicked tormentors were expelled from the womb, births were induced, babies were protected, husbands were returned to their wives, the dead were conjured up, nightmares were sent to sleepers, distances were shortened, treasures were found, Torah was studied, love was forcibly attained. All brought about through a few words (some of them meaningless), incantations, and holy names; actions (gestures and ritual acts, at times strange); and some odd materials (a lion's heart, water that has not seen the light of day, a donkey's bone, a palm needle and a human effigy, olive oil and rose oil, laurel leaves, a nail from a crucifixion, a waste pipe segment, a burnt potsherd, dust from a holy ark, tablets of gold and silver and precious stones, human semen, blood, a black dog's head—all these and

PREFACE

many others were used in the charms). An entire culture of knowledge and action was downloaded from heaven and delivered to humans. Vast powers were granted to them by divine command. Guides were written and handed down from one to another and from one generation to the next. Charms were compiled, collated, and uttered, adjurations were written, amulets were scripted and borne, gems were engraved and worn, incantation bowls were buried in the corners of the house and under the threshold, and skulls were covered in spells.

I learned all this from the magic texts. Magic culture is certainly fascinating. But what is it? What, in fact, are magic writings, magic artifacts? I soon learned that this culture, magic, can be found in other writings as well, some of them "magic" writings that are not Jewish, some of them Jewish writings that are "not magical." Each of these groups posed a different challenge. The non-Jewish magic writings reveal cross-cultural similarity and at times even cooperation and professional contacts between neighboring magicians—mutual borrowing, an outside cult that wandered in, penetrated, and stayed. These cases are relatively easy. The culture's borders are unquestionably breached. Magic is a pragmatic matter, and when a child is burning with fever, curled up and dying of exhaustion, it is irrelevant who will heal him and how, yet Jewish identity was preserved. But whose identity was this? What kind of Jews were these sorcerers and who were their clients? I was never seduced by the delusion that had satisfied the scholars who founded the study of Jewish magic, who assumed that these people were simple, ignorant, and uneducated. This perception is definitely wrong insofar as the magicians themselves are concerned—the masters of knowledge, the literate figures reflected in the magic writings that they created and bequeathed to us. So, were they not properly educated? Did they not know that "When you come to the land that the Lord your God gives you, you shall not learn to do after the abominations of those nations. There must not be found among you anyone that makes his son or his daughter to pass through the fire, or that uses divination, a soothsayer, or an enchanter, or a witch, or a charmer, or a medium, or a wizard, or a necromancer. For all that do these things are an abomination to the Lord"? Had they not heard, "You shall not suffer a witch to live"? Had they not learned, "a witch—this applies to both man and woman"? Did they not fear that they would thereby "deny and diminish the heavenly household"? Did

x

they not understand that "were all the world's creatures to gather together, they could not create one fly and place a soul in it"? (By the way, they did understand. Jewish magic is amazingly pragmatic!) What part did they play in Judaism? Or indeed, what is *the* Judaism within which we should look for their share? Who does *the* Judaism belong to?

At this point, the second group of texts emerged, posing the other and far more complicated challenge, because, as soon as I looked at the Jewish texts that are not magical, I found the magic culture in them as well. Or perhaps, to begin with, I lacked a true concept of magic. Whenever I was asked about my study and mentioned Jewish magic, someone would invariably say something along the lines of, "Jewish magic? No such thing! Either magic or Jewish." And charms? and amulets? and blessings? and curses? and use of holy names? and reversing bad dreams? and reciting psalms? and mezuzot? and holy men? and miracle workers?— "Well, that's another matter." (By the way, that is true. Magic is always the "other" matter). And maybe it is merely a question of rhetoric? of the use of words? But can we indeed put everything in one basket? Is it right to do that? And perhaps also (and inevitably), is it worth doing that? And actually, what is this "everything"? What singles it out? How do we examine it so that it seems that something does single it out, and compared to what? And what is the relationship between the "worth it" and the "wherefrom"? Or maybe that—the range between the "worth it" and the "wherefrom"—is the very gist of the matter. After all, no one is ultimately exempt from dealing with this relationship. Neither am I.

What, then, was my concept of magic when I began to search for and investigate the "magic" texts? What did I mean when I said that I studied Jewish "magic," and why did my listeners have a concept of "magic" that prevented them from coupling it to "Jewish"? Have we inherited separate concepts from different sources of authority? If so, we should perhaps examine the discourse that shaped the distinction between the "matter" and the "other"—between a prayer and a spell, between a holy man and a magician, between *segulah* and *kishuf.* How was the term *kishuf* (magic, sorcery) used in the Jewish discourse of late antiquity and the early Islamic period? (By the way, the sorcerers did not use it. And I doubt that they would agree to being called sorcerers). How was magic perceived in this discourse? And here, alas, we come back to the original question: What exactly is the phenomenon—"magic"—the attitude toward which we wish to examine? And not only we. The study of Jewish magic has been ongoing for more than 150 years. The researchers must have had some concept of the object of their inquiry! And indeed, the concept that they—the creators of academic, normative knowledge—had of magic plays an important role in the shaping of our own concept. Hence we must consider how they understood magic—and perhaps not only they, because, in turn, they were influenced, as is everyone, by the trends and the research of their time. These trends, then, should also be examined.

Rather than preceding my work, this move accompanied it, and still does. And I find it no less fascinating than magic per se. All that time, however, I went on dealing with "magic" texts and with Jewish "magic." In my view, as I will clarify, it is possible (and indeed, we have no choice but) to do so even without entirely unraveling the methodological entanglement.

This book emerged from these two concerns. The first part is devoted to the methodological question that touches on the understanding of magic and its definition and is an inquiry into the research. Because I do not believe in "truth" but in its self-interested social-subjective representations, I hold that it is crucial to examine the genealogy of these representations within the institution (to which I belong) entrusted with the formation of knowledge in our culture—academia. The second part of the book deals with Jewish magic as such and, more specifically, with the magic evidence and with additional Jewish sources that are a platform for understanding the culture of Jewish magic before the rise and expansion of Kabbalah. I do not, in this book, paint a general picture of Jewish magic culture. I have proposed elsewhere modest parts of such a description in the past, and I hope to complete this endeavor in the future. But many aspects of it are evident here too, both regarding the culture as such—actions, beliefs, agents, and aims of the activity—as reflected in insider magic sources, and regarding the social and political aspects of the discourse about it, as reflected in outsider, nonmagical sources. In this way, I hope to introduce the reader to the methodological foundations of the study of ancient Jewish magic—to present at length the methodological complication of defining magic and the ways of disentangling it, as well as to suggest a solution for it, and to expose and clarify the nature of the sources for the study of Jewish magic in late antiquity and the early Islamic period, thereby shedding some light on the culture reflected in them.

—

The study of magic in general and that of Jewish magic culture in particular is a dynamic pursuit. Many years have gone by since I finished writing the original version of this book. Since then, new findings have been published and new views have been proposed. Once the decision was made to offer an English edition of this study, I realized that I could not confine myself to its translation and would need to refine and update the entire book. The fruits of this effort are woven throughout and are evident in both the research and sources chapters. This, then, is a better, broader, and more up-to-date version of my original book.

The research work at the basis of this book began many years ago, when I wrote my dissertation at the Hebrew University of Jerusalem, "Early Jewish Magic: Methodological and Phenomenological Perspectives" (1998). I had two excellent teachers—Prof. Shaul Shaked and Prof. Moshe Idel. Their inspiration imbues this work. The breadth of their knowledge is embedded in it. Their regard and their generosity enabled it. I thank them both deeply. Special thanks are due to my friend, Prof. Gideon Bohak, who meticulously read the (Hebrew) draft of the book and whose comments left a real mark on it. The writing of our books on ancient Jewish magic at the very same time, each following his own method and in a spirit of friendship, openness, and cooperation, was for me a gratifying and productive experience.

The English edition of the book would not have seen the light were it not for the insistent invitation of Prof. Dan Ben-Amos to publish it in the Raphael Patai Series in Jewish Folklore and Anthropology, and his sustained encouragement to bring the task to completion. I am deeply indebted to him for leading me along this course. Many thanks to Batya Stein for her committed, accurate, and professional translation, for her endless patience with my whims, and particularly for the superb results that she achieved. Mimi Braverman has further polished the text by means of her careful and meticulous editing, for which I am grateful. Thanks also go to Kate Mertes for preparing the detailed indexes. I am thankful to

Kathryn Wildfong, Editor in-Chief and Associate Director of Wayne State University Press, who accompanied the process, and to the wonderful team at the publishing house, particularly Kristin M. Harpster, the editorial, design, and production manager, who brought it to completion.

Several research funds supported the study and research that enabled the writing: the Charlotte and Moritz Warburg Fund, the Memorial Fund for Jewish Culture, the Kreitman Fund, the Koret Fund, and the Alon Fund. The publication of the English version was generously supported by the Israel Science Foundation and by Ben-Gurion University of the Negev. I am grateful to all these institutions for their backing.

Thanks go also to the Israel Antiquities Authority; the Institute of Archaeology at the Hebrew University of Jerusalem; the Vorderasiatisches Museum im Pergamonmuseum, Berlin; the Kelsey Museum of Archaeology, University of Michigan; the Cambridge University Library; la Bibliothèque de Genève and Fondation des Comites Latentes; and Segre Amar and the late Shlomo Moussaieff for their permission to publish the plates in the book. Thanks to Yael Barashek, Dr. Joachim Marzahn, Michelle Fontenot, Ben Outhwaite, and Barbara Roth for their help in obtaining these plates and the permits to publish them, and to Gaby Laron and Matthew Morgenstern for the photographs they placed at my disposal.

Finally, and above all, I owe deep thanks to Gaby, my wife. Without her love and help, I would not have completed this task. It is questionable whether I would have even embarked on it. This book is dedicated to her with all my love.

Introduction

The historical research of Jewish magic is basically textual research. Its fundamental assumption is that we have access to magic writings that reflect the magic practice of Jews who held a magic worldview, and the research is founded on these writings. But what are these writings? What singles them out? How can we retrieve them from the multitude of available texts? In other words, what defines the worldview and the practice reflected in these texts, as a result of which we could call them magic? Seemingly, if we had a clear definition of magic, we could answer these questions. If we could point to the characteristics of magic thought and magic action, they could serve us as criteria for selecting magic writings. By relying on these writings, we would be able to successfully describe the magic culture they reflect.

The methodological difficulty of this approach is immediately evident: To characterize and describe Jewish magic on the basis of magic writings, we must first define them as such. The process of choosing the writings to be used in the research is thus marked by our approach to the phenomena they purportedly represent. This problem arises because neither the writings nor the society in which they were created provides the tools for defining them as magic. Obviously, the writings do not define themselves as such, either by using terms derived from the word *magic* or from the root *kšf*. *Kishuf*, whatever the practice that this term points to, was forbidden, first in the Torah and later by the rabbis.[1] The chance that a Jewish text will explicitly note or even hint that its concern is magic is therefore extremely slim. Nonmagic Jewish literature does not help in this regard either. The Jewish literature of the period discussed in this book does not

---

1. See Deuteronomy 18:10; Exodus 22:17; M. *Sanhedrin* 7:4, 11; TB *Sanhedrin* 67a–b; and PT *Sanhedrin* 7:11.

have a general definition of *keshafim*, *kashfanut*, or *kishuf* that could have enabled us to decide precisely what is and what is not included in this realm.[2]

By contrast, we do have a variety of narrative and halakhic statements, most of them in rabbinic literature, touching on *keshafim* (acts of magic) and *mekhashfim* (sorcerers) and especially *mekhashefot* (witches) as well as discussions of actions that are—or are not—placed under the rubric of "ways of the Amorites" (*darkei ha-'Emori*) and hence forbidden or allowed, respectively. None of these discussions offers an essentialist definition of *kishuf*, just descriptions and evaluations of concrete acts concerning the "ways of the Amorites" category that, as such, is devoid of informative content. Nor do the discussions on *mekhashfim* suggest a general characterization of their actions as a basis for labeling them as such. The rabbis did not adopt an overall conceptual definition of *kishuf* as a distinct category of thought or of action. Their determinations are a product of their twofold involvement with it: on the one hand, agents of ritual power—a power attained through ritual means—that they identified as foci of a real and sociopolitical power alternative to their own; and, on the other hand, ritual practices that were widespread in their communities and required them to establish whether they were within the borders of the "normative" faith they sought to fashion and impose.

The specific character of the discussions on magic, sorcerers, and ways of the Amorites in rabbinic literature does not enable us to trace the rules that the rabbis relied on to label them as such, if any such rules actually existed.[3] Had the rabbis, or their successors, suggested a solid conceptual view of magic or a detailed set of criteria for determining the magic character of beliefs and actions, as many modern theologians and scholars have

---

2. The closest statement to such a definition is the description of the *siḥr* (magic, *kishuf*) by the Karaite Ya'qub al-Qirqisani in *The Book of Lights and Watchtowers* (*Kitab al-anwâr wal-marâkib*). See the discussion on polemical Karaite writings in chapter 6.

3. A single attempt to formulate a rule concerning the ways of the Amorites was attempted by negation and was based on the consequence rather the essence of the action: "R. Shmuel R. Abbahu in the name of R. Yoḥanan: Anything that heals is not deemed ways of the Amorite" (PT *Shabbat* 6:10). Cf. TB *Shabbat* 67a and TB *Hullin* 77b. Veltri sought to base the rabbinic attitude toward the ways of the Amorites on an empirical principle. In his view, the rabbis allowed actions found to be beneficial and rejected those that were dangerous (Veltri 1998, esp. 308–11).

attempted to do, we could try to locate such beliefs and actions in Jewish writings and define them as magic texts, at least according to the authoritative and influential establishment of Jewish society.[4] But in the absence of such external rules and lacking an intratextual definition, we must turn in another direction and shift the starting point of the entire discussion from the contemporary Jewish texts that concern us to the current magic discourse.

To describe ancient Jewish magic on the basis of magic texts, we must first define, even if in the most general terms, what magic is. That is, we must clarify what we mean when we use such terms as *magic* or *kishuf* and note at least the type of phenomena we wish to discuss. Such a definition might direct us to texts that reflect phenomena of the requested kind and, by relying on them, we might be able to study the phenomena in detail. Although this solution could seemingly further the attempt to determine the research method, it is a mixed blessing. A definition of magic in general, as a kind of phenomenon, emerges as a task no less difficult and perhaps even more complicated than its detailed description. At the end of a study on Jewish magic, we might be able to say, "These and these were the magic beliefs and acts of the Jews who wrote the texts we studied," but how will we define the phenomenon in general from the beginning? At first glance, the terms *kishuf* and *magic* seem to have a clear denotation. Yet when we seek to go beyond the stereotypical perception of the phenomena denoted through these words, to understand *kishuf* or magic and to describe them precisely as the basis for choosing the textual foundation of a study on the culture of magic, we face a real difficulty.[5] The borders of acts and beliefs called magical and the distinction between them and other acts and beliefs, particularly those included in the category

---

4. A similar approach, relying on Yaʿqub al-Qirqisani, was the one endorsed by Schiffman and Swartz (1992, 12–15). But although al-Qirqisani's brief statement on the *siḥr* in *The Book of Lights and Watchtowers* fits the contents of Jewish magic texts well, it does not offer a basis broad enough to define them.

5. Definitions of *kishef, kishuf, keshafim, kashfan,* and similar words derived from the same root in modern Hebrew dictionaries are close to one another. The two main components of an act of *kishuf* according to these definitions are (1) being outside nature and (2) being performed by means of "unnatural" or "mysterious" powers, particularly demons and spirits. See Ben Yehuda (1948–1959, 5: 2540); Even-Shoshan (1988, 2: 569); and Knaani (1960–1989, 7: 2303–4).

of beliefs and acts called religious, are not at all clear. Determining a sound set of phenomenological criteria that will allow the classification of ritual phenomena as magical or religious emerges as an almost impossible or even insurmountable task. Consequently, we have no basis for identifying the Jewish writings that could be of interest to us for the purpose of this study.

Two key questions emerge at this stage. First, is the problem of distinguishing magic from religion specific to Jewish culture? If so, why? And if not, does magic have any unique characteristics in the Jewish context? Second, how can we overcome this difficulty, identify the writings that interest us, and create the necessary textual foundation for the study and description of ancient Jewish magic? These were the questions I faced as soon as I began dealing with Jewish magic, and my interest in them was both theoretical and practical. Concerning the first key question, it is quite clear. The mode of using language and the relationship of language with the world (and in my view, the way that a society constitutes the world through language and imparts it to its members) is one of the most fascinating riddles in the history of human thought. Regarding the second key question, like researchers who preceded me, I too knew well what kind of texts I wanted to study, but I also wanted to justify my choice. I knew that the problem could be ignored or circumvented in various ways, as had indeed often been the case in the past. Yet I wanted to find a solution to the riddle of magic's elusiveness and to the question of its complicated relationships with religion before approaching the study of Jewish magic culture itself.

I thought that a good way of coping with the definition of magic would be to explore the development or variation[6] of the research in this area outside Jewish studies and then clarify the relevance of the suggested solutions to the object of my own research. This exploration, the results of which are presented in the first part of the book, taught me that the problem of defining magic and the question of its differentiation from religion are not necessarily a "Jewish problem." Arriving at a clear and precise identification of the area of human beliefs and acts denoted through the term

---

6. Here and wherever I refer to the "development of the research," I do not intend any value evaluation but merely its history—its change over time.

magic or *kishuf* (and their parallels in the scholars' various languages) emerged as a complicated and controversial issue in almost all the fields of research that attempted to do so—the comparative study of religion, history, sociology, anthropology, and culture studies.[7]

The beginning of the scientific attempt to define magic and delimit its boundaries in relation to other realms of culture, particularly religion and science, is at the root of the comparative study of religion. Over the 150 years that have elapsed since the first modern anthropologists began paying attention to religion as a universal phenomenon and turning it into an object of comparative study, magic has been a concern to many scholars who have tried to understand it and characterize it from several

---

7. A number of reviews on research approaches to magic and its place vis-à-vis cultural systems such as religion or science have been published in recent years. The most comprehensive is that by Randall Styers (2004), who seeks to trace the emergence of the concept of magic as a scientific object of modern research. This is the deepest and most extensive study on the "invention of magic" (and perhaps, more precisely, inventions of magic) in modern times, and of its deep connection to social, political, and philosophical processes that have unfolded in the West in the twentieth century. A concise and interesting discussion appears in Tambiah (1995). Stanley Tambiah, one of the most important theoreticians of magic among anthropologists, traces the historical development of the thought on the relationships between magic, religion, and science in modern research and concludes by pointing out the need for a moderate relativistic position in order to understand other cultures and describe them fairly. The brief discussions by Graham Cunningham (1999) offer a matter-of-fact account of the views of thinkers and scholars on the "sacred," that is, on religion-magic (and, where relevant, the distinction between them), but without placing them in a theoretical context. Frederick Cryer and Rüdiger Schmitt summarize the main positions concerning magic in the introductory chapters to their books on divination and magic in the Hebrew Bible (Cryer 1994, 123–42; Schmitt 2004, 1–42). And finally, Jesper Sørensen (2007) introduces a concise survey of scholarly perceptions of magic arranged according to four modes (thinking, living, acting, and being) at the opening of his cognitive study of magic. Although these studies have made a large and significant contribution to a clarification of the view of magic in modern thought and research and although together they offer more sources than those to be presented later (though not additional approaches), none of them are focused on, confined to, or organized around the question discussed here—the definition of magic in relation to religion—in the way to be suggested.

perspectives.[8] It proved attractive for two reasons. On the one hand, magic was identified as an essential component of the worldview and ritual activity of preliterate tribes—"primitives" or "savages" in the language of the time—who were perceived as representing a primeval stage in the development of the human race. Magic thus appeared to scholars as the beginning of human thought and action. On the other hand, remnants of this "shared beginning" survived also in "developed" cultures, foremost among them, according to these scholars, European Western culture. This channel of human thought and action, whose ontological assumptions and practical effectiveness scholars refused to accept, required explanation in both regards. Scholars needed to understand how and on what grounds magic had developed to begin with and why it had remained in place, even if in a weakened version, in a society that had embraced a new, scientific-rational worldview.

The first to address these questions was the British ethnographer Edward Tylor. Like other ethnographers of the time, Tylor is usually referred to as an armchair anthropologist, because, before the emergence of anthropological field research, these researchers never lived in the communities they studied, did not learn their languages, and were not acquainted with the full range of the cultures, segments of which they sought to describe and explain relying on a comparative method. Their theories relied on data compiled through "scissors-and-paste," as Edward Evans-Pritchard sarcastically noted, and data gathered from travelers, army and administration personnel, and missionaries.[9] The "survivals" (as Tylor called them) of magic faith in European society attracted Tylor's attention, and his attempt to understand them and trace their origin can be viewed as the beginning of the comparative study of magic. I therefore open chapter 1, which is a historical review of the study of magic and the question of its relationships with religion, with Tylor's studies and the evolutionist worldview that characterizes them. After Tylor, I focus on

---

8. The comparative study of religion began in the 1860s to 1870s. For a good historical review of its development, see Sharpe (1975). For a detailed review of research schools in this field during the nineteenth century, see L. H. Jordan (1986).

9. For an approach decrying the gathering of data and other methodological mistakes that characterized anthropological research before field studies became its basic method, see Evans-Pritchard (1965, 1–19). The quotation is from p. 9.

the views of Herbert Spencer and James Frazer, the other prominent spokesmen of the evolutionist school. In their wake, the discussion moves on to consider the views of Wilhelm Wundt and Sigmund Freud, whose psychological analysis of magic was also pinned on this approach. The section concludes with the alternative to the evolutionist position formulated by Robert Marett, the most prominent of its early opponents.

Along with the continued influence of the evolutionist school and the controversy it evoked, a completely antithetical view on the character of magic and its place with respect to religion developed in France at the beginning of the twentieth century. Strongly influenced by Émile Durkheim, who himself was influenced by the work of William Robertson Smith, members of this school tried to explain the relationship between these cultural phenomena with the tools of the social sciences. This method soon transcended the borders of Durkheim's circle and became a crucial component of the description and discussion of magic and religion in focused and comparative studies. In the second part of chapter 1 I explore the views of magic held by the most important sociologists of religion: William Robertson Smith, Émile Durkheim, Marcel Mauss, Max Weber, and Daniel O'Keefe. Special attention is paid to the two broadest and most significant works in the field: Mauss's *General Theory of Magic* and O'Keefe's *Stolen Lightning: The Social Theory of Magic*.

The next significant change in the study of magic was characterized by a shift from general theoretical studies to specific field studies. The data generated through systematic fieldwork and participant observation allowed anthropologists (particularly between the 1930s and the 1960s) to understand how magic functioned in the life and beliefs of the tribes they had chosen as objects of their studies. Some of the anthropologists confined themselves to limited, context-bound conclusions. Others sought to reopen a general theoretical discussion, relying on their findings. The discussion of the anthropological study of magic, concentrated in the third section of chapter 1, focuses on scholars who placed magic at the center of their work: Bronislaw Malinowski, Alfred Radcliffe-Brown, Edward Evans-Pritchard, and Stanley Tambiah. I also present the views of Lucien Lévy-Bruhl and Claude Lévi-Strauss, who influenced the anthropological interpretation of magic. The discussion closes with the central solutions that have been suggested concerning the relationship between magic and religion in anthropological and cross-cultural research after the 1950s.[10]

In chapter 2, the discussion shifts from the study of magic in living societies to the historical study of magic in late antiquity and the early Islamic period (up to the time covered by evidence from the Cairo Genizah). I begin the chapter with a concise discussion of the research on the essence of magic in the Greco-Roman world and its role in the ritual activities of this culture to attain power. This context for the main discussion, which focuses on the magic-religion question in Judaism, was chosen for two reasons. First, researchers of Jewish magic have tended to approach magic in the Hellenistic world as a natural parallel and as a comparative horizon for their findings, both because Hellenism was the neighboring culture for Jews in Palestine and its surroundings and because real information about magic in Sassanid Babylonia in the talmudic period was lacking.[11] Second, the study of magic in the Greco-Roman world precedes its Jewish parallel and is also far broader in all areas. Hence it is useful to examine the theoretical changes in it as a historical-textual field of study before attempting to do so in the relatively limited study of magic in Judaism. As I show, traces of the theoretical change in the study of magic in comparative and anthropological-cultural research during the twentieth century are evident in the changed attitude toward this topic among researchers of the Hellenistic world. This change anticipates a similar move later recorded in the study of magic in Judaism.

---

10. A new scientific approach to the study of magic has emerged in recent years in the rapidly developing field of cognitive studies. This trend, originating in the psychological study of magic, is not presented in the survey in chapter 1 because, in general, it does not deal with the issue at stake here—the magic-religion question—and has no concrete applications to the study of Jewish magic, which is the horizon of the research overview presented in that chapter. For a summary of recent achievements in the cognitive study of magic (and a detailed bibliography), see Bever (2012). For major theories in this field, see Sørensen (2007), Subbotsky (2010) (for Subbotsky's view concerning magic, science, and religion, see chapter 1, note 99), and Vyse (1997).

11. The main information available originates in non-Jewish incantation bowls, except that the magic of bowls, beyond being a cross-cultural phenomenon, is also a closed phenomenon that we have nothing to compare with in the geographic-historical area of Babylonian Jews. On Babylonian incantation bowls, see chapter 5.

Chapter 2 is focused mainly on the study of magic in Judaism in late antiquity and the early Islamic period and is divided into three parts. In the first part I deal with the study of magic in rabbinic literature since the beginning of this research in the 1850s. In recent decades a revolution has been recorded in the perception of magic in rabbinic literature, the understanding of its place in Jewish society, including in rabbinic circles, and the explanation of the rabbis' resolute opposition to it. This revolution is exposed here in full. As I show, its essence is the almost complete abandonment of phenomenological and essentialist elements in favor of sociopolitical criteria as the foundation of the distinction between magic and religion.

In the second part of chapter 2 I consider the study of magic in the context of ancient esoteric Jewish literature—the *Hekhalot* and *Merkavah* literature. The role of adjurations—performative formulas through which people seek to impose their will on supernatural entities—is so central in this literature that researchers have been split concerning its main essence. Some consider the *Hekhalot* and *Merkavah* literature a visionary literature, where adjurations serve only as an auxiliary tool for attaining the religious-mystical goal of envisioning God and adoring him with the angels, which is its main purpose. Others propose viewing it as magic literature, where mystical visions are merely one channel, even if central, for the many uses of adjurations suggested in it. The controversy in this regard has obviously not been settled, but the ongoing discussion, in and of itself, has significantly helped to focalize the question about the essence of magic and its place in the spectrum of ritual beliefs and practices that characterize early Jewish mysticism.

In the last part of chapter 2 I deal with the study of Jewish magic literature itself. The broad review of the research on magic findings—the direct products of professional Jewish magic activity in late antiquity and the early Islamic period—focuses on the essence of magic and on the way its researchers attempted to understand it. In the whole of chapter 2 I try to point to a similar trend of change in the perception and place of magic in Judaism in relation to close (and no less vague) areas of culture, such as religion and mysticism. This trend resembles similar developments in the comparative and anthropological study of religions in general and the study of magic in the Greco-Roman world in particular.

In chapter 3 I outline my own approach concerning the magic-religion question in Judaism. I first present the difficulties posed by the suggested solutions regarding the Greco-Roman world and Jewish culture in late antiquity. I then attempt to suggest a new solution that rests on the linguistic theory of Ludwig Wittgenstein. Finally, I deal with the problem of defining ancient Jewish magic and present my view concerning the location of magic texts based on our current mode of using language. I propose a dialectic move that begins by reducing *magic* to a Jewish *adjuration text*, then focuses on the identification of such a text's linguistic characteristics, and culminates in the expansion of magic-Jewish textual circles based on these characteristics. The purpose of this move is to enable substantive justification for the choice of a textual foundation in the study of Jewish magic culture (in defined contexts of time and place) and to explicate my methodological proposition to abandon a dictionary definition of magic in favor of a quasi-ostensive definition of ancient Jewish magic.

Chapter 4, the last chapter in part 1, is devoted to the standing of magic language as a performative language. Since John Austin published his book *How to Do Things with Words*, his insights concerning the performative aspects of the speech act have served as a tool for explicating the performative character of ritual language. The discussion opens with a presentation of the principles of Austin's method, tracing the adoption of his theory to anthropological research of magic language and its applications to the textual study of performative language in Judaism. Finally, we come to the problem entailed in giving in to the temptation of endorsing the superficial resemblance between speech act theory and the perception of language in Jewish magic culture and the mistake involved in basing one on the other.

In part 2 of this book I deal with sources for investigating the early Jewish culture of magic. These sources split roughly into two: (1) primary (or *insider*) sources, that is, products of Jewish magic activity (writings that are themselves adjuration texts in the most distinct sense and the artifacts these texts are written on, and writings that include texts of this type); and (2) secondary (or *outsider*) sources, that is, writings that are not magical by nature but contain references to spells, adjurations, and other matters that characterize the primary sources. In chapter 5, then, the discussion considers primary sources, among them amulets, gems and magic jewelry, adjuration bowls, spell skulls, magic recipes, and books of magic. All this inventory, originating in the eastern Mediterranean and in Babylonia and dating back mainly to the third to the thirteenth centuries CE, has been published mostly since the 1990s and is discussed extensively and systematically according to the types of findings.

The last two chapters of this book deal with secondary sources. In chapter 6 I consider all the sources outside rabbinic literature. The discussion opens with the Apocrypha, the Dead Sea Scrolls, and the writings of Flavius Josephus (where references focus on the harmful effects of demons and on exorcising devices). I then review the magic aspects prominent in *Hekhalot* and *Merkavah* literature, discuss statements touching on magic in Karaite and Geonic writings, and conclude with the stance of Maimonides, who was a contemporary of the Cairo Genizah. I integrate the description of these sources and their interpretation in a systematic register that points to the close link between ritual power and sociopolitical power.

This register is also prominent in chapter 7, which expands its topic beyond magic to what I call the rabbinic discourse of the occult. In this chapter I review key aspects in the perception of magic, demonology, and divination in rabbinic literature, including the interpretation of dreams and astrology. The discussion spreads across two levels that are never really separate: the textual and the hermeneutical. At the textual level I extensively illustrate conceptual perceptions, practices, and narratives related to these topics. At the hermeneutical level, I consider the political character of the rabbis' use of these terms as an expression of their drive to monopolize knowledge and power.

All these sources, particularly the primary ones, are the basis for a description of early Jewish magic as a culture, in all its four components: beliefs, actions, goals, and social contexts. I have already examined several aspects of early Jewish magic in previous publications.[12] A comprehensive description of the phenomenon is a matter for another book.

12. See Harari (1997a; 2000; 2001; 2005c).

I

Research and Method

Magic and the Study of Religion

EVOLUTIONIST THEORIES

The comparative study of religion, including that of magic, began in the mid-nineteenth century, when an evolutionist worldview was almost completely dominant in Western thought. At the core of this research were such concepts as development, progress, and advancement, used as central tools for explaining life, society, culture, and the individual.[1] Early scholars of religion also adopted this approach and tried to view magic as an initial stage in the process of spiritual and cultural advancement that humanity undergoes in the course of its development (the paragon of "developed society," "developed culture," and "developed thinking" obviously being that of the educated late-nineteenth-century Western European white male). This trend developed in various directions as scholars attempted to characterize magic activity per se and the various

---

1. The scholarly literature on the evolutionist theory of Charles Darwin, who is most often identified with evolutionism as a method, is vast. For a good example, see G. Himmelfarb (1962). From the range of studies on evolutionism, I note briefly the following: For a review of evolutionist theories since the pre-Socratic philosophers and up to the beginning of the twentieth century, see Gaudant and Gaudant (1971); for a detailed discussion of the evolutionary approach in the hundred years before the publication of *The Origin of Species*, see Glass et al. (1959). On the development of evolutionism in the nineteenth century (before and after Darwin), see Eiseley (1958); on the influence of Darwinist theory on scientific thinking in almost all fields of research, see Ellegard (1990), Glick (1975), and Tax (1969).

courses of human development following from it in the direction of religion and science.

The forerunners of the evolutionist school in the study of religion were Edward Tylor, Herbert Spencer, and James Frazer. These scholars, whose heirs later referred to them as armchair anthropologists, sought to understand and analyze the development of the human spirit by combining testimonies from travelers, merchants, missionaries, and representatives of colonial powers on the practices, beliefs, and rituals of tribes that they considered living exemplars of the beginning of human development.[2] This approach, especially in the strict historical pattern adopted by Frazer, was tremendously influential at the end of the nineteenth and beginning of the twentieth centuries, for reasons far deeper than theoretical agreement with then dominant evolution principles. By arranging all human societies in hierarchical order along one developmental axis, from the primitive to the enlightened, evolutionist ethnographers ostensibly put a scientific stamp on the West's supremacy over the colonial subjects and indirectly contributed to its justification.[3] These relationships between knowledge and power in the late nineteenth and twentieth centuries

---

2. This approach, which for many scholars was unquestionable, was already being contested in the early twentieth century by R. R. Marett, who claimed that it was impossible to reconstruct an ancestral archetype of humanity on the basis of contemporary "primitive" societies (Marett 1979, 247). Adam Kuper's critique is even more scathing. He argued that the attempt to characterize a unified human origin by projecting current findings onto the past is not only methodologically unjustified but also not based on evidence. In his view the "primitive society" described by the early anthropologists never existed outside their writings (Kuper 1988).

3. A similar critique targeted anthropological research too, particularly its British version. Initial variations of it appear in a seminal anthology compiled by Tallal Asad (1973), which was preceded by a critical article by Kathleen Gough (1968). More such writings have appeared since. See, for example, Clifford and Marcus (1986), Pels and Salemink (1995), Stocking (1992), and N. Thomas (1994). For a concise review and further references, see N. Thomas (1996). Edward Said's celebrated book, *Orientalism* (1978), is a crucial and notable example, exposing the link between the construction of a low negative image of the colonies' subjects, which relied on various knowledge and power mechanisms that included academia (and its anthropological studies departments), and the political interests of the colonial rulers. On Frazer's patronizing view of primitive peoples, see Douglas (2002, 29–30). On Malinowski's attitude toward the Trobriand Islanders, as conveyed in his personal diary, see Geertz (1988b, 103–29).

were certainly not intended or even deliberate. Frazer, like the evolution-ists who preceded him and the many researchers inspired by him,[4] was not employed in the service of colonialism. He and his colleagues naïvely believed in the organizing and explicative power of the evolution principle and, out of the deep sense of superiority that is typical of Western scien-tific thought in our times as well, located every individual and every nation on a uniform scale of human development. Tylor is the one who blazed this trail for them.

Tylor was not especially interested in magic. He considered it a part of religious thought in general and of the ritual behavior connected to it that characterizes "primitive tribes."[5] In the few places where he does consider magic, he does not distinguish it from religion and treats both as mutually related or mutually complementary.[6] When referring to religion, Tylor coined the term *animism* (from *anima*, meaning "spirit" or "ghost"), to denote belief in the existence of bodiless spirits. This belief is for him the minimal definition of religion and, in its simplest form—the one that characterizes "tribes very low in the scale of humanity"—it is natural religion.[7] According to his view, the origin of animistic religion is the experience of "being personal," that is, the notion of a distinction and a

---

4. See, for instance, Benedict (1933), Jevones (1896), King (1892), and Radin (1957). See also the works of Malinowski, Weber, Wundt, and Freud discussed later in this chapter.

5. When relating to the scholars' views, I allow myself to use the terms they resorted to when dealing with communities commonly referred to as preliterate or pre-industrial. For the sake of clarity, I wish to establish unequivocally that my use of these terms (e.g., *primitive, savage*) is a repetition of the original uses and *in no way conveys a judgment on my part* as to the cultural development of these societies compared with Western culture.

6. For a comparison between Tylor's examples of religion and magic, see Tambiah (1995, 49). Roland Robertson claims that Tylor emphasized the personal character of powers related to religion, contrary to the impersonal character of magical powers (Robertson 1970, 48), but I have found no evidence for this in Tylor's works or in the studies about him. Robertson's reference there is general, and his source for this claim is unclear.

7. Tylor (1874, 1: 424–27). Tylor first introduced the notion of animism in 1866, in an article titled "The Religion of Savages" (Sharpe 1987, 107), and he developed it exten-sively in his book (chaps. 11–17). For succinct summaries of his method, see Bolle (1987), D'Alviella (1951), and Tambiah (1995, 42–51).

separation between body and soul, whose source Tylor identified in the experience of death, the visions of dreams, the projection of human spirituality on nature, and the anthropomorphization of natural phenomena.[8] Religion emerged out of the "savage's" contemplation of the world and of himself and out of his attempt to understand and explain his impressions. Tylor therefore considered the "savage" a primitive philosopher whose religion was a product of his thoughts about the world.

Similarly, Tylor considered the magic of "savages" as based on a thinking that involved a measure of rationality. Yet he thought this rationality was mistaken because it rested on the confusion between subjective and objective connections—between connections that are typical of human thinking and connections between actual objects. A person of "low intellectual condition" (Tylor's words) connects in his thought things that he has found to be actually connected. In the next stage he reverses the process and seeks to create actual associations between things that are connected in his thought. That is magic.[9] Magic, therefore, should not be seen as some kind of random hocus pocus but as an action based on a dialectic process of thought. The process begins with the identification of connections between objects and their classification and ends in a transition—mistaken from a Western scientific perspective—from associative connections between objects to their actual connection in reality. The linking of magic to this rational process led Tylor to view it as the first sign of scientific thought.[10] In any event, from an evolutionist perspective, magic "belongs in its main principle to the lowest known stages

---

8. Tylor (1874, esp. 1: 436–50).

9. Tylor (1874, 1: 115–16 and the examples in the pages that follow); and Tylor (1964, 111, 114–15). In a critical study of the English intellectualist interpretation of magic, Evans-Pritchard claimed that Tylor had been mistaken when assuming that the confusion between associative and actual ties was based on a psychological rather than a social reality (Evans-Pritchard 1933). Tambiah also stressed the social aspect in the preliterate tribes' perception of reality and argued that Tylor's view is most vulnerable precisely on this point: Why should members of these communities confuse associative and actual connections in one specific realm of their activity but not in others? Tambiah answered that the explanation of their ritual-magic activity must be based on the social context of its performance rather than on their distorted view of reality (Tambiah 1995, 51).

10. Tylor (1874, 1: 112, 119). Tylor refers there to magical practices as "occult sciences."

of civilization, and the lower races, who have not partaken largely of the education of the world, still maintain it in vigour."[11] Yet magic does not precede animism but coexists with it, complementing it from the practical angle. It is "the strategy of animism," as Solomon Reinach later defined it.[12] Together, then, primitive animistic religion and the magic that accompanies it constitute the first stage of human faith and its concomitant activity.

Several years after Tylor published his studies, Herbert Spencer completed his extensive work, *The Principles of Sociology* (1893), in which he sought to implement the principle of evolution as an explanation of the development of human society.[13] In this work Spencer discusses at length

---

11. Tylor (1874, 1: 112). Such formulations are no longer acceptable, but they are frequent in Tylor's writings, which are marked by a typical and in some sense even naïve Western elitism. They are certainly not exceptional in the context of contemporary evolutionist formulations. Julius Kollman, for instance, relied on the Pygmies' short stature to determine that they are a remnant of the "childhood peoples of humanity." Georg Schweinfurth tried to rest this view on the fact that the Pygmies' back is covered in fine, downy hair, like that of a newly born child. Wilhelm Schmidt went even further and tried to connect the Pygmies' physiology to their mentality in order to prove (in the context of the *Urmonotheismus* theory) that they also represent an infantile stage in the mental development of humanity (Wundt 1916, 77–78, 353). Cf. Freud on this matter later in this chapter. Signs of this kind of evolutionist elitism were still widespread in the study of magic decades later. The work of Hutton Webster in the mid-twentieth century is a good example. Webster ranked tribes as high or low in the "culture" spectrum and held that "religion and moral teaching, together with instruction in elementary science, may be counted upon, slowly but surely, to get rid of much white magic among primitive peoples, or to reduce it, as among ourselves, to pale and inconsequential survivals" (Webster 1948, 505). A real change in the perception of preliterate peoples occurred only when postmodernism began to influence research. A reverse view to that of Webster has been suggested by psychiatrist Ori Schwartzman concerning magic and its agents in Ghana. See Schwartzman (2007).

12. Reinach (1905–1923, 2: xv). On magic as the performative aspect of religious theory, which is inseparable from it, cf. van Gennep (1960, 13).

13. *The Principles of Sociology* is part of Spencer's synthetic philosophy, an enormous endeavor that he devoted to an attempt to explain the world, human beings, and culture relying on the evolution principle. Spencer adopted this approach even before Darwin's publication of *The Origin of Species*, and he should be seen as one of the most important harbingers of evolutionism. For concise reviews of Spencer and his thought, see Elliot (1951), Kaminski (1967), and Trompf (1987).

the beliefs and practices of preliterate tribes, including the beginning of magic and religion. Spencer's views are close to Tylor's, though he seems to have developed them independently.[14] Spencer also saw "the savage" as an ancient thinker who observes the world and weaves in his mind intellectual conceptions about his surroundings, and he too located the source of the distinction between body and spirit that underlies both religious and magic faith in the human reflection about sleep and death.[15] But he went further. He tried to offer a description and explanation of the development and progress of this faith.

According to Spencer, the source of magic is the belief that physical and spiritual problems result from a spirit settling in a person's body and from the conclusion warranted by this belief—the remedy is to cast it out. Basic magic practice, then, is exorcising spirits. At a later stage the savage comes to imagine that if a maleficent spirit can enter a person, so can a beneficent one. So why not use the latter against the former? Magic thus developed from rituals of exorcism to the use of spirits to expel other spirits. The idea then emerged of using spirits for broader purposes, such as revenge, and so gradually, through logical thought and inference, magic developed into a general phenomenon of taking over spirits and using them for various human needs. Religion, according to this method, was merely one logical step further: Humans came to believe that it was preferable to replace the recurrent process of taking over spirits with a permanent positive connection with them. They decided to propitiate them in advance and in this way merit the spirits' goodwill to help them. Thus was religion born.[16]

According to Spencer, then, magic and religion rely on the same principles for understanding reality. The difference between them is only in the developmental level of the primitives' rational thought. In this sense, Spencer's theory traces a clear course of religion's development from magic, even if indeed beside it rather than instead of it. This development, though fundamentally philosophical, soon assumed practical contours.

14. Evans-Pritchard (1965, 23).

15. Spencer (1893, vol. 1, chaps. 9–17).

16. For a description of the process concisely summarized here, see Spencer (1893, vol. 1, ch. 18). See also Spencer (1893, vol. 1, ch. 19) about the beginning of religion's development.

Beside continued attempts to rule the spirits, a new—religious—practice was born, meant to propitiate them and satisfy them. According to Spencer, this distinction regarding supernatural powers would also characterize, at later stages of human evolution, the difference between the healer-sorcerer and the priest. Both turn to supernatural powers and try to enlist them for the same ends. The difference between them is in the attitude toward these powers. The sorcerer approaches them pugnaciously and belligerently, whereas the priest does so sympathetically and amicably.[17] This attitude would recur in the research as one of the essentialist criteria through which scholars would determine the border between magic and religion.

The approach suggested by Tylor and Spencer was strictly and methodically formulated in the monumental endeavor of James Frazer, the most prominent evolutionist scholar in all that concerns the relationships between magic, religion, and science, and the most influential among them. Frazer adopted the intellectualist-evolutionist approach of his predecessors to explain the roots of magic and religion, but he radicalized it to the point of determining three historical stages in the development of human thought: the magic, the religious, and the scientific.[18] He ascribed the shift from one stage to the next to disappointment with the solutions suggested for day-to-day problems in each of the stages in turn.[19] Thus, according to Frazer, magic is the original form of human thought, which is accompanied by specific characteristic action.[20]

---

17. Spencer (1893, 3: 37–43).

18. Evans-Pritchard notes that Frazer may have relied for this division on the method of French philosopher August Comte, who defined three stages in the development of science: the theological, the metaphysical, and the positive (Evans-Pritchard 1965, 27). On Comte's method, see Mazlish (1967) and references there. Mary Douglas emphasized the connection between Frazer and William Robertson Smith, except that in her view Frazer adopted a secondary and negligible assumption of Robertson Smith's dealing with the ethical advantage of the Jewish people over their neighbors "and sent comparative religion into a blind alley" (Douglas 2002, 23).

19. Frazer (1900, 1: 75–76)

20. Frazer (1900, 240–43) and, more concisely, Frazer (1925, 11–12, 20). The reliability of the data that Frazer relied on for his theory is quite dubious, as noted. See, for example, Middleton (1987, 84) and J. Z. Smith (1973).

Frazer drew a distinction between theoretical magic, which he called pseudoscience, and practical magic, which he saw as pseudo-art.[21] In his view, taboo laws were also part of magic, and he viewed them as negative magic that, together with positive magic, covered the entire realm of practical magic.[22] Beyond these distinctions, Frazer founded the elements of both practical and theoretical magic on the same basic principles. These principles, identified through his method, are the sympathetic laws of magic: the law of similarity and the law of contact. Magic, in Frazer's view, is sympathetic magic, that is, an attempt to manage the world according to the laws of the mutual ties and influences that prevail between similar (and at times opposite) objects or of objects that have come into contact with one another.[23] Seeking to explain the source of these laws, Frazer adopted Tylor's approach connecting mental associations and magic and developed it into a system that views sympathetic laws as resulting from the projection of these modes of association onto the real world. In relying on the sympathetic laws, Frazer drew a distinction between two kinds of magic: homoeopathic and contagious. The source of both kinds is the associative connection between ideas on the basis of similarity or contact. Homoeopathic magic assumes identity, representation, and mutual influence between similar things. Contagious magic, which is usually also related to homoeopathic magic, assumes that things that come into contact are mutually influenced even after their separation. He summed up: "Both branches of magic, the homoeopathic and the contagious, may conveniently be comprehended under the general name of Sympathetic Magic."[24]

In his writings, Frazer discusses at length the relationship between magic and religion. Contrary to Tylor and Spencer, he viewed them as antithetical methods of thinking. He identified magic thinking as essentially close to science, because it considers nature a closed system that works according to fixed and necessary cause-and-effect laws. By contrast, in his definition, religion is "a propitiation or conciliation of powers superior to

---

21. Frazer (1925, 11–12, 20).
22. Frazer (1905, 52–57; 1925, 19–20). Marett attacked the association of taboo laws with magic and sought to equate them instead with negative mana (Marett 1979, 73–98).
23. Frazer (1905, 37–40; 1925, 11–12).
24. Frazer (1925, 12).

man which are believed to direct and control the course of nature and of human life,"[25] which perceives the course of events in the world as flexible and amenable to change. "The distinction between the two conflicting views of the universe," notes Frazer, "turns on their answer to the crucial questions, Are the forces which govern the world conscious and personal, or unconscious and impersonal?"[26] Contrary to religion, which views supernatural powers as personal beings, magic views them as an impersonal system of laws, just as science would do later. As such, magic is a primeval human attempt to understand and use the laws of nature.[27] The problem with this attempt, according to Frazer, is that it is based on a distorted perception of reality and is thus fundamentally mistaken. This is the reason that Frazer viewed magic as a "spurious system of natural law as well as a fallacious guide of conduct; it is a false science as well as an abortive art."[28]

---

25. Frazer (1925, 50).

26. Frazer (1925, 51). See also an extensive discussion on this question in Frazer (1925, 48–60).

27. Ruth Benedict would later suggest a similar approach. She also identified magic with science and viewed it as a technical activity devoid of feeling that is performed according to rigid rules. It thereby differs from religion, which, in her view, is based on animism, that is, on the anthropomorphization of nature, and on behaviors typical of human relationships. Benedict saw the difference between magic and science in those areas where both systems apply rigid laws of causality. Whereas science is interested in the natural realm and operates within its context, magic activity is based on the laws of causality in the domain of the supernatural (Benedict 1933).

28. Frazer (1905, 11). In a series of comments on Frazer's *Golden Bough* recorded around 1931, Ludwig Wittgenstein categorically dismissed Frazer's notion of magic (Wittgenstein 1993). As usual, his formulations take the form of aphorisms and are not easy to decode. I do not deal with them in detail, but it does appear that the core of Wittgenstein's critique of Frazer is Frazer's description of magic as based on thoughts, views, or beliefs. Wittgenstein suggests viewing magic as expressive and compares it to an instinctive beating of the ground or of a tree with a walking stick when angry (this approach closely resembles Malinowski's). As such, magic cannot be tested through the true-false criterion that Frazer uses, and presenting its adherents as wrong or foolish is pointless: "No opinion serves as the foundation for a religious symbol. And only an opinion can involve an error" (Wittgenstein 1993, 123). The mentality that is represented by magic is not a mistaken or silly rationality from which the correct, Western scientific rationality developed. It is a different mentality, which characterizes not only the "primitive" but also the "civilized individual." These comments may be related to

Frazer's version of historical evolutionism gained considerable influence among scholars of religion at the end of the nineteenth and beginning of the twentieth centuries. A special expression of this evolutionism came to the fore in the psychological research conducted by two of the discipline's forerunners: Wilhelm Wundt and Sigmund Freud. The working methods of these two researchers were different and so were their conclusions, but both shared a common aim. They tried to show that the human development from magic to religion (and to science) was based on psychological motives. Wundt was the first to draw a systematic link between ethnographic and psychological research, and he used the tools of psychology to explain the development of peoples, which he divided into four historical stages.[29] The first stage, which he called primitive man, was ruled by faith in magic and demons.[30] Up to this point, Wundt does not deviate too far from the earlier approaches. His main contribution was the explanation about the source and essence of this belief.

Wundt viewed magic as a product of feelings rather than of rational thought, as his predecessors had. He proposed viewing magic beliefs as the emotional reaction of primitive man to the anxiety evoked by the surrounding world that threatened him. The first reason for this anxiety

---

Wittgenstein's thoughts in *On Certainty* twenty years later, stating that, although proving a mistake is indeed possible, the idea of proof assumes a scheme of thought resting on *axiomatic* assumptions that define the conditions for verifying a claim and thus enable the very act of casting doubt. Casting doubt on the correctness of an idea, or refuting an idea, is thus possible only when both the one stating the idea and the one objecting to it share the same epistemological starting point. This claim, which in its religious context is part of the approach known as Wittgenstein's fideism, together with Wittgenstein's opposition to the fact that magic is based on thoughts and ideas, clarifies his opposition to Frazer's definition of magic as a false science. See Tambiah (1995, 54–64, 159–60). For an extensive discussion of Wittgenstein's remarks on *The Golden Bough*, see Clack (1999, esp. 21–50, 107–37). See also Cioffi (1998, 80–106), Clack (2001), and Wolfson (2001, 78–93). On Wittgenstein's fideism, see Lemberger (2003) and Nielsen (1967). On Wittgenstein's view of religion in light of *On Certainty*, see Vasilios (2001). For further aspects of Wittgenstein's conception of religion, see Arrington and Addis (2001).

29. On Wundt's method and his motivations for using it, see Wundt (1916, 1–6).

30. One should not confuse the impersonal powers that Wundt called demons with the maleficent personal beings denoted by that word in Christian tradition.

was, in his view, death. The very change that occurs in the dead evoked a terror that, in turn, led to a belief in the resurrection of the spirit. From here it was only a short step to a belief in demons. And once demons took up their place in the world, humans began to tie to them other threatening phenomena, above all, illness and natural disasters, weaving an intricate system of magic beliefs and causal links around them. Magic, then, was initially feeling, an emotional response. Magic ideas and beliefs developed only at a later stage. According to Wundt, the intellectualization that magic underwent in the works of Tylor and Frazer was an unfortunate and fundamentally mistaken consequence of projecting Western scientific thought on "primitive man."[31] In his view, causality in the sense accepted in our culture does not exist at all in the thought of primitive man, whereas the magic causality that rules early man's life does not originate in the laws of his thought but in his feelings. Rational thought developed only at a later stage and was related to the neutralization of feelings that accompanied the shift in the objects of human attention. Rather than focusing on the different and the strange and hence the threatening and frightening, human attention shifted to the stable and common in nature. Logical causality, then, developed out of the early stage of "emotional magic causality" and, according to Wundt, it is questionable whether this development of human rationality would have been at all possible had it not been anticipated by the magical stage.[32]

Because magic is essentially an emotional matter, it was connected in practical terms to the development of art, particularly dance, which primitive man, according to Wundt, brought to perfection.[33] From a theoretical perspective, magic preceded religion, for only in the third stage of human development, in the "age of heroes and gods," did the belief in

---

31. Gilbert Chesterton slightly anticipated Wundt in his critique of the "man of science," who projects logical thinking onto the objects of his research. This projection led, in his view, to a complete misunderstanding of the ritual's meaning. Forcing the logic of rituals "done without reason" yielded an approach that founds them on an absurd logic, except that this logic is absurd precisely "because it originates not in the simple mind of the barbarian but in the sophisticated mind of the professor" (Chesterton 1905, 144; see also 142–52).

32. Wundt (1916, 75–94).

33. Wundt (1916, 94–109). See also Marett's similar position discussed later in this chapter.

demons typical of magic advance to the belief in gods that is essential to religion. In certain senses, "the god also is only a new form of demon."[34] It is born from the impersonal power that originates in primitive feelings and developed in human thought into a fixed personal figure. This development took place in two stages. In the first stage the demon turned into a hero and assumed personal form. In the second stage the hero's qualities intensified and it became a suprahuman figure, the god. The origin of religion can thus be seen as the personalization process of the magic demons: "The various forms of pure demon-belief are preparatory to religion; religion itself begins with the belief in gods."[35] Wundt, then, distinguished magic from religion by relying on the essence of the supernatural powers, the objects of human belief. He tied the change in their perception to the historical evolution of peoples.

Sigmund Freud, Wundt's younger and more famous contemporary, suggested a different though still evolutionist-psychological explanation. Freud dismissed the work of Wundt, whose assumptions and research methods were based on nonanalytical psychology, and replaced them with his psycho-ethnographic method, in which he applied the principles of psychoanalysis to magic and to the magic-religion-science relationship.[36] Freud endorsed Frazer's three-stage historical evolutionism as the basic assumption of his research. He presented animism, the earliest system of thought that "is perhaps the most consistent and exhaustive,"[37] as a psychological theory. For Freud, magic was the practical side of animism, a technique meant to implement the aspiration to rule the world.

The basis of Freud's analysis of magic was Tylor's theory of associations, though Freud thought this theory was not sufficiently developed. This theory can explain the magic phenomenon per se but fails to address the reasons for confusing associations in thought with associations in reality. Freud tried to provide this missing layer in the theory by

34. Wundt (1916, 284).

35. Wundt (1916, 284). See also the discussion in Wundt (1916, 281–86).

36. Freud (1985, 49). On the contribution of Freud and his disciples to the understanding of the function of magic in the context of analytical psychology, see O'Keefe (1982, 264–77).

37. Freud (1985, 134).

resorting to the psychoanalytic conceptual framework he had developed.[38] He argued that constructs of human thought are projected onto reality because of the overestimation of mental powers that characterizes primitive man. In this regard, Freud held, the tribesman resembles the child. Like the child, he places his trust in the power of his wishes and is convinced that his will is a sufficient warranty and even a necessary condition for their realization. He differs from the child in his motor ability and, therefore, whereas children's wishes are satisfied through illusions, primitive man can use his will not only to describe the requested satisfaction but also to experience it: "This kind of representation of a satisfied wish is quite comparable to children's play, which succeeds their earlier purely sensory technique of satisfaction."[39] The primitive man's childish overestimation of his wishes and his will extended, at a later stage, to all the mental powers subordinate to the will and eventually covered mental processes in general, including thought.

It is precisely at this point, in the overestimation of thought, that Freud locates the confusion between the laws of association and the laws of nature: "The principle governing magic, the technique of the animistic mode of thinking, is the principle of the 'omnipotence of thoughts.'"[40] In Freud's view, this principle is the key to Frazer's three-stage characterization of the development of the human worldview, including the distinction between the stages: magic, religion, and science. Each one of these stages rests on a different notion of the omnipotence of thoughts. In the animistic stage the individual ascribes omnipotence of thoughts to himself. In the religious stage he assigns this feature to the gods, reserving for himself the power to influence them and direct them to fulfill his will. In the scientific stage he denies this omnipotence altogether and comes

---

38. This critique is different from the one that Evans-Pritchard and Tambiah later directed against Tylor. Freud accepted the notion of confusion between the two types of associations (in thought and in reality) and tried to explain it, unlike Evans-Pritchard and Tambiah, who rejected the very idea of confusion. In their view, social circumstances rather than confusion were responsible for the temporary replacement of rational thought that is also typical of tribes with magical thought. Cf. Douglas (2002, 72–90).

39. Freud (1985, 141).

40. Freud (1985, 143). On this idea and the surrounding debate, see also Styers (2004, 170–76).

to terms with the existence of impersonal natural laws that rule the world and his life.

Freud's interest in magic was not confined to the question of its place in the development of human thought and extended to an additional psychological aspect: the function of magic for the individual personality as a means of protecting and strengthening the ego. Contrary to the developmental theory that he had presented methodically and in detail in *Totem and Taboo*, Freud did not formulate his position on the second question in conclusive terms. Daniel O'Keefe, who suggested such a synthesis, summed it up by determining that Freud's writings clearly point to the role of magic in protecting the individual from psychic death. Relying on the entirety of Freud's statements on magic, O'Keefe suggests viewing Freud's approach toward magic as entailing three different modes: "(1) negative (the narcissistic theory of magic as infantile thinking); (2) neutral (his explorations of sympathetic magic); and (3) positive (how magic helps the ego)."[41]

The positive function of magic in the protection of the ego and in its preservation from psychic death was a continued concern for several of Freud's heirs. Prominent among them are Géza Róheim and O'Keefe himself. Róheim adopted Bronislaw Malinowski's view that magic helps the individual to overcome situations of crisis and uncertainty and to act rather than despair, and he supported this view with a psychological analysis. His conclusion was that magic is the element that actually makes human action possible: "Magic in general is the counterphobic attitude, the transition from passivity to activity. As such, it is probably the basic element in thought and the initial phase of any activity."[42] Magic, argued Róheim, thus serves not only "the primitives" but everyone. The whole of humanity operates mainly according to magic principles in the sense that we desire and then act.[43] O'Keefe extensively developed the view that magic helps the ego contend with pressures from society, the superego, and religion. His theory is discussed in the next section.

---

41. O'Keefe (1982: 264–69).

42. Róheim (1955, 3). See also the discussion in Róheim (1955, 3–91). Cf. O'Keefe (1982, 271–75).

43. Róheim (1955, 82–83).

As is true of all scientific theories, however stirring and appealing, the evolutionist theory also evoked opposition. The main critique of it, and certainly the most crushing one, was that formulated by Edward Evans-Pritchard and his successors, though they had been preceded by several others, among whom Robert Marett features most prominently. Although Marett was not altogether free of evolutionist inclinations, his theory was more moderate than Frazer's and he attacked some aspects of Frazer's work in his articles. In any event, magic in Marett's theory occupied a completely different position from the one it held in the theories of his predecessors. Marett's critique was based, above all, on opposition to what he considered Tylor's and Frazer's excessively intellectualist description of the savage: "Savage religion is something not so much thought out as danced out."[44] At its foundation are not only a primitive worldview but also feelings, aspirations, and actions.

In his article "Pre-Animistic Religion," Marett questioned the perception of animism as an adequate definition of religion and an explanation of its initial development and suggested viewing animatism as a stage that, logically and historically, precedes the animistic stage of religion. This stage was characterized by the belief in *mana*—a supernatural and impersonal magic-religious power. Rather than the belief in personal incorporeal spirits, this belief is the one that, in Marett's view, was the minimal definition of religion and thus also of magic. Marett tied all the phenomena touching on the human attitude toward the supernatural to a common source—the belief in mana—thus actually rejecting any distinction between them at the initial stage of their development. In his view, this was the "magico-religious" stage.[45]

---

44. Marett (1979, xxxi).

45. Marett (1979, 1–28). This thesis was first presented in 1899; see Marett (1979, xxii, note 1) and cf. Marett's article "The Conception of Mana" (Marett 1979, 99–121). On the magic-religious realm, see van Gennep (1960, 1–13). The notion stating that at the basis of magic is a belief in an impersonal supernatural power had been suggested earlier by John King. See King (1892, 1: 4–13, 101–31). Later, Evans-Pritchard was extremely critical of the use that Marett and others had made of the Melanesian term *mana*, leading, he believed, to "disastrous results" (Evans-Pritchard 1965, 33). His critique is part of his consistent opposition to historical generalizations based on local findings. On *mana* and similar terms in other cultures, see Webster (1948, 1–37). Webster held that belief in an "occult power" of this kind is indeed the foundation of

Marett developed his view concerning the beginning of magic religion in another article, where he disputed Frazer's theory. He rejected the idea about the role that human disappointment with magic played in the emergence of a new, religious historical stage. Instead, he tried to show that the contribution of magic to religion, with which it coexists without any separation, had actually been positive rather than negative. Here, too, Marett contested the intellectualism of his predecessors when he placed the performative aspect at the center of the magic phenomenon. The magic act, he argued, precedes the magic theory. The analysis of magic acts and their contribution to religion brought Marett to determine two stages in magicoreligious activity. The first, which he called basic magic, is characterized by action on a symbol out of emotional intentions toward the symbolized. At this stage the performers are unaware of the symbolism in their actions, which originate in the emotional (and not the intellectual) dimension of their personality and, at the psychological level, join the other ways they rely on to cope with the world. Magic functions as a means of liberation from oppressive feelings caused by the distress and difficulties the performers encounter in life, easing and improving their ability to act. The relief that follows the liberation from negative feelings is at the basis of magic activity and was therefore preserved in the second stage of magic's development as well, when magic activity was accompanied by awareness of its symbolism. Its performers, who understood that their actions fail to attain anything, developed instead a theoretical system whose role was to justify and preserve the liberating symbolic activity. This system deeply persuaded the "savages" of magic's effectiveness and helped to preserve it, until they not only became its users but also were influenced by it.[46] This presentation of magic made Marett the first scholar to view magic positively and to claim that it made a concrete contribution.

---

magic. He ascribed it to the primitive contemplation of the world and to the division of events within it into ordinary and exceptional. In his view, the need to explain the exceptional gave rise to a belief in an occult power, whereas animist beliefs were a second stage of development. This trend becomes stronger as culture advances, "and reaches its height in the great polytheistic religions of antiquity" (Webster 1948, 38–59; quote on 38).

46. Marett (1979, 29–72). Cf. Marett (1951, 247–48).

Marett's positive attitude toward magic moved him to seriously examine its components. He determined that the spell is the core of the magic ritual and explained it as a turn to a personal power, a turn meant to hasten the realization of a wish. In doing so, Marett emphasized the psychological purpose of magic talk and negated the impersonal, scientific character that Frazer sought to ascribe to magic. The mana idea, which Frazer ascribed to the religion stage, is already present, according to Marett, in the stage of developed magic. The transition from developed magic to religion, from spell to prayer, does not involve the anthropomorphization of the powers that operate the word but rather a change in the human attitude toward the supernatural power. Whereas the spell acknowledges the arbitrariness of this power and seeks to impose magic necessity on it, prayer turns to its will and seeks to influence it to be so kind as to help the petitioner. In the transition from spell to prayer, then, will replaces necessity and request replaces imposition in the relationship between humans and the supernatural whose help they seek.[47]

Marett opened up a new way of looking at magic that quite a few adopted, rejecting the historical distinction between magic and religion as separate stages of human development.[48] Scholars, then, were divided concerning the origin of these cultural phenomena and their mutual relationships, but all based their inquiry on phenomenological foundations. They sought to rest the distinction between magic and religion on essentialist differences between the phenomena themselves. The real change in the treatment of this question came from an entirely different direction.

---

47. Marett (1979, 55–71). Marett's conclusion that the mode of addressing supernatural powers changes according to the change in their character is close to that of Spencer. In another article, Marett extended his view to cover the taboo as well. He rejected Frazer's view of the taboo as negative magic and claimed that it extended further than the sympathetic laws that Frazer had made the basis of magic. In his view, the taboo should more accurately be viewed as negative mana (73–98).

48. See, for instance, Crawley (1909), Hartland (1914), Lang (1901), Lowie (1924), and van Gennep (1960). Evolutionist theories were still in use in the second half of the twentieth century for describing and explaining religion and magic, but they were no longer used for determining the relationship between them. Robert Bellah, for instance, offered an evolutionist theory of religion (Bellah 1964), whereas Milton J. Yinger suggested examining magic in similar terms (Yinger 1971, 72).

SOCIOLOGY OF MAGIC

At the beginning of the twentieth century, a school of thought evolved in France that sought to explain religion and magic by resorting to sociological tools, placing society rather than the individual at the focus. The most prominent researchers in this school were Émile Durkheim, Henri Hubert, Marcel Mauss, and Lucien Lévy-Bruhl.[49] These and other scholars, such as the German sociologist Max Weber and the British anthropologist Alfred Radcliffe-Brown, viewed religion as, above all, a kind of social activity. They based religion's origin, function, and aims on a social system, which was so deeply necessary that, without it, religion would simply be impossible. Therefore, according to this view, religion's explanation should be sought and formulated in social terms.[50] This shared basic view, on which these scholars also founded their respective attitudes toward magic, derived directly or indirectly from William Robertson Smith. Besides being a classic evolutionist, Robertson Smith is also considered the founder of the sociology of religion.[51]

Robertson Smith, whose main concern was ancient Semitic cultures, was the first to claim that religion should above all be seen as a collective practice, a social parallel to government institutions: "Religion was a part of the organised social life into which a man was born, and to which he conformed through life in the same unconscious way in which men fall into any habitual practice of the society in which they live."[52] Elsewhere, he explains, "Thus a man was born into a fixed relation to certain gods as surely as he was born into relation to his fellow-men; and his religion, that is, the part of conduct which was determined by his relation to the gods, was simply one side of the general scheme of conduct prescribed

---

49. On the Durkheimian circle, see Besnard (1938) and Webb (1916). Cf. Evans-Pritchard's reservations about including Lévy-Bruhl in this circle (Evans-Pritchard 1965, 78).

50. There is a vast body of literature on the history of the sociology of religion. See, for instance, Davie (2007), W. Davis (1987), O'Dea (1966), and Robertson (1970).

51. For an excellent summary of Robertson Smith's work, including a biography and a bibliography of his writings, see Beidelman (1974c) and Douglas (2002, 8–35).

52. Robertson Smith (1972, 21).

for him by his position as member of society."[53] Religion, then, is a social matter. Its objective is always collective, and it cannot serve individuals in their entirely personal turn to the gods. Hence there is an entire realm of human needs and aspirations that religion, by its very essence, cannot help to fulfill. This issue becomes particularly evident when these needs and aspirations clash with the good of the community. In such cases, when individuals require help from supernatural powers, they must create contact with them by other means. That is what magic is for.[54] Robertson Smith thus contrasted magic with religion, but not on the basis of an essentialist comparison between them but by reference to the social context of their respective aims. Although he does not define magic, it is clear that he views it as the set of means through which individuals seek to enlist the help of supernatural powers to fulfill their private wishes.

According to Robertson Smith, this fundamental distinction between religion and magic had an immediate consequence, which affected the standing and character of the powers that served individuals in their magic action. Religion addressed the friendly and beneficent powers: the gods of the community, which were considered the noblest in the supernatural hierarchy. These powers viewed the community favorably and wanted its best. Beside them, the community recognized the existence of additional entities, which were inferior to the gods. Religion adopted some of these and altogether ignored others, which only came to the fore "in private popular superstition, or by those who professed the art of constraining demonic powers to do them service and obey their commands."[55] The powers that were activated through magic were thus inferior to those that religion turned to. The conflict of interest between the welfare of the individual who activated the powers and the welfare of the entire community gave rise to the negative character assigned to these entities. For Robertson Smith, then, religion is a collective institution through which the entire community approaches its lofty and beneficent gods to seek their help, whereas magic seeks to enlist in its service inferior and negative entities to satisfy private needs that often contradict those of society.

---

53. Robertson Smith (1972, 30).
54. Robertson Smith (1972, 263–64).
55. Robertson Smith (1972, 90).

Robertson Smith's deep influence on the French school of the sociology of religion is also manifest in the attitude toward magic. The view of Durkheim, the school's founder, is actually a variation on the view of magic suggested by Robertson Smith. Durkheim hardly considers magic in his studies. In its few mentions in *The Elementary Forms of the Religious Life*, in which Durkheim sets out his position on religion, he suggests a definition of magic based solely on its social rather than its essentialist characteristics. In his view, differentiating between magic and religion by reference to the form or the content of their typical activity is impossible. Myths, rituals, songs, dances, sacrifices, and a turn to higher powers are common in both religion and magic, and their manifestations are not only similar but at times even identical. What distinguishes them is their place in the social setting: Whereas magic is an individual concern, religion is established by and serves the community as a whole.

Like Robertson Smith, then, Durkheim also identifies magic through its contrast with religion's collective character, but he shifts the contrast from the aims of actions to their performative standing. Religion is always performed in distinctly social settings. Religious beliefs belong not only to each community member but to the collective as such. They define the community's unity and create a sense of participation among its members when they translate these into a shared ritual. Magic, by contrast, is personal by its very essence and is therefore realized individually. The belief in it, even if shared by community members as individuals, does not constitute or consolidate the community as a collective because magic-related activity is invariably performed between individuals: the sorcerer and the client he serves.[56]

In his approach, which grants precedence to the society over the individual, Durkheim suggests viewing religion as a phenomenon that fundamentally precedes magic. He views magic as a secondary branch of religion and as based on religious principles. Durkheim absolutely rejects Frazer's version of the evolutionist theory and casts doubt on the possibility that any sorcerer would think along the lines of sympathetic

---

56. Durkheim (1967, 57–63). Anthropological evidence often contradicts Durkheim's view. For a factual, persuasive critique of his view of religion, and indeed that of Robertson Smith as well, see Horton (1960, esp. 203–4, 218–19). See also Winkelman (1992, 3).

laws, when reality and experience neither justify nor encourage such a hypothesis. In his view, these laws have their source in religion, where they serve as part of the perception of holiness and the holy powers. Only at a secondary stage was their scope of application expanded from the holy to the profane, and they then turned into "magic natural laws."[57]

Durkheim's view concerning the collective essence of religion decisively influenced several contemporary scholars of religion and magic, as evident in the shared endeavor of Henri Hubert and Marcel Mauss, who attempted to analyze the magic phenomenon with sociological tools in *Equisse d'une théorie générale de la magie* (An Outline of a General Theory of Magic).[58] Later, this work appeared in a revised English translation authored solely by Mauss and bearing a more assertive title: *A General Theory of Magic.*[59] This work is an attempt to analyze magic as a universal and homogeneous cultural phenomenon, resting on a discussion of its manifestations in different cultures at various times and weaving them into one common picture.

Mauss did use the methodological tools developed by Durkheim for the analysis of magic, but he did not accept Durkheim's conclusions. Mauss clarifies already at the start that magic, like religion, submits to social rules and that magic also is a defined social realm of action, an agreed-on and stable traditional ritual under strict social control. Hence no random or entirely personal action can be considered magic. Underlying his view of magic are three principles: activity, communality, and definability. Mauss held that this realm of activity can be defined as social and yet as still different from and even opposed to religion. Mauss agreed with Durkheim's claim that the form or the content of a ritual activity does not help to distinguish magic from religion, and he rejected the attempts to do this by identifying magic with sympathetic action, the character of the human turn to the supernatural powers, or the automatic measure of their response. In Mauss's view, all these are incapable of clearly and sharply differentiating magic rituals from religious rituals.

---

57. Durkheim (1967, 398–405 and note 26).
58. Hubert and Mauss (1902–1903).
59. Mauss (1972).

The method, Mauss argued, must be different. We must point to a distinctly magic ritual—*the* magic ritual—and, through it, characterize the phenomenon as a whole. In his view, a type of such rituals that clearly convey the magic phenomenon is available. These are the rituals of maleficent magic, intended for harming others. These rituals are the antithesis of the classic religious rituals that, according to Mauss, deal with sacrifice: "We have, in other words, two extremes which form the differing poles of magic religion: the pole of sacrifice and the pole of evil spells."[60] The reason for identifying maleficent rituals as the clearest expression of magic as a whole is neither their content nor their mode of performance. Religion also contains such rituals at times. What turns them into magic is the social prohibition to perform them. Mauss sums up: "A magical rite is *any rite which does not play a part in organized cults*—it is private, secret, mysterious and approaches the limit of a prohibited rite."[61] By contrast, religion is the commanded ritual. This method, which establishes the distinction between magic and religion solely on the social legitimation of the ritual's performance, entirely detaches the issue not only from the essentialist aspects of rituals but also from those social aspects of their performance that Robertson Smith and Durkheim pointed to. The only demand tied to the act itself is that it should be a ritual.[62] The only element that dictates the ritual's essence as being either magic or religion is the attitude of the society toward it (or more precisely, the attitude of the social institutions that dictate the limits of what is permitted within it).

---

60. Mauss (1972, 22). See also Mauss (1972, 7 and the entire discussion on 18–24). Mauss does not justify the choice of "black magic" as the distinct expression of magic. It would appear that, unwittingly, he inquired into the accepted use of the terms *magie* and *religion* in his own language and culture as a basis for the universal definition of the phenomena denoted by these terms.

61. Mauss (1972, 24; emphasis in original). The private character of magic is not mentioned as a criterion for determining its essence, as Durkheim had suggested. Rather, it is dictated by the social prohibition on the performance of the ritual and from the secrecy attached to it.

62. Although Mauss does not mention this explicitly, this demand excludes from the realm of magic acts such as theft or murder, which are also performed privately and secretly and are contrary to social authorization. Nevertheless, Mauss does not explain what is a ritual.

Determining magic's social character was only the first part of Mauss's general theory. In the second part he offered a meticulous description and analysis of its components. Except for O'Keefe's comprehensive work, no other study as detailed and ambitious as Mauss's has ever attempted to map the formal and thematic components of magic. Mauss had two aims: (1) to demonstrate that all the elements of magic activity (the sorcerer, his rituals of initiation, the personal and impersonal foundations of ritual, the rituals of entry and exit from it, the role of its spectators) are a result of social conventions and are never arbitrary or personal, and (2) to demonstrate that all these conventions have only one purpose: to remove the magic ritual, with all it entails, from the realm of the normal. Mauss tied this removal to the "magic potential" he identified as the basis for the belief in the efficacy of magic. After showing that the three elements commonly included in descriptions of magic—sympathetic relationships, magical properties, and demonology—are insufficient to explain the belief in it, Mauss turned to the mana, the universal supernatural power, which he presented as the basis for the belief in magic's efficacy and even for its very existence.

According to Mauss, magic power is the key concept of the magic worldview. Believers in this power view it as a potential for action in an environment with laws different from ours that, under certain abnormal conditions, can be implemented in our world as well. All the components of magic are therefore directed to the abnormal. Their purpose is to create in the world a kind of vacuum from normality, an abnormal space that will draw in the magic power and enable its action.[63] Hence the magic claim, the magic principle, anticipates experience. Magic power is an a priori concept that serves as the foundation of the belief in the efficacy of magic beyond any specific performance and beyond any practical success or failure of magic rituals. The belief in magic power is what prevents criticism of magic's efficacy and extracts it from the realm of doubt. According to Mauss, this belief is a universal category of thought. In some societies it is externalized, and in others it exists below the threshold of consciousness. Magic power is also the platform of religion, because "not only is the idea of *mana* more general than that of the sacred, but . . . the

---

63. On the elements of magic, see Mauss (1972, chaps. 3 and 4).

sacred is inherent in the notion of *mana* and derives from it. It would probably be fair to say that the sacred is a species of the genus *mana*."[64]

Members of the *Année sociologique* circle, who were inspired by Durkheim, neglected the evolutionist aspect of the magic-religion relationship in favor of social aspects. Max Weber tried to integrate these two options of interpretation. In *The Sociology of Religion*, he proposed viewing religion as a historical stage that succeeds magic and is based on the development of the society's perception of God. The transition to the religious stage did not lead to any essential changes in the means that served society to attain its aims, that is, in the form or the contents of the rite. The two main features of the religious rite, prayer and sacrifices, rest on magic rituals and at times are even identical to them. Nor did the aims change. Both magic and religion mean to improve life in this world. What did change, according to Weber, is the social organization of those responsible for performing the rituals. The expansion of God's power in human thought and his transformation into a supreme ruler of personal character distanced God from magic means. New means meant to propitiate him, such as prayer and gifts, penetrated the ritual and were added to existing ones. This development of metaphysical thought and its related ethics led to the most essential change: the growth of a priestly class, which replaced sorcerers in the rituals used to connect with God. The difference between priests and sorcerers does not come forth in their attitude toward God, their areas of knowledge, or their levels of erudition but in their social class. The character of the priesthood as an organized establishment, including a ritual activity that shifted from a series of one-time attempts to affect God to a fixed and ongoing cultic order, established the priesthood as a social class. Instead of individuals occasionally busy with rites, each one for himself, an organized and stable priesthood routinely maintained traditional ritual. This is the meaning of the transition from magic to religion.[65] This transition, however, was not apparent in any absolute change. Beside the priestly rituals and institutions, meaning the community religion, a broad and important area remained open for the sorcerer's actions as well. Like Robertson Smith, Weber also held that the religious ritual, collective by its very essence, does not address

64. Mauss (1972, 119). See also the discussion of mana in Mauss (1972, 108–121).
65. Weber (1965, 26–31).

individual needs. Sorcerers therefore survived even after the growth of the priesthood and continued serving the personal needs of community members "on demand."[66]

The sociological comparative method used in the study of magic was replaced in the twentieth century by concrete social considerations, which originated in anthropological fieldwork (see the next section). Toward the end of that century, however, another comprehensive, scholarly, and ambitious study was published; in this work Daniel O'Keefe presents what he calls the social theory of magic.[67] O'Keefe formulates, specifies, and seeks to demonstrate in his book thirteen postulates that constitute the social (more precisely, asocial) function of magic. They amount to a social-psychological theory that presents magic in a light different from that previously suggested by any single scholar.

O'Keefe formulates his definition of magic by relying on a synthesis of features and definitions suggested by his predecessors. He integrates the views of Weber, Hubert and Mauss, Durkheim, and Freud and presents magic as

> well-known sacred institutions . . . which are widely designated as magical in many societies, which are derived from religion, associated with religion or respond to religion, which are often of a secret or illicit or peripheral nature, or tend at least to organize themselves separately from (or within) religion, more often on a professional-client rather than community relationship, and which tend to serve fractional rather than fully collective ends, especially those of individuals and of subgroups in any collectivity.[68]

This broad and detailed definition serves as the foundation of O'Keefe's theory, one tier over another. I present O'Keefe's thirteen postulates, in order, briefly in the following discussion.[69]

---

66. Gerth and Mills (1958, 272).

67. O'Keefe (1982). O'Keefe does not see any of the discussions that preceded him as a general theory of magic. For his attitude toward the work of Hubert and Mauss and the work of Malinowski, see O'Keefe (1982, xv–xvi).

68. O'Keefe (1982, 14–15).

69. For a concise summary of the first two books (postulates 1–8), see O'Keefe (1982, 240–44). For a summary of the entire theory, see O'Keefe (1982, 502–8).

1. Magic is a social mode of action. For O'Keefe, magic is above all a kind of action. He rejects Jean-Paul Sartre's claim that magic is passive (and tied to feelings) and merely a pseudo-activity[70] and asserts that, socially, magic involves real action and even creates a new reality.

2. Magic social activity is based on symbolic actions, and linguistic symbolism is central to it. An intricate network of connections ties magic language to all the symbolic representations involved in magic.

3. Symbolic magic activity, and most prominently its linguistic component, is rigidly scripted. Magic speech is unique among all linguistic modes of human expression and is characterized by a rigid imperative of performance. Its source should therefore be sought in a special kind of human activity—religious activity. O'Keefe argues that magic draws its symbolic activity from religion but makes two main changes in it: Magic tightens the performative script down to the finest details and replaces the collective safety intended by the religious ritual by giving individuals the courage to speak, to act and to think, and thereby to hope.

4. Magic scripts draw their social efficacy largely from preexisting or prefigured agreements ("synthesized a priori"). Their power stems from a dialectic process founded on two elements: a temporary relaxation of normal social directives that makes room for deviant activity and an overvaluation of this deviant activity that turns it into a paragon, as part of the community's social agreement: "Magic continually recycles itself back into religion and social consensus by . . . relaxing the frame to produce exceptional experiences and then interpreting and patterning them according to the traditional agreements of the culture."[71]

5. Magic borrows its symbols from religion and then uses them to attack religion and argue with it, as part of a dialectic process that renews religion itself. The change in religion, which is thus compelled to answer magic's challenge, is expressed in both social and ideological aspects. Magic, for its part, develops at times into a new religious sect, but because such a sect is only meaningful in the context of the symbolic and conceptual framework of the religion it attacks, it should be viewed as part of the entire religious whole. Indeed, religion sometimes absorbs the magic sect and institutionalizes it within its own framework so that it can serve

---

70. Sartre (1948, 50–91).
71. O'Keefe (1982, 96).

its own needs. O'Keefe identifies the source of the magic protest not in the contents or the procedures common in religion but in the fact of magic's absence from religion. When religion is absent ("in the sense of sacral-magical religion")[72] or excessive (referring to antimagical overintellectu-alism or overmoralism or to a monopolistic takeover of magic activity by the religious establishment), the human need for *personal magic* cannot be satisfied and seeks fulfillment in various magic sects. In these cases, magic offers itself in concentrated form within religion's symbolic system.

6. Logically, and in the few cases where the developmental sequence can also be traced historically, magic follows from religion rather than vice versa. O'Keefe prepared the ground for this claim in postulate 5. Here, he substantiates it and seeks to demonstrate that the fact that religion includes magic a priori does not contradict the fact that magic develops from religion and as a response to it.[73]

7. Magic is a by-product of the projection of society in its religion. O'Keefe adopts the anthropological-sociological claim that religion reflects the values and the structure of the society or of its ruling groups. He therefore concludes that magic's challenge to religion is also partly directed against the society and its structure, values, and laws.

8. Religion is the institution that creates and shapes magic for society. O'Keefe argues that, despite the close mutual relationships and the great similarity between magic and religion, the two should not be equated, not even in essentialist terms. He determines that the core of religion's various expressions—sacrifice, mysticism, myth, prayer—is magic in the weak sense and claims that religion enables magic by shaping the magic symbolic potential and by presenting it openly as part of its own practice. This symbolism becomes magic in the strict sense when it is institutionally used in instrumental terms outside religious frameworks.[74] In O'Keefe's view, sacrifice and initiation are the most salient instances of this process. He discerns at their basis the key concept shared by both religious and

---

72. O'Keefe (1982, 132).

73. O'Keefe devotes considerable attention to the decadence theory of Wilhelm Schmidt and of the *Urmonotheismus* school. On this issue, see also Brandewie (1983) and Henniger (1987).

74. For the distinction between the weak sense and the strict sense of magic, see O'Keefe (1982, 11–13, 213–14).

magical practices—the group, as based on membership within it—and explains that both sacrifice and initiation "are born together when membership [in the group] becomes problematical. They smooth transitions for the group . . . ; they also strengthen group members. . . . In this, they are *preludes to the birth of the individual*."[75]

9. Magic protects the self. This is the heart of O'Keefe's theory. O'Keefe examines at length, with psychological tools, the positive functioning of magic and emphasizes its contribution to the individual: "What it comes down to is a matter of life or death. At a limit, in a show-down, what magic defends the self against is death."[76] He determines that the influence of magic focuses on psychic processes tied to the semiconscious self and that these processes are related to repression and to unconscious pressures that the individual is exposed to. O'Keefe also points to the link between strong social pressures and the repression of the self. He analyzes the reciprocal relationships between acts of magic and the psychological processes through which these acts exert their influence, protecting the self from the death implicit in the social pressures that target it.

10. Magic helped to develop the institution of the individual. O'Keefe relies on his previous conclusions to expand on the contribution of magic in the social context as well. A clear parallel prevails, in his view, between the development of magic and the advancement of the social structure. He views the tribal era as a decisive stage in this regard, because it was then that the main realms of magic activity took shape. The reason is the expansion and enhancement of the social structure, processes that obstructed the individual's inclusion in it. In turn, this obstruction gave rise to the concept of the individual, and magic rituals henceforth served as "the agency that performs the social manufacture of individuals."[77] Society itself, then, creates the means for strengthening the individual within it. Individuals then use these means to rebel against society and resist the pressures it imposes on them, but

---

75. O'Keefe (1982, 249; emphasis in original).
76. O'Keefe (1982, 277).
77. O'Keefe (1982, 363).

society ultimately benefits from this rebellion, which stimulates development and progress.

11. Magic, especially black magic, is a key to the social pressures exerted on individual selves. Like Mauss, O'Keefe holds that black magic is the earliest, most radical, and most distinct of all magic practices. In his view, however, magic in its simplest form—witchcraft—lacks any magic characteristics. This fact and the close link of witchcraft to totemism drove O'Keefe to assume that belief in witchcraft and the fear of it are earlier than magic. He identifies their source at the social level: "Witch fears are religious projections of society's power to kill. The witch accusation is the individual's first magic, his first counterattack on social consensus. Voodoo death is experienced in dreams and hallucinations as an attack by a totemic animal. The victim beats off the attack by accusing the moral entrepreneur . . . of being the exact opposite of every social value, of being a witch."[78] The historical persistence of the dread of witchcraft in many different societies is a product of their consistent recourse to witchcraft as a tool for exerting pressure on the individuals within them. The existence of magic practices for contending with witchcraft shows that magic is indeed meant to protect the individual from such pressure.

12. The persistent presence of magic in modern culture is a product of social pressures that continue to prevail and endanger the self in contemporary society.

13. Magic symbolism travels easily and accumulates in the course of history. O'Keefe uses the claim that the sociological category of mobility characterizes magic knowledge and symbolism. In its light, he reviews the development and the functioning of the occult sciences, clarifying the standing of magic in relation to the other cultural realm to which it is often linked—science.

O'Keefe, then, took elements from sociological research and from the psychological study of magic and tied them together into a dialectical psychosociological theory. His method seeks to consider the place of magic in religion and its vital role in protecting individuals from the

---

78. O'Keefe (1982, 422). For the distinction between magic and witchcraft, see the next section.

pressures of society and even rescuing them from the death that could befall them as a result of these pressures. At the social level, O'Keefe's theory points to the role of magic in the birth of the individual. The birth of the individual threatened society but ultimately contributed to its development. The symbiotic relationship between religion and magic reflects a similar pattern in the relationship between society and the individual. Just as society precedes the individual, who is born into it and draws the contents of his own self from the culture, so religion is related to magic. And as the individual, who is born into a rigid coercive framework, defies it and struggles for existence as a separate personality and is finally contained within the collective and affects it, magic does so in relation to religion. But this is not only a reflection. Essential relations of cooperation prevail between social and symbolic systems. Society symbolizes itself in its religion and thereby imposes itself on its individual members. Individuals, for their part, use magic to protect themselves from society and to defy it. Finally, both magic and individuals are contained within these broader frameworks and leave their impression on them. According to O'Keefe, this dynamic dialectic has recurred in waves since the dawn of history.

As noted, O'Keefe published his book toward the end of the twentieth century, when dozens of anthropological fieldwork reports dealing with the phenomena he had researched had already been published. Those findings and the methodological reflections that followed were before him and he used them, even though they were not always in agreement, to fashion his method. Let's return to that period at the beginning of the twentieth century when the study of magic ceased to be an object of general theoretical hypotheses and became focused and observation based. The scholars who preceded anthropological fieldwork had all been partners to the same methodological fallacy: The research data they used had been collected by others, mostly without proper method or control. The researchers had no immediate knowledge of the objects of their research and were thus unable to trace the role of magic in their cultures' web of life, myth, and ritual. This situation underwent a fundamental change in the early decades of the twentieth century with the development of anthropological fieldwork.

MAGIC, RELIGION, AND RATIONALITY
IN ANTHROPOLOGICAL RESEARCH

Bronislaw Malinowski's fieldwork in the Trobriand Islands, east of New Guinea, marked a breakthrough in anthropological research, and magic played a significant role in it.[79] Malinowski was the first anthropologist to focus attention on magic in the lives of the "primitives" he studied closely for a long period and the first to formulate a general theory of magic relying on his acquaintance with its function in the society he researched. His views on this subject were thoroughly articulated in 1925 in his article "Magic, Science, and Religion," in which he sought to describe the origin, function, and mutual relationships of these three cultural phenomena.[80] Right at the start, Malinowski calls for removing magic from the realm of thought and knowledge exclusively and viewing it as, above all, a kind of human behavior. This behavior is based on thought, feeling, and will and is related to all aspects of "primitive man's" life: faith, action, personal experience, and social organization.[81] Malinowski's course, then, leans toward Marett and Durkheim, though Frazer's influence is also evident in it. Malinowski adopted Frazer's triple distinction between magic, religion, and science and the connection of magic to science.[82]

---

79. See Malinowski (1932; 1935; 1964, esp. chaps. 5, 10, 17, 18). On Malinowski's contribution to the study of cultural anthropology, see Firth (1957). For an excellent and critical review of Malinowski's attitude toward magic and religion, see Tambiah (1995, 65–83).

80. Malinowski (1948, 1–71). Tambiah points out that Malinowski's analyses of his observations in the Trobriand Islands do not spell out how he differentiates magic from religion and, in Tambiah's view, not by chance. The islanders did draw a clear distinction between "gardening," meaning physical agricultural activity, and "magic," but the category of "religion" did not exist in their culture. Hence Malinowski could not draw distinctions between the islanders' religion and their magic. The sharp separation between magic and religion that characterizes *Magic, Science, and Religion* belongs to a later stage in his thought, when he shifted from local conclusions to a universal theory of magic (Tambiah 1995, 68).

81. Malinowski (1948, 8).

82. Despite his explicit critique of Frazer, Malinowski adopted his ideas on this count. See, for example, Malinowski (1966, 196–210). Middleton's claim that Malinowski was, above all, Frazer's heir, is exaggerated (Middleton 1987, 86).

On this point, Malinowski created a unique synthesis, combining a functionalist view of magic activity (and of religious and scientific activity) with an emphasis on its personal-emotional foundations.[83]

Like Wundt and Marett, Malinowski saw magic as an expression of feelings, but he explained the phenomenon differently. He claimed that magic follows from the human need to confront the distress, frustration, and despair accompanying the impotence that human beings often experience in their lives. The examination of human behavior taught him that, at these times of crises, we unwittingly tend to express our feelings through symbolic words and acts. He judged that the similarity of this spontaneous behavior to spells and magic rituals was too great to be just random chance. He therefore concluded that the basis of magic ritual was the social ritualization of the spontaneous human reactions accompanying the strong emotional responses evoked by crisis, failure, and distress. From this perspective there is no room for identifying every magic ritual with sympathetic activity, as Frazer suggested, given that it often functions in an entirely different realm—the emotional one. In these cases the components of the ritual are not intended to represent the target of magic sympathetically but to externalize the performers' feelings toward the object of their action.

Malinowski's claim about the emotional importance of magic was based on observations concerning its function in the daily lives of the Trobriand Islanders. He discovered that some actions in their lives abounded in "magic support," whereas others lacked such "support." The key to the difference was the degree of danger attached to the actions and the degree of anxiety about their performance. Malinowski concluded that "primitives" use magic as a means to help them overcome anxiety and to enable them to function in crisis situations. In this realm, magic plays an infinitely important existential role.

---

83. On the functionalist school in the study of religion, see Robertson (1970, 17–24, 38–42; 1987). On Malinowski's functionalism, cf. Malinowski (1966, 147–76). In any event, Malinowski was opposed to the radical approach that identified the divinity with the society, and he therefore viewed religion as solely a social matter (Malinowski 1948, 37–41).

Magic supplies primitive man with a firm belief in his power of succeeding; it provides him also with a definite mental and pragmatic technique wherever his ordinary means fail him. It thus enables man to carry out with confidence his most vital tasks, and to maintain his poise and his mental integrity under circumstances which, without the help of magic, would demoralize him by despair and anxiety, by fear and hatred, by unrequited love and impotent hate.[84]

In Malinowski's terms, "The function of magic is to ritualize man's optimism, to enhance his faith in the victory of hope over fear."[85]

Malinowski's findings match Marett's view not only concerning the emotional character of magic rituals but also concerning the central standing of the spell in them. Malinowski argues that for primitive man, magic knowledge means knowledge of the spell to be uttered in the course of the ritual, a spell where the ritual's performative power is concentrated. In every important magic ritual the spell includes mention of the tribe's mythological forefathers and of their role in the transmission of magic to the tribe. Every event of this kind is therefore tied to the tribe's magic

---

84. Malinowski (1948, 116). See also Malinowski (1948, 114–19).

85. Malinowski (1948, 70). Opinions concerning this claim are divided. Radcliffe-Brown definitely opposed it (Radcliffe-Brown 1965, 174–75). By contrast, Clyde Kluckhohn found that, among Navajo Indians, faith in witchcraft and the ritual activity related to it was a key tool for contending with anxieties and aggression at the social level (Kluckhohn 1967, 95–110). Harold Fallding suggested an original interpretation of Malinowski's findings. In his view, the religious ritual presents humans as victors, whereas the magic ritual presents them as defeated and impotent creatures that, lacking any other option, prefer to do something rather than nothing (Fallding 1974, 82–83). Tambiah was extremely critical of the way Malinowski interpreted his own findings. He showed that Malinowski's field data contradict his theory and that he had been mistaken in linking danger to the use of magic. According to Tambiah, magic is not related to dangerous areas of actions or to situations that no longer allow operating technology but to actions of special social importance, where the need for success is extremely strong. According to Tambiah, Malinowski's important contribution to the study of magic was the discovery of the social mechanism of its functioning, not the psychological explanation he offered (Tambiah 1995, 72–73). See also Tambiah's renewed analysis of the links between myth, magic, and social structure in Malinowski's reports (Tambiah 1985a).

myth and rests on it. Usually, the magic myth is integrated into the core of the ritual and tied to myths about the sorcerer's power and the magic powers he controls. The myth is thereby excluded from the realm of historical hypotheses and is assigned an entirely different social role, attesting to the validity of the tribe's magic and strengthening faith in its efficacy.[86] Malinowski's analysis of the Trobriand Islanders' historical myth showed him that, when the myth related to magic, it told the story of magic's entry into the tribe and its transmission within it but not the story of its emergence. Malinowski explained this by claiming that the islanders do not perceive magic as a human invention but as an ancestral power that has forever been present in the world, for their sake. In the tribe's perception, magic's significant starting point is its actual entry into the tribe and, for this reason, its mythical history is always related to human history. This insight, together with his view concerning magic's emotional foundation, moved Malinowski to question the notion that magic is related to mana. Magical power, he argued, is the opposite of this mighty and arbitrary natural power. This is a special human power meant to serve humans when confronting the powers of nature. In the tribal consciousness it is tied to the traditional ritual practice that the founding fathers bequeathed to the tribe.[87]

---

86. Malinowski (1948, 54–64). For a broad clarification of magic language among Trobriand Islanders, see Malinowski (1935, 2: 213–50). On the central role of the spell in the magic ritual, cf. also Firth (1967, 195–212) and Tambiah (1968). Tambiah held that Malinowski failed to keep a sufficiently sharp distinction between magic language and everyday language and that, at times, he did not distinguish between them at all (contrary to the locals themselves). Tambiah sought to complete this picture and to characterize magic speech, and for this purpose he pointed out its links to the performative utterance, as described by philosopher John Austin in speech act theory. See Tambiah (1968; 1995, 74–80). On speech act theory and its implications for the study of magic and anthropology, see chapter 4. Evans-Pritchard altogether negated the universalist perception about the centrality of the spell in magic activity and claimed that this is a culture-bound phenomenon (Evans-Pritchard 1929).

87. Gerard Zegwaard pointed to an additional mode of relationship between the tribe's founding fathers and its magic in the shape of magical artifacts believed to have served the tribe's forefathers, who then bequeathed them to their heirs (Zegwaard 1968, 438–39).

Malinowski endorsed a functional approach concerning magic. He traced its role and assessed its contribution to the proper course of life in the community he examined. His attitude toward religion and science was similar. He based the differences between the three phenomena—magic, religion, and science—on the way each of them served the individual and the society. This view drove him to determine that magic is a pseudoscience. Like the aims of science (or, more exactly, technology),[88] the aims of magic are always geared to the satisfaction of limited and well-defined needs. The deception that this pseudoscience is founded on is that its set of assumptions and principles is not based on normal everyday experience but on strong emotional situations. Magic is characterized by the belief that a wish expressed with strong passion cannot disappoint, rather than by (scientific) recognition of the validity of logic and experience.[89] Religion is different from magic in that it does not serve for the attainment of goals outside it but is instead a collection of actions whose very goal is their performance.[90] The religious ritual is performed for performance's sake, whereas the magic ritual seeks to attain something beyond. This is not the only difference between them. The solutions that magic and religion offer humans differ in almost every possible regard: Magic offers faith in human beings and in their ability to contend with nature through the magic charm in their possession, whereas religion

---

88. Several anthropologists have tried to replace the view of magic as science with one that views it as a kind of technology. See, for instance, Benedict (1933, 40; 1938, 537–639), Firth (1956, 152–85), and Norbeck (1961, 50). See also Wolfson (2001, 96n80). On the other hand, see the reservations of Dorothy Hammond regarding this claim (Hammond 1971, 1354).

89. Nevertheless, Malinowski rejected Lévy-Bruhl's binary distinction between primitive and rational thought. Malinowski acknowledged the primitives' rationality and ascribed a significant role to it in both their thought and their actions (Malinowski 1935, 1: 75–80; 1948, 8–18). On Lévy-Bruhl and the issue of rationality in "primitive peoples," see later discussion in this section.

90. Malinowski (1948, 68). On the function of religion in the primitives' lives, see Malinowski (1948, 35–50). In a later article, Malinowski presented the difference between magic and religion in different terms: "Religion refers to fundamental issues of human existence, while magic always turns round specific, concrete, and detailed problems" (Malinowski 1966, 200). His view of magic, however, did not change.

offers faith in providential supernatural powers, whose help humans must obtain; magic requires defined and limited action, whereas religion is characterized by general and complex action; magic has a restricted myth with only one concern—previous magic successes—whereas religion has a broad and diversified myth. But religion and magic also have something in common: Humans resort to them in the same circumstances of crisis and grave emotional distress.

Malinowski determined that these differences enable us to identify the singular contribution of each cultural domain—magic, religion, and science—to the proper functioning of the tribe and its members. Science is the source of knowledge about the environment. It gives humans an advantage over animals and helps them to survive. Religion serves as a tool for social harmonization. It encourages desirable beliefs and helps the tribe to function properly as a community. Magic strengthens the individuals' belief in their power to overcome crises that their scientific knowledge cannot help to solve. All three, then, uniquely contribute to the proper functioning of the society and to its members' existence.[91]

Alfred Radcliffe-Brown, also a functionalist and indeed one of the most radical, suggests a scheme different from Malinowski's for describing the social function of magic and religion. In his study of the Andaman Islanders in the Gulf of Bengal, Radcliffe-Brown found no grounds in their culture for a distinction between magic and religion. He presents their religious and magic beliefs as part of one conception and describes in similar terms the interpretation of the rituals related to

---

91. Hutton Webster also held that magic is close to science. He argued that its use in productive contexts is accompanied by defined activities based on knowledge and does not replace them. On the one hand, he saw magic as a pseudoscience because, in his view, it is "an inchoate, unorganized mass of beliefs and practices, traditional in character and uncontrolled by experience" (Webster 1948, 497). On the other hand, he praised the role of magic in developing knowledge and crafts among primitive peoples (esp. 497–510). Francis Hsu added his findings to the criticism of several other scholars, above all Evans-Pritchard, concerning the universal generalization of local findings of the type Malinowski had engaged in. In his view, the Chinese community that he studied in the Hunan area made no distinction between magic and scientific behavior, a distinction that fits Malinowski's description. Hsu believed that the reason for this lack of distinction did not lie in the mental difficulties of the community members but in the accepted behavioral dictates of their culture (Hsu 1952, 7–8, 85–96).

them.[92] His comment on the impossibility of defining Andamanian religion on essentialist grounds and on the consequent difficulty of distinguishing religious phenomena from others in their society explicates this trend.[93] His perception of magic rituals as part of religious ritualism and his location of their function in the context of religion at the level of preserving society (rather than the individual) are based on this state of affairs.[94] Radcliffe-Brown confronts Malinowski on two counts. First, he refuses to recognize magic rituals as the source of the individual's psychic strengths and hopes when facing a threatening world. In his view, not only do magic-religious rituals often fail to reduce fears, but they also patently create them and enhance them.[95] He also rejects the very notion of magic functioning at the individual level and entirely removes magic-religious activity in preliterate tribes from the personal level (be it at the technical practical level or at the emotional one). For the first time in the study of magic, Radcliffe-Brown limits its function to the social level: Magic religion, by its very rituality, serves the harmonious existence of the society and thereby its very existence.[96]

About a decade after Malinowski and Radcliffe-Brown returned from their pioneering research voyages in the Indian Ocean islands and began to publish their findings, the talented British anthropologist Edward Evans-Pritchard began his studies in East Africa. Evans-Pritchard's imprint can be detected in almost every anthropological study of magic

---

92. Radcliffe-Brown (1948, 136–85, 229–329). Radcliffe-Brown hardly mentions magic per se in these discussions.

93. Radcliffe-Brown (1948, 405–6).

94. Radcliffe-Brown argued that every society creates for itself a religious pattern that reflects its social structure and thereby turns itself into the object of its members' religious activity. The role of religion, including magic, is therefore to strengthen the social context and to enhance its members' loyalty to the community (Radcliffe-Brown 1958, 108–29; 1965, 117–32). This approach relies on Durkheim-like principles, radicalizing them in a functionalist trend that, as noted, leaves no room for the distinction between individual and community (magic and religion). For an extensive discussion of Radcliffe-Brown's views, see Kuper (1983, 51–88). For a serious critique of them, see Evans-Pritchard (1965, 73–75).

95. Radcliffe-Brown (1965, 148–49). John Beattie also held this view (Beattie 1964, 208).

96. Cf. Middleton (1987, 88–89).

written since he published his book *Witchcraft, Oracles, and Magic Among the Azande* in 1937. Many view this work as the most important and certainly the most influential anthropological study in the area of magic and perhaps in modern anthropology in general.[97] Evans-Pritchard's starting point for the study of magic is entirely different from that of his predecessors. He attempts to examine in the field the view of the French philosopher-sociologist Lucien Lévy-Bruhl about the special mentality of "primitive peoples," of which magic was a prominent manifestation.

Lévy-Bruhl held that attempts to understand the primitive mentality by relying on personal and Western thought ("Why would I act so if I were in their place?") were unfounded to begin with. He claimed that thinking is never private and is always the product of a set of mental and linguistic collective representations of the society a person lives in. These shared representations anticipate private thinking and impose themselves on it. Humans absorb these in their childhood, and their assimilation into their consciousness shapes their worldview according to the collective model within which they grew up. Each society's mental pattern is slightly different, hence the differences in their worldviews. Beyond this, however, humanity can be divided into two main types of societies—primitive and civilized—which are essentially different in their characteristic mental patterns. Western rational thinking is based on logical-scientific categories, whereas primitive thinking operates within a "supernatural," "prelogical," "magic-religious" category. In primitive societies this category of thinking creates a world entirely different from ours.

> The reality surrounding the primitives is itself mystical. Not a single being or object or natural phenomenon in their collective representations is what appears to be in our minds. Almost everything that we perceive therein either escapes their attention or is a matter of indifference to them. On the other hand, they see many things there of which we are unconscious.[98]

---

97. On Evans-Pritchard's scientific endeavor, see Beidelman (1974a; 1974b), Douglas (1980), and Geertz (1988b, 49–72). On Evans-Pritchard's study of the Azande, see Douglas (1980, 46–60) and Kuper (1983, 98–105).

98. Lévy-Bruhl (1985, 38).

The difference between these two types of thinking is evident in both content and structure. Concerning the content, primitive thinking is pervaded by basic assumptions about reality that are entirely alien to Western thought. Concerning the structure, this thinking displays great toleration of factual contradictions within it.

Lévy-Bruhl emphasized that the source of the difference is not biological, as many of his contemporaries then held, but social. A different agreed-on scheme of collective representations developed in each of these types of society, which fashioned different worldviews and different behavior patterns. Hence we cannot describe primitive thinking as irrational or as rationally mistaken, in the sense attached to "rational" thought in Western culture. Primitive thinking has a rationality of its own. At its basis is the law of participation, which implies a linkage between the individual's personality and things in the world. In the primitive mentality the borders of the personality and its links with other parts of reality are different from those accepted in "civilized logic." Hence matters that civilized logic identifies as separate from one another are linked and identified with one another in primitive thought to the point of being perceived as one entity. Rather than retarded development, then, it is the law of participation that is responsible for the essential difference between "primitive" and "civilized" mentality.[99]

---

99. See Cazeneuve (1972), Evans-Pritchard (1965, 78–79), Littleton (1985), Needham (1972, 161–85), and Tambiah (1995, 84–88). Many studies have since been conducted on magic thinking and belief (e.g., Bever 2012, Sørensen 2007, and Vyse 1997). The most relevant to our discussion is Eugene Subbotsky, *Magic and the Mind* (2010). Subbotsky, whose study is based on cognitive and behavioral experiments with children and adults, shows that magic thought, faith, and behavior are dominant in the world of children. At an early age the children's readiness to rely on magic to explain real events equals their readiness to rely on explanations based on scientific causality, even when they have already acquired the latter. Unlike Jean Piaget and other developmental psychologists, however, Subbotsky does not tie the change in the children's worldview to the natural development of their thinking and understanding of the world, which accompanies growth. Rather, he ascribes it to pressures exerted by socialization agents (parents, educators, and other adults), who represent society's scientific and/or religious conceptions. This action is completed in the schooling period, when these pressures succeed in pushing magic thinking and faith to the unconscious, fixating scientific or religious views in the children's consciousness. Subbotsky, then, draws a distinction between science and magic first and then one between magic and religion. He distinguishes

Evans-Pritchard took Lévy-Bruhl's theory seriously but felt uneasy about it in principle. First, he dismissed the notion of all "primitive" contents of thought as "mystical," that is, as involving a belief in the influence of supernatural powers in all matters. At a more fundamental level, Evans-Pritchard was troubled by the idea of mental differences between various human societies touching on the very process of thought. The claim concerning the tolerance of primitive peoples toward contradictions seemed to him especially unfounded.[100] He also held that we should not generalize and speak about primitive thinking. Instead, we should examine in detail the conceptual world of the societies purportedly sharing this type of thought, an endeavor that is only possible by considering how the language, and the concepts it represents, function

---

magic from religion on the basis of their goal as cognitive systems: "Viewing magic as a 'false science' is misleading; magic is more akin to art than to science. . . . Both art and magic imply a fusion between mind and nature. They aim at a different goal than that of science; whereas the ultimate goal of science is product, the ultimate goal of art and magic is meaning" (Subbotsky 2010, xx). By contrast, religion is itself suffused with magic, and the distinction at this level is social: "Two types of magical beliefs can be distinguished from one another. *Non-institutionalized magical beliefs* (NIMBs) are magical beliefs that are unrelated to any 'official' religious doctrine. Most beliefs in mind-over-matter and mind-over-mind in everyday magic (witchcraft, curse powers, astrology, palm reading, and everyday superstitions) belong to NIMBs. In contrast, *institutionalized magical beliefs* are magical beliefs that are accepted by an official religious ideology" (12). The abandonment of magic faith in the Western world, then, is due to the pressures of scientific and religious systems demanding a monopoly on the way individuals explain the workings of the world to themselves and to those surrounding them. When the protection that individuals set up against magic faith begins to crumble under pressure, or when the individuals participating in the experiment have not been educated in Western settings, the growing tendency is to explain events incompatible with the routine working of reality on a magical basis. According to Subbotsky, then, magic is a cognitive system for explaining reality embedded in humans, and its disappearance in Western society is a result of the oppression that other interpretative systems imposed on its members. For Jean Piaget's notion of magic in children's view of reality and for its correlation with Lévy-Bruhl's idea of the primitive's law of participation (but not with animism in general), see Piaget (1997, 123–68, esp. 131–33). Cf. Subbotsky (2010, 18) and Vyse (1997, 139–68).

100. Evans-Pritchard (1970; cf. 1965, 88–90; 1981, 23–34, 128–29).

in the day-to-day life of the society at stake.[101] His fieldwork among the Azande in Sudan was directed precisely to this aim.

Evans-Pritchard chose for his study a society in which witchcraft (meaning maleficence through spiritual means, including divination and the healing magic related to it) was a central concept of the culture and thus a key for understanding its thinking and its worldview. His study proved that, in Azande culture, witchcraft, divination, and magic create a consistent spectrum of beliefs and behaviors whose components are mutually related through logical ties. The views underlying this spectrum are indeed strange and alien to Western thinking, but assuming that they are the given, the internal structure of the theoretical and practical conclusions derived from them do rest on consistent rational thinking. Evans-Pritchard agreed with Lévy-Bruhl that the contents characteristic of this thinking are a social matter. The Azande, then, differ from us in their belief in witchcraft. But once we become used to these contents and accept them as a basis for understanding mishaps and failures in human life, we find that the thinking and the behavior that the Azande derive from them are rational and consistent: "In Zandeland one mystical idea follows on another as reasonably as one common-sense idea follows on another in our own society."[102] This claim, which is the basis for Evans-Pritchard's conclusions on witchcraft among the Azande, is his most important contribution to the comparative study of magic. Although he was in principle opposed to the expansion of local conclusions to a universal theory[103] and although he suggested that his

---

101. Douglas has pointed out the strong similarity between this claim of Evans-Pritchard's and Wittgenstein's method in *Philosophical Investigations* (Douglas 1980, 26–32). Peter Winch, who was influenced by Wittgenstein's fideistic approach, criticized Evans-Pritchard for going only part of the way and leaving the entire linguistic-religious system of the Azande exposed to Western-oriented criticism concerning its fit to "objective reality" (Winch 1964). See also Nielsen (1967).

102. Evans-Pritchard (1937, 541). On the importance that Evans-Pritchard ascribed to the demonstration of this claim, cf. Evans-Pritchard (1951, 98).

103. Evans-Pritchard presented this position in an early study in which he compared his findings on the Azande with those of Malinowski in the Trobriand Islands. He pointed out essential differences between magic activities in these two societies and exposed the problem of generalizing local findings (Evans-Pritchard 1929; cf.

conclusions concern the Azande alone, his findings did put an end to the discussion on the alogical character of magical thought.[104]

Evans-Pritchard's work and his influence on the anthropological study of magic were not limited to the question of rationality. His insights concerning both the method and the contents became corner-stones of anthropological research. Concerning magic, a distinction that he drew based on the language and concepts of the Azande themselves is singularly important. He separated witchcraft, a congenital psycho-physiological feature that enables people to exert maleficent influence on their neighbors through spiritual means, from sorcery, a kind of ritual activity that, among the Azande, is based on the use of plants and is usu-ally accompanied by the uttering of a spell.[105] This distinction splits the broad area of magic into two subareas, which the studied community itself views as different because of the methods typically used in each one of them. This distinction between two subareas in the field of magic was welcomed and yielded extensive anthropological research

---

1931, 23). Evans-Pritchard recurrently argued that the magic phenomenon must always be described and understood in the specific cultural-social context where it is examined.

104. The dispute over the existence of "another" way of thinking obviously did not wane but was denied the element of eliminating rationality among preliterate tribes. Douglas, for example, sought to revive the Lévy-Bruhl type of distinction between primitive and modern perceptions of reality, which had lost all appeal in the second quarter of the twentieth century. In Douglas's view, the term *prelogical* that Lévy-Bruhl used to describe the primitive mentality was the source of the problem and thus so was the comparative method that Lévy-Bruhl adopted. Lévy-Bruhl's definition of *prelogical* and his method no longer seemed appealing because of Evans-Pritchard's scathing cri-tique, but Douglas thought that this was unjustified. In her view, comparative research is justified and shows that primitive societies do indeed perceive reality in terms essen-tially different from those accepted in modern society. The reason is these societies' level of differentiation, which is unlike that in the West: "Progress means differentia-tion. Thus primitive means undifferentiated; modern means differentiated" (Douglas 2002, 96). The advantage of Douglas's method is that she exchanges the binary distinc-tion between cultures for a perception that places them on a developmental continuum on the differentiation axis. Douglas holds that we should acknowledge the existence of this development, in which social, economic, and intellectual differentiation processes occur simultaneously, but without adding patronizing Western judgments to it (91–116).

105. Evans-Pritchard (1937, mainly 9, 21–39, 387).

on witchcraft throughout the world.[106] One significant implication of this development was an analysis of the social contexts of witchcraft accusations. The contributions of Stanley Tambiah, Edmund Leach, and Mary Douglas to this analysis are especially interesting.

By re-decoding the data presented by Malinowski, Tambiah pointed to the distinction that Trobriand tribes draw between female witchcraft and male sorcery. Female witchcraft is inherited, based on an inner power related to childbearing and tied to threatening supernatural capabilities, such as disappearance and flight, as well as to cannibalism. Its action is always destructive. It is dangerous, subversive, and hence illegitimate. Male sorcery, by contrast, is scholarly knowledge. It is an acquired legitimate asset whose use is a source of pride and displayed social power, which serves to preserve the established social order and is in turn supported by it. The danger entailed by it is accepted as part of its general constructive function that, inter alia, serves for protection and salvation from the witches' harm.[107]

Leach clarified the topology of links between the two kinds of "supernatural influence"—controlled or uncontrolled—and the social position of the possessors of these powers in the political system of a given society. His claim was that controlled supernatural power is to be found at the foci of the political authority that define the society's structure, whereas uncontrolled powers are ascribed to elements that are not part of the social power structure as defined through the kinship ties common in the society. Accusations of witchcraft (i.e., of possessing an uncontrolled supernatural power that at times erupts from the person holding it without ill intentions and even without this person's knowledge) occur in the society between subgroups joined by kinship ties, which leave the accused outside the accusers' authority structure. Controlled supernatural power, which can be identified with sorcery, is the

---

106. This segment of the supernatural emerged as an essential component of almost all tribal cultures in Africa as well as in North America. The research on this issue is extensive. On witchcraft in Africa, see, for example, Crawford (1967), Marwick (1970; 1987), Middleton (1967), and Middleton and Winter (1963). On witchcraft in North America, see Kluckhohn (1967) and Walker (1970). Cf. in the context of the Trobriand Islands, Tambiah (1985a).

107. Tambiah (1985a).

opposite of witchcraft, because it is ascribed to those in authority in the society's kinship structure.[108]

Douglas developed this view into a claim about the connection between accusations of witchcraft and the accused's social standing. An accusation of possessing uncontrolled maleficent powers is tantamount to a call to order of elements whose social status is vague. Douglas identifies witchcraft with blurred social belongingness, pollution, lack of structure, and margins whose power threatens the structure and the individuals in authority who guide it and officiate. These individuals hold the controlled supernatural power that is the antithesis of witchcraft. This contrast does not reflect the aim of using power—benefit as opposed to harm. Controlled power can harm too. Rather, the contrast between the two types of power lies in the social membership of their bearers. Social ambiguity is identified with uncontrolled and hence threatening supernatural power. The structure (and its political representatives) protects itself from this ambiguity through controlled, restrained, and organized power.[109]

Evans-Pritchard's conclusions concerning the social function of the beliefs and behavioral systems related to witchcraft also had a decisive influence on the research.[110] One of his most significant conclusions was that the belief in witchcraft and all it entailed functioned as an element that endowed reality with meaning. Evans-Pritchard showed that the Azande belief that an act of witchcraft was behind every mishap or crisis excluded these events from the realm of arbitrariness and random causality, explaining them in a way that facilitated coping with them actively and satisfactorily. Evans-Pritchard recurrently emphasized that the Azande understood the direct and natural cause of the negative event. They identified the link between the snakebite and the illness or between the obstruction on the track and the injury inflicted, but they were not satisfied with this level of understanding and sought an explanation of

108. Leach (1966, esp. 21–27).
109. Douglas (2002, 125–40).
110. See, for example, Leach (1966), Norbeck (1961, 188–212), O'Keefe (1982, 414–75), Swanson (1960, 137–52), Tambiah (1985a), Wallace (1966, 180–184), and Whiting (1950). See also Crawford (1967), Kluckhohn (1967), Marwick (1970; 1987), Middleton (1967), Middleton and Winter (1963), and Walker (1970).

the event's occurrence: Why did the snake bite *me*? How did it happen that *I* was the one involved in an accident? The Azande answered such questions as "Why here?" "Why now?" "Why me?" on two levels: One details the natural circumstances of the mishap, and the other determines that, in the background of the event, there is an act of witchcraft. Once the Azande determined this, they could deal with the problem to prevent painful occurrences in the future.[111]

Claude Lévi-Strauss expanded this claim into a theory of magic in general. In his article "The Sorcerer and His Magic," he traces the source of the belief in magic held by the tribe members and by the sorcerer himself. He concludes that this belief rests on a deep psychological need to organize the chaos that prevails in reality and in the human soul and to endow it with meaning. In his view, magic thinking is an intermediate path between normal thinking, which seeks meaning in the world, and pathological thinking, which suffers from an excess of internal meaning: "For only the history of the symbolic function can allow us to understand the intellectual condition of man, in which the universe is never charged with sufficient meaning and in which the mind always has more meanings available than there are objects to which to relate them."[112] Magic bridges this gap. It provides a stable social pattern that enables humans to organize the chaos of reality and, more important, enables them to organize the closed and painful feelings evoked by the encounter with the external chaos.

Although Evans-Pritchard does not explicitly discuss the connection between religion and magic, his works and the method he adopted reveal his view on the matter. He felt no need to connect these phenomena, as evidenced by the facts that he devoted a comprehensive study to witchcraft and sorcery in the Azande tribe without tying it to a discussion of their religion and that he wrote a profound analysis of the religion of the Nuer without dealing with their magic.[113] In truth, this was

---

111. Evans-Pritchard (1937, 63–83). Jeanne Favret-Saada pointed to a similar mechanism, widespread among peasants from the Bocage area of France in the 1970s, for explaining recurrent incidents of mishap and pain as well as their treatment (Favret-Saada 1980).

112. Lévi-Strauss (1963, 184).

113. Evans-Pritchard (1956).

not a feeling but a strict and consistent research method, which required the scholar to determine such links based only on their existence in the inner conceptual world of the society examined. In his book on the Azande Evans-Pritchard writes, "Magic is the chief foe of witchcraft, and it would be useless to describe Zande magical rites and notions had their beliefs in witches not previously been recorded."[114] But their religion, according to their worldview and their conceptual framework, is not related to their magic and therefore the discussion of witchcraft and sorcery in their culture does not require Evans-Pritchard to address their religion or to determine its place in their regard.

Precisely the same method guided Evans-Pritchard in his study of the Nuer tribe: "The rites these people perform might be classed, according to some definitions of the term, as magic, but in the Nuer classification, which is the one we have to follow if we are to delineate their thought and not our own, we are still concerned with a relationship between man and *kwoth*."[115] Evans-Pritchard, then, demands that cultural phenomena be discussed only according to the inner conceptual world of the society studied. A general theory about the relationship of magic and religion is impossible, because the question—and the answer to it—must always depend on a specific cultural context. Any deviation from this rule means a mistaken and misleading projection of concepts from one culture to another or, even worse, a projection of the researcher's concepts onto the objects of the research.[116]

This demand of Evans-Pritchard's deeply influenced the types of solutions that anthropologists suggested to the problem of the magic-religion relationship but did not lessen the controversy between them. Before examining this change, however, we should briefly consider the development of the discussion on the rationality of magic thinking. Stanley Tambiah is among the more prominent scholars concerned with this question.

---

114. Evans-Pritchard (1937, 387).

115. Evans-Pritchard (1956, 95). *Kwoth* in the Nuer language means "god" or "spirits."

116. This methodological problem concerned anthropological research in general. Leach, for example, formulated a critique similar to that of Evans-Pritchard concerning the study of kinship ties (Leach 1966, 1–27).

Tambiah is one of the most distinguished contemporary anthropologists to offer a new and original view of magic. His main concern was decoding the magical mentality and its relationship with the scientific mentality. At the basis of his method is a moderately relativistic approach, which led him to a discussion of rationality, the ability to evaluate cultures on a commensurable basis, and the possibility of translating one culture into another's concepts.[117] Tambiah's starting point for the discussion of sorcery is that we cannot examine magic mentality with the criteria of scientific mentality. In his view, analogical thinking, which is a conspicuous feature of magic mentality, is one of the modes of human thinking in general, including scientific thinking. The difference between magic analogical thinking and scientific analogical thinking is the kind of analogy that appears in each of them. Scientific thinking uses predictive analogy, whereas in magic thinking persuasive analogy is common. This difference creates different thinking patterns, and therefore examining and hence judging magic analogical thinking using the criteria of scientific thinking is pointless. From this perspective, Tambiah criticizes Evans-Pritchard for examining Azande healing from a perspective that is too Western. In his view, the basis of the problem is Evans-Pritchard's attempt to understand and classify the phenomenon according to the Western criteria of "ritual" and "empirical." This way of looking at magic healing and the negligible value that Evans-Pritchard assigned to the semantics of the ritual led him to disregard the unique analogical thinking of magic healing, even though his findings patently attested to its presence. Tambiah is even more critical of Robin Horton's attempt to expose the rationality underlying the thinking of indigenous Africans and compare it to Western scientific thinking.[118]

---

117. On Tambiah's place in the relativism scale, see his statement in Tambiah (1995, 129); for a discussion of relativism in the context of the study of culture, see Tambiah (1995, chaps. 5 and 6). The studies of Clifford Geertz are prominent expressions of this approach. See, for example, Geertz (1973; 1988a). On the relativistic approach in general, see Brandt (1967), Harre and Krausz (1996), and Popkin (1987). For a focused discussion on the question of rationality and relativism, see, for example, Hollis and Lukes (1982) and Tambiah (1995, 111–39, 166n7).

118. Tambiah (1973; 1995, 90–93, 131–32). Cf. Horton (1967; 1968; 1973). Raymond Firth also suggested an approach similar to those of Evans-Pritchard and Horton concerning the rationality of primitive thinking. He absolutely rejected Lévy-Bruhl's

The implications of this approach for the magic act are clear. Because the magic ritual rests on a thought pattern that differs from the scientific one, there is no room for examining it through such concepts as correct/incorrect or true/false. These concepts were created in scientific thinking, and they therefore suit only this type of thinking. Their use in the study of magic, which is ruled by another type of analogical thinking, necessarily leads us to describe magic as an incomplete science—an act that fails to generate causal influence. But this conclusion is irrelevant to magic. It follows from mistakenly including magic in a domain of thought that is alien to it and from judging magic as though it were part of this domain. The semantics of magic rests on persuasive analogy and must therefore be examined by comparison to another cultural domain where such an analogy does exist rather than by comparison to science. Performative speech, according to Tambiah, is such a domain. Tambiah, then, enlists the speech act theory developed by John Austin to examine magic and seeks to show that the most appropriate way of describing the magic ritual is to present it as a performative utterance.[119] As such, judging the ritual by the criteria of Western technology is obviously pointless; instead, we should evaluate it in light of prevailing social norms. The only significant question bearing on the validity and the results of magic speech is the extent to which it fits the social convention that defines the proper mode of expressing performative utterances within whose context it is performed.[120]

In his book *Magic, Science, Religion, and the Scope of Rationality* (1995), Tambiah sums up his view on the link between rationality and the ways of organizing reality, as he puts it, of which magic thinking is one of the most prominent. He argues that these ways, which were observed and

---

approach and opposed the distinction between magic and religion relying on the rationality criterion, claiming that the magic thinking and actions of preliterate tribes are based on rational thought (Firth 1956, 152–85). Tambiah does not refer to this chapter in Firth's studies, but it is plausible that he would reject its conclusions too.

119. On speech act theory and its applications to the study of ritual (including Tambiah's view), see chapter 4.

120. Tambiah (1973, 218–27). Tambiah adopted the performative approach in his research on ritual as well. See Tambiah (1985b).

presented in many anthropological studies, are always a result of the culture in which people acquire their conceptual world. Tambiah proposes recognizing at least two such ways, which differ sharply from one another according to the central thought category at their respective bases: causality or participation. Given that, in his view, the commensurability of cultures is limited, Tambiah determines that explaining and evaluating one system of organizing reality through the concepts of another is impossible. This applies to religion, whose "metaphysical springs and conceptions . . . cannot be explained in terms of the positivist tests of truth falsity,"[121] no less than to magic. For Tambiah, both these phenomena convey participatory thinking, which establishes in human consciousness an organization of reality alternative to the scientific one.

The mutual relationships between magic and religion continued to occupy scholars of culture—historians, anthropologists, and sociologists—in the second half of the twentieth century. Although the lion's share of this work was conducted in the first half of the century, its echoes resonate in everything that has been written about magic up to today. Both trends—distinction and unification—remained in place, but the balance of power between the supporters of each trend changed drastically. Suggestions about essentialist distinctions between magic and religion came up repeatedly. The more prominent among them are the works of Misha Titiev and William Goode.

Titiev suggests distinguishing between magic and religion according to their performative contexts. Religion is the ritual activity that is performed cyclically. Its performance, which recurs and is based on the yearly calendar, is detached from concrete needs and communal or personal events. As such, it always serves the entire community. By contrast, magic is the critical ritual activity that follows from crises or concrete and actual needs. It serves those who experience such needs: the entire community or, as is usually the case, individuals in it. Titiev holds that even when the cyclical rituals of a society disappear and are replaced by others as a result of the weakening of its identity (as was the case in many African societies, for instance), the critical rituals common in the society remain

---

121. Tambiah (1995, 154).

in place. He takes this as evidence of the real distinction between these two kinds of ritual activity.[122]

Goode's suggestion is less radical. He holds that magic and religion should be viewed as phenomena on a continuum of ritual behavior. The dichotomous distinction between magic and religious rituals is therefore pointless. Both are invariably found at some point in the magic-religion continuum and combine elements from both phenomena. The amount of magic and religious elements in each given ritual determines its location on the axis whose extremes are magic and religion.[123]

At the same time, opponents of this view became more dominant. William Warner and Raymond Firth, for instance, report that in the communities they studied (Australian and Polynesian) no essential difference could be discerned between magic and religion.[124] Robin Horton identifies both phenomena when he defines religion "as an extension of the field of people's social relationships beyond the confines of purely human society. . . . This extension must be one in which human beings involved see themselves in a dependent position vis-à-vis their non-human alters."[125] Melville Herskovits argues that, for the Dahomey (in West Africa), magic is an integral part of religion.[126] Peter Worsley

---

122. Titiev (1960). To corroborate his claim, Titiev showed that preliterate tribes also have a calendar, even if extremely simple. He also tried to show that the essentialist criteria that had traditionally been used to distinguish magic from religion were all derived from the distinction he suggested. In this context, note Crawford's claim concerning the Shona tribe in Zimbabwe, that their religion had significantly changed after seventy years of Christian missionary work but that their magic had remained unaltered (Crawford 1967, 90–91).

123. Goode (1949; 1951, 52–54). Goode developed a suggestion similar to that of Benedict. See Benedict (1933, 40; 1938, 647). Cf. also Firth (1956, 152–58). Peter Schäfer attempted to apply Goode's suggestion to Jewish magic. See the discussion in chapter 2. The problem with Goode's elegant solution is obviously the assumption of the a priori essences "religion" and "magic" at the extremes of the continuum, essences that dictate the place of any ritual at some point in between. On additional suggestions for an essentialist distinction between magic and religion, see Middleton (1967, ix) and Munday (1956, 18).

124. Firth (1967, 196); Warner (1958, 223–42, esp. 229).

125. Horton (1960, 211, 218–20).

126. See Herskovits (1938, 2: 262). Herskovits later developed his claim into a generalized approach on the function of magic within religion (Herskovits 1952, 359–60).

argues (in the wake of his study in Melanesia) that magic and religious aspects are invariably found together and, in the ritual domain, are mutually complementary.[127] John Beattie states that all attempts to distinguish religion from magic are arbitrary; he limits the difference between them by suggesting that magic-religious activity can be distinguished from technical activity according to the presence of symbolic elements.[128] Francis Hsu (in the context of his study in China) writes that any criterion we choose will bring us to the recognition that magic and religion must always be treated as one phenomenon—magic-religious.[129]

Hsu's approach goes beyond the analysis of specific fieldwork findings and culminates in methodological and cross-cultural research. One notable example of it is the work of Rosalie Wax and Morrie Wax, who argue that underlying the distinctions between magic, religion, and science is a Western, modern conceptual system that scholars bring with them to the field of research rather than the conceptual system of the societies they study.[130] Dorothy Hammond sharpens this approach in her statement that the magic-religion question is merely a "semantic problem." She criticizes scholars' use of these terms in the denotation common in their culture to create universal theories on the subject. In her view, magic is neither different nor opposed to religion but part of it. Hence the relevant question is, What is the place of the part in the whole? Hammond's solution is a view of religion as a system determined by three concepts of power: personal power, impersonal power (such as mana), and magic power. Magic represents the human power to act in order to

---

127. Worsley (1968, xxviii).

128. Beattie (1964, 202–12). Despite his claims about the arbitrariness of the distinction between magic and religion and despite being aware of the methodological complication entailed, Beattie preserves the distinction and discusses magic (symbolic activity in relation to an impersonal power) separately from religion (symbolic activity in relation to a personal being) (Beattie 1964, 212–40). In any event, Beattie's view concerning the expressive function of magic distinguishes his perception from those of Frazer and Benedict, who, as noted, also distinguished magic from religion on the basis of the personal or impersonal character of the powers that humans seek to activate.

129. Hsu (1952, 1–8).

130. Wax and Wax (1961–1962; 1963).

influence and change reality. In that, it differs from other areas of religion, such as prayer or sacrifice, which represent other kinds of power.[131] Other scholars, among them Karl Rosengren and Michael Winkelman, support the view denying any essential distinction between magic and religion.[132]

We can therefore sum up and determine that, in the second half of the twentieth century, the view seeking to dismiss the distinction between religion and magic overrides the one seeking to preserve it and specify it. Fundamental to this trend are Evans-Pritchard's methodological claims. They set in motion a process of scholars reconsidering the terminology they use in their studies and an awareness of the danger entailed by the projection of their conceptual world onto the objects of their research. Tambiah successfully showed that the roots of this semantics are deeply embedded in Christianity's puristic views. The Protestant distinction between philosophical and ethical elements, as opposed to the performative system of sacraments and other Catholic power symbols, gave rise to a judgmental view of all manifestations of Christianity. This view relies on the determination of a border between the spiritual true inner essence of religion and alien appendices that Christianity absorbed from pagans and barbarians, corrupting itself in the process. This distinction, intertwined with the identity of the scholars and with their educational background, is the basis for the semantics they use in their studies to describe phenomena such as magic and religion.[133] And it is this semantics they

---

131. Hammond (1971) relies on Edward Norbeck's view of religion (Norbeck 1961, 49).

132. See Rosengren (1976) and Winkelman (1982). Winkelman rejected the basic scholarly assumption denying any direct causal link between magic action and a specific result. He argued that blending anthropological observations in the realm of magic with findings and theories of experimental parapsychology suggests the possibility that magic does have concrete influence. This influence follows from the universal human ability related to the psi power (Winkelman 1982, 44). On the psi, a central term in the theory of experimental parapsychology, and on the way magic powers can be connected to it, see Winkelman (1983). For reflections in this regard concerning Judaism, see Bazak (1972).

133. Tambiah (1995, 16–31). Cf. Douglas (2002, 8–35). For an excellent concise review of magic in the medieval Catholic Church and the change brought about by the Reformation, see K. Thomas (1971, 25–77).

want to deny altogether. Olof Pettersson formulates this demand in particularly extreme terms.

> The study of comparative religion would win on clearance, honesty and stringency, the aspects of valuation would be avoided etc. if the term "magic" were "given a decent burial" . . . in the scientific debate of the nature of religion.[134]

This insight, like many of the others presented in this chapter, found its way into the historical study of magic as well. Scholars of antiquity were indeed enclosed in libraries and in museum warehouses in search of sources for their studies, but they were extremely attentive to developments outside. As I will show in chapter 2, echoes of the increasingly diversifying controversy on the essence of magic and its place with respect to religion resonate strongly in writings about magic in late antiquity in general and about Jewish magic in particular.

---

134. Pettersson (1957, 119).

Magic, Mysticism, Religion, and Society

The Study of Early Jewish Magic

The study of Jewish magic in late antiquity and the early Islamic period—a time span extending from the Mishnah to the "classic" Genizah period— has changed profoundly in recent decades, both textually and method- ologically. Textually, the number of publications dealing with primary magic literature—particularly incantation bowls, amulets, and books of magical recipes—has grown dramatically. Methodologically, the apolo- getic approach that had sought to exonerate Judaism (or at the least the rabbis who founded its talmudic version) from any concern with such "nonsense" has been replaced with an approach that favors reexamining the role of magic in the rabbis' web of life, creativity, and controversies, applying the tools used in social and cultural studies. These changes are not detached from one another or from the study of magic outside Juda- ism. Publication of magic findings, including or beside the Jewish mystic/ magic ancient texts of *Hekhalot* and *Merkavah* literature, reveals the exis- tence of a developed and scholastic magic that is specifically Jewish. This culture could no longer be marginalized as a set of folk superstitions or a foreign influence that had gained access to Judaism by exploiting the ignorance of backward social strata. These primary (*insider*) writings pro- vide firsthand knowledge about a Jewish culture of magic, enabling the reexamination of secondary (*outsider*) sources and, above all, the rabbinic literature that in the past had been the main and almost sole source for the study of the subject.

In turn, this research was influenced not only by the primary evidence but also by the general spirit dominating the study of culture in general and its expressions in the study of magic and religion in particular. More restrictive views of the gap between magic and religion replaced the presumptuous approach determining an absolute distinction between them, which viewed "Judaism" as a (sublime) religion and magic as wild weeds growing on its margins. This change reflects the penetration of trends prevalent in the study of culture into Jewish studies—the study of the "other," of power, of the body, of gender—and their growing impact on the deconstruction of the unifying and judgmental (true-false, proper-improper) traditional discourse dominating the study of Judaism in general and rabbinic literature in particular. Thus, holding the picture of Jewish magic in one hand and methodologies from social and cultural studies in the other, several scholars turned to the traditional sources and shed new light on their perception of magic. In so doing, they followed a trail parallel to the one that had been blazed several decades earlier in the comparative study of magic, whose principles had already been adopted and applied to the study of magic in the Hellenistic world.

In this chapter I review the history of the study of magic in Judaism in late antiquity and the early Islamic period from the perspective of the definition of magic and its relationship to religion in three realms: rabbinic literature, ancient mystical literature, and magic literature.[1] By way of introduction, I briefly present the main trends in the study of magic in the Hellenistic world, which is a constant horizon of reference and comparison for scholars of Jewish magic. This review will point to local expressions of the broader changes discussed in chapter 1.

---

1. For an updated annotated bibliography on ancient Jewish magic, see Bohak (2012a). The periodization terminology used throughout this study refers to the geographic and cultural contexts of its sources. I have systematically favored the term *early Islamic period* over the *early Middle Ages* for referring to the period from the rise of Islam to that of the classical Genizah period (seventh–thirteenth centuries) in the area between Babylonia and North Africa.

CHAPTER 2

MAGIC IN THE GRECO-ROMAN WORLD: AIMS OF THE RESEARCH

In chapter 1 I discussed the changes recorded during the twentieth century in the understanding of magic's essence as such and of its relationships with other systems of knowledge and action—religion and science. The diverse research methods mentioned include ethnography, sociology, psychology, anthropology, and the comparative study of culture. All these studies share one feature: They are based on testimonies about rituals and beliefs in use in living societies. But the study of magic in antiquity is fundamentally different. The only sources where we can learn about it are textual remnants and objects tied or related to phenomena that interest the scholars. Fundamentally, scholars of magic in late antiquity are philologists and epigraphers, trained in deciphering writings in the languages of the ancient world and in offering translations of the original texts in modern languages.[2] At this stage, either they or others can add their own interpretations of these writings and turn them from textual raw material into stones in the historical mosaic of the cultures they study. It is at this stage that scholars must choose their course and their words and decide on the question, what is the phenomenon that the text expresses? That is, what beliefs, values, or acts does it reflect? To what realm of the culture does the text belong? These are the questions that guide and enrich the discussion of magic as a live phenomenon, but with one essential difference. Cultural anthropologists, if they are working as they should, to some extent assimilate into the society they examine. They can form their own impressions about the elements of the culture, ask members of the society for explanations concerning the meaning and the broader context of elements that interest them, and even examine these members' reactions to their own hermeneutical insights (within the well-known limitations of participatory observation). Researchers of magic and religion in antiquity know the cultures that they study mainly through the mediation of writing. The information available to them is fixed,

---

2. Objects also play a significant role in the exposure and description of ancient cultures. Their meaning, however, is always determined through an interpretive process based on the scholar's previous knowledge of the culture in whose context they are discussed, a knowledge based on texts.

70

partial, and detached from its natural context in life. A further obstacle is that in antiquity not everyone could write. The beliefs, rituals, and controversies recorded in the texts of the period are those of the writing classes—the political and religious establishments and the scholars who attached themselves to them. The "common people" did not write and, by definition, had no part in the processes of fixating and preserving the records of their culture in the cumulative textual knowledge of the West. Although this issue does not generally bother researchers, it does at times create a bias in the description of ancient cultures, which is structured by the character of the sources.

Evolutionist approaches of the type discussed in chapter 1 also encouraged the thinking that, religiously, ancient culture developed from low to high, that is, from idolatry to monotheism and from a carnal to a spiritual covenant. On the other hand, secularization and the development of science increased admiration for the Greco-Roman culture that had been eradicated by the medieval church, elements of which became a cultural paradigm for European elites from the Renaissance onward. Many European libraries hold writings originating in the Greco-Roman world, and dealing with them means diverting perspectives and making new choices concerning the "worthy" corpus. Here, too, the higher classes mediate between the culture studied and its exposed or constructed picture, on two levels. First, literature, philosophy, law, and science were created and written by the highly educated class and preserved (in the context of the evolution of knowledge) in institutions that wielded economic and political power. Second, scholars dealing with Greco-Roman culture themselves belong to such strata and institutions, which are highly interested (not necessarily explicitly or even consciously) in fixating class distinctions. The identification of European learned elites with the culture of the educated strata in the ancient world and the clear distinction between the elites and the "vulgar culture" of the masses derived from elitist approaches and, in turn, served them. "Classic culture" was thus the culture of the higher classes in the Greco-Roman world (actually only part of it). Their religion did have a pagan orientation, but in all other regards they were perceived as the harbingers of the latest and most "developed" stage of the culture—the stage of secularization, beauty, and science.

This picture began to change in the nineteenth century. The European concern with the treasures of the past, particularly in its economic aspect, encouraged widespread local interest in the search for antiquities and in their sale. A growing stream of texts and objects, among them many forgeries that deceived both collectors and scholars, made their way to the West. Beside personal initiatives, archaeology began to take its first steps. A long series of organized excavations yielded a vast quantity of findings, which were carefully recorded and studied. These findings contributed to the development of new research fields, such as Egyptology and Oriental studies. Regarding the Greco-Roman world, these research fields enriched and diversified existing knowledge. The picture of classic culture broadened, and new questions found their way to center stage. The magic evidence was among the most prominent and intriguing of these questions. Thousands of magic objects and hundreds of magic recipes and passages from magic writings were found and deciphered. Thus a broad area of ritual activity that had been known only indirectly until then (i.e., from outsider description) merited its own definition: Hellenistic magic.

The more the corpus of primary insider sources expanded, the less researchers required the external, familiar classic sources (which mentioned magic and magicians, described them, expressed their views on them, or determined their legal status) to describe Hellenistic magic. The classic sources became used mainly in the reexamination of the cultural and social contexts of magic activity: What was the role of magic rituals, objects, and agents in Greco-Roman culture? How can we explain the gap between the legitimate status of the official (meaning religious) ritual practices and the repudiation of magic and the legal prohibition to perform it? Was the difference between religion and magic a matter of essence or of place in the web of power and social interests? The answers to these questions will be shown to correlate significantly with the thought methods touching on them in the broader comparative context (discussed in chapter 1).[3]

---

3. The study of magic in Mesopotamia focuses mainly on the publication of texts and on their textual and linguistic study. Comprehensive reviews of Mesopotamian magic and witchcraft are rare, and the discussion of the relationship between magic and religion in Mesopotamia is only beginning. See Schmitt (2004, 51–57) and Thomsen (2001, 22–23, and 18–95 for an extensive discussion of this topic). Also cf. Geller (2010), Erica Reiner (1995), and van Binsbergen and Wiggermann (1999). Magic and adjacent

Hellenistic magic was a complex system of rituals, beliefs, objects, and power agents. We learn about it from Greek and Coptic magical papyri, from curse tablets (*defixiones*) and voodoo dolls, from amulets, gems, and jewelry for protection and healing, and from literary testimonies.[4] Its foundations can be traced back to the dawn of Greek culture, but its image in the Greco-Roman world was decisively influenced by Egyptian magic.[5] In late antiquity, Egypt was considered the cradle of magic,

---

areas (demonology, divination) in the Bible have been the subject of relatively extensive study. A comprehensive review had already appeared by the beginning of the twentieth century: Thompson (1908). For early discussions of biblical magic, demonology, and divination, see Kaufmann (1955, vol. 1, 286–303, 350–96, 425–35, 458–532). Cf. the concise English translation: Kaufmann (1960, 21–24, 40–53, 63–101). For updated studies and further bibliography, see Cryer (1994; 2001), Jeffers (1996), and Schmitt (2004). On magic in ancient Egypt, see later discussion.

4. The research literature on these sources is vast. The following bibliography is merely the tip of the iceberg. For extensive reviews and detailed bibliographical research (until the mid-1990s) of the Greek and Coptic magical papyri, see Brashear (1995) and Pernigotti (1995). For annotated editions of the texts, see Betz (1986), Kropp (1930–1931), and Preisendanz (1973–1974). On the later Egyptian magic recorded in Demotic magical papyri from late antiquity, see Betz (1986), Dieleman (2005), Johnson (1986), and Ritner (1995). On Coptic Christian magic texts, see Meyer and Smith (1994). For large collections of *defixiones* and the main discussions on them, see Audollent (1904), Gager (1992), Graf (1997, 118–74), D. Jordan (1985a; 1985b), Preisendanz (1972), Tomlin (1988), and Wünsch (1897). For collections of amulets, see Daniel and Maltomini (1990–1992) and Kotansky (1994; 1995). On collections of magic gems, see Bonner (1950), Hamburger (1968), Simone (2001), and Spier (2007); see also Aune (1980, 1517n33). On magic in Greco-Roman literature and its research, see Caro-Baroja (1971, 24–40), Dickie (2001), J. Ferguson (1989, 147–58), Graf (1997, 175–204), Lowe (1929), Luck (1986), and Ogden (2002).

5. On the antiquity of Greek magic, see Luck (1986) and Ogden (2002). See also Burkert (1995, 41–87), Burn (1966, 82–102), Faraone (1993), and Lain-Entralgo (1970). Chester Starr points to the escalation of magic at the end of the eighth and beginning of the seventh centuries BCE and ties it to the anxiety and the tension that, in his view, characterized this period (Starr 1991, 279). Eric Dodds points to a similar process during the fourth century BCE. He holds that the growing strength of magic at this time should be explained on two levels: (1) a reaction of the "second generation" to the intellectual flowering of the previous century and (2) the continued struggle in the Peloponnese, which gave rise to anxiety and superstitions on the one hand and the weakening of traditional religion on the other (Dodds 1959, 194–95). Martin Nilsson connects the strengthening of magic in the fourth century BCE to the weakening of traditional religion (Nilsson 1940, 115). Christopher Faraone, however, suggests viewing the apparent

"the mother of poets, and wise men, and magicians, the inventor of every kind of sorcery and propagator thereof among all others."[6] Already at the beginning of the sixth century BCE, we find evidence of Egyptian influence on Greek magic healing. As the ties between the two cultures became stronger, so did the Greek processes of absorbing and elaborating Egyptian magic practices and beliefs, culminating in the creation of a new, vital Hellenistic magic layer atop the foundations of ancient Egyptian magic.[7]

Scholars claim that pointing to any conceptual or practical difference between magic and religion in these two sources of Hellenistic magic, the Greek and the Egyptian, is difficult and at times impossible. The broad consensus on ancient Egyptian magic is that its worldview and its practice were pervaded to such an extent by what we tend today to call magic that it can be described as magic performed in the temple by priests.[8] As for ancient Greek culture, agreement is not as broad. Several views have been suggested to explain the blend that emerged between magic, rite, and myth. One line of thinking holds that there was a his-

---

waves of growth and decline of magic in the Greek world as an artificial product of the written sources' irregular pattern in their approach to an ongoing phenomenon (Faraone 1992, 114).

6. As spoken by John Chrysostom, the Archbishop of Constantinople at the end of the fourth century CE, in his homilies on Matthew (homily VIII, 6). See Schaff (1978, 53). A similar view prevailed among Jews as well. The saying "Ten measures of witchcraft descended to the world, nine were taken by Egypt [and the remaining one by the entire world]" (TB *Kiddushin* 49b) succinctly sums it up. Additional sayings of this kind appear throughout rabbinic literature. See Blau (1898, 37–49) and Bohak (2000, 220–21). On this view among Greeks and Romans, see Brashear (1995, 3390n3).

7. See, for example, Betz (1991, 253–54), Brashear (1995, 3390–95), Burkert (1987, 20–21), Fowden (1993, 65–67, 79–87), Lane-Fox (1987, 36–37), and Ritner (1995, 3358–71; 1993, 99–102). On Babylonian influences on Greek magic, see Burkert (1995, 41–87).

8. See, for example, Budge (1934, 113–36; 1991, xi–xix and passim), Gardiner (1951), Pinch (1994, 9–17, 47–60), and Ritner (1992; 1995, 3353–55). Scholars did not always accept this approach. At the end of the nineteenth and beginning of the twentieth centuries, we find attempts to differentiate between magic and religion in Egypt and even to determine various courses for their separate historical development. See Budge (1934, 114–18 and 130) for his distinction between the priests-magi and the charlatans and his determination that the priests-magi sought to institutionalize their practices as a "religious science." Cf. Schmitt (2004, 42–51).

torical development from the stage of magic practices to a religious stage, where performance of these practices was transferred to an official establishment. Other scholars suggest that the basis for the blending is the absorption of remnants from the magic layer, which the Hellenes inherited when invading Greece, into the institutionalized religion that they brought with them. Yet others suggest that the source is the decline of religion to the level of magic customs originating in *theurgia* (controlling and activating the gods) and ending up with *goêteia* (witchcraft). All agree, however, that already by an early stage in the development of Greek culture, we find an indistinguishable blend of the official, established religion with magic practices within or around religion.[9]

The claim that magic cannot be distinguished from religion in Greek culture obviously assumes their separate, discrete existence at the theoretical level that serves the discussion. Indeed, the words *mageia* and *magia* do appear in Greek and Latin writings and hint at the existence of a separate magic phenomenon. But what was this phenomenon? In particular, what distinguished it from other close phenomena (such as religious ritual) so that it merited its own name? Scholars naturally resort here to the usual, stereotypical images of magic and religion, suggesting such criteria as automatism (as opposed to addressing the supreme will) or aggressiveness (as opposed to submission and gratitude). The theoretical level, as expected, reflects the conceptual system of the scholars themselves, an insight that evokes wide criticism. More and more claims have stated that nothing useful would come from the a priori projection onto Greco-Roman culture of the magic-religion dichotomy typical of Western modern thought. Scholars who endorsed this position did not dismiss the distinction between magic and religion because these had native names of their own. They did hold, however, that this distinction should be understood by tracking down the speakers' own use of these terms, and even this use should be understood only in the concrete contexts where the terms *magia* or *mageia* appear. As Charles Philips indicated, "The antithesis of magic and religion has value only if qualified by an

---

9. On the historical development option, see Dodds (1973, 148), Nilsson (1940, 7, 29; 1964, 87–89, 97), and Starr (1991, 179). On the absorption of magic remnants option, see Luck (1986, 7–9). On the decline of religion option, see Barb (1963, 100–101).

understanding of the ways a particular social group employed the distinction."[10]

An examination of how *magia* and *mageia* are used in late antiquity shows that they are tied mainly to individual or official hostility. Their clear context was legislative: laws against sorcery on the one hand and accusations of sorcery, meaning transgressions of these laws, on the other.[11] A comparison between the forbidden magic practices described in these sources and the official religious practices shows that the difference between them was not a matter of essence but of their place in the established laws of the ritual. Religion was allowed and magic was, by definition, forbidden, so the allowed ritual was religion and the forbidden one was magic. Kirby Smith described this as follows: "Religion, then, is the orthodox, magic is heterodox, it being understood, of course, that for the Greeks and Romans the criterion of orthodoxy was the official recognition of their own State. The god must be officially recognized by the State, and his ceremonial must be the one prescribed by the official experts of the State."[12] A cult performed outside this mechanism of authority was magic.

The problem attached to the legal use of such terms as *magia* and *magus* (and, respectively, *mageia* and *magos*) is reflected in the remarks of Lucius Apuleius, from the second century CE. Apuleius delivered a speech at his trial for a charge brought against him by the relatives of Emilia Pudentilla, a wealthy widow much older than him. Her kinsmen accused Apuleius of causing her to fall in love with him and marry him by casting a spell on her, and they demanded compensation from him. He wrote:

> I should therefore like to ask his most learned advocates how, precisely, they would define a *magus*. For if, as I read in many authors, *magus* is the Persian word for priest, what is there criminal

10. Philips (1986, 2731). Also see Aune (1980, 1516–23), Betz (1991), Faraone (1991, 17–20; 1992, 11), Graf (1991), Nilsson (1964, 88), Nock (1972, 2: 310–23), Philips (1986, 3711–32), and A. F. Segal (1981).

11. On the legal status of magic in the Roman Empire, see Kippenberg (1997), Liebeschuetz (1979, 126–39), McMullen (1966, 95–127), and Ritner (1995, 3355–58). See also Ogden (2002, 286–99) for passages from the legal proceedings on accusations of witchcraft against Apuleius and Libanius.

12. K. Smith (1951, 269).

in being a priest and having due knowledge, understanding, and skill in all ceremonial law, sacrificial duties, and the binding rules of religion?[13]

Apuleius, who in his defense speech displayed broad knowledge about the area he was accused of and its social contexts, obviously did not admit to witchcraft. Had he done so, he would have risked not only a heavy fine but even death. Hence he dodged the accusation by alluding to the link between religion and common sense, pointing to the problematic character of the label that had been attached to him at this trial.[14]

In an article that became a milestone in the study of magic in the Greco-Roman world, Peter Brown shows that accusations of sorcery were not a matter of content but of order. He proposes distinguishing between acts of magic and the ascription of such deeds to the "other" and analyzing the other deeds separately from acts of magic. Brown suggests that the growing number of accusations of witchcraft in the Roman Empire between the fourth and sixth centuries CE was not a result of increased magic activity in this period but a reflection of the weakening of the old social order as a result of the inner pressures of a new power system. In his view, the collision and struggle between the traditional, Roman-pagan power system and that of the Christian church led to fear of the "other" and encouraged attacks on its legitimacy. These attacks

---

13. Apuleius (1909, 55, with slight changes). For the original, *Apologia*, sec. 25, see Apuleius (1994). On the source and meaning of the words *magus*, *magos*, and other close terms in Greek and Latin, see de Jong (1997, 387–413). Cf. Bremmer (2002), Graf (1997, 20–60), and Janowitz (2001, 9–16).

14. Obviously, his defense did not end there. Apuleius rejected one by one all the charges brought against him, including Emilia's infatuation with him, paying the fisherman for special fish, and the collapse in a trance of a child and a woman in his presence. Fritz Graf successfully shows that, throughout his line of defense, Apuleius strives to distinguish between (sublime) knowledge and (despicable) sorcery and to present himself as a learned philosopher who belongs to the former sphere rather than the latter. In so doing, argues Graf, Apuleius sought not only to acquit himself of the legal offense of witchcraft but also to dispel the rumors that had been spread about him in Oea, the small town where he lived, and particularly among the local elite whom he was seeking to join (Graf 1997, 65–88). On this matter, see also Ogden (2002, 286–90 and his bibliography at 313).

assumed the form of witchcraft accusations.[15] Magic was identified in the Roman Empire with the power of the "other." Accusations of sorcery were a symbolic means for expressing fear of that "other" and were, at the same time, an effective legal tool for contending with it. The difference between magic and religion was thus a matter of title, though highly significant politically, legally, and economically. This perception of magic in late antiquity has dominated the historical study of it, almost unchallenged, for the last two decades. John Gager formulated it clearly and succinctly.

> Magic, as a definable and consistent category of human experience, simply does not exist. . . . The beliefs and practices of "the other" will always be dubbed as "magic," "superstition," and the like. . . . The sentence, "X is/was a magician!" tells us nothing about the beliefs and practices of X; the only solid information that can be derived from it concerns the *speaker's* attitude toward X and their relative social relationship—that X is viewed by the speaker as powerful, peripheral, and dangerous.[16]

Hence, like O. Pettersson several decades earlier, Gager recommends that researchers avoid using the term *magic* altogether. Jonathan Z. Smith reinforced this view when, in a highly influential article, he pointed out that the use of *magic* in second-order theoretical academic discourse was inefficient in terms of its explanatory value. Indeed, the neutral term *ritual power*, referring to power attained through ritual means, has replaced *magic* in many later publications in the field.[17]

---

15. Brown (1970). Cf. also A. F. Segal (1981). Kimberly Stratton broadly develops this attitude in her book on magic, ideology, and stereotype in the ancient world (Stratton 2007). Resorting to Foucault's method of discourse, she analyzes various magic discourses in antiquity to expose their function as tools of power and as means for marginalizing and othering (especially in the context of gender).

16. Gager (1992, 24–25). See also Gager (1992, 39n114).

17. On Pettersson's suggestion, cf. Pettersson (1957) and the quotation at the end of chapter 1 (from Pettersson 1957, 119). For Smith's stance, see J. Z. Smith (1995). Investigating the Greek magical papyri corpus, Smith proposes an alternative explanation for its "magic" character and claims that the core element of these texts is "miniaturized sacrifice." See also Bernd-Christian Otto's discussion on this topic, which turns toward

The most prominent figure who objected to this trend in principle was Henk Versnel.[18] Versnel explicitly rejects the demand to refrain from using the term *magic* in research. He argues that pointing to the legal-social status of magic and of those involved in it in the Roman Empire does not offer answers about the essence of magic as a ritual phenomenon. In his view, just as researchers have some kind of concept about magic that they refer to when using the term, people in Greco-Roman culture had some concept concerning the phenomenon denoted through such terms as *magus, magia, magos, mageia,* and additional terms such as *goês* and *goêteia* (sorcerer, sorcery), which were part of their semantic field. Versnel insists that, in antiquity, these terms had essential rather than only social or legal meaning. Whoever accused an adversary of magic acts or described the actions of saints such as Apollonius of Tyana or Jesus Christ as free from it had something definite in mind that listeners knew how to identify. Versnel holds that that something, "the perception of the deviant forms of religion or outside religion *and* the practices they were consistently associated with," can be described without locating it along the distinguishing line between magic and religion.[19]

Versnel's view is exceptional against the background of a plethora of publications in this field that recurrently claim that, insofar as the Hellenistic world is concerned, it is not the act that attests to itself as magic but those who call it or accuse it of being so. Magic, according to this view, is not a special kind of acts that is essentially different from the religious kind. Among all the practices performed for the sake of attaining ritual power, acts are classified as magical because they are performed by people who are not official agents of such a power, appointed and recognized by the civil authority and the religious establishment tied to it. Not the "what" but the "who" defines magic in the Greco-Roman world.

---

a historical-semantic analysis of magic in antiquity (Otto 2013). References to "ritual power" are frequent in many articles in the anthology, for example, Meyer and Mirecki (1995). See also Meyer and Smith (1994). Rebecca Lesses explicitly adopts this view in her studies of Judaism in antiquity (Lesses 1998, 59–66).

18. See also Hoffman (2002).

19. Versnel (1991b, 190; emphasis in original). Versnel rests his claims on his findings in a study comparing curses and prayers for justice in the Hellenistic world (Versnel 1991a. I return to this theory in chapter 3.

CHAPTER 2

RELIGION, MAGIC, AND MYSTICISM
IN JUDAISM IN LATE ANTIQUITY
AND THE EARLY ISLAMIC PERIOD

More than 150 years have elapsed since the publication of the first studies on magic in Judaism, and this research is still in its infancy. Despite a thin, if steady, flow of publications throughout this period, only in recent decades and with the growth in the publication of magic artifacts and literature—amulets, incantation bowls, and books of magic recipes—have scholars become more aware of this area of Jewish culture. Fruits of this awareness are visible on the bookshelves and in the journals dealing with Jewish studies, but a significant task is still ahead.[20] Many texts still await publication, and the research work that must accompany their publication is even greater. We still lack a phenomenological description of Jewish magic, as it is reflected in the magic writings themselves, and a description of its historical development.[21] Next to nothing has been written about its social aspects. The ties between magic and other areas of Jewish thought and behavior in late antiquity and the early Middle Ages, such as rabbinic Halakhah and Aggadah or early Jewish mysticism, have been explored only partly, as is also true of the mutual relationships between Jews and their neighbors in all that concerns witchcraft. Yet the study of Jewish magic did not stagnate. Dozens of studies have appeared in the last 150 years, and in the last 25 years "Jewish magic" has actually prospered. The explosion in the publication of ancient texts of Jewish magic accompanied by research, together with the undermining of conventional notions of center and periphery, substantive and trivial, and at times even worthy and contemptible, rescued magic from the backyard of Jewish studies and pushed it toward the main street.

In this section I review the study of Jewish magic in late antiquity and the early Islamic period from the methodological perspective that organizes the entire discussion in this part of the book: How did researchers understand the essence of magic and its place in relation to additional phenomena in Jewish culture at the time? The discussion is divided into

---

20. See Bohak (2009b).
21. For an initial history of Jewish magic, see Harari (2012a).

80

three parts: (1) magic in rabbinic literature, (2) magic and early Jewish mysticism, and (3) Jewish magic literature.

Kishuf, Halakhah, and Aggadah: Magic in Rabbinic Literature

The systematic research of Jewish magic (*kishuf* in Hebrew) begins with two relatively large works written in the second half of the nineteenth century by Gideon Brecher and David Jöel.[22] Brecher's book was published in 1850. His concern was magic and particularly magic healing in the Babylonian Talmud. Jöel's treatise, published about thirty years later, was broader and was devoted to "superstition and the view of Judaism" from the Bible up to Geonic literature. In the chapters on the Mishnah and the Talmud, Jöel discusses the main issues that would later concern scholars in the field: beliefs touching on demons and spirits, the fear of the pairs, witchcraft, divination, astrology, necromancy, ritual healing, and the rabbis' attitude toward all of them. His discussion of these subjects in Geonic literature is the broadest review devoted to the subject up to today. Jöel relates all these issues to "superstitions."[23] In this spirit, he points to the Persian origin of some of these (foreign) beliefs and seeks to clarify the attitude of "Judaism" toward them. In the spirit of nineteenth-century *Wissenschaft des Judentums*, he also discusses Jewish mysticism in similar terms. For Jöel, Judaism is ethics and rational philosophy.[24]

---

22. The two works are Brecher (1850) and Jöel (1881–1883). Another mid-nineteenth-century work was a brief study on "foreign sciences" in the Talmud published by Kilair (1841). He mentions healing by means of spells, the danger posed by harmful agents and by the pairs (TB *Pesahim* 110a–b), and a few talmudic matters on healing. But these issues are not discussed beyond the claim that their source is "Greek wisdom."

23. In this regard, note Salomon Rubin's *Geschichte des Aberglaubens bei allen Völken mit besonderem Hinblicke auf des jüdische Volk*, where he deals with various kinds of "superstitions." Rubin tries to point out their non-Jewish origin and their alienation from Judaism on the one hand and their encroachment on the margins of Jewish culture on the other (Rubin 1887). See also Moritz Steinschneider's view of magic, though not specifically in antiquity, in Veltri (2011).

24. On the same inclination among the handful of scholars who discussed magic in their studies in the second half of the nineteenth century, see Veltri (2011). This view of Judaism reflects not only the accepted view of the contemporary *Wissenschaft des Judentums* but also fits, as shown, the view of religion common among the first ethnographers.

The studies of Brecher and Jöel, as well as the studies of Alexander Kohut on demonology in the Babylonian Talmud (which were published at the midpoint between them),[25] deal with two rabbinic bodies: the Mishnah and the Babylonian Talmud, without any mention of the Palestinian Talmud and the local midrashim. This neglect was partly corrected by Ludwig Blau in his book *Das Altjüdische Zaubervesen* (Ancient Jewish Magic), which since its publication at the end of the nineteenth century and until recently had been the main source for the study of magic beliefs and practices in rabbinic literature.[26]

Blau draws no distinction between his sources according to their geographic origin or their date of composition. He relates to rabbinic literature as one corpus, which expresses a uniform worldview. His only distinction in this regard is the famous determination that Jews in Babylonia were more infected (*angesteckt*) by magic than their brethren in Palestine. The declared basis for this claim is the quantitative comparison between mentions of magic in Babylonian and Palestinian works. But this distinction also seems to reflect Blau's view that the source of Jewish magic is in foreign influences on the people of Israel, which in his view were more pronounced in Babylonia than in Palestine. Blau's determination that Jews in the Hellenistic diaspora were more involved with magic than their Palestinian brethren probably rests on similar grounds.[27]

At the opening of his book, Blau considers the definition of magic and its connection to religion in general and Judaism in particular. He concludes that magic is above all practice, a mode of action, the performance of an act. As such, it is a set of actions in the supernatural realm closely related to demonology and faith in the human power to control

---

25. Kohut (1866, 48–96).

26. Blau (1898). Giuseppe Veltri's *Magie und Halakha* (1997) is the only monograph published since then on magic in rabbinic literature. Gideon Bohak's *Ancient Jewish Magic: A History* (2008) includes an extensive review of magic in rabbinic literature in a broad cultural and historical context. See also chapter 7.

27. Blau (1898, 23, 37–49, 96). Several decades before Blau, Shlomo Rapoport claimed that Jews in Palestine had relatively less faith in "unnatural charms and spells" than Jews in Babylonia; he relied on a comparison between the Talmuds (Rapoport 1852, 1: 227). Saul Lieberman refuted this claim, and scholars no longer accept it (Lieberman 1942, 109–11).

demons. This is also true of magic in Judaism.[28] Yet Blau does expand his discussion far beyond the praxis of Jewish demonology. The sources of Jewish magic and its expansion—the image of the sorcerer, magic means, and beneficent and maleficent means—are reviewed knowledgeably and at length in his study. The incantation, which Blau views as the gist of the magic ritual, and the holy names included in it are the subject of a particularly broad discussion. Blau discusses two adjuration texts in Greek in his book—one for love and the other for exorcising a demon—that he views as an expression of Hellenistic Jewish magic. Although his conclusion may be questionable, this is the first example of a comparative study that seeks to identify significant links between Jewish and Hellenistic magic.[29]

Between Blau's study and Joshua Trachtenberg's renowned *Jewish Magic and Superstition*, published about forty years later, little was written on magic in rabbinic literature.[30] Trachtenberg's goal in his book, which until recently had been the last significant landmark in the phenomenological study of Jewish magic, was to describe the magic beliefs and

---

28. Blau's claim concerning the practical character of magic in Judaism relies on the Mishnah: "A sorcerer—one who carries out a (real) act (*ha-'oseh ma'aseh*), is liable, but one who merely creates illusions (*ha-'ohez 'et ha-'einayim*) is not" (M. *Sanhedrin* 7:11). Blau rightly highlights the explicit aspect of action in this determination, but some clarification and qualification is required. First, The word *ma'aseh* (act or action) does not denote here the sorcerer's deed (after all, the illusionist also does something) but its result. The rabbis distinguish action causing real change in the world (*ma'aseh*, hence magic) from action that seduces the observer into believing that such a change has taken place, even though it is no more than a sophisticated ruse (*'ahizat 'einayim*, which is not magic). Second, the Mishnah does not discuss the essence of magic (unfortunately, no rabbinic discussion on the subject is available). It discusses the sorcerer, who had previously been included among transgressors whose offenses are punishable by stoning (M. *Sanhedrin* 7:4), and provides a legal criterion for determining his guilt. In this halakhic-legal context, defining a sorcerer by his actions is only natural.

29. Blau (1898, 96–117). Philip Alexander rightfully opposed the claim that a love charm from Hadrumetum, which Blau quotes, was written by a Jew (Alexander 1986, 358). On Jewish elements in Greek magical papyri, from which the incantation for exorcising the demon was taken, see chapter 5.

30. Trachtenberg (1970). See also Blau (1904), Daiches (1913, 7–12), Lewy (1893a), Marmorstein (1923), and Preus (1983, 149–50). For magic, incantations, and spells, see also Preus (1983, 638, 641).

practices of Ashkenazic pietists. He did so methodically and thoroughly, and, by consistently relying on rabbinic sources, he shed light on a long series of issues, some of which had hardly been discussed until then.

At the same time, Jacob Lauterbach published his article on the power of the word in rabbinic thought. Lauterbach begins by emphasizing the difference between the rabbis and the "primitives" described by Frazer, for whom "the word becomes fact," and suggests exploring the rabbinic belief in the power of the word in the context of their ideology as a whole. He briefly expounds on his view that the rabbis, or at least some of them, had themselves endorsed "popular superstitions." Yet, where principles essential to their faith were concerned and when they did "recognize [these superstitions] as dangerous to the religious life of the people," they fought against them and tried to eradicate them; if they failed, they at least tried to make them "theologically less harmful."[31] In any event, the rabbis did believe in the performative power of the human word, and Lauterbach attempts to explain this. Without relating to the details of his interpretive move (which, at best, rests on flimsy foundations), I note that he aimed to prove that the rabbinic belief in the word's performative power is free from any magic elements, and that was Lauterbach's conclusion. This cleansing trend is compatible with Zeev Yavetz's claim from decades earlier regarding the well-known talmudic story about R. Shimon b. Yohai and Ben Temalion, who came to the rabbi's aid when the rabbi was traveling to Rome in order to revoke the emperor's edicts (TB Me'ila 17a–b). Yavetz cleanses the story of its demonological element when he states that Ben Temalion was the son of a Roman Jewish rabbi by the name of Temalion, who was close to the emperor's court.[32]

A similar approach was also endorsed by the prominent talmudists Ephraim Elimelech Urbach and Saul Lieberman, and it still appears in the current scholarship. The studies of Lieberman and Urbach, published around the mid-twentieth century, place the study of magic in rabbinic literature on a more solid basis. Lieberman offers a scholarly interpretation of the Tosefta discussions on "the ways of the Amorites" (*Shabbat* 6–7) and relies on his extensive knowledge of Greco-Roman civilization to expose the Hellenistic influence on Jewish magic tradition.

31. Lauterbach (1939, 287, 289).
32. Yavetz (1963, 6: 318–20) On this story, see chapter 7.

It is fundamentally an error to generalize and say that in Palestinian Talmudo-Midrashic literature fewer "superstitions" are
found than in the Babylonian. To adhere to this view would mean
to maintain that the Palestinian Jews were less civilized than
the Babylonian, that they were not men of their time and place.
Palestine, situated between Egypt on the one hand and Babylonia on the other, could not escape the influence of the wisdom of
that time. The rabbis did their utmost to combat the superstitions which were forbidden by the Written Law, to eliminate the
magic which smacked of idolatry, but they had to accept those
charms which were sanctioned by the "scientists" of that time.
The power of love charms was recognized by all nations of the
ancient world, and the Palestinian Jews were no exception.[33]

This passage patently attests to Lieberman's view of magic in Judaism.[34]
First, he rejects attempts to play down the extent of its spread among
Palestinian Jews. Second, he relates it to part of the "culture," "wisdom,"
and "science" of the Mishnaic and talmudic era and views believers in it
as people who have adopted this culture. In other words, Lieberman
holds that, as is the case everywhere at all times, Jews in Palestine in late
antiquity adopted parts of the surrounding culture, especially because
those parts represented the wisdom of that time and were approved by
the "scientists." Magic, then, did not originate in the Jewish people. It
wandered around in the cultural realm between Egypt and Babylonia
and infected the people. In this area one could not escape its influence,
unless one were one of the rabbis. The rabbis, according to Lieberman,
remained free from magic's hold. As far as they were concerned, these
superstitions were vain beliefs forbidden by the Torah and therefore had
nothing to do with them. If, moreover, these superstitions also smacked
of idolatry, the rabbis did their utmost to eradicate them.

Lieberman does not exonerate Palestinian Jews from magic. Instead,
he distances them from religion. According to his description, Jewish
religion is the religion of the rabbis. The values of truth (correct or mistaken) and morality (worthy or objectionable) in their religious faith are

---

33. Lieberman (1942, 110). See also Lieberman (1942, 91–114; 1991; 1992, 3: 79–105).
34. Cf. Gruenwald (1996, 24–26).

antithetical to the values of magic, and supporting both is consequently impossible. The representatives of religion identified the invasive pollution and hastened to combat it but failed. The power of magic's scientific wisdom overrode the power of religion in the struggle for the people's heart. For lack of other options, the rabbis reconciled themselves to the existence of some beliefs that were particularly prevalent. At least, they tried to Judaize them by pouring religious-Jewish content into the foreign shell of magic practices and incantations.[35]

Elsewhere in this discussion Lieberman hurls an accusation of magic at Hellenistic culture, which drew the people to the "external brilliance and the superficial beauty of Gentile life."[36] Here too, the rabbis struggled for and preached religious values.

> But it is hardly possible that the great masses of the Jewish people in the big towns conducted themselves in conformity with the idealistic views of the rabbis. It is unlikely that they kept consciously refusing to imitate the manners and life patterns of their neighbors, so attractive at first sight. The ignorant people of the country, on the other hand, whose economic status made it impossible to emulate the middle class in the pursuit of pleasure and elegance, adopted their neighbors' belief in magic, astrology, and all kinds of superstitions in defiance of Written and Oral Law.[37]

A clear distinction separates "the idealistic views of the rabbis" and the magic and superstitions forbidden by religion, accompanied by a further dimension. Lieberman ties magic to ignorance and poverty. The explanation, I must admit, is slightly strange. It suggests that the masses of the people sought Hellenization. Those who could afford it adopted standards of Greek beauty. Those who could not endorsed superstitions. The ascription of magic to the lower classes appears to be the most prominent

---

35. Lieberman (1942, 91; 1991). Lieberman's view closely resembles Lauterbach's description of the popular adaptation process of foreign practices and the rabbis' attitude toward them (Lauterbach 1925, 2–5).

36. Lieberman (1942, 91).

37. Lieberman (1942, 91).

indication that Lieberman projected his own views about a dichotomy between magic and the religion of truth and its representatives' idealistic faith onto the society he so skillfully studied and described. Magic, then, was first pushed out of the rabbis' circle and ascribed to the masses and then pushed out even further to the distant, poor, and ignorant margins of Jewish society.

Urbach's view is close to Lieberman's. Urbach devotes two chapters of his book on the sages' concepts and beliefs to magic and miracle and to the performative power of God's name. He reviews the subject expansively, as part of a systematic clarification of the rabbis' comprehensive and integrated worldview. His opening remarks are revealing.

> The Rabbinic doctrine concerning God's all-embracing power has a bearing on other concepts. It excludes the possibility of the existence of magic power capable of influencing the laws of nature and the decree of God. . . . The same reasoning applies to magic—it is impossible to reconcile it with the existence of an All-Powerful God. . . . Opposition to sorcerers is in keeping with the spirit of the Torah, only in Rabbinic literature it is much more detailed and is discussed with emphasis, indicating the actuality of the issue. . . . But there is ample evidence of the widespread practice of sorcery, not only among women and simple folk, but also among the scholars in Eretz-Israel and even more so in Babylon. . . . In actuality, even the Sages of the Talmud and Midrash—despite their fundamental recognition that there is none besides God and that consequently witchcraft does not exist—could not ignore the facts, to wit, that broad masses of the people believed in and made use of these practices. They sought to find a compromise.[38]

Urbach's view of magic, which he ascribes to the rabbis, follows from logical considerations. The argument is the following: Divine omnipotence precludes the possibility of human magical influence on the natural order. The rabbis believed in God's omnipotence. Therefore the rabbis did

---

38. Urbach (1975, 97–101). See further, Urbach (1975, 97–134).

not believe in magic.[39] Furthermore, they could not believe in magic. Had they believed in it, they would have been expressly irrational.

Rabbinic opposition to magic, then, follows from common sense, and this common sense fits the spirit of the Torah. Jewish religion cannot contain magic by virtue of logical principles. Hence, in its pure form, it is clean of it: "There is none besides God and . . . consequently witchcraft does not exist." Unfortunately, however, rabbinic literature is pervaded by traditions about men and women endowed with magic powers. At this point, the "masses of the people" enter the picture. Among "women and simple folk," who we can assume were not properly educated, magic beliefs and even magic actions were widespread.[40] Again, unfortunately, aggadic writings explicitly attest to the rabbis' belief in human ritual power (not to say magic) and to the rabbis' use of it! Furthermore, according to Halakhah, a sorcerer is defined as one who "carries out a (real) act" ('oseh ma'aseh), as opposed to one who merely creates illusions. Thus, contrary to his strong opening lines, Urbach half-heartedly admits that rabbis also had a share in magic. In his terms, this was a kind of compromise between their "fundamental recognition" and the pressure of the people, between religion as is and the foreign elements that had gained a foothold in it.

Just as the rabbis compromised, Urbach also appears to be inclined to do so, but he masks this inclination. He presents at length sources that deny magic and systematically disregards those who challenge his approach.

---

39. Urbach's first assumption is obviously a logical fallacy. The author of *Harba de-Moshe* (The Sword of Moses), a Jewish book of magic from the second half of the first millennium CE, easily solved this problem. He explains at the beginning of the book that the holy names used in the adjuration of angels, which is the basis for the Jewish practice of magic, were given by the angels to Moses and his descendants following a divine command. Human control over the angels, which is the power of human magic, follows from an explicit divine command to the angels to obey all those adjuring them by his names. On this issue and on parallel versions of this tradition, see Harari (2005b).

40. Cf. also Urbach on this point: "Witchcraft and magic, which were a kind of international faith, made deep inroads into popular belief. The rabbis, however—even those who adopted a more moderate view and chose to Judaize or at least temper practices and views originating in magic, who took reality into consideration—never ceased to struggle against acts of witchcraft and magic, which indeed have no place among the forty eight ways that Torah is acquired by" (Urbach 1967, 27).

Urbach chooses the story about a heretic asking R. Yoḥanan b. Zakkai concerning the practice of purification from the dead with the ash of the red heifer as a paradigm of the rabbis' attitude toward magic. This choice, however, is itself paradigmatic. R. Yoḥanan, who evades the heretic's question, tells his disciples, "By your life! Neither the dead person defiles nor does the water purify; only this is the decree of the Holy One, blessed be He."[41] This answer distances the rabbis not only from a belief in magic but also from a belief in the existence of any human ritual power. If this is the paradigm, then rabbinic religion is a pure, rationalist-ethical faith based on the principle of God's omnipotence.

This is also the source for the distinction between miracle and sorcery that Urbach identifies in rabbinic thought. Miracle is a result and an expression of God's omnipotence. Magic (which, as noted, is not possible) is a human action. The rabbis sanctified the miracle, but they feared the popular blurring of its borders with magic. "The common people were, of course, interested in one thing only—in the result of the action, without differentiating its source."[42] The rabbis were so determined to emphasize God's omnipotence that at times they preferred to recognize Gentile wonders as an expression of God's power rather than proclaim them as sorcery. Hence, claims Urbach, the social distinction between miracle and sorcery (religion and magic) on the basis of a distinction between what we do and what others do, which has often been suggested in the scholarship, tends not to fit the rabbinic position. The rabbinic distinction between miracle and magic is one of essence.

Urbach then moves on to another matter essential to magic: the power of the Name. The problem is clear: Rabbinic literature points to a widespread belief in the performative power of God's name and in the possibility of implementing it that ostensibly appears to be incompatible with the rabbis' absolute negation of the human ability to interfere with the natural order. Urbach attacks the problem on two levels. First, he detaches the discussion about the power of the Name from the discussion about magic, and then he deals with it according to the same principles that had guided his treatment of magic. Here as well, therefore, he is forced into similar compromises.

41. *Pesikta de-Rav Kahana* 4:7. See also Urbach (1975, 99).
42. Urbach (1975, 103).

Urbach's discussion on the rabbis' belief in the power of the Name relies on a study about the perception of the Name in the Bible and in Egyptian and Babylonian cultures. According to Urbach, Egyptians and Babylonians made magic use of names and tried to overpower the gods by using their names. By contrast, in the Bible "God's name is called, it is mentioned, when there is a desire for His blessing, for His response; but He that responds and blesses is God, not the priest by mentioning the Name."[43] Jewish religion thereby extirpated all magic elements from the use of the Name and enabled its existence within it. This distinction, however, was not so rigorously preserved among "simple folk," and the rabbis were therefore extremely careful in their use of the Name. Beside traditions attesting to its vast power to protect and also to harm, which Urbach broadly illustrates, he emphasizes the rabbis' desire to play it down in order "to prevent the blurring of the distance between God and man and the use of the Name for magical purposes."[44] Urbach, then, predicates the rabbis' attitude toward the Name on an ideological-didactic foundation based on the popular use of it and designed to limit it. At the same time, he unwittingly contradicts the determined view he had presented in his opening remarks, which set the terms for the discussion of the entire subject. If magic is altogether impossible, why the fear displayed here?

The studies of Lieberman and Urbach excel at conveying one way of dealing with the distinction between magic and religion. These scholars project onto the research not only modern approaches concerning magic and religion but mainly their own views of religion and religiosity, a view that attempts to identify the rabbis as its forerunners. "Opposition to sorcerers is in keeping with the spirit of the Torah," writes Urbach, and this spirit appears to have joined the impressive erudition of these two scholars when they formulated a comprehensive view on the essence of magic and its role in rabbinic literature and culture.[45]

Only a few scholars joined this trend. Prominent among them are Joshua Efron, Abraham Weinroth, and Yehuda Liebes. Efron links

---

43. Urbach (1975, 124).

44. Urbach (1975, 134).

45. For a similar view in a broader discussion about the "people" in the study of the rabbis, see Stein (2009).

together witchcraft and foreign ritual in his explanation of the story about Shimon ben Shetaḥ's struggle against the witches in Ashkelon (PT *Sanhedrin* 6:4, PT *Hagigah* 2:2): "Shimon ben Shetaḥ, therefore, hastened to act in accordance with the commandment of the Torah and Halakhah to uproot the source of the sin. . . . The distinguished *nasi* (leader) of the Pharisees rushed to eradicate a dangerous nest of foreign, pernicious cultic customs liable to poison his nation's soul. . . . A group faithful to the covenant broke forth and fulfilled the commandment of zealousness."[46] Weinroth has recently strongly attacked "spiritualism," as he calls it, for returning to Judaism, "through the back door," idolatrous fears of arbitrary powers from which Judaism had liberated human beings by basing their fate on rational moral principles of reward and punishment. He sums up: "The rabbis' war against sorcery is, therefore, an all-out war. . . . A review of the sources . . . reveals that, in fact, what is at stake is a war of the rational motif against varieties of charlatanism, as well as the war of the hopeful believer against the fatalist."[47] Both Efron and Weinroth hold that magic was essentially different from Jewish faith, that it penetrated Judaism from the outside and polluted it, and that the rabbis waged ideological war against it.[48]

Liebes has recently drawn a categorical distinction between magic and religion, which he ties to an explicit value judgment. In his articles he contrasts magic with what he calls "major writings" and suggests distinctions concerning the rabbis' attitude toward it. Liebes's starting point is a recognition that "hierarchy is of the essence in the religious phenomenon."[49] "Major and minor" (religion and magic) do coexist but, in order to estimate the real, specific value of the minor, we must consult the major. In his view, "It is right to see in magic as such a lower kind of religiosity," a kind that cannot possibly be integrated into major religious texts without

---

46. Efron (1988, 305, 318–19). For a critique of his interpretation of the story, see Ilan (2006, 214–23, esp. 218–20). On this story, see chapter 7.

47. Weinroth (1996, 21–22). Weinroth's distinction between magic and religion is based on the strength of the active power: "Whereas faith in heavenly powers [meaning religion] supports a view of them as omnipotent, magic operates through technical accessories and is thus limited to the technical powers of the artifact or the means creating the charm" (Weinroth 1996, 22).

48. Cf. Herr (1979, 64–65).

49. Liebes (2004, 3).

cleansing it and eliminating its original, technical-manipulative essence.[50] As Liebes understands it, magic can be summed up as "the adoption of technical procedures, far removed from love or fear, in order to force God or his angels to fulfill the wishes of those using them." And he adds, "This definition fits the rabbis' position concerning the essence of magic."[51] As evidence of the rabbis' position, Liebes cites the well-known tradition: "Why are they called sorceries (*keshafim*)? Because they deny/diminish (*makhishin*) the heavenly household" (TB *Hullin* 7b; TB *Sanhedrin* 67b). And when pointing to the case of Ḥoni ha-Meʻagel, the rainmaker, Liebes states:

[Ḥoni] seemingly uses for this purpose [making rain] the well known magic procedure of tracing a circle around himself, but his manipulation of Heaven by means of this circle, rather than technical, is personal-emotional. Even Shimon ben Shetaḥ, a stern member of the establishment, acknowledged that, . . . and Shimon ben Shetaḥ was well acquainted with sorceries and fought them zealously. . . . Other rainmakers, who are also described in rabbinic literature, replace magic with love of God and love of their fellows.[52]

---

50. This view is explicitly expressed in Liebes (2004; 2005). The quotation is included in the following passage: "It is right to see in magic as such a lower kind of religiosity (not only according to my evaluation but also according to the view of prominent religious authorities over generations). When integrated into the *Zohar* literature, however, magic, technical, and manipulative elements actually serve to elevate antithetic religious elements: the personal myth and individual devotion" (Liebes 2005, 22–23).

51. Liebes (2004, 4).

52. Liebes (2004, 5–6). Liebes questions my suggestion to define magic by relying on the linguistic characteristics of an "adjuration text" (see chapter 3; first published in Hebrew in Harari 2002). In his view, my suggestion "also stigmatizes as magic major religious texts that integrate magic elements within them and, in so doing, change their essence and become part of the first, religious trend, while adding their own nuance to it" (Liebes 2004, 4). Liebes's view, as noted, rests on a distinction between magic and religion as mutually exclusive, accompanied by the determination that these two opposite phenomena are never together in any text. As will become clear in the next chapters, I find entirely unacceptable the essentialist perception of magic and of the rabbinic approach to it at the basis of Liebes's (and his predecessors') view. I certainly object to

Thus (high) religious feelings of love and fear on the one hand and (low) magic procedures on the other are separated by an abysmal gap: "Major religious works do contain magic elements too but, in that context, they lose the essence of their magic."[53] Magic and religion are incompatible. Religion either repels magic or incorporates it while purifying it from its basic essence.

This radical view did not develop in a vacuum. Unlike Efron and Weinroth, Liebes was well aware of new research trends attempting to deconstruct the distinction between magic and religion, pointing to magic elements in Jewish religiosity in general and rabbinic religiosity in particular. He responded by openly and steadfastly supporting the purity of Jewish religion, formulating his claims in an explicit attempt to avoid "tarnishing it with the stain" of magic. Although he was not alone in this struggle, most scholars in recent decades have not favored puristic tendencies of this kind and have held that the question of magic in rabbinic literature should be solved in other ways.

Jacob Neusner's studies mark the beginning of change. In some of the works he published at the end of the 1960s, Neusner claims that the figure of the rabbi outlined in the Mishnah and both Talmuds is in many ways closer to that of the *magush*, the priest-magus of Persian religion.

> It must be stressed, however, that the rabbi was far more than a political figure. . . . The rabbi emerges, therefore, as a wonder-working sage, master of ancient wisdom both of Israel and of his native Babylonia and privy to the occult.[54]

How did Neusner develop an outlook so different from that of his predecessors? The answer lies in his sources. Neusner shifts the center of the discussion from Halakhah to Aggadah. His predecessors had taken as their starting point the halakhic ban on magic, sensing that everything

---

the rigid approach by which textual religious elements cleanse the magic ones and uproot their original, merely technical, essence.

53. Liebes (2005, 5).

54. Neusner (1966–1967, 170–172). Cf. also Neusner (1969, 10–11). It may be worth noting that Neusner was a student of Morton Smith, the author of *Jesus the Magician* (M. Smith 1978).

else had to be adapted to it. Neusner does not deny the ban's existence but suspends it in order to examine stories about the rabbis' actions. He points to many sources (unquestionably known also to his predecessors) that ascribe to the rabbis supernatural powers, such as reciting blessings or curses, possessing far-reaching sight, interpreting signs, killing with looks, conversing with the dead, and dabbling in medicine and astrology. He compares these features to those of the *magush*, the Zoroastrian fire priest who was a contemporary neighbor of talmudic rabbis, and claims that both share many characteristics.

Neusner expanded this discussion in two more articles, in which he highlighted the rabbis' magic features on the one hand and the problem attached to the term *magic* in this context on the other. At the basis of the discussion is a fundamental distinction between two perspectives—one from outside society and one from inside (equivalent to what is frequently termed in anthropology the *etic* and *emic* perspectives). From an external, anthropological-scientific perspective, the Babylonian rabbi is a legislator-sorcerer. But even if he is no different from other Gentile sorcerers active in his time and his surroundings, the Jewish community in Babylonia might still have viewed him as different.

> Jewish society, including the rabbis, was not primitive. It had long since distinguished sharply, by its own standards, between what *it* considered magic, and what *it* considered religion—neither identical with what we should class under these terms—and by *its* standards, the rabbis were not magicians. . . . Some of them did practice magic on the side, but this is a different matter. . . . The rabbis never called themselves magicians. On the contrary, they consistently and explicitly disapproved of "magic." . . . But many of the things they did, especially the supernatural character alleged to have been imparted to them by their knowledge of Torah, must be seen in the context of antiquity as appropriate to divine-men or magicians.[55]

By addressing the categories that the examined society used when relating to itself, Neusner solves the contradiction between the rabbis'

---

55. Neusner (1969, 11–13; emphasis in original).

consistent opposition to magic and the fact that an external examination of the traditions about them shows that they themselves had been sorcerers. He adopts a social distinction between magic and religion based on the way the Jewish community itself—and in this case the religious-political establishment of the rabbis, whose writings are the source of the discussion—perceived the relationship between center and periphery. Neusner argues that in the intrasocial context it is not the act that defines its performer but the social status of the performer that determines the character of the act. In the circles where rabbinic literature was created, no acts of magic were ascribed to the rabbis and they were not perceived as sorcerers because they themselves were the religious establishment. For this reason, they could condemn and forbid supernatural activity of the kind they themselves performed, referring to them as sorcery. In this view, saint and sorcerer (miracle and witchcraft, religion and magic) are examined on two parallel levels: external and internal. Even though externally they do not appear to differ, from an inside perspective they are sharply distinct, and the demarcation between them rests on the person's place in the social-political order of the community.

Neusner returned to this question about twenty years later, in an article where he extended the social-political distinction between magic and miracle to the realm of knowledge. In his view, not only is the essence of the act determined by the performer's social status, but so is the truth of the knowledge in whose name the act is performed. The distinction between magic and science, meaning true knowledge, systematically follows from the social context of the knowledge: "Science is what I know; magic is what you know. . . . In every case . . . the distinction between miracle and magic and the distinction between science and magic is precisely the same. In both cases the distinction flows from the system's larger systematic judgment on who and what are inside, who and what are outside."[56] Neusner examines the rabbis' distinction between true knowledge and magic knowledge according to this principle and states that, in this context, religion and science are on one side and magic is on the other. The rabbis' distinction of miracle and science from magic acts follows from the distinction between the people of Israel and the

---

56. Neusner (1989, 62–63).

Gentiles and indeed marks it. Both miracles and true knowledge are a product of the Torah. The rabbi's ideal figure is indeed equipped with both, and they are mutually tied. His miraculous powers follow from his intellectual and practical internalization of the Torah through a ritual life of study and through the commandments he observes.[57] By contrast, magic refers to Gentile knowledge and the acts that accompany it. According to this principle, the rabbis do not belong to the realm of magic in rabbinic literature by definition! They are the spiritual heroes of their literature; they are its "us," and therefore their acts are miracles and the knowledge they possess is the truth.[58]

Neusner, then, sets the study of magic in rabbinic literature on foundations entirely different from those proposed by his predecessors. He replaces an essentialist-dichotomous view of magic and religion with one seeking to clarify the terms prevalent in the society itself concerning ritual power phenomena and with an analysis of these terms in a social-political context. This view resonated broadly in the scholarship and, as will be shown, underwent progressive refinement.[59]

In an article published in the mid-1970s, Judah Goldin applied (for the first time in the study of Jewish magic) insights of the Edward Evans-Pritchard and Peter Brown variety concerning the social use of categories such as magic or witchcraft. Goldin claims that, according to the

---

57. Neusner (1970). See also Neusner (1969–1970, 4: 351–62).

58. Cf. Charles Philips's similar claim concerning the sociology of knowledge in the Greco-Roman world (Philips 1986).

59. Not everyone saw a need to pay attention to this problem. Many studies published in recent decades have dealt with limited aspects of what is generally referred to as magic, or with its textual manifestation in rabbinic literature, without adding methodological reflections of the kind that concern me here. See, for example, Avishur (1979), Bar-Ilan (1988; 1995), Bazak (1968a; 1968b; 1972, 63–104), Bohak (2003b), A. Cohen (1978, 260–97), Gafni (1990, 167–72), Hadas-Lebel (1979, 454–77), Herr (1979, 62–76), Idel (1990, 27–43), Levene (2003b), Ratzaby (1992), Shinan (1983; 1992, 120–48), Sperber (1994, 118–47), Ulmer (1994; 1996), and Verman and Adler (1993). In some of these articles, the authors do note something about the essence of magic or its relationship with religion, and the use of terms such as *magic* or *religion* in their works at times suggests their essentialist perception of it, but they rely mainly on a descriptive method.

rabbis, "what is magic and what is not, the authorities determine. . . . One is simply to obey and trust the authorities."[60] In his view, the religious establishment rejects magic in search of reaffirmation. The establishment acknowledges the sorcerer's power and fears the threat entailed by his activity, which offers believers profits attained through a course alternative to its own. It therefore uses its authority to push sorcerers and their actions beyond the pale of the social norm. According to this description, faith in the power of sorcery was widespread in late antiquity not only among the people but in society as a whole. The rabbis were never contemptuous of magic. They recognized the performative power of witchcraft and were well aware of the social power advantage that magic ensured its performers. Their duality regarding magic, which Goldin recognizes—absolute rejection or, for lack of any other option, incorporation into religion while tempering magic features—resulted from political considerations: They hastened to preserve their status as an authoritative leadership.

In the early 1990s this insight was extensively applied in the research of female witchcraft in rabbinic literature. The first to present studies in this direction was Jonathan Seidel. In an article that went unnoticed by scholars, Seidel links anthropological research on witchcraft to the methods of Brown and Neusner, applying anthropological insights into the realm of body-gender-magic to the study of witchcraft in rabbinic literature. He states that the rabbis' testimonies indicate that Jewish society, particularly in Babylon, fits Mary Douglas's definition of the "witchcraft society,"[61] and he traces the political constructs related to the triangular connection between women, pollution, and witchcraft. In his view, the rabbinic sources dealing with female witchcraft express the rabbis' fears of independent women who challenged their ideological and political authority. Such women could rebel, for example, by breaching the laws of marriage and menstrual purity, thus spreading pollution

---

60. Goldin (1976, 122). In the notes to his article, Goldin suggests the following broad definition of magic (together with other "forms of superstition"): "belief in the efficacy of the object or act of the recital in compelling supernatural forces to perform in some desired way if the act or recitation is carried out properly" (Goldin 1976, 138n1).

61. See Douglas (2003, 115–31, esp. 115–18).

in the community. This is a close, intimate threat, which women could spread deliberately and even unwittingly.

Douglas suggests seeing the human body as a symbol of society and examining its perception, including its holiness and/or the prohibitions of pollution related to it in a specific society, as a symbolic expression of social matters.[62] Hence the image of women as witches in general and the image of witches in particular convey anxiety about the danger of pollution in the entire society (meaning male society), as embodied in their independence: "Women's impurity can defile the male body and mind and can infect the Rabbis' system. . . . Witchcraft in the literary culture of the Rabbis becomes the psychic component and counterpart to bodily invasion and violation."[63] The purpose of witchcraft stories is to publicize the danger, bring it to the public arena, and struggle against it there. Secrecy is a cover for the breaking of boundaries, for lack of control. The rabbis therefore sought to make female witchcraft explicit, expose it, and uproot its power. Seidel skillfully analyzes traditions of witchcraft and exposes their depth structure. He shows that they are tied to independence, to knowledge, to openness, to the organization of women on the one hand and to malicious powers on the other. The accusation of witchcraft is a kind of warning about the social danger latent in women who are not under halakhic control, as dictated by the rabbis. The stories of struggle against women expose the deviation, oppress it, and remove it. These are stories about leadership and proper social order.[64]

Simha Fishbane and Meir Bar-Ilan also apply gender and political insights to their discussions of rabbinic views of female witchcraft, but they adopt a feminist rather than an anthropological perspective. Fishbane proposes examining the attitude toward witchcraft in the Babylonian Talmud according to three concentric social circles: rabbis, men, women (from center to periphery, in that order). In his view, the Talmud attests that ritual activity involving supernatural forces takes place in all these circles, but the attitude toward it is different in each case. Supernatural actions by rabbis are presented as miracles that follow from their special

62. Douglas (2002).

63. Seidel (1992, 50).

64. These ideas were developed in Seidel's dissertation. See Seidel (1996, 157–221).

closeness to God. Similar actions by men who are not part of the rabbis' circle are decried as a sin, whereas women engaging in such actions are accused of witchcraft. Fishbane deals first with the gap between the rebuke of women and that of men. He determines that the reason for identifying the ritual activity of women with witchcraft and the usual connection of their witchcraft with harlotry—an additional focus of illegitimate feminine activity—is their threat, as a group, to the social order centering on men. Men, although they can weaken rabbinic authority, do not fundamentally threaten the social order. Hence a man who is not part of the rabbis' circle and performs miracles is a sinner. Women, by contrast, are perceived as liminal, as social margins posing a definite threat to the male center. Supernatural female power, therefore, is not merely a sin. Men view such power as a genuine threat and hence as intolerable. Fishbane illustrates this trend well when exploring stories about struggles between rabbis and witches. These symbolic expressions of male anxiety about the power of women end with the victory of the rabbi, who, in the eyes of the narrator, holds legitimate authority over the woman. Fishbane clarifies that *witchcraft* is a label expressing male fear of the female gender, regardless of the essence of the women's actions and even regardless of whether such acts are actually performed.[65]

Bar-Ilan presents a similar claim. In his view, accusing women of witchcraft at the time of the rabbis and even earlier, in the Bible and the Apocrypha, serves as a political means to "suppress a lower class" and fixes the hierarchical relationship between ruler and ruled (as similar accusations against Jews were used, for example, in Christian society). The essence of the act, then, is not at all relevant to its labeling as witchcraft (*kishuf*). The only thing that determines this is the performer's social membership: "If Rabbi Simeon bar Yohai carried out actions beyond the realm of the laws of nature, that was a miracle, but if a woman carried out the same action, that was witchcraft."[66]

In their studies Fishbane and Bar-Ilan convey a sociological conception of magic and religion. But there is an essential difference between them. Fishbane presents the female witchcraft dimension as a structured cultural expression of collective male anxiety about the social power of

65. Fishbane (1993).
66. Bar-Ilan (1993, 20).

women.[67] Bar-Ilan claims that the rabbis did indeed have good reason to fear them. Because rabbis distanced women from any leadership role, women tried to control society by means of witchcraft and to dictate to men what to do: "To a certain extent one can regard this as a type of 'revenge' by the woman against the male world which forced her to act in this 'non-conventional' manner."[68] These remarks explicitly deal not only with women's actual attempts to activate supernatural means in order to attain control but also with the effectiveness of these attempts. According to Bar-Ilan, then, witchcraft is an oppressive political term reflecting struggles that had been related to supernatural power and were actually waged between men and women.

In recent years, several scholars have shed further light on gender aspects of witchcraft traditions in rabbinic literature. Tal Ilan offers a feminist reading of the "witch hunt" in Ashkelon as a basis for a renewed understanding of the historical events recorded in it.[69] Rebecca Lesses examines the place of the female gender in three layers of the Jewish culture of witchcraft: clients, witches, and she-demons. She sees the actual connection between talmudic traditions and magic traditions in Babylonian incantation bowls and bases her approach on a study of these two bodies of sources. She also notes that the female character of witchcraft in rabbinic literature reflects a gender politics struggle. Yet, by relying on traditions about general medicine and magic healing conveyed by Abaye's foster mother, as transmitted and preserved in the Talmud through her son, Lesses claims that the rabbis' gender ideology in this regard is not uniform. Women are indeed perceived as "engaged in sorcery"

---

67. Fishbane's example of the *zar* illustrates another way of male dealing with this anxiety (which is related to the oppression of women) through the category of the supernatural. He presents the *zar*, a kind of possession widespread in Sudan and Ethiopia, as a means for tension release in the oppressed female group within a structured and well-demarcated context (Fishbane 1993, 35–37). On the *zar* among Ethiopian Jews, see also Bilu (2003), Edelstein (2001; 2002), and Grisaru and Witztum (1995).

68. Bar-Ilan (1993, 21). On the role of the actual performative power of miracles (or sorceries) in historical considerations, cf. Bar-Ilan (1995, 23–24).

69. Ilan (2006, 214–23). Ilan challenges the interpretations of Joshua Efron and Martin Hengel, which she presents briefly. See Efron (1988) and Hengel (1984). On this story, see also Amir (1994) and Yassif (1999, 156–58).

but also, at times, as possessing knowledge vital for protection and healing from it. This kind of knowledge was valued and preserved by the rabbis in their literature, despite its female origin.[70]

Kimberly Stratton, who emphasizes the social-political aspect of sorcery accusations in antiquity, including in rabbinic literature, extensively discusses the feminine dimension of the discursive practice of othering. Stratton points to the deep connection between women, food, and magic typical of both Palestinian and Babylonian sources: "If there is a single ideology regarding magic in rabbinic writings, the association of women, food and magic might be it."[71] She excels at illustrating this connection through traditions linking magic and cooking and, pointing to the rabbinic use of food as a metaphor for sex, she states, "The fear of women preparing food, expressed in many rabbinic presentation of magic, may mirror a deeper anxiety over controlling women's sexuality."[72] Sex and magic, then, intertwine in the rabbinic discourse on magic as two facets of a female power that the rabbis feared and sought to restrain.

Joshua Levinson, who sharpens the differences between stories on magic in the Palestinian and Babylonian Talmuds, explains the stories in the Babylonian Talmud in light of his determination that "Babylonian magic—and particularly female magic—is presented as a carnivalesque threat to the *beth midrash* culture. Not surprisingly, the carnivalesque also includes a gender component: while the world of the *beth midrash*, which is distinctly male, symbolizes the desirable normative order, its opposite is characterized by female characteristics."[73] Levinson then discusses at length the carnivalesque character of the magic stories in the Babylonian Talmud and the women's share in the rabbis' structuring and staging of the "anti-culture."

Feminism and gender are only one channel for developing the discussion about the social aspects of magic in rabbinic literature, and scholars deal with them from several directions. Eli Yassif contributes a

---

70. Lesses (2001). See also Janowitz's review of magic and gender in the rabbinic and Greco-Roman worlds (Janowitz 2001, 86–96).

71. Stratton (2007, 169).

72. Stratton (2007, 174).

73. Levinson (2006, 312).

literary-folkloristic approach to the discussion.[74] He suggests separating Halakhah from Aggadah and concentrating on the latter. In his view, latent in the narrative structure are solutions to the many problems that concerned scholars regarding the rabbis' attitude toward magic and demons. Yassif holds that the rabbis shared the belief in demons and spirits; however, he is puzzled by the relatively large number of demon stories in their literature. He shows that these stories had didactic aims. As usual in all religious establishments, the rabbis also enlisted the society's deepest fears to impose their views on it, and they did so through exemplary demonological stories, among other things. The plots of these stories, which were purportedly real, attest to the superiority of the religious and ethical values preached by the rabbis in the struggle against demonic evil and in gaining protection from it. Incidentally, these stories also corroborate the relative superiority of the bearers of these values, that is, the rabbis themselves.

Yassif adopts a similar attitude concerning rabbinic witchcraft stories. He suggests distinguishing the rabbis' pronouncements from the stories about them. In this model the rabbis' pronouncements point to their opposition to magic (and at times even to interest in it) and reflect the rabbis' historical image. By contrast, the witchcraft stories about the rabbis are a collection of popular fabrications that were created many years after the rabbis' death.[75] These exemplary fabrications, which glorify the miraculous-magic power of the rabbis, the community's heroes, found their way naturally into rabbinic literature. The didactic form they were given in its context served the rabbis' ideological and political aims.

An additional direction in the development of the sociological discussion of magic touches on the halakhic category of "ways of the Amorites," which in the past had been mainly a topic of philological and historical research.[76] Giuseppe Veltri and Jonathan Seidel separately claim that this

---

74. Yassif (1999, 144–66).

75. Yassif discusses the figure of R. Joshua b. Ḥanania (Yassif 1999, 162–63). Cf. Neusner's discussion of R. Joshua b. Peraḥia, where he points to the rabbi's duality as a sage in rabbinic literature and as an expert on exorcism in Babylonian magic bowls (Neusner 1969, 13–17; 1969–1970, 5: 235–41). See also chapter 5.

76. See Avishur (1979), Hadas-Lebel (1979, 454–77), Lewy (1893a), and Lieberman (1992, 3: 79–105). See also the discussion in chapter 7.

notion, in which rabbis distinguish permitted from forbidden, does not relate to the essence of the acts defined through it but only to their social ascription. The problem with the foreign elements that spread among the people did not concern the elements themselves but only their foreignness. Seidel holds that, for the rabbis, the "ways of the Amorites" category denotes acts that were less significant in the category of magic. Their foreignness was less problematic to the rabbis than the "abuse of divine/human boundaries,"[77] as they presented magic, because magic posed a direct threat to the exclusivity the rabbis demanded for themselves in the use of these powerful boundaries. The ways of the Amorites were forbidden as idolatry. Magic was described as hostile to and as weakening heavenly powers (TB *Sanhedrin* 67b and parallel versions) and was thus transformed from an enemy of the establishment into an enemy of society.[78]

Veltri emphasizes the authority-dependent relativity of what is meant by the ways of the Amorites, because, barring an essentialist principle, each case is decided ad hoc.[79] He later develops the idea of empiricism concerning the rabbis' view of witchcraft, particularly concerning healing, and applies it to the ways of the Amorites as well. His central claim in these studies is that, regarding "Greek wisdom" (*ḥokhmah yevanit*), meaning contemporary scientific knowledge and its accompanying praxis, the rabbis were suspicious but open. Their attitude was based on pragmatism and empirical investigation. What had proved empirically useful was accepted. The rest was rejected as idolatry. Veltri thus shifts the discussion from the magic-religion realm to that of magic versus science.[80] In his view, whatever proved to be "science" was excluded from the category of

---

77. Seidel (1995, 150).

78. Seidel (1995). In his recent discussion on this issue, Gideon Bohak also emphasizes the rabbinic distinction between magic and the ways of the Amorites but still stresses the difference between these ways and idolatry: "Such a category [the ways of the Amorites] had one great advantage, as it could serve as a repository to all those contemporary Gentile practices which could not easily be subsumed under the category of 'idolatry' . . . since they were not directly related to any specific idol, temple or pagan cultic activity" (Bohak 2008, 384).

79. Veltri (1994).

80. For a brief discussion of the problem related to the term *magic*, the opposition to the suggestion of abandoning it, and the deliberate avoidance of defining it, see Veltri (1997, 18–20).

magic, even if it did derive from a foreign source. The ways of the Amorites category served the rabbis precisely for drawing a distinction between what had proved useful and thus was accepted as ours, and what had failed to pass the empirical test and had been rejected as foreign magic (TB *Shabbat* 67a and TB *Hullin* 77b). According to Veltri, the empirical thought seeking direct ties between cause and effect in reality is also at the basis of the distinction between a sorcerer, "who carries out a (real) act" (*'oseh ma'aseh*), and one who merely creates illusions (M. *Sanhedrin* 7:11). Rabbinic empirical thought did not exclude the possibility of action through supernatural powers. It examined such actions suspiciously and affirmed them or rejected them ad hoc. In any event, no place was found for their agents outside rabbinic circles. The rabbis' aspiration to monopolize all the knowledge tied to supernatural powers led them to reject whomever they suspected of possessing any ability to genuinely affect reality, through a power they sought to preserve solely for themselves.[81]

In recent decades and particularly since the 1990s, a trend of social-political gender analysis has become prominent in the study of magic in general and in the inquiry into accusations of witchcraft and stories about the rabbis' struggles against it in particular. This trend seeks to exclude the rabbis' opposition to magic from the realm of ideology and to link it instead to their aspiration to monopolize truth, the supernatural power derived from it, and the social leadership related to both of them. This insight is tied to the scholars' view that all beliefs and rituals related to the supernatural are part of one system. Distinctions between religion and magic, between miracles and sorceries, between saints and witches, and so forth are perceived as an intracultural expression of

---

81. Veltri (1997; 1998; 1998–1999; 2002). In his article "On the Influence of 'Greek Wisdom'" (1998), Veltri further argues that the rabbis' openness to magic healing, which was the practical science of late antiquity, extended also to astrology, the theoretical science of the time, which they supported on the basis of a rational, empirical-pragmatic examination. In another article, Veltri (1998–1999) attempts to show that the rabbis' empirical approach parallels that of Pliny the Elder to contemporary medicine and that the ways of the Amorites described in the Tosefta, which Avishur (1979) links to Babylonian beliefs, often resemble Pliny's descriptions of the ways of the Persian *magush* (priest). Cf. Janowitz (2001, 13–16). For a distinction between magic and healing in rabbinic thought, see also Bar-Ilan (2002). And see the discussion of rabbinic "medical science" in Bar-Ilan (1999).

gender and political struggles using ideological language and symbols. Yet not all scholars adopt this approach. Approaches seeking to unify, separate, or link magic and religion in rabbinic literature have also been discussed without paying attention to the power fields generated and demarcated by language.

Ithamar Gruenwald, for example, ascribes definite "mystical-magic" overtones to rabbinic spirituality. His starting point is essentialist. Gruenwald views magic as a "cognitive modus that organizes the religious person's perception of reality" and determines both his conceptual and actual world.[82] The distinction, then, is not between the religious and the magic phenomenon but between different types of cognitive modes: a magic one on the one hand and a rational-scientific one—I presume—on the other. From an external perspective, that of a researcher in Western culture, religion is a way of expressing the cognitive magic modus. This was also the religiosity of the rabbis. Indeed, as Gruenwald indicates, "This is not the usual pagan magic, but a magic denoting a special spirituality," even though mystic-magic elements are still prominent within it.[83]

Gruenwald identifies the core of magic as the attempt to influence natural or supernatural external powers through the human spirit. He relies on this insight to point out the magic character of the rabbis' miracles and to determine that the main Jewish religious ritual, prayer, is an expression of a magic worldview.

> The human spirit operates in magic through words, magic names and other accessories. . . . Words have inherent power. . . . In this sense, words used in prayer are no different in principle from those used in magic. . . . In other words, the religious ritual—particularly one accompanied by words and special formula—fundamentally bears a magic character.[84]

---

82. Gruenwald (1996, 20).

83. Gruenwald (1994, 93). Gruenwald does not clarify what he means by "usual pagan magic," but he is clearly trying to differentiate the magic religiosity of the rabbis from views that he identifies as another magic. His definition of magic still fits the anthropological descriptions of the phenomenon in preliterate tribes as well as magic in the Hellenistic world.

84. Gruenwald (1994, 94). This claim is compatible with that of Yitzhak Baer concerning the theurgic perception of sacrifices during the Second Temple period (Baer

This conclusion goes well beyond the scholarly discussions on the rabbis' knowledge and their miraculous or magic deeds[85] and touches on the essence of the religious act taking place between an individual and God, which the rabbis established and shaped.

Moshe Idel's approach is even more radical. He defines Jewish magic as "a system of practices and beliefs that presupposes the possibility to achieve material gains by means of techniques that cannot be explained experimentally."[86] In Idel's view, the most significant category in the discussion of magic is empirical explanation, and the productive distinction in such a discussion is the one between magic and scientific-empirical thought. Idel also adopts an approach that defines magic in essentialist terms by comparing it with the empirical category (a category that is a fundamental principle in the cultural system that organizes reality in his own world, as a researcher). This approach blurs almost entirely the border between Jewish systems of faith and action, usually referred to as magic and religion. It does exclude from the broad scope of magic limited aspects of religious "rationality" (and possibly perceptions that shift the entire gain from this to the next world) but still leaves within it the absolute majority of Jewish manifestations of religiosity. Moreover, "The phenomenologies of some forms of Judaism, with the exception of some few, though sometimes influential exceptions . . . [are] magic at the core, because of the centrality of performance acts—ritualistic and liturgical— over knowledge and faith."[87] This magic core, fundamental to most expressions of Jewish religiosity, enabled the penetration of similar magic elements from the surroundings. Rather than creating Jewish magic ex nihilo, these elements were absorbed into and enriched its core.

1985, 1: 399–457). Nevertheless, Baer took exception to the use of the term *magic* in the context of acts performed in "developed and explicitly theistic cults" (435 and note 90).

85. The scholarly literature on the wondrous figures of rabbis is extensive. Mostly, this literature is either descriptive or comparative and does not address the methodological questions discussed here. See, for instance, Bokser (1985), Green (1979), Kalmin (2004), L. I. Levine (1989, 105–9), Lightstone (1985), Patai (1939), Rosenfeld (1999), Safrai (1965; 1985), Sarfatti (1957), and Vermes (1972; 1973).

86. Idel (1997, 195). Idel's article examines magic in broad contexts of Jewish religious culture, but his conclusions touch directly on rabbinic literature. Cf. Idel (2004).

87. Idel (1997, 206).

Idel applies this view of magic in his many studies of Kabbalah and Hasidism, which exceed the scope of this survey. For my current concern, what matters is his discussion of ancient Jewish "theurgy," as he put it, including the "theurgic elements" in rabbinic faith. In *Kabbalah: New Perspectives*, Idel defines theurgy as "the ritualistic and experiential way of relating to the divinity in order to induce a state of harmony."[88] Often, however, such attempts to influence the divinity are ultimately directed to the attainment of some material gain. Hence, even though "in contrast to the magician, the ancient and medieval Jewish theurgian focused his activity on accepted religious values," his actions are actually magical.[89] Idel shows that rabbinic sources expressing a theurgic vision of the commandments attest that they were perceived not only as a means of intensifying divine power but also as a way to bring down God's *Shekhinah* upon the world. Some of the sources link the world's existence to the commandments. According to these sources, then, the official Jewish system of ritual, as shaped by the rabbis, is, in Idel's definition, a kind of magic activity.[90]

Dinah Stein deepens these insights and adds a further layer to them, the latest so far. If magic had thus far invaded the rabbis' religiosity and the religious praxis they had established, then, according to Stein, magic is tied to the uniqueness of Jewish faith. She makes this connection from an original perspective that traces the meaning of magic as a cultural symbol in general and in the context of the monotheistic experience in particular.

The nucleus of the magic experience is the sense of a gap. . . . The gap is the basic experiential paradigm in a disjointed and fragmented world: there is a semiotic (including a verbal) gap

---

88. Idel (1988, xi). See also Idel (1997, 156–72) for a discussion of ancient Jewish theurgy. Gershom Scholem was the influential source of the term *theurgy*, which was adopted by scholars of Jewish thought and mysticism (such as Moshe Idel, Ithamar Gruenwald, and Rachel Elior) from the 1950s onward. In one way or another, they all endorse the cross-cultural, ritual-practical denotation ascribed to it by Scholem.

89. Idel (1988, 157–58).

90. Idel does not explicitly formulate such a claim in his 1988 book, but the determined view he would develop in his later studies is already discernible here between the lines.

between sign and signified, a gap between humans and their surroundings and between humans and God. Furthermore, the power of the magic language, which flows from its simultaneous ascription to three generally separate categories—God, humans, and the object itself (language itself)—also hints at a (longing for) a uniform undifferentiated system. Magic, then, expresses a longing for a non-differential, "non-gapped" state: fantasy. We should therefore understand the centrality of the magic experience especially within the monotheistic context, which seeks to bridge what Goldin had referred to as "the empty space between God and man." Magic praxis then, in a way realizes the experience that is also at the basis of the miracle.[91]

This suggestion is diametrically opposed to the logical argument that Urbach turned into the basis of the rabbinic view of magic and to the views of Lieberman, Weinroth, and others who tried to cleanse Judaism, in its "pure form," from any hint of magic. According to Stein, it is in monotheistic faith that magic acquires a particularly deep meaning. Where the gap between God and humans is especially broad, where the concealing of God is remarkably large, and where the human loneliness that follows from them is exceptionally harsh, a particularly strong yearning arises for a magic that will bridge the gap. Stein, then, anchors magic in a mentality founded on an existential gap experience. This mentality has distinct performative expressions, such as the magic treatises and the adjuration texts in *Hekhalot* and *Merkavah* literature, but also has literary expressions that are not expressly practical (such as those in *Pirke de-Rabbi Eliezer*, on which Stein focuses her study). This mentality does not identify magic as a separate phenomenon and does not detach it from other phenomena. The border between incantation and prayer, between magic and miracle, and between magic and religion is therefore blurred. All are part of a broad cultural system, founded on a painful experience of gap and on a deep yearning for a way of bridging that gap.[92]

---

91. Stein (2005, 184–85). Cf. Goldin (1976, 131).

92. Stein (2005, 178–86). See also Stein (2005, 262–67) for Stein's remarkable analysis of the "shortening of the way" (*qefiṣat ha-derekh*) as a concrete symbol of closing gaps.

Research, pendulum-like, tends to oscillate between theoretical extremes. Earlier in this chapter I discussed a radical reaction to the prevalent research view: the position of Yehuda Liebes. A more moderate response is that of Peter Schäfer. Schäfer's work marks the beginning of a retreat from the almost absolute unification of magic and religion in the thought and the praxis bequeathed by the rabbis.[93] His is not a sharp movement. Schäfer fine-tunes the distinction between magic and religion on the basis of nuances rather than separate categories. He rejects the demand to refrain altogether from the use of the term *magic* in the study of ancient culture. He is also opposed to its understanding as merely a political term, whose meaning is summed up by pointing to power struggles between individuals or groups in the community. Instead, Schäfer suggests adopting William Goode's view and sees magic and religion as phenomena separated by a fine distinction rather than as a dichotomy, given that they are on a continuum.[94] Schäfer finds Dorothy Hammond's proposition to view magic as one of the powers operating within religion especially fruitful, because it enables him to discern magic within rather than against religion. In his view, which resembles Gruenwald's, magic in Jewish religion is the part of it that emphasizes human supernatural powers of action and influence in the world. By contrast, other perceptions in religion emphasize the absolute power of God.

Schäfer refrains from weaving in the thin and defined strains of essence, which are necessary to capture magic phenomena in religious culture in general. His discussion of magic in rabbinic literature, however, is based on such a web. He ties the rabbis' absolute rejection of magic and the struggle they waged against magic practices that he claims were widespread to an ideological stance: The rabbis viewed them as idolatry. Schäfer's study of sources dealing with healing led him to the conclusion that the rabbis' distinction between legitimate and illegitimate healing practices rests on the character of the act. Healing through prayer did not contradict faith and was therefore recognized as miraculous

---

93. Efron and Weinroth do not represent a reaction to the development of the discussion on the question that concerns me here. Theirs are independent reflections that completely ignore the results of this discussion.

94. Cf. chapter 1.

healing and practiced by the rabbis. Healing through witchcraft was rejected because it was idolatry. Magic elements were adopted only if compatible with the rabbinic values of faith and were allowed only to the rabbis.[95]

Another approach, recently endorsed by Philip Alexander, makes a similar but far stronger claim, stating that the rabbis' attitude toward magic rests on their theological view. Alexander points to a trend marked by the breakup of the magic category and the rabbis' "decriminalization" and "liberalization" of magic actions in relation to the biblical view. This trend is evident in the creation of the illusion (*'aḥizat 'einayim*) category in the realm of magic on the one hand and in a somewhat lenient view of "true" (effective) magic, referring to the one performed by the rabbis with God's help, on the other. Alexander ties the opposition to magic noted in the Talmud to another kind of "true magic," which relies on help from demons. In his view, the rabbis' opposition to magic (meaning demonic true magic) follows from a prekabbalistic view concerning the cosmic power of evil forces and its theurgic aspect, which is the meaning of the statement that sorceries (*keshafim*) "deny/diminish (*makhishin*) the heavenly household" (TB *Hullin* 7b; TB *Sanhedrin* 67b). Ultimately, argues Alexander, the struggle between the rabbi-sorcerer who relies on God and the sorcerer who uses demons suggests that both sides not only are strengthened through the cosmic powers that assist them but also strengthen these powers in turn. The "Torah-magic" of the rabbis is thus not only a personal and national privilege in the struggle against evil powers but a true obligation meant to strengthen God's power in the world. For this theological-theurgic reason, argues Alexander, the rabbis did not entirely break up the category of magic, and therefore they both participated in and opposed "true magic" at the same time.[96]

Alexander's and Schäfer's views lead the current discussion to its last stop: Gideon Bohak's broad study, *Ancient Jewish Magic: A History*, and the chapter he devoted to rabbinic literature. Echoes of their views resonate in the position of Bohak, who traces the course of Jewish magic as a unique cultural phenomenon (although without defining it and without any judgmental baggage) and discusses the rabbinic halakhic discourse

---

95. Schäfer (1997).
96. Alexander (2005).

on the subcategories of Jewish magic and the related terminology. Bohak is, above all, a historian of Jewish magic, and he invests his main effort into the careful search, systematic classification, and lucid presentation of magic findings from antiquity, which he discusses both per se and in their historical intracultural and cross-cultural contexts. And he does so also in a chapter dealing with the traditions about magic and magicians in rabbinic literature. His aim is "to re-examine the rabbinic evidence in light of the 'insider' sources, produced by the Jewish magicians who were the rabbis' own contemporaries."[97]

Bohak, then, refrains from defining magic in the context of rabbinic literature. For the collection and classification of relevant materials on the perception of Jewish magic in the Jewish culture surrounding the rabbis, he relies on the cumulative magic evidence he refers to as *insider* sources, which he describes at length.[98] He seeks—and easily finds— various aspects of this cultural perception of magic in the plethora of rabbinic traditions that he gathers, classifies, presents, and analyzes. For Bohak, the reality of magic in rabbinic culture is a simple fact, discernible in the open existence of many traditions expressing worldviews and practices similar to those emerging from the magic finding: bowls, spells, use of the Ineffable Name and of biblical verses, and so forth. And although he declares that his aim is "narrow" and focused on the inquiry into rabbinic literature in light of the magic finding, his discussion extends far beyond the shared foundations of these two bodies of sources and covers questions touching on phenomenological, halakhic, and social aspects of the rabbinic traditions per se.

The prominent advantage of this discussion is the breadth of its scope. Bohak does not deal with one or another aspect of magic in rabbinic literature but with all the traditions bearing on this matter. At the same time, he does not seek to discuss this broad range as a monolithic expression of *the* magic of the rabbis or *the* rabbis' stance on magic. Instead, he examines it as a multihued mosaic, whose various tiles must be illuminated

---

97. Bohak (2008, 352).

98. The study of insider magic evidence, which is Bohak's main concern, does not rely on a definition of magic either. On his choice of a course opting for nondefinition, see the last section of this chapter ("Artifacts, Recipes, and Magic Treatises (Mainly) from the Eastern Mediterranean").

from different directions according to the matter at hand. This approach, which seeks to encompass all the information and at the same time focuses on its components, leads the discussion to many specific conclusions about, for example, the rabbis' halakhic discourse on licit and illicit magic in their religious legislation, stories about rabbis engaging in (forbidden) sorcery, the use they made of the fear of witchcraft and demons to exert social control, the social contexts of their struggles against heretics and witches, their familiarity with magic practices widespread in their Jewish and Gentile surroundings, and the magic knowledge (mainly apotropaic and antidemonic) that was absorbed in their literature. All these conclusions do not add up to one uniform trend in the rabbis' perception of magic or in their attitude toward it, which Bohak strives to formulate. Quite the opposite. From the gathering together of the many facts, sayings, attitudes, and rabbinic stories, we learn that "the rabbis had mostly undermined their own anti-magic legislation."[99]

Methodologically, Bohak relies on a distinction between what is and what is not magic in rabbinic literature (as discernible in the contemporary Jewish "magic evidence"). Using this distinction, he points out the variety of magic elements in rabbinic culture and their place in it. By doing so, he rejects the two extreme positions that had been articulated in the past regarding Jewish magic in antiquity: "We may conclude that both the claim that the Jewish magical texts we have examined belong to heretical Jews and the claim that they belong at the heart of rabbinic Judaism are false."[100] Bohak, then, seeks to propose a cautious, impartial view concerning the place of magic in rabbinic literature. The wealth and scope of the sources revealed and discussed in his study no longer leave any doubt concerning the depth of magic's hold on the rabbis' thought and on their world. Although perhaps not always compatible with the halakhic rulings they issued and possibly not entrenched at the heart of rabbinic Judaism, magic was definitely a central component of Jewish culture in late antiquity. Not only did the rabbis not fully reject it, but they also actually seized from it by the handful.

---

99. Bohak (2008, 386).
100. Bohak (2008, 425).

In sum, we can clearly see that the study of magic in rabbinic literature underwent a true revolution in the second half of the twentieth century, manifest in the attention devoted to the subject and mainly in the scholars' treatment of it. Approaches that now seem apologetic, which had sought to place magic outside the rabbis' religious world, ceded ground to sociological views of religion that do not differentiate religion from magic on essentialist grounds. The dichotomous stance by which religion and magic, miracles and sorceries, saints and witches, are antithetical, a stance that served scholars in their explanations of the rabbis' absolute repudiation of magic and of anyone involved with it, was replaced by new approaches grounded in politics and gender. The political approaches reveal the rabbis' rejection of magic as an expression of their desire to monopolize knowledge and power in the community they wished to lead. The gender approaches tie to magic a fear of women as a gender and as an oppressed group.

The rabbis' religiosity has itself been recently presented as marked by magic aspects and even as yearning for magic by its very essence. The discourse on rabbinic magic may find it hard to contain such radical views, and initial signs of explicit and deliberate opposition to them have already appeared. Beside them, echoes of the old voices occasionally resonate as well. The change, however, does not appear to have happened by itself. It is part of a broader change in the self-perception of the Western world and in the absolute value it tended (and still tends) to ascribe to its culture. The beginning of the sociological discussions of magic in rabbinic literature is tied to a change in the perception of magic in anthropological research and in the historical study of the Greco-Roman world. Their ending, so it seems, lies in postmodern and postcolonial thought, which dismisses absolute values and founds morality, faith, and ideology on relationships of power and control. Were the strong hold of this thought in the Western world to become weaker, magic in rabbinic literature may change its place yet again and even return to the place allocated to it at the start of these discussions.

Visions and Adjurations: Magic in *Hekhalot* and *Merkavah* Literature

The growing interest in magic expanded to include scholars dealing with early Jewish mysticism. This religious trend developed in Palestine and

Babylonia mainly between the third and eighth centuries CE and reached us in the form of a few works commonly known, collectively, as *Hekhalot* and *Merkavah* literature.[101] I do not discuss this literature per se, but, in general, it can be described as conveying a complex set of relationships between humans and angels and as reducing the gap between them in one of two ways: (1) through humans ascending to heaven (which is populated by an infinite number of angels and other heavenly entities) in a journey driven by the longing to contemplate the divine surroundings and God sitting on his throne and, through them, participating in and even leading the angelic ritual of God's glorification and learning the heavenly mysteries; or (2) through humans drawing down angels to the earthly realm in order to learn from them and use them.[102] Although this is obviously not an exhaustive description of early Jewish mysticism, it does clarify the course along which the power structures between humans and angels developed. These structures are the basis for the researchers' concern with magic in *Hekhalot* and *Merkavah* literature.[103]

The study of magic in *Hekhalot* and *Merkavah* literature has its roots in Gershom Scholem's work. In his 1950s studies, which deal with

---

101. Early Jewish mysticism preceded Kabbalah, which developed in Europe mainly from the thirteenth century onward. *Hekhalot* and *Merkavah* literature survived mainly in relatively late texts, originating in circles of Ashkenazic pietists. Fragmented sources of it were also found in the Cairo Genizah. The standard edition is Schäfer (1981). For compilations of *Hekhalot* fragments from the Genizah, see Schäfer (1984) and Bohak (2014b). The scope of the research literature on early Jewish mysticism is vast. For reviews and extensive discussions, see Arbel (2003), Boustan et al. (2013), Dan (1993), Elior (2004a), Halperin (1988), Schäfer (1992), and Scholem (1946, 40–79; 1965). On Babylonian elements in *Hekhalot* literature see, for example, Gruenwald (1969, esp. his comments on 356 and in note 7; 1988, 253–77), Halperin (1988, 362, 434–37), Swartz (1992, 216–20; 2000), and Vidas (2013).

102. Further gaps between humans and angels are also reduced in ancient Jewish mysticism—in the ritual and in essence. The compilation known as *Book of Enoch III* distinctly expresses the absolute elimination of essential differences between humans and angels. See Schäfer (1981, secs. 80–81) and Odeberg (1928). See also Alexander (1983), Dan (1993, 108–24), and Elior (2004b, 88–110). On the narrowing of ritual gaps, see Elior (2004b, 232–65; 1997).

103. Lesses has reviewed this topic (Lesses 1998, 24–56). I will be brief on topics that she expanded on and add to her findings.

Jewish mysticism,[104] Scholem points to the magical and theurgic features typical of this literature. He hardly refers to these features, however, nor does he seem to ascribe great significance to them. He views them as a secondary element that was added to the vital core of *Hekhalot* and *Merkavah* literature—the experience of ascending to heavenly heights and contemplating God.[105] For Scholem, theurgy, meaning the adjuration of the angels, was only a means for attaining the true end, a tool serving mystics to carve their upward path to the longed-for contemplation of the divine throne, and definitely not an essential interest. The rejection of magic as an essential element of ancient Jewish mysticism is also evident in Scholem's attitude toward the Prince of Torah (*sar shel Torah*) traditions. The explicit concern of these traditions is to adjure the angel in charge of the Torah and use him to attain absolute knowledge and remembrance of it. In Scholem's view, we can distinguish the early layers of these traditions, where the magic element is absent, from the later layers, where its presence is decisive.[106] Scholem, then, relegates magic to the margins of *Hekhalot* and *Merkavah* literature. He views it as an element of minor importance to the essence and the concern of

---

104. Boaz Huss suggests abandoning the notion of "mysticism" in general and of "Jewish mysticism" in particular. In the wake of postmodern and postcolonial critiques of the study of "religion," such as those of Tallal Asad, Jonathan Z. Smith, Timothy Fitzgerald, and Russell McCutcheon, he suggests that "mysticism" is the theoretical structuring of a universal phenomenon that does not actually exist. Its theoretical existence results from the ideological projection of Western cultural conventions onto a set of human activities that lack unifying essentialist foundations and onto communities that do not use the semantics of mysticism research and that probably do not identify their activity as fitting this semantics in their modern Western meaning. See Huss (2007).

105. For Scholem's studies on the magic and theurgic foundations of *Hekhalot* and *Merkavah* literature, see mainly Scholem (1946, 50–51; 1965, 75–83). On his perception of the visionary experience as the core of this literature, see Scholem (1946, 40–79, esp. 43–44). On this issue, see also Schäfer (1988, 277–81; 1993, 59–64). On Scholem's attitude toward magic in his studies on Kabbalah, see Bohak (2012c).

106. See Scholem (1946, 12–13). On the traditions of the Prince of Torah, see Schäfer (1981, secs. 281–306). For an extensive discussion of them, see Swartz (1996). See also Dan (1992b). See also Schäfer's claim against Scholem that one cannot simultaneously hold that *Hekhalot Zutarti* is an ancient work and that the magic elements in *Hekhalot* literature are late (Schäfer 1993, 73).

this literature, one that gained a hold in it only in the later stages of its development.[107]

Magic aspects were hardly considered in the research of *Hekhalot* and *Merkavah* literature in the two decades that followed. Moshe Idel and Ithamar Gruenwald are the most notable contributors to the discussion. Gruenwald, who describes this literature as "technical guidebooks" for mystics, sees two facets in it: descriptions of heavenly journeys and descriptions of drawing down angels. In his work he ascribes far greater importance to the magic-theurgic aspect in both these areas than Scholem did. Gruenwald points out the magic elements common in the practices described in *Hekhalot* and *Merkavah* literature and examines their ties with the magic found in Greek magical papyri. Nevertheless, he cautions against the perception of this literature as magic-theurgic or as an expression of such an experience. To judge by Eric R. Dodds, whom he quotes, Gruenwald draws a distinction between popular magic, which uses holy names and wordings from a religious source in order to attain secular ends, and theurgy, which uses popular magic rituals for religious purposes. The purpose of adjuring the angels, then, is what determines whether the action is placed under the rubric of popular magic or religious theurgy.[108] Gruenwald later refines this distinction in an article where he points to "mystical-magic" layers in rabbinic religiosity. Idel deepens even further the significance of magic in the worldview of the descenders to the heavenly chariot (*yordei ha-merkavah*)[109] by pointing out that the view of the Torah as a "mystery" (*raz*), which their literature endorses, is equivalent to a view of the Torah as names endowed with a performative power that humans can activate.[110]

---

107. For a detailed analysis of Scholem's view on the stages of magic's penetration of mysticism, see Schäfer (1993, 59–64).

108. Gruenwald (1980, 98–123).

109. In *Hekhalot* and *Merkavah* literature, and especially in *Hekhalot Rabbati*, the visionary journey to heaven is termed *yeridah* (descent) rather than *'aliyah* (ascent). Scholars have offered various explanations for this puzzling terminology. See Boustan (2005, 11n24). On *yeridah* texts in *Hekhalot* and *Merkavah* literature, see Kuyt (1995).

110. Idel (1981).

The publication of Peter Schäfer's *Synopse zur Hekhalot-Literatur* in 1981 and the consequent surge in the research of this literature widely broadened the inquiry to include the issue of magic within it. Rachel Elior is one of the more prominent participants in this discussion. She notes the importance of holy names in *Hekhalot* and *Merkavah* literature and the particular interest of *yordei ha-merkavah* in them. In her view, this interest results from the magical and theurgic potential of these names. Although Elior holds that the main concern of the early mystical treatises is the heavenly vision, heavenly learning, and poetry, she clarifies that the holy names, which are the essence of the heavenly revelation, became a mystical-magical means to determine the possibility of a mystical experience.[111] This experience is infeasible without knowledge of holy names and without the mystic activating the performative power hidden in them. Separating mystical from magical layers in this literature, then, is impossible.[112] Elior develops this view extensively at a later stage. She argues that the uniqueness of ancient *Hekhalot* and *Merkavah* literature is the close integration of mysticism, magic, and angelology. She identifies the magic component as "the adjuration of angels, secret incantations, knowledge of the names, and the use of magic spells within a specific ritual framework," regardless of whether they serve for an ascent

---

111. On Elior's suggestion about linking the sources of the traditions on the heavenly ascent, vision, and ritual traditions to the Sadducean priesthood and on her attempt to point out their foundations in biblical and postbiblical literature, see Elior (2004b, esp. ch. 10). Elior succinctly formulates her view on these traditions: "Merkavah tradition readily switched to and fro between an inanimate cultic object, reflecting a celestial pattern, and a living visionary entity, reflecting a cosmic order as represented in cultic and numerical terms, a luminous reality of a mythical and metamorphic nature, a celestial liturgy performed ceremonially in the supernal sanctuaries. In so doing it essentially invoked creative imagination, the poetic power of memory embedded in language, to combine remembrance of song and sacred service in the earthly Temple, their immortalization in the visionary Temple, and the renewed experience of them in the mystical *hekhal*, the world of the ministering angels and the descenders of the Merkavah" (Elior 2004b, 258–59). The historical theory introduced in Elior's book evoked widespread criticism. See, for example, M. Himmelfarb (2006) and S. Stern (2005).

112. Elior (1987).

and a mystical vision or for drawing down heavenly powers: "The use of meaningless names to create a link with a supernatural force is a mainstay of magical thought, of mystical elevation, and of ritual worship."[113] All forms of direct contact between the human and the supernatural in Judaism, then, assume magical overtones.

In another article, in which Elior discusses the difference between mystical language (the divine, creative language that turns chaos into essence and that eventually turned into communicative [Hebrew] human language) and magic language (meaningless names and meaningless letter combinations that resist semantic decoding), Elior describes Jewish magic as follows:

> In Jewish culture, the magical element implies using meaningless names, nonsensical sentences, or letter combinations lacking a common semantic denotation in a ritual context related to a tradition of using names in order to attain supernal powers, to shift to supra-sensual forms of being, or to acquire hidden knowledge granting some form of influence over supernal and nether worlds.[114]

This is an essentialist definition that views Jewish magic as (1) a practice (2) of using a language lacking a known semantic meaning (3) in a ritual event (4) in the context of a knowledge tradition (5) to attain supernatural powers (6) in order to realize through them aspirations bearing on heavenly and earthly matters. According to this definition and in line with the perception of mystic language suggested by Elior, integrating descriptions of heavenly visions in the communicative language of humans with the use of meaningless names is the classic manifestation of how mysticism and magic are interwoven in *Hekhalot* and *Merkavah* literature.

In this context Joseph Dan's brief discussion of magic language in ancient mystical writings deserves mention. As a rule, Dan hardly refers to the magic aspect of *Hekhalot* and *Merkavah* writings in his studies. He confines himself to noting the existence of magic elements

---

113. Elior (1993, 11–12).
114. Elior (1998, 83).

within them (particularly when dealing with *Sefer ha-Razim*, *Ḥarba de-Moshe*, and *Havdalah de-Rabbi Aqiva*, which he includes in this category) and to emphasizing the importance of the Prince of Torah traditions.[115] At a later stage, he devotes attention to the essence of magic language and its relationship to religious and mystical language. In his view, Jewish magic texts in the corpus of ancient mystical writings convey a view of language that is both semantic and semiotic. The semantic element is evident in the magic instructions, which are formulated in clear and precise terms resembling the language of scientific research. In this sense, magic literature is a kind of ancient scientific literature, recommending performance of certain defined actions for the purpose of attaining specific results. Yet it involves a semiotic element that comes forth in names, which are meant to denote the powers addressed in the adjuration in precise and exact terms. This function of the names follows from the magic approach that identifies language and the reality it signifies. According to Dan, this feature is unique to magic language and essentially distinguishes it from both religious and mystical language.[116]

David Halperin's extensive study on *yordei ha-merkavah* sheds a different light on the picture. Halperin holds that the main concern of *Hekhalot* and *Merkavah* literature is not a mystical ascent to heaven but an earthly struggle over knowledge of Torah and the rivalry between the rabbis and those they called ʿam ha-ʾaretz (uneducated). According to Halperin, *yordei ha-merkavah* are the ʿam ha-ʾaretz that the rabbis despised and banished.[117] These mystics borrowed the idea of the ascent to heaven from the tradition of the synagogue and "made it into a paradigm of their own struggle with the rabbinic elite for a place of honor in Jewish

---

115. See, for example, Dan (1987b; 1992a; 1992b; 1993). On the mentioned works, see chapter 5.

116. Dan (1998, 127–30).

117. Halperin (1988). The foundations for the theory that Halperin develops in his book were set in a previous study (Halperin 1980). The ʿam ha-ʾaretz are mentioned in rabbinic literature as ignoramuses who do not know Torah and Halakhah and as people one should refrain from drawing close to and marrying. Scholars disagree on their identity. For an extensive study on this topic, see Oppenheimer (1977). For a concise discussion and additional bibliography, see L. I. Levine (1989, 112–17). And see Halperin (1988, 437–39).

society—an unequal and frustrating struggle which they waged with magic as their chief weapon."[118] Halperin holds that the Prince of Torah traditions are the crux of both the interest and the activity recorded in *Hekhalot* literature. He therefore stresses the centrality of magic (which is the gist of these traditions) in this literature in general and points out how *yordei ha-merkavah* used it to gain access to the key Jewish religious value in late antiquity—knowledge of Torah.

When Halperin published his book, Peter Schäfer published the first in a series of articles suggesting a fundamental revolution concerning the essence of *Hekhalot* and *Merkavah* literature. Already in this first article, Schäfer rejects Scholem's view about the central role of the mystic-ecstatic experience in this literature and argues that it is fundamentally magical. In his view, the constitutive texts of early Jewish mysticism are "eminently magical. . . . The entire literature is permeated by such adjurations, and the means by which these adjurations are carried out are the same as those needed for a successful completion of the heavenly journey."[119] The goal of adjurations is to draw down an angel in a way that reverses the heavenly journey of humans, and its purpose is usually to attain absolute and permanent knowledge of the Torah. Schäfer emphasizes the tie between knowledge of Torah and the descent to the heavenly chariot and ties together the adjurations' explicit aims: drawing down angels and heavenly ascent.

> In both cases, the means of achieving this is magic. The world view which informs these texts is thus one which is deeply magical. The authors of the Hekhalot literature believed in the power of magic and attempted to integrate magic into Judaism. The central elements of Jewish life—worship and the study of Torah—are determined, in these mystics' understanding of the world, by the power of magic.[120]

---

118. Halperin (1988, 450).

119. Schäfer (1988, 282). Also see Schäfer (1988, 277–95). Cf. the confrontation with Scholem's position (Schäfer 1993).

120. Schäfer (1988, 290). On the connection between knowledge of the Torah and the heavenly journey, see Schäfer (1988, 257). Cf. Schäfer (1981, sec. 234).

This is the most radical view in the scholarship regarding the place of magic in *Hekhalot* and *Merkavah* literature. Schäfer dismisses almost entirely the importance of the mystical experience as a constitutive element of this literature, which he founds instead on the use of adjurations. Like Halperin, Schäfer points to the importance of adjurations for the purpose of studying and remembering the Torah and emphasizes that magic was a legitimate means of attaining religious values.[121] He nevertheless draws a distinction between magic elements in rabbinic literature and in *Hekhalot* and *Merkavah* treatises and definitely rejects the possibility that the *Hekhalot* and *Merkavah* works were created in rabbinic circles. He proposes viewing this corpus as suggesting a magic alternative to the rabbinic model, an alternative seeking to realize the accepted religious values in the realms of knowledge and ritual.

Schäfer formulates this view at length in further studies. He repeatedly claims that "the form of the heavenly journey, which since Scholem normally has been allotted the center of the Hekhalot literature, is found *only* in Hekhalot Rabbati."[122] He also shows that both this pattern of ascent to heaven and the other one (the "Moses/Aqiva" pattern) point to a significant interest in adjurations and at times are also entirely based on magic. In the first pattern of ascent, magic elements are at times entwined in descriptions of ascent to heaven and at times vice versa. In the Moses/Aqiva pattern, interest centers "around the magic-theurgical potency of the divine name and using the heavenly journey for the purpose of obtaining knowledge of this name."[123] In this context Schäfer clarifies his method by which magic is one of the powers active in religion and, in this light, determines that *Hekhalot* literature is a classic expression of a religiosity with magic at its core. The religious values are preserved but assume magic overtones, conveying the belief of *yordei ha-merkavah* in the human ability to act effectively to hasten historical processes. This is

---

121. Schäfer, however, explicitly opposed the social-historical context of magic knowledge of Torah at the focus of Halperin's method. See Schäfer (1992, 157–60; 1993, 77–78). On the controversy surrounding the role of *yordei ha-merkavah* in the Jewish society of the time, see Dan (1995). See also Davila's view in the later discussion.

122. Schäfer (1992, 143; emphasis in original). See also Schäfer (1992, 139–48).

123. Schäfer (1993, 71).

precisely the approach that distinguishes their worldview from that of the rabbis.

> The boundaries between "prayer" and "adjuration" are torn down, and the classical form of Torah study is transformed into magical adjuration. . . . The mystic of Merkavah mysticism is not satisfied with following the approved rules of Rabbinic Judaism (although he does not relinquish them), he has lost the patience to wait for redemption in the world to come. By his coercive powers he forces God, in the true sense of the word, to do his will and to bring about complete comprehension and fulfillment of the Torah—which is nothing less than the redemption here and now.[124]

Hence we find the essential difference between the rabbis' attitude toward magic and that of *yordei ha-merkavah*. Normative Judaism, that of the Bible and the rabbis, confronts magic. It tries and, in Schäfer's view, largely succeeds in domesticating it and making it part of its special set of values. For the mystical approach, however, magic is an essential element built into religious thought that requires a restructuring of traditional value approaches.[125]

The means-and-ends criterion that Schäfer uses for determining that *Hekhalot* literature is an expression of magic religiosity (the activation of magic means to achieve religious ends) also helps him to distinguish this literature from contemporary magic literature. In his view, rabbinic literature and mystical literature convey a partnership of ends (religious values) and a difference in means, whereas mystical literature and magic literature share means (adjurations) but differ in their ends. Magic literature also suggests using adjurations, but not for religious ends. It does not

---

124. Schäfer (1992, 76–77). Schäfer holds that belief in a direct cause-and-effect link concerning the effectiveness of adjurations is an expression of magic thinking, and he ascribes this belief to *yordei ha-merkavah* (Schäfer 1992, 78). His method is based on Hammond's suggestion to view magic as an expression of one of three forces at work in religion. In any event, he clarifies that Judaism leaves no room for an impersonal supernatural power and therefore acknowledges only God's power and human power.

125. Schäfer (1997, 42–43).

show the same special interest in the Torah that is the main concern of the adjurations in mystical literature.[126]

Schäfer's approach concerning the magic character of *Hekhalot* literature was not universally accepted and even evoked opposition in principle. Philip Alexander, who had already briefly discussed theurgy in *Hekhalot* literature and had pointed out its magic foundations,[127] responded to Schäfer's article with a methodological critique that had been proposed in the comparative and historical study of religions and demanded that "internal" and "external" descriptions be separated. He pointed out the negative value of magic in the ancient world in general and in Judaism in particular and stated that *yordei ha-merkavah* would have rejected outright a description of them as religious-magicians supporting a worldview pervaded by charms. Like others, Alexander also held that the distinction between magic and religion was a social-political matter rather than an essentialist one. He suggested renouncing the use of the term *magic* altogether in the study of early Jewish mystical texts and describing the works, each one separately, as located at various points on an axis having mystic contemplation at one end and theurgy at the other. Alexander also negated the Schäfer-type distinction between rabbinic and mystical Judaism on the basis of their attitude toward magic. In his view, just as normative rabbinic values have a place in mystical thought, so do magic values have a place in rabbinic thought. Hence magic cannot be used, as Schäfer tried to do, as a criterion for distinguishing between these two expressions of Jewish religiosity.[128]

---

126. Schäfer (1990, 77). The ends criterion would later serve Schiffman and Swartz (1992, 26) and Naveh and Shaked (1993, 19) in distinguishing magic from mystical literature. Note, however, that such a claim is actually a case of petitio principii. Schäfer himself edited *Geniza-Fragmente zur Hekhalot-Literatur* (Schäfer 1984) and *Magische Texte aus der Kairoer Geniza* (Schäfer and Shaked 1994–1999). But these fragments did not proclaim themselves as mystical or magic. Schäfer was the one who decided on this classification and compiled them in separate volumes. He used his own judgment concerning the religious or secular character of the use of magic as an a priori criterion for their classification. And obviously, so did all the other scholars.

127. Alexander (1986, 361–64).

128. Alexander (1993). Alexander extensively developed his view concerning the place of magic in the world of the rabbis in an article he devoted to this issue (Alexander 2005). Contrary to the political stance he adopted in his response to Schäfer, in the

Beside the external academic dispute over the mystical-religious, religious-magic, or mystic-theurgic character of *Hekhalot* and *Merkavah* literature, several scholars have dealt with the internal perception of adjurations. Meir Bar-Ilan points out a further use of magic by the mystics. In his view, traditions from tannaitic and mystical literature attest to a practice of inscribing sacred names on the mystic's body. Bar-Ilan holds that this was a set way of attaining a mystic vision and that the seals, which the descender to the chariot had to show to the guarding angels at the gates of the heavenly palaces (as explained in *Hekhalot Rabbati*), were inscribed on his body. These seals were not meant just for protection or transit. By inscribing them on the body, the mystic imitated the angels and even God, who also had names inscribed on their bodies, and to some extent became part of the supernal world.[129]

Naomi Janowitz discusses the performative power of the *Hekhalot* adjurations. She emphasizes the performative character of the poetic language used to describe the ascent to heaven and claims that, through it, the language of mystics creates the ritual framework for the ascent itself. In her view, stories of ascent to heaven are not merely descriptive. They actually create the act by speaking about it—to speak about ascent is to ascend.[130] Janowitz, however, objects to a view of this as magic. In her view, the "linguistic strategy" of the early Jewish mystics is neither religious nor magical but focused on the specific problems that need to be solved in order to ascend to heaven.[131] Hence Janowitz tries to extract the heavenly ascension from the discussion of whether it should be considered religion or magic, claiming that pragmatism, which is the category in whose light this work should be judged, is not exclusive to either of them.

A similar approach is suggested by Rebecca Lesses in her book on ritual practices to gain power in *Hekhalot* literature.[132] So far, her study is

---

article on magic in rabbinic literature he endorses an essentialist view of magic (Alexander 2005). Also see the first section of this chapter ("Magic in the Greco-Roman World: Aims of the Research").

129. Bar-Ilan (1988). On this tradition in *Hekhalot Rabbati*, see Schäfer (1981, secs. 219–24).

130. Janowitz (1989, 83–111).

131. Janowitz (1989, 104–5).

132. Lesses (1998).

the most comprehensive work in this corpus devoted to magic elements, though Lesses consistently and systematically refrains from calling them magic. In the following discussion I focus on her contribution to the subject that concerns me here: her view of adjurations as "performative utterances" and her abstention from using the term *magic*. Lesses views adjurations as only one facet of *Hekhalot* literature rather than its core.[133] She extensively analyzes many texts of adjurations in this literature and considers the conceptual and practical characteristics of the ritual culture they express. She deals with the ecstatic preparations required for the successful performance of adjurations, broadly reviews their aims, exposes the linguistic structures used in them, and points to the relationship between them and similar practices described in Jewish magic literature and in Greek magical papyri. Finally, she examines the use of adjurations in light of the speech act theory developed by the philosopher John Austin.[134]

Lesses endorses speech act theory and suggests viewing adjurations in *Hekhalot* and *Merkavah* literature as performative utterances. She bases their potential for action in the heavens on the view that Jews in antiquity perceived reality in a way that broadened society's borders to include God and the angels. In this broad society, adjuration rituals are effective performative rituals.[135] Lesses relinquishes the term *magic* in favor of the phrase "ritual practices to gain power," claiming that the dichotomous categories religion/magic or mysticism/theurgy are not useful as explanations. The alternative terminology enables her to connect adjuration rituals to practices usually referred to as religious or mystical. Lesses, then, suggests that the use of holy names and incantations in *Hekhalot* and *Merkavah* treatises should be understood as part of a broad realm of religious ritual activity. This is a kind of religious ritual meant to grant power to its performers.[136]

A similar approach is endorsed in the work of Michael Swartz. Swartz, who has dealt at length with Jewish scholastic magic, tightens

---

133. Lesses (1998, 53).

134. Lesses relies mainly on the works of Tambiah (1985b) and Sullivan (1986). But see also Lesses (1998, 161–73). On speech act theory and its applications to the study of religion and magic, see chapter 4.

135. See Lesses (1998, 161–278).

136. Lesses (1998, 55–61).

even further the connection between magic practices and normative religious values. Like many of his predecessors, he also points to the vital role of the Prince of Torah traditions in ancient mysticism and to the special magic-religious concern they denote. He also deals with the ritual aspects of scholastic magic performance and stresses traditions on the giving of the Torah—traditions alternative to the rabbinic one—that appear in *Hekhalot* and *Merkavah* literature. Furthermore, Swartz ties the Prince of Torah traditions to the broad concern with Torah knowledge and remembrance, which is also widely reflected in the magic literature that does not take part in the "mystical" Prince of Torah narrative. In this context, Swartz deals with charms for "opening the heart" (*petiḥat ha-lev*) and with the magic use of angels for knowledge in general, pointing to the significant similarities between Judaism and the Hellenistic world in their perception of magic as a means for knowledge acquisition.[137] Swartz examines the Prince of Torah traditions in connection with three issues—magic, mysticism, and scholasticism—and suggests viewing magic as the part of the ritual religious complex designed for personal purposes.[138] Yet he holds that the personal use of a ritual does not define it as magic; rather, it is only one characteristic of it.

Swartz bases the identification of Jewish magic and its definition on an original approach: an analysis of the rhetoric of adjurations in magic rituals. For this purpose he limits the definition to the contexts of place, time, and culture of these texts' creation. Swartz uses the magic texts created by Jews in Palestine and its surroundings in late antiquity and the early Middle Ages to define the phenomena that they reflect. In his view, three elements characterize Jewish magic:

---

137. Swartz (1996). On practices for opening the heart (i.e., for improving the learning and memory) in magic literature, see Harari (2005c).

138. Swartz (1996, 18–22). Swartz emphasizes that the delivery traditions of scholastic magic hinder its perception as a personal and antisocial activity in the extreme sense of the term. Like other important bodies of knowledge, Halakhah and mysticism, magic was also perceived by those who put it in writing as a body of knowledge whose standing rests on the agreed authority of whoever delivered it. Regarding the tradition and the delivery of magic knowledge, cf. Harari (2005b). On the connection between religion and magic, see also Swartz (2001b) and the discussion in the next section.

"(1) the emphasis on the power of the name of God; (2) the intermediacy of the angels in negotiating between divine providence and
human needs; and (3) the application of divine names and ritual practices for the needs of specific individuals."[139] In this light, Swartz
emphasizes the ritual character of magic. Ritual and ritual power are
key concepts in his perception of religion in general and, in its context, of magic as well.

The relationship between *Hekhalot* literature and the literature of
Jewish magic adjurations, which Swartz discusses in the scholastic context, were reexamined by Joseph Naveh and Shaul Shaked in their own
discussions of magic literature. These two scholars assume a mutual relationship between these two types of writings as well as a mutual inter-
penetration of their components: "The *Hekhalot* books use the magical
style of incantations and amulets, while the magic texts of Late Antiquity, for their part, were deeply impregnated by the *Hekhalot* tradition."[140]
They also trace a historical course in the development of their relationship: To start, they note that magic traditions had already existed in
Palestine from an early period. Thus mystical-theoretical literature—
Hekhalot and *Merkavah* works—developed while borrowing elements
from magic literature. Finally, theoretical foundations from *Hekhalot* literature in turn influenced magic literature, which continued to exist
throughout. At the same time, broad sections of magic literature remained
outside the scope of mystical influence.[141]

An extreme formulation of the trend assuming mutual connections
between *Hekhalot* and *Merkavah* literature on the one hand and Jewish

---

139. Swartz (1996, 20). For previous versions of Swartz's method, cf. Schiffman and
Swartz (1992, 60–62) and Swartz (1990).

140. Naveh and Shaked (1993, 19). See also the discussion in Naveh and Shaked
(1993, 17–20). This shared view is a kind of compromise between Shaked's view, which
holds that the influence of *Hekhalot* literature on magic literature is limited (Shaked
1995, 197–98), and Naveh's view, which holds that these two bodies of literature are
intertwined and draw on the same source. For Naveh, the mystical approach uses magic
tools to discover the mysteries of the world, whereas magic literature mobilizes supernatural powers to help the troubled individual (Naveh 1992, 171).

141. Naveh and Shaked (1993, 19). This hypothesis should also be examined against
the claim of Schiffman and Swartz (1992, 16), who state that the clear inner links
between these literary bodies need not be interpreted as one's dependence on the other.

magic writings on the other is found in the work of James Davila, who views *yordei ha-merkavah* as shamans. Davila's discussion of shamanism per se and the precise shamanic character he ascribes to Jewish mystics is not relevant to my interests here. My discussion focuses on his perception of the social reality underlying these writings, which leads the trend positing the unification of mysticism and magic ("ritual power," as he prefers) to what seems its most radical articulation.[142] Davila's work aims to demonstrate that *yordei ha-merkavah* fit the shamanist model, and he anchors the visionary journeys and magic powers ascribed to them in *Hekhalot* literature in a historical reality in which they served their community as shamans.[143] This concern drove Davila to deepen the discussion on the performative aspects of *Hekhalot* literature, tying them together with magic writings close to them into one whole that, in his view, attests to the *sitz im leben* of the mystical practices of the *yordei ha-merkavah*. Thus he points out conceptual and linguistic connections between *Hekhalot* and *Merkavah* texts and the contemporary magic literature—amulets, Babylonian adjuration bowls, and incantations from the Cairo Genizah—turning them into one whole, cultural products of the very same circles.

The comparative discussion is, as such, not new. Not so its consequence and conclusion, however. The parallel bordering on unification that Davila assumes between Jewish circles of mystics and magicians serves his wish to prove the existence of a historical reality underlying *Hekhalot* and *Merkavah* literature and to show that the best way to understand it is to see its protagonists as shamans. According to his method, performance instructions in the *Hekhalot* and *Merkavah* literature are practical and their end is the personal empowerment of the Jewish mystic-magician-shaman, who ultimately uses his power for healing, protection, and exorcising demons in the service of the community as a whole. This historical reality also came to the fore in the social context of using ritual power, which was exposed in both mystical and magical literature.

The self-image of *yordei ha-merkavah* is one of people with access to powers dangerous to their surroundings. *Hekhalot* literature, particularly the Prince of Torah traditions and the opening of *Hekhalot Rabbati*,

---

142. See the discussion on the definition of mysticism, magic, and shamanism in Davila (2001, 25–54).

143. Davila (2001, 49 and passim).

explicitly shows that *yordei ha-merkavah* aspired to social-political power based on their knowledge advantage in both overt and occult realms. It also suggests an ideology that upholds the spread of knowledge—the Torah—to the entire Jewish people, by spreading the mystery of adjuring the Prince of Torah, but also hints at a confrontation with rival circles (apparently rabbinic ones) and fear of harm from them, perhaps because of this ideology. Magic texts complete the picture and point to the self-perception of mystics/magicians as able to realize their ritual power to inflict physical harm on their rivals. According to Davila, all the characteristics he reviews point to the openness of *yordei ha-merkavah* to their community (instead of the closure of secrecy that the research had tended to point to in the past), an openness that is the basis of their shamanic character.[144] So, were *yordei ha-merkavah* sorcerers? According to Davila, the answer is no. His answer is based on the two criteria that, relying on anthropological research, he sets for witchcraft: a deliberate deviation from social norms and an accusation of witchcraft. *Hekhalot* and *Merkavah* literature shows no deliberate deviation from the Jewish norm but rather the opposite, and no evidence suggests that *yordei ha-merkavah* were the target of witchcraft accusations. They may have been suspected and the public was probably apprehensive about them, but they were still part of the collective and enlisted their ritual power in its service.[145]

The unification that Davila suggests between mystical and magical texts, and even more so between the circles that created them, marks the peak of a research process seeking to highlight the magic element in *Hekhalot* and *Merkavah* literature. Gideon Bohak sought to challenge this trend in a discussion he devoted to the ties between magic and Jewish mysticism in late antiquity. This discussion is unique in the type of data that Bohak places at its center and, accordingly, in the resolution level of the answers he proposes to the question. Here as well, as in his discussion of magic in rabbinic literature, the foundation of the discussion is the Jewish magic phenomenon as it is reflected in insider testimony—magic texts with typical linguistic characteristics that reflect a typical activity. Relying on their comparison with ancient texts of Jewish

---

144. Davila (2001, chaps. 8 and 9).

145. In particular, see Davila (2001, 290–92). Also see Davila (2001, 292–302) on the shamanistic model—shaman/healer—that fits *yordei ha-merkavah*.

mysticism, Bohak first determines that, regarding two prominent works, *Sefer Yezirah* and *Shi'ur Qomah*, no real link can be established with Jewish magic. Concerning *Hekhalot* and *Merkavah* works—those dealing with the ascent to heaven and the bringing down of angels—he points, above all, to the difference between the two phenomena. Starting from a stance that, in principle, seeks to distinguish between them, Bohak turns to the links between these two bodies of knowledge and, through them, to the modes in which magicians and mystics influenced one another. Bohak's fundamental claim is that Jewish magicians and mystics (as they appear in the magic and mystical bodies, respectively) belonged to separate circles, reflected different social patterns (self-oriented mystics as opposed to client-oriented magicians), and had different objectives, even if part of their actions were shared.

> The *Hekhalot* mystics seem to seek either to ascend to the celestial *hekhalot* or to bring an angel down to earth, mainly in order to discover divine secrets and master the entire Torah. . . . The magicians, on the other hand, rarely thought of revelations of cosmological or angelological secrets . . . and their interest reveal[s] much interest in being of service to (paying) clients with the widest possible range of needs and desire. . . . Seen from this perspective [i.e., the type of purity demanded from the mystic as opposed to the materials used by the magician and also his contacts with women], the mystical and the magical texts point to two distinct types of religious personalities and social contexts.[146]

Bohak, then, revives Scholem's position that magic elements are marginal in *Hekhalot* and *Merkavah* literature. However, he does so by setting magic on concrete foundations characteristic of its operators and expressed in the performative texts and artifacts they created rather than on a general phenomenological perception of it. He restricts magic's place, as I will show, to the technical aspect of action performed by means of sacred names and adjurations. Indeed, after emphasizing the distinction between these two bodies and the social-conceptual surroundings where they emerged, Bohak turns to discuss the links between them. For this

---

146. Bohak (2008, 333–34).

purpose he argues that the (widespread) discussion about shared elements lacking a magic dimension must be abandoned and that the focus must instead shift to the most characteristic element of magic texts and techniques, the magic names: "We must once again leave the ritual aside and focus on the 'sheer gibberish of magical abrakadabra.'"[147] This inquiry reveals that these two religious professional types shared a technique based on the use of adjurations (usually in a ritual context), which included God's names, attributes, and descriptions, and a considerable number of *voces magicae*. In this context, Bohak points to vectors of influence between the groups—linguistic elements that were absorbed from the Greco-Roman environment by Jewish magicians and, through them, reached circles of mystics, or elements created in circles of mystics that found their way to magicians as well: "We certainly should not assume that Jewish magic and Jewish mysticism flowed from the same source or that one was a by-product of the other. It seems quite clear that these were independent activities, with different aims and methods and often performed by different people."[148]

Bohak's view regarding the links between magic and mysticism (magicians and mystics) rests on the same principles he relied on to examine the place of magic in rabbinic literature and culture. This approach places at the center a deep knowledge of a broad magic finding and examines the role of its typical elements—linguistic, tangible, and conceptual—in other contemporary Jewish bodies. The time has come, then, to move on to a discussion of this finding and to the scholars' approach to the phenomena revealed in it, but first, let me briefly summarize the discussion in this section.

The *Hekhalot* and *Merkavah* writings offer a firm view on the use of holy names and adjurations. In some traditions they are used in heaven in the context of a visionary journey; in others they are used on earth. For the use in heaven, the mystic employs adjurations and seals to overcome the angels blocking his passage to God and enlist their help. For the earth-bound use, adjurations are part of the ritual that aims to control angels and draw them down to earth to fulfill the adjuror's wishes. At times, *yordei ha-merkavah* use a series of adjurations to protect themselves

---

147. Bohak (2008, 335).
148. Bohak (2008, 339).

from the angels' wrath by activating the performative power of holy names. Names, then, emerge as a main focus of interest in *Hekhalot* and *Merkavah* literature, both in stories of ascent to heaven and in traditions of adjurations on earth. Scholars are no longer in dispute about this and have rejected Scholem's view on the marginality of magic elements in this literature as opposed to visionary ones. Yet the approaches that have emerged regarding the adjurations that appear in this literature are diverse: Some scholars consider the performative character of adjurations, their activation contexts, and the rituals related to them; other scholars emphasize the value context of their use (knowledge of Torah and the social and political background of this act); another group points to ancient elements of magic thought and action that assumed unique forms in them; and still others turn adjurations into the basis of the entire corpus of *Hekhalot* and *Merkavah* literature. In all these discussions, scholars have often implicitly or explicitly referred to the essence of magic and at times to its relationship with mysticism and religion. Views differ, and although some researchers point to significant differences between magic and mysticism (mainly concerning the ends of mystics and magicians in their use of adjurations), others believe that no clear distinctions prevail between magic and religion or between magic and mysticism insofar as *Hekhalot* and *Merkavah* literature is concerned and that research would not profit at all from such distinctions.[149]

Jewish Magical Literature

The scientific study of Jewish magic findings from late antiquity, that is, of artifacts and texts that reflect magical activity or professional interest in it, began in the mid-nineteenth century with the publication of the text written on five adjuration bowls in Jewish Aramaic from an excavation next to the ruins of Babylon (Iraq). The publication of Babylonian magic bowl texts has continued ever since, particularly since the end of the nineteenth century, accompanied by the publication of texts from magic artifacts, such as amulets, jewelry, and gems, and of magic recipes and treatises originating in the eastern Mediterranean. Whatever has been published in this field is obviously relevant to my concern here. Nevertheless,

---

149. For further discussion of the main adjuration texts in *Hekhalot* and *Merkavah* literature, see chapter 6.

I do not offer a detailed description of the history of this research but instead point to its development, especially to its prevalent perceptions of magic.

Scholars of Jewish magic texts have naturally paid attention, above all, to the reading and decoding of the findings that reached them. Their work was fundamentally philological and yielded editions of the inscriptions (which were often amended and improved at a later stage), their linguistic analysis, and parallel versions in other sources. This necessary basic research was often accompanied by discussions about the general cultural phenomenon reflected in these writings. My main interest here is in studies of this kind, and my discussion of them is split into two sections. I consider first the study of Aramaic incantation bowls from what is today Iraq and western Iran.[150] I then move on to the study of other magic findings, most of them from the eastern Mediterranean.[151] In this discussion my perspective is the understanding of magic and its place in Jewish culture in general.

JEWISH INCANTATION BOWLS

The study of Babylonian incantation bowls began in the mid-nineteenth century. In Austen Layard's book *Discoveries in the Ruins of Ninveh and Babylon* (1853), Thomas Ellis read and published the texts from five incantation bowls in Jewish Aramaic and one in Syriac found in Tel Amarna, next to the ruins of Babylon.[152] Not long after (1955), M. A. Levy published

---

150. Concise reviews have been published in the past. See Levene (2003a, 1), Naveh and Shaked (1987, 19–21), and J. B. Segal (2000, 21). For a detailed list of the publication of the texts from 152 bowls, updated until almost the end of the twentieth century, see Sokoloff (2002, 62–66).

151. Exceptions to this geographic ascription are magic treatises such as *Ḥarba de-Moshe, Sefer ha-Yashar, Sefer ha-Malbush*, and *Havdalah de-Rabbi Aqiva*, which are basically, and at times entirely, based on late (fourteenth century and later) Ashkenazic manuscripts so that their time and origin remain unclear. On all these works, see chapter 5.

152. Layard (1853, 509–23). For a detailed review of the nineteenth-century study of bowls, see Montgomery (1913, 13–22). Of the 2,000 bowls known so far, among them about 400 that have been studied and published, most include inscriptions in Jewish Aramaic. Other bowls bear inscriptions in Syriac, Mandaic, and Pahlavi. These were not written by Jews and are not discussed here. For a basic bibliography, see V. P. Hamilton

an article in which he offered a new reading of one of these texts together with an extensive study of its language and contents. This work marks the beginning of systematic research into magic bowls.[153] Incantation bowls continued to reach museums and private collectors in Europe, and by the end of the nineteenth century scholars had dealt with several dozens of them. Their apotropaic, antidemonic context was exposed and clarified.[154]

The work of James Montgomery, which appeared at the beginning of the twentieth century, was the significant breakthrough. In his book *Aramaic Incantation Texts from Nippur* (1913), Montgomery published the texts from 40 bowls (out of 150) found in archeological excavations in Nippur, southern Iraq. Thirty of them were written in Jewish Aramaic. Montgomery offers in this work transcriptions of the bowls' texts, translations, indexes, and a broad inquiry into their language, their social and historical relationships, and the magic-demonological culture reflected in them.[155] Although all these aspects in the research of bowls were widely developed in later works, Montgomery's 1913 work remains to this day the most exhaustive study on the subject.

Montgomery's view of the bowls' magic and its place in relation to Jewish religion is typical of his time. He drew a sharp distinction between religion and magic in general—the institutionalized cult of the gods as part of a sin and atonement conception as opposed to their mechanical coercion through adjurations—and in the Jewish monotheistic context in particular. He saw in the bowls a sign of foreign influences, Babylonian and Hellenistic, which changed the religious incantations that had been prevalent in the ancient Babylonian cult into an "absolute magic" that used adjurations technically and impersonally. At the same time, he detached the bowls from Jewish religious tradition, minimizing the

---

(1971), McCullogh (1967), Morony (1984, 384–424), Pognon (1979), J. B. Segal (2000, 103–50), and Yamauchi (1967).

153. Levy (1855).

154. Moïse Schwab suggested tying incantation bowls to the hydromancy practices that were in use in Babylonia in antiquity and later in the Muslim world, as Ellis suggests in Layard (1853, 511). This view has long been rejected. Both the contents of the bowls and the state of the script's preservation attest that they are in no way connected to hydromancy. See Montgomery (1913, 40–41) and Schwab (1890; 1891).

155. Montgomery's readings should be updated according to the emendations in Epstein (1921, 1922). Cf. B. A. Levine (1970).

importance of biblical motifs in them and stating that "the passages of real religious import are not employed."[156] Montgomery took a far-fetched view and claimed that even the Jewish elements in the language of the bowls should not necessarily be seen as an expression of Judaism, given that these motifs had also been appropriated by other cultures. On this basis, he concluded that these bowls do not express typical Jewish magic but the eclectic religiosity of late antiquity. This view is no longer common in the scholarship, which actually seeks to focus on the cultural-religious ascription of the bowls, beyond their characteristic syncretism.

Half a century after the publication of Montgomery's book, Cyrus Gordon emerged as the most influential figure in the research on bowls. In a series of articles published since the 1930s, he discusses more than twenty of them as part of his broad scientific work on cultures of antiquity.[157] Summing up the demonology of the bowls, Gordon points out the pragmatic ends common to science and magic and draws two fundamental distinctions: one between science and superstition and the other between science and magic. He suggests separating science from superstition from the perspective of the sociology of knowledge: "If something appears plausible at a certain time, it may fairly be classified as scientific; but if it is later disproved and yet people adhere to it, it is then superstition."[158] People in antiquity, then, should not be judged as lacking rationality because of beliefs that today are considered superstitions. The distinction between science and magic should be based on their attitude toward the causality principle. Gordon claims that magic disregards this principle, which is the basis of science. The demonology and the anti-demonic magic reflected in the bowls are not a science of antiquity in the modern and rational sense of science, because they derived from a worldview that ignored proven causal relationships. Yet from a historical perspective, they cannot be dismissed as superstitions. They had been part of the science of antiquity in the sense that they expressed common and acceptable knowledge about the world and about ways of dealing with it. Gordon offers an elegant solution to the question of magic that enables a

---

156. Montgomery (1913, 112). See also the entire discussion on the question in Montgomery (1913, 106–16).

157. For detailed references, see Sokoloff (2002, 63–64).

158. Gordon (1957, 160). See also the entire discussion in Gordon (1957, 160–74).

categorical distinction between magic and science but also allows for a tolerant view of those who had believed in magic before the development of modern science.

Texts from incantation bowls in Jewish Aramaic and other dialects continued to be published occasionally throughout the twentieth century, and broader summaries began to appear. William Rosell published a guide to the language of the bowls and to their Aramaic grammar.[159] Charles Isbell compiled a corpus of seventy-two incantation bowl texts, which had already been annotated by the end of the 1960s.[160] The study of the bowls' texts acquired renewed impetus with the publication of twenty-eight of them (mostly in Jewish Aramaic) in two books by Joseph Naveh and Shaul Shaked.[161] In these books, Naveh and Shaked publish texts from Babylonian incantation bowls, amulets from Palestine and its surroundings, and magic fragments from the Cairo Genizah, accompanied by extensive philological discussion and by introductions that discuss general aspects of Jewish magic culture in late antiquity. The gist of their discussions touches on the amulets and their magic (see the next subsection). Yet what deserves note here is their statement that, insofar as shifts of traditions between Palestinian and Babylonian communities are at all traceable on the basis of the magic artifacts that they created, the direction is from Palestine to Babylonia. This determination relies mainly on a comparison between versions of the historiola about Semomit (Semumit, Semumita), Sideros (the killer of Semomit's sons), and the three protectors that appear in an amulet and in two bowls. Their publication together affords a rare glimpse into the potential link between the two magic genres, the Babylonian and the Palestinian.[162]

159. Rossell (1953). See further B. A. Levine (1970).

160. Isbell (1975). On bowls that were not included in his compilation, see Naveh and Shaked (1987, 21n21). Isbell includes in his work ten bowls that had been discussed in Isaac Jeruzalmi's dissertation (Jeruzalmi 1964). Other students of Gordon, Edwin Yamauchi, and Victor Hamilton prepared compilations of bowls in Mandaic and Syriac. See V. P. Hamilton (1971) and Yamauchi (1967).

161. Naveh and Shaked (1987, 124–214; 1993, 113–43). The text on Bowl 8 had been published before; see Naveh and Shaked (1987, 174).

162. Naveh and Shaked (1987, 104–22, 188–97; 1993, 20–22). A historiola is a short story that is interwoven in the incantation and functions as part of it.

These studies, and Shaked's ongoing work on the bowl collection of Martin Schøyen, numbering about 650 items, yielded a series of articles in which Shaked points to various aspects of the bowls' magic, including cross-cultural ties bearing on their writing, their use, and their underlying demonology on the one hand and their ties to rabbinic literature, Jewish liturgy, and *Hekhalot* and *Merkavah* literature on the other.[163] Many of the articles present new bowls, which serve as the basis of the discussion. In almost all these articles, Shaked touches on questions bearing on the essence of bowl magic and on its place in the religious culture of late antiquity. His analysis indicates that this phenomenon was based on the foundations of a popular religion common to people from different cultures in Mesopotamia, which crossed the borders separating the official religions and assumed a different form in each one of them according to its special character.[164] His view concerning the definition of magic is pragmatic. At the opening of one article, he notes that, despite the difficulty of defining magic as a general phenomenon, definition is relatively easy once we encounter a magic text. Even though we do not know the precise borders of the area denoted by the term *magic*, we can use it reasonably when confronting its actual expressions. These expressions, that is, the magic texts, rest on the personal character of the practice proposed in them, which is opposed to the collective character of what he calls the "usual" ritual, referring to the religious.[165]

Other scholars have also paid attention to these questions, particularly to the considerable cross-cultural commonalities of demonological traditions and the incantation formulations on the bowls. Mandaic, Christian, Persian, and "pagan" elements found in them have been progressively revealed,[166] clarifying their demonology in general and the place of "famous" she-demons, such as Astarte and Lilith, within it in

---

163. Shaked (1985; 1995; 1997; 1999a; 1999b; 2002; 2005a; 2005b; 2010; 2011). See also Shaked et al. (2013, 1–27).

164. Shaked adopts a similar approach concerning the relationships between Judaism and Islam in the realm of magic.

165. Shaked (1995, 197).

166. See Greenfield and Naveh (1985), Harviainen (1993; 1995), Levene (1999), and Shaked (1999a). Pagans in this context are those who were not Jews, Christians, Mandaeans, or Zoroastrians.

particular. In the course of this discussion, further attention was also devoted to the ties between the Lilith mentioned in the Talmud and possibly hinted at in Midrash allusions to Adam's first wife and the Lilith mentioned in the bowls, who, it has been suggested, was the wild-haired she-demon often painted in them.[167] Hardly any attention had been paid to this iconographic aspect of the bowls until recently. Elliot Wolfson claims that, according to magic thinking, the drawings are actually the essence of the bowls and the crux of their power and that the visual symbols, iconography, and pictography in them are more important than the contents.[168] Erica Hunter and Michael Swartz have made initial suggestions concerning the images on the bowls and their function.[169] Only recently, however, has the iconography of the bowls been made the subject of a comprehensive study. In her dissertation Naama Vilozny systematically analyzes this topic, centering on three main aspects: (1) the link between content and form in the bowls themselves, (2) visual patterns common to the entire corpus, and (3) connections between this visual language and the cultural environment in which the bowls were produced.[170]

The study of the bowls as artifacts is at even a more preliminary stage. Most scholars conclude this issue by noting their simple shape and their dimensions. Hunter offers a pioneering typological investigation on the bowls, and Michael Morony's study, which includes comparative data on the types of material and the shapes of the bowls, can now be added to it.[171] This work's main importance is that it marks a breakthrough in the sociology of the bowls, another topic that has also merited scant attention so far. Morony's treatment of this topic relies on data gathered on the bowls' users, who are mentioned in them by name in contexts of gender, family

---

167. Fauth (1986); Hunter (1995b); Lesses (2001). For a discussion of rabbinic traditions on Lilith in their Mesopotamian context and their medieval development, see Gaster (1971b), Hurwitz (1980), Krebs (1975), and Yassif (1984, 63–71, 231–34).

168. Wolfson (2001).

169. Hunter (2000a, 202–4; 2000b); Swartz (2006a).

170. See Vilozny (2010). Cf. Vilozny (2011; 2013).

171. Morony (2003); Vilozny (2010; 2011; 2013). For an earlier discussion on the bowls and their visual characteristics, see Morony (1984, 384–96). Dan Levene's discussion of the *qybl'* bowls (prepared for overturning evil sorceries) also touches on the materiality of these objects (Levene 2011).

relationships (marriage, relatives, clans, polygamy), and cultural-religious belongingness (on the assumption that the language of the bowls reflects the clients' origins), and he presents their statistical segmentation. All were collected from a corpus of about 900 bowls in all the known writing languages.

The last aspect of the research that should be mentioned is the language of the bowl texts, a matter that has indeed been the focus of more attention than any other aspect. In this regard, Hannu Juusola's comprehensive and systematic study, based on a textual inventory far broader than the one that served William Rossell about fifty years earlier for his philological handbook, stands out.[172]

In recent years, several interesting theoretical developments have been recorded in the study of the bowls. Matthew Morgenstern suggests examining the grammar of adjurations for the appearance of "nonstandard" Aramaic in bowls, which he thinks are phonetic spellings (i.e., the written expression of spoken language). Concerning the structure of the adjurations, Shaul Shaked has coined a terminology for the morphological analysis of the spells in the bowls and suggests examining the various combinations of similar fundamental constructs from a *langue* and *parole* perspective. Avigail Bamberger looks at the social-cultural context of the adjurations and offers the first extensive discussion of the connections between magical *get* (divorce) bowls and the rabbinic sources dealing with the divorce writ, pointing to the contribution of the bowls' language to the understanding of the halakhic texts.[173]

The publication process of the bowls, which has gained momentum in the last few decades, culminated in five large works that have recently been printed. Judah Segal published the texts from seventy-five Aramaic bowls (as well as forty-one Mandaic bowls and four Syriac bowls) from the British Museum collection. He preceded this edition with a brief discussion of the bowls' language, their writers and the clients mentioned in them, the religious background of their creation, and the antidemonic

---

172. Juusola (1999a). Sokoloff includes the bowls in the textual inventory he used as a basis for his dictionary of Babylonian Aramaic (Sokoloff 2002).

173. See Bamberger (2012), Morgenstern (2007b) (cf. Morgenstern 2013), and Shaked (2011). For the magical *get*, see chapter 5. For a broad collection of *get* bowls, see Shaked et al. (2013, 103–275.)

praxis that they record.[174] Dan Levene published the texts from twenty bowls from the Moussaief collection (numbering over 100), which join those that had been published in his recent articles. This volume by Levene has recently been followed by another one, in which he edited and published thirty curse and countercharm bowl texts, many of them for the first time. His effort focuses on the deciphering of the bowls' texts and on linguistic inquiries, but he also discusses broader cultural contexts.[175] Christa Müller-Kessler published texts from fifty-one bowls (some broken and fragmented) from the Hilfrecht collection and from other bowls originating in Nippur in Babylon, including bowl texts in Aramaic, Mandaic, Syriac, and Pseudoscript. Her work focuses on the philological aspect of the incantations.[176] Shaul Shaked, James Nathan Ford, and Siam Bhayro have recently edited and published sixty-four bowl texts from the Schøyen collection, focusing on two major groups: texts that relate to R. Ḥanina b. Dosa and divorce texts.[177] As noted, relatively little attention in the study of bowls has been devoted to questions beyond the artifacts as such. We do not have a comprehensive and up-to-date summary of the Jewish bowl culture, and the inquiry into the relationship of the bowls with rabbinic and *Hekhalot* traditions is still in its early stages. The studies of Shaked, Levene, Lesses, and Bamberger herald such a trend in the scholarship, which is sure to expand in the future. As we will soon find, the situation is entirely different in the study of "western" (i.e., Palestine and its vicinity) magic.

ARTIFACTS, RECIPES, AND MAGIC TREATISES (MAINLY)
FROM THE EASTERN MEDITERRANEAN
Shortly before Blau published his book on ancient Jewish magic at the end of the nineteenth century, Moses Gaster published the treatise called *Ḥarba de-Moshe* (The Sword of Moses).[178] This is one of the most significant sources for the understanding of Jewish magic in late antiquity

---

174. J. B. Segal (2000). For notes and emendations of his readings, see Ford (2002) and Müller-Kessler (2001–2002).

175. See Levene (1999; 2002; 2003a; 2003b; 2003c; 2013).

176. Müller-Kessler (2005).

177. Shaked et al. (2013).

178. Gaster (1971a). On Gaster's edition, see Harari (1997b, 12–14).

published so far. The manuscript that Gaster relied on in his edition was indeed late (from the eighteenth century at the earliest), but he viewed it as a Palestinian work dating back to the first to fourth centuries CE. The edition included a translation, indexes, and an extensive discussion of textual and contextual aspects of the work, dealing mainly with God's names and the magic use of them. Gaster pointed to theurgic "Gnostic" elements of the tradition on God's names on the one hand and to its parallels in rabbinic and Geonic literature, magic adjuration bowls, *Hekhalot* writings, and Greek magical papyri on the other. In so doing, he shed light on the place of magic traditions and practices in *Harba de-Moshe* within the broader cultural context of the work, in both its Jewish and magic "international" dimensions.[179]

The second important magic treatise from late antiquity, *Sefer ha-Razim* (The Book of Mysteries), was published by Mordechai Margalioth about seventy years later. Throughout this period, only few magic findings whose Jewish origin were certain were published: texts from seven Aramaic amulets; two gems with Hebrew or Aramaic inscriptions; a magic medallion with a Greek inscription engraved on one side and Jewish symbols (menorah, shofar, and *lulav*) on the other; a brief passage from a book of magic recipes in Aramaic (which was not identified as such) on a papyrus; and two Cairo Genizah fragments.[180] The decisive issue in

---

179. In the second half of the nineteenth century, Greco-Roman scholarship equated "magical" with "Gnostic," particularly because of the image of Gnosticism in the writings of the church fathers. A prominent example in this regard is provided by the Gnostic gems, as magic gems from the Greco-Roman world used to be called. This tendency declined as the research of Gnosticism (mainly following the discovery of the Nag Hammadi papyri) and the study of Hellenistic magic widened. Cf. Bonner (1950, 1–2). Gaster and Margalioth adopted such an approach concerning potential sources of the view expressed in the Jewish magic writings that they published (*Harba de-Moshe* and *Sefer ha-Razim*); see Gaster (1971a, 1: 289–99) and M. Margalioth (1966, 17–22).

180. The Aramaic amulets of known origins are from Aleppo, Irbid, and Agabeyli (Turkey). See Duppont-Sommer (1950–1951), Montgomery (1911), Schwab (1906), and Vincent (1908). All the amulets were reread and have been compiled by Naveh and Shaked (1987, amulets 4, 5, 7a–b; 1993, amulets 27–29). On the magic medallion, which seems to originate in Syria, see Schwabe and Reifenberg (1946). For a photograph of it, see Reifenberg (1950, 143). Cf. Goodenough (1953–1968, 2: 218–19 and vol. 3, plate 1023). The fragment of the Aramaic papyrus was found in Oxyrhyncus, Egypt. See Cowley

these publications had been to present a linguistically precise and annotated version and to point to the sources of Jewish symbols, when such were found.

Margalioth's study on *Sefer ha-Razim* is different. He skillfully presents a "mosaic" edition of the work that is based on a combination of passages from many manuscripts, particularly from the Cairo Genizah.[181] He views *Sefer ha-Razim* as a Palestinian work from the third to fourth

---

(1915, 212 and plate 28), Geller (1985), and Sirat (1985, 121 and plate 76). The source of the magic gems is not certain. One is written in Greek Hebrew, and the seller claims it was found in Ephesus. See Keil (1940) (and see Scholem 1990, 29n8). On the second gem, whose origin is unknown, seven lines are inscribed in Hebrew letters that are hard to read, and they are surrounded by a circle in the shape of a snake with its tail in its mouth (*ouroboros*). See Reifenberg (1950, 143), and cf. Goodenough (1953–1968, 2: 219 and vol. 3, plate 1024). These and other gems are discussed at length in Spier (2007, 163–67). On the Genizah fragments, see Gottheil and Worrel (1972, 76–81, 106–107). The many publications of amulets and magic gems from the Roman Empire, which began in the Renaissance and expanded widely over the last two centuries, has also included many items with inscriptions of symbols or formulas of Jewish origin, but whether the magic items themselves were created by Jews is questionable. Linguistic formulas (*nomina barbara*) and various symbols that were thought to have performative power were passed around in late antiquity and made their way among professionals without consideration for ethnic or religious borders. And as Greek elements penetrated Jewish magic, so did Jewish elements gain a hold in Hellenistic magic culture. In the Greek to Jewish direction, see, for example, Bohak (1999; 2008, 277–90) and Rohrbacher-Sticker (1996); and in the Jewish to Greek direction, see Bohak (2003a) and M. Smith (1996). Also see Bohak's discussion of asymmetry in the mutual borrowing between cultures (Bohak 2007). On these grounds, we cannot establish with any certainty that amulets containing Hebrew formulas in Greek transcription or other hints at a Jewish origin were indeed created by Jews (e.g., Kotansky 1994, amulets 32 and 51). We may nevertheless include the gems (and other medallions) containing a drawing of a seven-branched candelabrum (menorah) in this corpus of Jewish magic objects. This is a distinctly Jewish symbol, and even though the magic function of these gems is not certain, they may have been used for magic purposes (though they obviously could have served merely as jewelry). See Simone (2001, items 472 and 473). Cf. Bonner (1950, 29) and Goodenough (1953–1968, 2: 221–22 and vol. 3, plates 1032 and 1033). Cf. Goodenough (1953–1968, 2: 214–22, and vol. 3, plates 1019–1022, 1026, and 1027), M. Smith (1981, 191), and Spier (2007, 161–62). On the menorah as a Jewish symbol in late antiquity, see Hachlili (2001, esp. 109, on the gems containing this symbol); see also L. I. Levine (2001).

181. For notes on the character of this edition, see chapter 5.

centuries CE that was written on the margins of Judaism and under strong foreign influence. Margalioth precedes his edition with a broad introduction in which he discusses the manuscripts of the treatise, the magic Hellenistic elements prevalent in it, what he identifies as Gnostic influence on the author, the considerations for determining its time and place, and its ties to later Jewish literature. As he attests, he invested a great deal of effort in this endeavor, and this effort was apparently not only academic. His explicit statements concerning the contents of the work and its author are a clear expression of the desire to discuss Jewish magic, drawing a sharp distinction between "magic" and "Jewish." In his view, the author of *Sefer ha-Razim* had certainly "not received a proper Jewish education."[182] His work does show that there were Jews who dealt in witchcraft and worshipped angels, but "the Jewish public in general, which obeyed its teachers and rabbis, the talmudic sages, had no concern with such matters."[183] He sums up in a preaching, self-justifying tone.

> Although the content of the book is magic and witchcraft, which the soul abhors, I thought it wrong to ignore it and felt compelled to bring it before the public of knowledgeable scholars so that we might learn what the trends of thought were in rabbinic times, what were the views of ancient heretics, and, by contrast, what was the rabbis' endeavor in their war against them. Now, confronted with the folly we found in this work, the rabbis' words will shine even more brightly and we will know how to appreciate their work and their success in cleansing and purifying Judaism from its dross, and refine it from all dust of idolatrous cult. Only the rabbis prevented the imposition of this heresy, which had been widespread among the spiritual dwarves brainwashed by magic and witchcraft, on the entire people.[184]

Such comments would hardly ever be found today in studies of Jewish magic.

---

182. M. Margalioth (1966, 27).
183. M. Margalioth (1966, 16).
184. M. Margalioth (1966, xvi).

CHAPTER 2

The publication of *Sefer ha-Razim* exposed a reality unknown so far: The Jewish people in antiquity had created magic literature in Hebrew that based on the conceptual and practical merger of both Jewish and Hellenistic components.[185] To judge by *Sefer ha-Razim*, its authors were deeply involved in the world of Greek magic and Jewish angelology, knowledgeable in such works, and professionally interested in them. The question was where exactly to locate this work and its author in the Jewish cultural context. In this regard, views were and are divided. Hen Merchavya, for instance, holds that *Sefer ha-Razim* copies Gentile wisdom, without any conceptual identification or practical intention on the author's part. In contrast, Joseph Dan (justifiably) refutes Margalioth's suggestion about the Gnostic-Jewish origin and character of the work. Ithamar Gruenwald points to the conceptual elements common to *Sefer ha-Razim* and to *Hekhalot* and *Merkavah* works; Naomi Janowitz narrows the gap between this work and the rabbinic world, and Philip Alexander holds that the author had surely been educated in a rabbinic *beth midrash*. Other scholars point out the astral foundations of the work, which they consider central, and suggest viewing it as a Jewish expression of the astral-magical tradition prevalent in the Greek and Roman world in late antiquity.[186]

Jans Niggermeyer's study on the rhetoric of *Sefer ha-Razim* is its broadest analysis so far. Niggermeyer, who also translated this work into German, divides it into its prominent elements (names, angels, ends, acts, and adjurations) and devotes most of his energy to a detailed typological analysis of the adjurations.[187] Later, Janowitz and Alexander dealt with

185. As Margalioth notes, Jews had been described as dealing with witchcraft and the cult of angels in the Christian and pagan literature of late antiquity, but here was insider Jewish evidence. See M. Margalioth (1966, 15–16) and Simon (1986, 339–68). For a description of Jewish love witchcraft in the writings of church father Epiphanius, see Harari (1997a, 250–52). On Jewish witchcraft in general in Epiphanius's story, see Elchanan Reiner (2004). On the reverence for Moses as a sorcerer in the Greco-Roman world, see Gager (1972, 134–161; 1994).

186. See Alexander (2003b, 184–90), Dan (1968), Gruenwald (1980, 225–34), Janowitz (2002, 104–8), and Merchavya (1967). For astral elements in this work, see Charlesworth (1987, 636–37), Ness (1990, 206–17), and von Stuckrad (2000b, 523–32).

187. Niggermeyer (1975). The detailed typology that Niggermeyer suggests is an excellent starting point for an analysis of the rhetoric of adjurations in a broader textual context as well.

the worship of angels and with "black magic" in the book, respectively.[188] The last phase so far of the research on *Sefer ha-Razim* is the synoptic edition of the treatise (together with its second, later macroform) and a commentary by Bill Rebiger and Peter Schäfer. Their interest is mainly textual and so is the comprehensive introductory discussion, but the detailed commentary touches on and examines almost every aspect of the book.[189]

The publication of amulet texts and fragments of magic writings continued throughout, though in limited form. In the fifteen years after the publication of *Sefer ha-Razim*, two more amulets, six pieces of Aramaic magical papyri, and three Genizah fragments appeared.[190] At this time, Gershom Scholem published his edition of a work known as *Havdalah de-Rabbi Aqiva* that he claimed appeared in Babylonia in the Geonic period and possibly even before. Scholem attached to his edition a long and scholarly study in which he pointed to the work's literary structure,

---

188. Alexander (2003b); Janowitz (2002, 85–108).

189. See Rebiger and Schäfer (2009).

190. On the amulets, see Klein-Franke (1971), Milik (1967), and Testa (1967). The two amulets are included in the compilation by Naveh and Shaked (1987, amulets 8 and 9). For the Genizah fragments, see Mann (1972, 2: 91–94). On the Aramaic magical papyri, see Marrassini (1979). Marrassini studied five fragments with few readable letters. In the first fragment, four "framed" words or names are discernible and circled and among them are possibly *krwb* (cherub) (Marrassini read *kbwd*, "honor") and *whw* (Marrassini read *zhw*). The second fragment contains a few fragmented words that do not join into a meaningful text, but at the end is the abbreviation commonly found at the end of adjurations: *'s* ('amen, 'amen, Selah). Marrassini may be correct in assuming that this abbreviation is preceded by the letters *yy*. In the space between this abbreviation and the written line below is the drawing of a square split into four. Passages 3–5 are dark and nothing can be read in them. Marrassini reads in one of them a combination of letters that is also typical of incantations: *zzzqqqw*. All these indications, and the fact that these passages were found together with passages from Greek and Coptic magical papyri, suggest that these are magic texts. For more on the Aramaic magical papyri, see Sirat (1985, 106, passage E 7020 and plates 32 and 33). On one side of the papyrus Sirat studied, the following words, which are endings of two lines at the end of the papyrus, are clearly written: [ ] *bot qdwš* / / [ ] *bqwl 'wfnym*. On the other side are drawings of *charactères*—signs made up of lines with circles at their ends, typical of magical incantations. Cf. Norman Golb's brief review on magic writings and ideas in the Genizah (Golb 1967, 12–15).

that is, to the incantation units within it. He also considered at length the linguistic and conceptual parallels in Babylonian magic bowls, *Hekhalot* and *Merkavah* treatises, rabbinic literature, and magic Hellenistic writings. In this fashion he wove the magic in *Havdalah de-Rabbi Aqiva* into the broader web of the Jewish culture of its purported time.[191] Several years later, Franco Tocci published an annotated version of the long apotropaic adjuration called *Pishra' de-Rabbi Ḥanina ben Dosa* (The Spell-Loosening of Rabbi Ḥanina ben Dosa). Influenced by Scholem, he stated that it had originated in Babylon, in the sixth or seventh century.[192]

At this time, Shaul Shaked published an unassuming article dealing with Jewish magic literature in Islamic countries, which constituted a turnabout in the attitude toward Jewish magic findings. Shaked pointed to the connection and continuity between Palestinian magic traditions and those in the writings of the Cairo Genizah—the first time this had been done—and looked for evidence of the penetration of Muslim elements into Jewish magic literature. By doing so, he also pointed to the openness of Jewish magic to such elements *precisely* because they were alien, stating that it showed evidence "not only of significant readiness to unwittingly accept influences from a nearby culture but, seemingly, also actual recognition of other religions' legitimacy, at least insofar as the magic realm is concerned."[193] He stated that Jews had been considered skilled sorcerers in their foreign surroundings and pinned this on the tendency to ascribe witchcraft to marginalized social groups, thereby conveying the suspicions and anxieties about them. Later, Shaked developed this social perception of magic in other writings as well.

I noted earlier Shaked's view of magic as a ritual with a personal purpose. Here I wish to direct attention to another matter. In another article on the relationship between Islam and Judaism in the realm of magic, Shaked points to the duality of magic in both these cultures—its official denial on the one hand and its constant presence, even among spiritual leaders, on the other. In his view, the source of this phenomenon is the

---

191. Scholem (1981). On Scholem's studies on Jewish magic, see Bohak (2012c).

192. Tocci (1986). Cf. Tocci (1984). Tocci relies on Scholem's sweeping ascription of magic works in Aramaic—*Havdalah de-Rabbi Aqiva*, *Sefer ha-Yashar*, *Sefer ha-Malbush*, *Ḥarba de-Moshe*, and so forth—to Babylonia of the time (Tocci 1986, 101n).

193. Shaked (1983, 19).

social place of those who use ritual activity, as opposed to those who relate to them and describe them. Because Shaked holds that it is hard to draw essentialist distinctions between religion and magic, he suggests defining the latter in this social context.

> I suggest that, simply, magic and the theurgic realm be defined by negation, as including everything that was not part of the accepted worship. . . . This definition is thus entirely arbitrary from a theoretical perspective, from the researcher's perspective, but highly convenient in practical terms. It releases us from the complicated and hopeless task of stripping every liturgical text down to its components in order to decide what and how much magic it contains, or of the other material, which is even harder to define: religion.[194]

This proposition implies two conclusions: (1) Magic must always be examined and characterized within a defined social-cultural context, and (2) in the Jewish context, every ritual or turn to heavenly powers that is not included in the official framework as determined by the religious establishment belongs to the realm of magic. This is an expansion of Marcel Mauss's proposal to see magic as the forbidden cult, perceiving it as including all the nonofficial rituals. As Shaked explicitly states, his proposal is guided by practical motives. He holds that identifying a magic text when one meets it poses no practical problems. Because his main concern is the texts as such, he dismisses the "hopeless" concern with definitions by means of an ostensibly "simple" and "arbitrary" definition that he himself creates. This paradox is essential to my concern, and I return to it in chapter 3.

A review that Philip Alexander wrote in the mid-1980s is the first summary on magic in Judaism (including demonology) in late antiquity.[195] This is a good and comprehensive summary of magic findings and related research available up to his time. The timing of the publication was appropriate because, simultaneously, Joseph Naveh and Shaul Shaked published their first volume that marked (and largely caused)

---

194. Shaked (1994, 9). On Muslim connections in medieval Jewish magic, cf. Shaked (2000b).

195. Alexander (1986).

the deep change in the study of Jewish magic that we have witnessed over the last twenty-five years. In this volume and in a second one, published several years later, Naveh and Shaked reveal a broad corpus of amulets and magic Genizah fragments (and incantation bowls).[196] Altogether, they edited and published texts from twenty-nine Jewish metal amulets and one clay one (and two more Christian ones) and dozens of Genizah pieces, which included texts from ten amulets and many magic recipes. Naveh and Shaked annotated the texts, translated them, and provided a broad linguistic apparatus. In the introductions to their books, they discuss broader aspects of the textual finding. First, they point to the distinct Jewish elements of the ancient amulets, such as biblical verses, the formulas "Amen" and "Selah," or the client, "Rabbi Elazar the son of Esther, the servant of the God of Heaven" on the one hand, and the cosmopolitan context of the amulets on the other. In their view, we have no reason to doubt the orthodoxy of the amulets' creators and users, and we have no justification for pushing them to the margins of Judaism or seeing them as members of lower classes. Their involvement in magic is a typical Jewish expression of a worldview common to all in the ancient world. Naveh and Shaked later expanded this claim to the adjuration literature in general and reinforced it when they pointed to the strong links of adjurations to Jewish liturgy and *Hekhakot* literature and to the medicine of the ancient world.[197]

Naveh and Shaked's first book was the beginning of an awakening in the study of Jewish magic. Naveh himself continued to deal with Palestinian amulets and their connection to contemporary manifestations of religion. He points to the presence of magic in the synagogue—the place of "institutionalized religion"—in three areas: the placing of amulets in the synagogue, the integration of linguistic elements typical of adjuration literature in the dedication inscriptions, and the zodiac and Helios ornamentations on the mosaic floors of several Palestinian synagogues.[198] Elsewhere, he expands on the connection between incantation and prayer.

---

196. See Naveh and Shaked (1987; 1993).

197. Naveh and Shaked (1987, 35–38; 1993, 17–39).

198. Naveh (1989). See also Naveh (1992, 145–76). Helios is among the most important deities in the Greek magical papyri and is addressed in many of the adjurations. He

The various types of adjurations are merely prayers. But contrary to the institutionalized prayer, to the liturgy, the adjuration turns directly to the supernatural powers and asks, and even demands, from them to help the individual in his personal sorrow. Contrary to the prayer at the synagogue, the adjuration is a personal prayer in the full sense of the term, seeking urgent solution to a burning problem. . . . As we separated the institutionalized prayer from the adjuration, one could seemingly distinguish religion from magic: religion is the institutionalized faith and ritual, whereas the direct address to God and his angels, which is not included in institutionalized worship, belongs to magic.[199]

What counts, then, is the place of the ritual within the institutionalized framework of worship. If it is included, it is religion, and if not, it is magic. This was also Shaked's view. This criterion, however, proves insufficient, given that Naveh showed that many elements of magic penetrated both official religion and its prevailing praxis. Naveh, then, ultimately appears to have endorsed an approach that combines two principles, one essentialist and one social: Magic texts have essentialist characteristics, which are clearly revealed in the adjuration literature and reflect rituals that are not part of the official one. Hence we can identify (essentialist) magic elements in institutionalized religion as well and still preserve its (social) distinction from magic. In further articles, Naveh dealt with the antiquity of magic recipes and with the magic perception of illness. He also published texts from several new amulets but did not return to deal with the essence of the phenomenon he studied.[200] This has been the prevalent trend in the publication of ancient Jewish amulets in recent years. Scholars decipher

---

is also mentioned in *Sefer ha-Razim*, in a charm seeking knowledge by talking with the sun (M. Margalioth 1966, 99). Yet note that the Helios/Sol ornamentations in synagogues have also been interpreted in other ways. On the study of Helios/Sol mosaics in synagogues, see England (2000), Irshai (2004, 91n65), L. I. Levine (1998, 149–60; 2000, 561–79), Mack (1998), Magness (2005), Ness (1990, 218–77); and Z. Weiss (2005, 104–41, 231–35).

199. Naveh (1992, 51–52).
200. See Naveh (1985; 1996; 1997a; 2002).

and annotate the writings but do not discuss them in broader contexts.[201] The study of magic in Genizah writings was handled differently.

At the beginning of the 1990s, Steven Wasserstrom wrote a programmatic article on the study of magic writings in the Cairo Genizah in which he complained about the paucity of research on the topic and its character and pointed to its required directions: typological, historical, social, and cross-cultural: "The history of the scholarship of magical texts found in the *Genizah* may be accurately and succinctly summarized: a handful of texts have been edited and translated."[202] This situation has changed. Although most of Wasserstrom's "demands" are yet to be met, the number of writings since published has greatly increased and the methods of inquiry have diversified.

One prominent example of the comprehensive and diversified approach to magic in the Cairo Genizah is a small book by Lawrence Schiffman and Michael Swartz in which fourteen incantations from the Genizah are published, most of them from amulets.[203] Schiffman and Swartz precede their discussions of amulets with introductory chapters, where they point to the links between adjurations in the Genizah and adjurations in Babylonian magic bowls and Palestinian amulets, examine their place in relation to rabbinic and *Hekhalot* traditions, and devote an extensive description to "the magic of the amulets." In this context they discuss the rhetoric of the adjurations, the amulets' performative practices, the views on angels and demons that are revealed in them, and the social aspects related to their preparation and use. This introductory survey is a first attempt to engage in the comprehensive study of ancient Jewish magic literature and of the cultural phenomenon it reflects. In the course of it, Schiffman and Swartz also question the definition of magic. Their approach to this topic is original, as was the conclusion that emerged from it. Schiffman and Swartz claim that the fact that Jewish magic was recorded textually must be at the basis of any attempt to define it. Hence they proposed

---

201. See Geller (1997, 331–34), G. J. Hamilton (1996), Kotansky (1991a [which is the same as Kotansky 1994, amulet 56]; 1991b); Kotansky et al. (1992), McCullough and Glazier-McDonald (1996; 1998), and Tsereteli (1996).

202. Wasserstrom (1992, 161). Cf. Wasserstrom (1991).

203. See Schiffman and Swartz (1992). Five of the amulets (TS K1 18+30, 42, 68, 127, 137) were also published and discussed by Naveh and Shaked (1987; 1993).

to analyze the philological and literary elements of the texts, and from them to endeavor to arrive at a picture of the mechanics, theory of operation, and social situation of mediaeval Mediterranean Jewish magic. For this reason . . . it is not necessary for our purposes to produce a general definition of "magic." Rather, we shall identify characteristics our texts have in common, and point to how they relate to other elements of the religion of their authors and their contemporaries.[204]

Schiffman and Swartz, then, suggest replacing an a priori definition of magic with an outline of its contours. Instead of determining a priori what magic is and, in this light, describing its manifestations in Judaism, they point to the characteristics of the phenomenon reflected in the incantations they investigated and state that all these characteristics are what can be called Jewish magic at defined times and places. Tracing the contours of magic, which was based on the rhetoric of the adjurations, led them to isolate three main elements in the theory of magic as reflected in the Genizah amulets: (1) expression of holy names and the drawing up of lists of such names, (2) the address of demands to mediating supernatural forces—angels or demons—and (3) the linkage between the two previous elements and human material welfare, both in general and of specific individuals.[205]

Schiffman and Swartz's method is indeed a proper starting point for a suitable description of magic in Judaism, but it raises a significant difficulty: What are the writings where we must search for the characteristics of the phenomenon we are trying to describe? What were the grounds for choosing the 14 "incantations" they analyzed in their book from among the 200,000 available Genizah fragments? What makes these fragments and not others magic literature? To justify their choice of magic texts, Shiffman and Swartz use the description of the forbidden act of magic by the Karaite Ya'qub al-Qirqisani, who was (more or less) a contemporary of the literature discussed by them. In their view, al-Qirqisani's description,

---

204. Schiffman and Swartz (1992, 13).

205. Schiffman and Swartz (1992, 61). This approach and the analysis entailed by it were suggested by Swartz (1990). Its conclusions were formulated, with slight changes, in Swartz (1996).

based on a claim about the ability to perform supernatural actions by means of incantations, fits the picture that emerges from the incantation fragments in the Cairo Genizah.[206] Schiffman and Swartz therefore base the description of magic in the Genizah on a move that begins with a contemporary definition that founds magic on the use of incantations, continues through the location of incantation texts, and culminates in the tracing of the phenomenon they reflect. This method is a new and important step in the attempt to solve the question of defining Jewish magic. It seeks to detach itself altogether from the notion of "magic" in the language of scholars and to base the study solely on medieval Jewish rhetoric. I hold that this is impossible. My method, which I propose in chapter 3, is indeed close to Schiffman and Swartz's method, but I disagree with them regarding the justification for choosing the textual corpus that the description of Jewish magic rests on. I propose basing this choice on our own perception of magic rather than on the writings' fit with an incidental (external and hostile) definition of magic.

The rhetoric of the magic writings found in the Cairo Genizah and a range of aspects of the phenomenon they express have been discussed in other studies published in recent years.[207] Unquestionably, the pinnacle is the series of volumes edited by Peter Schäffer and Shaul Shaked, which include dozens of Genizah fragments, among them, according to the methodical division they adopted, amulet texts, incantations and remedies, passages from books of magic recipes, adjuration prayers, practices for controlling demons, liturgical-magical texts, and fragments from theoretical books of magic.[208] The broad textual findings that these volumes make available to scholars and the linguistic and intertextual research that accompanies them greatly enrich our knowledge of the Jewish magical tradition—both theoretical and practical—that prevailed in the eastern Mediterranean in the early Islamic period. These writings, together with the rest of the amulets, recipes, and magic works reviewed in this chapter, have been the basis for the series of articles I have

---

206. Schiffman and Swartz (1992, 13–14).

207. See Bohak (1999; 2005), Schäfer (1990; 1996), Shaked (1983; 1994; 2000b), Swartz (1995; 2001b), Veltri (1993; 1996b), and Wasserstrom (1991; 1992).

208. See Schäfer and Shaked (1994–1999). A fourth volume of this work is in preparation.

published in recent years. In these articles I seek to shed light on specific aspects of Jewish magic culture—harm, love, economic success, and knowledge.[209] The writings are also the core evidence for Ortal Paz-Saar's broad research on ancient Jewish love magic.[210]

Four magic works have recently been published in new editions: *Ḥarba de-Moshe* (The Sword of Moses), *Sefer ha-Yashar* (The Book of the Right [Way]), *Sefer ha-Malbush* (The Book of the [Magic] Dress), and *Sefer Shimush Tehillim* (The Book of the Use of Psalms). My edition of *Ḥarba de-Moshe* relies on a relatively late (sixteenth-century) manuscript, but one that is earlier and better than Gaster's. Beside the work itself, I include new fragments from the Magical Sword literature, a literary layer that treats the magic formula as a powerful sword, and Genizah fragments of the work attesting to its practical uses. I also deal at length with the structure of the work, with questions touching on the author's world-view and the magic practice he suggested, and with Moses's magic figure.[211] Irina Wandrey edited *Sefer ha-Malbush* and *Sefer ha-Yashar* relying on their fragments in the Cairo Genizah and their later versions in Ashkenazic manuscripts. In her study Wandrey deals at length with the various versions of these works and with the role of the Genizah versions in their elaboration and expansion. She also discusses magic in them and their place in the magic discourse of the early Islamic period.[212] Bill Rebiger edited (and translated into German) two relatively late (fifteenth–sixteenth century) versions of the ancient *Sefer Shimush Tehillim*. He introduces the book with a general discussion of its characteristics and contexts and studies every detail of its content in a broad apparatus that sheds light on the magic views and practices typical of it.[213]

Finally (so far), two comprehensive thematic studies should be noted. One is Reimund Leicht's study on Jewish astrological literature, which

---

209. See Harari (1997a; 2000; 2001; 2005c).

210. Saar (2008). See further, Saar (2007; 2013).

211. Harari (1997b). Cf. also Harari (2005b). On *The Sword of Moses*, see chapter 5. See also Rohrbacher-Sticker (1996), where she deals with Greek traces in the work. For Genizah fragments of the book, see Harari (2014).

212. Wandrey (2004).

213. Rebiger (2010). Cf. Rebiger (1999; 2003). Many fragments of *Sefer Shimush Tehillim* have also been found in the Cairo Genizah. See Schäfer and Shaked (1994–1999, 3: 202–375). See also chapter 5.

deals at length with astromagic writings (i.e., writings that tie together magic and astrology and suggest magic activity that relies on astrological elements). The writings that Leicht discusses are from a later period than the one considered here. Nevertheless, when tracing the sources of these works (*die astrologische Kleinliteratur* in his terms, as opposed to scholarly, theoretical-systematic astrology) and the progression of the traditions and the practices they offer, Leicht sheds broad light on this special channel of Jewish magic activity, tying it to Jewish and non-Jewish theoretical astrological approaches from late antiquity and the early Islamic period.[214] The other study is Dorothea Salzer's comprehensive research on biblical quotations and their function in the magic texts of the Cairo Genizah. In this thorough work, Salzer introduces hundreds of biblical references and quotations and, relying on the theoretical platform of intertextuality, she systematically analyzes their magic use. Because the Bible is dominantly present in Genizah magic pieces, this work actually touches on almost every angle of the magic culture reflected in these texts.[215]

The magic finding reviewed here in general (and presented in detail, according to their various genres, in chapter 5) has recently been discussed by Gideon Bohak in a chapter devoted to insider evidence in his book on ancient Jewish magic.[216] As noted, in his approach to magic in the context of both rabbinic literature and Jewish mystical literature in antiquity, Bohak refrains from defining magic in general and focuses instead on the presence of textual elements and action patterns typical of the magic finding on the one hand and the clear demarcation of this presence on the other. Abstention from defining characterizes his discussion of the textual and tangible products of Jewish magic activity as well and appears to be deliberate. In the introduction to his book, Bohak discusses the problem of defining his field of research and points to the absence of emic signifiers in the way that Jews in antiquity demarcated magic in their culture. In his approach, "we must resort to an etic definition of magic at least as a heuristic device for setting aside those phenomena

---

214. Leicht (2006a).

215. Salzer (2010).

216. Bohak (2008).

in our sources which we would like to study in the present book."[217] Bohak is well aware, however, of the difficulties posed by the attempt to agree on the meaning of the term *magic* in our language and therefore chooses "to focus less on the identification of magical *practice* and more on the identification of magical *texts and artifacts*."[218] But what are these texts and artifacts? Bohak clarifies this matter elsewhere.

> If we decide to focus on the magical dimensions of the Jewish religion we may certainly adopt any intuitive definition of magic and search for all aspects of Jewish culture which fall under that definition. But if we wish to study *Jewish magic*, we must adopt a somewhat different strategy, in order to separate Jewish magic from Jewish religion. Luckily, this is not so difficult, for there exists an extensive body of ancient Jewish texts which would fall under our intuitive category of "magic," and which certainly were not part of the standard (or "normative") Jewish religion at the time or even that of some specific inner-Jewish group or sect.[219]

He concludes: "Rather than looking into the phenomenology of Jewish ritual and praxis and classifying parts thereof as 'magical,' we should focus on those bodies of non-normative Jewish texts which could only be classified as 'magical,' and use them as a starting point for any study of Jewish magical tradition."[220]

Bohak clearly distinguishes here between magic and "normative" religion (on theoretical grounds and without a judgmental slant). For this purpose and contrary to his explicit wish, he is forced to resort to phenomenological criteria. On the one hand, he relies on intuition about the phenomenon reflected in the magical texts: "No reader . . . would fail to

---

217. Bohak (2008, 4).

218. Bohak (2008, 4; emphasis in original).

219. Bohak (2008, 65).

220. Bohak (2008, 67). For this approach, see Harari (2005d). Instead of identifying a text as magic by relying on arbitrary intuition, my study makes this identification by focusing on the cumulative presence of several typical linguistic characteristics. See chapter 3.

note their 'magical' *contents*."[221] On the other hand, he is forced to define (intuitively?) the borders of normative Jewish religion in order to separate from it what he calls magic. In any event, he does so with full awareness of the problem involved in this move, an awareness that relies on deep knowledge of the various components of Jewish culture in late antiquity and the early Islamic period that do not fully fit his mold.[222] Elsewhere, Bohak indeed erodes this fundamental distinction when he seeks to characterize Jewish magic as Jewish. Whereas it is convenient to point out in various writings (rabbinic literature or *Hekhalot* and *Merkavah* literature) the presence of elements from non-Jewish texts intuitively, which are identified as magic, "the distinction between what falls under the rubric of Jewish 'magic' and what falls under that of Jewish 'religion' can become quite blurred."[223]

The obstacle confronting Bohak in his study, then, is not the lack of a definition of magic per se or the unease with the problematic border between what is and what is not magic in Judaism. His main concern is the description of the cultural segment reflected in texts and artifacts identified as "magical" while rigorously examining their Jewish and non-Jewish components. Once he describes these artifacts and the beliefs, practices, and aims they reflect as insider evidence, he does not refrain from expertly using these insights to examine the scope and the character of magic's penetration also into the world of Jewish rabbis and mystics in late antiquity.

CONCLUDING REMARKS

The study of Jewish magic writings has greatly advanced in recent decades, gradually revealing a Jewish magic culture. The growing interest in this area is not specific to Jewish studies, as attested by the extent of the research devoted to magic in general and to the study of its place and nature in the Greco-Roman world in particular. Scholars of Hellenistic magic have benefited from an abundance of texts that, for many years now, have placed at their disposal a broad and well-established

---

221. Bohak (2008, 65; emphasis added).

222. Bohak (2008, 67).

223. Bohak (2008, 297).

corpus of magic writings. Hence it is only natural that they have often channeled efforts to an inquiry into the culture and the sociology of magic. Developments in the anthropological and cultural research of magic have left a deep impression on these scholars. Their views on the term *magic* and on the caution required in its use became so extreme that the beginning of a pendulum move in the opposite direction is already discernible.

The study of Jewish magic, by contrast, is still in its cradle. No wonder, then, that scholars invest most of their efforts in the location, study, and publication of the magic texts themselves. The importance of this scientific work can hardly be exaggerated. Without a broad, credible, and clear textual basis, no real discussion of Jewish magic is possible (and indeed, where such a basis is found, as in rabbinic literature or in *Hekhalot* and *Merkavah* literature, scholars turned to the phenomenology or sociology of magic). The textual focus, however, has not diverted attention from questions of essence. Most scholars have related, either explicitly or indirectly, the characteristics of the phenomenon that concerned them and their place in the broader context of Jewish religious culture. Scholars disagree about the definition of magic and even about the proper methodological tools to be used for its study. But the discussion that has unfolded on this question in Jewish studies, the growing awareness of the problem evoked by the talk about magic or magic texts and their distinction from contemporary religion or mysticism, is extremely important. The advantage that the tools used in anthropology, sociology, and the comparative study of religions have placed at our disposal for the clarification of this question and the way these tools have served the historical study of magic and the discourse about it in the Greco-Roman world have also gradually percolated into the study of Jewish magic.

The discussion surrounding the definition of magic does not lead to a defined goal, and to expect that a universally agreed-on solution can be found seems pointless. But even without reaching such results and even if the vague contours of "magic" fail to become entirely clear, the process leading to it, the continued inquiry, and the emerging discourse are interesting and important on their own merits. My suggestion in chapter 3 should be viewed in this context. I do not hold that my position is the only one possible, that it offers indispensable answers, or that its conclusions exclude all others. Magic can be defined and described from different perspectives and with diverse methods, thus shedding light on it from several directions. Yet I do hold that my view has one relative advantage: It shifts the discussion from the essentialist realm of "magical" and "religious" phenomena in the Jewish culture of late antiquity to the use of terms that describe these phenomena in the language of scholars. I thereby suggest in chapter 3 reasonably clear criteria for the use of the term *magic* or *kishuf,* first in a textual context and then in the context of the cultural phenomenon that the magic writings reflect.

3

Religion, Magic, Adjuration, and the
Definition of Early Jewish Magic

The discussion in chapters 1 and 2 shows that, although (and possibly because) research on magic has been ongoing for close to 150 years, we are not nearing agreement on the essence of magic and its definition.[1] Almost everyone believes they understand what they and others mean when they use words such as *magic, magie,* or *Zauberwesen.* The academic discourse on the subject has indeed proceeded unhindered, but both explicit clarifications and implicit insights emerging from the research show that we are far from a uniform perception of magic. In this chapter I wish to present a new solution to this problem. First, I point out the difficulties evoked by the currently prevalent trend concerning the use of the term *magic* and by the attempt to understand the essence of the phenomenon it denotes solely by examining its use in the texts of the culture being studied. I then present my view concerning the use of the term through a proposition that relies on Ludwig Wittgenstein's later writings on the philosophy of language; I suggest replacing a dictionary definition of magic with a quasi-ostensive definition of the cultural realm it denotes.[2]

---

1. For an early version of this chapter, see Harari (2005d).
2. By "ostensive definition" I mean a definition that explains the meaning of a term by pointing to something, accompanied by a statement such as "this." When trying to define red, for example, we can (and this is indeed the most successful definition in this case) point to a variety of red objects and say, "this." This mode of definition is obviously not free of problems. For instance, how will the listener know exactly what we mean by the word "this" out of all the features of a given artifact?

In the course of this discussion, I also look at the relationship between magic and religion. Finally, as part of the dialectic move adopted in the definition of magic suggested here, I formulate a set of textual rules for determining whether (or better, to what extent) any given Jewish text is a magic text. My proposition should help to untangle the complexity surrounding phenomena called magic or religion and their mutual relationship. More significantly, I provide methodological tools for justifying the choice of texts that may serve as the foundation for a phenomenological description of ancient Jewish magic.

MAGIC-*MAGEIA*: INTRODUCING THE PROBLEM

Among the prominent contemporary scholars of Hellenistic magic, Fritz Graf best summed up the discussion on the definition of magic.

> There are only two possible attitudes: either a modern definition of the term is created and the ancient and Frazerian are resolutely cast aside, or the term *magic* is used in the sense that the ancients gave it, avoiding not only the Frazerian notion, but also all the other etymological notions of the term.[3]

Graf chose the second option. He stated that *magic* was a term that originated in Hellenistic culture, which he studied, and that the proper course was thus to examine its meaning and the scope of its denotation in this culture according to its usage in Hellenistic writings. This approach, however, appears to be fraught with considerable difficulties.

When studying magic as a phenomenon or writing a book titled *Magic in the Ancient World*, we address our readers in a language we share. In Graf's case, that language is English (or, originally, French), reflecting

---

And if we try to reduce ambiguity by saying "this color," we now have to define "color" and we are back where we started. These and other questions have been discussed in contemporary linguistic philosophy, and I do not elaborate on them here. When I use the term *quasi-ostensive definition*, I am trying to convey my reservations about the use of the term *ostensive definition* in the present context because the pointing at the conclusion of the process is not at an artifact but at a cultural phenomenon that is described textually.

3. Graf (1997, 18).

a conceptual-cultural system in which *magic* denotes a specific range of phenomena. Even if the limits of this range are not clear and even if the differences leading us to refer to a particular phenomenon as religion and to another as magic are not easy to point out, we cannot ignore the common use of these terms in our culture. When Graf attempts today to describe magic in the ancient world by relying on the usage of the word *magic* in Hellenistic literature, he performs a dual move. First, he assumes that the word *magic* in our language denotes a specific phenomenon (which he wishes to investigate) and that his readers, just like him, more or less know what this phenomenon is.[4] And second, he assumes that a sufficiently meaningful connection prevails between the modern English usage of *magic* and the ancients' usage of a variety of terms through which they denoted the phenomenon that he describes.

The first assumption is self-evident. This is the basis for all linguistic communication. The fact that the boundaries of the concept of magic (and hence also the conditions for using the term *magic*) are not sufficiently sharp does not preclude a meaningful discourse about magic. True, as the discussion attains greater precision and refinement, it is incumbent on us to clarify the terminology, but lack of clarity is not really an obstacle to the possibility of discussion.

The second assumption is more problematic in that it creates a dangerous illusion of authenticity. Even without recalling the whole range of Greek and Roman terms through which we might examine the essence of magic as a phenomenon in the ancient world, the question arises, What is the criterion for selecting them? What is the source for the confidence in any links connecting the English use of *magic* and the Greek use of *mageia*? The basis for this connection is certainly not the similarity between the two words. First, say that they are similar. So what? Second, scholars also rely, for instance, on mentions of *pharmakeia*, *theurgia*, and *goeteia* in Greek or *defixiones* and *magus* in Latin for studying the area in which they are interested. The assumption of a shared meaning or even of any connection of meaning between the English *magic* and the Greek *mageia* follows from a necessary precondition: knowledge of the conceptual baggage attached to the usage of the term *magic*. It is only through

---

4. Henk Versnel offered a similar argument in the past. See Versnel (1991b, esp. 181, 185).

an understanding of the usage of *magic, sorcery, witchcraft*, and the like in our languages that we might determine that specific Greek or Latin terms were used by the speakers of those languages to denote, more or less, the same phenomena we denote through these terms. By identifying the common use of terms then and now, we can refine the discussion and point to more precise borders of, for instance, the usage of the term *mageia* in the ancient world, including both the concept it represented and the phenomena it denoted. The idea that the term *magic* could be used "in the sense that the ancients gave it, avoiding not only the Frazerian notion, but also all the other etymological notions of the term," as Graf proposed to do, is an illusion. Not even the ancients themselves could do this. The term *magic* did not exist in their vocabulary. The terms *magie, magic, Zauberwesen*, or the Hebrew *kishuf* or *keshafim*, and so forth serve members of our communities and bear a semantic baggage given to them in our culture. Without knowledge of this baggage, these terms cannot be used in day-to-day speech or to describe magic in the ancient world.

Even if we need to clarify the conditions for the use of these terms, that is, their meaning, and even if this is a particularly challenging task, these are still the only tools available for any kind of dialogue. The starting point in any definition of magic (and of religion) must necessarily be our mode of using the terms denoting these phenomena. Only after clarifying this matter will it be possible to search for the characteristic usage in antiquity of the terms denoting the phenomena that we have defined in our own language as magic.

MAGIC AND RELIGION: A CASE OF FAMILY RESEMBLANCE

In his *Philosophical Investigations*, Ludwig Wittgenstein proposes a new and revolutionary theory of meaning, with the principle of family resemblance as one of its central foci.[5] Wittgenstein points to the difficulty of defining precise limits of applicability for terms in a language and to the

---

5. Wittgenstein (1953, secs. 65–88). These and the following sections of Wittgenstein's philosophy of language have been discussed at length. See, for instance, Baker and Hacker (1983, 185–227), Hallett (1977, 14–157), and Rundel (1990, 40–63). I do not

fact that, although these limits are blurred, we are still capable of using them well. The example he uses to explain this linguistic principle has become a cornerstone in twentieth-century philosophy of language.

[66] Consider for example the proceedings that we call "games." I mean board-games, card-games, ball-games, Olympic-games, and so on. What is common to them all? Don't say: "there *must* be something common, or they would not all be called 'games'"—but *look and see* where there is anything common to all. For if you look at them you will not see something that is common to *all*, but similarities, relationships and a whole series of them at that. To repeat: don't think, but look! Look, for example, at board-games, with their multifarious relationships. Now pass to card-games; here you find many correspondences with the first group, but many common features drop out, and others appear. When we pass next to ball-games, much that is common is retained, but much is lost . . . and we can go through the many, many other groups of games in the same way; can see how similarities crop up and dis-appear. And the result of this examination is: we see a complicated network of similarities overlapping and criss-crossing: sometimes overall similarities, sometimes similarities in detail.

[67] I can think of no better expression to characterize these similarities than "family resemblances"; for the various resem-blances between members of a family: build, features, color of eyes, gait, temperament, etc. etc. overlap and criss-cross in the same way. And I shall say: "games" form a family. And for instance the kinds of number form a family in the same way. Why do we call something a "number"? Well, perhaps because it has a—direct—relationship with several things that have hith-erto been called number; and this can be said to give it an indi-rect relationship to other things we call the same name. And we extend our concept of number as in spinning a thread we twist fibre on fibre. And the strength of the thread does not reside in

---

mean to expand on this issue beyond Wittgenstein's presentation of the family resem-blance principle.

the fact that some one fibre run through its whole length, but in the overlapping of many fibres.[6]

I hold that the principle of family resemblance is a particularly efficient tool for clarifying the relationships between the phenomena we refer to through the terms *magic* (or *kishuf*) and *religion*.

Henk Versnel, in an article that, as noted in chapter 2, is unusual in the context of the scholarly tendency to dismiss essentialist distinctions between magic and religion in general and in the Hellenistic world in particular, rejects Olof Pettersson's suggestion to give the term *magic* a decent burial. Instead, Versnel proposes characterizing magic according to phenomenological criteria.[7] The starting point of his research is his recognition of the need for the term *magic* in the scientific study of the phenomenon of magic and hence the impossibility of ignoring the conceptual baggage attached to the term in scholarly culture and language. Because avoiding this use altogether is impossible, Versnel holds that it would be better to attempt a definition of this term, even at the cost of some vagueness. Following William Alston's definition of religion,[8] Versnel proposes using the family resemblance principle to characterize the whole range of phenomena called forth by the term *magic*. In his view, one can point to several crucial features characterizing magic in the commonsense perception prevalent in our culture: instrumental, manipulative, mechanical, nonpersonal, coercive in the short term, with defined and generally individual goals, and so forth. By relying on the family resemblance principle, we can say that, when enough of these features are present in a given phenomenon, that phenomenon is magic.[9]

The adoption of the family resemblance principle with regard to the range of phenomena we wish to characterize through the term *magic* is to be welcomed. No better way seems available for defining the applicability of such terms. Yet the problems hindering such a definition are

---

6. Wittgenstein (1953, secs. 66 and 67; emphasis in original).

7. Versnel (1991b).

8. Alston (1967). Alston's definition of religion is based on the principle of family resemblance between phenomena called religion.

9. Versnel (1991b, 186).

obvious and common to Wittgenstein's later theory of language in general: Is there indeed commonsense agreement regarding the essentialist features whose presence will determine the magic character of any given phenomenon? Who are those endowed with this common sense? the average speakers of a language? the scholars? Even more problematic: Who determines whether and which of these characteristics are present in the given phenomenon? And what is the basis for this decision? Are not the borders of concepts such as manipulative, coercive, and mechanical themselves blurred? Finally, do these characteristics indeed help us to distinguish between religion and magic?

Of all these questions, Versnel considers only the last one, expressing reservations about the importance ascribed to it in scholarly research. In his view, rather than the distinction between magic and religion or between elements within religion, what matters is the distinction between magic and nonmagic, that is, the identification of magic per se, regardless of whether it is found within or outside religion.[10] This stance is a good starting place in the search for a definition of magic and its relationship with religion. My approach begins from a similar viewpoint, but I seek to expand it, refine it, and thereby remove some of the difficulties it raises.

The inquiry into the connection between magic and religion assumes the existence of two separate phenomena, or possibly two separate concepts, warranting two separate terms. Whatever the reason for the existence of these two terms in our culture, each with its own conceptual baggage, their coexistence in the languages of Western culture is a fact. Obviously, this fact cannot serve as a final conclusion in a discussion on magic and its relationship with religion, but obliviousness to it and even attempts to circumvent it do not help to clarify the question. From a scientific perspective, this obliviousness is potentially disastrous. It drags into the scholarly research one or both of the following: distinctions originating in intrareligious (Christian or Jewish) perceptions concerning the ideal essence of religion, to which magic is compared to determine its character and role; and/or elitist Enlightenment perceptions

---

10. Versnel (1991b, 187).

concerning ideal science as the sole source of a true description of reality, to which magic is compared to determine its character and role.

These approaches have been challenged in the past and have now been almost entirely abandoned. Their shadow, however, and with it perhaps the fear of unwittingly holding onto something in them, hovers persistently over the skies of research and disturbs the scholars' peace. These scholars, particularly those specializing in magic in the Hellenistic world, have not confined themselves during the last two decades to an awareness of the problems entailed by the use of such terms as *magic* and *religion* but have attempted to solve the problem by relinquishing the use of the term *magic* altogether. The use of this term, they claim, laden with the conceptual baggage it bears in our culture, is a methodological mistake that is likely to hamper the discussion about the phenomenon we are seeking to denote through it. Yet this tendency has in turn created new problems. Relinquishing the term *magic* resulted in a vacuum into which other, no less problematic terms have inevitably been drawn. In the final analysis, Hellenistic magic cannot be studied without recourse to the concept of magic, that is, without some general concept, however broad and vague, about the phenomenon to be examined. Not by chance, matters of agriculture, sailing, architecture, army, administration, economy, theater, philosophy, and many other similar areas of Greco-Roman culture are not discussed in studies of Hellenistic magic. These studies focus on a specific area of this culture, even when its precise parameters are hard to trace.

The choice of texts that scholars rely on in their works attests to a preconceived perception of the specific phenomenon in which they are interested. If this phenomenon is not called magic, then new terms are necessary. In the last decade many researchers of ancient magic have indeed tended to define their field of research in other terms. They have not dealt with magic but with artifacts or with specific texts, such as curse tablets (*defixiones*) or adjurations, or with specific rituals, such as "rituals for gaining power," or with a phenomenon they have tended to refer to by the general term of *ritual power*.[11] These solutions are indeed efficient

---

11. See, for instance, Davila (2001), Gager (1992), Lesses (1998), and Meyer and Smith (1994) as well as many of the chapters in the volume edited by in Meyer and Mirecki (1995).

in that they release us from the yoke of "magic," but only on condition that the researchers clarify precisely what it is they intend by each one of these terms. What is unique about an adjuration text? What characterizes a curse tablet as an artifact and a text? What distinguishes a ritual for gaining power from one that is not so designed? What is meant by "power"? Finally, should all these terms be understood in the context of our own language or in the context of their parallel use in the languages of the cultures studied? No discussion has yet been devoted to the problems raised by the new terminology.[12]

The perplexity and uncertainty entailed by the use of the term *magic* are well understood. Like many other terms in our language, such as *love, happiness, art, ritual, religion,* and *game,* it covers a wide range of phenomena and the borders of its applicability are blurred. I do not, however, share in the sense of distress entailed by its use, even in the research literature. The fact that the boundaries of its applicability are vague need not deter us or prevent us from discussing the phenomenon we wish to denote through it. Nor should it preclude the examination of magic's relationships with additional phenomena that we denote through such terms as *religion, mysticism,* or *ritual,* whose borders are no less vague. Versnel's approach on the family resemblance between phenomena called magic conveys this type of view. It recognizes the difficulties raised by the use of the term *magic* but does not refrain from doing so. The phenomena that we call magic do indeed share a family resemblance. Each one resembles each one of the others in some features and differs from it in others. There is no one essential feature or any particular combination of essentialist features that constitutes magic as a phenomenon in the sense of a necessary and sufficient condition. What we have is a number of features that, when combined in one way or another, create one or another expression of magic. The identification of these features, in varying doses and compositions in certain phenomena, is what leads us to call them magic.

Accepting the family resemblance principle means forgoing the objective of a precise dictionary definition of magic and shifting to a looser perception of it based on a quasi-ostensive definition, that is, a descriptive

12. For the beginning of this discussion, see J. Z. Smith (1995).

definition pointing to what we wish to refer to as magic and a statement that these and other similar phenomena are magic. We replace the attempt to delimit phenomena on the basis of essentialist, defined, and fixed features with a continuing learning and refining of the usage of the term *magic*, which is based on pointing and describing as broadly as possible the phenomena we wish to denote by this term. The boundaries of use for the term *magic* will remain vague. Some phenomena will always have looser links with other magic phenomena mutually linked together in a tight net of resemblances on the one hand and partly tied through resemblance to phenomena from other realms, such as those called religion, mysticism, ritual, and so forth, on the other. Phenomena from these realms are not defined through any essentialist unifying characteristic but according to the principle of family resemblance, as Alston, for example, applied to religion.

This is also the best way to explain the relationship between magic and religion. Not only are there phenomena linked in a network of partial resemblances to other phenomena from both the magic and religion categories (thus misleading researchers who wish to classify them into one or the other of these categories), but also many phenomena that fit paradigmatically into the spheres we denote through these terms are in relationships of partial resemblance. The move that Alston developed in the realm of religion and Versnel in the realm of magic should be complemented with the statement that a family resemblance prevails between religious and magical phenomena. This appears to be the most efficient way to describe the complex relationship between the phenomena that we naturally denote through these terms. It is better than perceiving them as phenomena separated in essentialist ways (an approach that scholars have abandoned almost entirely) or perceiving them as a continuum, as proposed in anthropological research and also in the study of Jewish magic by Peter Schäfer.[13] A continuum implies a transition between two poles that ultimately must be defined as found in an essentialist opposition. Family resemblance, by contrast, does not define essentialist poles of magic or religion. Instead, it states that a partial resemblance prevails between all the components of the set of phenomena we call magic and

---

13. See Schäfer (1997).

religion. Each one resembles others in certain features and differs from them in other features. The density of the web of partial resemblances between them is what determines the realms that are more or less distinctively magical or more or less distinctively religious. Nothing, however, precludes resemblance ties between phenomena from the dense areas of magic and religion. The network of partial resemblances creates a web of varying density, within which religious and magical phenomena are linked together.

FROM MAGIC TO JEWISH MAGIC

My concern has thus far focused on the fundamental question of the relationship between magic and religion. I have tried to show that the family resemblance principle can function as an efficient means for describing the boundaries of phenomena described by us as magical or religious and even to describe the connection between them, despite the lack and even the impossibility of essentialist definitions of either magic or religion. Nevertheless, note that the use of the family resemblance principle is justified only insofar as we, as speakers, have some notion, however general, of what we mean by magic or religion—in Wittgenstein's formulation, when we know how to use these terms. This is the starting point in the dialectic move I wish to propose now.

Shaul Shaked opens one of his articles on incantation bowls with the following remark:

> Anyone working within the field of magic in Judaism in Late Antiquity and the early Middle Ages knows the difficulties besetting any attempt to define it. Despite these difficulties . . . there are not many cases of hesitation when one tries to identify magic texts in practice.[14]

This statement accurately describes the situation in which we know what we mean by the terms *magic* or *magic text* even though we cannot define them precisely. The general, hazy concept of magic that prevails in contemporary Western culture, including the academic community, still

---

14. Shaked (1995, 197).

enables broad, profound, and continuous discussion on the subject. As a starting point, then, this is not at all bad. But if we wish to advance beyond it, we must search for tools that will allow us a more precise and refined use of its referent. The way to do this is not to search for more precise dictionary definitions but rather for the opposite: a description as wide-ranging and detailed as possible of the phenomena that constitute the field in question. Subsequently, a quasi-ostensive definition will enable us to state that these and similar phenomena are magic. That is the ultimate goal we should aim for.

Attempting a detailed phenomenological description of magic as a universal phenomenon would be unwise. An ostensive definition of magic will be effective only within a limited and well-defined cultural context. My focus is indeed on such a cultural-geographic-historical context: Jewish culture in Babylonia and the eastern Mediterranean in late antiquity and the early Islamic period. The starting point for the methodological move I propose is therefore a natural, ordinary, and more or less agreed-on use of the general and hazy term *magic* regarding this culture, this time, and this area. In the first stage I identify through this use Jewish "magical" texts from the relevant period. In the second stage I examine these texts and point out that adjuration is the central rhetorical motif in them. In the third stage I characterize the textual foundations of the adjuration and define a Jewish *adjuration text*. In the fourth stage I determine the wider cycles of Jewish *magical texts* based on the definition of a Jewish adjuration text. Last, I suggest describing ancient Jewish magic by relying on the entire corpus of magical texts created by Jews in this area at this time.

Although the move proposed here may appear circular, this is not the case.[15] This is a dialectic move that begins and ends with magic as a cultural phenomenon, but in contexts entirely different from one another. At the beginning of this move, magic, as perceived in our culture, serves as a general delineation of the discussion. At its end, magic is described in detail in the context of a defined culture, time, and place that are different from ours. The dialectic is also evident in the attitude toward the texts. We progress from the general notion of *magic* to Jewish *magical*

---

15. See Liebes (2004, 4).

texts, then proceed to a Jewish *adjuration text*, then to Jewish *magical texts*, and finally to *Jewish magic*. This move allows us to (1) justify the choice of the texts used as a basis for the phenomenological study of magic in the specific cultural context, (2) expand the textual platform based on the family resemblance principle, and (3) offer a broad phenomenological description of ancient Jewish magic based on Jewish magical texts (in both a narrow and broad sense).

Almost all our knowledge about Jewish magical activity in antiquity and the early Islamic period stems from surviving texts. Material findings attest to the use of precious stones and magic jewelry as well as metal and clay amulets in Palestine mainly between the fifth and seventh centuries and of clay magic bowls in Babylonia at more or less the same time. Archaeological findings indicate that the Palestinian use of amulets was occasionally connected to the synagogue and that Babylonian Jews used bowls mainly in their homes. A love amulet that was written on soft clay and thrown into the fire attests to the ritual burning of amulets to achieve a sympathetic effect: kindling the beloved's heart with the fire of love. Findings in the Cairo Genizah show that Fostat Jews used cloth, parchment, and paper amulets in the first centuries of the second millennium.[16] The rest of the available information about ancient Jewish magic—its objectives, the actions adopted to attain them, and the belief system in whose context these actions were meaningful to their users—comes from the contents of texts we define as magical.

The study of ancient Jewish magic, then, is above all textual.[17] For a suitable description of it, we must point to the texts we wish to call magical and, through them, describe the cultural phenomenon they express. The initial selection of Jewish magical texts, as I tried to clarify, must be based on the prevalent usage of the general and vague term *magic* in our culture. As Shaked notes, the choice may be hard to justify but is easy to make. Knowing the conditions for the use of the word *magic* on the one hand and the difficulty of defining them precisely on the other are the reasons for this situation. At this stage, then, we will not define those texts but will only select them and examine them.

---

16. On the magic finding, see chapter 5.
17. Cf. Schiffman and Swartz (1992, esp. 32–62).

An examination of Jewish magical texts from Babylonia and from Palestine and its environs dating back to antiquity and the early Islamic period reveals that their fixed and most prominent rhetorical characteristic is the appeal to some supernatural power (or powers) in order to enlist it for the benefit of a certain person (or group). This address is usually referred to as an adjuration or incantation.[18] Adjurations are the focus of magic texts and, as far as can be judged by them, they are also the heart of the magic acts described in them or performed by means of them. I therefore hold that a Jewish magical text, in the most limited and distinct sense of the term, is an adjuration text. Hence, if we wish to create a solid basis for selecting Jewish magical texts in a broader sense of the term, we must define an adjuration text in the clearest possible terms.

I should stress that, at this stage, venturing beyond the textual framework of the discussion and characterizing an adjuration text based on the phenomenon it expresses is pointless. Such an attempt requires a definition of adjuration as a phenomenon, and in a textual study this means interpreting the text for the purpose of its phenomenological description. Although such an interpretation is the goal of the methodological move proposed here, at the present stage the focus should be only on the text per se and on its definition as an adjuration based on its rhetorical features. I suggest eight such features as the basis for determining whether (or better, to what extent) any given Jewish text from the time and area under discussion is an adjuration. These are the prevalent rhetorical characteristics of adjurations in texts identified as magical in the scholarly literature according to the current use of the term *magic*. My suggestion at this stage, then, is to rest the vague and hard-to-define concept used for choosing magic texts on rhetorical elements in these texts, whose presence leads us to categorize them as magic. I do not claim that all those features must be present in a text for it to be considered an adjuration. Indeed, the cases that do contain all of them are rare. Yet I hold that *the greater the number of such features in a Jewish text, the more distinctly will we be able to consider it an adjuration.*

---

18. I do not consider the distinction between adjuration and prayer at this stage. The examination of adjurations in magic texts enables us to make such a distinction, even if not unequivocally, by relying on the adjurations' rhetorical characteristics.

The following eight features are the rhetorical features on whose basis we can identify a Jewish adjuration text:

1. The self-definition of the text or of the artifact on which it is written as an adjuration (*hashba‘ah*), writ (*ketav*), seal (*hotam*), amulet (*qame‘a*), ban (*shamta’*), incantation (*lahash*), or counter-magic (*qibla’*).

2. An appeal to supernatural powers, usually angels (*mal’akhim*), princes (*sarim*), names (*shemot*), letters (*otiyot*), or demons (*shedim*), to operate according to the supplicant's will.

3. An address to these powers in the first-person singular.

4. Using verbs derived from the roots *šb‘*, *zqq*, *gzr*, or *qym*, or using expressions of restriction and expulsion generally derived from the roots *’sr*, *kbš*, *qm‘*, *htm*, *gdr*, *g‘r*, or *btl*, in the formulation of the appeal to supernatural powers.

5. Use of the language "in the name of" (*be-shem*) followed by the names of God, names of angels, or other holy names made up of combinations of letters, divine attributes, or biblical verses that describe God's actions (and that generally attest to his power).

6. Use of hastening and threatening formulations toward the supernatural powers.

7. Absence of formulations of request, as in formulations derived from the roots *bqš*, *hnn*, and *pll*, or the words meaning "please" (*’ana’*, *na’*) from the address to these powers.

8. Indicating the name of the party interested in this appeal as well as that of his or her mother or, in the instructional literature, with the label NN (so-and-so, the son/daughter of so-and-so; *pbp, peloni ben/bat pelonit*).

Not all these features are equal in value, and some are more significant than others for determining whether a given text is an adjuration. Nevertheless, measuring their relative value is not only impossible but also, according to the method of cumulative definition proposed here, not required. I am not seeking to set some minimal threshold to distinguish between what is an adjuration and what is not. On the contrary, I am interested in pointing to a dynamic situation in which the accumulation of the listed rhetorical features is what creates the extent to which a specific text is an adjuration. The greater the number of these textual features in a text, the more clearly and distinctively we can say that it tends to be an adjuration.

Having determined that adjurations are at the focus of Jewish magic texts and having set a foundation for a textual definition of adjuration, we can now proceed to the next stage and redefine Jewish magical text. I propose setting three concentric circles of such texts, all based on the definition of adjuration text. A magical text is, in the most distinct and limited sense of the term, an adjuration text. This is the innermost circle. Such texts are found in amulets, magic bowls, the *Hekhalot* literature, and, occasionally, rabbinic literature. In a broader sense, a magical text is one that includes adjurations. This circle, which is broader than the first, includes mainly magic guidebooks but also sections of *Hekhalot* literature and Midrash. In the widest sense, a magical text is one that expresses a worldview and practices typical of magical texts in the more narrow senses or one that includes literary components that characterize these texts. This is a first breakthrough (which is always dangerous) beyond the strict linguistic aspect and entering comparative dimensions. Determining the magic dimension of texts of this kind rests on familiarity with the more classic magic texts. Indeed, this circle includes many texts that are not part of magic literature, such as rabbinic traditions about the powers of rabbis, their struggles with heretical sorcerers and witches, demonological beliefs and related acts, and even parts of the liturgy, such as the bedtime recitation of the Shema prayer, which are of magic character. All these texts can be used in the phenomenological description of ancient Jewish magic.

Relying on this definition of Jewish magic texts as resting on their definition as adjuration texts, we can now expand and state that the more textual features of adjuration a Jewish text contains, the more this will attest to its greater tendency toward magic. This statement enables us to capture, even if not exactly (which, in any event, is not required in my method), the extent of magic in texts, regardless of whether or not they are included in the Jewish textual canon, literary or liturgical. It enables us, on the one hand, to identify and point to magic features in the entire written corpus of the Jewish culture discussed in this study and, on the other, to choose the texts on which we can rely for a comprehensive description of the cultural phenomenon called ancient Jewish magic.

The notion of magic that I propose opens with the identification of Jewish texts as magic according to the perception of magic in our culture, detects adjuration as the focus of these texts, characterizes it as a text, and defines through it the range of Jewish magical texts. These texts can be the basis for a description of the beliefs, actions, objectives, and cultural contexts that characterized ancient Jewish magic. This course of definition in general and the definition of adjuration in particular is not a simple one, because it does not provide a clear-cut answer to such questions as, Is *this* magic? Is *this* not magic? But such an answer is also hard to provide to such questions as, Is *this* love? Is *this* art? Is *this* illness? Ultimately, the meaning of these words derives from their use, which, in turn, is tied to the conceptual baggage they bear in the discourse that they serve. Avoiding or ignoring the use of terms such as *magic, kishuf, magie,* or *Zauberwesen* in our culture in a discussion about Jewish magic in antiquity is therefore impossible. On the other hand, projecting their conceptual baggage onto the Jews of antiquity is not proper either. The dialectic move I propose seeks to tie these ends together by exposing the rhetorical foundations of the texts we perceive as magic and by setting up a broad textual platform that rests on these foundations in order to describe the phenomenon at stake. When we arrive at such a description, we will be able to point to it and determine, This is Jewish magic in late antiquity and the early Islamic period.

How to Do Things with Words

Speech Acts and Incantations

In chapter 3 I offered my view concerning the central role of the adjuration (or the incantation) in Jewish magical texts and of the adjuration act in the Jewish culture of magic reflected in them. This proposal concludes the discussion on the definition of magic developed at length in chapters 1 and 2. The discussion in this chapter also touches on the essence of ancient Jewish magic but from a different perspective: a systematic consideration of the performative nature of the adjuration act. For the discussion of this question I rely on John Austin's speech act theory and consider to what extent its adoption has been useful in the understanding of the magic language in use among Jews in late antiquity and the early Islamic period.[1]

In the early 1960s a slim volume appeared titled *How to Do Things with Words*.[2] In this work Austin exposes and analyzes a special aspect of the use of language. The philosophy of language, a field that had significantly expanded since the end of the nineteenth century, focused mainly on the structure of utterances, the logical relationships between them, and the association between language and the world. Austin, by contrast, addresses in his book the performative aspect of language, that is, the power of human linguistic utterances to act in the world and change it. In his view, certain utterances, when stated properly in a given

---

1. This chapter is based on Harari (1997–1998).
2. Austin (1962).

and compelling set of circumstances, change the state of affairs in the world. Austin points to three performative aspects of the speech act—locutionary, illocutionary, and perlocutionary—and clarifies and illustrates their character. In the discussion that follows I focus on illocutionary utterances. According to Austin, the execution of such an utterance (in the conditions mentioned) is an act that creates change in the world.[3] The Jewish magic worldview rests on a similar foundation: Certain linguistic utterances performed in the context of a compelling ritual have a performative power that acts on reality and changes it. This approach is not specific to Judaism. Other studies show that an approach assuming the active power of words prevails in many cultures.

The possibility of acting through speech is thus at the basis of two worldviews that are entirely different from one another: one magical and one philosophical. Is it possible to discern an essential link between them? Or is this perhaps an illusion, a superficial misrepresentation that leads us to draw a connection between a modern language theory and magical ideas? This issue is at the focus of the discussion in this chapter. In the first part I deal with the main characteristics of the speech act theory as formulated by Austin. In the second part I describe several prominent attempts to apply this theory to the study of ritual and magic language in general and of Jewish magic language in particular. In the last part I try to clarify the relationship between speech act theory and the perception of magical Jewish language. I point out the difficulties that follow from the simplistic use of Austin's theory in the study of Jewish magic and set forth the reasons that justify caution in the application of the philosophical model to the study of magic culture.

SPEECH ACT THEORY

Speech act theory was first presented systematically in the William James Lectures delivered by Austin at Harvard University in 1955 and published several years later as a posthumous book. The starting point for Austin's philosophical reflections is the inadequacy of the rules through which philosophers of language had attempted to define a statement.

---

3. Austin does not speak of change in the world but of the "doing of an action" or "doing something" (e.g., Austin 1962, 5, 12), but this is what he means.

Austin rejects the view that, unlike other utterances, a statement describes a fact and can therefore be verified, at least theoretically, and must be either true of false. He also claims that the grammatical structure of a statement is a sufficient criterion for defining it as such. Furthermore, he notes that not all true or false statements are indeed descriptive and that it is therefore more accurate to call them constative: "Many traditional philosophical perplexities have arisen through a mistake—the mistake of taking as straightforward statements of fact utterances which are *either* (in interesting non-grammatical ways) nonsensical *or else* intended as something quite different."[4] Speech act theory deals with one kind of such utterances: performative utterances.

A performative statement is one through which the speaker does something by the very act of uttering it (obviously beyond the act of speaking). Mostly, and in its most distinct form, this utterance resembles the constative statement. It should not, however, be confused with a description of a situation, an action, or an intention of action. Through its utterance, the statement is itself the performance of an act that changes the state of affairs in the world. Austin illustrates his intention in a series of examples.[5]

"I do (sc., take this woman to be my lawful wedded wife)"—as uttered in the course of the marriage ceremony.[6]

"I name this ship the Queen Elizabeth"—as uttered when smashing the bottle against the stem.

"I give and bequeath my watch to my brother."

"I bet you sixpence it will rain tomorrow."

These statements do not describe the speaker's situation or intention. They act. Through their very utterance, the speaker performs an act.

---

4. Austin (1962, 3; emphasis in original).

5. Austin (1962, 5).

6. In the appropriate circumstances, the Jewish parallel formula "Behold, you are consecrated unto me by this ring, according to the Law of Moses and of Israel" is also suitable.

The reader has probably discerned that the circumstances of the act's performance appear next to some of the examples, and not by chance. Uttering the words is indeed the decisive step in the actualization of the speech act, but the statement assumes its performative character only in the defined circumstances that society determines for this purpose. These circumstances touch on two aspects of the performative statement: (1) the speaker, who should be defined as a person appropriate for acting through words (e.g., that he or she be at least a certain age, of sane mind, own the bequeathed property [in case of a legacy], or be male [in case of a Jewish Orthodox wedding]); and (2) the particular context of the utterance, which is defined in terms of time, place, ritual, or social activities during which the speech act is to be performed, and at times even the physical activity of the speaker, which accompanies the utterance as a necessary condition for turning it into action. Beyond these two aspects, a basic condition is required from the speaker: a serious intention to perform the act through speech, which should be received with the same measure of seriousness by the listeners.[7] This web of external and internal circumstances is what grants the words their performative character, turning them from mere speech into action. Any deviation from the accepted and known process in whose course the words are to be uttered or from the prescribed formulation or performance of the speech by an unsuitable subject or by someone with no serious intention to act through the words makes the utterance "infelicitous," as Austin says, and denies it any performative validity.

The central principles of speech act theory, as presented here succinctly, are suggested in the first two lectures in Austin's book. The subsequent lectures are devoted to discussions of various aspects of the theory, the related philosophical difficulties, and their possible solutions. Particularly important for my current pursuit are Lectures 8 and 9, in which Austin defines the three types of action discernible in a performative speech act: locutionary, illocutionary, and perlocutionary. In the present context the distinction between them can be summed up as follows:

---

7. An interesting attempt to define the web of circumstances required for the fulfillment of a promise was made by John Searle, one of Austin's most prominent disciples and unquestionably the most profound. See Searle (1970). On performative speech, cf. Searle (1974; 1985).

A locutionary act is the act of speaking. An illocutionary act is the act that the speaker performs through his utterance. For instance, when saying, "I promise" (in specific circumstances and with serious intention and so forth), he or she promises, and when saying, "I bequeath" (in the same terms), he or she bequeaths. Uttering the words is the locutionary act, whereas the promise (or the bequeathing) is the illocutionary act.[8] A perlocutionary act is the influence, if any, that the speaker achieves through his or her words.[9] When a boy says to his friend, "You should come on this trip. All the guys are coming, it's a great place, and it will be fabulous" and he succeeds in persuading the friend, then the speaker, besides making a locutionary act, has also performed a perlocutionary act of persuasion. A similar act is performed by a commander who tells her soldiers, "Thirty seconds and you're there," and they obey her.

Austin recurrently emphasizes the importance of the distinction between an illocutionary act that the speaker performs through his or her words, which is the classic expression of performative statements and thus concerns him most in his lecture, and the perlocutionary act that results in influence on another person. He also draws a distinction between the two of them and the locutionary act that is the actual act of speaking. Beyond these distinctions, which are significant in the context of applying speech act theory to the study of religion and ritual, Austin's claims about performative statements can basically be summed up as follows: There are statements that, when suitably uttered in the appropriate circumstances by the appropriate person and with serious intention, act and create by their very utterance a new state of affairs in the world.

SPEECH ACT THEORY AND MAGIC SPEECH

Students of magic, whether as an active pursuit or based on textual evidence, will easily discern that Austin's description of performative speech

---

8. Austin enumerates other kinds of illocutionary actions, for example, to ask or to answer a question, to provide information, to declare an intention, or to set a meeting. See Austin (1962, 98–99). See also the list of verbs pointing to illocutionary intention in Searle (1974, 23).

9. Austin (1962, 101). See also the discussion on these three actions in Austin (1962, 94–107).

is remarkably similar to magic linguistic activity. Magic speech, regardless of whether or not its contents are understood, functions primarily as the execution of an intention to act and is supposed to perform, through its very utterance, a certain requested change in the world. Magic words, like the performative statement, acquire their performative quality by virtue of the special circumstances in which they are uttered, and these circumstances are surprisingly similar to those that Austin described. The speaker must be the person deemed appropriate to perform this act. The time, the place, and the social and ritual matrix that accompany and frame the utterance are exactly described and should be performed as prescribed. The incantation should be uttered precisely, according to a set and defined formula. This similarity turns the possibility of relying on Austin's theory for a better understanding of magic activity into a tempting option that scholars have indeed made use of.

At the end of the 1960s and during the 1970s, several researchers examined the implications of speech act theory for anthropology. Magic was not always the focus but was discussed, at times directly and at times indirectly. This method has recently been applied to textual studies of Jewish mysticism. Its use in the scholarship is presented in the discussion that follows.

Ruth Finnegan was the first to apply Austin's theory to anthropological research. Her work does not necessarily focus on the ritual realm but on utterances such as "I agree," "I declare," and "I insist," which function as performative statements in the language of the Limba tribe in Sierra Leone.[10] Finnegan thus points to the existence of linguistic activity of this type in tribal societies and dismisses Austin's approach that the emergence of the speech act is a later stage in the development of language.[11] Although aware that, through the words "primitive or primary forms of utterance," Austin could have been referring to a hypothetical stage in the history of language development, Finnegan clarifies, "But if Austin is using 'primitive language' in the more popular (and misleading) sense which would cover present-day African languages, then his point does not hold of Limba at least."[12] Furthermore, the analysis of Limba

---

10. Finnegan (1969).

11. Austin (1962, 72).

12. Finnegan (1969, 547).

language shows that Austin's speech act theory is a significant and fruitful tool in the exploration of the status of language and the attitude toward it in tribal societies. At the end, Finnegan hints at the great potential advantages of applying Austin's theory to the realm of religion. She shows how religious language is related to social performative utterances among the Limba and suggests seeing religious utterances not only as expressive or symbolic, as had been the case in the past, but often as performative speech. This proposal was implemented by Benjamin Ray, but consideration of his work should be preceded by Stanley Tambiah's view on this theme.

Tambiah applied speech act theory to an analysis of the structure and meaning of magic activity. He begins with Edward Evans-Pritchard's study of medical magic among the Zande, particularly the systematic mistake that he identifies in Evans-Pritchard's attitude toward these findings: "Evans-Pritchard had clear clues that much of Zande magic was based on analogical thought and action, but rather than investigate its semantics deeply, he, being at this stage of his thought unable to liberate himself from the influence of the observer's distinction between things empirical and things mystical . . . simply subjected Zande magic and leechcraft to the Westerner's criteria of induction and verification."[13] Tambiah uses this study to illustrate what he views as the flaw that characterizes the study of magic in general and that results in it being studied (and at times judged) by the criteria and concepts of scientific causality. In his work, he refutes the possibility of understanding magic through these criteria and offers an alternative based on speech act theory.

After emphasizing that analogies are a prominent characteristic of magic thought and activity among the Zande, Tambiah examines the relationship between this type of analogy and scientific analogy. His analysis leads him to conclude that they are entirely different from one another and that scientific analogy is predictive, whereas magic analogy

---

13. Tambiah (1973, 203). On his debt to Finnegan concerning speech act theory, see Tambiah (1973, 219). Indeed, Tambiah dealt with magic language in an earlier article while ignoring Finnegan's approach. See Tambiah (1968). On Evans-Pritchard's study of magic, see chapter 1.

is persuasive. This essential difference between magic thought and action and scientific thought and action is what makes it futile to analyze the mechanism of causality in magic in scientific terms of empirical verification, that is, by considering its validity in terms of truth and falsity. Such an analysis, seeking to consider magic in the terms of another realm, cannot serve the attempt to understand it. Other tools are necessary for this purpose, and Tambiah indeed devotes part of his discussion to their clarification. He describes magic positively using speech act theory. His starting point is the Austin-like distinction between locutionary, illocutionary, and perlocutionary acts.

> Now adapting these ideas for our purposes, we can say that ritual acts and magical rites are of the "illocutionary" or "performative" sort, which simply by virtue of being enacted (under the appropriate conditions) achieve a change of state, or do something effective. . . . The vast majority of ritual and magical acts combine word and deed. Hence it is appropriate to say that they use words in a performative or illocutionary manner, just as the action (the manipulation of objects and persons) is correspondingly performative.[14]

Tambiah then expands this idea and applies it to magic ritual as a whole, relying on Austin's distinction between the pairs of categories true/false and felicitous/infelicitous[15] appropriate to the locutionary and illocutionary aspects of the speech act, respectively: "Now it is *inappropriate* to subject these performative rites to verification, to test whether they are true or false in a referential or assertive sense or whether the act has effected a result in terms of the logic of 'causation' as this is understood in science."[16] This approach is, in fact, a first instance of using speech act theory to clarify and describe the essence of magic language. Tambiah's analysis, by which this language is an illocutionary kind of performative action, successfully serves the general conception proposed in his article,

14. Tambiah (1973, 221–22).

15. Austin (1962, 14).

16. Tambiah (1973, 223; emphasis in original).

which distinguishes magic from science and denies the methodological legitimacy of examining magic causality through scientific criteria.

Tambiah formulates his notion about magical language as an illocutionary act of speech quite succinctly and without really entering into a discussion about the general relationship between philosophical theory and magical linguistic action. Ray's article on performative speech in African Dinka and Dogon rituals, the most profound attempt to apply Austin's theory in the realm of cultural anthropology, fills some of the gaps. Ray explains his intention as follows:

> My purpose in applying Austin's notion of "performative utterances" to Dinka and Dogon rituals will be to illuminate their meaning by noticing what is being *done* through the use of *words*. I intend to show that the "performative" approach enables us to see not only that language is the central mechanism of these rites but also how the belief in the instrumentality of words (their causal "power") may be intelligibly understood without consigning it to the sphere of the "primitive," the "magical," or the "symbolic," as so frequently done.[17]

Ray, then, uses Austin's theory to propose a new conception of ritual, liberated from what he considers the problematic necessity (identified with John Beattie's view) of classifying ritual expressions into one of two categories: expressive or symbolic.[18] His controversy with Beattie on the one hand and with Tambiah on the other is at the focus of his attempt to explain the tribal rituals he examines in light of speech act theory.[19] Contrary to both scholars, Ray does not confine the discussion to the illocutionary realm but extends it to all the linguistic performative powers identified by Austin. Ray emphasizes that, according to Austin, the meaning of a performative utterance derives from its special character.

17. Ray (1973, 17; emphasis in original).
18. For this classification, see Ray (1973, notes 3 and 18).
19. Ray's controversy is mainly with Tambiah's (1968) article, which was written before Tambiah became acquainted with speech act theory and incorporated it into his research.

Hence, ignoring its character hinders the chances of understanding it properly: "I intend to show that we can grasp their [Dinka and Dogon rituals] full meaning only by noticing what is being done through the illocutionary and perlocutionary acts involved."[20] In support of his position, Ray describes a Dinka ritual for healing the sick. By relying on the tools of Austin's theory, he analyzes what is done and said in the ritual and shows that the ritual fits the demands and the characteristics of illocutionary acts.

> The speech act itself performs the same conventional function as any institutionalized command. It gives an order. Its object, a spirit, may be described as "symbolic," but the speech act itself is not. . . . From the Dinka point of view, the command does not "symbolize" the expelling of spirits, it *does* it.[21]

Ray also points to perlocutionary aspects in Dinka ritual language and tries to demonstrate that, in this realm as well, the tribe's concepts and demands are compatible with the theory.[22] Ray's discussion of the Dogon focuses on an analysis of their language of prayer that, in his claim, rests on a perlocutionary conception. He expands the parameters of the discussion in the summary and determines that illocutionary acts are at the foundation of the entire Dogon ritual system.[23]

The last anthropological study I want to mention is that of Sam Gill. This study is essentially an attempt to characterize the prayer of Navajo Indians as a performative speech act. Gill replaces the set of magic terms that scholars tended to rely on to describe the Navajo belief in the operative power of their prayer with one drawing on speech act theory: "I want to show that it is due to the semantic structure of the prayer act, rather than to its magically compulsive character, that Navajos see it as an active agent in their world."[24] In his view, then, the Navajos themselves

---

20. Ray (1973, 19).

21. Ray (1973, 26–27; emphasis in original).

22. The discussion focuses mainly on the performer's authority.

23. Ray (1973, 32).

24. Gill (1978, 144).

perceive their prayer as a "performative utterance," according to the criteria set for it by Austin. Gill illustrates and analyzes various aspects of Navajo prayer and determines that it "bears an illocutionary force of an 'exercitive type' in Austin's categorization," because it creates a commitment to respond on the part of the Holy Person to whom the prayer is addressed.[25] He then broadens the scope and determines that prayer as a whole, including all its gestures and utterances, functions in a perlocutionary mode: Through the repetition of a number of actions and utterances, the one praying is healed.[26] Gill thus seeks to show that all three aspects of the speech act—locutionary, illocutionary, and perlocutionary—characterize the performative aspect of Navajo prayer. In his judgment, the insight about prayer as a performative act is not only the result of contemplation from the outside but also a foundation of Navajo religious thought.

Austin's theory was also used to discuss the language of prayer in the study of Kabbalah. Abraham Elkayam presents the theurgic-magic discourse in the medieval kabbalistic treatise *Ma'arekhet ha-'Elohut* as a speech act à la John Searle and John Austin. This interpretation of the symbolic system of the treatise supplements its analysis according to referential approaches.[27] Underlying Elkayam's view is the following claim:

> Their [i.e., the kabbalists of various Spanish schools] theurgic-magic approach to theological language can be directly ascribed, *inter alia*, to their interest in the behavioral-performative aspect of language. . . . In other words, the core of theurgic-symbolic language is not the fact that it includes declarative sentences but rather that it includes performative sentences, whose utterance is the performance of an action upon the "supernal world."[28]

---

25. Gill (1978, 150).

26. Gill (1978, 154).

27. Elkayam (1990). See Elkayam's methodological discussion in Elkayam (1990, 6–7, 29–30).

28. Elkayam (1990, 34).

Elkayam demonstrates how all aspects of the speech act can be applied to the analysis of prayer in *Ma'arekhet ha-'Elohut*.[29] He states that, according to this treatise, there are prayers in which the act of speech itself (i.e., the locutionary act) affects the supernal powers without the addition of the illocutionary act. In this sense, "According to *Ma'arekhet ha-'Elohut*, there is no difference whatsoever between the very act of uttering the prayer and ordinary operational magic."[30] Elkayam equates the illocutionary addition to the utterance with the special (mystic) intention that accompanies prayer. Through intention the worshiper turns his prayer from ordinary liturgical language into a symbolic text of holy names and invests it with theurgic-magic quality. Elkayam further locates the perlocutionary act in the influences of this symbolic prayer on the heavenly realm: increasing the flow of the emanation between the *sefirot*, bringing them together into a dynamic unity, and even affecting the mundane world according to the mystic's will. In sum, the characteristics of the symbolic discourse in *Ma'arekhet ha-'Elohut*—memory, intention, and emanation—enable the identification of this discourse as a performative speech act in terms of speech act theory.

The latest attempt to apply speech act theory to the study of Jewish ritual language is that of Rebecca Macy Lesses in her research on adjurations in *Hekhalot* and *Merkavah* literature.[31] The uniqueness of this work is that Lesses does not rely solely on Austin but also, and mainly, on later views regarding the performative meaning of rituals and their language. Lesses's main contribution to the discussion is the use of the concept of *cosmology*, which Tambiah used in the study of ritual. According to Tambiah, every ritual is performed and acquires its meaning within a given cosmology, that is, "the body of conceptions that enumerate and classify the phenomena that compose the universe as an ordered

---

29. Note that Elkayam disregards the issue of the conditions for successful performative utterances, to which Austin ascribes great importance.

30. Elkayam (1990, 35).

31. Lesses (1998, esp. 161–278). Cf. also Lesses (1995). For a similar and (earlier) approach concerning the performative character of language in *Hekhalot* literature that does not rely on Austin, see Janowitz (1989). On the view of the efficiency of language in late antiquity, see also Janowitz (2002).

whole and the norms and processes that govern it."[32] Cosmology may be different in different societies, but its relativity becomes evident only from an external vantage point. Members of the society never doubt that their own cosmology conveys reality as is rather than their personal or social outlook.

Lesses states that, in order to understand the rites described in *Hekhalot* and *Merkavah* literature—specifically, in order to understand how they were effective—we should first understand the cosmology within which they were significant.

> The culture that composed and used these adjurations saw an intimate connection between the human and divine realms. Society extended beyond humanity to include angels (and in principle demons, who do not, however, feature prominently in the *Hekhalot* texts) and God. Ritual utterances could thus have an effect on extrahuman hierarchies.[33]

Speech acts in human society, as Austin describes them, can serve as a model for understanding the efficiency of adjurations that address angels. The reason is that, from a performative perspective, there is no essential difference between them once the borders of the society have been determined in this fashion.[34]

These studies describe present attempts to apply a certain philosophy of language to an analysis of verbal utterances in anthropological and historical-textual research. The parallels that scholars identify between performative statements according to Austin's (and Searle's) speech act

---

32. Tambiah (1985b, 130).

33. Lesses (1998, 164). The dead should be added to those included in the broader Jewish society in late antiquity and the early Islamic period, surely in the context of a magic culture.

34. Following Jacques Derrida and Stanley Fish, Lesses expresses reservations about Austin's intentionality condition as necessary for successful performance of the speech act, because the thoughts and feelings of the speaker and of his or her listeners cannot be known. These reservations are important for her concerns because "the Hekhalot adjurations . . . provide no information about the expected or real state of mind of the adjurer" (Lesses 1998, 170). For Derrida's criticism, see Derrida (1977) and Norris (1982, 108–15).

theory and the statements they themselves examine are indeed impressive. But are they truly relevant? Is it right in principle to draw this comparison, or does this perhaps involve the same fallacy that these very scholars had warned against: the projection of modern Western distinctions and concepts onto societies and worldviews far removed from them?[35] Is it right to claim that the Dinka and the Dogon engage in performative speech acts and that Zande medicine is based on the performance of illocutionary actions in the same sense that Austin ascribed to these terms? Is it justified to describe the theurgic-magic prayer of a fourteenth-century kabbalist and the adjurations of one who in the first millennium CE "descends to the chariot" as performative utterances in the sense of Austin's terminology? This question is the focus of the discussion in the next section. It is not my intention, however, to enter into a controversy over one or another of these scholars' specific conclusions but rather to consider the actual methodological legitimacy of using Austin's philosophical theory to understand magic activity. Ancient Jewish magic serves as a test case.

PERFORMATIVE UTTERANCES AND ACTS OF ADJURATION: EARLY JEWISH MAGIC AS A TEST CASE

Ancient Jewish magic culture is recorded in hundreds of magical artifacts and texts from the end of antiquity and the early Islamic period. Performative artifacts, such as amulets and incantation bowls, join a literature of magic prescriptions and treatises and together provide a broad picture of the beliefs, acts, and aims of magic's agents and consumers. As I will show in chapter 5, each component of the magic inventory is uniquely important. The performative artifacts attest to the actual execution of spells for the benefit of specific clients and for a specific purpose. The recipes provide evidence of the inclusive ritual that constitutes the act of magic, whereas the treatises add the conceptual framework within which these actions and the beliefs related to them had inner logic and meaning. The following are four examples of magic acts taken from four different

---

35. See especially Ray (1973, 35) and Tambiah (1973, 200–203).

sources: *Sefer ha-Razim, Ḥarba de-Moshe, Havdalah de-Rabbi Aqiva*, and a book of recipes from the Cairo Genizah. Each example represents one of the four central areas in Jewish magic culture: harming, healing, love, and knowledge.[36]

The "first firmament" of *Sefer ha-Razim* offers a long list of harmful acts that can be performed with the help of the angels dwelling in this firmament. Action and speech join here in the execution of the longed-for aim.

> These are the names of the angels of the second encampment who serve TYGRH: 'KSTR, MRSWM. . . . These are the angels who are full of anger and wrath and who are in charge of every matter of combat and war and are prepared to torment and torture a man to death. And there is no mercy in them but (they wish) only to take revenge and to punish him who is delivered into their hands. And if you wish to send them against your enemy . . . take yourself water from seven springs on the seventh day of the month, in the seventh hour of the day, in seven pottery vessels that have not seen daylight, and do not mix them together one with another. And place them under the stars for seven nights; and on the seventh night take a glass vial for the name of your adversary[37] and pour the water (from the vessels) into it, then break the pottery vessels and throw (the pieces) to the four winds [directions], and say thus toward (the) four winds: "HHGRYT who dwells in the east, SRWKYT who dwells in the north, 'WLPH who dwells in the west, KRDY who dwells in the south, please accept from me at this time in which I throw to you for the name of N son of N to break his bones to crush all his limbs, and to shatter the vigor of his strength, as these

---

36. The variety of sources is deliberate but not imperative. Many examples are found in every single one of these books. On these works, see chapter 5. For a discussion of these realms in early Jewish magic, see Harari (1997a; 1998, 139–50; 2000; 2005c).

37. Doing something "for the name of" someone means doing it with deliberate intention to generate a firm (sympathetic) connection between the artifact (or the deed) and the named person, so that the named individual will be influenced by the artifact.

pottery vessels are broken. And may there be no recovery for him[38] as there is no repair for these pottery vessels." Then take the vial of water and recite over it the names of these angels and the name of the overseer, who is TYGRH and say thus: "I deliver to you, angels of anger and wrath, N son of N, that you will strangle him and destroy him and his appearance, and make him bedridden, and diminish his wealth, and annul the intentions of his heart, and blow away his thought and his knowledge so that he will waste away continually until he approaches death." And if you wish to exile him (conclude and) say thus: . . . ; and if he is one to whom you are in debt (conclude and) say thus: . . . ; and if (the rite is) for a ship (conclude and) say thus: . . . ; and if (you wish) to fell a fortified wall (conclude and) say thus: . . . ; and (do) the same for each and every matter. And act in a state of purity and then you will succeed.[39]

The omitted passages refer to further harmful acts that the book's user can perform through these angels and the special incantations corresponding to each one of them.

A characteristic healing incantation, which connects healing to the eradication of demons and evil spirits from the body appears in *Havdalah de-Rabbi Aqiva*. This work, a successful testimony of the mutual relationships between magic and liturgy in Judaism,[40] weaves incantations and holy names into the Havdalah prayer, which marks the end of the Sabbath, and thus turns the event of Havdalah into a ritual of protection from demons and maleficent sorcery. At its opening, the treatise sets the guidelines for a purification ritual required from its performer.[41] It then

---

38. In the original, "for them."

39. M. Margalioth (1966, 69–71). Cf. Rebiger and Schäfer (2009, I, secs. 40–54). On harmful magic in *Sefer ha-Razim*, see Alexander (2003b). For further discussion of magical practices in *Sefer ha-Razim*, see Dan (2008–2014, 3: 1060–92), Janowitz (2002, 85–108), and Niggermeyer (1975).

40. On this matter, see Harari (1997b, 92–101), Levene (2005), Naveh and Shaked (1993, 22–31), Schäfer (1996), and Schäfer and Shaked (1994–1999, 2: 1–6).

41. This part of *Havdalah de-Rabbi Aqiva* is apparently late. See Scholem (1981, 248). Magic sources, however, indicate that the requirement of purity in Jewish magical culture is ancient. See later discussion.

presents the usual version of the Havdalah prayer, incorporating verses from Psalm 91 and combinations of holy names.[42] At the end of this compounded version, the performer of the Havdalah should utter the following adjuration:

> I adjure, and I bind a binding, and I limit a limitation, and I vow a vow on (every) spirit, and demon, and shadow spirits, and sorceries, and (magical) bindings, and acts of magic and evil deeds, and every evil eye, and all evil women, and every evil word, and every evil creature in the world—may you be expelled and annulled from all two-hundred and forty-eight limbs of N son of N from this day onward, in the name of 'DYRYRWN Lord of the hosts, Holy Holy Holy Amen Amen Amen Selah.[43]

More protective adjurations appear later in the work. Together with instructions for ritual actions, they establish the ritual move required for the successful performance of the Havdalah.

Recipes for love charms appear in several places in magic literature.[44] The following example is taken from a series of recipes in *Ḥarba de-Moshe*:

> If you wish a woman to follow you, take some of your blood and write [with it] your name and her name on her gate, and write her name and your name on your gate and say in front of her gate from *'LYHWS* up to *GSKY'*.[45]

Charms for knowledge often make use of supernatural agents, including angels and the dead, to obtain information unattainable through ordinary channels. At times, as in the following event, the angels are invited into a person's dream to disclose the answer to a question.

---

42. On the magical use of Psalm 91 and of psalms in general, see later discussion.

43. Scholem (1981, 252–53).

44. See Harari (2000) and Saar (2008).

45. Harari (1997b, 41, sec. 64). *'LYHWS* and *GSKY'* are words in the sword of magic names that demarcate the specific passage to be uttered for the implementation of this rite. On this sword and the mode of using it in *Ḥarba de-Moshe*, see Harari (1997b, 115–21).

Another one [meaning another spell for a dream inquiry],[46] which is good and fair and tested and true. Fast for three days and on the third night go to sleep without eating, dress in pure clothes, keep away from the house where a woman is found, and say seven times "God is my shepherd I shall not want," the entire psalm [Psalm 23], and say, "I adjure you to show me what I seek and answer my question and my request." And go to sleep and you will see the wonder—they will come, fulfill your wish, and (answer) your question.[47]

These four examples present a ritual-performative practice that is based on faith in the power of words to change reality in the world by their very utterance. They thereby faithfully reflect the *Weltanschauung* of ancient Jewish magic in its entirety.[48] This faith in the power of words is not surprising, given the status of language in Jewish thought and in Jewish religion in particular. Prayer, which since the destruction of the Temple had become almost the sole way of contacting God, the liturgical poetry (*piyyut*) that accompanied it, the mysticism of the *Merkavah* and *Hekhalot* circles where holy names were a major focus of interest and study, the Midrash and commentaries—all attest to the enormous importance that Jewish culture ascribed to the holy tongue. It is thus not surprising that language merits this highly significant standing in magic thought as well, to the point that all that is at times required for the performance of magic is to pronounce a verbal formula.[49] In almost all the rituals described in ancient Jewish magic, the incantation is the core of the ritual and all the other components are organized around it. Stored in this core is the power of magic action and, without it, the accompanying acts will be useless. In the magic rite, words are the operative element that generates a new reality.

---

46. This recipe follows another titled *she'elat ḥalom* (dream inquiry), which aims at summoning "Michael the great prince, come to me and faithfully show me everything I will ask from you tonight." See Schäfer and Shaked (1994–1999, 1: 136).

47. Schäfer and Shaked (1994–1999, 1: 136).

48. On this viewpoint and its parallels in Greco-Roman culture and in Christianity in late antiquity, see Janowitz (2002).

49. See, for instance, Harari (1997b, 44–45, secs. 113–16) and Naveh and Shaked (1993, 184–85, 197, 216).

The power and range of adjurations was almost limitless,[50] but not so the conditions of their use. A complex system of instructions and restrictions set up the exclusive and precise context of circumstances that could allow human speech to turn into an operative power. These circumstances, as anthropologists have also found in their research, fit Austin's theory well. The first requirement is the precise uttering of the magic formula. Each spell requires a special formula specified in a recipe.[51] Performative utterances also rest on the conception that, in each case, only certain defined statements have operative power. To promise is possible through the saying "I promise," to bequeath through the saying "I bequeath," and to marry through the set formula in the marriage ritual that compels the parties. In these cases precision need not be as rigorous as in magic speech, but in all of them (and in others like them) an act can be performed through speech only by means of the linguistic formula specific to its performance.

Magic speech and performative utterances are also similar with regard to the ritual context of speech. Magic recipes show that the adjuration must be performed in a defined ritual context, which is a sine qua non for realizing the performative potential latent in the incantation.

---

50. Ancient Jewish magic is usually focused and pragmatic but also includes several all-purpose recipes. See Harari (1998, 136–38; 2001).

51. A comparison of parallel versions of incantations in amulets and incantation bowls written by the same person shows that, at times, the writers took some license in formulating the final version of the incantation. In any event, the extreme precision in detailing the components of the ritual in general and the incantation to be uttered in its course in particular patently attest to an approach that ascribes great importance to exact performance. Hence it is plausible that, even if the writers wove together incantation elements from different sources, they did not do so arbitrarily but in a belief that they were creating the right combination, that is, the most appropriate adjuration from a performative perspective for solving the problem facing them. Furthermore, the warnings that occasionally accompany magic recipes show that a mistake in a spell means not only a performative failure but even an actual danger. Not only does the erroneous execution of an adjuration act fail to submit the angels to human will, but it also opens up the possibility of an attack by them. For expressions of fear from the angels and adjurations of protection and threat addressed to them, see, for instance, Harari (1997b, 100, 104–5). For a discussion of this issue in *Hekhalot* and *Merkavah* literature, cf. Dan (1987a, esp. the references in note 1; 1993, 93–107), Liebes (1990), and Scholem (1946, 49–54).

The ritual matrix for the performance of the adjuration in each magic act is also rigorously determined. This demand is illustrated in the recipes in the four examples. At different levels of complexity, all four detail the ritual acts that should accompany the act of adjuration. According to Austin, performative utterances acquire their special standing only if uttered in defined circumstances. The words as such do not create a performative utterance, nor does every word do so in these defined circumstances. For an utterance to be performative, what is required is a combination of speech and the circumstances of its utterance appropriate to the performance of the requested action by means of speech. As in magic, different aims require different utterances and different ritual conditions.

The third prominent resemblance between the magic deed and the performative speech act is the definition of the performer. According to treatises and manuals on magic, not everyone can cast a spell. This statement requires no further explanation if we assume that this literature is a priori meant only for professionals. But even when partly meant for personal use, in a do-it-yourself variation,[52] ritual preparations are required to carry out the spell. Preparation and purification rites considered as rites of entry are detailed in *Ḥarba de-Moshe* and in *Havdalah de-Rabbi Aqiva* and mentioned in the demand to "act in a state of purity" in *Sefer ha-Razim* and in many other sources.[53] The purpose of these rites is to extract individuals from the ordinary course of their lives and fundamentally change them in a way that will prepare them to use the adjurations successfully. Unless they are in a ritual-personal situation suited to the execution of the spell, their deeds will fail to help. Speech act theory also defines a similar condition: Only one who, at the time of the utterance, is in a situation that authorizes him or her to perform the required act can realize the potential latent in the performative utterance and act through it.

Ostensibly, then, Austin's theory (or, more precisely, his notion of illocutionary utterance) is remarkably similar to the view of magic in

---

52. This trend is evident in some of the recipes in *Ḥarba de-Moshe*, for instance. See Harari (1997b, 73–76).

53. See, for instance, Naveh and Shaked (1993, 216, 220) and Schäfer and Shaked (1994–1999, 1: 20, 136). Cf. Harari (1997b, 90–91).

Jewish magical texts. The idea of speech endowed with action powers and, even more so, the parallel demands for a suitable ritual context and for the speaker's special standing tempt us to think that ideas and acts common in ancient Jewish magic culture can be explained through the concepts of mid-twentieth-century philosophy of language. Yet it is not so.

Ancient Jewish magic practice has its roots in a *Weltanschauung* conceptually far removed from the one underlying Austin's theory. Speech act theory is a philosophical theory dealing with consensual language. It clarifies that, in the set of social agreements that institutionalize language, there are agreements that endow certain utterances with a different standing. This theory, then, deals above all with the exposure of the hidden social agreements bearing on language and with their description. Language is perceived in it as a social activity, and its consequences are therefore always social. Whether they are constative or performative, linguistic statements function within a human system of communication and interpersonal contacts. The consequences of the performative statements, that is, the changes that they create in the world's state of affairs, invariably take place within this system and are only social. Marriages, bequests, promises, and bets (in illocutionary utterances) and seduction, persuasion, deceit, and command (in perlocutionary utterances) are part of the range of social relations. In the context of this range, and only within it, an action may be realized through speech based on a social agreement. To preclude mistakes, the power of these performative utterances should be redefined in more limited terms. When Austin claims that there are cases when "*by* saying or *in* saying something we are doing something,"[54] he should be understood only in social terms. Performative statements change the *social* state of affairs in the world. This formulation in no way weakens Austin's claim, nor does it detract from its beauty, because social action is action for all intents and purposes and social change is real change in the general state of affairs in the world for every person involved. This presentation of speech act theory, however, prevents illusions about its application to inappropriate areas.

---

54. Austin (1962, 12).

Jewish magic, unlike the case of a performative utterance, seeks to introduce limitless change. Its consequences transcend the realms of human society and its valid social agreements to actually affect the world. Sinking a ship, winning a horse race, healing a fever or a snake bite, improving memory, killing or banishing a man from his home, boosting a crop or a catch of fish, sustaining pregnancy and easing delivery, and many other issues common in Jewish magic literature have no bearing on the social consensus that underlies the possibility of speech acts. The possibility of attaining these wishes through speech rests on a view of life and language entirely different from that conveyed by Austin. According to this view, the power of a magic incantation is not derived from the consensual character of language but from its opposite—its holy divine character. The twenty-two letters of the Torah were perceived not only as preceding reality in general and human reality in particular but as actually generating them.[55] The holy standing of language in general and of the divine names that embody its omnipotent potential in particular is what granted human magic speech its special power. According to the magic worldview, this potential can be used to control various occult powers—angels, names, letters, bindings, demons and other harmful spirits—whose influence on human destiny is permanent and decisive. Controlling angels and other supernatural powerful beings and harnessing them to the will of their user are elements so essential to ancient

---

55. The formula repeatedly used to describe creation in Genesis 1, "And God said . . . and there was," is presented as an explicit outlook concerning creation through speech in Psalm 33:6: "By the word of the Lord were the heavens made; and all the host of them by the breath of his mouth." Later, it found expression in rabbinic traditions, such as "By ten sayings the world was created" (M. *Avot* 5:1); "R. Abbahu said in R. Yoḥanan's name: He created them [heaven and earth] with the letter *heh* . . . not with labour or wearying toil did the Holy One, blessed be He, create His world, but by the word of the Lord were the heavens immediately made" (*Genesis Rabbah* 12:10; cf. 3:2); "Bezalel knew how to combine the letters by which the heavens and earth were created" (TB *Berakhot* 55a). See also Urbach (1975, 184–213). This approach is particularly emphasized in *Sefer Yeẓirah*, which describes creation as an act of combining letters. On the magic context of *Sefer Yeẓirah*, see Bar-Ilan (2011), Dan (1998, 234–68), Hayman (1989), and Idel (1990, 9–26). See, however, Yehuda Liebes's objections to this view in Liebes (2000, 63–71). On the development of *Sefer Yeẓirah* and on the ancient foundations of the version that has reached us, see Hayman (2004).

Jewish magic that it cannot be described without them. This is how magic action is actually performed. Only in this context, that is, in the context of faith in the power embedded in the holy names of God on the one hand and the worldview that grants supernatural beings a central role in the shaping of human destiny on the other, can the magic act of speech be understood correctly. And in this context the magic use of language is indeed entirely different from Austin's performative speech act.

The conditions of the speech act in Austin's theory and in ancient Jewish magic do not appear to be genuinely parallel either. According to the philosophical theory, the required conditions for a successful implementation of an illocutionary act are social. Austin's examples—marrying, bequeathing, christening, betting, and promising—attest to this well. Furthermore, these conditions are not defined with the precision that characterizes the magic ritual but serve as a general denotation of the situation's character, that is, a social definition of its essence. Establishing an illocutionary meaning depends on the social recognition of the unique circumstances surrounding the performance of the utterance. Beyond it, it is what determines the fact of its being felicitous or infelicitous. According to Jewish magic literature, the standing of the magic ritual—meaning whether the speech performed in its course will or will not have operative power—does not depend on social recognition of it (which is often impossible because of the secrecy that is required as a condition of its success) but on the magician's success in creating it properly. A Jewish magic ritual is not a social situation but a concrete reality that the adjurer must create in all its intricate detail according to a rigorous model prescribed a priori. Magic action through speech will fail without precise execution, not because implementation of the required ritual lacked social recognition but rather because of worldly laws stating, for instance, that coffee cannot possibly be sweetened with a teaspoon of salt. A magic act requires a defined ritual to attain a defined aim.

Like the incantation, the ritual is also a tool of action, a special and precise means adapted to the attainment of a specific required aim. A deviation from explicit ritual demands, that is, an attempt to perform a certain act through the tools of another, will lead the sorcerer nowhere.

The magic ritual, then, does not define the social standing of the magic act through speech and therefore does not need witnesses for proper performance. This is a set of objective conditions, which strengthen the performative power of the incantation by creating the unique environment that will enable its transformation from ordinary speech into active power. The success of the entire endeavor, including its verbal aspect, is not tested in the social terms that Austin's theory requires but in objective terms of cause and effect: If the ritual instructions are properly followed, the magic will work and bring about the requested result. Failure to attain results is proof of failure to comply with the instructions.

The difference I present here between the conditions for a performative utterance and those of magic speech also characterizes the question of the speaker's authority and its relationship with the success of the speaker's action in both cases. According to Austin's theory, an action cannot be successfully executed through an illocutionary utterance unless it is performed by the appropriate person. A woman cannot bequeath her neighbor's assets to her children even if she writes this in her will. A married man cannot marry a woman even if he performs the appropriate wedding ritual unless society recognizes bigamy. Similarly, society does not recognize the validity of oral commitments made by babies or mad individuals, and so forth. The society, whose laws define the proper standing for concretizing action through speech, determines in all these cases the failure of illocutionary utterances performed by people who were found to be unsuited to the task.

The question of the speaker's serious intention when expressing an illocutionary utterance is also related to this matter. Austin holds that serious intention is the fundamental quality required from the speaker as a necessary condition for being qualified to perform action through speech. The speaker's authority to act through words, then, follows from and is determined by the social conventions within which illocutionary utterances are performed. In ancient Jewish magic, by contrast, one's authority to act through words is perceived as part of the general ritual matrix. The available literature on magic does not point to the importance of the sorcerer's social recognition, and his authority to act through incantations does not follow from it. Rather, it derives from his unique physical and spiritual situation, whose mode of attainment is also dictated by the recipes of magic. *Harba de-Moshe*, for instance, prescribes a three-day ritual of purity, prayer, and adjuration for attaining control over the "sword" of magic names. Here are some of the instructions:

> One who prepares himself to manipulate it [the sword] should sanctify himself (free) from nocturnal pollution and from (ritual) impurity for three days and should only eat and drink in the evening. And he should eat (only) bread made by a pure man or by his own hands with clean salt and drink (only) water. And no one should be aware that he is doing this deed for the purpose of manipulating this sword. . . . And on the first day of your seclusion, perform ablution(s) and you need not (do so) again. And pray three times a day[56] and after each prayer say this prayer: Blessed are You QWSYM our God, King of the world. . . . Whoever wishes to manipulate this sword should recite his (daily) prayer and upon reaching *Shome'a Tefillah*[57] he should say: I adjure you the four princes. . . . And he should not touch or use this sword until he has carried out these things; and afterward he may perform everything that he desires according to that which is written [in the last part of the treatise], each matter according to its proper order.[58]

The validity of this ritual does not rest on social consensus but on its essence as heavenly knowledge.[59] It does not grant its performer a social status that authorizes him to execute a speech act, but it fundamentally changes his personality. Furthermore, not only is a preliminary social status required for the successful performance of magic not intimated in the text, but also its necessity is negated through the general formulations "one who prepares himself to manipulate it" and "whoever wishes to

---

56. Apparently the Amidah prayer, which is to be recited three times a day.

57. *Shome'a Tefillah* (You who hearkens unto prayer) is the sixteenth benediction (out of nineteen) in the Amidah prayer.

58. Harari (1997b, 24–31). See also the discussion in Harari (1997b, 70–73, 79–114).

59. According to *Harba de-Moshe*, Moses received the magic mysteries from the angels. See Harari (1997b, 23–24, 58, 62–66). According to *Sefer ha-Razim*, the mysteries were delivered to Noah or to Adam. On traditions of transmission in magic literature, see Swartz (1994; 1996, 173–205).

manipulate this sword." What enables a person to act by means of the sword of names is the ritual situation that is attained through the performance of the instructions, not his social status.

Another treatise, which is concerned with a magic test for a woman suspected of adultery, explicitly clarifies this matter.

> You should realize and understand that if, at this time, a person were to fear God and cleanse his soul from all sins and wickedness and step on the path of purity—purity in his body and purity in his flesh—and were he to attend to these names and amend his soul through (the)se paths, he will be as an angel and a High Priest. Whatever he may act will be fulfilled.[60]

The purity ritual, then, extracts a person from ordinary life and confers on him a supernatural status that is part of all the conditions of the adjuration rite, one of the requirements in the unique situation allowing the power stored in the incantation to be released.

A comparison of the three central elements that generate the possibility of action through speech according to speech act theory (the linguistic formula, the circumstances of the utterance, and the speaker's authority) and their parallels in ancient Jewish magic suggests that the conceptual foundations of Austin's theory and the magic worldview discussed here cannot be tied together. They are in two different realms, not only in their perception of the essence of the language and the source of its performative power but also insofar as it concerns the very action through speech and its mode of realization. The attempt to use Austin's terms to describe magic, or at the very least ancient Jewish magic, proves impossible. The price for succumbing to the temptation to adopt the superficial similarity between them is to ignore the essential gap separating them as two distinct systems of thought and action. Ancient Jewish magic, contrary to illocutionary utterances, was not a means for attaining social change by virtue of social agreements. Rather, it was a technique whose effectiveness was perceived as anchored in objective conditions

---

60. Schäfer and Shaked (1994–1999, 1: 20). On this treatise, which offers an alternative test to the biblical ordeal of a suspected adulteress (Numbers 5:11–31), see the "Magic Treatises" subsection in chapter 5.

and circumstances: the divine power of God's holy names, which was bestowed on the incantation in a suitable ritual context by one who had been made fit to do so through ritual preparation.

A question could emerge at this point: Should we indeed relate so seriously to the worldview of the research subjects and to the way they perceive their activity? Should the fact that they themselves do not view their actions in the same way we explain them indeed prevent us from ascribing to these actions the meaning emerging from our insights about them? In other words, are we not allowed to ignore their (emic) self-perceptions and explain their cosmology according to our (etic) insights? My answer is that, at least regarding my current pursuit, this is impossible. The reason is not only the way users of magic perceive their actions but also Austin's conception of the performative speech act. These are the only two possible ways of examining magic speech acts, and choice is imperative. Speech act theory, as noted, states that some utterances, when uttered correctly, each one as such and in defined circumstances, constitute acts that change the state of affairs in the world. This link between means and results is the gist of Austin's view about the illocutionary utterance and its very essence. I have shown that, according to the worldview of the study's subjects, the magic incantation does indeed change things in the world, but not because it essentially corresponds to the conditions set by Austin for its being an illocutionary speech act.

From this perspective, then, a magic speech act cannot be viewed as an illocutionary utterance in Austin's terms. On the other hand, if we attempt to disregard the worldview of the research subjects and explain their action by resorting to Austin's concepts, will we indeed admit that any real action was performed through this act? Will we indeed claim that the magic incantation for lighting an oven, opening a locked door, expelling crickets from the house, or walking on water, for instance, achieved the desired result? In other words, is there room for acknowledging a direct causal link between magic speech and its results in the world in the cosmology within which Austin formulated his theory? I do not think so. We must therefore choose within what cosmology we examine this issue. If, to understand ancient Jewish magic, we use our cosmology, we will have to recognize the inefficiency of the act and will thereby pull the rug out from under the claim that uttering an incantation is a speech act. In the cosmology of adjurers, however, an incantation is indeed thought to operate in the world, but they perceive it as fundamentally different from a performative utterance à la Austin. The integration of the two cosmologies, taking performative conditions from one and efficiency from the other, seems to me to be the fallacy characterizing attempts to use Austin's theory to explain ritual and magical language.

II

Sources

5

Jewish Magic Literature

Magical Texts and Artifacts

The available sources for understanding and describing the culture of ancient Jewish magic split into two main kinds: insider (primary) and outsider (secondary).[1] The insider sources are magic sources in the more distinctive sense of the term: adjuration texts, or texts that include adjurations, created and used in circles of sorcerers or by people interested in witchcraft that supply internal evidence of a Jewish magic culture. Outsider sources are Jewish sources that are not distinctly magical but express direct or indirect interest in magic as known to us from the insider sources. This interest is found in many Jewish sources from late antiquity and the early Islamic period. As noted in chapter 2, in the past the main and almost sole source for describing Jewish magic was the secondary, outsider evidence, particularly rabbinic literature, a corpus that is obviously basically flawed. Not only are rabbinic texts in no way magic literature, but also the rabbis, who acknowledged the power of magic, were hostile toward it. The actual knowledge about magic culture that can be retrieved from these sources is limited and is usually not explicit. Most of it touches on two mutually intertwined areas: demons

---

1. In citations from magical sources in the form of manuscript, I use the following conventions: [ ], lacuna or illegible text; <aaa>, gloss written above the lines or in the margins; [aaa], reconstruction of missing text; (?), uncertain reading; (aaa), grammatical or clarifying intervention in the text. My own comments appear in brackets and are prefaced with "i.e."

and healing. Although rabbinic literature includes many (largely narrative) traditions concerned with such matters, occasionally including important information about demonological conceptions and magic healing, the rabbis' real interest in them was didactic rather than informative. Hence, rather than teaching us about the essence of magic and demonology in their circles or their surroundings, the rabbis' statements often attest to their use of these issues to promote their public, moral-halakhic, and sociopolitical agendas.

The discovery and publication of primary magic literature made possible a systematic transformation in the study of Jewish magic, resembling the transformations in the study of Gnostic sects after the discovery of the Nag Hammadi scrolls and in the study of Greco-Roman magic following the discovery of the Greek magical papyri. Here too we can replace hostile outsider literature with primary insider sources, though rabbinic traditions should not be underestimated or ignored. Precisely against the background of the findings emerging from magic literature itself, we can now reevaluate these traditions, assess how they fit or deviate from the magic findings, enrich our knowledge regarding magic wherever possible, and mainly, consider the broader social context where these magic beliefs and acts should be located. Scholars are confronted with a challenge, though: The rabbinic hagiography that ascribes to biblical heroes and to the rabbis themselves the power to operate the world by means of rituals and linguistic formulas, as sorcerers do, also categorically rejects magic (*kishuf*) and anyone involved in it. In light of the clear evidence from magic literature, however, this challenge is no longer focused on the clarification of essentialist differences between the actions or beliefs of the rabbis and those of the sorcerers, as it had been in the past. Instead, it centers on the political meaning of the didactic use of elements from magic culture and on the rejection of magic and its agents in the rabbinic discourse as part of the rabbis' struggle for exclusive control of the truth and the power derived from it in Jewish society of late antiquity.

Rabbinic literature is only one of three bodies of sources showing traces of Jewish magic culture and its role in the conceptual and political web. Jewish texts from the Second Temple era, *Hekhalot* and *Merkavah* literature, and Karaite and Geonic texts also offer extensive and valuable textual evidence on these matters. Directly or indirectly, these sources touch on the origin of magic, its legitimation, its human agents, and the social power advantage latent in it, on performance issues concerning control of angels and demons through linguistic and ritual means, and on theoretical concerns about the origin of evil spirits and their opera- tion in the world. I present and discuss all these testimonies, from rab- binic literature and other bodies, in chapters 6 and 7. In this chapter I focus on primary magic sources: texts and artifacts created in Jewish culture for magic purposes and as an expression of its operation; these should be the basis for describing early Jewish magic.[2]

The magic literature discussed in this chapter splits into three bodies of sources: artifacts with performative power, magic recipes, and magic treatises. Each of these sources highlights a different aspect of the inter- est in magic and of the attitude toward it. The first group includes sev- eral dozen amulets, hundreds of adjuration bowls, and a few magic gems. These artifacts provide direct testimony of living magic activity in the service of clients who are usually mentioned by name and for a defined purpose, which is also explicitly noted in the incantation. The second group, magic recipes, is a large corpus of professional, technical litera- ture that has survived in a small number of works and in hundreds of Genizah fragments. Together, these works and fragments contain hun- dreds of magic recipes attesting to the practice and performance of sor- cery and the preparation of performative artifacts. The third group is more limited. It includes a few magic treatises, a more developed version of the magic recipe literature. Beside recipes, they also contain highly valuable information about the sorcerers' worldview. When integrated, these three sources trace a broad picture of all the components making up Jewish magic culture: beliefs, rituals, aims, and historical and social contexts.

The main magic finding that concerns me here spreads over a period of about a thousand years that begins in the third to fourth centuries CE. Textually, this corpus begins with *Sefer ha-Razim* and ends with documents from the Cairo Genizah. The uniting element in this corpus is the genre; all these texts reflect a persistent cultural phenomenon rest- ing on a stable picture of reality and of performative patterns, based on

---

2. For a concise survey of early Jewish magic based on both insider and outsider evidence, see Swartz (2006b). For a broad, historical study, see Bohak (2008). For a use- ful, updated bibliography, see Bohak (2012a).

the use of adjurations. Rather than meeting theoretically, the historical borders intersect methodologically. On the one hand, few findings anticipate the corpus that is discussed here.[3] On the other hand, the adjuration literature continued to exist and develop after the beginning of the second millennium. Magic texts were created, copied, and printed throughout the second millennium and are offered for sale even today. It is indeed possible to point to a culture of Jewish magic with stable characteristics that has persisted since the end of antiquity to the present.[4] Nonetheless, most magic manuscripts originating in the Cairo Genizah are from the early centuries of the first millennium, and the upper limit of my inquiry has been set accordingly.

Beyond the cultural cohesiveness of the findings discussed here is their diversification according to time and place. Concerning place, the uniqueness of Babylonian magic bowls, as opposed to the evidence of "western" (i.e., west of Babylonia) magic findings, deserves particular note. Prominent in this context are the links of these bowls to the local foreign culture in general and to the prevalent cross-cultural practice of incantation bowls in particular. At the same time, deep commonalities must be stressed between the perception of reality and the power means used to contend with it that are evident in the findings from Babylonia and Palestine. A prominent example of such commonalities is the historiola (brief magic story)[5] about Semomit (Semumit, Semumita). Her

---

3. The findings include two silver amulets from Jerusalem, magic passages from the Dead Sea Scrolls, and most probably some magic gems. They are discussed in the first section of this chapter ("Performative Artifacts").

4. For an overview of Jewish magic from the Bible to the Internet, see Harari (2012a). Kabbalah has left its mark on several areas of magic thought and literature. But beside texts on practical Kabbalah (*Kabbalah ma'asit*) in the strict sense, a traditional magic literature bearing no traces of kabbalistic thought has also survived, for example, in broad sections of the *segulot u-refu'ot* (charms and healing) literature. On this literature, see Matras (1994; 1997; 2005). On practical Kabbalah and the Kabbalah of the holy names as a continuance of earlier magical perceptions and practices, see, for example, Idel (1993) and Scholem (1974, 182–89).

5. A historiola is a brief story included in an incantation to ensure the sympathetic realization of linguistic or conceptual elements within it. Historiolas were used in Jewish magic and in magic of other nations. See Frankfurter (1995). And see, for example, the historiola about R. Joshua b. Peraḥia and the divorce deed from a lilith (discussed in

children were murdered by evil Sideros, who then took an oath to refrain from killing, choking, and hurting others whenever the names of his persecutors (Sa'uni, Sassa'uni, Sangro, and 'Artiko) were mentioned.[6] This historiola was used for protection in magic Babylonian bowls and on a typical western metal amulet (probably from Palestine) and is concrete proof of the links between Palestinian and Babylonian traditions and of their shared magic culture. These links are found in many other forms and contents, even in the absence of such explicit linguistic expression.[7]

Commonality of this type is also evident in the historical examination of magic findings. Here too we find that Jewish magic diversifies according to the cultural environment: Whereas early texts at times reflect the influence of Hellenistic surroundings, Genizah texts often reflect Muslim influence.[8] This diversification, however, does not blur the explicitly Jewish, traditional, and stable character of Jewish magic throughout this period. Jewish magic in Genizah texts is without doubt a continuation of an earlier Palestinian (and sometimes even Babylonian) tradition.[9] This conclusion is the result not only of a general impression but also of explicit parallels between Palestinian amulets and magic recipes from the Genizah, previous patterns of which had been in use centuries before for the preparation of amulets. One suitable example is a clay amulet for love from the fifth or sixth century

---

the "Incantation Bowls" subsection) and the developed historiola about a lilith in a Mandaic bowl (Müller-Kessler 1996).

6. See Naveh and Shaked (1987, 104–22, 188–97).

7. For another example of linguistic parallels between Palestinian amulets and Babylonian incantation bowls, see Naveh and Shaked (1987, 51–52).

8. A prominent example of the influence of Greek magic is *Sefer ha-Razim*. See M. Margalioth (1966, 1–16). For Greek elements in *Ḥarba de-Moshe*, see Rohrbacher-Sticker (1996). Bilingual (Hebrew-Greek or Aramaic-Greek) amulets also attest to the influence of Greek magic. On the ties between Judaism and Islam in Genizah magic, see Kahn (1986, 58–59), Shaked (1983; 1994; 2000b), and Wasserstrom (1991; 1992). Both kinds of cross-cultural contacts in the field of magical signs are discussed in Bohak (2011a).

9. On this conclusion, cf. Bohak (2009a; 2012b), Naveh and Shaked (1987, 30), Schiffman and Swartz (1992, 22–32), Shaked (1983, 15–16); and Swartz (2001a). On the Babylonian tradition of magic in the Cairo Genizah, see Levene and Bohak (2012).

that was found in Ḥorvat Rimon in the northern Negev and the recipe for the preparation of such an amulet that was found in a Genizah fragment. The love amulet was engraved in the clay while still soft, etched along its length and breadth, and then fired. The firing, or human intervention, broke it along the incisions, and the five broken shards that were found join together into a fragment of the amulet (Plate 5). At the top are the following five names, written within frames: HR'WT, 'TB'WT, QWLHWN, SPTWN, and SWSGR. Under them, the following words can be made out: "You ho[ly] angels [ ] you, just a[s] [ ] shall burn the heart of [ ] after me, I [ ] her kidney [ ] my desire in this [ ]."[10]

A love recipe in a fragment from a Genizah grimoire enables us to trace the full text of the adjuration as well as ritual aspects of the amulet's preparation and its operation. It turns out that the words of the incantation and the firing ritual in the Ḥorvat Rimon amulet reflect an approach that seeks to create reality by comparing it to power images, in line with the sympathetic pattern: "As . . . so . . ."[11] Here is the wording of the recipe:

> Write on an unbaked clay: HR'WT 'YTB'WT QWLHWN <QLHWN> SPTWN <SPWNYN> SWSYG <SWSG> MKMR. You, the holy angels, <I adjure you> just as this piece of clay burns <in the fire>, so shall the heart of N son of N and his kidneys burn after me and after my fortune and after my lot. His heart shall not sleep. They shall turn to me <until he[12] follows [me]>, I, N daughter of N, with great love and affection. By the name of Nebiel the Angel, and you, Sama'el the Satan, ABṢLḤ, and you, Ashmedai the swift, perform my desire

---

10. See Naveh and Shaked (1987, 84–89 and plate 9). A sixth name was written in a frame, the upper part of which is evident in one of the shards.

11. This formulation is a classic expression of the law of similarity, one of the two sympathetic laws (similarity and contact) that Frazer made the basis of magical thought and action. See chapter 1. On the symbolism of fire in Jewish erotic magic, see Saar (2013).

12. *She* is mistakenly used in the original. The recipe aims at burning a man's heart in love for a woman.

at this hour, quickly, at once, from now till eternity, QYNW QYNW, Amen, [Amen, Se]lah, Hallelujah.[13]

Further examples of such a textual connection are the amulet for suppression cited later in the "Amulets" subsection of this chapter and recipes for preparing amulets for this purpose found in the Genizah that resemble it in their language and style.[14]

A close link between early and late is exposed in these cases in unequivocal ways.[15] These records also reveal another important link—that between theory and performance. These parallels point to the professional and practical character of the magic recipe literature and to the way it served writers of charms in their creative activity. Although the writers often took liberties when determining the final version of the amulet, they definitely based the text of the adjuration on the professional literature available to them, which detailed the rituals and incantations appropriate for each specific purpose. On the one hand, then, is the literature that serves as a professional foundation for the performance of magic practice. On the other, contrary to the widespread image of the witchcraft act whose success purportedly depends on the exact performance of every single detail, the contents of this literature are indeterminate. The contrast is illustrated in the comparison of an amulet and a recipe for prosperity that were found in the Genizah. The following table shows the differing texts side by side:

---

13. Naveh and Shaked (1993, 216–17). Cf. Naveh (1996, 453–57), where another parallel to the clay amulet is discussed.

14. Cf. Naveh (1985; 1996) and Naveh and Shaked (1993, 43–50).

15. Note also the similarity between a cloth amulet for love found in the Cairo Genizah (Naveh and Shaked 1987, 216) and the instructions for preparing such an amulet in Ms New York Public Library, Heb 190, a manuscript of magic recipes (and a few other issues) written in Oriental script in the mid-fifteenth century (Bohak 2014a, 1: 223, 2: 181). The comparison between these sources (in this case the Genizah is the older source) shows that the amulet was prepared exactly according to the recipe's instructions. As is the case in recipes, the instructions also add details about the ritual context of the amulet: The piece of cloth on which the adjuration for love was written was meant to turn into a wick and be burned with a new candle full of rose oil. If the amulet was indeed written according to an early version of this recipe, we could assume either that this amulet was indeed prepared to be burned but for whatever reason was not or that the writer gave the client instructions for a different use for it and that is why it was not burned.

The recipe

[For] commerce (and) for (finding) grace. Write on the hide of a deer:

I adjure you, Raḥmiel, Ḥasdiel, Ḥaniel, Kafš[iel]. Give power and grace to N son of N

in front of all sons of Adam and Eve, and may there assemble in his [pre]sence every one who wishes to conduct a bargain, to buy and sell any thing in the world.

None of the children of Adam and Eve shall have the authority to open the mouth, to speak or to answer this N son of N.

In the name of Barqiel and in the name of Qedošiel and in the name of ḤSYN YH, may you grant N son of N grace and favor and mercy in the eyes of all those who see him and his hand will find like a nest the wealth of peoples.[17]

The amulet[16]

[ ] and in the name of HWYH b[ ] health, and in the name of 'ṢQ [ ], I adjure you, Ṣedq[iel] on the fifth day to do all I ask in this amulet concerning Shalom ben Zuhra. In the name of 'H 'YH 'WHW Alef Bet Gimel

I adjure you, Raḥmiel and Ḥasdiel, and Ḥaniel and Kanšael to grant favor and grace to Shalom ben Zuhra

so that he may transact business with every person in the world

None of the children of Adam and Eve shall have the authority to open (the mouth) or to speak or to distress Shalom ben Zuhra

In the name of Barqiel and in the name of Qadšiel and in the name of ḤSYN YH, may you grant grace and favor and compassion to Shalom ben Zuhra. "My hand has found like a nest the wealth of peoples; as one gathers

---

16. The upper left half of the amulet, which contains eight lines and two frames containing magic signs, is missing. The remaining fragmented text details names of angels in whose name Ṣadkiel is adjured, before the adjuration of the other angels.

17. Cf. Isaiah 10:14: "My hand has found like a nest the wealth of peoples."

abandoned eggs, so I gathered all the earth: Nothing so much as flapped a wing or opened a mouth to peep" (Isaiah 10:14).

"And Joseph found favor in his eyes, and he served him. And he made him overseer over his house, and all [that he had] he put into his hand" (Genesis 39:4) served he and eyes his in [favor] found Joseph and.[18] And may God be with N son of N and may he give him favor and grace in the eyes of all.

"And Joseph found favor in his eyes, and he served him. And he made him overseer over his house, and all that he had he put into his hand." "God was with Joseph " (Genesis 39:2). So shall Shalom ben Zuhra find (favor).

In the name of Kerubiel the angel (who is appointed) over [ ] "And Noah found favour in the eyes of God" (Genesis 6:8), [so sha]ll N son of N find [fav]or and grace in the eyes of both God and Man.

In the name of Barqiel, the angel who is enthroned upon the wings of the wind. "And Noah found favor in the eyes of God."

Amen, Amen, Amen, Selah. [19]

Blessed be the name of His Majesty's glory for ever and ever.[20]

The connection between these two texts is unquestionable, but its essence is still hard to grasp. The amulet is certainly based on a recipe of the kind presented here, but the differences between the versions are no less clear. Two explanations for this situation are possible: Either the amulet is based on the recipe and the writer made his own decisions about additions and deletions, or the amulet was prepared according to another recipe, similar to this one, which is unavailable to us. Both possibilities

---

18. The first five words of the verse *Va-yimṣa' Yosef ḥen be-'einav va-yesharet* are repeated backwards: *va-yesharet be-'einav [ḥen] Yosef va-yimṣa'*. Thus in the translation, instead of "and Joseph found [favor] in his eyes and he served," we have "served he and eyes his in [favor] found Joseph and."

19. See Naveh and Shaked (1993, 235–36, with slight changes).

20. Schiffman and Swartz (1992, 137–42, with slight changes).

point to professional flexibility, be it at the stage of preparing the amulet or at the time of copying magic texts and recipes. In both cases we are speaking about the same group: members of a professional community who collected theoretical magic knowledge and implemented it according to the clients' needs. The professional liberties the writers took when changing and adapting ad hoc suggestions for incantations from the recipe books available to them prove even greater in the comparison of parallel but different versions of amulets (in the Genizah) or magic bowls (from Babylonia), some of them even written by the same scribe (judging from the handwriting). In these cases the incantation formulas obviously served the charm writer as raw material, which he shaped and edited anew each time.[21]

A general examination of the inventory of magic texts and artifacts, then, points to cultural cohesiveness and continuity concerning both faith and action. East and West, early and late, theory and performance—all come together in the Jewish literature of adjurations discussed here, beyond the local colors, into a single broad expression of the magic culture widespread among the Jewish people in late antiquity and the early Islamic period. I present this literature here according to its two basic patterns: performative artifacts and instructional literature.

PERFORMATIVE ARTIFACTS

Amulets

An amulet (*qameʿa*), in the broad sense of the word, is an artifact possessing a performative power meant to serve the one who uses it. In general, and most distinctly in the context of the sources discussed here, an amulet draws its power from the words of the adjuration and other signs written on it.[22] In this sense, magic gems and incantation bowls

---

21. See Levene (2003a, 24–30) and Swartz (1990).

22. The Tosefta, and in its wake the rabbis of the Babylonian Talmud, draws a distinction between an "amulet in writing" (*qameʿa shel ketav*) and an "amulet of roots" (*qameʿa shel ʿiqarin*), clearly attesting to the existence of amulets whose power lay in the roots placed in them rather than in incantations (Tosefta *Shabbat* 4:9; TB *Shabbat* 61a–b). On the belief in the magic power of roots in late antiquity, see the discussion in the "Second Temple Period Literature" section in chapter 6. These amulets did not survive because they were a mixture of organic materials. The Mishnah mentions a

should also be viewed as amulets and, indeed, many incantation bowls are viewed as amulets, as evident in the adjurations written on them.[23] For the purpose of this discussion, however, I draw a distinction between various kinds of performative artifacts common in the culture of early Jewish magic, reserving the term *amulet,* as is commonly done, to pieces of paper, vellum, cloth, leather, clay, or metal on which adjurations are written. Amulets are usually identified with preservation, protection, healing, and success, but, as I show, they also served aggressive and harmful purposes.

The word *qame'a* derives from the root *qm'*, which means "to tie." In its use in rabbinic language the word has three close meanings that are not always easy to differentiate in a specific context. First, the word can denote a small leather pouch or a small metal box that contains roots or a text and is tied to or hung on its user's body. Precisely in this sense, the word *qame'a* denotes also the leather pouch of the phylacteries (tefillin), which also hold written parchment and are tied on the head and the arm when in use. Second, the word can denote the contents of the pouch: the roots or the text, which, according to the Babylonian Talmud (*Shabbat* 115b), include "letters of the [divine] name" and biblical verses, that

broad range of additional apotropaic artifacts: knots, bells, a grasshopper egg, a fox tooth, a nail from the crucified (M. *Shabbat* 6:8–9; cf. TB *Shabbat* 66b–67b and PT *Shabbat* 6:9–10). Only one archaeological finding can be tied with some certainty to these artifacts in their Jewish context. I am referring to a child's shirt and additional pieces of cloth that were found in the Cave of the Letters in Naḥal Hever (in the Judean Dessert); it can be dated precisely (together with the rest of the cave's findings) to the Bar-Kosibah (Bar-Kokhba) revolt in 132–135 CE. Yigael Yadin, who published the findings of the excavation, directed attention to pockets of small "knots" that were tied in the cloth with a thread and were filled with salt grains, seeds, and shells. Two such knots were found in a child's well-preserved shirt, four others on the edge of two pieces of cloth, and one on its own. Yadin was probably right when he suggested that these are the knots mentioned in the Mishnah—"Boys go out with knots and royal children go out with bells" (M. *Shabbat* 6:9)—of which Abaye's foster mother later said, "Three stop [illness], five cure [it], seven [work] even against witchcraft" (TB *Shabbat* 66b). See Yadin (1963, 256–58 and plates 89 and 90; 1971, 79–81). For a comprehensive survey of Palestinian performative artifacts in late antiquity, see Saar (2003).

23. See the "Incantation Bowls" subsection in this chapter. See also Montgomery (1913, bowls 1, 10, 29) and Naveh and Shaked (1993, bowls 22, 24).

are the actual operative power of the artifact. Last, the word can denote the entire artifact—the wrapping and the content together.[24] In magic literature, as noted, the second denotation is the more common one.

An amulet is an artifact bearing an adjuration text. Many of the amulets that have survived, which are small to begin with, were folded or rolled into even smaller sizes and often placed in small metal boxes or wrapped in cloth.[25] The amulet was thereby preserved and could be

---

24. On the root qm' in the sense of tying, see Tosefta *Kelim, Bava Metsia* 6:1; *Demai* 2:17; and TB *Bekhorot* 30b. On *qame'a shel tefillin* (phylacteries), see M. *Shabbat* 8:3; and Minor Tractates, *Tefillin* 1:9, 12. On *qame'a* as a leather pouch not for a phylactery, see M. *Mikva'ot* 10:2. A "metal amulet" mentioned in the Tosefta (*Kelim, Bava Metsia* 1:11) is probably a small metal box for storing the wording of the amulet, as mentioned in the discussion about the impurity of its parts, upper and lower, when it fell apart. When the rabbis discuss permits for going out on the Sabbath with amulets "of roots" and "of writing," they are referring to the entire artifact that the person bears (M. *Shabbat* 6:2; M. *Shekalim* 3:2; Tosefta *Shabbat* 4:5, 9–10; TB *Shabbat* 61a–b; cf. *Sanhedrin* 21b–22b). But when they discuss an "expert amulet," they are definitely referring to the active element of the artifact (M. *Shabbat* 6:2; TB *Shabbat* 53a, 57b; PT *Shabbat* 6:2). This is also the denotation of *qame'a* (amulet) as being written on or wrapped in leather (Tosefta, *Kelim, Bava Metsia* 1:12; TB *Pesahim* 111b). See also Kohut (1926, 7: 123, s.v. קמע).

25. Many amulets have been found in such small metal boxes. See, for example, Naveh and Shaked (1993, amulets 17, 25, 30). Rolled and folded metal amulets wrapped in cloth were found during excavations in the ancient synagogue of Ma'on (in the northwestern Negev). One of them was found with the bearing thread tied to its end (Rahmani 1961, 83). No amulet in a leather pouch has yet been found, but this appears to be merely accidental. For a picture of a rolled amulet that was preserved with its bearing threads, see Plate 6. A rolled box for an amulet is mentioned in PT *Shabbat* 6:2 and called *siloneh* (from the Greek σωλήν, meaning "tube" or "roll"). The same name is used in *Sefer ha-Razim* (M. Margalioth 1966, 88). The Babylonian Talmud (*Shabbat* 56b) refers to a copper roll into which one is supposed to place an ant, seal it with lead and with sixty seals, shake it, and then bear it on the body after saying a certain spell. It is hard to determine with any certainty whether or not minute metal rolls that were found empty or full of some unidentified material in excavations served as amulet boxes. When these boxes have loops for bearing, however, that was probably the case, and the boxes were amulets of roots or contained a vellum amulet that crumbled. See, for example, Baramki (1932, plate 5, finding 15) (only the author's initials are mentioned in the publication, and I relied on Gudovitz for Baramki's name), Gudovitz (1996, 68–69), and Harding (1950, 88–90, items 244, 289 and their pictures in plates 27–28). See also Saar (2003, 57–58).

hung on its user, person or animal, or at the place where it was meant to act.[26] Not all amulets were tied or hung. Instructions for their preparation and places where they were found attest that, at times, users were supposed to hide them—in the doorpost of the house where the people they wished to influence lived or passed through, on the river bank, on a grave, on an animal's yoke, under a pillow, at a synagogue—or even throw them into the sea, a river, or a fire.[27] All amulets were meant to bind. Their purpose was to take control of supernatural entities addressed in the texts—angels, demons, holy names, letters, planets, the sun and the moon, and even God[28]—and coerce them, through the power of the adjuration, to act in favor of the amulet's beneficiary.

An amulet was prepared for a defined purpose and in most cases was to be used by a particular client, man or woman, specifically mentioned in the adjuration by his or her name and by his or her mother's name. The matronymic denotation of the client, possibly for the purpose of definite identification, was also common in Greco-Roman magic and in both Jewish and non-Jewish Babylonian incantation bowls and is still in use today in Jewish traditions of amulet writing.[29] The amulets that have

---

26. See, for example, Harari (2012b, 83, sec. 14), Naveh and Shaked (1993, 193, 231), and Schäfer and Shaked (1994–1999, 3: 115, 175, 193, 368). For additional recipes, see Schäfer and Shaked (1994–1999, 3: 56 [hanging an amulet on a white cock for finding a lost treasure], 130 [hanging an amulet on a dried-out tree for it to bloom], 368 [hanging an amulet for success on the doorpost]).

27. These examples can be found in the following works: hiding a harming amulet at the house of the victim, Naveh and Shaked (1987, 232; 1993, 231); hiding an amulet in a grave, Naveh and Shaked (1987, 232 [an egg amulet]); hiding an amulet on a river bank, Naveh and Shaked (1987, 230); placing an amulet on an animal's yoke, Schäfer and Shaked (1994–1999, 3: 146); placing an amulet under the pillow, Schäfer and Shaked (1994–1999, 3: 369); and placing an amulet at the synagogue, Harari (2012b, 93, sec. 105) and Schäfer and Shaked (1994–1999, 3: 69) (many amulets were indeed found in excavations of ancient synagogues and, at times, on the presumed location of the ark). For an amulet that was thrown into the fire, see Naveh and Shaked (1987, 87–88 [shards of this amulet were also found in the synagogue area]; cf. Schäfer and Shaked 1994–1999, 2: 58–59). For throwing an amulet into the sea, see Harari (2012b, 89–90, sec. 72).

28. For references, see Harari (2001, 14–15).

29. Cf. Abaye's comments on this matter: "My mother has told me: All the countings must contain the mother's name" (TB *Shabbat* 66b). The magic denotation of countings (*minyanei*) emerges from the context, and Rashi, commenting on TB *Shabbat*

survived were used for various purposes—love, economic success, healing, finding favor with someone, suppressing other people, and causing
harm.[30] The following three examples illustrate the language of amulets
and the way it served their performative purpose.

The first amulet was written for the healing of Simon, son of Kattia,
from various types of fever, evil spirits, and evil eyes.[31] The amulet was
meant to expel all these evil entities from Simon's body by means of
incantations and holy names. The amulet was found in Ḥorvat Kannah
(in the Galilee). It was a bronze lamella, rolled after the text was engraved
on it. The end is cut off. It says:

An amulet proper to expel[32] the great fever and the tertian
(fever) and the chronic (?) fever and the semi-tertian (fever)[33]

66b, explains: "'All the countings'—all the incantations, and because they are multi-
ples, three times or more, they are called countings." Matriarchal indication of individuals also prevailed in Hellenistic magic. See Curbera (1999) and Gager (1992, 14
and notes 70–72). Also see anthologies of amulets and cursing tablets, such as Gager
(1992, 14), D. Jordan (1985b), and Kotansky (1994). This manner of indicating the amulet beneficiary was essential also in the Jewish tradition of magic during the Middle
Ages and up to the modern period. For modern amulets (mainly those written on vellum or paper, not on metal, where the name of the client does not usually appear),
see E. Davis and Frenkel (1995) and Shachar (1981). Cf. Harari (2005a; 2007a). For a
similar practice on the Mi She-berekh (He who blessed) prayer for a sick person, see
Golinkin (2002).

30. On some of these areas, see Harari (1997a; 2000; 2001). Cf. also Harari (1998,
136–222; 2005c).

31. For an overview of antidemonic Jewish adjuration texts from late antiquity, see
Shaked (2005b).

32. On the rendering of the Hebrew *lig'or* (from the root *g'r*) as expelling or
exorcising an evil spirit, see Sokoloff (1990, 134). This use appears already in the
Dead Sea Scrolls, in the Genesis Apocryphon, and in the War Scroll. See Fitzmyer
(2004, 120, 211–12), Greenfield (1980, 38–39), and Yadin (1962, 329). In this sense, the
root *g'r* is widespread in Jewish magic literature. See, for example, Naveh and
Shaked (1987, 268; 1993, 266). See also Macintosh (1969). A formula using this term
had already appeared in one of the silver amulets from Ketef Hinom. See Barkay et al.
(2004, 65, 68).

33. Tertian fever is a fever that rises in 72-hour cycles. Semitertian fever is a fever
that rises in 36-hour cycles. In both cases it appears that the writers are speaking of
malaria. On these medical terms, their Greek context, and their meaning, see Naveh

and any spirit and any misfortune[34] and any (evil) eye and any (evil) gaze from the body of Simon, son of Kattia, and from all his limbs, to heal him and to guard him. In the name of all these holy names and letters which are written in this amulet, I adjure and write in the name of Abrasax[35] who is appointed over you that he may uproot you, fever and sickness, from the body of Simon, the son of Kattia. In the name of the engraved[36] letters of the Name ṢṢṢṢṢṢṢṢṢṢṢṢṢṢṢṢṢṢṢṢ El El El and in the name of this great angel 'RBYḤW Neḥumiel Shamshiel LLWZBH MRP'WT MR'WT . . . (magic names and signs).[37] May there be driven away the evil spirit, the fever, the tertian (fever), and all evil spirit from the body of Simon, son of Kattia, and from all his limbs. Amen Selah. And in the name of . . . (magic names) your name, I adjure and write: You, heal Simon son of Kattia, from the fever which is in him. Amen Amen Selah. I make an oath and adjure in the name of YŠR Tamnuel who sits on the river whence all evil spirits emerge; and in the name of Yequmi'el who sits on the roads, [Na]hari[el], who sits over [ ] Tomi'el, who sits [ ] and in the na[me of] [ ].[38]

The second amulet is meant for subjugation (*kibush*). The root *kbš* is widespread in recipes, amulets, and adjuration bowls in the denotation of aggressive control, which the wording of the adjuration seeks to establish.

---

and Shaked (1993, 36–37, 64). For further discussions on medicine in Jewish magic, see Harari (1998, 139–150), Naveh and Shaked (1993, 31–39) and Wandrey (2003).

34. In the original, *mishpat*. Naveh and Shaked suggest that this word is related to *shoftin* (*shiftin, shivtin, shivtei*), which is mentioned in adjuration bowls as a spirit that brings disease. See Levene (2003a, 36 [M59]), Montgomery (1913, 92 and the bowls on pp. 174, 185 [Aramaic], and 236 [Syriac]), and Naveh and Shaked (1987, 134; 1993, 64, 115, 124, 132).

35. On this name, originally Greek Αβρασάξ (or Αβραξάς), see Brashear (1995, 3577).

36. This phrase probably hints at the tradition about the name of God that had been engraved in Moses's staff. See Harari (2005b).

37. By magic names, I mean combinations of letters of the sort quoted here. By magic signs, I mean graphic signs which are intertwined in the adjuration text, most commonly *charactêres*.

38. Naveh and Shaked (1987, 60–66).

In the bowls, where the Aramaic *kibsha'* at times serves to refer to the entire incantation or even to the bowl, this use addresses mainly the evil spirits as part of the verbal means used to take control of them, suppress them, or remove them.[39] Elsewhere, the desire for subjugation is directed to human society in general, at times for the purpose of self-protection and at times for gaining an advantage by ruling over others. Ruling over others is the purpose of the amulet in question, and it seeks to attain this goal by resorting to sympathetic language—establishing power relationships in the world according to the pattern of relationships described in the adjuration. The amulet offers two domination patterns: One is God's rule over nature, and the other is the chain of power hierarchies prevailing in reality. The amulet, engraved in a bronze sheet probably at the beginning of the seventh century CE and rolled after the writing, was written for Yose, son of Zenobia, for him to rule over the inhabitants of some village.[40] It was found in the excavations of a synagogue at Ḥorvat Marish, northwest of Tel Ḥazor. It says:

> "For your mercy and for your truth" (Psalms 115:1; 138:2). In the name of YHWH we shall do and succeed. Strong and mighty God! May your name be blessed and may your kingdom be blessed. Just as you have suppressed the sea by your horses and stamped the earth with your shoe, and as you suppress trees in winter days and the herb of the earth in summer days, so may there be supp[ressed] [ ] before Yose son of Zenobia. May my word and my obedience be imposed on them. Just as the sky is suppressed before God, and the earth is suppressed before people, and people are suppressed[41] before death, and death is suppressed before God, so may the people of this town be suppressed and broken and fallen before Yose son of Zenobia. In

39. See, for example, Levene (2003a, 145–46), Montgomery (1913, 291), Naveh and Shaked (1987, 271; 1993, 268); and J. B. Segal (2000, 213).

40. Cf. the recipe in *Sefer ha-Razim* titled "If (you wish) to bring around the citizens of the city." Its purpose, as detailed there, was to bring around "all the citizens of this city, great and small, old and young, poor and honorable, so that the fear and terror of me be over them. . . . Let all of them obey me and let none of the children of Adam and Eve be able to speak against me" (M. Margalioth 1966, 74).

41. This word is repeated in the original.

the name of ḤṬW" the angel who was sent before Israel I make
a sign. Success, Success, Amen Amen, Selah, Hallelujah.[42]

The third amulet was meant to cause harm. Harm to others is
recorded in many magic recipes, but evidence of actual damage is rare.[43]
The following amulet was found in the pages of the Cairo Genizah. It
was written (on paper) to expel "'Ali, who is of the Ishmaelite religion,"
from a house that, according to the amulet, "he had taken by robbery."
The amulet beneficiary, who wrote it himself in first person but without
mentioning his own name, asked to deprive Ali of sleep, food, and drink,
to separate him from all other human beings, to deny him all pleasure, to
burn a fire in his heart, to fall ill in all his limbs, and to cause his death.
For this purpose the writer sought to recruit angels and "great and
mighty" names, which he adjured to assist him immediately. The amulet
is written in three languages: Hebrew, Aramaic, and Arabic (Plate 16).
It says:

> In the name of Shaddai who created the heaven and the earth. I
> adjure you, holy angels, that you should come and help me, and
> support me, and fortify me, and not hold me back from doing an
> uprooting, a chasing away, a crushing, destroying, annihilating,
> of Ali son of Nuḥ, who is of the Ishmaelite religion, at this hour,
> him and all those who help him. (magic sign) In the name of
> 'HY YH' [ ] Amen (magic sign). This is by the name of He who
> sees hidden things, he sees and does the will of those who fear
> him. In the name of the fearsome, NWR' NWRH NRWR
> NWR' NUR . . . (magic names). You, the names that are
> appointed over evil and over all criminal things, expel, banish
> and separate from all sons of Adam and Eve, whether male or
> female, from this place, Ali the Ishmaelite, from this place. May
> he never see love, but only great hatred. May he be pushed away
> and expelled from this valley where he is. May conflagration be
> made to burn in his heart, when he sees this place where Ali the
> Ishmaelite resides B'HWH B'DYRYRWN. Amen, Amen,

---

42. Naveh and Shaked (1993, 43–50). Cf. Naveh (1985; 1996).
43. On harm in early Jewish magic, see Harari (1997a).

Neṣaḥ Selah, tomorrow, fast. Amen. This writing is appointed for Ali the Ishmaelite, so that he may be cursed (?) and wander from one place to another, and that there should be no standing to this 'Ali, and that he should have no comfort in this dwelling which he has taken,[44] and the place which he has taken by robbery until they go and fall to bed, in illness, all the days of their lives, when he sits in the place which he has robbed, with the 248 limbs that are in the body of this 'Ali. In the name of ŠM' M'WT 'BR MR'WT . . . (magic names), you glorified, great and mighty names,[45] expel and banish this evil Ali from my neighbourhood, so that he should not stay there even one hour, but that he may fall ill with a serious illness, that he should not eat or drink or sleep until he goes away from this stable and throne.[46] By the truth of His great name, move him away from my neighbourhood (magic signs). Amen, Amen, Selah.[47]

These three amulets are examples of the way that charm writers asked to enlist the power of angels and holy names and even the power of God to help them or their clients in order to rescue them from distress or to fulfill a desire. Most amulets, as noted, represent a magical response to an actual crisis or to a desire arising in someone's life, yet not all of them fit this category. At times, amulets were intended from the start to serve many potential clients. In such cases the client's name is obviously not mentioned and the purpose is noted only in general terms. Such an amulet was found in Sepphoris (in the Galilee) (Plate 4). It was engraved on a bronze sheet and rolled. The excavation layer where it was found dates it to the fourth or fifth century CE. Its purpose was to heal a high fever, and the following text was written on it: "An amulet against

---

44. The original is probably a miswriting of *lekaḥah* (he took it), as rendered in this translation.

45. In the original, singular rather than the plural warranted by "names."

46. In the original, *misnad* or *masnad*, a large cushion used as a sofa (see Goitein 1967–1993, 4: 108). "Stable and throne" is a strange expression in this context and should probably be understood as denoting the house and possibly other buildings that this Ali had "taken by robbery."

47. Naveh and Shaked (1993, 164–66). This reading is more accurate than the one suggested by Schiffman and Swartz (1992, 83–92).

protracted fever that burns and does not cease (magic signs) NNN WHYH'W ''' ŠŠŠ. An amulet against protracted fever that burns and does not cease (magic signs) NNN WHYH'W ''' ŠŠ[Š]."[48] An amulet of this kind would probably be preserved within a family and used repeatedly, whenever necessary.[49]

Further examples of such amulets were found in the Cairo Genizah. One of them is an amulet that was designed for "the bearer of this writing" (Plate 17). This inscription, which appears twice in the wording of the incantation, explicitly attests that the text was a priori meant for use by any potential client and perhaps even for recurrent use of the amulet.

> Upon your name and upon your might, Lord of the world YH YH, a rock! May the bearer of this writing depart[50] from all sickness, from all affliction, from every evil thing and from all evil jealousy (magic signs) YH 'HH ḤSYN YH YḤYŠH (magic signs) YH 'HH ḤSYN YḤYŠH and ŠMTYH. You, holy angels, YH 'HH ḤSYN YḤYŠ. Take away and save the bearer of this writing (from) evil sorceries and all evil curses YH 'HH YḤYŠ and PRḤYH (and) evil demons and from all evil plagues and all evil spirits, night, day and noon. May they be expelled, go far away and depart from the bearer of this writing and from his two hundred forty-eight limbs, in the name of the living and enduring God, who injures and heals.[51] "The Lord will ward off from you all sickness" (Deuteronomy 7:15) "and He

---

48. McCullough and Glazier-McDonald (1996, 161). Cf. McCullough and Glazier-McDonald (1998).

49. Such an amulet is referred to by the term *expert amulet* (*qameʿa mumḥeh*) in Tosefta *Shabbat* 4:9: "What is an expert amulet—any that served to heal twice or three times." The Mishnah mentions "an amulet made by an expert" (*qameʿa min ha-mumḥeh*) and talmudic rabbis later consider the question of who the "expert" is—the amulet or the writer. The Tosefta, however, is unequivocal. An expert amulet was almost certainly one that proved helpful at least three times, was passed around, and thus was recognized as effective.

50. The original Aramaic *vyzʾ* poses a problem. Naveh and Shaked suggest deriving it from the Aramaic root *ʾzl* and reading it as "go away from" (Naveh and Shaked 1987, 240).

51. Cf. Deuteronomy 32:39.

said: 'If you will heed the Lord diligently, doing what is upright in His sight, giving ear to His commandments and keeping all His laws, I will not bring upon you any of the diseases that I brought upon the Egyptians for I am the Lord your healer'" (Exodus 15:26). MR MR'WT ŠMYRWT QRWBY WHW' G'RH 'H 'H Selah, forever, Amen Amen. For his health: TSGWG' heal! WTY'W WTYY'W WTYN'W WYRGYH.[52]

Another instructive example of this professional option is a long and narrow page (26 cm×9 cm) on which a brief incantation for removing scorpions was recorded in identical form twenty times. About a quarter of the page, its lower right section, is missing. The page was split lengthwise into two with a line, and on each side the incantation was written and signed twice with an iconic drawing of a scorpion. Under every two such copies, a line was drawn across and, at times, the two copies were separated by a faint line. The page, then, was divided in the course of the writing into extremely small units (each about 2.2 cm×4 cm), each one being an amulet ready for use. Clearly then, the writer in this case prepared a board of generic amulets, intending to give out one or a few at a time, as requested. The missing part of the page, which was cut off along the splitting lines, probably attests that use of these amulets had already began.[53]

Instructions for the preparation of amulets in the recipe books show recourse to a broad variety of materials used in the writing of incantations. The materials include leaves, glass, egg, bone, papyrus, cloth, paper, leather, and various metals—lead, copper, silver, and gold.[54] Although sorcerers probably did use all these materials, the inventory of the amulets that have reached us does not attest to this. The absolute majority of known amulets are made of either metal or paper, a result of a combination of the survivability of the materials that served for the writing of amulets and the climatic conditions in the places where they

---

52. See Schiffman and Swartz (1992, 131–36); cf. Naveh and Shaked (1987, 239–40).

53. On this manuscript (Ms Cambridge, Cambridge University Library, T-S AS 143.26) and other "mass-produced" scorpion amulets, see Bohak (2009c).

54. Amulets of parchment, leather, and metal are mentioned in rabbinic literature as well. See M. *Shabbat* 8:3, M. *Kelim* 23:1, and Tosefta *Kelim, Bava Metsia* 1:11.

remained. Only amulets written on a highly survivable surface or amulets that survived in conditions of extreme dryness were preserved over the long period that elapsed from the time of their writing to today, and even they show definite traces of the passing of time. When seeking to track the use of amulets in late antiquity and the early Islamic period, one should beware of drawing conclusions based on existing material findings. In this regard, the information found in the professional recipe literature seems preferable to the evidence of its practical implementation.

About eighty Jewish amulets from late antiquity and the early Islamic period have so far been annotated and published. They split into two main and almost equal groups: amulets that were excavated and amulets that were preserved in the Cairo Genizah. The excavated amulets have been found in the places of their use throughout the eastern Mediterranean and at times farther away. Given the climatic conditions in these areas, the fact that almost all of them are made of inorganic materials should not surprise us. Most of these amulets are lamellae—small metal sheets, most of relatively cheap metals such as lead, copper, bronze, silver, and rarely gold.[55] They are seldom bigger than 10 cm long and 5 cm wide. They apparently rely on an old tradition of apotropaic writing on metal sheets, as attested by two silver amulets from the sixth to the fifth century BCE that were found in a burial cave in Ketef Hinom (in Jerusalem), where the priestly blessing (Numbers 6:24–26) serves as part of the incantation.[56]

---

55. This inventory fits what we know from Hellenistic magic. See Kotansky (1994). The cursing tablets (*defixiones*) were prepared mainly from lead and lead alloys. See Gager (1992, 3–4). Mandaic metal amulets that were found in Mesopotamia were also engraved in lead, silver, and gold. See Müller-Kessler (1998, 83; 1999, 197–99). See also the Jewish lead amulet from Mesopotamia discussed later. Note, however, the few leather amulets written in Syriac that were also preserved. See Gignoux (1987) and Naveh (1997b). Gignoux's claim of a Jewish origin for the three amulets he published is hard to accept. As is true of Greek amulets and incantations, here too the "Jewish elements" (which are mostly recorded in the Christian Syriac literature) do not necessarily attest to Jewish sources. The mention of the Holy Trinity at the top of two of them actually tilts the scales in a Christian direction. See Brock (1989).

56. See Barkay et al. (2004). See also Barkay (1989), Haran (1989), Na'aman (2011), and Yardeni (1991). In his study, Na'aman dated these lamellae to the fifth century BCE, contrary to the other scholars who ascribed it to the seventh–sixth century BCE.

In general, the adjuration was written on metal amulets by engraving it with a sharp tool (Plates 3 and 4). One exception is a Jewish amulet from Babylonia written with ink on a lead board. This amulet differs not only from the usual pattern of western metal amulets (both Jewish and Hellenistic) but also from the inventory of Mandaic metal amulets from Babylonia.[57] We also have two clay amulets from Palestine. In one, as noted, the adjuration was engraved on soft clay and then fired. The other—meant to counteract harmful sorcery (by repeatedly stressing the drying of the wet—sea, saliva, weeds, and so forth)—was dried after it was engraved.[58]

As noted, the metal amulets were found rolled or folded, at times in small metal boxes or wrapped in cloth. Some of them were hidden in synagogues, perhaps even where the holy ark was (Plate 2).[59] Most were written in Hebrew, Aramaic, or a combination of both. A few of them were written in Greek or in a combination of Greek and Hebrew or Aramaic.[60] The names of the clients mentioned in the amulets show them to be mainly Jews. In one of them, the client is called "rabbi" ("Rabbi Elazar, son of Esther").[61] In at least one case, however, a trilingual amulet found in Egypt, we have evidence showing that a Jewish charm writer provided professional services to a client who was most probably a Christian (Joannes, son of Benenata).[62] In this context, note also the Greek-Hebrew amulet written for the healing and saving of Cassius, son of

---

57. See Geller (1997).

58. See G. J. Hamilton (1996) and Naveh and Shaked (1987, amulet 10).

59. See Naveh (1985, 368) and Naveh and Shaked (1987, 90–92). For instructions about hiding amulets in the synagogue, see Harari (2012b, 93, sec. 105) and Schäfer and Shaked (1994–1999, 3: 69).

60. For Jewish amulets in Greek, see Kotansky (1994, amulets 2, 33) and Kotansky et al. (1992). See also the later discussion on the magic bronze medallion, and note the caution required when determining that magic artifacts and texts in Greek are Jewish.

61. Naveh and Shaked (1987, amulet 3). The title "rabbi" may not bear the special meaning attached to it in rabbinic literature and could be used here as a general honorific address. See S. J. D. Cohen (1981). And cf. the adjuration bowl written for "Rav Yosef son of Imma de-Imma" in Harviainen (1981).

62. Kotansky et al. (1992). Cf. Bohak (2008, 231–35). Relationships of this kind between clients and charm writers from other cultural-religious communities are also recorded in the Babylonian incantation bowls.

Metradotion, which was found near Kibbutz Evron (in the western Galilee).[63] In the transition between the names of God written in Hebrew at the top of this amulet and the contents of the incantation written in Greek below them are two graphic signs. One is a circle divided into four (through the intersection of two lines), and in each section is one of the four letters of the tetragrammaton. The other is most probably a combination of the Greek letters *I* and *X* one over the other—a Christian symbol founded on the acronym of Jesus's name: ΙΕΣΟΥΣ ΧΡΙΣΤΟΣ. The wide use of the names of God in Hebrew in the amulet shows that this is not an amulet from a Christian source but a Jewish amulet, whose writer included in it a Christian symbol.[64]

The location of amulets that were found in archaeological excavations, in combination with polygraphic data, enables us to date the amulets in Hebrew and Aramaic to the fifth to seventh centuries CE. The amulets written in Greek preceded them by about two centuries.[65]

The second group of amulets originates in the Cairo Genizah. So far, about forty amulets from the Genizah have been published. Most of them were written in ink on paper or vellum (and in one case on cloth),

---

63. On the name Metradotion (Μητραδώτιον), see Kotansky (1994, 320). Also see the discussion on this amulet in Kotansky (1991a; 1994, 312–25).

64. On the Christian monogram in the Evron amulet, see Dauphin (1998, 1: 220) and Saar (2003, 52–55). For another Jewish amulet including an apparently Christian sign, see Naveh and Shaked (1987, amulet 4). On Christian elements in Jewish adjuration bowls from Babylonia and their possible meaning, see Levene (1999) and Shaked (1999a; 2000a, 6).

65. For updated editions of amulets, see Eshel and Leiman (2010), G. J. Hamilton (1996), Kotansky (1991a [1994, amulet 56]; 1991b), Kotansky et al. (1992); McCullough and Glazier-McDonald (1996; 1998), Naveh (2002), Naveh and Shaked (1987, 40–62, 68–122; 1993, 43–107), and Tsereteli (1996). See also the second–third century CE golden leaf excavated near Halbturn (eastern Austria), on which a Greek transcription of the Hebrew *Shema' Yisra'el* formula (Deuteronomy 6:4) is engraved (Eshel et al. 2010). If this lamella was indeed a Jewish amulet, as its redactors assume, then this is the earliest artifact from late antiquity currently available. Beside these, note also the Babylonian Jewish lead amulet described in Geller (1997). Despite the caution required concerning the cultural origin of Greek amulets containing "Jewish elements," two of them do seem to be Jewish: an amulet written for Yehuda (ΙΟΥΔΑ) and an amulet including God's names and passages from Jewish liturgy. See Kotansky (1994, amulets 2, 33).

mostly on one side of the surface and at times on both.[66] The Genizah amulets are larger than the Palestinian metal amulets. They are between 5 cm and 12 cm wide and about double that in length. They are written in Hebrew, Aramaic, and Arabic. Some were folded or rolled, definitely for the purpose of hiding them or bearing them on the body. They probably originate in the Fostat (old Cairo) community, and that was clearly the last place where they were used (though we cannot entirely dismiss the possibility that one or another amulet was written somewhere farther away and reached Fostat with whoever had used it). In any event, the names of the clients mentioned in the amulets and at times even the wording of the incantation attest to the Arab surroundings where both the writers and the users lived. Their date, as far as it can be traced, is the first centuries of the second millennium CE.[67]

Magic Gems and Pendants

Magic gems were widely used in late antiquity, as attested by about 5,000 such gems known today found mainly in the eastern Mediterranean (in most cases, we do not know exactly where).[68] They are small

---

66. For the cloth amulet, see Naveh and Shaked (1987, 216) and note 15 in this chapter.

67. For scientific editions of amulets in the Cairo Genizah, see Bohak (2009c; 2010a), Harari (2011), Mann (1972, 2: 91), Naveh and Shaked (1987, *Genizah* 1, 3, 4, 7, 8; 1993, *Genizah* 10, 12, 19, 27, 29), Schäfer and Shaked (1994–1999, 1: 151–98, 206–34, and 2: 240–63, 266–73, 305–11), and Schiffman and Swartz (1992, except for the texts on 93–98, 129–30, and 160–64, which may not be amulets). Jewish amulets from the Genizah in Arabic are yet to be published, but see Kahn (1986, 58–59). Four ink on paper prints of amulets in Arabic that were found in the Genizah are discussed by Schaefer (2001). Schaefer considers eleven prints in this article, all but one of which are amulets. This is an interesting example of an early stage in the production of print amulets in the West. These are Muslim amulets addressing Allah in search of help and protection, using the *bismillah* formula and names of Allah, quoting Quran verses and at times drawing graphic signs. The amulets are generic, and the potential client is mentioned in them in general terms, such as "the bearer of this writing." An interesting question is how these amulets came to be stored in the Cairo Genizah, and one possibility is that they may have been used by Jews, though this is merely a guess.

68. In line with the large number of magic gems, the scope of the research on them is vast. The best and most comprehensive study is still that of Bonner (1950). He based

stones from a variety of rocks and minerals: lava, carnelian, a variety of jasper stones, lapis lazuli, sard, hematite, magnetite, limonite, and more. Some are also made of glass. They are usually elliptical, and mostly no longer than 2 or 3 cm. The gems were usually polished on one or both sides into a flat surface, where magic letters and symbols were engraved. Often, these gems were worn by threading a chain through a hole drilled in their upper part; at times, they were set in a metal piece of jewelry. Their dimensions did not allow for the writing of detailed contents in them, as was usual in amulets or on curse tablets (*defixiones*). Their power derived mainly from visual symbols and from the few names and letters engraved on them, which in most cases attest to the integration of Egyptian and Greek elements typical of Hellenistic magic (Plate 7).

Jewish elements appear in the magic gems as well, but they do not usually attest to the Jewish origin of these stones. The situation is similar regarding amulets in Greek and the extensive recipe literature in Greek magical papyri, where Jewish contents are evident—usually the names of God, the angels, and the patriarchs, often distorted as, for example, Σαβαώθ (for *ṣeva'ot*, "hosts"), Ιστραήλ (for *Yisrael*), and Αδωναϊος and Ελωαϊος (for *Adonai* and *Elohai*), which in most cases reflect cultural (or at times professional) borrowing by "pagan" sorcerers from Jewish or Christian sources. We have no reason to assume that the writers' use of this knowledge implied awareness of the original context of these names or symbols or that their use in any way attests to the Jewish origin of the recipe's author or the amulet's writer. Quite the contrary. Often, when these elements were woven into Egyptian and Greek elements, Jewish contents were used not only disregarding this context but also in ignorance of their original meaning. These contents, some of which apparently began their course as sources of ritual power through the work of Jewish sorcerers, wandered into the cross-cultural (Jewish-Christian-Gnostic-"pagan") magic arena of late antiquity and there joined the

---

his study on about 375 gems (and about 30 medallions and magic metal bracelets). Two other useful, extensive anthologies are Simone (2001) and Spier (2007). Jewish gems are reviewed at length by Spier (2007, 159–70). Cf. Bohak (2008, 158–65). For ancient Iranian magic gems, see Gyselen (1995).

spectrum of performative elements that established the magic praxis of the Hellenistic world.[69]

This approach should also guide the handling of the special challenge that the visual richness of the magic gems adds to the question about their creators' cultural and religious identity. Here too we must beware of automatically determining that every gem on which biblical symbols are engraved is of Jewish origin.[70] The number of gems with Jewish elements is quite small, and the number of those whose Jewish origin can be determined with any certainty by relying on the language of the inscription or on such symbols as a menorah, a shofar, or a *lulav* is perhaps only a few dozen. Unfortunately, many of the Jewish gems lack any inscription, so it is hard to determine whether they served magic needs or only ornamental purposes. The few remaining stones bearing Hebrew, Aramaic, or Hebrew and Greek inscriptions contain names of angels and letter combinations typical of adjuration texts, indeed linking them to the inventory of Jewish performative magic artifacts from late antiquity.[71]

The most prominent among these artifacts is a carnelian stone about 3 cm long with a Greek inscription engraved on one side ending with the letters ET BOC ΓAP ΔAK AC OOΦ Z[A] AC TAN IAN XAΛ. As Ludwig Blau noted, this combination is a transcription of the abbreviated pronunciation that obtains from combinations of letters from the Hebrew alphabet in a mode known by the acronym *'atbash ('aleph-tav, beth-shin, gimel-resh,* etc.). This formula does appear (almost) in full in Hebrew on the other side of the stone. This side is entirely covered by five concentric circles of writing in Hebrew letters. The text is dense and hard to decipher. At the center are the words *'eheye 'asher 'eheye* (I am that I am) (Exodus 3:14). In one of the lines we can identify the words "that you

---

69. See Bohak (2003a; 2004b) and M. Smith (1996). Bohak (2007) emphasizes the asymmetry of mutual borrowing as reflected in Jewish and Hellenistic magic sources. As will be shown, cross-cultural cooperation is also well reflected in Babylonian magic bowls.

70. See Bohak (2004b, 102–3) and the examples there. See also Bonner (1950, 26–32).

71. Spier (2007) counts thirteen such gems (items 953–965), some of which have not yet been published.

may fear this glorious and fearful name YHWH" (Deuteronomy 28:58) and on the margins of the writing, the word *Israel.*[72] Unquestionably, then, this is a Jewish magic gem. Hence the Greek text that invokes "O heaven-form, darkness-form, sea-form, and all-form, eternal, leader of myriads, leader of thousands, inconceivable, (at whose side) myriads of angels stand, eternal, Adônaios, the One who Is" affords us a glimpse into the incantation language of Greek-speaking Jews.[73] The full decoding of the Hebrew inscription will hopefully provide information on the purpose of this adjuration.

The Jewish magic medallion made of bronze bearing the Greek inscription "for the welfare of Madam Matrona" also belongs to this genre. This is a metal sheet about 4½ cm in diameter, with a hole apparently drilled on its upper part so that it could be tied and worn. The brief inscription and the symbols of the menorah, the shofar, and the *lulav* engraved on both its sides resemble magic gems and are far closer to them than to the rolled metal amulets.[74]

Given the enormous number of magic gems from late antiquity, which definitely attests to their great popularity throughout the eastern Mediterranean, including Palestine, the small number of Jewish gems is even more significant.[75] It should perhaps be interpreted as conveying Jewish reservations about the use of apotropaic artifacts of this kind. Indirect confirmation of this hypothesis can be found in the Jewish literature of magic recipes, which does not contain even one recommendation for writing on a gem.[76]

---

72. See Keil (1940). Cf. Bohak (2008, 161–62) and Scholem (1990, 29n48).

73. Elements of this language, such as οὐρανοειδῆ (heaven-form) and θαλασαειδῆ (sea-form) can also be traced in Greek magical papyri (PGM IV 3063–64). See Keil (1940, 80).

74. See Reifenberg (1950, 143) and Schwabe and Reifenberg (1946).

75. Only relatively few magic gems have been found in authorized excavations, and their source has been recorded with certainty. For a detailed list, see Kotansky (1997). The greatest Palestinian finding is a group of more than 160 gems in Caesarea (Hamburger 1968). For more than ninety other gems, apparently originating in Palestine and its surroundings, see Manns (1978). Cf. Bohak (1997), Dauphin (1993), Elgavish (1994, 140), Kotansky (1997), Raffaeli (1920), and E. Stern and Sharon (1995, 32).

76. Using a gem for easing birth pains is mentioned by the Karaite Ya'qub al-Qirqisani as part of the "natural things wielding extraordinary influence." He claims

Incantation Bowls

The corpus of Babylonian incantation bowls known today numbers more than 2,500 items.[77] Not all of them have been studied and published, but the current inventory clearly shows that at least two-thirds of the texts on the bowls are written in Jewish Aramaic. This is a vast textual corpus and, besides the Babylonian Talmud, the only one to have reached us from Babylonian Jewry before the Muslim conquest. The hundreds of additional bowls originating in other cultures and religions show that in Babylonia, as in the eastern Mediterranean, various nations shared a common set of magic beliefs and customs. Each one colored it with its special hue and conveyed it in its own language. The way Jews did this leaves no doubt concerning the shared cultural foundation of Jewish magic traditions in Babylonia and Palestine.

The earliest testimony of the apotropaic use of bowls in Mesopotamia dates back to the beginning of the second millennium BCE. In the Nippur excavations in southern Iraq at the end of the 1980s, archaeologists found bowls (without writing) in all the excavation layers, from the time of the first dynasty in the first half of the eighteenth century BCE until the Achaemenid period in the seventh to fourth centuries BCE.[78]

---

that when this stone, whose essence he does not mention, is placed under a woman experiencing a difficult birth, it causes her to give birth immediately. This issue is cited in al-Qirqisani's long discussion against witchcraft and in support of the wonders of true prophecy. Clearly, he is referring to the stone's "natural" influence, as he understands it (such as magnetic power or the power of healing herbs and poison), rather than to the power stored in magic symbols engraved in it. See Nemoy (1986, 338–39).

77. Michael Morony counts at least 885 bowls. More than half of them (565) were in the National Museum of Iraq, with 142 more in the British Museum; the rest are in various museums and private collections (Morony 2003, 87–93). Five large private collections were not included in this estimate: the Schøyen collection (Norway), which includes about 650 bowls; the Gil Shaya Moussaieff collection (Israel), with about 300 bowls; the Shlomo Moussaieff collection (England), with more than 100 bowls; and the collections of Samir Dehays (Jordan) and Barakat Gallery (England), each with about 75 bowls. On the publication of the Jewish bowls and their study, see chapter 2.

78. Two of the bowls contained animal bones. According to the excavation findings, in this case we are not speaking of an animal's burial in the bowl but of the ritual use of a limb, of which only the bones remained. Fulvio Franco reports that an incantation

Usually, the bowls (thirty-nine in number) were found in pairs, beside one another, and placed against the walls of buildings or under the floor next to entrances. According to the excavators, the location of the bowls is not random. It points to their ritual burial as a homage tied to the construction of buildings or designed to remove pain and illness from their dwellers. It thus seems that the use of bowls in the Sassanid era and the beginning of the Muslim era as a place for writing adjurations for protection from demons, witchcraft, and illness is a cultural variation of a magic practice that had been widespread in Mesopotamia for thousands of years.[79]

Babylonian adjuration bowls are dated to the fifth to seventh centuries CE. This assessment, based on the location of bowls that were found in orderly excavations, has now been corroborated by the discovery of six dated bowls. The dates of the writing, mentioned in the bowls as part of the divorce deed formulation that appears in them, indicate that they are from 544–687 CE.[80] The contents and the spread of the bowls (throughout central and southern areas of contemporary Iraq) point to the broad

---

bowl from the Sassanid era was found in Tel Baruda together with the bones and skull of a cat (Franco 1978–1979, 233). In the Venco Ricciardi article to which he refers, however, the bones are mentioned without any connection to the bowl, and therefore it is not clear whether this is indeed evidence of the use of animals in the context of the incantation bowls (Venco Ricciardi 1973–1974, 19). Sacrifice was a widespread element of magic practice in late antiquity. In the context of Jewish magic, see Swartz (1995). In the context of Hellenistic magic, see Johnston (2002). On the use of a human skull in Jewish magic, see the next subsection ("Magic Skulls").

79. See Gibson et al. (1998, 24–26). On the most ancient bowls ever found in the Nippur excavation, cf. Gibson et al. (1978, 56–67). For a summary of the excavation findings according to the layers, see Gibson et al. (1978, 7, 88–106, 107). Six later bowls (from the sixth and seventh centuries CE) were also found in this excavation. See Hunter (1995b and note 2 therein). So far, no evidence is available about the existence of this magic practice beyond the Middle East. Cyrus Gordon's suggestion that the bowls from Knossos are a Minoan cultural parallel to the Babylonian bowls is purely speculative and should not be accepted. See Gordon (1964) and the critique of Hägg (1993, 394n56).

80. See Shaked (2000a, 58n1; 2005b, 10; 2010, 221). Obviously, this relative restriction in the dates of these bowls' writings does not dictate a sweeping restriction in the dating of all bowls. Several scholars even extend the period of their writing for more than a century in each direction, based on paleographic and other considerations.

dissemination in the use of this type of performative artifact, both in geographic and cultural-religious terms.

As noted, most bowls were written in Jewish Aramaic, and their adjuration formulas contain distinctively Jewish contents. Among them are names and attributes of God, biblical verses, biblical figures and contents, Mishnah passages that include a liturgical passage from tractate *Zevahim* (5:3) and quotations from tractates *Gittin* and *Shevu'ot*, and talmudic motifs. Among the talmudic contents are hints to a midrash on a dispute between Moses and the angels (TB *Shabbat* 88b–89a), to the story of Solomon and Ashmedai (TB *Gittin* 68a–b), and to the story about the encounter between Rabbi Hanina b. Dosa and Agrat, daughter of Mahalat (TB *Pesahim* 112b–113a). Mentioned in the bowls are also the names of R. Joshua b. Perahia, Rav Aha b. Rav Huna, and several clients bearing the title "Rav." Although their first names are mentioned in rabbinic literature, it is impossible to identify them as those rabbis, given that in the bowls they are referred to by their mother's name.[81]

R. Joshua b. Perahia is mentioned in the bowls as an archetype of an exorcist who could ban demons and remove them by means of a divorce writ (*get*).[82] The magical divorce activated by R. Joshua b. Perahia is

81. On literary features of the bowls, see Shaked et al. (2013, 13–27). On talmudic motifs, see Shaked (2005a; 2005b) and later discussion. On Hanina b. Dosa, see Shaked et al. (2013, 53–96). Cf. Shaked (2002, 68). On the story of Solomon and Ashmedai in the context of the magic bowls, see Levene (2003b) and Ten-Ami (2013). On bowls for clients titled "Rav," see Ford and Ten-Ami (2012) and Harviainen (1981). An early (and at times problematic) attempt to tie together rabbinic literature and the magic bowls was done by Irving Teitelbaum (1964). For a unique bowl whose entire content is five verses from Ezekiel and Jeremiah and the translation of some of them into Aramaic, see Kaufman (1973). Unlike Kaufman, I doubt whether this bowl was indeed written for a performative end. In any event, it does not meet the list of criteria for an adjuration text that I suggested in chapter 3.

82. For an anthology of bowls with the divorce theme embedded in their incantations, see Shaked et al. (2013, 99–275). For discussions of the magic divorce writ in bowls, see Bamberger (2012), Levene (2003a, 18–21; 2003b), and Shaked (1999b). On the magic divorce theme in a magical fragment from the Cairo Genizah, see Levene and Bohak (2012). The only hint in rabbinic literature at any connection between R. Joshua b. Perahia and magic might be the tradition in TB *Sanhedrin* 107b, which states that he had been the teacher of Jesus (who was accused of witchcraft) and stayed with him in Alexandria. On this matter, cf. also the tradition about "ben Stada" (probably a name

mentioned in many bowls, at times as a magic historiola whose power their writers sought to apply to exorcise the spirits that they themselves confronted. A good example of such a historiola appears in the writing in the following bowl:

[By] your name I make this amulet that it may be a healing to this one, for the threshold of the house [ ] and any possession which he has. I bind the rocks of the earth, and tie down the mysteries of heaven, I suppress them [ ], [I r]ope, tie and suppress all demons and harmful spirits, all those which are in the world, whether masculine or feminine, from their big ones to their young ones, from their children to their old ones, whether I know his name or I do not know it. In case I do not know the name, it has already been explained to me at the time of the seven days of creation. What has not been disclosed to me at the time of the seven days of creation was disclosed to me in the deed of divorce that came here from[83] across the sea, which was written and sent to Rabbi Joshua bar Peraḥia. Just as there was a Lilith who strangled human beings, and Rabbi Joshua bar Peraḥia sent a ban against her, but she did not accept it because he did not know her name;[84] and her name was written in the deed of divorce and an announcement was made against her in heaven by a deed of divorce that came here from across the sea;

---

for Jesus Christ) bringing in witchcraft from Egypt (TB *Shabbat* 104b). See also Neusner (1969–1970, 5: 235–41, esp. 239) and Shaked et al. (2013, 103, with further bibliography).

83. The original is miswritten.

84. "Lilith" in this case and in the incantation bowls in general is not a first name but a generic one, a term for a kind of demon, of which there are many, both male and female (*lilin* and *liltin*). At times, the personal names of certain liliths are mentioned in bowls. See, for example, Müller-Kessler (1996; 2001). A ban, like a divorce writ and like adjuration formulas, must note the specific name of the addressee. In this case, although R. Joshua may have shared with the narrator the knowledge that the she-demon was a lilith, he did not know her name, and consequently she did not receive the ban and was not banished. Other bowls referring to the story of the divorce writ that arrived from across the sea spell out the identifying names written in them. See, for example, Montgomery (1913, bowls 8, 11, 17), J. B. Segal (2000, bowl 13A), and Shaked et al. (2013, bowls 15, 19, 24).

so you too are roped, tied and suppressed, all of you under the feet of this Marnaqa son of Qala. In the name of Gabriel, the mighty hero, who kills all heroes who are victorious in battle, and in the name of Yehoel who shuts the mouth of all [heroes]. In the name of YH YH YH Sabaoth. Amen, Amen, Selah.[85]

The magic *get* clearly and explicitly illustrates the connection tying Jewish halakhic and legal elements to magic praxis—a sympathetic channeling of the legal and social power of the divorce deed to the demonic. This connection comes forth not only in the application of the legal principle of expulsion by means of a divorce writ but also in the actual expulsion through the wording of the divorce deed itself. Evidence is found, for instance, in the wording of the following incantation addressing demons:

> I cast a lot and take it. And a (magical) act I perform. And that (which) was in the court-session of R. Joshua bar Peraḥia. I am writing them a divorce deed (*get*), to all the male and female liliths who appear to this Uri daughter of Maroshita and to this Qaqai son of Ṣiporta in the dream of the night and the sleep of the day. A divorce writ, a *get* of releasing and sending away. In the name of a character out of a character and characters out of characters and a name out of the names [ ] a hollow out of an empty space.[86] [ ] Therefore, I ascended against you to the heights. I have brought against you a harmer to destroy you and remove you from her house and from every bedroom of this Uri daughter of Merushita and this Qaqai son of Ṣiporta And may you not appear to them, not in the dream of the night and not in the sleep of the day. For I have released you from them by a document of divorce, and by a deed of release and by a letter of dismissal (*be-sefer gerushin uve-get piturin ve-'igeret shivukin*) according to the law of the daughters of Israel from this day and

---

85. Naveh and Shaked (1987, 158–63). Cf. the parallel version of this text in Shaked et al. (2013, 140–43).

86. For this expression, the meaning of which is uncertain, see Shaked et al. (2013, 103).

forever. Amen, Amen Selah, Hallelujah. For Your namesake
I have done (this act). Gabriel and Michael and Raphael are
sealed[87] upon this *get*.[88]

The ending of the incantation is based on R. Judah's reference to the
wording of the divorce deed as cited in the Mishnah (*Gittin* 9:3): "The
essential formula in the *get* is, 'Lo, you are free to marry any man.' R.
Judah says: 'Let this be from me your document of divorce and letter of
dismissal and deed of release (*sefer gerushin ve-'igeret shivukin ve-get pitu-
rin*), that you may marry any man you wish.'" In this case, then, the
bowl's scribe seeks to apply to the liliths the legal-performative power
of the specific formula determined by R. Judah stating that a man has
divorced his wife to expel demons from his clients.

Another example illustrating the channeling of legal-performative
power to the area of human-demon relationships appears in another
bowl, which cites a passage from tractate *Shevu'ot*. The Mishnah discussion in chapter 4 of this tractate deals with testimony oaths, meaning the
oaths of witnesses who are required by a person involved in a civil suit to
testify for him concerning a financial affair but who know nothing about
this affair. The halakhic deliberation seeks to clarify, among other things,
what linguistic formulas compel a person to attest to the truth of someone's claim of damages and what formulas release him from doing so (and
accordingly, what to do when the witness is guilty if it emerges that he
lied in his oath). The Mishnah states (*Shevu'ot* 4:13):

> [Should someone turn to witnesses and seek to compel them to
> testify for him by stating] "I adjure you (*mashbi'a 'ani 'alekhem*), I
> command you, I bind you" [and it is later found they lied when
> swearing they had not known] they are liable. [If he seeks to com-
> pel them to testify for him by stating] "by heaven and earth"—
> they are exempt. [And if] "by *'alef dalet*" [i.e., by Adonai], by *yod*

---

87. The original is miswritten.

88. Levene (2003a, 32). Cf. bowls M50, M59, M113, and M119 and the discussions
on them in Levene (2003a, 18–21, 35–37, 51–61). For more parallels to this *get* formula,
see Shaked et al. (2013, bowls 13, 14, 19, 20, 21, 24). For a detailed discussion of it, see
Bamberger (2012).

he' [i.e., by YHWH], by *Shaddai*, by *Ṣeva'ot* [hosts], by merciful and gracious, by the long-suffering one, by the one abounding in kindness or by any of the substitutes [for the name], they are liable.[89]

The last option, which presents a case in which a person seeks to compel the witnesses to testify by mentioning the names of God and their substitutes and states that this act is indeed legally compelling, is the one that interests me. The reason is that this is precisely the legal-performative validity that the writer of one of the bowls sought to realize in the incantation for exorcising demons.

Again, I put under oath and adjure you evil demons, (and) strong and powerful sorceries that you shall depart and go out of the house of Abandad son of Batgada and from the dwelling of Sami daughter of Parsita. . . . If you appear as a pig I adjure and put you under oath by means of YHW YHW. If you appear as a ram I adjure and put you under oath by *'alef dalet*, by *yod he'*, by *Shaddai*, by *Ṣeva'ot*, by merciful and gracious, by the long-suffering one, by the one abounding in kindness or by any of the substitutes (for the name). If you appear as a dog I adjure and put you under oath by means of I am that I am.[90]

The list of names in the Mishnah (including the concluding reference to "any of the substitutes [for the name]"), which in the original serves to denote linguistic formulas endowed with legal (human) enforcement powers, becomes here an incantation formula endowed with performative (supernatural) power, addressing the demons in order to expel them. In this case too, then, we see an attempt to have elements from Halakhah brought into play in the magical act of writing incantation bowls.

Beside these issues and the other biblical and talmudic elements mentioned, typical names of angels and linguistic formulas that appear

---

89. Reimund Leicht has attempted to trace the development of the magic adjuration formula *mashbi'a 'ani 'alekha* (I adjure you) from the formula of the legal oath, historically tying the adjuration to the oath. See Leicht (2006b).

90. Levene (2007, 61–62).

in the liturgy and in *Hekhalot* and *Merkavah* literature also occur in the bowls.[91] All of them together reflect the *sitz im Kultur* of the Jewish bowls. Beside them, bowls in Syriac, Mandaic, and Pahlavi that include Christian, Mandaic, Manichean, Zoroastrian, and "pagan" cultural and religious elements attest to their creation and their use in these communities.[92]

Babylonian magic bowls are made of fired clay. They are usually 15–20 cm in diameter, though bigger and smaller ones have also been located. They are simple and usually do not have any patterns or ornamentations. Most are entirely concave, and a minority are flat-bottomed.[93] The adjuration, usually a reasonably long text, is written in ink on the inner side of the bowl, usually in a spiral pattern from the center to the margins. Less widespread forms of writing are in a spiral pattern from the margins to the center, dividing the surface of the bowl and then writing in lines in each part, writing in concentric circles, and writing in the shape of rays radiating from the center to the margins (Plates 8–10).[94] At times, an illustration is added at the center of the bowl that resembles,

---

91. On these characteristics of magic bowls, see Lesses (1998, 351–65), Levene (2005; 2007); B. A. Levine (1970), Montgomery (1913, 51–66), J. B. Segal (2000, 26–27), Shaked (1995), and Shaked et al. (2013, 23–27).

92. For an excellent discussion of bowls in the context of their cultural-religious origin, see Shaked (2002). For his hypothesis on the Zoroastrian origin of the Pahlavi bowls, which have not yet been read and published, see Shaked (2002, 71). On Manichean bowls and the identity of the scribes who used a proto-Manichean script, see Shaked (2000a). For more on religious-cultural syncretism in the bowls, see Harviainen (1993) and Shaked (1985; 1997). On the identity of the bowl writers using Syriac (Christian or "pagan"?), see Harviainen (1995), Juusola (1999b), and Naveh and Shaked (1987, 18). For a corpus of Syriac bowls, see V. P. Hamilton (1971) and Moriggi (2014). Mandaic bowls were published and discussed mainly by McCullogh (1967), Pognon (1979), and Yamauchi (1967). Cf. Morgenstern (2012) and Morony (1984, 384–430), and see J. B. Segal (2000, 103–50) for the Mandaic and Syriac bowls in the British Museum collection. Adjuration bowls in Arabic are also found in the British Museum collection. They have not yet been the subject of a scientific study.

93. See Hunter (2000a, 189–202; 2000b, esp. 165–72). The existence of additional magical containers in the form of a goblet or a vase, although rare, is also worth noting. See Levene (2002, 11, 19–20). See also Gordon (1934a).

94. See Levene (2003a) and Morony (2003, 85 and plates 6–9).

reveals, and presents the demon or demons addressed in the adjuration. Some look human and some monstrous. The human-like demons are often drawn with their hands, feet, and neck tied in chains and surrounded by a circle—a visual performative expression of their subjugation, binding, isolation, and removal from the human realm (represented by the word/speech/writing/adjuration that constrains them all around, overwhelms them, and coerces their expulsion), complementing and strengthening the power of the incantation (Plates 11–13).[95] The contents of the adjurations show that most of the bowls were used in a struggle against demons and harmful witchcraft, which were viewed as the force behind all human calamities and failures. A few bowls were also written for other purposes: sending harmful witchcraft, attaining love, finding favor with someone, and commercial success.[96]

A few pairs of bowls, bearing signs of their mutual tying and with tar seal marks still recognizable on their sides and bases, attest to the practice of protection from harmful witchcraft. These bowls bear the name *qibla'* (from the root *qbl*, meaning "against," in the sense of a countercharm) and were meant to return the harmful witchcraft to the sender, thereby preventing harm to the client for whom they had been written. The sealing together of the bowls facing one another is a powerful

---

95. On the iconography of the bowls, see Hunter (1998; 2000a, 202–4; 2000b) and Vilozny (2010; 2013). Some scholars have suggested that, at times, the paintings in the bowls resemble the sorcerer raising his hand to exorcise the demons. See Gordon (1951, 98), Montgomery (1913, 55), Morony (1984, 390, 411; 2003, 98), Vilozny (2010, 202, 251–60), and Yamauchi (1967, 5). For a bowl that is altogether a painting of a she-demon surrounded by drawings of "waves" resembling the lines of an adjuration text, see Franco (1978–1979, 240). Elliot Wolfson has suggested that the magic power of the bowls rests mainly on their visual symbols—the iconography and the pictography. In his view, which I do not share, they are more important than the contents (Wolfson 2001).

96. For an overview of the antidemonic character of the bowls, see Shaked (2005b). On incantation bowls for other purposes, see the following: for harm, Levene (2013) (in which thirty bowls, bearing curses and countercharms, were published) and Morgenstern (2007a); for love, Montgomery (1913, 213); for finding favor (combined with love and blocking rivals' mouth from generating evil sorceries, Montgomery (1913, 178); and for economic success, Levene and Bhayro (2005–2006).

symbolic expression of their purpose, which is made explicit in their adjuration formulas.[97]

The bowls, then, were intended mainly to protect clients, their homes, their families, and at times their households from harmful agents or to expel the harmful agents when unfortunate life circumstances suggested that they had invaded the life space or the bodies of the bowl users.[98] As in the case of the amulets, the bowls also drew their power from the adjurations written on them. The visual icons, however, probably had some performative (and not necessarily aesthetic) significance as well. The circle motif was also probably important and actually dictated the choice of a bowl as the basis for writing adjurations and the mode of the writing.[99] Several examples of incantation formulas in bowls are given in the following discussion.[100]

The first bowl was written to heal Maḥoy, son of Imma, from various demons and injurious spirits and to protect him from them. Its language points to a desire to seal any possible crack in the magic protection wall by, on the one hand, precisely detailing all aspects—the name of the client, the time, the place, the harmful agents removed, and their mode of appearance—and, on the other, generalizing them. The text reads:

Healing from heaven to Maḥoy son of Imma, who is named Barshuti, and any other name he (may) have from childhood.

___

97. For an anthology and study of *qibla'* bowls, see Levene (2011; 2013, bowls 1–6, 19–21).

98. The incantation, which details the realm of protection and the names of the individuals and their mutual family ties, provides a broad arena for the sociological study of the bowls. For the beginning of such a study, see Morony (2003, 100–107).

99. The choice of bowls as magic artifacts results from a cultural preference, the roots of which, as noted, go back to the second millennium BCE. Erica Hunter tied it to the apotropaic cult of the *zisurrû*, or flour circle, widespread in Babylonia in the first millennium BCE (Hunter 2000b, 176–80). Gordon tied the choice of bowls to their similarities with skulls (Gordon 1957, 162). David Frankfurter anchored the choice in a practice for trapping scorpions (Frankfurter 2015). On the circle in Jewish magic and as a universal magic symbol, see Harari (2005b, note 81).

100. For a formal analysis of the incantations in the Aramaic bowls, see Shaked (2011) and Shaked et al. (2013, 8–13).

May he be healed from the *baroqta'* (cataract demon),[101] male
and female, and from the evil spirit that appears in appearances
and the *nida'* (uncleanness?) spirit and from the *deiva'* (a type
of demon) and the *nidra'* (vow) and the *sheda'* (demon) and the
ṭulin (shadow-spirits) and from [ ] and from the evil affliction
(demon) and from the blast (demon) and the tormentor (spirits)
and from every evil thing, so that they should not come upon
him, Maḥoy son of Imma, from this day for ever. Amen Amen
Selah. A song and praise and deeds (?) and might for the king
of the kings of kings, may He be blessed. By His great name, I
adjure and invoke against you, the male and female cataract,
demons, dēws, evil spirit, *nidra'* by witchcraft,[102] and all other
spirits and all other (demonic) tormentors that the God of Israel
created in the world.[103] May you not bind Maḥoy son of Imma
from this day for ever. Amen Amen Selah. I adjure and invoke
against you, male and female cataract, that you should not come
against Maḥoy son of Imma, and that you should not tie him
up or chain him. That you should not come in through the way
he comes or go out the way he goes out, and you should not
turn (after him) at the place where he turns, and that he should
not have a misfortune either by day or by night, and that you
should not subdue him, you, the male and female cataract, (him,)
Maḥoy son of Imma, either from his right side or from his left
side, and you should not sit upon the house (?) [ ] that appear to
him in evil appearances and in evil thoughts and in terrifying
fears. And that you should not appear to him in any form or
appearance as you appear to people. And that you should not [ ]
[male and] female from Maḥoy, son of Imma, from the way he
enters and the way he goes out, and his residence and from the

101. For the Aramaic *baroqta'* (*baraqti, barqit*), see Jastrow (1903, 197) and Sokoloff
(2002, 247).

102. The original *nidra' be-ḥirshei* apparently refers to the demonization of maleficent sorceries, that is, to the embodiment of the harmful adjuration in a demonic power
called *Nidra'*.

103. On the views concerning the origin of demons in the world, see Chapter 6.

four corners of his house, of Barshuti son of Imma, and that you should go to [another?] place [ ]. By the name of [ ] Amen Selah.[104]

This bowl is an expression of a precise and rigorous trend in the writing of incantations that is meant to ensure the client as hermetic a defense as possible. Many bowls are written in this kind of detailed style, but not all.

The next bowl is an example of a brief and succinct incantation. This one too was written for healing purposes, except that in this case the illness was tied to injurious witchcraft cast upon the client. The purpose of the bowl is to cancel the effects of this witchcraft. It seeks to do so through the combined power of holy names and a biblical verse (Numbers 10:35) dealing with God's power to overcome his foes and enemies and make them flee.

Healing from heaven to Mādar-Āfri daughter of Anushay. May there lie in the dust the injuries of vows of every place and every shaded place.[105] And every evil thing, and whatever oppresses Mādar-Āfri daughter of Anushay,[106] the sorcery and the charms which are cast, (all) will be pressed and hidden in the earth before her. By the power of his army! "And it came to pass, when the ark set forward, that Moses said Rise up, YHWH, and let Your enemies be scattered, and let flee before You" (Numbers 10:35). 'QDD W'BR' Amen Amen Selah.[107]

Anyone reading this brief incantation in its original language will immediately notice the numerous errors in it. They point to the writer's limited literacy on the one hand and to his professional strategy on the other. He undoubtedly mastered Aramaic but negligently and unintelligibly garbled

104. Naveh and Shaked (1993, 137–38).

105. Literally, "shadow." On the danger of the shadow, see TB *Pesahim* 111b.

106. Manushay in the original. For this alternation of Anushay, see Naveh and Shaked (1987, 148–50).

107. Naveh and Shaked (1987, 146–51). On bowl incantations for blocking evil sorceries, see Montgomery (1913, 83–89).

the name of the client and her mother. He cited the verse correctly but could not write in Hebrew. He may have copied it from a garbled source, but, more likely, he knew it by heart. In any event, the space left in the verse after "let" is not a mistake but a deliberate act. The omission of "them that hate You" (*mesan'ekha*) is a sympathetic act meant to omit, erase, and dismiss Mādar-Āfri's enemies, against whose witchcraft the bowl was meant to work.[108]

The character of this type of sorcery is also revealed in the bowls' language. The next bowl, which makes extensive sympathetic use of aggressive biblical verses, including the curse verses in Deuteronomy, is a good example of the way the plot was devised. At the beginning of the incantation, surrounding the drawing of a person or a demon, are several words, including unclear names, surrounded by a circle. After them, the following text appears:

And all the vomit (?) and spittle of Yehudah son of Nanay, that his tongue may dry up in his mouth, that his spittle may dissolve in this throat, that his legs may dry, that sulphur and fire may burn in him, that his body may be struck by scalding, that he may be choked, become estranged, become disturbed to the eyes of all those who see him, and that he may be banned, broken, l[o]st, finished, vanquished, and that he may die, and that a flame may come upon him from heaven, and shiver seize him, and a fracture catch him, and a rebuke burn in him. May the following verse apply to him: they shall fall and not arise,[109] and there will be no power for them to stand up after their defeat,[110] and there will be no healing to their affliction. "Their eyes will darken, so that they see not, and their loins will be made by you continually to shake" (Psalms 69:24). "Let their habitation b[e]

---

108. The scribe omitted the last five letters of the word משנאיך, which compose the word שנאיך, "your enemies" (literally "those who hate you"). The space between the words, which is insufficient to insert all the missing letters, shows that this is not a word that had been written in the original and is no longer readable (see Naveh and Shaked 1987, plate 20). The precise quote of the verse and the written letter *mem* show that this was not a scribe's mistake.

109. See Jeremiah 25:27. Cf. also Jeremiah 8:4 and Amos 8:14.

110. Cf. Leviticus 26:37.

desolate, and none dwell in their tents" (Psalms 69:26).[111] May
the following verse apply to him: "And my wrath shall wax hot,
and I will kill you with the sword, and your wives shall be
widows and your [children] fatherless" (Exodus 22:23). And the
following may apply to Yehudah son of Nanay: "The Lord shall
smite you with a consumption and with a fever and with an
inflammation and with an extreme burning and with the sword
and with blasting and with [mildew] and they shall pursue you
[until you per]ish" (Deuteronomy 28:22). "The Lord shall smite
you in the knees and in the legs with a fes[tering eruption] that
cannot be healed from the sole of your foot on to the top of your
head" (Deuteronomy 28:35). "The Lord shall smite you with
madness and blindness and astonishment of heart" (Deuteronomy 28:28). "And you shall eat the fl[esh of your s]ons and the
fl[esh of your d]aughters" (Leviticus 26:29). The throat of Yehudah son of Nanay shall not swallow and his [g]ullet shall [n]ot
eat, choking shall fall on his palate, and paralysis shall fall on
his [?]. The following verse will ap[ply to h]im: "The nations
shall see and be confused at all their mig[ht. They shall l]ay
their h[and on their mou]th, their ears shall be dear, they shall
lick [the dust] like a serpent. [They shall move] out of their
holes like worms of the earth" (Micah 7:16–17). "The Lord will
not spare him but then the anger of the Lord and his jealousy
shall smoke against that man and [all the curses that are written
in this] book [shall lie upon him] and the Lord shall blot out his
name from under heaven" (Deuteronomy 29:19). So shall the
name of Yehudah son of Nanay be blotted out and [his memory
(?)] shall be uprooted from the world just as was blotted out the
name of [Amalek (?)] may his members be pressed down and
may there be done to him and come (upon him) judgment, omen
and misfortune swiftly, with an inflammation, ear purulence,[112]

---

111. Two words in the original Hebrew in these verses, which were changed by the
writer of the bowl while still keeping their assonance, *ham'ed/ham'et* and *neshamah/
leshamah*, show the version of the psalm known to him, apparently by heart.

112. See Sokoloff (2002, 1127, s.v. שחליא). A spirit of ear infection (*ruaḥ shaḥalniaʾ*) had
been mentioned already in the Genesis Apocryphon scroll. See Fitzmyer (2004, 102, 210).

an itch, with lice and black illness, and with shivering and lice [ ] a pirate and a satan. And in the name of ŠŠ‘RB the angel, and in the name of MWT and YRWR[113] and ’NHYD and ‘YSṬR ṬWR’ and ŠṬYWY and the spirit which resides in the cemetery, all should lean on Yehu[dah son of Nanay].[114]

Bowls' writers, then, made a good deal when they made their professional services available for the benefit of the collective. On the one hand, they functioned as agents of harmful magic in the service of whoever wanted to harm another. On the other, they offered protection from such acts of witchcraft with the same linguistic and ritual means, but this time to offset the witchcraft. We need not assume that the same writer was responsible for both aspects in any particular case, but in the broad social perspective reflected in the bowls, as professionals skilled in the activation of ritual power in the service of the individual, they served the interests of both parties.

Information concerning the professional aspects of writing bowls is limited. It is based mainly on bowls whose incantation formulas, all or some of them, are parallel. These parallel versions exist in bowls written by the same scribe (and at times for the same client), by different scribes from the same culture, and even in bowls written in different languages (i.e., in different cultural and religious communities). They attest to the existence of set incantation formulas, passed from generation to generation either orally or in lost magic texts. At the same time, they also attest to the writer's freedom to use them for the purpose of adapting them to the circumstances of the writing.

Bowls written by the same person point to two methods of writing. At times the writers copied the same incantation into several bowls, and at times they displayed professional independence and creativity in their writing. In the latter case, they chose passages of adjurations, powerful verses, names of demons and angels, and opening and closing formulas from the available pool of oral or written professional material and wove

---

113. On the YRWR demon, cf. Levene (2003a, 40), J. B. Segal (2000, 213), and Sokoloff (2002, 514).

114. Naveh and Shaked (1987, 174–79). For more curse texts in the Aramaic incantation bowls, see Levene (2013).

them together, according to the circumstances of the bowl preparation, into a unique incantation formula. Parallels between bowls by different writers, at times from different religions, point to the transfer of magic knowledge in professional circles of bowl writers, within as well as outside the religious community.[115]

Most of the surviving bowls have reached the West through antique dealers, and they lack context. Those that were found in archaeological excavations shed light on the use that was made of them. Almost all the bowls located in situ were found in living quarters and placed either inversely or in pairs—one inside the other or one against the other—mainly in the corners of living quarters or under the threshold and at times in the courtyard.[116] The bowls may have served as traps for demons, which were assumed to dwell in the corners and on the threshold, as indicated by the wording of some of the incantations.[117] It is more likely,

---

115. See Levene (2003a, 24–30) and Shaked (2011).

116. Shaul Shaked pointed out to me that several bowls in the Schøyen collection were found one inside the other, possibly with the wish of making the complex more powerful. Mandaic bowls that designate the cemetery in the context of their use (*debeit qubraya'*) attest that this too was a preferred site for this purpose. Several bowls were indeed found in an excavation in an area of graves. See Montgomery (1913, 14, 43–44), Pognon (1979, 30, 88) (=Yamauchi 1967, 208, 162), and Naveh and Shaked (1987, 15–16, 152–53).

117. The idea that the demons enter the house through corners had appeared already in the *Testament of Solomon* 7:5 (Duling 1983, 969). On the evidence from bowls in this regard, see, for example, the following formula, meant to tie the demons to the four corners of the house: "Suppressed are you! Bound are you, bound! Bound are you and sealed are you in [ea]ch one of the four corners of the house" (Montgomery 1913, 133). See also Montgomery 1913, 41–42 and note 13). Cf. also the incantation discussed earlier where the demons are adjured to go away from the four corners of the client's house. The threshold is also mentioned in the incantations. For example, "O Lilith Ḥablas, the granddaughter of Lilith Zarnai, who dwells on the threshold" (Gordon 1934a, 470). The wording in another bowl requires Lilith to be "suppressed and sealed away from the house and from the threshold" (Gordon 1951, 307); cf. Segal's comments on this bowl (J. B. Segal 2000, 99, bowl 68A). See also Naveh and Shaked (1987, bowls 5, 11; 1993, bowls 15, 19) and Shaked et al. (2013, 281). A similar approach is also found in Mandaic adjuration bowls. For the threshold, see, for example, Yamauchi (1967, 230, 234). For the four corners of the house, see Harviainen (1995), J. B. Segal (2000, bowl 76M; cf. bowl 82M, with a drawing of a house with its four corners and the power of *Hiyya'* ["life," the god invoked for help in most Mandaic bowls] therein), and Yamauchi

however, that their users sought to delimit this space from the beginning, so that injurious agents would not enter the house. The bowls obviously could have performed a dual function: delimiting and curbing from the start and entrapping and removing after the fact. In any event, instructions for use that appear on the outside of some of the bowls—"for the center of the threshold," "for the middle gate of the entrance," "for the lower vestibule," "for the inner room of the eating house"—show that they were not randomly hidden. Their placement was deliberately planned by those who produced them, and those people also guided their clients on how to use them.[118]

The names of clients (and those of their mothers) mentioned in the Jewish incantation bowls and the language of the instructions for their location that were sometimes written on the outside to guide the clients are valuable information sources. Names of women, for instance, denote their share in the public of bowl consumers as opposed to the men mentioned in them, whereas clients referred to as Rav may point to the client's social status. Yet the names and the language of the instructions attest that the clients may not have belonged to the same community as the bowls' creators. Writers of Jewish bowls whose magic practice attained renown served a broad community of both Jews and non-Jews.[119] Cooperation was not just one way, nor was it confined to the bowls' use; it also came forth in the bowls' creation.

So far, we have no evidence of Jewish clients using bowls from a different cultural and religious origin (i.e., we do not know of bowls written in languages other than Jewish Aramaic mentioning names of clients who proved to be Jewish). Clearly, however, writers of Jewish bowls did not refrain from using foreign performative languages or even supernatural

---

(1967, 154, 156, 290). On the four corners of the house in antidemonic rituals in Islam, cf. Sviri (2002, 206–7).

118. On the location of the bowls, see Hunter (1995b, 62), Montgomery (1913, 13–14, 40–45), Naveh and Shaked (1987, 15), and Shaked (2000a, 54–65; 2005b, 8). For a summary on the use of the bowls, see J. B. Segal (2000, 27–29) and Shaked (2005b).

119. This phenomenon is not specific to Jewish bowls. The names of the clients and the instructions for use reveal a widespread use of bowls by clients belonging to cultural-religious communities different from that of the bowl writer. See Levene (1999, 291), Montgomery (1913, 49–50), Naveh and Shaked (1987, 18), and Shaked (1997; 2000a, 64–66; 2002, 65–66).

powers foreign to Judaism known to us from other sources. In doing so, they participated in the cross-cultural magic syncretism of Babylonia in late antiquity, which we also find in the cultures of the eastern Mediterranean. This cross-cultural mutual borrowing, which was based on a shared magic approach on the one hand and on pragmatic motivations on the other, is manifest throughout the corpus of Babylonian bowls, regardless of their cultural and religious origin.[120]

Magic Skulls

Adjuration skulls became known at the beginning of the twentieth century, when Montgomery first discussed an item of this kind that had been preserved at the University of Pennsylvania Museum. Because of the state of the skull, particularly of the written signs on its external smooth side (and so in all the skulls), the writing could not be deciphered. Yet, on the basis of the few readable words—*ruḥin*, *lilta'*, *'ant ruaḥ*, and several first names—the skull is presumed to have served in the struggle against demons, probably in the way incantation bowls had.[121]

Clearer evidence of this use of a human skull has become available recently in the shape of a particularly small skull, probably of an elderly woman, which is in the Shlomo Moussaieff collection. We have no information about the location or the circumstances of this finding except that the skull was apparently found between two clay bowls tied facing one another. The incantation that appears on it is jumbled, but the

---

120. On Mandaic influences on the Jewish version of the bowl, see Greenfield and Naveh (1985) and Harviainen (1981). For a Jewish use of the adjuration "By the name of Jesus . . . and by the name of his exalted Father and in the name of the Holy Spirit," see Levene (1999) and Shaked (1999a). In the opposite direction, see the case of bowl writers in Syriac borrowing the theme and the divorce deed of R. Joshua b. Peraḥia for exorcising a lilith in Montgomery (1913, 225–30, bowls 32, 33), and cf. Shaked (2002, 68). Hellenistic influence, though relatively rare, is also evident in the bowls (Shaked 2002, 71–72).

121. See Montgomery (1913, 256–57). Montgomery does not mention where the skull came from. He published its finding as an appendix to his study on the Nippur bowls, and the skull could be part of the Nippur archaeological findings. Levene, who has recently examined the remnants of the skull, determined that almost no readable traces remain and that Montgomery's readings can no longer be corroborated or improved. See Levene (2006, 364–65).

words "Healing from heaven . . . may there be for Marta" are clearly visible. This wording and the rest of the readable components in the adjuration are extremely similar to incantations in Babylonian magic bowls.[122]

These findings join two adjuration skulls and a fragment from another incantation skull that are relatively well preserved and kept in the Pergamon Museum in Berlin (Plates 14 and 15). No information is available on the location or circumstances of their finding either. One of the skulls is covered in what seem to be meaningless writing signs, and on its front is a drawing of an iconic figure similar to figures that often appear in the bowls. On the other skull, the text of a long, though jumbled, incantation has been preserved, similar in character to the bowls' texts. Angels and other entities are mentioned in it by their names and titles, although the purpose of adjuring them remains vague. The fragment of the third skull contains several broken words.

Altogether, then, we know about remnants of five magic human skulls. In all of them an Aramaic incantation was written on the upper part of the skull, and in one case a figure was also drawn. The linguistic and visual contents of the skulls seem to locate them in the world of the magic bowl writers. Unfortunately, none of the texts are continuous or broad enough to enable us to learn about unique aspects of their use, if any, in the context of Jewish Babylonian magic activity in general, which is widely recorded in the incantation bowls.[123]

The Babylonian Talmud tells of a skull with the inscription *zot ve-'od 'aheret* (this and something besides) that R. Ḥiyya bar Abuya found at the gates of Jerusalem. The skull's "refusal" to be buried despite R. Ḥiyya's recurrent attempts to do so (a refusal that led R. Ḥiyya to determine that this was the skull of King Yehoyakim) is a magic narrative motif that may hint at the author's insight into the power of such artifacts. In any event, even if the story relies on familiarity with written

---

122. On the other hand, this similarity and the relatively good state of the skull, which Shlomo Moussaieff acquired in an antiquities market, raise the suspicion that it could be a forgery.

123. For a detailed study of all these skulls and their photographs, see Levene (2006).

skulls, it does not reveal any magic use of them or any fear of a potential harmful power that they might bear.[124]

The use of human limbs, though extremely rare in Jewish magic practice, is not entirely absent from it. In the Magical Sword literature, for example, it is suggested to seek guidance from the dead by whispering in his left ear, that is, through his corpse (presumably before the burial). In a book of recipes from the Cairo Genizah, a "bone from the fingers of a dead human hand" or possibly the entire hand (together with "virgin wax," sulfur, and a rope used in a hanging) is required for a charm applied to the finding of a treasure.[125] Writing on human skulls is not mentioned in the professional magic literature (just as writing on bowls is not mentioned!), but the incantation skulls are themselves incontrovertible evidence of the Jewish use of human limbs in the performance of magic.[126]

Summary

The unique contribution of performative artifacts to the study of Jewish magic culture is manifest at several levels. First, the objects attest to the actual performance of magic, which can often be located quite precisely historically and geographically. The silver lamellae from Ketef Hinom are the earliest insider evidence of Jewish magic culture available to us, and, except for a few passages of magic writings from Qumran, performative artifacts are the sole testimony of that kind until the time of the Cairo Genizah.[127]

---

124. In the end, the skull was brought to R. Ḥiyya's house and his wife burned it in the oven. See TB *Sanhedrin* 82a.

125. See Harari (1997b, 142, sec. 174) and Schäfer and Shaked (1994–1999, 3: 93). The indicated manuscript in Schäfer and Shaked's work (Ms Cambridge, Cambridge University Library, T-S K1.3) was written in the late-sixteenth-century, but its contents match recipe books in earlier manuscripts. This is probably a later copy of an earlier work, though so far we cannot prove this. On the magic-therapeutic use of mummies in the Ottoman Empire, including among Jews, see Ben Naeh (2000, 98, 104) and Patai (1983, 308–12).

126. On magic and the dead in later Jewish culture, see Harari (2007, 75n72; 2015).

127. Although some of the magic works are dated to the middle of the first millennium or even before, their surviving manuscripts are much later.

Second, although the available performative artifacts constitute a random sample, they do enable us to point out realms of the Jews' practical interest in magic as they actually existed. Obviously, this information is not comprehensive, but what was recorded in the surviving amulets and bowls—protection and healing from demons and evil spirits, preventing miscarriages, gaining love, finding favor, improving trade, finding a treasure, overall success, protection from enemies and suppressing and harming them—is decidedly factual.

Third, these artifacts provide direct knowledge about nontextual aspects of magic—the substance, form, mode of writing, visual aspects, ritual (such as throwing into fire), location of the artifact, and so forth.

Fourth, the performative artifacts allow us to trace the connections between magic instructions and their actual performance. Such a comparison and the comparison of the adjuration versions that orthographic analysis indicates were written by the same person point to set patterns of Jewish magic practice over centuries and to the freedom of professional creativity that sorcerers took for themselves when they used these set patterns to create amulets or incantation bowls for their clients. The commonly held view of magic as an absolutely precise technique, compelling charm writers to abide rigorously and precisely by the detailed instructions if seeking success, had apparently been based on the magic instructional literature. This literature details the magic actions required for every specific matter in great detail and thereby creates the justified impression that no deviance is allowed at all. The performative artifacts show that their writers, who surely used magic guidebooks, did not approach them with awe and allowed themselves professional improvisations when writing incantations. Several cases even attest to the carelessness of incantation writers concerning the recipes they used. Thus, for example, the owner of the trilingual amulet from Egypt copied twice, in both Aramaic and Greek, the instructions for preparing the amulet as though they were part of the adjuration.[128]

Last, the performative artifacts contain extensive sociological information concerning the users of magic. The names of the clients and the

---

128. Kotansky et al. (1992, ll. 20, 32). Cf. also on this matter Naveh and Shaked (1993, amulet 30, ll. 7–8). For a similar phenomenon in a Greek amulet, see Kotansky (1994, amulet 32).

names of their mothers expose their gender, religious, class, and family ties. Through them we learn about the proportion of men and women clients and about their goals in using magic support, about the relationships between Gentile clients and Jewish sorcerers, about a certain client turning to sorcerers of different religions, about family ties between clients, and about family problems manifest in groups of incantations that were written for members of the same family. The drawback of performative artifacts lies precisely in what singles them out: their being the end product of magic activity, that is, focused, targeted products containing relatively little textual information. We cannot learn from them the entire ritual process involved in their preparation (purification rituals, the time and place of the preparation, rituals tied to the writing, and so forth). Information about the worldview in whose context they were ordered, created, and used is also quite limited. These shortcomings are offset by the other magic writings, guidebooks, and treatises that greatly enrich our knowledge on these subjects.

INSTRUCTIONAL LITERATURE: MAGIC RECIPES AND TREATISES

Magic guidebooks are the professional literature of Jewish practitioners, who offered their services to the community. The scope of this rich body of literature, as known today, includes hundreds of suggestions for performing magic in almost every area of life. Many of these magic recipes survive as fragmented lists in the Cairo Genizah. At times, these lists seem to have been torn off from a body of magic literature whose only organizing principle had been to ensure effective searching (and at times even this principle is not evident). Another part of this instructional literature was created or collected and organized in structured treatises, arranged according to one of the following patterns: (1) a professional principle, such as systematic use of psalms or of the liturgical blessings of the Amidah prayer (*Shimush Tehillim*, *Shimush 18 Berakhot*); (2) a performative nucleus, that is, a powerful name or an artifact capable of performing various actions (such as *Sefer ha-Yashar*, *Sefer ha-Malbush*, *'Arba'ah Yesodot*, and the Magical Sword literature) or having a defined purpose (such as *'Inyan Sotah* and *Havdalah de-Rabbi Aqiva*); or (3) a coherent literary framework (*Sefer ha-Razim* and *Harba de-Moshe*). These are magic books above all, with notes suggesting specific actions at their core. Framing these operational suggestions in theoretical and literary contexts, however, occasionally yielded writings through which we can track down the foundations of a worldview in which magic not only had an anchorage but was also logical and meaningful.

Magic Recipes

The Dead Sea Scrolls provide the earliest evidence of a Jewish magic literature. Among the thousands of fragments found in the Qumran caves are several segments dealing with adjurations for exorcising evil spirits and for protection from them.[129] Although all are extremely fragmented and reading them requires much filling-in of blanks, their magic-exorcising context is unquestionable. In one case (a vellum fragment), we seem to be reading a partial text from a book of recipes of the genre discussed here.[130] This vellum fragment contains two columns of six fragmented lines dealing with the expulsion of various kinds of illness, fever, and pain that are demonically personified: "male *lḥlḥy'* and female *lḥlḥyt* . . . fever and shivering and the fire of the heart . . . male *prk* and female *pkyt*" (4Q560). Possibly, the same applies to scroll 11Q11, which, despite its particularly bad state, appears to be a collection of adjurations for exorcising demons.[131] The brief fragment 8Q5, which includes four fragmented lines of which the first is "[ ] by Your name [m]ighty one I scare

---

129. On demonology in Qumran, see chapter 6. On the exorcising texts, see also Bohak (2008, 105–12), Eshel (2003), and Lange (1997).

130. See Naveh (1998) (cf. Naveh 1996). Naveh's position seems preferable to the other hypothesis, which claims that the vellum fragment is a fragment from an amulet. See Penny and Weise (1994).

131. For the latest edition of this text, see Martínez et al. (1998, 181–205). See also Eshel (1999, 270–83) and Puech (1989–1990). The textual inventory in the scroll is too limited and fragmented. The scholars' completions are impressive, but they should be approached with care. Although explicit exorcist wordings are few, the text as a whole does appear to constellate into what is seemingly a remnant of a collection of adjurations against demons. And indeed, at least one passage from this scroll made its way into later exorcising praxis, as can be seen from a Genizah magic fragment (Ms Cambridge, Cambridge University Library, T-S K1.123) that includes a slightly different version of the Qumran formula. See Bohak (2012b).

and [ ]," also seems to be part of an adjuration.[132] The hymns of the *Maskil*, designed "in order to frighten and terr[ify] all the spirits of the raving angels, demons, Lilith, owls, and [jackals]," which were preserved in two parallel versions (4Q510 and 4Q511) and provide the first testimony of the use of Psalm 91 for protection from demons and evil spirits, are also part of the antidemonic Qumran literature and, in that sense, also of the magic literature discussed here.[133] These passages from the scrolls afford a glimpse into the practical aspect of the belief in demons and evil spirits in the Judean desert sect: the existence of linguistic performative practices for the protection of the sect's members. If this is indeed a passage from a magic book of recipes, then this is the earliest concrete testimony of the Jewish people having such a literature.

An additional link in the chain of evidence pointing to the existence of Jewish magic recipe literature is two fragments from Aramaic magical papyri that were found in Egypt, dated to the fifth to sixth centuries CE. One was found in Oxyrhyncus and contains fragmented traces of at least two recipes. One recipe mentions the binding and adjuration of demons. The other recipe opens with the words "For a dog who bit a person" and is meant as a cure for the bite of a rabid dog. The other papyrus fragment is one of five found together in an unknown location. The readable part of the text is extremely fragmented, but the organization of the script (which contains many magic allusions) on the papyrus and the context of its finding (together with magic recipes in Greek and Coptic)

---

132. If *myr'* is indeed a technical term for one who exorcises (scares) demons, then this is indeed an explicit version of an exorcist adjuration. See Baumgarten (1991–1992, 136) and Eshel (1999, 286–88).

133. For the text, see Baillet (1982, 215–62), and Martínez and Tigchelaar (1998, 2: 1029). For its study, see Nitzan (1986; 1994, 227–72). Cf. Baumgarten (1986) and Ta-Shma (1986). Psalm 91, known in the Talmuds as *shir shel pega'im* (the song for tormentors) or *shir shel hanega'im* (the song for afflictions) (TB *Shevu'ot* 15b; PT *Eruvin* 12), was also copied at the end of the exorcist scroll (11Q11). Additional scroll passages (4Q444, 6Q18) have been read and interpreted as protection hymns, but the information they contain does not appear to be sufficient for concretely tying them to the current discussion. See Chazon (1999) and Eshel (1999, 313–16).

strengthen the hypothesis that this is indeed a passage from a Jewish book of recipes.[134]

The gist of the magic instructional literature from late antiquity and the early Islamic period survives in later manuscripts. The earliest were found in the Cairo Genizah. According to codicological and paleographic data, they are dated to the eleventh to thirteenth centuries and at times even later (up to the sixteenth century), but their contents are probably earlier. So far, a few dozen pages from recipe books found in the Genizah have appeared in print. This is only a small part of the magic literature in the Genizah, but the hundreds of recipes contained in it and in the large magic treatises *Sefer ha-Razim* and *Ḥarba de-Moshe* are a trove of information touching on almost all aspects of Jewish magic culture.[135]

The surviving manuscripts show that the lists of recipes for performing magic rituals collected in grimoires were often organized on a professional and practical basis so as to facilitate the search for them. Related matters were placed contiguously and in order (a prominent example is the list in *Ḥarba de-Moshe*) (Plate 21). Recipes for the same purpose were placed together and, at times, instructions for the performance and annulment of an act were joined.[136]

---

134. See Cowley (1915, 212 and plate 28), Geller (1985), and Sirat (1985, 121 and plate 76).

135. Shaul Shaked indicates about 2,000 magic Genizah fragments in a list he built, most of them found at the University of Cambridge Library. This list has been recently expanded by Gideon Bohak. For a preliminary survey of this inventory, see Bohak (2010c) and the bibliography in Shaked (2000b). Anthologies of these texts were published by Naveh and Shaked (1987; 1993) and Schäfer and Shaked (1994–1999). More fragments were published by Bellusci (2011), Bohak (2011b; 2012b), Gottheil and Worrel (1972, 106–7), Levene and Bohak (2012), Mann (1972, 2: 91–92, 94) Saar (2007; 2008; 2013), and Schiffman and Swartz (1992, 93–98, 129–30, 160–64). My preference is to include in the instructional literature incantation passages that have not been identified for sure as amulets (through a mention of the client by name and by his or her mother's name or through such phrases as "the bearer of this text" or "the bearer of this amulet"). Some of them, such as those cited in Mann (1972, 2: 94) or Schäfer and Shaked (1994–1999, 2: 264–65), could be ready-made amulets for use by passing clients.

136. On the groups of sorceries included in the list that appears in *Ḥarba de-Moshe*, see Harari (1997b, 126). For additional instances, see, for example, Naveh and Shaked (1993, *Genizah* 11, 3–4 [on fertility, pregnancy, and birth], 24 [two pairs of recipes for two purposes: for expelling crickets from the house and for a scorpion bite]) and

All these recipes have a similar linguistic pattern. Their title, which is often preceded by greater spacing or by a graphic sign visually denoting the beginning of the section, declares their purpose: "for a crying boy," "for hatred," "for a woman who has not become pregnant," "for a spirit stirring in the body," "for depriving an officer of his rank," "for a woman to follow you," "for the opening of the heart" (i.e., for improving one's study and memory), and so forth. Another linguistic pattern common in recipe titles is, "if you wish to/that" plus the purpose of the act, such as, "if you wish the earth (meaning a distance) to shorten before you," "if you wish to walk on water without your leg drowning," "if you wish to see the sun," and "if you wish to kill a person."[137] They are followed by performance instructions in imperative, male, singular wordings, such as "take," "give," "write," and "immerse."[138] These instructions detail the acts to be performed (including the determination of the time, the place, the materials of the sorcery, and the order of the actions), the words and the names to be uttered or written, and the magic signs—the *charactēres*—that sometimes accompany them.[139] These instructions sometimes open

---

Schäfer and Shaked (1994–1999, 1: 58–59 [four recipes for love]; 1: 136–38 [two pairs of recipes on matters of knowledge—for finding a thief and for interpreting a dream—and a pair of recipes for turning hatred into love]; 3: 145–47 [two recipes for returning a fugitive, three for fishing a big fish. The correct order of the pages there should be 1b, 1a, 2a, 2b]).

137. Examples of the first pattern are taken from several sources. Examples of the second pattern are all from *Ḥarba de-Moshe*, where this is the prevalent pattern in both Hebrew and Aramaic.

138. Jewish magic literature bears no trace of the widespread image of women as witches and is worded entirely in male language. A claim could be made that male-gendered formulations are meant as gender-neutral ones (although this claim seems unpersuasive to me) or that women had an oral magic tradition. My view is that the accusation of witchcraft hurled at women is anchored in a historical reality unrelated to women's ritual involvement but touching on gender relationships in the accusing society. Its sources lie in the male desire for social hegemony and in the fear of threatening female power, which is labeled dangerous and illegitimate. On this matter in the context of the Second Temple and rabbinic literature, see chapters 6 and 7.

139. The *charactēres*, which are also known as ring letters, are made up of a combination of lines with circles at their ends. They originated in the Greco-Roman world and were also widespread in Christian and Muslim magic. For their function in Hellenistic magic, see, for example, Frankfurter (1994, 205–11) and Gager (1992, 10–11).

with a description of a preliminary ceremony of purification to be performed by the adjurer to ensure success and may end with a general requirement, such as "do this in purity and you will succeed" (Plates 18–20).

Many recipes also include, usually at the end, a recommendation bearing on their quality and their proven powers through wordings such as "tested and proven," "clear and absolutely true," "good and proper and tested and true." This evaluation, when accompanying a recipe, highlights its special quality, according to the book's author (or whoever he copied the recipe from). In some books, however, such evaluations are so common that almost all the suggested actions are highly recommended. In such cases, what we witness is the style of the author, whose professional personality is imposed on all the material collected and edited in the book.[140]

Books also differ in the complexity of the suggested rituals and in the detail concerning their mode of performance. *Ḥarba de-Moshe* and *Sefer ha-Razim* are good examples of recipes that differ in what appears to be their authors' professional style. *Ḥarba de-Moshe* suggests simple actions, at times merely uttering a few holy names (but only following a three-day purification ritual!). *Sefer ha-Razim* details at great length complex rituals that often require unusual materials and performance at unusual times and places. Magic rituals often differ in the details of the

---

They were named after the Greek term χαρακτῆρες, which was distorted over the course of time. In the Middle Ages they were also known as the Alpha Betha of Metatron, angels' script, and *setumot*. In *Sefer ha-Razim* they are called *karakṭerim* and *kalakṭerim* (M. Margalioth 1966, 4, 83–87). In the Genizah we find *kalakṭiraya'* (Naveh and Shaked 1993, 148, 196). When the word was no longer understood, it was split into two (*kol qṭiraya'*, "all the knots"), and thus the following version emerged: "You, all the holy knots" (*'atun kol qṭiraya' qadishaya'*) (Naveh and Shaked 1987, 216–17). In the Muslim world these signs were sometimes called *qalafṭeriat*. For a discussion of this and other similar terms, see Winkler (1930, 160–63). On these and other magic signs in Jewish magic, see Bohak (2008, 270–78; 2011a). On their meaning as the angels' alphabet in a brief treatise from the circle of the medieval rabbi Neḥemia ben Shlomo (the prophet from Erfurt), see Idel (2006) and Weinstock (1982).

140. See, for example, Schäfer and Shaked (1994–1999, 1: 135–39). On the linguistic pattern of recipe books, see also Schäfer (1990, 85).

performance instructions and in the required modes of performance. In such cases, however, when the rituals in a particular treatise are characterized by a similar performative style, differences not only touch on specific details but also extend to the professional style of the magicians who wrote them. Let me demonstrate with the following three examples of recipes.

The first recipe is brief and simple.

For pain in the stomach and for pain in the intestines, say over water from YYHQLTYH until YYSWSWGYH and he should drink (it).[141]

The second recipe, of "proven" effectiveness, is more complex.

For a theft. If you suspect that a man has stolen something from you but you do not know who took it, if you know the names of the suspects, take clay of the kind used to make pottery and write the suspects' names on paper, each one separately, according to the number of the suspects. And make as many rolls from the clay as there are written names of the suspects, and place the name of each suspect in a roll, and the roll should be (shaped) like a nut. And put all the rolls in a recipient full of water, in a bowl or a glass, and say over the glass containing the rolls the entire psalm, "A Maskil of Asaf. Give ear, O my people, to my Torah" (Psalms 78), and you will then see the roll containing the written name of the thief splitting into two or three, and the written text will be floating on the water. You should catch him because [he] is the thief. And this is a great wonder because the roll containing the written name of the thief will split and others will not. And this is true.[142]

---

141. Harari (2012b, 84, sec. 22). The words "from YYHQLTYH until YYSWSW-GYH" refer to a precise sequence of names in the magic sword of names that is specified in the second part of the work. On this method of the author of *Ḥarba de-Moshe*, see Harari (1997b, 115–21, 129–31).

142. Schäfer and Shaked (1994–1999, 1: 136–37).

The third recipe is detailed and hard to perform, and at the end is a sign
of its success.

> If you wish to turn the king's opinion to your favor, or (that of)
> the chief of the army, or a rich man, or a ruler, or a judge of a
> city, or all the citizens of the state, or (if you wish to turn to your
> favor) the heart of a great or wealthy woman, or the heart of a
> beautiful woman, (do this). Take a lion cub and slaughter it with
> a bronze knife and catch its blood and tear out its heart and put
> its blood in the midst (of the heart) and write the names of these
> (above mentioned) angels in blood upon the skin between its
> eyes; then wash it out with wine three years old and mix (the
> wine) with the blood. And take three of the chief spices, istor-
> gon and myrrh and musk,[143] and stand clean and pure, facing
> the star Venus and put the spices on the fire; then take in your
> hand the cup in which are the wine and the blood and call on[144]
> the name of the overseer and the names of the angels of this
> encampment. (Do this) twenty-one times over the blood and
> over the wine and say to the star Venus, the name, which is
> Aphrodite . . . and the angel Ḥasdiel: I adjure you in the name
> of the angels of the fourth encampment who serve QLMY' that
> you bring around for me (the heart of) King N and the heart of
> his army and the heart of his ministers (and put them under) my
> hand, I, N son of N, and I will find favor and mercy before him
> and he will do my wish and desire whenever I ask (anything)
> from him." And when you finish repeating the adjuration twenty-
> one times, look up and you will see (something) like a coal of
> fire descending into the blood and wine.[145]

The importance of the magic recipe literature lies in its trove of
information concerning all performative aspects of magic. First, it
exposes the strains and aspirations that Jews in antiquity and the early

---

143. On these spices, see M. Margalioth (1966, 11, 73), Morgan (1983, 33), and
Rebiger and Schäfer (2009, 2: 216–17).

144. In the original, "and say and call," which is apparently a scribal mistake.

145. M. Margalioth (1966, 73–74).

Islamic period tried to deal with through this practice, revealing the broad spectrum of life realms where these emerged and attesting to the deep penetration of magic into the daily life of this Jewish society. Second, it exposes the range of means in use in this society to attain ritual power, which was channeled to deal with all these aims: preliminary rituals required from the sorcerer (especially abstention rituals in contexts of sex, food, and impurity as well as immersion, prayer, and adjuration) and elements of the magic ritual itself (the materials required for it, its time and place, the actions to be performed, the mode of uttering or writing the adjurations and their wording, the mode of using performative artifacts, and other such matters). Finally, it points to the supernatural entities that the sorcerer seeks to suppress or enlist into action through his charms and to the worldview in whose context this action is considered possible.

Some of these aspects can also be found to a lesser extent in the performative artifacts, as noted earlier. Others, as will be shown, are discussed at great length in the literary framework of the magic treatises. The recipes' unique contribution is the broad scope they present to the reader of the detailed ritual acts involved in implementing the adjurations. The quantity and diversity of the magic recipes—the breadth and vast amount of information they hold—add to the information found in the performative artifacts concerning the language and the aims of the adjurations. Contrary to these artifacts, however, which are products of actual magic activity, we cannot be sure that the magic instructions of the guidebooks were indeed ever implemented. Yet I find no reason to assume that the opposite is true, certainly not as a sweeping assertion.[146] This is a professional literature whose performative contexts have been demonstrated through its parallels in amulets. Hence, even if not every detail of it can be seen as an expression of concrete ritual activity, this literature does reflect the theory of Jewish magic as developed and preserved in circles charged with its realization. Questions such as how to find a young lion or how to use the blood of a man and a woman (to tie

---

146. In light of the evidence collected in recent decades, we can clearly reject hypotheses, such as that of Hen Merchavya, that touch on the pure theoretical interest of the author and copiers of *Sefer ha-Razim* in the book's material (Merchavya 1972).

them in love without their knowledge)[147] or how to determine whether someone wrote on an egg with his semen[148] obviously dictate the terms of the discussion on the possibility of implementing the practice suggested in the recipes. They do not, however, undermine recognition of the professional and substantive level of this literature on the part of those who chose to preserve this information in their books.

This should also be the attitude toward magic deeds whose objectives may appear unreasonable, such as speaking to the dead, shortening voyage distances (*qefiṣat ha-derekh*), walking on water, or speaking with the sun to gather hidden knowledge or to coerce it (as a persona) to act according to the adjurer's will.[149] Although most of the aims suggested in the recipes touch on more mundane matters, we have no reason to assume that no attempts were made to realize desires of this type as well. Magic is a serious professional matter for one who believes in its efficacy and certainly for one applying it for clients who reward such performance with money and gratitude. Even without knowing what part of the professional literature was actually implemented, the potential of aims and actions in Jewish magic culture is widely evident in the magic recipes. The theoretical framework of the magic treatises anchors this potential in a cosmology that grants it internal coherence and rationality.

Magic Treatises

Jewish treatises on magic from the period discussed here split into several groups according to their organizing principle: a methodological-professional principle, a performative nucleus, or a literary structure.[150] Some of them, as will be shown, are broad and well organized, whereas others are fragmented. I briefly review these works according to the suggested division. The division is fundamentally methodological, and some of these works do not entirely fit into it.

---

147. Schäfer and Shaked (1994–1999, 1: 135–36).

148. Naveh and Shaked (1993, 216–17).

149. See Harari (2012b, 90–95, secs. 78, 93, 126) and Morgan (1983, 67–72).

150. All these works have some literary structure, but only in two that are included in the last group—*Sefer ha-Razim* and *Ḥarba de-Moshe*—is this structure the organizing principle of the work and not merely the product of another organizing principle.

The first group, based on the organization of the work around some methodological-professional principle, includes two works and two genres (by genre I refer to a range of works or fragments of works that share the same professional principle and reflect more than one manifestation of it). The genres are the (magical) use of psalms and the (magical) use of the liturgical blessings. The works are *Sheva' Ma'alot* (Seven Steps) and *'Arba'ah Yesodot* (Four Foundations). The organizing principle of the two genres is a systematic use of the canonical texts according to the order of the psalms or of the blessings. The performative use of psalms was already known in Qumran. It is mentioned in both Talmuds and was widespread in Jewish and medieval Christian magic.[151] The uniqueness of the magical literature on the use of psalms in general and of *Sefer Shimush Tehillim* (The Book on the Use of Psalms) in particular lies in the systematic use of the psalms for performing various types of sorcery, in a pattern familiar from the beginning of the second millennium up to the printed versions that are sold today.

Writings on the use of psalms offer a broad range of options for action. A specific psalm (or, at times, a verse from a psalm) is assigned for each purpose and is to be uttered or written as an incantation in a certain, defined ritual context. For example:

> Chapter 33, "Rejoice in the Lord O you righteous," for one who would expel (an evil spirit?),[152] and for a woman whose sons die, write it and whisper it over olive oil and rub it (on her). Chapter 33, "Rejoice in the Lord O you righteous," and Chapter 34, "when he changed his demeanour," two psalms for one who comes before a ruler—utter seven times. And another (use), if you wish to release your friend from pressure, say it and go with him to a distinguished (person). And another, Chapter 34, "when he changed his demeanour," for fever—whisper (it) on olive oil, and he (i.e. the sick) should anoint it. Chapter 35,

---

151. On the antidemonic use of Psalms 3, 29, and 91 in the Babylonian Talmud, see chapter 7. On the Christian use of psalms, see Rebiger (2010, 33–34) and Schäfer and Shaked (1994–1999, 3: 10–13).

152. The original is miswritten. See the parallel versions in Schäfer and Shaked (1994–1999, 3: 214, 242n, 279n).

"Strive, O Lord, with those who contend against me," and Chapter 36, "transgression speaks to the wicked," write them and hide them before the gate of the cattle. And another one, "Strive, O Lord, with those who contend against me," if someone oppresses you or hates you, say it in your prayers three days, three times a day. Chapter 37, "Fret not yourself because of evil doers," if a man is drunk, take a glass of water and salt and say (the psalm) over it and let him drink a bit and pour (the remaining water) on his head and on his face.[153]

Genizah fragments from the use-of-psalms literature reflect two historical layers in the prolonged editing process of *Sefer Shimush Tehillim*, from the tenth century onward. A comparison between these fragments and between them and the versions that were the basis of the first printing (in the mid-sixteenth century) points to a long process of integrating various magic sources onto the structural-systematic scaffold of the use of psalms, intensified by means of adjuration prayers and holy names.[154]

The use of liturgical blessings appears in two patterns: use of the eighteen blessings of the Amidah prayer and use of the seven Sabbath blessings. The first pattern—*Shimush Shemoneh 'Esreh*—consistently and systematically uses the eighteen blessings of the Amidah version that was in use in Palestine (contrary to the Babylonian version, which includes nineteen blessings). This structure, together with the names of the blessings used in this work, attests to its Palestinian source.[155] Each section in the book opens by noting the blessing that is used in it and details the defined ritual framework for its performance. The number eighteen is itself a ritual-performative component in this context, because

153. Schäfer and Shaked (1994–1999, 3: 204–5).

154. For a discussion of the work—its literary components, the history of its editing—see Rebiger (2010, 1–43) and Schäfer and Shaked (1994–1999, 3: 2–17). The manuscripts from this genre were annotated in Schäfer and Shaked (1994–1999, 3: 202–375). Cf. also Schäfer and Shaked (1994–1999, 1: 138–39). See also Barkai (1987, 71–77) and the studies of Bill Rebiger on later redactions of *Sefer Shimush Tehillim* (Rebiger 1999; 2003; 2010).

155. On this matter and on the possible connection between this work and *Hekhalot* literature and its creators, see Schäfer (1996).

the use of the blessing requires that it be recited eighteen times. The purpose of the recipes often fits the contents of the blessing, and in the later and more developed versions of the book, this is a fixed and systematic characteristic of it. Thus the *Gevurot* ("You, who revive the dead") blessing is used to "bring the dead back from his grave," the *Teshuvah* ("delight in repentance") blessing to bring back apostates, the *Ḥonen ha-Daʿat* ("favor man with knowledge") blessing for "opening the heart" (meaning for knowledge, understanding, and recollection), the *'Ohev Ṣedaqah* ("love righteousness and justice") blessing for winning in court, and the *Ha-Minim* ("humble the arrogant") blessing to harm the enemy, and so forth.[156]

The use of the seven Sabbath blessings, set forth in the work known as *Shevaʿ de-'Eliyahu* (Seven [Blessings] of Elijah) or *Shevaʿ Zutarti* (The Minor Seven [Blessings]), is an essentially different work and can also be included in the second category (which includes works organized around a uniting performative nucleus). This is a long adjuration whose aim is "to chase away every spirit and every demon" from the body of its user and, for this purpose, among other incantations and holy names, also includes the seven Sabbath blessings in their order.[157]

The two other works in this group, *Shevaʿ Maʿalot* and *'Arbaʿah Yesodot*, are systematic treatises that tie the magic praxis suggested in them to a theory and organize it accordingly. Fragments from *Shevaʿ Maʿalot* point

---

156. For Genizah fragments of *Shimush Shemoneh 'Esreh*, see Schäfer and Shaked (1994–1999, vol. 2, texts 26, 29). See also Schäfer and Shaked (1994–1999, vol. 2, text 30), which expands the liturgical blessings through the use of names but without suggesting action through them. Cf. also the parallels in Ms Michael 9 (=Ms Oxford, Bodleian Library 1531), and see also Ms Bibliothèque de Genève, Comites Latentes 145 (formerly Sassoon 290), pp. 265–67 (secs. 627–647). These manuscript versions of the work are broader and more complete than those in the Genizah fragments. The examples of the blessings' purposes are from Ms Bibliothèque de Genève, except for the first, which is from Schäfer and Shaked (1994–1999, 2: 103).

157. Schäfer and Shaked (1994–1999, vol. 2, texts 22–24). Some of these fragments were first published in Schäfer (1984, 140–51). For a discussion of this work, see Lesses (1998, 260–78) and Schäfer (1996). On the use of the liturgical blessings, see also Schäfer and Shaked (1994–1999, 2: 1–14) and Schäfer (1990, 80–81). The use of the Amidah prayer and its blessings is also mentioned in *Ḥarba de-Moshe*. See Harari (2012b, 90, sec. 77; 95, sec. 127). Also see Harari (1997b, 25, 98–99).

to the organization of the work according to the order of the *ma'alot* (steps or strata) containing holy names, from the first onward, suggesting use of the names according to this order. The texts available are fragmented and the information they contain too limited to afford a perspective on the broad theoretical context of these steps and on the general structure of the work.[158]

'Arba'ah Yesodot opens with a clarification of the "four foundations that exist in the world"—a name in purity, a name in impurity, conjuring, and witchcraft—and their place in the ethical system.[159] A name in purity and conjuring are "good," their ways (or they themselves) are "solemn," they "entail no transgression" and they "will only be found in the hand of one who is experienced in abstinence, innocent, and upright before his Lord, and who is clean and pure all his days." A name in impurity and witchcraft are "bad," their ways (or they themselves) are "heedless," "one who carries them out them is liable to *karet*," and "you will find them in the hand of every bad man and bad woman." The writer bemoans the fact that the substitutes of the names (*kinuyim*) of the "foundations" are known to people but that "their very essence and the way to carry them out are far removed from them."[160] This is precisely the task he sets himself (regardless of the moral value of the *yesodot*).

I will begin by explaining several deeds you may do by a name in purity and what is its power to control, and after that I will

---

158. See Schäfer and Shaked (1994–1999, 2: 105 [2b], 119–20 [1a–b]).

159. The Karaite Daniel al-Qumisi refers to the use of "a pure name and an impure name" (*shem tahor ve-shem tame'*) as a Rabbanite sorcery. Ya'qub al-Qirqisani ascribes to the Rabbanites a belief in the power of a "name of purity" (*shem taharah*) and a "name of impurity" (*shem tum'ah*). See the discussion in chapter 6. According to the work known as *'Inyan Sotah*, "a name in purity and a name in impurity" (*shem be-taharah ve-shem be-tum'ah*) had been known "to the Sanhedrin of Israel, which were familiar with the seventy names (of God), and a name in purity and a name in impurity, and (concerning) all the main deeds (based on these names) they knew everything" (Schäfer and Shaked 1994–1999, 1: 19, 32). "[Members of] the Sanhedrin of Israel" are also mentioned in the treatise *'Arba'ah Yesodot* as knowers of names (Schäfer and Shaked 1994–1999, 1: 69).

160. Schäfer and Shaked (1994–1999, 1: 46–54). Cf. Schäfer and Shaked (1994–1999, 1: 57 [T.-S. K1.37, 1a–1b]).

return to explain a name in impurity, several deeds you may do . . . and what is its power [to control and then], I will return to explain the other two sides, that of conj[uring] . . . wit[chcraft] and what are the deeds regarding it, so that you will know and understand each and every way of all these.[161]

Some possibilities for using these names are given fragmentarily in this passage of the work, but so far we lack a full version of it that would point to a systematic division of the purposes of use according to the four *yesodot*.

The second group of works, including works with a unifying performative nucleus, can be split into two: works that focus on one particular action, which are actually no more than one long and particularly complex recipe; and works that essentially detail one linguistic formula through which several aims, or even any desired goal, can be attained. The first group includes works such as *Sheva' de-'Eliyahu*, which deals with protection from demons and spirits and their removal from the adjurer's body, and *'Inyan Soṭah* or *'Eseq Soṭah* (The Praxis Concerning the Adulteress). This brief work suggests a magic test, an alternative to the biblical one, for testing a woman who is suspected of adultery (the defiled woman in Numbers 5:11–31) for when "we have no priest and no holy water and no Tabernacle."[162] First, it clarifies:

Know and understand that, if a man at this time is God-fearing, cleanses his soul from sin and wickedness and steps in the path

---

161. Schäfer and Shaked (1994–1999, 1: 69). The quoted passages are from two additional fragments of the work found in Schäfer and Shaked (1994–1999, 1: 47–48, 57–58). Schäfer and Shaked draw a distinction between the two parallel passages from the opening mentioned here last (T.-S. K1.2, T.-S. K1.37) and the first (JTSL ENA 2643.6–7), and saw them as passages from separate works (Schäfer and Shaked 1994–1999, 1: 8). My view is that these are fragments from the same work or, at least, from the same magic genre.

162. Schäfer and Shaked (1994–1999, 1: 20). See the entire text and the discussion in Schäfer and Shaked (1994–1999, 1: 15–28, 32 [passage 1b]). See also Schäfer (1996, 541–44), Swartz (2002, 307–11), and Veltri (1993). A hint at the existence of an alternative ritual to the biblical test appears also in *Megilat 'Aḥima'aṣ* (The Scroll of Aḥima'az, from mid-eleventh-century Italy). See Harari (2006b).

of purity—purity in his body and purity in his flesh—and takes care of these names and amends his soul through [the]se paths, he resembles an angel and a High Priest. Whatever he does will not go without consequences.[163]

The writer thereby takes this ritual away from the priesthood (as demanded in the Bible) and solves the problem of the professional mediation required for its performance by pointing to an available substitute. A replacement was also found for the material components of the test.

Instead of the required holy water, take flowing water from a flowing source in a new recipient, and instead of the Tabernacle dust, go to the synagogue and take dust from the four corners of the temple of Torah.[164]

The replacement of the biblical curse with an adjuration that relies on it but closely corresponds, in its style in general and in its use of holy names in particular, to the incantation common in the magic literature completes the alternative ritual. The author thus sets a new course for dealing with the suspected woman. On the one hand, he completely ignores the (broad) halakhic discussion of this issue in the Mishnah and both Talmuds and returns directly to the Bible. On the other hand, he omits from the biblical ritual all the elements that are not related to the technical-performative operation of the incantation. He thereby sets up a viable magical alternative to the biblical test for the *Soṭah*.

Another work in this group is *Havdalah de-Rabbi Aqiva*. Gershom Scholem, who annotated the work based on Ashkenazic manuscripts from the fourteenth–sixteenth centuries, describes it as a product of a haphazard compilation of various issues originating in Babylonia during the Geonic period or even before.[165] Note also that the work includes

---

163. Schäfer and Shaked (1994–1999, 1: 20).

164. Schäfer and Shaked (1994–1999, 1: 20).

165. Scholem (1981). On the geographic and historical origin of this text, see Scholem (1981, 245–46). Hannu Juusola (2004) points to linguistic closeness between the Aramaic dialect widespread in Babylonian incantation bowls and the Aramaic sections of *Havdalah de-Rabbi Aqiva*.

several Palestinian traditions and that in its current form, all these elements have been compiled into a long and detailed adjuration writ meant to protect and heal the user of the *Havdalah* from harm by demons, spirits, and harmful witchcraft—all mutually connected issues.[166] The opening of the work sets the ritual context required for the successful performance of the incantation in terms of time, place, audience, and the purity status of the person and the artifact in the ceremony of uttering the required text over the cup. Its ending details the ritual acts required, after its uttering, for its successful operation in the patient's healing. The compilation date of the magic traditions appearing in the volume in the form available to us is unknown, and thus so far, deciding whether it was compiled in Babylonia, later in Italy, or perhaps even in Ashkenaz, is impossible.

The work *Pishra' de-Rabbi Ḥanina ben Dosa* also belongs in the category of works that focus on one particular action. This adjuration work is found almost complete in fourteenth- and fifteenth-century manuscripts, but an earlier fragment of it was also found in the Cairo

---

166. On Palestinian elements in the work, see Harari (2001, 35). The purpose of the work is explained at its end: "And after he finishes reciting this *havdalah*, he should let the sick drink from it . . . and say . . . thus should all the maladies of N son of N leave him and never ever return to him" (Scholem 1981, 281). The wording of the adjurations attests to the connection between sickness and harmful witchcraft or demonic attack. The opening of the work mentions additional purposes, among them, "for one removed from his wife and for opening the heart" (Ms Oxford, Bodleian Library, 1539 is far more detailed). Magic literature shows that all the issues mentioned are related to harmful sorcery and to demonic afflictions. On harmful magic aimed at inflicting sexual impotence ("for one removed from his wife"), see Ratzaby (1992). "Opening the heart," meaning improving the ability to learn, recollect, and understand, is mentioned at the opening of the *Havdalah de-Rabbi Aqiva* as a result of the inclusion of an adjuration of Potah, the prince of forgetfulness (*Sar ha-Shikheḥah*) at its end. In this context, the editing of the *Havdalah de-Rabbi Aqiva* may hint at an approach whereby harm to the intellectual ability, which the opening of the heart is meant to take care of, is also a result of harmful sorcery. Recipes for such an injury are indeed known. See, for example, Harari (2012b, 96, sec. 129). In any event, the recommendations at the opening are hard to reconcile with the instructions at the end, and the recommendations, in all their different versions in the manuscripts, do not seem to be part of the work's original editing but are rather additions by later copiers (cf. Scholem 1981, 248).

Genizah.[167] This work, which apparently originated in Babylonia in the Geonic period and which is specifically concerned with healing, is a good example of a discharge text, that is, an adjuration meant to annul and grant release from a harmful sorcery. At the opening, after the title that attests to its name, is a request or demand for healing: "May healing from heaven be granted to N, son of N, so that he shall be healed soon, through heavenly mercy." This is followed by a detailed enumeration of many kinds of fever, spirits, injurers, evil sorceries, bindings, knots, satans, liliths, and so forth whose effects the adjurer seeks to annul, remove from his body, and be healed from. The possibility is then raised that the distress originates in "an act and a knot that were performed against him, N, son of N." The gist of the incantation is a long and detailed explanation of such a possible act, noting dozens of options for its performance according to three criteria: the place of the act, the means used, and the time of the performance.

The last criterion takes up more than half the work and includes four possible time references—the day of the week, the day of the month, the month, and the influence of stars—each one fully specified in rigorous detail. Each possibility of the supposed action is formulated in the same terms: If on T (indication of the time possibility), it (the sorcery) was done to him, (angel) X will release and untie him. For example: "And if on the fourth day of the week it was done to him, Gabriel will release and untie him . . . and if in (the month) Tamuz and Scorpion it was done to him, Ḥasdiel will release and untie him . . . and if on the hour of Venus it was done to him, Arbiel will release and untie him."[168] A systematic and detailed list is thereby attained, tying angels to (mainly) times or modes of witchcraft performance. The rigorous specification of demons and evildoers on the one hand and of potential harmful sorceries on the other is meant to untangle any (magic) knot tied against the client, to unravel any witchcraft cast upon him or her, to release the client from any possible foreign control, and thus to heal him or her.

Three broad adjurations in *Hekhalot* and *Merkavah* literature also belong to this group: the adjuration of the Prince of Torah (*Sar ha-Torah*),

---

167. For the later manuscripts, see Bohak (2014a, 1: 229–31) and Tocci (1984; 1986). On the Genizah fragment, see Schäfer and Shaked (1994–1999, 2: 30–31).

168. Tocci (1986, 103–4).

the adjuration of the Prince of Presence (*Sar ha-Panim*), and the adjuration of the Prince of Dream (*Sar ha-Ḥalom*). The adjuration of *Sar ha-Torah* concerns swift and exhaustive study of the Torah by using the Prince (angel) of the Torah. The adjuration of *Sar ha-Panim* is designed to bring down the Prince of Presence to earth, to reveal to the adjurers whatever they wish. The adjuration of *Sar ha-Ḥalom* is meant to bring about the revelation of the Prince of Dream, in order to learn from him during sleep. To preserve the unity of the discussion, I present these works in detail in chapter 6 when dealing with *Hekhalot* and *Merkavah* literature.

The use of one formula for several purposes—the second type of works with a unifying performative nucleus—is clarified in the two brief works known as *Sefer ha-Yashar* (The Book of the Right [Way]) and *Sefer ha-Malbush* (The Book of the [Magic] Dress). These two works, which are linked by textual and conceptual ties, were created in the course of an editing process and perhaps in a prolonged process of elaboration, thickening, and tying of magic, angelological, astrological, and liturgical elements of unknown dating. Passages from these works, or from the elements on which they are based, have been preserved in manuscripts from the first half of the twelfth century in the Cairo Genizah, but in their more developed and complete version they are found mainly in manuscripts from the sixteenth century onward.[169] As I show in chapter 6, *Sefer ha-Yashar* is mentioned as a book of magic by the Karaite Daniel al-Qumisi and by Rav Hai Gaon. In his genealogical chart (written in Italy in the mid-eleventh century) R. Aḥimaʿaz b. Paltiel mentions it together with *Sod ha-Merkavah* (The Secret of the Merkavah) and with knowledge of mysteries as part of the celebrated esoteric knowledge of his ancestors in Oria, southern Italy.[170] Clearly, then, a magic book by this name had been known in Babylonia from at least the ninth century,

---

169. For critical editions of these works and extensive discussion of their textual history, see Wandrey (2004).

170. Bonfil (2009, 237). In this context the work is also mentioned later, in Midrash *Leqaḥ Tov*: "No one should wonder about the *hekhalot* of R. Ishmael and about the words of R. Aqiva who, in *Sefer ha-Yashar*, talk about the act concerning the chariot (*maʿaseh merkavah*), since all are clear to one who understands that all are powers and glories of the Creator" (Midrash *Leqaḥ Tov* on Deuteronomy 4:12 [vol. 2, 14]).

but we cannot determine what version of it was known to them and what of that version can be found in the version available to us. *Sefer ha-Malbush* is not mentioned in sources older than the Genizah writings, but its origin could also be in Babylonia or Palestine in the late first millennium CE. If so, these mystical-magic traditions were probably conveyed by migrants from Babylonia to Italy at the turn of the first and the second millennia and from there found their way to circles of Ashkenaz pietists who elaborated, edited, and preserved them in their writings.[171]

In its complete version, *Sefer ha-Yashar* details a purification ritual and the use of a complex holy name made up from many biblical verses for the attainment of the many aims specified in it: ruling over predatory animals and poisonous reptiles, the sun and the moon, and spirits and demons; freezing the sea; putting out a fire; victory in battle; and so forth. Furthermore, it specifies at length magic, astral, and angelological information that includes the names of the angels who rule during the four seasons; the names of the sun, the moon, the sky, the earth, the winds, and the sea at these times; and the names of the hours and the angels in charge of these seasons. This information is necessary for the successful performance of adjurations according to the time, place, and purpose requested. God's help, which is also required to "one who wishes to utilize the great name," is enlisted by means of a long prayer "that he should recite before the ark having washed with water at dawn before sunrise." The idea of wearing the holy name, which is the gist of *Torat ha-Malbush*, is mentioned in *Sefer ha-Yashar* but is not its main terminological or substantive concern.[172] Part of this work, as noted, was found in a Genizah fragment and, at least in this part, the later version is close to the early one.

Sefer ha-Malbush is now available in two different, though not wholly unrelated versions. One version, *Torat ha-Malbush*, part of which is found in the Cairo Genizah in a manuscript from the first half of the twelfth century, is a recipe for writing "a holy and pure name" on a gold plate (*ṣiṣ*). The adjurer must tie the plate to his neck after performing rigorous purification rituals, whose success is recurrently confirmed through a figure that appears on the water. If this figure is seen, the adjurer will be

---

171. See Wandrey (2004, 8–19).

172. For the edition of the work, see Wandrey (2004, 200–205).

able to use the power he has gained for any desired purpose. The other version, *Sefer ha-Malbush*, is apparently a medieval Ashkenazic development of traditions close to *Torat ha-Malbush*. This work suggests preparing a vellum attire, which includes a wrapping for the top part of the body down to the hips and a hat that is tied to it. The holy name should be written on the front and the back of this "coat of righteousness" and on the hat in a circle, and "better yet, make a gold plate (*ṣiṣ*) and write the name on it." Here too meticulous purification ritual preparations are required before wearing the garment, and the rituals attached to its wearing are specified. In this case the garment's user is granted power "to make the rain fall and the wind blow" or to fight his enemies with the help of a "great and powerful troop" of angels who will be seen by them but not by him. These angels can be employed for seven days, once every day, for a period of three or four hours. This (relatively late) version of *Sefer ha-Malbush*, however, exceeds the scope of the current study.[173]

The third group of magic works, where the prominent organizing principle is the literary structure, includes two large treatises: *Sefer ha-Razim* (The Book of Mysteries) and *Ḥarba de-Moshe* (The Sword of Moses). Despite the significant differences between these works, both show strong evidence of an author or editor who attempted to integrate the magic recipes he had compiled (some of them probably originating in earlier compilations) into a comprehensive theory of magic. The integration of these recipes creates a text with a clear and consistent structure, which leads the reader from beginning to end, and enriches it not only with magic means of action but also with extensive theoretical knowledge. In these works too the main purpose is to convey the practical information contained in them. Contrary to recipe books and to the smaller volumes, however, these works also show signs of a broader

---

173. For versions of *Torat ha-Malbush* and *Sefer ha-Malbush*, see Wandrey (2004, 97–182). On the editing of these works, see also Wandrey (2004, 30–32). On the ritual of the wearing of the name, see Wandrey (2004, 41–96). On the gold plate in Jewish magic, see Swartz (2001b). Scholem holds that *Sefer ha-Malbush* originated in Babylonia at the beginning of the Geonic period and that its sources are even earlier (Scholem 1990, 20, 180; cf. Alexander 1986, 344–45). Wandrey's text criticism, however, denotes that two separate works existed, only one of which (*Torat ha-Malbush*) was included within the time and place constraints discussed here.

notion that touches on conceptual aspects of magic no less than on the performative ones, particularly on a magic that places the theoretical aspect at the center of the work's general structure.[174]

In its printed version *Sefer ha-Razim* is a mosaic-like work, compiling fragments from many manuscripts, a highly skillful endeavor by Mordechai Margalioth. Most of the manuscripts that Margalioth's edition relies on were found in the Cairo Genizah. The rest are later and more complete. Bill Rebiger and Peter Schäfer, in their recent synoptic edition of the available manuscripts of *Sefer ha-Razim*, which includes dozens of Genizah fragments and a few later redactions and is accompanied by a profound study of the text and the history of its redactions, have considerably expanded the textual basis for the study of this work and its variant copies.[175] But despite their intensive search into the textual history of this book, they could not find even one ancient manuscript containing the entire printed version or even a large part of it. Hence, even though Margalioth's work is consistent and generally persuasive, we must beware of the illusion that the final result reflects an ancient version, identical in its contents or scope to the first one that appeared in print.[176] This limitation and the critiques concerning textual imprecisions in Margalioth's edition[177] compel great caution regarding *Sefer ha-Razim*. Nevertheless, they cannot preclude the assumption that underlying all the passages collected from the many manuscripts is an ancient Jewish magic work, with clear and defined textual and literary characteristics.

---

174. The makeup of *'Arba'ah Yesodot* seems to resemble this description and should perhaps be included in this group. The fragmented version that has reached us, however, is insufficient to understand the general structure and the scope of the information included in it, beyond the reference to four *yesodot* and a few magic acts related to them.

175. Rebiger and Schäfer (2009). My interest is in version I.

176. On the editing and the manuscripts at its basis, see M. Margalioth (1966, ix–xvi, 47–51). For reservations about the mosaic-like character of Margalioth's edition and the version of the text that he annotated, see Gruenwald (1980, 226–27), Merchavya (1967, 301–2), Niggermeyer (1975, 16–17), and Schäfer (1988, 15). Philip Alexander holds that it is entirely justified to believe that a work such as that Margalioth constructed did exist once (Alexander 1986, 349; 2003b, 172). For an English translation of Margalioth's redaction of *Sefer ha-Razim*, see Morgan (1983).

177. Gruenwald (1980, 226–27, notes 6–7).

Sefer ha-Razim draws together cosmological, angelological, astrological, and magic elements and organizes them, in a fluent Hebrew register, into a text containing seven parts that correlate to the seven firmaments. The work opens with a preface that ties together a tradition of delivering magic knowledge with praise of its wonders. According to the preface, the entire work is celestial knowledge that was given to Noah by the angel Raziel. Noah wrote it down and placed it in a gold cabinet.

And he learned from it how to do wondrous deeds, and (he learned) secrets of knowledge, and categories of understanding and thoughts of humility and concepts of counsel, (how) to master the investigation of the strata of the heavens, to go about in all that is in their seven abodes, to observe all the astrological signs, to examine the course of the sun, to explain the observations of the moon, and to know the paths of the Great Bear, Orion, and the Pleiades, to declare the names of the overseers of each and every firmament and the realms of their authority, and by what means they (can be made to) cause success in each thing (asked of them), and what are the names of their attendants and what (oblations) are to be poured out to them, and what is the proper time (at which they will hear prayer, so as) to perform every wish of anyone (who comes) near them in purity. (Noah learned) from it acts of death and acts of life, to understand the evil and the good, to search out seasons and moments, to know the time of giving birth and the time of dying, the time of striking and the time of healing, (and he learned) to interpret dreams and visions, to arouse combat, and to quiet wars, and to rule over spirits and over demons, to send them so they will go like slaves, to watch the four winds of the earth, to be learned in the speech of thunderclaps, to tell the significance of lightning flashes, to foretell what will happen in each and every month, and to know the affairs of each and every year, whether it will be for plenty or for hunger, whether for harvest or for draught, whether for peace or for war, to be as one of the awesome ones and to comprehend the songs of heaven.[178]

---

178. M. Margalioth (1966, 65–66). Cf. Morgan (1983, 17–18). An additional version of the preface appears in a partial copy of it that Margalioth had not been

After leaving the Ark, Noah used the book throughout his life, and at the time of his death,

> he handed it down to Abraham, and Abraham to Isaac, and Isaac to Jacob, and Jacob to Levi, and Levi to Kohath, and Kohath to Amram, and Amram to Moses, and Moses to Joshua, and Joshua to the elders, and the elders to the prophets, and the prophets to the sages, and thus generation by generation until Solomon the King arose. And the Books of the Mysteries were disclosed to him and he became very learned in books of understanding, and (so) ruled over everything he desired, over all the spirits and the demons that wander in the world, and from the wisdom of this book he bound and released, and sent out and brought in, and built and prospered. For many books were handed down to him, but this one was found more precious and honorable and strong than any of them.[179]

The list of possible uses of the information in the book, which is suggested in the preface, does not overlap its contents. It does match it when it mentions such issues as knowledge about the existence of overseers in the firmaments and the names of their attendants, what oblations will be poured out to them and at what times in order to activate them, and its repeated demand of purity. But although the preface deals at length with many questions that are never mentioned in the book, it also disregards important areas of action, such as love and healing, which the book does refer to. Essentially, this list is a combination of angelological, astral, and mundane knowledge—the revelation of mysteries in heaven and their divination on earth. Notes on such knowledge are widespread in the Apocrypha, and *Sefer ha-Razim* may have originated in a close tradition.[180] Its author combines characteristic realms of desired knowledge

---

aware of, on the margins of pages 16–17 in Ms Bibliothèque de Genève, Comites Latentes 145.

179. M. Margalioth (1966, 66). Cf. Morgan (1983, 19).

180. M. Margalioth (1966, 56–57). Mysteries and their revelation are a key issue in the Apocrypha, the Qumran scrolls, and *Hekhalot* and *Merkavah* literature. See, for example, Elior (2004b, passim) and Gruenwald (1988, 65–123). On lists of mystical knowledge revealed to the chosen, see Stone (1976).

with technical matters related to the activation of angels (which are mentioned in the work) and ties all of them together in a tradition of delivery meant to anchor the knowledge offered in the work to a heavenly source, thus investing it with the authority of truth.[181] Unfortunately, control of demons, for example, which is twice mentioned in the preface, never appears in the work itself! On this basis, then, we must assume either that the work available to us is not complete and that some of the actions suggested in it are missing from the available manuscripts, or that the preface was added by some copier-editor after the stage of collecting and editing the magic materials in the body of the work.[182]

Sefer ha-Razim has seven chapters, according to the ascending order of seven firmaments. Each chapter opens with the description of the firmament, which includes details from various realms. (1) What is in the firmament. For example, the second firmament has "frost and fog and treasuries of snow"; the third firmament has "storerooms of mist from which the winds go forth, and inside it are encampments of thunder from which lightning emanates"; the fourth firmament "is pitched upon a storm wind, and stands on pillars of fire, and is held up by crowns of flame, and full of treasuries of strength"; the sixth firmament's "storehouses are full of honey. Within is the place prepared for the spirits of the righteous."[183] (2) The inner structure of the firmament, for example, the number of the *ma'alot* (stairs), meaning its inner strata and the angelic camps that populate it. (3) The glory, the might, and the awe of the angels dwelling in the firmament. For example, "encampments filled with wrath"; "angels of fire and angels of trembling and spirits of terror and spirits of dread"; "they are like fire in their strength and their voices are like the roar of a peal of thunder. And their eyes are like sunbeams, and they rule over the wheels of flame and fire. They have wings to fly, the whinnying of their mouths is as horses, their appearance like torches; when they speak

---

181. As we know, the rabbis also anchored their teachings in a similar tradition (M. *Avot* 1:1). On delivery traditions in mystical-magic writings, see Swartz (1996, 173–205).

182. A third option—the author who collected and edited the sorceries suggested in the work wrote a preface far removed from its contents—appears much less plausible to me.

183. M. Margalioth (1966, 81, 92, 96, 104). Cf. Morgan (1983, 43, 61, 67, 77).

and tremble, they roar and flutter, they soar in every direction and fly to every corner (of the world)"; "the angels of water, their bodies like the sea and their voices like the voice of waters."[184] (4) The hierarchical order in which the angels are arranged in their encampments under the *shotrim* (overseers) who control each stratum. The names of the first three firmaments—*Shamayim*, *Shmei ha-Shamayim*, and *Ma'on*—are also given. This setting of firmaments and angels, with all its components, is close to the common conception of the heavenly world, which is specified at length in *Hekhalot* and *Merkavah* literature. Its roots are in traditions of apocryphal visions and, prominent among them, the descriptions of heavenly voyages in *1 Enoch* and *2 Enoch* and the Syriac *Apocalypse of Baruch*.[185]

After describing the firmament, enumerating its stairs, and presenting the overseers and their encampments, the author moves on to the practical part. First, he enumerates the names of the overseers and the angels that serve them. He then notes the potential uses of these angels and describes in detail the rituals required for this purpose. These include preliminary purification rituals and rituals for activating and releasing the angels after the act. Most rituals are complex; some are complicated and hard to perform. Performance instructions are strict and touch on dimensions of time, place, materials, actions, and the adjuration formula. The adjurations always include the names of the angels (which were mentioned previously) whom the sorcerer seeks to control.[186]

The seven literary units are not equal in size, and they progressively shrink the higher the number of the firmament. Thus the first firmament includes many strata and many actions for various goals: healing, harm, knowledge of the future, favor, success with the authorities, love, speaking with the sun, necromancy, sending spirits on to act, bringing back a thief or a slave who escaped, knowledge of a person's thoughts, and interpreting dreams. By contrast, the sixth firmament offers only

184. M. Margalioth (1966, 67, 81, 92, 96). Cf. Morgan (1983, 21, 43, 61, 67–68).

185. On these and other visions in the pseudepigraphic literature, see Dean-Otting (1984), Gruenwald (1980, 29–72), and M. Himmelfarb (1993). On the firmaments and angelology in the *Hekhalot* literature, see, for example, Dan (1996) and Elior (1993).

186. On the magic practice of *Sefer ha-Razim*, cf. Janowitz (2002, 85–108).

one option: "If you wish to go on a journey (or) to war and if you wish to return (safely) from the war or from the journey, or (if you wish) to flee from the city and you want it to appear that a large and powerful company is with you, so that all who see you will be afraid of you, as of one who has with him a military escort armed with swords and spears and all of the implements of battle."[187] The seventh heaven is exceptional. This is God's dwelling.

> He alone sits in the heaven of His holiness, seeking out judgment, evening the scales of justice, judging the truth and speaking in righteousness. And before Him books of fire are open, and from before Him flow rivers of fire. When he rises the gods are afraid, and when He roars the pillars shake, and from his voice the doorposts tremble. His soldiers stand before Him but they do not gaze upon His likeness for He is hidden from every eye and none can see Him and live. . . . He sits on a throne of light and light is a wall around Him. The *ḥayot* and *'ophanim* bear Him up as they fly with their wings. . . . Troops upon troops stand one above another before Him and immerse themselves in rivers of purity and wrap themselves in garments of white fire and sing with humility in a strong voice: Holy Holy Holy is the lord of Hosts, the whole world is full of His glory.[188]

This is the place for the celestial worship of angels who praise, glorify, and bless God at all times. According to the version of *Sefer ha-Razim* available to us, magic never enters this place. The seventh chapter focuses solely on the description of the firmament where God dwells and on God's praise.[189]

Sefer ha-Razim is apparently the oldest surviving magic treatise and so, obviously, are the magic recipes included in it.[190] The words "these

---

187. M. Margalioth (1966, 105). Cf. Morgan (1983, 79).

188. M. Margalioth (1966, 107–8). Cf. Morgan (1983, 81–83). The use of biblical verses is particularly prominent in this passage.

189. On the angels' celestial cult in *Hekhalot* and *Merkavah* literature and its roots in ancient priestly traditions, see Elior (2004b).

190. The magic fragment from the Qumran scroll that was discussed at the beginning of this section attests to the existence of earlier books of magic recipes. Its

are the angels who are obedient in every matter during the first and second year of the fifteen year cycle of the reckoning of the Greek kings"[191] relate to the system of dating based on a fifteen-year indiction cycle that was in use in Egypt from the end of the third century and in the Byzantine world from the middle of the fourth century. This mention is the foundation of Margalioth's suggestion to date the work to the talmudic period, which is a plausible determination, although its limitations deserve note. Like many other authors of sorcery books, the author of *Sefer ha-Razim* also uses inventories of recipes he already had, which he incorporates into the general literary structure of his work. The mention of the indiction in one of the recipes attests to *terminus post quem* for the writing of this recipe and the dating of the work's editing. This mention, however, cannot determine the timing of all the recipes found in this work, some of which could have been earlier, and certainly not the timing of their integration into one treatise, which could have been later.[192] In any case, Margalioth persuasively points to the link between *Sefer ha-Razim* and Greco-Roman magic literature. Technical magic terms that were transcribed from Greek to Hebrew, ritual acts, and material means known from Greek magical papyri, dated to the second–fifth centuries CE, are common in *Sefer ha-Razim*. We can hardly assume that the author relied on materials far earlier than his own time or distant from

---

contents, however, are not sufficient even to ascertain the act that is required to struggle against the spirits mentioned in it. This is also the case concerning the papyrus fragments found in Egypt.

191. M. Margalioth (1966, 68). Cf. Morgan (1983, 23).

192. M. Margalioth (1966, 23–26). Margalioth bases his early dating estimate on the Hebrew language of the text and on the Greco-Roman magic environment reflected in the book. Other scholars rely on allusions to later textual and cultural elements for much later dating estimates of its composition: fifth to sixth centuries in Alexander (2003b, 188), sixth to seventh centuries in Gruenwald (1980, 226), and seventh to eighth centuries in Rebiger and Schäfer (2009, 2: 3–9). So far, no clear-cut evidence has been suggested for a definite, or even agreed on, dating of this work. The dispute on the question of what is the earliest literary layer in the work, the magical (Morgan 1983, 8–9) or the cosmological-angelological (Merchavya 1967, 297; 1972, 1594), seems futile. Both these elements were common in Jewish culture in late antiquity, and, in the absence of concrete information, attempting to decide on this question is pointless.

his own world, which he no longer understood. Plausibly, then, we can posit that the author lived in the eastern Mediterranean in the late Roman or early Byzantine period, was well acquainted with Greco-Roman magic in general and with contemporary astral magic in particular, and successfully integrated them into theological, angelological, and cosmological Jewish traditions.[193]

Sefer ha-Razim is mentioned by its name among the Rabbanite books of magic and abomination in the polemical writings of the Karaites Daniel al-Qumisi and Salmon ben Yeruhim, from the end of the first millennium. In the absence of any hint to the book's contents, however, we cannot be sure that they were actually referring to the book currently available to us. Rav Hai Gaon did not mention *Sefer ha-Razim* in his famous responsum to the sages of Kairouan (see chapter 6), but Maimonides could be hinting at it in his allusion to necromancy (*ma'aseh ha-'ov*).

> How is communing with the dead practiced? The practitioner stands up, offers a certain kind of incense, holds in his hand a myrtle twig, and waves it. He pronounces softly certain words known to them [i.e., the practitioners of this art], till the one who consults him fancies that someone is conversing with him, and answering his questions.[194]

Such an act, including holding a myrtle twig, is described in *Sefer ha-Razim*.

> If you wish to question a ghost (*lish'ol ha-'ov*); stand facing a tomb and repeat the names of the angels of the fifth encampment (while holding) in your hand a new flask (containing) oil and honey mixed together and say thus: 'I adjure you . . .' When

---

193. On astrological elements in *Sefer ha-Razim*, see Charlesworth (1987, 936–37) and von Stuckrad (2000b, 523–32). Margalioth's suggestion to anchor the work in Gnostic-Jewish views was, justifiably, rejected immediately after publication. See Dan (1968).

194. *Mishneh Torah, The Book of Knowledge*, Laws of Idolatry 6:1 (Maimonides 1962, 1: 72a–b).

he [i.e., the dead] appears set the flask before him and after this speak your words while holding a twig of myrtle in your hand.[195]

The many manuscripts of *Sefer ha-Razim* found in the Cairo Genizah, in Hebrew and in translations into Arabic, attest to the vast popularity of this work and to the great interest it held for Jews in Egypt at the beginning of the second millennium. Maimonides was probably not oblivious to this fact, and, despite his resolute opposition to sorcery and necromancy, he may have known *Sefer ha-Razim* and may even have used it when requiring an example of this practice.[196]

The other magic treatise that has survived is *Ḥarba de-Moshe*.[197] One version of the complete treatise is known today, and it was copied into one branch of mutually dependent manuscripts, the earliest of which was apparently written in Greece or Turkey in the early sixteenth century.[198] Fourteen fragments related to this work have so far been identified in the Cairo Genizah. They include parts of four copies of the treatise, selected recipes that were copied from it, and a short magic text that bears its title. Except for one case—a Genizah fragment that attests to the existence of two recipes omitted in the complete version (but unfortunately almost nothing of their content)—these fragments are hardly different from the version known so far. Nevertheless, they are extremely important for several reasons. First, at least in the geographic-historical context of the Cairo Genizah, the interest evoked by *Ḥarba de-Moshe* was

---

195. M. Margalioth (1966, 76–77). Cf. Morgan (1983, 38).

196. Margalioth's view on this matter seems too clear-cut (M. Margalioth 1966, 40). Although the linguistic similarity between Maimonides' statement and *Sefer ha-Razim* is impressive, he could still be quoting a recipe from some other source that had relied on *Sefer ha-Razim*, or he could have been describing a practice common in his surroundings. On Maimonides' familiarity with sorcery books and witchcraft practices (not necessarily Jewish), see chapter 6.

197. *The Sword of Moses* uses the term *sword* to denote the magic formula. On rabbinic traditions concerning Moses's sword of the moth and on a Greco-Roman parallel (Ξίφος Δαρδάνου, The Sword of Dardanos), see Harari (2005a).

198. The work was published in two editions: Gaster (1971a) and Harari (1997b). On the manuscripts of this work and the relationship between them, see Harari (1997b, 11–16). On Ms Bibliothèque de Genève, Comites Latentes 145, which contains the earliest complete manuscript of the work, see Benayahu (1972). For an English translation of *Ḥarba de-Moshe*, see Harari (2012b).

far greater than had been thought. At least four copiers sought to profit from the recipes gathered in it. Second, one copy shows the personalization of the book, a phenomenon by which the owner of a magical manuscript seeks to become the beneficiary of the adjurations copied in it by replacing the "N, son of N" formula with his own name. In this instance, a passage citing the adjuration of the swift messenger for the benefit of N, the name Mariot b. Nathan appears.[199] Third, the copying of the recipes points to a focused interest in the professional knowledge suggested in the whole work. The Genizah passages attest to the version of the work (errors in the complete version can often be corrected in light of Genizah passages, though sometimes it is actually the latter that are mistaken) and perhaps also to the texts that were before the writer. Finally, one of these fragments is a much earlier testimony to the existence of the Magical Sword literature than those that have been available thus far.[200]

Ḥarba de-Moshe includes three textual units: (1) the investiture (or controlling the sword) rite; (2) the sword of holy names; and (3) the recipes. The investiture unit, at the beginning of the work, describes a complex three-day ritual composed of asceticism, purity, prayer, and adjuration of angels. The purpose of the ritual is to attain control of the sword, that is, to make the one who undertakes this rite ritually fit for using it for the performance of the charms specified in the last section. In the course of this, this section teaches about the power structure of the angels in heaven, the tie between magic and the Torah, the importance of liturgical prayer in the magic ritual, Moses's magic figure, and God's attitude toward magic and magic's attitude toward God.[201] The investiture part begins with theoretical information about the source of magic knowledge and the human power related to it. It opens with the description of a thirteen-angel hierarchy arranged in heaven one above the other.

> (There are) four angels who are appointed over the sword given
> from the mouth of 'H WH YH WH HYH, the Lord of the

---

199. On this phenomenon, see Saar (2007).

200. For a detailed study of these fragments, see Harari (2014).

201. For a broad discussion of the structure and contents of this unit, see Harari (1997b, 77–114). Cf. Harari (2012b).

mysteries, and they are appointed over the Torah. . . . And above them are five princes, holy and powerful . . . and (they) are appointed over a thousand thousands of myriads and a thousand chariots. . . . And the least (angel) in these chariots is a prince greater then all those four (above mentioned) princes. And above them are three (more) princes, chiefs of the host of 'H YWH WYW WYW, the Lord of all, who causes His eight palaces (*hekhalot*) to shake and be in commotion every day with tumult and quaking. And they have authority over all of His handiwork, and beneath them are double those chariots. And the least in (these) chariots is a prince greater then all those (five) princes. . . . The prince and master who is (the) king, named 'HYW PSQ-TYH, sits and all the heavenly hosts kneel and bow down and prostrate themselves before him every day, all together on the ground, after they are dismissed from prostrating themselves before NQS ŠL'H HW 'WHH, the Lord of all.[202]

Pragmatically, this hierarchical view of the angels is fundamentally different from the vision of the overseers and the angels arrayed over the firmaments' strata that we find in *Sefer ha-Razim*. It subordinates the inferior ones to those above them in a way that allows us control of the entire structure if we can control its top. And indeed, "when you adjure him [i.e., 'HYW PSQTYH] he is bound by you and he binds for you [all those three princes and their chariots and] all those five princes and all the chariots that are under their authority and the four angels that are under them."[203]

The four nether angels in this order are in charge of both the sword and the Torah. Cooperation between these two powerful bodies of knowledge is also evident in the narrative tie between Moses drawing down magic knowledge from heaven and the drawing down of the Torah. In this regard, *Ḥarba de-Moshe* is tied to talmudic and other traditions dealing with the angels' opposition to giving Moses the Torah, his triumph over them, and his receiving gifts from them, clarifying

---

202. Harari (2012b, 71–72).

203. Harari (2012b, 72). A copier's omission is probably the reason for the disregard of the other three angels and their carriages.

what had only been hinted at in other sources—the gifts were names for adjuring the angels.[204]

The author explicitly clarifies here God's attitude toward human magic and explains that this vast power over the angels was granted to humans through God's command.

> For he [i.e., 'HYW PSQTYH] and all those princes have been ordered so, to be bound by Moses, son of Amram, to bind for him all the princes who are under their authority. And upon their adjuration, they may not tarry or turn from it this way or the other, (but) should give all who adjure them power over this sword [and reveal to them] its mysteries and hidden secrets, its glory, might and splendor. And they may not tarry because the decree of 'BDWHW HWH ṢL 'LYH 'L YH is issued to them, saying: Do not impede any mortal who will adjure you and do not treat him otherwise than what you were decreed with regard to my servant Moses, son of Amram, for he adjures you by My Ineffable Names and it is to My Names that you render honor and not to him. But if you impede him I will burn you for you have not honored Me.[205]

By presenting God as the source of magic knowledge and the sovereign founder of the human use of this knowledge and by tying Moses to the drawing down of this knowledge to the world, the author not only seeks to enhance the authority of his treatise but also to substantiate the legitimacy of its professional use *within* Jewish tradition. This view of the practice offered in the work is also evident in the interweaving of the liturgical prayer and the adjuration act during the investiture ritual, as well as in several magic recipes in the last part of the work.[206]

The sword of magic names, which follows the investiture section, is a vast collection of names (generally meaningless combinations of letters), most of them arranged in groups according to a common characteristic.

---

204. See Harari (2005b).

205. Harari (2012b, 72). On God's attitude toward magic and on the attitude of magic toward God in this work, see Harari (1997b, 67–70).

206. See Harari (1997b, 92–101).

This is "the sword given from the mouth of 'H WH YH WH HYH, the Lord of the mysteries," which can be controlled by means of the ritual that is set down at the opening of the book and by which the magic actions suggested at its end can be carried out. The structure of the sword and the character of its ties with the list of the magic recipes unquestionably attest that this sword is a product of the author's editing work. The author combined and edited in it several lists of magic formulas, holy names and incantation fragments, to which he ascribed performative power. Originally, the sword had been a shorter formula used, as a whole, in the performance of many rituals (as we found in *Sefer ha-Yashar* or in *Sefer ha-Malbush*). Its expansion into its vast dimensions yielded a system for its use that is unique to *Ḥarba de-Moshe*, whereby each of the recipes suggested in the last unit resorts to a part of it in an orderly sequence. According to this method, the sword actually compiles magic incantations from all the recipes suggested in the work.[207]

The recipe unit consists of 137 sections of suggestions for dealing with many and varied areas of human desire and distress—physical and mental health, love, agriculture and crafts, enemies, relationships with the authorities, imprisonment, travel risks, and so forth (Plate 21). The internal organization of the list attests to the author's pragmatic professional approach. Beside a large group of forty-two healing sections arranged at the beginning according to the structure of the body from top to bottom,[208] it also includes smaller groups of recipes dealing with harm, agriculture, war and government, rescue from distress, protection, and knowledge and recollection. A few recipes are arranged in pairs, for the performance and the annulment of an act. In this list the author unquestionably includes information from various sources available to him. The connection between the list of recipes and the list of names (the sword) attests that the author created each list separately and that only afterward were these recipes tied to sequences of names from the sword according to the order of their appearance in the list. The end of this section (and with it of the entire treatise) is a set of general instructions concerning the manipulation of the sword and a dire warning

---

207. See Harari (1997b, 115–21).

208. For a list of organs and their treatment on a Greek magical gemstone (and its close parallel in a Hippocratic treatise), see Faraone (2011, 144–51).

against any amateur use of it. Such an act could end in disaster: "Angels of anger and rage and wrath and fury rule over him and torment his body . . . and his body will become disfigured."[209]

Ḥarba de-Moshe is the product of a complex and sophisticated editing effort of many textual elements. Its language combines Hebrew, Babylonian and Palestinian Aramaic, and even a passage in Greek that was transcribed into Hebrew and included in the work (without its author understanding it) together with its translation into Aramaic.[210] By relying on the Hebrew rendering of the performance instructions in the investiture section, which I think should be ascribed to the author of this work, we can quite plausibly determine that the editing was done in Palestine or its surroundings. This conclusion is supported also by the many fragments of the work that found their way into the Cairo Genizah. So far, we have no information that would enable us to decide on the dating of the editing. Nor do we have any sure information about the timing of its underlying materials. The work is mentioned by name and by its opening words in the responsum of Rav Hai Gaon to the sages of Kairouan (end of the first millennium), which is the earliest evidence of its existence.[211] Possibly, *Ḥarba de-Moshe* could be dated back several centuries before Rav Hai and, because it contains no signs of Muslim influence, it might even be cautiously traced back to the third quarter of the first millennium. However, these dates are merely speculations, and the materials edited in this work could definitely have been even earlier.

Beside the complete work, we also have many fragments of the magic genre to which I refer as Magical Sword literature. What all the fragments in this genre share in common is the use of the word *sword*, with or without any connection to Moses, as a technical-professional term for denoting an incantation formula. The scope of passages from this literature is limited by comparison with *Ḥarba de-Moshe*, which is the most complex and complete expression of it. Most of them do not contain much beyond lists of magic instructions for action. In all of them the sword is mentioned as an incantation to be uttered or written in full and not, as in the *Ḥarba de-Moshe* method, as a pool of names from

---

209. Harari (2012b, 97–98). Cf. the discussion in Harari (1997b, 123–33).
210. See Rohrbacher-Sticker (1996).
211. Emanuel (1995, 131–32).

which the incantations are derived. A textual examination of these fragments, particularly of the connection between them and the treatise, suggests that they reflect an earlier textual layer from which its author drew materials for his work.[212]

CONCLUDING REMARKS

Magic treatises are a literary and theoretical-systematic elaboration of the recipe literature. Witchcraft recipes and lists of recipes as such, which contain a great deal of information about adjuration rituals and their aims, were widespread in Jewish culture. Their elaboration into treatises anchored them in a broad and explicit perception of angels, firmaments, and holy names, of the source of magic knowledge and its unfolding in the world, of God's view on the power of human incantation, of the relationships between magic and other cultural elements such as the Torah, ritual, liturgy, and so forth. The authors thereby sought to establish the knowledge suggested in these works on a firm basis of legitimation and authority.[213] Legitimation was attained explicitly, as in the case of *Harba de-Moshe*, or implicitly, by relying on tradition chains. Authority also was established in two ways. The first determined a heavenly (divine or angelic) source for magic knowledge, ascribing its drawing down to earth to previous eras and to culture heroes such as Adam, Noah, Moses, or Elijah, and assumed its delivery through the accepted channels. The second worked through the process of methodical-professional elaboration of the recipes into a general theoretical context. Thus the performative artifacts (such as amulets and incantation bowls) point to the actual performance of magic charms and to potential ways of concretizing them, and the magic recipes offer information about all the elements of the magic ritual setup and the goals of its operation. The conceptual framework of the recipes expands and exposes the beliefs and

---

212. On these passages, which appear in relatively late manuscripts, see Harari (1997b, 139–52). Also see the early evidence in the Cairo Genizah in Harari (2014, 84–87).

213. A similar process of authority structuring at the editing stage of magic recipes into treatises occurred also in the Greco-Roman world. See Betz (1982) and Dieleman (2005, 185–284). Cf. Swartz (1996, 173–205).

outlooks that granted these acts their meaning and wove this meaning into the general Jewish perception of reality.

The adjuration literature and the magic culture reflected in it did not exist in an empty space. They were created in a Jewish society that sustained mutual relations with neighboring societies in the area of magic tradition among other things. They should therefore be examined in two main contexts: the Jewish nonmagic context and the magic non-Jewish context. Magic aspects in nonmagic Jewish literature from late antiquity and the early Islamic period are the concern of the last two chapters of this book. Here, I would like to note the existence of non-Jewish magic writings and artifacts that can point to the cross-cultural context of early Jewish magic. In this regard, three bodies of sources deserve mention: magic findings from the Greco-Roman world (magical papyri and treatises, jewelry and gems, amulets, curse tablets), non-Jewish bowls and adjuration tablets from Babylonia, and Muslim magic books and artifacts from the early Islamic period. In the first two cases, the reciprocal relationships between Jewish and Gentile findings have been studied and exposed.[214] In both we can point to commonalities in ritual views and practices between Jews and their neighbors and at times to mutual influences and exchanges of theoretical and practical elements, up to the emergence of an international magic culture with mythical and ritual elements common to all the nations in the region. This mutual cooperation and influence point to the openness of magic culture in late antiquity, which rests on the pragmatic character of this practice. Magic focused on successful results in a specific matter for the benefit of a specific client. As such, it ignored issues of morality, society, and collective identity and focused on the means that were perceived as most useful for dealing with the problem facing the sorcerer. These means usually and naturally drew on the surrounding tradition, but perhaps because of a professional pragmatism free from didactic considerations, sorcerers did not hesitate to borrow such means from their neighbors if they or their clients believed in their efficacy. In so doing, they did not renounce

---

214. Unfortunately, the question of ties and mutual influences between Jewish and Muslim magic, which is relevant to the study of the Cairo Genizah, has hardly been researched. See Harari (2005a) and Shaked (1994; 2005a). Cf. Wasserstrom (1992).

their cultural-religious identity. Magic treatises, which compiled charm recipes within a comprehensive conceptual framework, attest that this was not the case. In the performative context, however, both diagnostic and therapeutic, professionals drew support from one another. The fact that at times they also served each other's clients shows that pragmatism was not exclusive to the professionals but extended to far wider circles. In times of genuine distress, people are obviously less concerned with the identity and the means of those who can rescue them so long as they are successful.

Alien influences are highly visible in both Babylonian and western Jewish magic sources. Influence in the opposite direction is also found both in Babylonian magic bowls and in magic writings and artifacts from the Greco-Roman world. The meaning of "Jewish elements" in such cases is in dispute: Do they refer to the Jewish influence on Hellenistic magic culture, which was absorbed while losing its original identity, or is the writer perhaps a Jew expressing himself in a language that is neither Hebrew nor Aramaic? In the early stages of the research, the identification of Jewish elements in magical papyri and their explanation as a direct expression of Jewish magic culture in Greek was greeted with great enthusiasm. But this approach was targeted for extensive criticism and, in recent decades, the tendency to tie Jewish characteristics found in Greek magic texts to Jewish authors has diminished. This decline follows the development of stringent criteria for distinguishing what reached Hellenistic magic from a Jewish (or Christian) source and what was created by a Jewish writer who was part of Hellenistic culture. In light of this trend, the number of Greek magic artifacts and texts whose Jewish source can be identified with any certainty has significantly dropped.[215]

---

215. Prominent representatives of the first trend are Ludwig Blau, who, in his book on Jewish magic, cites two texts in Greek through which he illustrates what a Jewish work of this kind might have been like, and Erwin Goodenough, who endorses this approach as part of his vast efforts to expose the "Dionysian" Hellenistic Judaism that he believes existed. See Blau (1898, 96–117) and Goodenough (1953–1968, 2: 153–295). For a radical view of Jewish influence on the development of magic in the ancient world, almost up to a Jewish "role" in its development, see Simon (1986, 339–68). See also Alon (1950), Benoit (1951), Peterson (1948; 1953), Sperber (1994, 81–91, 99–114), and Veltri (1996a). Cf. Gignoux (1987, 3), and see the critique of Gignoux's determination concerning the Jewish origin of the amulets in Syriac that he published in Brock [1989] and

Be that as it may, the intercultural ties evident in the realm of magic belief and practice invite constant study of magic writings from neighboring cultures in an attempt to point out the characteristics of the shared conceptual and practical foundation and the unique mode of each culture's participation in these common grounds.

Having introduced the primary, insider magic sources and having pointed out their professional character and the cultural picture reflected in them, my focus now turns to an examination of prominent aspects of this culture and of the discourse related to it in the secondary, outsider evidence.

Wesselius [1991]). Morton Smith (1996) was the first to formulate a systematic critique of the approach assuming a Jewish source for every magic text with Jewish features, of which Gideon Bohak has also recently suggested a persuasive version (Bohak 2003a; 2004b; 2007). Cf. also Alexander (1986, 357–58; 1999b, 1067–78) and Nock (1972, 2: 889–92).

1. A fragment of a magic recipe book from Qumran (4Q 560). Israel
Antiquities Authority, Negative P.A.M. 43.602.

2. Five of the nineteen amulets found in Ḥorvat Maʻon (northwest Negev).
The adjurations were engraved on bronze sheets that were then folded or
rolled. The lamellae were all found in an ancient synagogue, dated to the sixth
to seventh century. Israel Antiquities Authority, Negative 19171.

3. An amulet for the healing of 'Ina, daughter of Ze'irti. The (Aramaic) adjuration was engraved on a silver sheet measuring 4 cm × 11 cm, which was then rolled and put into a small copper container. The amulet was found in a tomb near Tiberias, and it was probably produced in the fourth to sixth century. Institute of Archaeology, Hebrew University of Jerusalem. Photograph by Gaby Laron.

4. A bronze amulet, measuring 9 cm×3.7 cm, "for fever that burns and does not stop." The name of the client is not indicated, so this piece might be a generic amulet that was handed upon demand from one person to the next. It dates to the fourth to sixth century and was found in Sepphoris. The text, which was engraved on the bronze lamella, is presented in the picture as though it were protruding, an effect achieved by printing a mirror image of the negative. This technique helps scholars to read and decipher the engraved text. Israel Antiquities Authority, Negative 331414.

5. Pieces of an amulet for love. The adjuration, starting with framed names of angels, was engraved in soft clay. It was then thrown into the fire for the implementation of the sympathetic principle that was written on the clay (and that partly survived): "Just as this piece of clay burns, so shall the heart of N son of N burn after me." Ḥorvat Rimon (northern Negev), fifth to sixth century. Israel Antiquities Authority, Negative 138528.

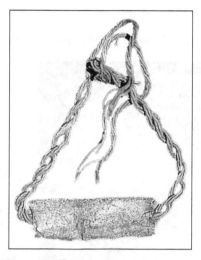

6. A lead amulet rolled on a rope (for wearing). Karanis, Egypt, third to fourth century. Kelsey Museum of Archaeology, University of Michigan, item KM 24255.

7. A gemstone from the Greco-Roman world. Kelsey Museum of Archaeology, University of Michigan, item KM 26054.

(a) This side of the gemstone shows a cock-headed, snake-legged god surrounded by magic words and signs, including (on the upper right) the angels' names Michael, Raphael, Gabriel, and Oriel. An *ouroboros*—a snake holding its tail in its mouth—encircles the entire complex.

(b) On the opposite side of the gemstone is a figure with an eagle head and six wings.

8–10. Aramaic incantation bowls from Mesopotamia, fifth to seventh century.

8. The adjuration, written in a spiral pattern from the center to the margins, encircles the image of a demon. The complex is surrounded and sealed by a circle line. Collection of Shlomo Moussaieff. Photograph by Matthew Morgenstern.

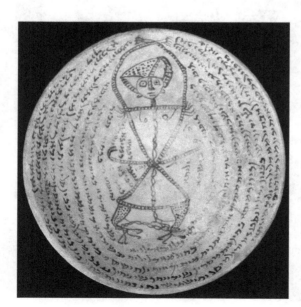

9. A she-demon bound with chains and surrounded by words of adjuration. Collection of Shlomo Moussaieff. Photograph by Matthew Morgenstern.

10. This long adjuration, written in a spiral pattern, is accompanied by two circle lines (a visual element typical of bowls), in the center and along the rim. Remains of tar on the rim indicate that this bowl was one of a pair that had been sealed together facing each other. Vorderasiatisches Museum im Pergamonmuseum, Berlin, item VA 2416. Photograph by Yuval Harari.

11–13. Images of demons in magic bowls: bound, chained, and encircled by adjurations. Fifth to seventh century. Collection of Shlomo Moussaieff. Photographs by Matthew Morgenstern.

11.

12.

13.

14. A human skull covered with spells from Mesopotamia, probably fifth to seventh century. On the front of the skull is an image of a demon surrounded by the words of a spell. Vorderasiatisches Museum im Pergamonmuseum, Berlin, item VA 2459. Photograph by Yuval Harari.

15. Parts of two magic skulls covered with spells from Mesopotamia, probably fifth to seventh century. Vorderasiatisches Museum im Pergamonmuseum, Berlin, item VA 2458. Photograph by Yuval Harari.

16. Trilingual (Hebrew, Aramaic, and Judeo-Arabic) curse for "uprooting, chasing away, crushing, destroying, annihilating, Ali son of Nuḥ." Found in the Cairo Genizah. Cambridge University Library, item T-S K1.42.

17. A Cairo Genizah amulet for safeguard and protection "for the bearer of this writing." The adjuration opens with a combination of *charactêres* (magic signs) and holy names and concludes with scriptural verses (Deuteronomy 32:39, 7:15; Exodus 15:26). Cambridge University Library, item T-S K1.137.

18–20. Four pages from a trilingual (Aramaic, Hebrew, and Judeo-Arabic) book of magic recipes from the Cairo Genizah. Typical graphic elements, such as *charactères* (magic signs), holy names written in frames or marked by short lines, and a pterygoma (a triangle of words, which results from omitting one letter of the magical name in each subsequent line), are discernible.

18. On the right-hand page are two recipes for delivery difficulties. The top of the page says, "For a dead fetus in his mother's womb," and is meant to initiate the abortion of a dead fetus. The bottom of the page reads, "For a woman whose placenta tarries," and is meant to extract the placenta from the womb after giving birth. On the left-hand page are two recipes related to aggression. The top of the page reads, "For releasing a bound person," and is meant for releasing a person from a binding spell, apparently from impotence imposed on him by means of a curse. The bottom of the page reads, "For blocking one's mouth," and is used to prevent a rival from harming through witchcraft. Cambridge University Library, item T-S K1.91.

19. At the top of the page is written, "Opening of the heart," which is meant to improve learning and memory. In the middle of the page, we find the words "If the sea is swollen," which is used for calming down a sea storm. The bottom of the page reads, "For the stinging of a scorpion," and is meant for healing a scorpion's bite. Cambridge University Library, item T-S K1.117 (1r).

שלוח אש ·

כתוב כדס עוף עלשמך חיים וקיימא בשמך
דבריך רוח סערה בימך וביבשתא קור קריר
עיר עד בשס חי ·: צבאות י: יה יושב הכרוביס
שלחשיקין מן זיקך ונורמן נורך כסתוב
בתורה יבה ·: בשחפת ובקדחת ובדלקת
ובחרחור ול כן יכה יתדפכ פ' כמה של
אדכעיס יכנולא יוסף פן יוסף להכותו עלולו
מנו, רכה וא' טבוב על פומא דקונצא יעני
ראס קצבה בנוקה דלך ערנל וטעמו יתיה
נקצר או קדס תרעיה דבית שנוך · יוכתב
פי קמץ עלוה בדס טיר ·
_____

לחסד ולשלטון ·
תסד ואמרת נפשו עדק ושלוס נשקו · טבוב
והב בשמאל · כי־ארך ימים ושנות חייס ושלוס
יוסיפו לך · כי לויתח הס לחשך ועניקיס לגנרותק
כי ב: ילבו ימך ויוסיפו לך ול ושמר ·: אלהיך לך ול

20. The top of the page says, "Sending out fire," and is meant to harm a person. The bottom reads, "For grace and for governing," which is used for gaining grace and favor in the eyes of others and for gaining control over them. Cambridge University Library, item T-S K1.117 (2r).

21. A page from the list of magic recipes in *The Sword of Moses*. Bibliothèque de Genève, Comites Latentes 145, p. 77.

6

Angels, Demons, and Sorceries

Beliefs, Actions, and Attitudes in Nonmagic Literature

In the last two chapters of this book I deal with references to sorcery and demonology (a main interest of Jewish magic culture) in sources not considered magical and whose geographic-historical origin fits that of the primary sources. On methodological grounds, the discussion will be split in two. Rabbinic literature, the richest and in the past the most influential source in the description of Jewish magic in late antiquity, is discussed in chapter 7. In this chapter I present the main elements that can be gathered from other texts—Second Temple period literature, *Hekhalot* and *Merkavah* texts, Karaite and Geonic writings, and, finally, the writings of Maimonides, who was a contemporary as well as a neighbor of the Cairo Genizah. Although these texts are not magic writings or professional magic products (with a caveat regarding ancient mystical literature), they surely enrich our knowledge in all that concerns magic beliefs and actions, particularly their cultural and social contexts.

My discussion in this chapter rests on sources from a large geographic area (Palestine and Babylonia), from a period lasting more than 1,000 years, and covering a broad range of genres: myth, theology, historiography, Aggadah, halakhic law, social guidelines, and polemics. Obviously, then, placing all of them under one rubric as the joint expression of a uniform ongoing phenomenon would be inappropriate. On the other hand, the character of these sources and their relative rarity would not justify engaging in a historical description of how beliefs, actions, or attitudes toward magic and demonology based on them developed in

Judaism. In my current pursuit, their importance for the description of early Jewish magic lies in their conceptual and linguistic ties with insider, primary magic literature. As such, they provide complementary elements for describing magic as a cultural phenomenon rather than being magic texts themselves. These outsider sources, however, can make a unique contribution by conveying external attitudes toward magic. Professional magic sources expose the phenomenon as such, whereas secondary sources point to the social implications. These implications, together with aspects of magical and demonological belief and performance conveyed through these bodies of literature, are at the focus of the discussion.

SECOND TEMPLE PERIOD LITERATURE

Demons

In Jewish writings from the Second Temple period, which precede by centuries the magic sources available to us, the culture of sorcery reflected in magic literature is hardly present except for one issue: demons and evil spirits. In this realm the sources offer a broad range of demonological perspectives and the actions that were tied to them.[1]

The developed demonology of the Second Temple period represents an innovation in relation to the Hebrew Bible—but not necessarily in Israelite culture in the biblical era!—rather than a continuation or an expansion of it. Although demons, evil spirits, and satans are mentioned in the Bible, they do not play a key role in it. Demons are mentioned as objects of a foreign cult that the children of Israel were accused of engaging in, without any details.[2] Various harmful agents, such as Ketev or Ketev Meriri, Negef, and Lilith, are mentioned by name but without specifying or precisely describing their injurious actions.[3] Several evil and misleading spirits were sent by God to cause harm and lead the people

---

1. For a comprehensive study on this topic, see Eshel (1999). For an inclusive collection of articles on demons in antiquity, particularly in late antiquity, see Lange et al. (2003). In the context of exorcism, cf. Bohak (2008, 88–114; 2012d).

2. For example, in Deuteronomy 32:17 and Psalm 106:37. See Loewenstamm (1976). The worship of satyrs (*se'irim*)—see Leviticus 17:7 and 2 Chronicles 11:15—could be tied to this. See van der Toorn et al. (1999, 732–33).

3. Van der Toorn et al. (1999, 520–21, 673–74).

astray: An evil spirit led to a dispute between Avimelekh and the men of Shekhem (Judges 9:23); a deceitful spirit misled the 400 Ba'al prophets to seduce Ahab to go into battle for Ramot Gil'ad (1 Kings 22:19–23); and an evil spirit tormented Saul (1 Samuel 16:14). If this last instance hints at possession, then David's playing his lyre to remove the evil spirit (verse 23) is the only biblical description of a healing act. Harmful angels were also sent by God to harm humans—"the destroying angel" brought the plague upon the children of Israel and the angel of God defeated Sanheriv's camp.[4] Finally, *Satan* or *ha-Satan*, an adversary angel, is mentioned in three places as an inciting and accusing figure.[5]

All these injurious emissaries, at times explicitly mentioned as part of the heavenly retinue, are hardly involved in national-historic events. When they are, they act as agents of God in his leadership of the world. This trend changes in the Second Temple period literature. First, the share of evil spirits and particularly that of their leaders—Satan, Belial, Mastema—both in the biblical history rewritten in this period and in day-to-day life, is far greater than in the Bible. Second, in some circles, evil spirits are no longer perceived as part of the ancient order of Creation but as a result of its subversion by rebellious angels.[6]

This expansion (by comparison with the Bible) of the role of evil spirits and their leaders in world events conveys a larger phenomenon, typical of broad areas of spiritual creativity in the Second Temple period. This expansion has two sides: (1) a broad interest in heavenly existence as a whole (its structure, the entities that populate it, the activities taking

---

4. On the destroying angel, see 2 Samuel 24:16 and 1 Chronicles 21:15–16. On the angel who defeated Sanheriv, see 2 Kings 19:35, Isaiah 37:36, and 2 Chronicles 32:21.

5. For *Satan*, see 1 Chronicles 21:1. For *ha-Satan*, see Job 1–2 and Zechariah 3:1–2. See also van der Toorn et al. (1999, 726–32).

6. These changes can be explained in one or both of the following ways: (1) release from the ideological censorship exerted over biblical stories, which had ignored views widely held by the people of Israel during the biblical period as well; and/or (2) a conceptual development in the Jewish people in the Second Temple era as a result of cross-cultural contacts or internal developments. Elaine Pagels (1991), for example, suggests tying the development of Satan's figure during the Second Temple era to the sectarianism typical of this period and to the social reality that emerged as a result, when the significant "other" is no longer the stranger (as in the Bible) but the one that is near—the "intimate enemy" in her terms.

place in it, and the knowledge hidden within it), and (2) the development of close mutual relationships between humans and angels. These ideas developed in different circles in separate ways, and their expression is therefore not uniform. Regarding my current concern, this is particularly prominent in the theological difference concerning the origin of evil spirits between *1 Enoch* and the *Book of Jubilees* on the one hand and the sectarian writings of Qumran on the other.[7] The Qumranites viewed the evil spirits and their leader—Belial, Mastema, Angel of Darkness— as part of pervasive divine predestination. Divine will created the two spirits, the spirit of truth and the spirit of injustice, including their leaders and their camps; and members of these camps, including the evil spirits, act according to divine predestination. The following text is the formulation in the *Serekh ha-Yaḥad* (Community Rule):

> From the God of knowledge stems all there is and all there shall be. Before they existed he established their entire design. . . . From the Angel of Darkness stems the corruption of all the sons of justice, and all their sins, their iniquities, their guilts and their offensive deeds are under his dominion in compliance with the mysteries of God, until his moment; and all their afflictions and their periods of grief are caused by the dominion of his enmity; and all the spirits of his lot cause the sons of light to fall.[8]

And in the War Scroll we read:

> You created Belial for the pit, angel of enmity; in dark[ness] is his [dom]ain, his counsel is to bring about wickedness and guilt.

---

7. *The Book of Enoch* (*1 Enoch*), also known as the *Ethiopian Book of Enoch*, is a compilation of five works. Views on its writing are in dispute, but I do not discuss this issue here (see, e.g., Dimant 1983; Greenfield and Stone 1977; Milik 1976, 4–107; and Nickelsburg 2001, 7–8, 21–26). For my current concern, the *Book of Watchers* (chaps. 1–36), which is among the earliest of these works, is particularly important. Aramaic fragments from the *Book of Watchers*, which were found in several Qumran scrolls, show that it was written in the beginning of the second century BCE, and its redaction was probably completed even earlier, in the second half of the third century BCE.

8. Martínez and Tigchelaar (1998, 1: 75–77).

All the spirits of his lot are angels of destruction, they walk in the laws of darkness; toward it goes their only desire.[9]

Everything, including Belial and his agents who lead astray and hinder the "Sons of Light," is rooted in God's previous thought, which is realized in all its details in the course of history. This predeterministic conception did not prevent human grappling with the supernatural agents of evil. This was the purpose of the Songs of the Master (*Maskil*)—"in order to frighten and terr[ify] all the spirits of the raving angels and the bastard spirits, demons, Lilith, owls and [jackals]"—and of additional ritual acts intimated in passages of magic recipes books from Qumran, discussed in chapter 5.[10]

1 Enoch and the *Book of Jubilees* present an entirely different approach concerning the origin of evil spirits. These works tie their appearance in the world to the hybrid mating of the Watchers (angels) and women. This act, to which the Bible refers briefly (Genesis 6:1–4), is developed in these books into a broad myth about the rebellion of 200 angels who united around their leader (Shemihazah, or Asael), deliberately disrupted the order of Creation, descended to earth, took women, and were defiled by them. Their sin of mixing what does not belong together— flesh and spirit, eternity and death, holiness and defilement, heaven and earth—engendered the giants. Some traditions hold that these giants were evil and violent spirits. According to other traditions, evil spirits came out of their bodies after the giants killed one another by divine decree.[11] Whatever the circumstances, these works do not view

---

9. Martínez and Tigchelaar (1998, 1: 135).

10. Martínez and Tigchelaar (1998, 2: 1029). On the demonology of the Judean Desert sect in light of all the writings found in Qumran (both sectarian and others), see Alexander (1997; 1999a), Duppont-Sommer (1950–1951), and Eshel (1999; 2003). See also Baumgarten (1991–1992), Bohak (2008, 105–12; 2012d), and Stuckenbruck (2003).

11. See *1 Enoch*, chaps. 6–15, and cf. also *1 Enoch* 19:1 and *Book of Jubilees*, chaps. 5 and 10. On the various traditions involved in the making up of the story in the *Book of Watchers* and on their final elaboration in this work, see Eshel (1999, 15–48) and Nickelsburg (2001, 165–73, 229–32). See also Collins (1978), Dimant (1974), P. D. Hanson (1977), Newsom (1980), and Nickelsburg (1977). For a broad discussion on this myth and its later appropriations in early Christian and rabbinic sources, see Reed (2005). A later echo of this tradition on the origin of demons may also resonate in the following passage

the appearance of evil spirits in the world as part of the divine program of Creation but as a flaw resulting from an essentially sinful mating of angels and women. Their action on earth is described as attack, battle, and destruction.[12]

The Book of Jubilees relates that, after the Flood, the evil spirits renewed their action. They bothered the sons of Noah, misled them, seduced them, and introduced envy and disharmony among them.[13] When turning to their father to pray for them, the sons describe the damage inflicted by the spirits as killing, misleading, and (moral?) blindness. Noah does indeed pray and mentions in his prayer the sin of the Watchers (the rebelling angels), which resulted in the birth of spirits in the world. He asks God to remove them and imprison them, so that they might not rule his sons and destroy them, "for they [i.e., the spirits] are savage and were created for the purpose of destroying" (*Book of Jubilees* 10:5). God agrees and orders his angels to imprison the evil spirits. Here, however, another figure enters the picture: Mastema, the chief of the spirits.

> When Mastema, the Leader of the Spirits, came, he said: "Lord creator, leave some of them before me; let them listen to me and do everything I tell them, because if none of them is left for me I shall not be able to exercise the authority of my will among mankind. For they are meant for (the purposes of) destroying and misleading before my punishment because the evil of mankind is great." Then He said that a tenth of them should be left before him, while He would make nine parts descend to the place of judgment.[14]

The *Book of Jubilees* ascribes to Mastema an ongoing and significant role in the history of the people of Israel. We are told that he incited God to

---

from *Pirke de-Rabbi Eliezer* 34: "The generation of the Flood . . . all their souls become spirits and harm the Israelites further."

12. *1 Enoch* 15:11–16:1.

13. *Book of Jubilees* 7:26–27, 10, 11. Cf. also Abraham's prayer, in which Abraham refers to evil spirits who lead astray (*Book of Jubilees* 12:19–20) and the notion that God imposed these spirits on foreign nations (but not on the Israelites) to "lead them astray from Him" (*Book of Jubilees* 15: 31–32).

14. *Book of Jubilees* 10:8–9 (VanderKam 1989, 59).

test Abraham by demanding the binding of Isaac, attacked Moses on his way from Midian to Egypt and sought to kill him (the "bridegroom of blood" incident), assisted the Egyptian sorcerers in their struggle against Moses, and even incited Pharaoh to pursue the children of Israel in the desert.[15] These traditions attest to the standing of Mastema as the spirits' leader on the one hand and to the limits of his power and his subordination to God on the other.[16] His spirits—"angels of hatred" (*mal'akhei mastemot*) or "angels of destruction" (*mal'akhei ḥevel*), as they are called in the Qumran scrolls—are granted to him but in limited measure, out of consideration for his role in Divine Providence. But no fairness or justice prevails in his kingdom. God, therefore, commanded that books of medicines be given to Noah, to help his sons in their struggle against Mastema's deceptive spirits.

> He told one of us that we should teach Noah all their medicines because he knew that they would neither conduct themselves properly nor fight fairly. We acted in accord with His entire command. . . . We told Noah all the medicines for their diseases with their deceptions so that he could cure (them) by means of the earth's plants. Noah wrote down in a book everything (just) as we had taught him regarding all the kinds of medicine, and the evil spirits were precluded from pursuing Noah's children.[17]

This is the first time we hear about the existence of books of medicines against demons, that is, books of recipes for exorcising demons and for protection from them, as well as a claim about their heavenly origin.[18]

Practical antidemonic knowledge, then, was familiar in the Second Temple period as part of an approach that ascribed human suffering to harm inflicted by demons and evil spirits and sought to grapple with it by exorcising them. Several narrative sources describe means adopted for

---

15. *Book of Jubilees* 17:15–18:12, 48:1–19. For more wrongs of Mastema, see *Book of Jubilees* 11:3–5, 11.

16. This matter is also emphasized in the tradition about his involvement in the Exodus from Egypt (*Book of Jubilees* 48:15–18).

17. *Book of Jubilees* 10:10–13 (VanderKam 1989, 60).

18. On the demonology of the *Book of Jubilees*, see VanderKam (2003).

this purpose. The Genesis Apocryphon, for example, speaks of afflictions and injuries, and perhaps even impotence, as resulting from the harm an evil spirit had inflicted on Pharaoh after he had taken Sarah, Abraham's wife, into his court. The healing is tied to prayer and the laying of hands, a practice already hinted at in the Bible (2 Kings 5:11).

> That night, the God Most High sent him [i.e., Pharaoh] a chastising spirit, to afflict him and all the members of his household, an evil spirit that kept afflicting him and all the members of his household. And he was unable to approach her [i.e., Sarah], let alone to have sexual intercourse with her, in spite of being with her for two years. At the end of two years, the punishments of plagues, against him and against all the members of his household, increased and intensified. And he sent for all the wise men [of] Egypt to be called, and all the wizards as well as all the healers of Egypt, (to see) whether they could heal him of that disease, (him) and all the members of his household. However, all the healers and wizards and all the wise men were unable to rise up to heal him. For the spirit attacked all of them and they fled. Then Hirqanos came to me and asked me to pray for the king, and lay my hands upon him so that he would recover. . . . I prayed that [he might recover] and laid my hands upon his [hea]d. The plague was removed from him; the evil [spirit] was banished [from him] and he recovered.[19]

Josephus tells how David, through his playing, exorcised the evil spirits that had troubled Saul, choking him so badly

> that the physicians could devise no other remedy save to order search to be made for one with power to charm away spirits and to play upon the harp, and, whensoever the evil spirits should assail and torment Saul, to have him stand over the king and strike the strings and chant his songs. . . . When he [i.e., David] came,

---

19. Martínez and Tigchelaar (1998, 1: 43). Cf. the reading of Fitzmyer (2004, 100–102, and notes on 193–216). See also Flusser (1979, 113–14). For the biblical source of this story, see Genesis 12:10–20.

Saul was delighted with him, made him his armour-bearer and held him in the highest honour, for his illness was charmed away by him; and against that trouble caused by the evil spirits, whensoever they assailed him, he had no other physician than David.[20]

Pseudo-Philo cites in *Biblical Antiquities* the wording of the song spell through which David exorcised the evil spirit from Saul. He thereby affords us a rare glimpse into the (potential) literary character of Jewish song spells from this period.[21]

Darkness and silence were before the world was made, and silence spoke and the darkness became visible. The foundation was created by the fastening together of what had been spread out; its upper part was called heaven and the lower earth. The upper part was commanded to bring down rain according to its season, and the lower part was commanded to produce food for all created things. After this was the tribe of your spirits made. Now do not be troublesome, since you are a secondary creation. Otherwise, remember Tartarus wherein you walk. Or is it not enough for you to hear that by means of what resounds before you, I sing to many? Or do you not remember that your brood was created from an echo in the abyss? But a new generation, from which I was born, will rebuke you, from which in time one will be born from my loins who will rule over you.[22]

---

20. Josephus, *Jewish Antiquities*, 6.166–168 (Josephus 1925–1965, 5: 249–51). Cf. also Josephus, *Jewish Antiquities* 6.211, 214. On this topic, see Deines (2003, 367–72).

21. *Biblical Antiquities* was originally written in Hebrew in Palestine, probably between the destruction of the Temple and the mid-second century CE. It was preserved in a Latin translation in manuscripts from the eleventh to the fifteenth centuries. See Jacobson (1996, 1: 195–280).

22. Jacobson (1996, 1: 82, 187–88), and see Jacobson's comments in Jacobson (1996, 2: 1177–81). I adopted the suggestion of Eshel (1999, 81–85, 209–10) in using "new generation" to correct the problematic rendering of *metra nova* as "new womb" in the last sentence. On this matter, see the comment in Jacobson (1996, 2: 1179–80) and the comments of Murphy (1993, 208–9). For a magical use of another (different) "version" of the exorcism hymn that David sang before Saul, see Kotansky et al. (1992).

As is common in later adjurations for exorcising demons, in this spell David turns directly to the evil spirit and seeks to expel it from Saul by means of rebukes, threatening hints, the mention of God's creative power and the relative inferiority of the spirits in the cosmic order, and, finally, the mention of Solomon, his offspring, who came to be known for his rule over demons.[23]

The *Book of Tobit* describes a more complex ritual practice, thereby adding to our knowledge on the perception of demons in its time.[24] For my present concern, what matters is a passage dealing with Tobias's marriage to Sarah, the daughter of Raguel, in the course of a voyage that Tobit, his father, had sent him on. The marriage takes places despite Tobias's apprehensions, which are founded on Sarah's past: She had previously been married to seven husbands, and the demon Asmodeus had killed one after another in the bridal chamber.[25] The *Book of Tobit*, then, exposes a defined (and gender-related) interest in the action of demons in the world and hints at the character of their action. When Sarah's family accuses her of her husbands' deaths (*Tobit* 3:7–9), we understand that Asmodeus has operated slyly and that his actions have been concealed. Unlike Sarah's family, however, Tobias understands not only the demonic foundation of the events but also the reason for the demon's action: "He [i.e., the demon] loves her. Her he doesn't hurt, but he kills

---

23. Some of the exegetes held that the reference is not to Solomon but to some future messianic figure. See Feldheim (1971, 1) and Jacobson (1996, 2: 1180). On Solomon and his rule over demons, see later discussion.

24. The *Book of Tobit* seems to have been written at the beginning of the second century BCE, at the latest. Its Greek translation is included in the Septuagint. The work was preserved in church writings in two main versions (one short and one long) and in translations to other languages. Aramaic fragments of it were found in the Qumran scrolls and they corroborate the hypothesis that it had originally been written in Hebrew. On these fragments, see Fitzmyer (1995a; 1995b). Many editions have been published. For recent ones, see Moore (1996) and Schüngel-Straumann (2000). Quotes from the *Book of Tobit* in the text refer to the Moore version.

25. *Tobit* 3:8. The origin of the Hebrew name Ashmedai (Asmodeus) is the Persian Aishma Daiwa (the demon of wrath). Asmodeus is also mentioned in the frame story of the *Testament of Solomon* and in a well-known talmudic story on Solomon's building of the Temple. On the figure of Asmodeus, see Pines (1982) and van der Toorn et al. (1999, 106–8). Cf. also its mention in the Talmud as the demons' leader (TB *Pesahim* 110a).

any man who comes near her."[26] A demonic eroticism and the demon-woman relationship are thus visible behind the overt plot.

Tobias's decision to marry Sarah despite the threat is tied to the promise of Azariah, the guide who had accompanied him on his way (and is no other than the angel Raphael), to help him exorcise the demon. He directs Tobias to do as follows:

> However, when you enter the bridal chamber, take some of the fish's liver and its heart, and place them on the embers of the incense. When the stench rises, the demon will smell it and flee, and will never again be seen near her.[27]

This ruse, which Tobias accomplishes successfully and through which he expels Asmodeus "to the uttermost parts of Egypt" (*Tobit* 8:1–3), is based on the deliberate collection of fish organs known for their antidemonic and medicinal properties. As the accompanying angel tells Tobias,

> As for the fish's heart and liver, you must burn them in the presence of a man or woman who is afflicted by a demon or an evil spirit; and the affliction will completely flee from him and will never again return to him. And as for the gall, rub it on a man's eyes on which white patches have developed and then blow on them, and his eyes will get well.[28]

And indeed, upon his return home, Tobias uses the gall and heals the white patches covering his father's eyes (*Tobit* 11:8–13).

The story of Tobias and Sarah, then, slightly expands our knowledge of Jewish demonology and of an exorcism practice attendant to it during

---

26. *Tobit* 6:15 (Moore 1996, 196). Cf. the parallel, fragmented version in Qumran scroll 4Q Tobit[a] ar (4Q196) (Fitzmyer 1995b, 20). On this issue, see Ego (2003). On gender aspects in *Tobit*, see Bow and Nickelsburg (1991).

27. *Tobit* 6:17 (Moore 1996, 196). Cf. fragments from the parallel version in the aforementioned Qumran scroll (Fitzmyer 1995b). A parallel version is found in the *Testament of Solomon* 5: 9–10, where Asmodeus himself tells Solomon that Raphael is the angel who thwarts him and that he can be exorcised by smoking the liver and the gall of a fish from the rivers of Assyria. See Charlesworth (1983, 1: 966).

28. *Tobit* 6:8–9 (Moore 1996, 195).

the Second Temple period. Several centuries later, the Jewish historian Flavius Josephus added a brief testimony that touches precisely on the same issues. Josephus ties his story, which he claims records a public event involving the exorcism of a demon performed in front of a large audience, to the wisdom of King Solomon and his rule over demons. The success of the exorcism attests to the credibility of the knowledge that Solomon bequeathed to his people.

> And God granted him [i.e., Solomon] knowledge of the art used against demons for the benefit and healing of men. He also composed incantations by which illnesses are relieved, and left behind forms of exorcisms with which those possessed by demons drive them out, never to return. And this kind of cure is of very great power among us to this day, for I have seen a certain Elazar, a countryman of mine, in the presence of Vespasian, his sons, tribunes and a number of other soldiers, free men possessed by demons, and this was the manner of the cure: he put to the nose of the possessed man a ring which had under its seal one of the roots prescribed by Solomon, and then, as the man smelled it, drew out the demon through his nostrils, and, when the man at once fell down, adjured the demon never to come back into him, speaking Solomon's name and reciting the incantations which he had composed. Then, wishing to convince the bystanders and prove to them that he had this power, Elazar placed a cup or foot-basin full of water a little way off and commanded the demon, as it went out of the man, to overturn it and make known to the spectators that he had left the man. And when this was done the understanding and wisdom of Solomon were clearly revealed.[29]

A seal (i.e., a performative magic icon), roots, and incantations serve together in this striking public performance of an exorcism that "draws out" the demon through the nostrils. All these means are mentioned in Jewish magic sources from later centuries.

---

29. Josephus, *Jewish Antiquities* 8:45–49 (Josephus 1925–1965, 5: 595–97). On this issue, see Deines (2003) and Duling (1985).

Josephus again refers to the magic properties of roots, hinted at in other places as well, when he tells about the legendary *baaras* root, which glows like fire and eludes anyone who approaches it, intending to pluck it, and could even be fatal to anyone touching it. He claims that, despite all the dangers attendant to plucking it and handling it, the root is prized and desired because of its power, "for the so-called demons—in other words, the spirits of wicked men which enter the living and kill them unless aid is forthcoming—are promptly expelled by this root, if merely applied to the patients."[30]

Josephus's view on Solomon's wisdom regarding his rule over demons is compatible with both Jewish and Christian traditions. The most significant for my present concern are the *Testament of Solomon*, a broad and detailed Christian astro-demonological guidebook from the first centuries CE showing clear Jewish traces, and the well-known talmudic

---

30. Josephus, *The Jewish War* 7.184 (Josephus 1925–1965, 3: 557–59). See also Josephus's reference to the Essenes, who, seeking to treat diseases, investigate "medical roots and the properties of stones" (Josephus, *The Jewish War*, 2.136 [Josephus 1925–1965, 2: 375]). Cf. the comments of Apion of Alexandria on the similar legendary properties of the cynocephalia (dog's head) plant, which he claims is a useful divination means and a hedge against witchcraft (cited in Pliny's *Natural History* 30.6.18). Josephus's comment is the only explicit reference in Jewish sources from antiquity about possession by a spirit of a deceased. The closest expression to it is the quote from *Pirke de-Rabbi Eliezer* 34 ("The generation of the Flood . . . all their souls become spirits and harm the Israelites further"). This tradition does not speak of evil men but of mythical evil-doers—ancients, the Flood generation—and accordingly of ancient spirits. Hence, rather than pointing to a belief in possession by the souls of the wicked, it seemingly echoes the story about the origin of the evil spirits found in *1 Enoch* and the *Book of Jubilees*. By contrast, in sources from the Greco-Roman world, the harm of restless dead spirits is widespread. See Johnston (1999) and Ogden (2002, 146–209). Possession by the spirit of a dead person is a phenomenon that spread under the name of *dybbuk* in Eastern European Jewish communities and in the Ottoman Empire from the sixteenth century onward. Research on the subject is extensive. See, for example Chajes (2003) and Goldish (2003). As for roots, see (1) the tradition in *1 Enoch* 7:1 and 8:3, tying the knowledge of roots to witchcraft; (2) the tradition of Solomon's knowledge about the properties of roots in *Wisdom of Solomon* 7:20, 172; and (3) "an amulet of roots," which is later mentioned in rabbinic literature (Tosefta *Shabbat* 4:9; TB *Shabbat* 61a).

tradition of Solomon and Asmodeus.[31] Josephus says nothing about the symptomatic expressions of possession, but the falling down of the possessed in reaction to the treatment is described in other sources dated close to Josephus's times. I am referring to New Testament stories of possession and exorcism by Jesus Christ.[32]

The activity of the historical Jesus, insofar as he can be a subject of discussion, did take place within the realm of Jewish culture, but the discourse about it in the New Testament is a selective and theological Christian discourse that exceeds the scope of the current discussion. Yet descriptions of possession and exorcism that relate to the figure of a Palestinian Jew living at the time discussed here and that preserve nuclei of Jewish traditions about him are not irrelevant to the current discussion and deserve at least a mention.[33] Stories of Jesus's life and death in the Gospels include many accounts of miracles and, among them, six events describing exorcisms.[34] In all of them Jesus exorcises evil spirits from the bodies of the sick and heals them. These stories obviously serve the parallel spiritual message related to Jesus that the Gospels intend to convey.

In two of the stories the narrators note that the possessing spirit is a spirit of impurity.[35] In two others, possession is tied to mutism, deafness,

---

31. On the *Testament of Solomon*, see Alexander (2003a), Duling (1975; 1983), and McCown (1922). On the talmudic story, see TB *Gittin* 68a–b, and Yassif (1999, 87–89). For a succinct summary of the traditions on the relationship of Solomon and the demons, see Särkiö (2004). On the later development of the traditions on Solomon's rule over the demons, see Torijano (2002).

32. On the affliction of demons and ritual ways to contend with it in Greco-Roman sources, see Kotansky (1995) and his bibliography.

33. The research literature on this topic is vast. See mainly Aune (1980, 1523–39), E. Ferguson (1984, 1–32), Hull (1974, esp. 61–72), Kee (1967–1968), Meier (1991–2009, 2: 404–23, 648–77), M. Smith (1978), Twelftree (1993), and Yamauchi (1986). I will obviously not dwell here on the character of the possession and exorcism stories, on philological or comparative aspects of their various versions, or on Jesus's figure as a miracle worker (or as an exorcist). All these topics are discussed at length in the studies mentioned.

34. Additional mentions of exorcisms, such as those in Mark 1:32–34 and Luke 4:40–41, should also be noted.

35. Mark 1:21–28 and Luke 4:31–37; Mark 7:24–30 and Matthew 15:21–28. In this context, see Jesus's comment (in response to the accusation that he had been helped by

and blindness.[36] The last two stories are the most interesting in the current context, because they provide relatively broad testimony of the kind of injury inflicted by the spirit and of a person thought to be possessed. One is the case of the epileptic boy. The description in Mark is the most detailed.

> Someone from the crowd answered him, "Teacher, I brought you my son; he has a spirit that makes him unable to speak; and whenever it seizes him, it dashes him down; and he foams and grinds his teeth and becomes rigid." . . . And they brought the boy to him. When the spirit saw him, immediately it convulsed the boy, and he fell on the ground and rolled about, foaming at the mouth. Jesus asked the father, "How long has this been happening to him?" And he said, "From childhood. It has often cast him into the fire and into the water, to destroy him." . . . When Jesus saw that a crowd came running together, he rebuked the unclean spirit, saying to it, "You spirit that keeps this boy from speaking and hearing, I command you, come out of him, and never enter him again!" After crying out and convulsing him terribly, it came out, and the boy was like a corpse, so that most of them said, "He is dead." But Jesus took him by the hand and lifted him up, and he was able to stand.[37]

This is a vivid description of an epileptic attack, which the surrounding society explained as the violent eruption of a demon that dwells in the boy and tortures him throughout his life.[38] The removal of the demon is

---

Beelzebub, the prince of demons, to exorcise demons from humans) that the exorcised spirit of impurity seeks to return and enter the person and even brings more spirits with it (Matthew 12:43–45 and Luke 11:24–26).

36. Matthew 9:22, 12:22, and Luke 11:14. Cf. the description of the possessed child in Mark 9:17 (below).

37. Mark 9:17–26 (New Revised Standard Version, 1989). Cf. Matthew 17:14–18 and Luke 9:37–43. Matthew also notes that the boy "is lunatic."

38. Epilepsy, "the sacred disease," was perceived in antiquity as a classic expression of possession. On this perception and on the Hippocratic school's opposition to it, see Longrigg (1998, 21–23) and Temkin (1994, 3–27).

accompanied by the boy screaming, shaking, and collapsing (loss of consciousness? quiet after the attack?). Similar descriptions appear in a story about the exorcism of an impure spirit from a congregant at the Capernaum synagogue. They too include shock, a powerful scream, and collapse.[39]

The other case is the celebrated exorcism in which Jesus shifts a legion of demons from the body of one possessed onto a herd of swine, which he then drives to their death in the Sea of Galilee. This time too, the version in Mark is the most colorful.

> They [i.e., Jesus and his disciples] came to the other side of the sea, to the country of the Gerasenes. And when he had stepped out of the boat, immediately a man out of the tombs with an unclean spirit met him. He lived among the tombs; and no one could restrain him any more, even with a chain; for he had often been restrained with shackles and chains, but the chains he wrenched apart, and the shackles he broke in pieces; and no one had the strength to subdue him. Night and day among the tombs and on the mountains he was always howling and bruising himself with stones. . . . Then Jesus asked him, "What is your name?" He replied, "My name is Legion; for we are many." He begged him earnestly not to send them out of the country. Now there on the hillside a great herd of swine was feeding; and the unclean spirits begged him, "Send us into the swine; let us enter them." So he gave them permission. And the unclean spirits came out and entered the swine; and the herd, numbering about two thousand, rushed down the steep bank into the sea, and were drowned in the sea.[40]

---

39. Mark 1:26 and Luke 4:35.

40. Mark 5:1–13. The versions in Matthew 8:22–32 and Luke 8:26–33 differ in many details. Matthew tells of two men possessed by devils and makes no mention of the legion, thus dismissing the idea of multiple possession (though in his story, the demons run the herd of swine into the sea).

My concern with this story is twofold. First, it points to an approach that ties social and behavioral strangeness (what we may call mental illness) to possession.[41] Second, it attests to the existence of a belief in multiple possession, which is also recorded elsewhere in the New Testament[42] and seems to tie the degree of strangeness to the number of underlying demons causing it. Stories of possession and exorcism in the Gospels, then, complete some of what is missing in the Jewish sources, enriching with additional details our knowledge about the possessed and the essence of the demonic harm inflicted on them.

These are the demonological sources from the Second Temple period that are not primary magic literature, and this is the picture that emerges from them—one far broader than could have been assumed relying on the few insider sources available—about the demonological worldview: the origin and role of demons, their character, ways of action, and modes of protection from them. This picture was widespread among contemporary Jews.

Angels, Women, and Witchcraft

Records from the Second Temple period enrich our knowledge on two other important issues: the origin of magic in the world and its ascription to women (by male writers and scribes, who most certainly represent male thinking in their community).[43] As for the origin of magic, we find an innovation in relation to the history of familiar traditions. As for the ascription to women, it is directly related to the prohibition on magic in the Bible, which refers to magic as one of the "abominations of those

---

41. The strangeness is evident in various expressions of inhumanity: the dwelling of the possessed among the tombs (Luke 8:29 adds that the man "would be driven by the demon into the wilds"), (animal) nakedness, and physical mutilation. Healing comes forth in the reverse of the inhuman behavior—a transition from nature to culture: "And they [who had heard about it] came to Jesus, and saw him that was possessed with the demon, and had the legion, sitting, and clothed, and in his right mind" (Mark 5:15; cf. Luke 8:35).

42. Matthew 12:43–45 and Luke 11:24–26.

43. We obviously have no way of knowing the attitude of women in the Jewish communities of late antiquity toward the male ascription of witchcraft to their gender, because men are the only mediators of knowledge in their regard.

nations" and, accordingly, as a sin[44] and commands the killing of those (the witches!) who engage in it.[45]

The negative attitude toward sorcery or, in other words, the use of labels such as *kishuf, keshafim,* and *mekhashef* for hostile labeling, particularly of the "other," is found in many places in the Bible[46] and was adopted in several sources of the Second Temple period. *2 Enoch,* for instance, numbers witchcraft among the crimes for which sinners imprisoned in the northern third heaven are punished and made to suffer cruel tortures. In the *Sybilline Oracles* we find that various magic practices are precisely the kind of deceit and evil that the Jewish people have abandoned, and Josephus emphasizes that Moses's miracles before Pharaoh were divine signs essentially different from (and more powerful than) manipulative Egyptian witchcraft. Finally, Philo notes that Mosaic law was meant to eradicate magic and divination, which are

---

44. Deuteronomy 18:9–11. Obviously, no implication is thereby intended that the Bible contains no distinctly magic traditions. Quite the contrary. When biblical figures are involved, however, these practices are no longer in the category of *kishuf* (magic), just as the man of God, the prophet, or the visionary are not categorized as *menahashim* (soothsayers). The literature on witchcraft and divination in the Bible is extensive. See Bohak (2008, 11–35), Cryer (1994; 2001), Jeffers (1996), and Schmidt (2002).

45. The specific admonition, "You shall not suffer a witch (*mekhashefah*) to live" (Exodus 22:17) is early evidence of the identification of witchcraft with the female gender. This identification stands out even more prominently against the general description of the forbidden Gentile abominations in masculine terms, as mentioned in Deuteronomy 18:9–11 (*kosem, me'onen, menahesh, mekhashef,* etc.). As usual, the normative principle is formulated in masculine terms, and this formulation is adopted regarding all agents of power and knowledge, including the wizard. It thereby concretizes and also fixates the masculinity of the normative and structural systems, which are the web that keep society together and enable its existence. The punishment law, however, dealing with sanctions for the actual breach of these codes, ascribes witchcraft to women.

46. Obviously, prominent here is the story of the struggle that Moses and Aaron conducted against Egyptian sorcerers and magicians (Exodus 7–8). Beside this tradition, see the negative references to sorceries and sorcerers (at times in a feminine context) by both chroniclers and prophets in 2 Kings 9:22; Isaiah 12:9, 12; Jeremiah 27:9; Mica 5:11; Nahum 3:4; Malachi 3:5; and 2 Chronicles 33:6. See also mentions of sorcerers beside other foreign, Babylonian agents of knowledge and power in Daniel 2:2.

fundamentally erroneous and conceal deviance and heresy.[47] Regarding magic and divination, Philo discusses magicians and potion makers (*magoi, pharmakeutai*) in his work on the special laws.

> Now the true magic, the scientific vision by which the facts of nature are presented in a clearer light, is felt to be a fit object for reverence and ambition and is carefully studied not only by ordinary persons but by kings and the greatest kings, and particularly those of the Persians, so much so that it is said that no one in that country is promoted to the throne unless he has first been admitted into the caste of the Magi. But there is a counterfeit of this, most properly called a perversion of art, pursued by charlatan mendicants and parasites and the basest of the women and slave population, who make it their profession to deal in purifications and disenchantments and promise with some sort of charms and incantations to turn men's love into deadly enmity and their hatred into profound affection. The simplest and most innocent natures are deceived by the bait till at last the worst misfortunes come upon them and thereby the wide membership which unites great companies of friends and kinsmen falls gradually into decay and is rapidly and silently destroyed.[48]

Philo draws a distinction here that was widespread in the Hellenistic world where he lived. On the one hand was the honorable "scientific" practice ascribed to the Persian priests from the Magush tribe (whose name was the source of the Greek word *magos*, "magician," hence *mageia*, "magic").[49] On the other hand were the despicable practices common in

---

47. 2 *Enoch* 6:10–13 (Charlesworth 1983, 1: 118–21); *Sybilline Oracles* 3: 218–34 (Charlesworth 1983, 1: 366); Josephus, *Jewish Antiquities*, 2.284–87 (cf. also Josephus's response to the accusation that Moses had been a "charlatan and impostor" [γόης] in *Against Apion*, 2.145, 161 [Josephus 1925–1965, 1: 351, 375]); Philo, *The Special Laws*, 1.60–63 (Philo 1929–1962, 7: 134–137). Cf. Philo's comment against divination in Philo, *The Special Laws*, 4.48–52.

48. Philo, *The Special Laws*, 3.100–101 (Philo 1929–1962, 7: 539–41). For parallels of this distinction in the Greco-Roman world, see Philo (1929–1962, 7: 635–37).

49. See Apuleius's comment on this matter, discussed in chapter 2. Cf. Philo's praise for the wisdom of Persian Magi, who study nature invoking knowledge of truth

his surroundings among those on the margins of the male intellectual society to which he belonged and for which he wrote: "charlatan mendicants and parasites and the basest of the women and slave population." In Philo's thought, then, (base) women, who perhaps because of their limited social power were often suspected by the hegemonic classes of seeking compensation through ritual power, belonged in the margins. Philo does not, however, tie witchcraft to femininity or to the female gender but rather to the ignorance and intellectual limitations common to both women and men. A different picture is presented in other sources of the Second Temple era and, above all, in *1 Enoch.*

The *Book of Watchers* that opens *1 Enoch* narrates at length the story of the rebellious angels who descended to earth in order to take women and the calamity they unleashed on earth and on themselves through this sin.[50] In the course of this story, we learn that, in their descent, the angels brought to the world heavenly but destructive knowledge, which they shared with humans.

> These [the angels' leaders] and all the others with them took for themselves wives from among them, such as they chose. And they began to go into them and to defile themselves through them, and to teach them sorcery and charms, and to reveal to them the cutting of roots and plants.[51]

We are later told that Shemihazah, the leader of the rebellious angels, taught the women incantations and root cutting, whereas Hermani, another one of their leaders, taught them sorcery for the loosing of spells.[52]

This account exposes the two sides of the attitude toward sorcery. On the one hand, its source is in heaven and it is therefore true and powerful knowledge; on the other hand, its existence in the world originates in sin. Magic knowledge is part of the corruption afflicting the

---

and are blessed with divine visions (Philo, *Every Good Man Is Free*, 74 (Philo 1929–1962, 9: 52–53).

50. See *1 Enoch* 6–16. Cf. Genesis 6:8.

51. *1 Enoch* 7:1 (Nickelsburg 2001, 182).

52. *1 Enoch* 8:3 (Nickelsburg 2001, 188). Astrological knowledge was also drawn down by angels (*1 Enoch* 8:3). The Asael tradition, of which a fragment was incorporated into the story at this point, bases learning on other matters.

world following the disruption of the order of Creation and the breach of the borders God had set to his creatures. The *Book of Watchers*, therefore, conveys a view of human witchcraft that is fundamentally negative. As such, it is tied to the transgression of the angels and their sexual defilement on the one hand and to women on the other. It originates in the theft of heavenly secrets and culminates in the growing power of humans in general and of women in particular to cause harm and destruction.

> You [angels] were in heaven, and no mystery was revealed to you; but a stolen mystery you learned; and this you make known to the women in your hardness of heart; and through this mystery the women and men are multiplying evils upon the earth.[53]

The Shemihazah tradition, which is the leading narrative in the story of the angels' descent in *1 Enoch*, does not as such explicitly label harlotry and witchcraft as two sides of the female transgression, as we find in many ancient Jewish sources.[54] The final editing of the work, however, which at this point weaves into the story a passage from the Asael tradition, tightens the connection between them. According to the story, Asael taught women and men how to enhance their power according to destructive gender patterns.

> Asael taught men to make swords of iron and weapons and shields and breastplates and every instrument of war. He showed them metals of the earth and how they should work gold to fashion it suitably, and concerning silver, to fashion it for bracelets and ornaments for women. And he showed them concerning antimony and eye paint and all manner of precious stones and dyes.[55]

---

53. *1 Enoch* 16:3 (Nickelsburg 2001, 267).

54. On harlotry and witchcraft in the Bible, see, for example, 2 Kings 9:21–22 and Nahum 3:4. On harlotry and witchcraft in rabbinic literature, see chapter 7. On the Shemihazah and Asael traditions and their redaction in the *Book of Watchers*, cf. Eshel (1999, 15–48) and Nickelsburg (2001, 165–73, 229–32).

55. *1 Enoch* 8:1 (Nickelsburg 2001, 188). On the integration of this tradition in the Shemihazah tradition and on the role of the learning traditions in the story of the angels' descent, see Nickelsburg (2001, 165–201).

The mutual interweaving of the various traditions of learning ties together the two kinds of female knowledge threatening the male gender (whose voice is heard in the story)—sexual seduction and witchcraft—and is thus destructive (in this gender's perception).

The *Book of Enoch*, then, explicitly formulates a substantiated accusation of witchcraft against women, tying it to their seductive sexual powers. This is a relatively early example of the hostile symbolization of the women's threatening power, as members of the "other" gender, by the threatened male gender. We find echoes of it later, in Josephus's description of the intrigues, conspiracies, and murders in Herod's court, which tie women in general and the court's women in particular to the concoction and use of aggressive brews (*pharmaka*): poisons and love potions.[56] The "exposure" of these deeds and their description by male writers, in this case Josephus, express (while also sharpening and intensifying) male anxiety about female power, which is presented as deceptive, concealed, and dangerous.[57] More explicit expressions of tying witchcraft to women and femininity appear later in rabbinic literature.

---

56. The meaning of the terms *pharmakos*, *pharmakov*, and similar terms was expanded from the realm of herbology (the science of preparing herbal substances both for healing and afflicting) to the realm of witchcraft—strengthening some liquid through rituals and incantations. See Liddell et al. (1948, 2: 1917) and Seidel (1996, 84–85). We cannot know for sure what Josephus intended by these words in these descriptions or whether he made any effort to draw a distinction a priori between potions whose power followed from the substance used and potions whose power followed from the ritual. Elsewhere, Josephus uses the word *pharmakeas* in a sense that is apparently no longer related to potions at all, when he speaks about the claim of people from Tarichaeae (northwest of the Lake of Galilee), whereby two noble vassals of the king, who had sought refuge with him, were "sorcerers who made it impossible to defeat the Romans." See *Life of Josephus*, 149–50 (Josephus 1925–1965, 1: 56–59).

57. For conspiracies and accusations about the use of love and death potions in Herod's court, see *The Jewish War* 1.572–73, 582–83; and *Jewish Antiquities* 15.221–29, 17.61–63. Cf. the accusation against Cleopatra about the use of love and death potions (*Jewish Antiquities* 15.89, 93). In one of these fragments (*Jewish Antiquities* 17.63), where Josephus tells that the potion was bought from a pharmacist-witch from an Arab land, he weaves in the comment that "the women from Arabia are the most skillful of all in the use of drugs." Not surprisingly, then, a woman who beside her gender "otherness" is also ethnically "other," was perceived as particularly powerful.

I discuss this issue at length in chapter 7, but for now, let's move on to consider other literary bodies.

HEKHALOT AND MERKAVAH LITERATURE

Hekhalot and *Merkavah* literature—a corpus that includes a few works which apparently represent diverse streams of what is known in the research literature as early Jewish mysticism—was written mostly in Palestine (and only partly in Babylonia), probably in the third to eighth centuries CE.[58] Insofar as their dating is concerned, these works are contemporaries of the magic literature available to us. In chapter 2 I discussed at length the relationship between these works—including the social phenomenon they represent—and Jewish magic, so I do not dwell further on this issue here. Whether adjurations are the gist of this literature or only an accompaniment to the visionary concern at its core, their presence in it is clear and essential. *Hekhalot* and *Merkavah* works convey a theoretical and practical interest in the power of seals, incantations, and holy names to enforce human will on angels in order to achieve human aims, be they heavenly or earthly.

The heavenly facet of this interest is prominently expressed in the use of seals at the entrances to the palaces, which R. Ishmael advises in *Hekhalot Rabbati* to ensure the success of the journey to the seventh palace.

> Rabbi Ishmael said: When you come and stand at the entrance of the first palace, take two seals in your two hands, one of ṬWṬRWSY'Y YHWH and one of Suriah, Prince of the Presence. (The one) of ṬWṬRWSY'Y YHWH show it to the ones standing to the right, and (the one) of Suriah, show it to the ones standing to the left. At once RHBY'L the prince who is head of the entrance of the first palace and who is appointed over the first palace and who stands to the right of the lintel, and ṬWPHY'L, the prince who stands to the left of the lintel with him—at once he takes hold of you, one from your right and one from your left, until they bring and they deliver you over and

---

58. On this literary corpus, see the "Visions and Adjurations: Magic in *Hekhalot* and *Merkavah* Literature" subsection in chapter 2.

introduce you and admonish ṬGRY'L concerning you, the prince who is the chief of the entrance of the second palace and stands to the right of the lintel, and MTPY'L, the prince who stands to the left of the lintel with him. Show to them two seals, one of 'DRYHRWN YHWH, one of 'WZHYY', Prince of the Presence. (The one) of 'DRYHRWN YHWH, show to the ones standing to the right. (The one) of 'WZHYY', Prince of the Presence, show to the ones standing to the left. At once they take hold of you, one from your right and one from your left, until they bring you and deliver you over and introduce you and admonish ŠBWRY'L concerning you, the prince who is head of the entrance of the third palace and stands to the right of the lintel, and RṢWṢY'L the prince who stands to the left of the lintel with him. Show them two seals, one of ṢWRṬQ YHWH and one of RHBYWRWN, Prince of the Presence.[59]

This journey, which culminates in the contemplation of "the King in His beauty" and participation in the exaltation ritual constantly unfolding before the heavenly throne, cannot take place without knowledge of holy names and their uses.[60] These are required not only for the passage from one palace to the other but also for protection.

The work known as *Ḥotam ha-Merkavah* (The Seal of the Chariot), which deals with the seal that Ozhayah gave to the descender to the chariot (*yored ha-merkavah*) to protect him in his voyage to the higher palaces, clarifies the dangers awaiting him and the importance of magic protection.

You must write and set down the seal of the descent to the chariot for those who enter the world, for you and for whoever seeks to descend to peer at the King and at His beauty. And (if) he has

59. Schäfer (1981, secs. 219–21) (=Davila 2013, 108–9).

60. A comprehensive review of *Hekhalot* and *Merkavah* works reveals that this knowledge and the use of it were necessary but not sufficient. Prayers, purification asce-sis (such as immersion and fasting), and abstention from seminal emissions, contact with women, and even conversation with them are detailed in various places in this corpus and point to the broader ritual context of the use of adjurations. See later discussion, and cf. Lesses (1998, 117–60) and Swartz (1996, 153–72).

taken hold of this path, so may he descend and see, and may he not be struck down, for I have put it on the scroll for you. . . . And (you are) not like those before you, whom great disgrace found, for they were like a man who got lost in a great wilderness, and a path took him along and he went, and they cast him into a fecund jungle. And he went and found there lair upon lair of lions and of young lions and den upon den of leopards and den upon den of wolves. He came and stood among them and did not know what he should do. And so one would smite him and tear him, and another smite him and drag him away. . . . They dragged him—Ben Zoma—a hundred times over the first palace, I am a witness, for I was counting the times he and his associate were dragged—whether they saved him or whether they did not save him, whether they were saved or whether they were struck down: two hundred times over the second palace, four hundred times over the third palace, eight hundred times over the fourth palace, a thousand six hundred times over the fifth palace, three thousand two hundred times over the sixth palace, six thousand four hundred times over the seventh palace. But you do not get even one scratch from the princes of the guardians of the palaces or from any angel of the angels of violence. And you come and arrive at the sixth palace:[61] regiments upon regiments of princes and of princes of princes and of bands and of bands of bands, since the entrance of the sixth palace thrusts and splashes and brings forth myriads upon myriads and camps upon camps and entourages upon entourages in a single hour. But there is no hindrance and you are not harmed for it is a great seal you take hold of and all the angels on high tremble at it.[62]

Ozhayah later describes "the fires that are stirred up, and go forth from the seventh palace to the sixth palace—fire of glowing coal and trickling fire and blazing fire and sweet fire—they go forth and enter like arrows."

---

61. A stringent test, which is not dependent on the power of names and seals, awaits the descender to the chariot at the entrance to the sixth palace. See Dan (1987a; 1998–1999, 1: 261–309).

62. Schäfer (1984, 103, ll. 24–38) (=Davila 2013, 406–7).

He warns the descender to the chariot of their danger and instructs him on how to protect himself from them and how to seal his body openings with wool, "so that there may be an obstruction for your soul so that it does not go out before I reach you and I come and I stand over you and fan you and your spirit returns and your soul is revived."[63] At their end, R. Ishmael attests about himself: "I did so in the first palace and on to the seventh palace . . . and saw the King in His beauty."[64]

Whether the heavenly voyage was, as some scholars think, merely an imagined reality and a literary fiction or whether, as others believe, *Hekhalot* works were practical guidebooks to mystic-shamanic visions of voyages, *yordei ha-merkavah* probably spent most of their time on earth. The *Hekhalot* and *Merkavah* literature shows that here too, in ordinary human society, mystical-magic knowledge yielded considerable advantages in the two areas of knowledge and power that, as is well known, are inseparable.

Adjurations in search of knowledge are the focus of the Prince of Torah traditions. These traditions have been discussed by several scholars, among them some who saw them as the focus of *Hekhalot* and *Merkavah* literature as a whole and as the key for decoding its social context.[65] The concern of these traditions, which are tied to the figure of R. Ishmael, is to attain knowledge of Torah through an alternative path to the scholarly rabbinic one, by adjuring the Prince of Torah. Of the act itself, R. Ishmael says,

> We wrote and we corrected and we established [for the gene]rations in order to make use of them, of the names and of these princes. Cheerful is the innocent one who has in him vigor and he makes use of this majesty and greatness and lordliness, who has made use of the King and of His attendants and of His servants and it was fine for him.[66]

---

63. Schäfer (1984, 103, ll. 39–46) (=Davila 2013, 407).

64. Schäfer (1984, 105, ll. 18–19) (=Davila 2013, 409).

65. See Halperin (1988). Michael Swartz discusses these traditions at length in contexts of knowledge, ritual, society, and witchcraft. See Swartz (1996). See also Dan (1993, 103–22) and Vidas (2013).

66. Schäfer (1984, 105, ll. 32–34) (=Davila 2013, 410).

These words rely on the approach whereby study and knowledge of the mystical content are explicitly willed by God, who granted "Israel" knowledge of his mystery and its uses.[67] At the end of that tradition, R. Ishmael clarifies the essence of the ritual required for this purpose and its assured results.

> R. Ishmael said: Thus said R. Aqiva in the name of R. Eliezer the Great: He who would bind himself to the Prince of Torah must wash his clothes and his garments and immerse (in) a strict immersion in case of a nocturnal emission. And he must enter and dwell for twelve days in a room or in an upper chamber. He may not go out and he may not come in, and he must not eat or drink. But from evening to evening (see) that he eats his bread, clean bread of his own hands, and he drinks clear water, and he may not taste any kind of vegetable. And he must insert this midrash of the Prince of Torah into the prayer, three times in every single day; it is after the prayer that he should pray it from its beginning to its end. And afterward he must sit and study it (for) twelve days, the days of his fasting, from morning until evening, and he must not be silent. And in every hour that he finishes it he must stand on his feet and adjure the servants by their King and he must call for every single prince twelve times. Afterward he must adjure him by the seal—every single one of them. He must adjure them for twelve days in the name of YWPY'L, who is the adornment of the height of his King; and in the name of SRBY'L, who is one of the princes of the chariot; and in the name of ŠHRRY'L, who is a beloved prince; and in the name of ḤSDY'L, who is called to might six hours in each day. And he must go back and adjure them, the latter four princes, with a great seal and with a great oath in the name of 'ZBWG', which is a great seal, and in the name of ṢWRṬQ, a holy name and a fearsome crown. When he completes the twelve, he will go forth to all the principles of Torah that he

---

67. On the question of who the "Israel" were who can use this mystic knowledge—the descenders to the chariot or the people of Israel—see Davila (2001, 269–77).

seeks, whether to Bible or to Mishnah or to the vision of the chariot.[68]

And he attests:

> R. Ishmael said: I bear this testimony for the generations, that as soon as I invoked the name of this beloved prince and delectable servant and by means of him I adjured the three princes, his companions, who are written in the word of the prince that is written in the Book of the Princes, at once I sat and I had a vision and feasted my eyes on the midrash and on the laws and on the message and on the interpretation of the laws, and I expounded and extolled the Torah, the Prophets and the Writings for a year and a half.[69]

Adjuring an angel to attain knowledge is mentioned in several places in the magic recipe literature under the title "opening the heart" and is anchored in a broader tradition of recourse to supernatural agents through adjurations.[70] The Prince of Torah tradition, then, is a particular instance of using adjurations to attain knowledge. Its uniqueness, beyond its literary context (with all its implications), lies in the character of the required knowledge.[71]

Broader, and indeed unlimited, knowledge is suggested in two additional passages of *Hekhalot* literature: the adjuration of the Prince of Dream (*Sar ha-Ḥalom*) and the adjuration of the Prince of Presence (*Sar*

---

68. Schäfer (1981, secs. 299–303) (=Davila 2013, 181–83).

69. Schäfer (1984, 105, ll. 34–37) (=Davila 2013, 411).

70. See Harari (2005c).

71. The scope of this desired knowledge is explained as follows: "I know what you seek and my heart has recognized what you desire: much Torah is what you seek, and a multitude of study and a great many traditions, and to inquire of the law is what you wish for, and a multitude of secrets is what you desire, to increase testimony in mountains upon mountains, to pile up sagacity in hills upon hills, to increase study in the courtyards and dialectic in the streets, and to multiply *halakhot* like the sand of the sea and mysteries like the dust of the earth" (Schäfer 1981, sec. 278 [=Swartz 1996, 95, with a slight change]). Early evidence of the Prince of Torah idea is found in several Babylonian magic bowls. James Davila sees this as one layer of the evidence on the shamanistic communal activity of the descenders of the chariot (Davila 2001, 220–22).

ha-Panim). "The adjuration of the Prince of Dream" is a long recipe that opens with general directives.

> Thus do: fast for three days and say to me these verses every night and sleep in your clothes. And on the third night, take this book in your hands and recite these names three times with the verses. And afterwards, lie on your shoulders, for immediately the image of a man will come to you and tell you all you wish to know, whether it be a great thing or a small thing.[72]

The following text is the precise wording of the incantation that includes names of God, biblical verses, and adjurations. The purpose of the adjuration is specified as follows:

> By your marvelous and wondrous name I command the Prince of Dream to hurry and come to me this night and tell me this night all of my desires. I adjure you RGŠ'L, the great prince of dream . . . to come to me this night in equanimity, in goodness, and not in anger, and speak to me and give me a sign or a miracle or a verse which will be in my hand, and tell me about a certain matter, and everything which will be about it, and will be with it in the future, whether for good or for something else. Do not hesitate to come now in the name of these explicit names which are engraved on the throne of glory.[73]

At the end of the incantation, the angel is again addressed directly. He is required to come calmly and without rage, to reveal to the adjurer whatever he wishes, and to inform him, in his dream, "whether I should reveal its interpretation or conceal its interpretation from others,"[74] so that he should not fail on this matter before God.

The adjuration of the Prince of Presence is also a matter of knowledge, but it is not related to a dream.[75] This tradition opens by emphasizing the enormous risk, up to the destruction of the entire world, entailed

72. Schäfer (1981, sec. 502) (=Lesses 1998, 395–96, with slight changes).
73. Schäfer (1981, secs. 504–5) (=Lesses 1998, 396–98).
74. Schäfer (1981, sec. 506).
75. Schäfer (1981, secs. 623–39). On this adjuration, see Lesses (1995).

by the adjuration act. However, careful performance of the purification instructions and of the protective adjurations will help to shield the user from the angels "whose charge is to hurt those who are not clean and pure and comes close to the use the heavenly servants."[76] The user will then be able to turn to the Prince of Presence himself and adjure him.

> By this name, in this language, I call to you, Ozhayah, Prince of the Presence, Youth attendant before the King of the world. And he is a prince and a commander over the whole host on high. I adjure you and I decree upon you that you should augment me so as to be bound to my will. And you shall accept the adjuration of my decree, and you shall do what I ask, and you shall fulfill my request. You shall not confound me, you shall not make me quake, you shall not perforate me, you shall not put my frame into a cold sweat, you shall not make my ankles slip, and you shall not make the speech of my lips err. But let me be strengthened and made valiant, and let the adjuration be made mighty, and let the name be in order in my throat. Let no convulsion seize me, and do not let the foot of your attendants make me wander so as to confound me and to make me fear and so as to make my hands slack. And let me not be drowned in the fire and in the flame, in the tempest and the storm that goes with you. . . . By them [i.e., by the names] I adjure you, I decree and establish concerning you that you must make haste and you must descend beside me—I am so-and-so, son of so-and-so— you, and not your emissary. And in your descent you must not prey on my mind. You shall reveal to me all the searches of the mysteries of above and below, and the secrets of the stored-up things of above and below and the mysteries of understanding and the shrewdness of abiding success, like a man who talks with his associate. For by the great and magnificent and wondrous

---

76. Schäfer (1981, sec. 624). The danger entailed by the adjuration of the angels is a common motif in the description of the relationship between humans and angels in *Hekhalot* literature. Cf. Schäfer (1981, secs. 224, 562–66, 681, and passim). On this matter in magic literature, see Harari (1997b, 46–47, 132–33).

and tested and arrayed names I have adjured you. . . . By them I adjure you that you know and recognize the praise and greatness of these names, such that mouth cannot praise and ears cannot hear the great praise of one of them. Upon them you are commanded and you are warned from the mouth of the Most High, that if you hear an adjuration by these names, do glory to His name and hasten and descend and do the will of the one who adjures you. . . . And you shall do my request: what I ask establish and my will fulfill. For in your hand is everything by the permission of 'NDYRW RD HW HYH, my God and your God, Lord of everything and your Lord. And by His names I have adjured you that you be bound to me and you hasten and descend and do my will and do not delay.[77]

Knowledge is power. And indeed, *Hekhalot* literature attests to several expressions of power that descenders to the chariot possessed on earth as well. In this context the mystical-magic tradition about Moses's ascent, found in a Genizah fragment, deserves special mention. It describes at length the hostile angels who blocked Moses's way in heaven and silenced him for three days. Moses eventually overcame them through "these three figures (*midot*), which are 'YSTYMH MSMH and KMDWT YGWR, and all the princes feared him, Moses, and they would not answer."[78] The importance of this tradition for my current concern is in the healing mysteries that the angels revealed to Moses after he defeated them.

The prince of the head came to him and told him, this is my adjuration. The prince of the eye came to him and told him, this is my adjuration. The prince of the ear came to him and told him, this is my adjuration. The prince of the mouth came to him and t[old] him, this is my adjuration. The prince of the whole body came to him and told him, this is my adjuration and this is my healing.[79]

---

77. Schäfer (1981, secs. 626–36) (=Davila 2013, 358–64).
78. Schäfer (1984, 175).
79. Schäfer (1984, 177).

Even though the formulas are not revealed in this work, they clearly rely on a conception that binds healing and the adjuration of angels in charge of body limbs and ties the knowledge necessary for this purpose to a heavenly voyage of vision and learning. The story of Moses's ascent to heaven to receive the Torah and the gifts he received from the angels serves in this version as an archetype of the mystical-magic voyage of the descenders to the chariot.[80]

A similar tradition is found at the end of *3 Enoch*. The revelation of the healing formula to Moses, notwithstanding the angels' opposition, is ascribed here to Metatron, who gives the following account:

> YWY, the God of Israel, is my witness in this thing, (that) when I revealed this secret to Moses, then all the hosts in each and every heaven on high raged against me. . . . And they were not appeased, until the Holy One, blessed be He, rebuked them and drove them away with rebuke from before Him saying to them: "I delight in, and have set my love on, and have entrusted and committed unto Metatron, my Servant, alone, for he is One [i.e., unique] among all the children of heaven. And Metatron brings them [i.e., the mysteries] out from his house of treasuries and commits them to Moses, and Moses to Joshua, and Joshua to the elders, and the elders to the prophets and the prophets to the man of the Great Synagogue, and the man of the Great Synagogue to Ezra and Ezra the Scribe to Hillel the elder, and Hillel the elder to R. Abbahu and Rabbi Abbahu to R. Zera, and R. Zera to the men of faith, and the men of faith to the masters of faith so that they should take care of it and heal by it all diseases that rage in the world.[81]

If the descenders to the chariot had magic-healing knowledge of this kind, perhaps they kept it for themselves or perhaps, as Davila suggests, they directed the power concealed within it for the benefit of the public in general.

---

80. On traditions of Moses's ascent, see Harari (2005b).
81. Schäfer (1981, secs. 79–80) (=Odeberg 1928, 178–79, with slight changes).

Another power, however, was explicitly reserved solely for them. I am referring to the advantage of the social power that the descenders to the chariot aspired to, which found propagandistic expression in their writings. This power was related to the absolute knowledge they possessed, anchored in the ongoing "life ritual" of ascesis and purification, mystical learning, and powerful personal contact with the supernal worlds. A declaration in principle regarding the social power concealed in the mystery of the Prince of Torah is issued by God himself.

> I know what you seek and my heart has recognized what you desire . . . to establish sessions in the gates of the tents, to expound in them the forbidden and permitted, to declare pure in them that which is pure, and to declare impure in them that which is impure; to declare fit that which is ritually fit, and to declare unfit that which is ritually unfit, to recognize in them types of blood, and to instruct the menstruant in what to do; to tie crowns on your heads, and the wreath of royalty on the heads of your children, to compel kings to bow down to you, and to obligate nobles to prostrate before you. To spread your name on every shore, and your renown in the ports of the seas, to enlighten your faces with the radiance of the day, between your eyes like the planet Venus. If you merit this seal, to make use of my crown, no ignorant person shall ever be found, and there shall not be a fool or simpleton among you.[82]

The actual realization of this power is the subject of R. Ishmael's words at the opening of *Hekhalot Rabbati*. At this point, the advantage of *yordei ha-merkavah* is tied to the beholding of the chariot. Ascent to the divine throne and proximity to it involve not only a strong spiritual experience but also absolute knowledge about all that will happen in the world: "who is made low, who is made lofty, who is weakened, who is made mighty, who is impoverished, who is made rich, who is killed, who is made alive, who is dispossessed of an inheritance, who is given an inheritance, who is made to inherit Torah, who is given

---

82. Schäfer (1981, secs. 287–88) (= Swartz 1996, 95–96).

wisdom."[83] Moreover, the descender to the chariot seeks what is hidden and penetrates the most intimate recesses. Nothing is hidden from him.

> Greatest of all it is that he has a vision of every deed that mortals do, even in inner rooms, whether fine deeds, whether corrupt deeds. He knows and recognizes the man (who is) a thief: he knows and recognizes the man who commits adultery; he knows and recognizes the slayer of a living person; he knows and recognizes the one who is suspected of (contact with) the menstruant; he knows and recognizes the one who tells gossip. Greatest of all is that he recognizes all sorcerers.[84]

As in all the other sources discussed, here too sorcery is the ritual-aggressive action of the other. In their own perception, descenders to the chariot are possessors of heavenly secrets, spectators of the chariot who master holy names, adjurers of angels, but not sorcerers. "Sorcerers" are those who threaten them and endanger their power and their status, and their community certainly included such people. Whoever boasts of such powers will obviously face opponents, all the more so when he threatens to expose not only the transgressions of individuals but also the shame of families.

> Greatest of all it is that all beings shall be before him like silver before a refiner, whether it be refined silver, whether it be unfit silver, whether it be pure silver. And also he will have visionary insight into a family: how many bastards there are in a family; how many sons of a menstruant, how many wounded by crushing, how many whose male organ is cut off, how many sons of slaves, how many sons of the uncircumcised.[85]

Having mentioned the existence of other power agents—sorcerers—around the descenders to the chariot and having dealt with the threat that they themselves pose, R. Ishmael next describes their advantage in

---

83. Schäfer (1981, sec. 82) (=Davila 2013, 51–52).

84. Schäfer (1981, secs. 83–84 (=Davila 2013, 52).

85. Schäfer (1981, sec. 86) (=Davila 2013, 53–54). Cf. Deuteronomy 23:2.

the explicit context of struggle. Protection from heaven, we find, is available to those living on earth as members of the heavenly retinue.

> Greatest of all it is that anyone who raises his hand against him and strikes him—they clothe him with plagues and cover him with leprosy and garland him with skin blemishes. Greatest of all it is that anyone who tells gossip about him—they attack and they cast on him all strokes, skin eruptions, and injuries and wounds from which has issued a raw ulcer. Greatest of all it is that he is set apart from all mortals and he is confounding in all his characteristics and he is glorified over the uppermost ones and the lowermost ones. And anyone who stumbles over him—great, evil, and harsh stumbling blocks fall on that person from heaven. And anyone who stretches out a hand against him with a legal document—the law court on high stretch out a hand against him. . . . Greatest of all it is that anyone who sets his face against him—they make dim the luminary of his eyeballs. Greatest of all it is that if anyone who despises him does not leave behind root or branch, nor does he leave an inheritance.[86]

The demand of authority and status culminates in R. Ishmael's concluding statement.

> The one who considers the chariot does not have permission to stand except before three figures alone: before a king, before a high priest, and before the Sanhedrin. The Sanhedrin at a time when it has in it a patriarch. Behold, if there is no patriarch in it, he may not stand even before the Sanhedrin.[87]

The advantages accruing to those who overcome the angels through the power of their adjurations on earth and above, which in *Hekhalot Rabbati* are limited to the social realm, are given far greater scope elsewhere. At the end of *Merkavah Rabbah*, immediately following the passages on *Shi'ur Qomah*, R. Ishmael says:

---

86. Schäfer (1981, secs. 84–91) (=Davila 2013, 52–54).
87. Schäfer (1981, sec. 93) (=Davila 2013, 55–56).

He who studies this great mystery—his face is sallow, his stature is fine to him, awe of him is imposed upon beings, and his good name goes into all the places of Israel. His dreams are easy upon him, his Torah is preserved in him, and he does not forget the words of Torah all his days. It is good for him in this world and restful for him with regard to the world to come. Even the iniquities of his youth He remits to him for the future to come. The evil inclination has no authority over him, and he is saved from spirits and demons and robbers and from all injurious animals and from snake and scorpion and from all harmful demons.[88]

Not only is this a succinct summary of almost all that was discussed earlier, but it also extends protection to other realms familiar from magic literature: harmful dreams, demons, robbers, predators, and poisonous reptiles, which are often identified in witchcraft literature with the deliberate infliction of magic harm.[89] Possibly, the intent was to acquire protection not only from their harm as such but also from the ritual power of their senders, an issue explicitly noted in a fragment from *Shi'ur Qomah* found in the Cairo Genizah.

Whoever knows this mystery is assured of life in the world to come, and saved from the punishment of hell, and from all harsh decrees, and from various sorceries and calamities.[90]

As noted, at the opening of *Hekhalot Rabbati*, R. Ishmael takes pride in the power of *yordei ha-merkavah* to identify and expose "sorcerers." His statement, conveying the struggle of descenders to the chariot against alternative agents of ritual power (meaning those they do not think of as "we"—partners to the holy mystery—but as "they"), suggests a new perspective. Not only can descenders to the chariot identify and denounce other power agents (who are illegitimate and hence sorcerers), but they are also protected from them. This kind of protection is a

---

88. Schäfer (1981, sec. 705) (=Davila 2013, 337). Cf. also Schäfer (1981, sec. 706).
89. Harari (1997a, 112n3).
90. Schäfer (1984, 101, ll. 41–45).

further, highly significant link in the web of power advantage, which in the self-perception reflected in ancient Jewish mystical literature was preserved for those who had been privileged with the ascent, the mystery, and the holy names of adjurations.

POLEMICAL KARAITE WRITINGS

Karaite sources (from the last centuries of the first millennium) dealing with sorcery and sorcerers are clearly polemical, essentially ascribing magical belief and action to the Rabbanites—the Karaites' significant "others."[91]

Karaites mention characteristic acts of magic and titles of magic books (some familiar from the magic literature), which they claim were part of the Rabbanite world. Thus, for example, Daniel al-Qumisi writes in his commentary on the minor prophets:

> And who is a sorcerer (*mekhashef*) today, surely the Rabbis that mention a pure name and an impure name, write amulets and carry out devices, and call their books *Sefer ha-Yashar* (The Book of the [Right] Way) and *Sefer ha-Razim* (The Book of Mysteries) and *Sefer Adam* (The Book of Adam) and *Raza Rabba* (The Great Mystery), and some books of sorceries: if you wish to bring close in love a man and a woman, or if you wish to cast hatred between them; if you wish to shorten voyage distances (*qefisat ha-derekh*), and such many [similar] abominations, may God keep us away from them.[92]

Karaites voiced such claims repeatedly.

---

91. The Karaite movement began its course in the eighth and ninth centuries CE, in an area east of the Tigris River (currently Iraq and Iran), as groups whose common denominator was their opposition to the Oral Law and to the rabbinic authority associated with it. Over the years these groups united under a shared leadership and a common set of texts and became a movement that, in the tenth and eleventh centuries, flourished particularly in Jerusalem and in Fostat (today's Cairo). At this time, the Karaite leaders engaged in a lively controversy with the Rabbanites, of which written records have partly survived. For comprehensive, detailed information on the Karaites, see Polliack (2003).

92. See Mann (1972, 2: 74–81; quote on 80–81).

A writer whose identity is uncertain, Salmon ben Yeruhim or Sahl ben Matsliah, also ascribed to the Rabbanites books of mysticism and magic and matters of demons and amulets found in them and also mentioned some of their goals: "and for (gaining) love and for (casting) hatred, and shortening voyage distances, and dream inquiry, and to stand at midday in front of the sun and make a request."[93] Similar issues are also mentioned in *Sefer Milḥamot Adonai* (The Book of the Wars of the Lord), a treatise written by Salmon ben Yeruhim as a polemic against R. Saadia Gaon in the first half of the tenth century, apparently in Egypt.[94] In chapter 14 of this work Salmon describes some of "all the abominations of your teachers which are (written) in *Sefer ha-Razim* and *Sefer Shem ben Noah* (The Book of Shem Son of Noah) and despicable and loathsome books."[95] Among these abominations, he mentions the use of explicit divine names for awakening love, improving knowledge, calling up demons, healing, banishing predators from settled areas, calming the sea, walking on fire, darkening the sun, and preventing the waning of the moon. Almost all these issues are indeed mentioned in the magic books of recipes from the Cairo Genizah, as are the ritual means described by Salmon.

> They [i.e., the Rabbis] wished to write amulets according to the way of the Amorites for love, they order that a white cock be brought in order to burn it in flame, and also blood of a turtle-dove and brain of a black ox in order to write with it, and the head of any black [animal] for carrying out abomination; spring water and old wine for pouring a libation and for fumigation, and a white tiger [?] to throw it into the furnace in order to gain authority for their words.[96]

Salmon's denunciation of witchcraft is tied to a critique of approaches widespread in *Hekhalot* and *Merkavah* literature, which in his treatise are

---

93. Mann (1972, 2: 82–83).

94. Salmon ben Yeruhim (1934, 5–7).

95. Salmon ben Yeruhim (1934, 111). On *Sefer ha-Razim*, see the "Magic Treatises" subsection in chapter 5. *Sefer Shem ben Noah* (The Book of Shem, Son of Noah) is mentioned in the preface to the *Sefer Assaf ha-Rofe'* (The Book of Assaf the Physician). See Yellinek (1938, 3: 155).

96. Salmon ben Yeruhim (1934, 112).

viewed as part of the Rabbanite literature represented by R. Saadia Gaon. Salmon focuses on the theory—the notion of descent to the chariot, *Shi'ur Qomah*, and Metatron—and does not consider the magic praxis of using holy names, so typical, as we have seen, of ancient Jewish mystical literature.

In a long chapter he devotes to the study of magic and miracles in *The Book of Lights and Watchtowers* (*Kitab al-anwâr wal-marâqib*), Ya'qub al-Qirqisani ascribes to the Rabbanites a belief in the power of holy names to effect magic. His concern, however, is different. His polemical stance is woven into his condemnations of sorcery and his claims about its implausibility. He opens with his succinct definition of sorcery (*siḥr*).

> The type of sorcery (*siḥr*) that is forbidden to be practiced . . . is the one which some people claim is miracle working— transforming the ways of nature, swaying (human) hearts towards love or hatred, imposing illnesses in (human) bodies and removing them without using such means as food or drink or tapping and so forth, as well as annulling all these by means of speaking and writing and other similar (means).[97]

This is an attempt to define magic categorically, unique in all the sources discussed in this book. Although not an actual definition, the combination of characteristics that al-Qirqisani ties together does suggest to the reader a cumulative impression of magic.[98] Some of the characteristics are descriptive: the principle (overturning the natural order); the purpose (aggressive magic, affecting the other's body and spirit); and the execution (through speech, writing, and "similar means," probably, we may assume, referring to incantations as well as to artifacts and acts of

---

97. See al-Qirqisani (1939–1943, 6.9.1 [3: 575]). I am grateful to Yitzhak Reiter for his help in translating the Arab source, in a version that is slightly different from that found in Nemoy (1986, 337). Some 200 years later, another Karaite, Judah Hadassi, also tied magic to the execution of incantations, speaking, in one breath, of magicians (*mekhashfim*) and whisperers of spells (*melaḥashei laḥash*). See Hadassi (1836, 152b [sec. 376.39]).

98. Schiffman and Swartz (1992, 12–15) suggest using this definition as a basis for characterizing magic in Genizah writings.

the kind related to the use of incantations). Some are legal—witchcraft acts whose use is forbidden. Some are polemical—some claim these are miracles (but they are not).[99]

This definition, particularly its legal and polemical aspects, is important to al-Qirqisani, who sought to outline in his book a Karaite moral code. The definition appears at the opening of a long chapter that is polemical on two fronts. On one front, against Rabbanites and other "people," he essentially draws a fundamental distinction between magic (human, forbidden) and miracle (divine, and possible only through God's prophets). The other and main front, confronting rationalists who are opposed to the possibility of miracle, is meant to demonstrate its feasibility as it is faithfully recorded in the Bible.[100] Al-Qirqisani, then, does not negate the possibility of overturning the natural order but pins it solely on divine action, meaning action meant to serve God's word as uttered by his true prophets. One who is not a true prophet cannot perform miracles but, at most, magic tricks.[101] Clearly, then, even though al-Qirqisani does not bother to say so, the rabbis are not miracle workers. Are they sorcerers then? Al-Qirqisani holds that they are, but not in the sense that they actually possess magic powers—he does not think such powers exist—but in the sense of negating the true prophecy, a negation conveyed in their belief in the feasibility of magic. The rabbis, he argues, believe in the human power to perform all that is mentioned in the definition of magic and even ascribe this power to the rule over two kinds of names—"Name of Cleanness" and "Name of Uncleanness"[102]—and join all "who hold this view that magic is valid

---

99. Nemoy ascribes this claim to the sorcerers trying to create the impression that their actions are miracles, but the original says "men" in general.

100. Al-Qirqisani invests a considerable apologetic effort in an attempt to prove that there is no magic in the Bible. He invests a similar effort in the context of discussing legitimate and illegitimate divination. See Nemoy (1986, 333–35, 357–61).

101. Al-Qirqisani devotes a broad and detailed discussion to distinguishing between the miraculous deeds of Moses and Aaron and the tricks of Egyptian magicians, proving that the woman of En-Dor did not really bring up Samuel's spirit from the dead, and explaining the text in Deuteronomy 13:2–3 concerning the realization of a sign given by a false prophet (Nemoy 1986, 337–56).

102. Regarding these names, see the discussion on the treatise *'Arba'ah Yesodot* (Four Foundations) in the "Magic Treatises" subsection of chapter 5.

and is capable of making miracles, such as the resurrection of the dead."
They thereby actually deny true prophecy,[103] because if the sole purpose
of miracles is not to serve as proof of God's word to his prophets, we no
longer have a basis for differentiating true from false prophecy. Magic is
forbidden, then, not because of its actual existence but because believing
in it undermines divine religion, divine prophecy, and divine law. In
al-Qirqisani's thought, it seems, such a belief is a breach of the first
commandment.[104]

THE RESPONSE OF RAV HAI GAON
TO THE SAGES OF KAIROUAN

Witchcraft issues of the kind the Karaites ascribed to the rabbis are also
mentioned in an exchange of letters from the early eleventh century
between the sages of Kairouan (in today's Tunisia) and Rav Hai Gaon.
These letters deal with the power of the holy names and their use, books
about the use of the names, and testimonies about wondrous deeds performed through them. This is the broadest and most important source
from Geonic literature for my current concern. Both the Kairouan sages'
question and Rav Hai's responsum afford a broad perspective of the
magic beliefs, actions, and writings of contemporary Jews, pointing to
their place in both the prevalent view and in the didactic normative view

---

103. Nemoy makes a claim that appears questionable. He states that al-Qirqisani
was well aware that magic was widespread in broad strata of the people but that the
"Rabbanite leadership—the professional scholars and the communal political and economic leaders—were no more believers in amulets and other superstitions than were
their opposite numbers on the Karaite side" (Nemoy 1986, 337). Nemoy relies for this
claim on the rare mentions of rabbis in this polemical chapter and on the frequent references to "opponents" (336) in general. Most of the chapter, however, is devoted to a
discussion of the feasibility of the biblical divine miracle and its uniqueness and never
refers to magic. In this context, al-Qirqisani's opponents may not have been the rabbis.
In the brief discussion at the opening and in the summary where al-Qirqisani contrasts
miracle with magic and with similar contemptible beliefs, such as requesting help from
the dead, rabbis *are* mentioned and the polemical target in this context appears to me
unmistakable. On the Karaites' claims concerning the cult of graves, cf. the epistle of
Sahl b. Matsliah to Ya'akov b. Shmuel in Nemoy (1952, 115–16).

104. Nemoy (1986, 333); al-Qirqisani's words are on page 338 in Nemoy (1986).

that Rav Hai sought to impose.[105] Rav Hai's first responsum to the sages, stating that "all these and the like are nonsense," failed to placate the sages of Kairouan, and they wrote to him again, thereby attesting to the strong hold of magic views among the local elite.[106] Explaining their repeated turn to him, they claimed that "some of the sages of Eretz Israel and of the sages of Edom [i.e., Islam], associates, wise and faithful people, say they saw this [i.e., the wonders they are asking about] in public."[107] In their letter, they detail several "known" acts, mention *ba'alei shemot* (masters of names), point to specific magic books, and attest to a widespread belief in sorcery and in the dangers entailed by its use.

> Such as one who hides himself from the robbers and one who binds them . . . one who takes [leaves] of reed and olive and writes on them and throws them at the robbers and they cannot pass; and there is one who writes it [i.e., the Ineffable Name] on a new clay and throws it into the sea and it calms down; and he throws it at a man and that man immediately dies. And many things are said by people about what they saw or heard from their ancestors and about shortening distances (*qefiṣat ha-derekh*); and several clear and humble people testified that they had seen a famous man, one of the masters of the Name, on the eve of the Sabbath at one place, and he was then seen at another place, a distance of a few days' away on the same Sabbath eve, and he was also seen on the same Sabbath at the first place . . . and in several books found with us, some of the names and some names of angels and shapes of seals are written, saying: "one who wishes to do this and one who wishes to attain this should write such and such on such and such and do such and such and his wish will be attained." And the old and pious ones who saw these books were frightened by them and did not

---

105. See Emanuel (1995, 121–46).

106. This responsum is quoted by Rav Hai at the opening of the letter available to us and, unfortunately, has not survived.

107. Emanuel (1995, 124). Cf. Ben-Sasson (1996, 275–78) and Sirat (1975, 42–46). See Sirat (1975, 41–42) for the responsum of Samuel ben Ḥofni, gaon of Sura at the turn of the eleventh century, on the woman of En Dor.

touch them; and they said that one man performed an act such and such as the one written in the books and his wish was attained but he became blind, and one did not live out the year, and another one did not live out the week because he had been unclean when he mentioned that Name.[108]

The sages of Kairouan also mention in their letter the magic use of the Amidah prayer, the practice of dream request, and divination through demons. All these matters are indeed mentioned in the available magic literature, parts of which were known to Rav Hai.

And the formulas that you saw: "one who wishes to attain such and such should do such and such," we have many of those, as (in the books) called *Sefer ha-Yashar*, and one called *Harba de-Moshe*, which opens with (the words) "four angels are in charge of the sword," for there are great powers and mysteries in it, and in the book called *Raza Rabba*, beside the fragments and the particular (recipes), of which there is no end.[109]

Rav Hai's responsum is detailed and scholarly. His rhetoric is interesting and convoluted, revealing a position fluctuating between two poles: recognition in principle of the power of words to act in the world and the absolute and scathing dismissal of such power manifestations in contemporary reality. Between them, he determines three degrees of plausibility concerning miraculous events: (1) "things not at all possible" (e.g., making someone disappear by citing the Divine Name); (2) things that are "not impossible" (e.g., shortening distances); and (3) things that are "very far from plausible" (e.g., calming the sea or killing a person by using incantations). Yet he sums up his attitude toward the rumors and testimonies that led the Kairouan sages to ask for his advice with the words, "In sum, a fool believes everything [Proverbs 14:15]."[110] The emphasis in this expression, then, is on the *every*. "A fool will believe everything" does not mean that none of it ever happened. Quite the

---

108. Emanuel (1995, 124–25).
109. Emanuel (1995, 131–32).
110. Emanuel (1995, 128–31; quote on 131).

contrary! There are things we definitely can and should believe in, but we should carefully consider what is and what is not possible. The sages of Kairouan, then, did well by turning to a spiritual authority like Rav Hai and seeking his help. And if they do not wish to be fools, they will do well to accept it.

Rav Hai relies mainly on rabbinic statements designed to structure a skeptical view concerning the existence of contemporary upright (normative) figures capable of miracles. The supernatural, then, is not dismissed but is actually presented as the ideal (and dangerous) horizon of a moral norm that no longer exists. Against this background, the theological discussion at the end of his responsum emphasizes the (spiritual and institutional) danger involved in admiration for the magic power of the "other."

Rav Hai Gaon does not deny the power of the holy names. He recognizes the efficacy of "expert amulets for healing, protection, and other things,"[111] but he qualifies their use. Rather than viewing ritual power as merely a performative technique, he pins it on the writer's (normative) personality. Beside his warnings concerning the dangers attached to writings and actions of this kind, he goes into some detail concerning the names of God but doubts the ability of his contemporaries to activate them: "And who is the one in these generations who pronounces the Ineffable Name over the sea and it calms down, on the living and he dies, and other such deeds? These are nothing but hollow words, do not believe in them."[112]

Rav Hai deals with many other issues: interpreting dreams, the normative gap separating the study of magic (*keshafim*) from its performance, trickery (*'aḥizat 'einayim*), and conjuring angels and demons and using them. He relies, as noted, on talmudic discussions on these issues. Finally, he seeks to clarify the difference between a divine sign of true prophecy and an act of magic, which is not at all a miracle. He points to a clear distinction between them.

Because acts of magic (*ma'aseh keshafim*) are found among the world's customs or are things that human creatures can perform,

---

111. Emanuel (1995, 132). On the "expert amulet" of proven efficiency, see chapter 7.
112. Emanuel (1995, 135).

but the miracle of prophecy through which we will know that this is God's messenger and emissary must have two attributes; if one is missing, this will not be a miracle of prophecy. One is that this should be an act of God, something that a creature cannot do and no one does except the Creator, and the other that it is not of the ways of the world but a change of the ways of the world.[113]

Rav Hai Gaon does not negate magic, but he clearly distinguishes it from God's power. Magic, however powerful, is limited to the power of created beings, "be it a man, or a demon, or a prince," and is confined to activity that does not exceed the laws of nature set by God. Disappearance does exceed them and is therefore impossible. Shortening distances, calming the sea, and killing a person through incantations are "very far" but not "impossible" within the ways of the world. Had there been spiritual giants in "these generations," that is, at the time of Rav Hai and the sages of Kairouan, they would certainly have known how to do this. But once such figures no longer exist, these acts are merely sorcery, not a "miracle of prophecy," and believing in them is therefore forbidden.

Magic and truth are antonymous categories. The power of magic is antithetical to the divine miracle. Idolaters have no "prophesying" power, and their power is therefore not miracle but magic. Seduction by it places us on the slippery slope of denying "prophecy" that, at this time, when divine prophecy is not revealed through miraculous signs on earth, is transmitted through the leaders of the scholarly halakhic establishment. Hence, "These are nothing but hollow words, do not believe in them."

MAIMONIDES' WRITINGS

Rav Hai Gaon's stance on magic seems conciliatory compared to that of Maimonides, who is the most prominent, extreme, and systematic spokesman of the Jewish rationalist elite in the medieval Muslim world. His uncompromising polemical, didactic stance regarding magic is anchored in a comprehensive philosophical conception of God's exclusive and absolute sovereignty in the world, conveyed in an unalterable natural

---

113. Emanuel (1995, 145).

order.[114] Maimonides attests that he had read many Muslim works on magic and astral magic,[115] and he is shown to be well acquainted with contemporary magic practices. In the chapter in *The Guide of the Perplexed* that deals at length with this issue, Maimonides describes idolatry (*'avodah zarah*) in the exact sense of the phrase: "actions that used to be performed by the Sabians, the Casdeans, and the Chaldeans; most of them were also found among the Egyptians and the Canaanites."[116] He draws a distinction between three kinds of magic: (1) material means (a plant, an animal, or a mineral), (2) astral definition of the time of the act, and (3) ritual gestures, "such as dancing, clapping hands, shouting . . . burning something, fumigating with a definite fume, or uttering a speech understandable or not." He describes the act as follows:

> Furthermore there are magical operations that can be accomplished only with the help of all these practices. For instance they say: This or that quantity of the leaves of a certain plant shall be taken while the moon is under a certain sign of the Zodiac in the East, or in one of the other cardinal points; also a definite quantity shall be taken from the horns or the excrements or the hair or the blood of a certain animal while the sun is, for example, in the middle of the sky or at some other determined place; furthermore, a certain mineral or several minerals shall be taken and cast while a certain sign is in the ascendant[117] and the stars in a certain position; then you shall speak and say[118]

---

114. Maimonides' attitude toward magic has been discussed at length in the past by several scholars. See Ravitzky (2010), Safran (1992), and D. Schwartz (2004, 21–34; 2005, 27–44). See also Lewis (1905), Nemoy (1954), Shapiro (2000), and Twersky (1980, 479–84; 1988–1989, esp. 135–40).

115. For example, *Guide of the Perplexed*, III:29 (Maimonides 1963, 514–22), and Twersky (1972, 465–66). See also D. Schwartz (2004; 2005, 33–37).

116. *Guide of the Perplexed*, III:37 (Maimonides 1963, 540–41).

117. The ascendant, *ha-Zomeaḥ* in the language of medieval astrologists, is the zodiacal constellation rising on the horizon at a specific moment. Its significance in the astrological considerations bearing on that moment is decisive. See Barton (1994, 86–142).

118. Dov Schwartz (2005, 31n7) suggests that the astral image speaks when the person worships it. Pines's translation here (in Maimonides 1963) as second person seems to me more reasonable.

these and these things and shall fumigate the cast-metal form with these leaves and similar things—whereupon a certain thing will come about. Furthermore, there are magical operations that, as they deem, may be accomplished with the help of only one of these kinds of practices.[119]

Magic is thus a foreign cult. In its developed form, it is an act of astral magic.[120] Its purpose is to draw down spirituality from the stars into a cast image specifically meant for this purpose by means of well-coordinated astrological rituals, weaving natural materials and human

---

119. *Guide of the Perplexed*, III:37 (Maimonides 1963, 541). An example of a magic act performed without an astral context is necromancy. Maimonides writes in the *Code* (*Mishneh Torah*), *Laws of Idolatry* 6:1: "How is communing with the dead (*ma'aseh ha-'ov*) practiced? The practitioner stands up, offers a certain kind of incense, holds in his hand a myrtle twig, and waves it. He pronounces softly certain words known to them [i.e., the practitioners of this art], till the one who consults him fancies that someone is conversing with him, and answering his questions in words that sound as if they came from beneath the ground in exceedingly low tones almost inaudible to the ear and only apprehended by the mind. Or he takes a dead man's skull, burns incense to it and uses arts of divination till one hears a sound as if a voice, exceedingly low, came from under his armpit and replied to him—all acts of such nature constitute communion with the dead" (Maimonides 1962, 1: 72a–b). On the myrtle twig in necromantic practice, see M. Margalioth (1966, 76–77). Cf. Morgan (1983, 38).

120. On the Sabians and their astral magic cult, cf. *Guide of the Perplexed*, III:29, particularly the following: "In conformity with these opinions, the Sabians set up statues for the planets, golden statues for the sun and silver ones for the moon, and distributed the minerals and the climes between the planets, saying that one particular planet was the deity of one particular clime. And they built temples, set up the statues in them, and thought that the forces of the planets overflowed toward these statues and that consequently these statues talked, had understanding, gave prophetic revelation to people—I mean, the statues—and made known to people what was useful to them. Similarly they said of the trees, which were assigned to the various planets, that when one particular tree was set apart for one particular planet, planted with a view to the latter, and a certain treatment was applied to it and with it, the spirit of that planet overflowed toward that tree, gave prophetic revelation to people, and spoke to them in sleep. You will find all this set forth literally in their books, to which I shall draw your attention" (Maimonides 1963, 516–17). See also *Guide of the Perplexed*, I:63 and III:30, 45 (Maimonides 1963, 133–36, 522–23, 575–81); and Maimonides, *Commentary on the Mishnah, Avodah Zarah*, 4:7 (Maimonides 1963–1968, 4: 357–59). See also Stroumsa (1999).

actions into a supernatural apparatus. Although not every act of magic requires the presence of all these components, all are linked in one way or another to the stars.

> In all magical operations it is indispensable that the stars should be observed. I mean, they deem that a certain plant should be assigned to the portion of a certain star; similarly they assign every animal and every mineral to a star. They likewise deem that the operations performed by the magicians are various species of worship offered to a certain star, which, being pleased with that operation or speech or fumigation, does for us what we wish.[121]

Although Maimonides writes about alien, Sabian magic, which "with regard to most of these magical practices, . . . pose the condition that those who perform them should necessarily be women,"[122] and although elsewhere he describes magic acts, incantations, and divination that were widespread among those "deficient in knowledge," his polemic targets scholarly astral magic in particular. Astral magic required extensive astronomical knowledge (which Maimonides valued and strictly distinguished from "chimerical" astrology) as a basis for magical activity. It relied on a developed theory, substantiated and accepted by the contemporary scholars. These characteristics, and astral magic's standing in the ranking of knowledge in the medieval Muslim world, made it particularly dangerous. The reason is that, beyond the halakhic and practical aspect about which Maimonides could rule overbearingly (as he indeed did, at times

---

121. *Guide of the Perplexed*, III:37 (Maimonides 1963, 542).

122. Maimonides (1963, 541). This description, as noted, relates to foreign (Sabian) magic, which Maimonides describes there. Later, Maimonides explains the biblical command "You shall not suffer a witch to live" (Exodus 22:17) as founded on the greater involvement of women in magic. Nevertheless, although he addresses here the gender issue in magic, he disregards the famous talmudic stance, "witch . . . because most women engage in magic" (TB *Sanhedrin* 67a). He interprets the biblical emphasis stating "man or woman" in reference to idolatry (Deuteronomy 17:2, 5) as based on the natural compassion that men, who are the executioners, feel for women, rather than as a sign that women are the chief agents of witchcraft, as the rabbis had held. Cf. D. Schwartz (2005, 32 and note 8). On the gender perception of magic in rabbinic literature, see later discussion.

offering an extreme one-sided version of the rabbinic position that he mostly relied on),[123] astral magic also posed a general philosophical and religious danger. Astral magic was part of the astrological conception stating that stars and planets influence the sublunar world and participate in directing its course. Maimonides thus consistently and resolutely presented astral magic as inimical to monotheism, true philosophy, and empirical thought, which were inseparably tied up in his system.[124]

Maimonides rejected astral magic as part of his general rejection of astrology.[125] Invoking monotheism, as he understood it, Maimonides sought to uproot from among Jews any belief stating that stars and constellations influenced the world, as well as the practices attached to it, both divination and magic.[126] To do so, he had to contend with two levels of idolatry, the scholarly and the popular.

> One consists of those who are well versed in the practice—that is the calculation of the constellation that is in the ascendant at the time of the act, and the bringing down by it of the power emanating from the stars,[127] and all the other delusions and

---

123. Maimonides resolutely objected to magic, to the point of ignoring magic elements in rabbinic literature. He used exegesis and obliviousness to subordinate "rebellious" rabbinic approaches in conflict with his system. Both his successors and his opponents noted this and often attacked him on this count to undermine his position or to dismiss it altogether. See Ravitzky (2010), D. Schwartz (2005, 49–54), and Twersky (1980, 479). See also the dispute on Maimonides' stance in this context in Halbertal (2000, 41–49, 162–69).

124. On the breaches in this resolute front and on its didactic purpose, see Kreisel (1994, 26): "Whether astrology is true or false is a secondary consideration in light of one of the implications of the belief in astrology on the perfection (of man, which is the perfection of reason). For example, it is better to set forth beliefs that are false but necessary for maintaining the belief in one God than to frankly tell the whole truth when it has negative effects."

125. On Maimonides' astrological conception, see Freudenthal (1993), Kreisel (1994), and Langerman (1991).

126. On the prohibition of acting according to astral divination, even if revealed accidentally, see *Code, Laws of Idolatry*, 11:8–9 (Maimonides 1962, 1: 79b).

127. On the term *rûḥaniyyât*, meaning the spiritual power that emanates from the stars, see Pines (1988). On the place of this concept in the development of Kabbalah, see Idel (1991, 83–104).

foolish things that soil the intellect and are imagined by those of this type. And the second type are those who worship those man-made images as they have learned to do, without knowledge of how they were made or for what purpose they were made, except for the stories of their sages alone—and such are the majority of idolaters.[128]

For Maimonides, the danger of astrology lay not only in the philosophical mistake it brought into the world but also, and indeed mainly, in the attractiveness of its practical aspects for the masses, leading them to idolatry. The struggle against the scholars of astral magic, then, involved ethical and political aspects no less important than the conceptual one. At this level, Maimonides acts to undermine the standing of these pseudoscholars as genuine philosophers.

> You must know that the perfect philosophers do not believe in talismans but deride them and those who believe in their influence, and the explanation of this matter should be lengthy. But I have said this because I know that most people, and perhaps all, are greatly tempted by them and believe in many things of that kind, and think that they are true things, but this is not so. And even good and pious men of our Torah think that these things are true, but that they are forbidden because of [the prohibition of] the Torah alone. And they do not know that these [i.e., the talismans] are empty and false things, against which the Torah has warned us just as it has warned us against falsehood.[129]

Maimonides emphasizes the epistemological aspect of his claims, the mistake and the falsity of astral magic that true—rational-empirical—philosophy demonstrates.[130] He addresses this claim to the "good and

---

128. Maimonides, *Commentary on the Mishnah, Hullin* 1:1 (Maimonides 1963–1968, 5: 173).

129. Maimonides, *Commentary on the Mishnah, Avodah Zarah* 4:7 (Maimonides 1963–1968, 4: 357). On potential addressees of this statement, see D. Schwartz (2005, 37–40).

130. In this context, the opening of his letter to the Provence sages dealing with astrology deserves mention: "Know, my masters, that it is not proper for a man to accept

pious people of our Torah," who believe in the theoretical foundation of astral magic but refrain from implementing it because of their wariness of idolatry. He does know, however, that not all are like them.

> "And ye shall not walk in the customs of the nation" [Leviticus 20:23]—these being those that are called by [the Sages], may their memory be blessed, ways of the Amorite. For they are branches of magical practices, inasmuch as they are things not required by reasoning concerning nature and lead to magical practices that of necessity seek support in astrological notions. Accordingly the matter is turned into a glorification and a worship of the stars.[131]

This is Maimonides' main fear and seemingly his key consideration in his polemical rhetoric against astrology.[132]

Philosophical and didactic considerations thus come together in Maimonides' thought and his writing for the purpose of systematically undermining astrology as a science, astrologists as scholars, and astral magic as a useful and legitimate activity. A similar picture emerges regarding Maimonides' attitude toward the more simple magic activity widespread in his community, which was not based on astral calculations. This

---

as trustworthy anything other than one of these three things. The first is a thing for which there is a clear proof deriving from man's reasoning—such as arithmetic, geometry, and astronomy. The second is a thing that a man perceives through one of the five senses—such as when he knows with certainty that this is red and this is black and the like through the sight of his eye; or as when he tastes that this is bitter and this is sweet; or as when he feels that this is hot and this is cold. . . . The third is a thing that a man receives from the prophets or from the righteous" (Twersky 1972, 465). On this letter, see also Lerner (1968) and Marx (1926). On scientific thinking in Maimonides, cf. also Bleich (1993).

131. *Guide of the Perplexed*, III:37 (Maimonides 1963, 543, with slight change). Cf. *Code, Laws of Idolatry*, 1:1 (Maimonides 1962, 1: 66a).

132. See Kreisel (1994). Almost all the scholars who have dealt with Maimonides' attitude toward astrology, astral magic, magic, amulets, *segulot*, and "superstitions" emphasize the empirical principle in his thought as the basis for his rejection of them. Although Kreisel does not deny this trend, he emphasizes that didactic considerations have been more significant than adherence to this principle in shaping Maimonides' public position in this regard.

activity, the theoretical and practical expressions of which I reviewed at length in chapter 5, was well known to Maimonides, and he was resolutely opposed to it as well on both scientific-empirical and halakhic grounds.

Maimonides' contempt for magic activity is tied to his attitude toward language. He holds that human language is conventional and lacks immanent holiness. Such holiness is at the basis of the performative conception of language in Jewish magic culture.[133] Its rejection, which founded language solely on its communicative function, automatically eliminates the performative power of words and with it the efficacy of uttered or written incantations.[134] Accompanying this approach of Maimonides' was a general conception of holiness as an essence external to and separate from things, which negates the possibility of transferring it as an effective performative power from humans to artifacts or from artifacts to humans.[135] Maimonides explicitly states his view in this regard when discussing two related topics: amulets and mezuzot. He considers amulets in *Guide of the Perplexed* when discussing the name of God.

> Do not let occur to your mind the vain ravings (*hadhayān*)[136] of the writers of charms or what names you may hear from them or may find in their stupid books, names that they have invented, which are not indicative of any notion whatsoever, but which they

---

133. See chapter 4.

134. See Maimonides' explicit statements on the conventionality of language in *Guide of the Perplexed*, II:30 (Maimonides 1963, 357–58): "And the man gave names and so on [Genesis 2:20]. It informs us that languages are conventional and not natural, as has sometimes been thought." On Maimonides' idea of language, see Kellner (2004), Septimus (1994), and J. Stern (2000). For a detailed discussion of the implications of Maimonides' conception of language for linguistic magic, see Ravitzky (2010).

135. Twersky (1988–1989, 138–39).

136. Pines, the translator of the 1963 edition of Maimonides' *Guide of the Perplexed*, translates *hadhayân* as "imaginings." On the rendering of this term as "ravings" and its denotation in Maimonides' writings, see Gellman (1991) and Stroumsa (2001). Gellman suggests seeing in this word, which is usually perceived as solely an expression of contempt, a polemical term intended against a specific mistake: a confusion between the attributes of substance and the attributes of form. Stroumsa rejects this stance and concludes that the word served Maimonides almost as a technical term "reserved for superstitious, nonscientific or pseudoscientific discourse that presumes to offer a coherent system" (Stroumsa 2001, 163).

call the names and of which they think that they necessitate holiness and purity and work miracles. All these are stories that it is not seemly for a perfect man to listen to, much less to believe.[137]

Scathingly, then, Maimonides dismisses the use of God's names together with the books giving directives on such use and states that they are based on a fabrication. This matter resembles his view on the hidden names of God: the Ineffable Name, a name of twelve letters, and a name of forty-two letters. In his view, these names, of which the longer ones are made up of several words, originally pointed to intellectual content touching on God. The problem evoked by this content led to "the corruption of beliefs," which in turn led to the concealment of God's names from the masses. Henceforth, events developed as follows:

> When wicked and ignorant people found these texts, they had great scope for lying statements in that they would put together any letters they liked and would say: this is a name that has efficacy and the power to operate if it is written down or uttered in a particular way. Thereupon these lies invented by the first wicked and ignorant man were written down, and these writings transmitted to good, pious, and foolish men who lack the scales by means of which they could know the true from the false. These people accordingly made a secret of these writings, and the latter were found in the belongings left behind them, so that they were thought to be correct. To sum it up: "A fool believes everything" [Proverbs 14:15].[138]

According to Maimonides, then, ignorance, lies, and naïveté are the foundation of the culture of using names and of the professional literature that goes with it. This is a silly and superfluous culture that is not confined to its constitutive lie but also entails a dangerous aspect of sin. Maimonides emphasizes this aspect when he warns against turning the mezuzah into an amulet, that is, displacing it from the realm of

---

137. *Guide of the Perplexed*, I:61 (Maimonides 1963, 149). In this context, see also Y. Schwartz (1996).

138. *Guide of the Perplexed*, I:62 (Maimonides 1963, 152).

commandments performed according to the accepted halakhic pattern (involving the worship of God) to the realm of personal apotropaic magic.

> It is a universal custom to write [the word] *Shaddai* on the other side of the *Mezuzah*, opposite the blank space between the two sections. As this is written on the outside, the practice is unobjectionable. They, however, who write names of angels, holy names, a Biblical text or inscriptions usual on seals, within the *Mezuzah*, are among those who have no portion in the world to come. For these fools not only fail to fulfill the commandment but they treat an important precept that expresses the Unity of God, the love of Him, and His worship, as if it were an amulet to promote their own personal interests; for, according to their foolish minds, the *Mezuzah* is something that will secure for them advantage in the vanities of the world.[139]

The issue of using names recurs in Maimonides' writings in other contexts, relying on the two elements noted: a fundamental negation of the performative power of words or artifacts and the sin entailed by their implementation. The sin aspect, anchored in Maimonides' role as legislator, is particularly prominent in his views on healing incantations, which thereby afford us a glimpse into the magic practices used in his surroundings.

> One who whispers a spell over a wound[140] and recites a verse from the Torah, one who recites a verse over a child to save it from terrors and one who places a scroll or phylacteries on an infant, to induce it to sleep, are not only in the category of soothsayers and sorcerers (*menaḥashim ve-ḥovrim*), but they are included among those who repudiate the Torah; for they use its words to cure the body whereas these are only medicine for the soul.[141]

---

139. *Code, Laws of Phylacteries, Mezuzah, and the Scroll of the Law*, 5:4 (Maimonides 1962, 2: 127a). On the Genizah evidence for mezuzot with magical additions, see Bohak (2010b).

140. Cf. M. *Sanhedrin* 10:1 and parallel versions.

141. *Code, Laws of Idolatry*, 11:12 (Maimonides 1961, 1: 79b).

Maimonides' concern with *segulot*—the properties of artifacts related to form rather than to matter—reflects his empirical-scientific thinking.[142] Maimonides acknowledges the healing potential of the *segulot* but sets it in nature rather than beyond it. Accordingly, he demands controlled use of an empirical method to prove their efficacy, each one separately, as a condition for allowing their use. This is also the basis for his interpretation of the well-known talmudic saying, which excludes whatever serves to heal from the category of "ways of the Amorites": "'All that pertains to medicine does not pertain to the Amorite usages' (TB *Shabbat* 67a). They mean by this that all that is required by speculation concerning nature is permitted, whereas other practices are forbidden."[143] Similarly, Maimonides justifies other hard to justify rabbinic licenses, such as the use of a nail from the cross and the use of a fox's tooth, and other ritual actions meant for healing. In his words, their benefit derives from experience rather than from logic.[144]

Surprisingly, and indeed leading to many exegetical problems, Maimonides applies this principle to amulets as well. Contrary to his explicit statement about the futility of amulets and the idiocy of their writers, he bows to the rabbis' dictum and, at least ostensibly, agrees to the existence of expert amulets (*qame'a mumheh*), whose efficacy or that of their writers has been empirically demonstrated. He allows these to be worn on the Sabbath for healing.

> One may also wear an expert amulet—that is, an amulet which has already cured three patients, or was made by someone who had previously cured three patients with other amulets. If one goes out into a public domain wearing a non-expert amulet, he is exempt, because he is deemed to have worn it as apparel.[145]

---

142. On Maimonides' scientific-empirical conception of the *segulot*, see Bleich (1993) and D. Schwartz (2005, 40–44).

143. *Guide of the Perplexed*, III:37 (Maimonides 1963, 543).

144. Maimonides (1963, 544–45). All the medical means mentioned there are solely material and their use does not rely on spells.

145. *Code, Laws of Shabbat*, 19:14 (Maimonides 1961, 120). Bleich (1993) bases this matter solely on the empirical principle—what has proven efficacious is allowed. Although emphasizing Maimonides' opposition to the performative use of names, Ravitzky (2010, 116–17) holds that Maimonides was not strongly opposed to expert

This is a puzzling but explicit deviation from Maimonides' resolutely consistent line against the use of holy names and amulets. It differs from the license to use materials whose healing efficacy has been proven, even though this proof lacks logical explanation and contradicts, in terms of its underlying rationale, his ruling allowing the use of an incantation for stings:

> If one was stung by a scorpion or a snake, it is permitted, even on the Sabbath, to whisper a spell over the part affected, so as to soothe the patient and give him reassurance. Although the procedure is absolutely useless, it has been permitted because of the patient's dangerous condition, so that he should not become distraught.[146]

An expert amulet is a performative artifact whose proven healing efficacy is the cause for allowing it to be worn. The incantation for the bite does not heal. It is allowed as a psychological placebo at a time of distress for one who holds it to have powers, not as a means of magical healing. The deliberate use of an incantation formula to counteract the effects of snakes or scorpions or for protection from them is, however, absolutely forbidden.[147]

The falsity and the sin that are the basis and the key to astral magic and to the simpler magic, the formula and the *segulot*, are what made magic so dangerous in Maimonides' perception. His handling of them, which is at the focus of his discussions on the various expressions of magic activity and the belief in it, conveys two main aspects of his personality:

---

amulets because, contrary to the astral magic talismans, these amulets did not lead to idolatry. In any event, even though Ravitzky correctly points out that his explanation "infinitely eases" the problem entailed by Maimonides' comment in this regard, the recognition of the efficacy of amulets is still puzzling. One possible solution is to assume that Maimonides is referring here to an "amulet of roots" rather than to a "written amulet" (TB *Shabbat* 61a–b). Had this been his intention, however, and given his absolute opposition to the use of incantations, he would probably have noted this explicitly. Also see references to the exegetic-halakhic discussion on Maimonides' ruling in Bleich (1993) and Ravitzky (2010).

146. *Code, Laws of Idolatry*, 11:11 (Maimonides 1962, 1: 79b).
147. *Code, Laws of Idolatry*, 11:10 (Maimonides 1962, 1: 79b).

thinker and leader. As a thinker, he knows magic theory from books and rejects it by relying on philosophical considerations. As a leader, he knows it from day-to-day life and rejects it by relying on religious considerations. These roles, which are mutually intertwined and integral to his personality and his writings, come to the fore in his succinct comments on the magic practice of necromancy.

> These practices are all false and deceptive, and were means employed by the ancient idolaters to deceive the people of various countries and induce them to become their followers. It is not proper for Israelites who are highly intelligent to suffer themselves to be deluded by such inanities or imagine that there is anything in them. . . . Whoever believes in these and similar things and, in his heart, holds them to be true and scientific and only forbidden by the Torah, is nothing but a fool, deficient in understanding, who belongs to the same class with women and children whose intellects are immature. Sensible people, however, who possess sound mental faculties, know by clear proofs that all these practices which the Torah prohibited have no scientific basis but are chimerical and inane; and that only those deficient in knowledge are attracted by these follies, and, for their sake, leave the ways of truth. The Torah, therefore, in forbidding all these follies, exhorts us, "Thou shalt be wholehearted with the Lord, thy God" (Deuteronomy 18:13).[148]

No one opposed the explicit biblical demand of wholeheartedness with God. Quite the contrary! But not everyone agreed with Maimonides' understanding of it.

Maimonides' extreme rationalistic stance reached realms that even the most stringent ancestors of rabbinic Judaism did not turn to. He based "wholeheartedness" on a form of religiosity that is particularly difficult to internalize and perform, leaving no room whatsoever for miracle and its human agents. Its conceptual foundations, and even more so some of its practical implications, were too difficult for collective digestion and hardly affected day-to-day Jewish religiosity in all that concerns

---

148. *Code, Laws of Idolatry*, 11:16 (Maimonides 1962, 1: 80a).

my current pursuit. Opposition to it assumed two forms: direct and open, and indirect and ignoring. Within elite circles, Maimonides' views gave rise to prolonged and profound debates. In this sense his rationalism was extremely influential both as such and mainly as a catalyst for opposite and more moderate trends. The people, however, were not overly impressed. Probably the most solid evidence is that provided by the hagiographies of Maimonides that evolved orally in the centuries after his death and were eventually written up in closely similar versions in many communities throughout the Muslim world.[149] If it was Maimonides' fate to serve the Jewish community as a folk hero, then community needs rather than Maimonides' thought shaped his image. The people, whose magic beliefs and actions Maimonides contemptuously dismissed, had no need for rationalist philosophers; they needed powerful and holy miracle men. And indeed, in Jewish folklore, Maimonides defeats sorcerers and sinks them in the ground, resurrects the dead, turns onions into gold, reveals hidden mysteries, shortens distances, and leads a ship into the sea by uttering the Ineffable Name. Even his coffin functions as a miraculous object after his death. In a Yemenite nineteenth-century manuscript dealing with amulets, *segulot*, and remedies, one of the pages bears the title: "A good amulet by the Sephardi rabbi Moses b. Maimon, of blessed memory, tried and proven for every spirit and fear and to protect a person anywhere." Under it is the required incantation.[150] Daily life in Jewish communities, where incantations and magic were practices in use for almost every purpose, together with magic imagination, gave rise to a fantastic and consoling folk literature that swallowed up and assimilated the Maimonidean rationalist spark.

CONCLUDING REMARKS

Magic beliefs and practices were part of the Jewish culture of antiquity and of the early Islamic period, and their traces are evident outside magic

---

149. See Avishur (1998). On the Jewish genre of hagiography, see Dan (1981; 1986).

150. Gross Family Collection, No. 42, 198a. In a photocopy of another Yemenite manuscript, from a private collection, I also found the title "for love; from Maimonides, may his merits protect us," followed by a brief recipe for love. I am grateful to Yisrael Almagor for sharing this information with me.

sources too. The unique advantage of testimonies of this kind lies in the fact that they are not part of the "system" but discuss it from "outside." On the one hand, they point to broad contexts of creativity and meaning in which a Jewish magic culture developed, which in turn contributed its share to them. On the other hand, they reveal the network of relationships between two complementary or conflicting power structures—ritual and political. The description of Jewish magic culture must be based, above all, on the insider magic evidence. Outsider bodies, however, can substantiate the information found in the insider sources and even expand it. The demonological theory of the Second Temple period and the angelological approach of *Hekhalot* and *Merkavah* literature (as well as the information found in rabbinic literature, discussed in chapter 7) are clear examples. This is one context where outsider sources serve the study of magic. Their main importance, however, is in the social context. This aspect of sorcery is hardly mentioned in magic literature, which does not concern itself with questions of society and morality, apologetics, or polemics. We can learn about all these aspects from the other literature, which "reports" on magic from the outside. At the focus, explicitly or in hidden ways of discourse, is the link between ritual power and social-political power. The demand of social-political power by the masters of names who descend to the chariot is an eye-opening example. No less impressive is the opposite trend—the attempt to diminish the social-political power of the "other" by labeling a person a sorcerer or a witch (*mekhasheflah*) and rhetorically symbolizing him or her as possessing a hostile, dangerous, and illegitimate power.

In this chapter I discussed theoretical, practical, and political aspects of Jewish magic in various bodies, quite different from one another in their character and their time. In the next chapter I expand the discussion beyond magic and demonology and consider these three elements in the rabbinic discourse of the occult in the broad, diverse, and most decisive corpus that was created in ancient Judaism: rabbinic literature.

7

Knowledge, Power, and Hegemony

Sorcery, Demonology, and Divination
in Rabbinic Literature

In this chapter I present a concentrated review of the rabbinic discourse in several interrelated areas, all connected to my pursuit here: sorcery, demonology, divination, interpretation of dreams, and astrology.[1] The discussion shifts between two poles: one phenomenological and one social. At the phenomenological level, I trace different views and practices in these areas as they come to the fore in the broad corpus known as rabbinic literature, including its two components, Halakhah and Aggadah. In this context I do not consider the value question involved in the rabbinic discourse about them, that is, whether they are mentioned with favor or disgust, denoting acceptance or rejection. At the social level the question is examined mainly from a political perspective: the rabbis' use of esoteric elements in their literature as part of their struggle for power and control in the (actual or imagined) community, where concealed knowledge, hidden powers, and their human agents played a central role. I outline the rabbis' perceptions of sorcery, demonology, and divination as realms of knowledge and action in order to examine their place in the rabbinic *Weltanschauung* and to discern the rabbis' attitude toward themselves and toward others as potential agents of knowledge and practices of this kind. I do not intend to determine, as

---

1. For an early and shorter version of this chapter, see Harari (2006a). Cf. the detailed account of magic in rabbinic literature in Bohak (2008, 351–435).

scholars have in the past, what the "rabbinic view" was on each of these topics. The rabbinic discourse on these questions is multifaceted and contradictory and a distinct expression of the multivocal character of rabbinic literature. This discourse brings together the views of many individuals from different periods, communities, and cultural areas of influence, which I see no reason to dismiss in favor of generalizations.[2] Instead, I expose the discourse unfolding in this literature, including the diverse views reflected in it and retaining the disputes and contradictions that are an essential part of its description.[3]

SORCERY

Affirming the Possibility, Negating the Practice

The rabbis are, in principle, explicitly opposed to magic (*kishuf, keshafim*). They thereby continue the determined biblical trend that rejects sorcery as a foreign cultural feature and sets a harsh sanction for those involved in it: "You shall not suffer a witch (*mekhashefa*) to live" (Exodus 22:17).[4] The rabbis state in the Mishnah: "Harlotry and sorcery have destroyed

---

2. In this context, I avoid further historical, geographic, or genre distinctions, which should definitely be taken into account in a broader and more profound discussion. Instead, I discuss rabbinic literature as a general corpus, despite the well-known drawbacks of such a discussion. For initial attempts at analyzing the differences in rabbinical attitude toward magic in Palestinian and Babylonian sources, see Levinson (2006) and Stratton (2007, 143–76).

3. In general, citations from the Babylonian Talmud rely on the printed version. For all citations, however, I also checked the manuscript versions that scholars of the Academy of the Hebrew Language assessed as the best for each particular treatise (according to the ranking in the *ma'agarim* database on the website of the Historical Dictionary Project (www.Hebrew-treasures.huji.ac.il). When the manuscript showed significant differences from the printed version, I referred to this or even based the entire citation on the manuscript and added a note to that effect. For the manuscript versions, I used the Talmud Text Databank of the Saul Lieberman Institute for Talmudic Research. Citations from the Palestinian Talmud followed the edition of the Academy of the Hebrew Language, and references follow their system (according to chapter and Mishnah rather than Halakhah). Citations from midrashim rely on the editions noted in the Bibliography.

4. On this question, see chapter 6 and later discussion in this chapter.

everything" (M. *Sotah* 9:3). Substantively, the punishment meted out to the sorcerer (or to the soothsayer [*ba'al 'ov*], the wizard [*yide'oni*], and others) is stoning (M. *Sanhedrin* 7:4). Yet sorcery (*kishuf*) is not precisely defined in the Mishnah beyond the statement that, contrary to trickery (*'aḥizat 'einayim*), sorcery is a real act (*ma'aseh*), that is, an actual change in reality. Accordingly, the punishments imposed on the sorcerer (*mekhashef*) and on the trickster (*'oḥez 'einayim*) are fundamentally different. The sorcerer is liable, whereas the trickster, who pretends to perform real acts but merely engages in deception, is exempt (M. *Sanhedrin* 7:11). In the Talmud the exemption is restricted. Beside the enumeration of several examples of trickery—extracting streamers of silk from the nostrils, cutting up a camel with a sword and putting it together again, turning a wooden board into a donkey—Abaye asserts:

> The laws of sorcerers are like those of the Sabbath: some [are punished] by stoning, some are exempt yet forbidden, while others are permitted *ab initio*. One who actually performs magic—is stoned; one who creates an illusion—exempt yet forbidden, permitted *ab initio*—such as [was performed by] R. Ḥanina and R. Oshaia. They spent every Sabbath eve studying the Laws of Creation, and a three-year old heifer was created for them and they ate it. (TB *Sanhedrin* 67b)

This distinction between sorcery and trickery attests to the rabbis' recognition of the sorcerer's power to perform tangible actions in the world, and this, not the deception of an illusory feat, is what they categorized as sinful and prohibited.

Furthermore, the examples of deception cited in TB *Sanhedrin* and elsewhere connect it mainly to Gentiles, conveying a trend of presenting "their sorcery" as mere conjuring and so denying it any supernatural performative power. Particularly prominent in this context is the attitude toward Yanai's eyewitness testimony concerning "a heretic who would take a bundle and toss it up into the air, and it would then land and become a calf" (PT *Sanhedrin* 7:11), essentially pointing out the obvious deceit in it. The rabbis cite there R. Elazar in the name of R. Yosi b. Zimra: "Were all the world's creatures to gather together, they could not create one fly and place a soul in it,"[5] as proof of this act's impossibility. They sum up: "[Surely] it does not say [that] he took a kind of bundle, tossed it up in the air and it landed and became a calf, but that he called upon a trickster who stole a calf from the herd and then brought it to him." Similar testimony by R. Ḥinena, son of R. Ḥanania, concerning such a "creation" concludes with his father's conceptual clarification: "If you have eaten from it—that is a proof [that a real act has indeed been carried out], and if not—it is a deception" (PT *Sanhedrin* 7:11). The concreteness of the creature, then, is the key to the distinction between an actual act of creation and a vain illusion. This is the context in which R. Joshua says about himself, "I am able to take gourds and watermelons and turn them into rams and deer who would produce rams and deer," when he seeks to boast about his actual power to perform an act of creation.[6]

The difference between sorcery and trickery, as opposed to the rabbis' holy learning that "produced" a calf they indeed ate, is now clearly evident. Because Torah study is the ritual that brought this creature into existence and because rabbis performed this ritual, not only is this act not one of forbidden sorcery (and certainly not at all a deception, as is the Gentiles' "creation"), but it is also categorically permitted *ab initio* under the rubric of sorcery laws. Indeed, the act is even desirable as a sign of ritual power derived from the proper religious norm, in which the rabbis are experienced.

Expressions recognizing the power of human magical manipulation for both beneficial and malefic purposes are widespread in many halakhic and aggadic traditions. Among the beneficial kind are traditions that recognize the power of circle drawers and utterers of incantations meant to

---

5. Similar versions of this claim appear in many places, usually in exegeses of the verse "and the souls that they had acquired [*'asu*, literally "created"] in Haran" (Genesis 12:5). See, for instance, *Avot de-Rabbi Nathan*, Version A, 12; *Genesis Rabbah* 39:14, 84:4; *Sifrei on Deuteronomy* 32; *Midrash Tannaim on Deuteronomy* 6:5; and *Pesikta Rabbati* 43.

6. As the concrete reality of the calf is summed up in the possibility of eating it, so the propagation ability of deer and gazelles is proof of the reality of the act. This tradition is cited after the two stories about R. Joshua's struggle against "foreign" sorcerers and his magical victory over them. His statements complete the picture and raise his powers up to the possibility of actual creation. For further discussion of the rabbis' creation capabilities, see later discussion.

bring about rain[7] and the effect of sympathetic acts on the fertility of trees (such as loading a tree with date clusters or with stones and painting it red, or hanging a shoot of wild figs on a fruitless fig tree).[8] One particular example concerns prescriptions for healing incantations and evidence of the healing and protective use of amulets, both written amulets (*qame'a shel ketav*) and amulets using plant roots (*qame'a shel 'iqarin*).[9] With regard to amulets, note mainly the discussion on the kinds of amulets that can be carried on the Sabbath for healing purposes, particularly the category of expert amulets, referring to amulets whose effectiveness or that of their

---

7. The tradition of Ḥoni ha-Me'agel (literally, "the circle drawer") is famous, and the gist of it that is relevant to the current context reads as follows: "People told Ḥoni the circle drawer, 'Pray that rain may fall.' He said to them: 'Go out and take in your Passover ovens so that they will not be damaged.' He prayed and no rain fell. What did he do? He drew a circle and stood within it and said: 'Master of the Universe, your children have turned to me because I am as a member of your house to you. I swear by your great name that I will not move from here until you have mercy on your children.' Raindrops began to fall. Said he: 'It is not for this that I have asked, but for rain [to fill] cisterns, ditches, and caves.' Tempestuous rain began to fall. Said he: 'It is not for this that I have asked, but for rain of good will, blessing and bounty'" (M. *Ta'anit* 3:8). See also TB *Ta'anit* 23a and PT *Ta'anit* 3:8. The power of incantation utterers is evident in the following: "If you see a generation over whom the heavens redden like copper and neither dew nor rain falls, [it is because] that generation has no incantations utterers [*loḥashei leḥishot*, also meaning "whisperers of whispers"]. What is their remedy? Let them go to one who knows how to utter incantations" (TB *Ta'anit* 5a). My personal view is that we should reject the interpretation ascribed to Rashi ad locum ("whisperers of whispers—for people do not whisper their prayers") and adhere to the literal reading of this phrase as incantation utterers. Following these two traditions, questions are raised as to the moral standing of these acts. These questions, which do not concern me here, definitely confirm the reading of these traditions as referring to performative incantations.

8. TB *Shabbat* 67a; PT *Shevi'it* 4:4. See also Harari (2001, 27–28).

9. On incantation prescriptions for healing, see TB *Shabbat* 66b–67a and TB *Gittin* 68b–69b. In my view the inclusion of incantations in a healing action justifies placing it under the rubric of magic healing. Many of the prescriptions mentioned in the cited sources are not in this category, however, and can be considered folk medicine that is not magical. On the Babylonian foundations of these prescriptions, see Geller (1991; 2000). Beside these practices, "scientific" medicine was also practiced in antiquity, originating in the school of Hippocrates and Galen. All these methods at times relied on astrological principles. On the term *qame'a* (amulet), see the discussion on amulets in chapter 5. For discussions of amulets in rabbinic literature, see Blau (1898, 86–96), Bohak (2008, 370–76), Trachtenberg (1970, 132–52), and Urbach (1975, 130–32).

writers has been demonstrated at least three times. Such an amulet can be carried on the Sabbath on a person but not on an animal.[10] Further evidence points to the use of therapeutic artifacts, such as a locust egg, a fox tooth, and a nail from one who has been crucified, which R. Meir permits to be carried on the Sabbath "for healing purposes" but the rabbis prohibit even on weekdays because these are "ways of the Amorites" (M. *Shabbat* 6:10). Another instance is the "preserving stone" (*'even ha-tequmah*), used to prevent miscarriages, which the rabbis allowed to be carried on the Sabbath (TB *Shabbat* 66b). Finally, note the magical healing prescriptions delivered in the name of rabbis.

These prescriptions are partly based on ritual acts founded on sympathetic principles[11] and partly on the healing power of incantations, the wording of which at times includes biblical verses and historiolas (brief stories hinting at well-known narratives, when the one reciting the incantation seeks to realize some quality being invoked in them—power, destruction, grace, love, and so forth).[12] Many of these prescriptions were meant to remove from the patient's body demons and other damaging agents that were perceived as the cause of illnesses (I return to this point later). Others were meant as treatments for fever, which were also at times perceived as resulting from possession. The following are examples of two such prescriptions that, like other items of information circulating in the house of study, are also part of the characteristic talmudic exchange. The first is cited by Abaye, as learned from his foster mother. The purpose is to transfer the fever from the body of the patient to the body of an ant.

For a daily fever[13] . . . he should sit at a crossroads and when he sees a big ant carrying something, let him take it and place it

---

10. M. *Shabbat* 6:2; Tosefta *Shabbat* 4:5, 9, 10; TB *Shabbat* 53a. Talmudic rabbis were divided on whether the effectiveness referred to the writer or to the amulet. See TB *Shabbat* 61a. On the empirical dimension of the rabbis' pragmatic approach to magic practices for healing, which is prominent in this discussion, see Veltri (1997, 221–82, 286–93; 1998; 1998–1999).

11. See Bar-Ilan (2002).

12. On the historiola in magic practice in late antiquity, see Frankfurter (1995). Cf. Bohak (2004b).

13. Possibly referring to a kind of malaria, where patients experience brief cycles of fever. Tertian fever is mentioned in a prescription discussed later. Tertian fever and

within a copper tube, close it [the tube] with lead, seal it with sixty seals, shake it, lift it up, and say to it [the ant]: "Your burden upon me and my burden upon you." R. Aḥa son of R. Huna said to R. Ashi: "But perhaps [another] man had [already] found it and stopped his with it [i.e., stopped his own illness through the ant, so that this person will take his predecessor's illness upon himself]? Rather let him say to it: "My burden and your burden upon you." And if not [offering another option], let him take a new pitcher, go to the river and say to it: "River river, lend me a pitcher of water for a guest that has chanced upon me." Let him then swing it [the full pitcher] seven times above his head, throw it [the water] behind him and say to it: "Take back the water you gave me, since the guest that chanced upon me came and left in one day!" (TB *Shabbat* 66b)

The second prescription for high fever is cited close to this one in the name of R. Yoḥanan. In this case the healing is based on the symbolic transformation of a thorny weed into a burning bush by means of ritual acts and biblical verses, transferring the special quality of the bush for burning without being consumed to a patient burning with fever. This ritual procedure is accompanied by a mention of the three friends of Daniel who were delivered from the burning furnace into which they had been cast (Daniel 3), all for the purpose of removing the fever from the patient's body.

For a burning fever,[14] he should take an iron knife, go to where a *vardina'* [thornbush][15] is to be found, and knot upon it a white

---

half-tertian fever are also mentioned in medical amulets. See the "Amulets" subsection in chapter 5.

14. In the Aramaic original, *le-'eshata' ṣemirta'*. Dictionaries are divided concerning the precise meaning of the term *ṣemirta'*. Jastrow (1903, 1288; cf. 1277, s.v. צימרא) explains it as a fever that spreads through the body generally (and so did Rashi ad locum), whereas Sokoloff (2002, 960–61, s.v. צימרא צימרתא) suggests that the term points to problems in the urinary tract.

15. At the conclusion of the ritual, the healer turns to the shrub and says, "Thornbush, thornbush!" TB *Avodah Zarah* (28a–b) mentions thornbush shavings and seeds as means of healing sword wounds and fissures, respectively. Possibly, then, *vardina'*

thread.[16] On the first day, he should carve a slight notch[17] and say: "And the angel of the Lord appeared to him . . ." (Exodus 3:2).[18] On the next day, he [again] carves a small notch and says: "And Moses said, I will now turn aside, and see this great sight . . ." (Exodus 3:3). The next day, he makes [another] small notch and says: "And when the Lord saw that he turned aside to see . . ." (Exodus 3:4). R. Aḥa son of Rava said to R. Ashi: "And [he should] say: 'Do not come near . . .' (Exodus 3:5)."[19] Rather, then, on the first day, he should say: "And the angel of the Lord appeared unto him . . ." [and also] "And Moses said . . ." The next day he should say: "And when the Lord saw . . ." And on the next day [he will say]: "Do not come near."[20] And when he has cut it [after three days], he should pull it down, cut it, and say: "Thornbush, thornbush! It is not because you are loftier than all the

---

is a name for the thornbush ('asana'), as Rashi comments in TB *Shabbat* 67a. In any event, the prescription opens with *vardina'* and ends with "thornbush," thereby illustrating and emphasizing the transformation of an ordinary shrub into the mythological bush. For further discussion of this matter, see Bohak (2004b, 118–20).

16. In the original, *nira' barqa'*. I have followed Jastrow's translation on this (1903, 197). Sokoloff (2002, 753, s.v. נירא) suggests "yellow thread." Rashi uses "hair of an animal" (Rashi on TB *Shabbat* 66b, TB *Avodah Zarah* 28b).

17. Ms Oxford 366 reads "tighten." In this case, the subject is the thread rather than the shrub, which is the subject when the action is carving a notch. Each day, the thread should be slightly tightened on the shrub.

18. These are the verses mentioned (Exodus 3:2–5): "(2) And the angel of the Lord appeared to him in a flame of fire out of the midst of a bush: and he looked, and, behold, the bush burned with fire, but the bush was not consumed. (3) And Moses said, I will now turn aside, and see this great sight, why the bush is not burnt. (4) And when the Lord saw that he turned aside to see, God called to him out of the midst of the bush, and said, Moses, Moses. And he said, Here I am. (5) And he said, Do not come near: put off your shoes from off your feet, for the place on which you stand is holy ground."

19. This suggestion seeks to enlist the rejection conveyed by the words "Do not come near" in the service of the patient and to apply them sympathetically to reproduce the rejection in the relationship between the patient and the fever.

20. The printed version, which is generally closer to Ms Oxford 366 than to Ms Munich 95, is clearer than both manuscripts concerning the verses to be recited on each day. On the various versions and the errors in them, see R. Rabinowitz (1960) on TB *Shabbat* 67a in the glosses.

other trees that the Holy One, blessed be He, brought his *Shek-hinah* to rest upon you, but because you are humbler than all other trees. And as the fire saw Ḥanania, Mishael, and Azariah and fled from them, so let the fever of [so-and-so], son of [the woman] so-and-so flee from him [i.e., leave his body]." (TB *Shabbat* 67a)

Additional healing prescriptions that combine incantations and ritual are also found elsewhere, formulated briefly and without discussion. For instance, here is a pair of prescriptions for extracting a fishbone stuck in the throat:

[For] one who has a bone in his throat, he should bring [another bone] of the same kind, place it on his [the former's] head, and say: "One by one go down, swallow, go down one by one."[21] . . . For a fishbone, he should say: "You are stuck in like a needle, you are locked up as a shield; go down, go down." (TB *Shabbat* 67a)

Also we have the following three prescriptions for healing the spleen:

For [diseases of] the spleen . . . he should take the spleen of an unopened she-goat [i.e., one that has not yet had offspring], smear it in the oven [and dry it], stand in front of it and say: "As this spleen has dried, [so] let the spleen of NN dry up." And if not [if he cannot do this or if it does not prove effective] he should smear it between the bricks of a new house[22] and say these words. And if not, he should look for the corpse of a man who has died on the Sabbath, take his hand, and place it on his [the sick person's] spleen and say: "As this hand has dried up, so let the spleen of NN dry up." (TB *Gittin* 69b)

---

21. *Ḥad ḥad neḥet belaʿ belaʿ neḥet ḥad ḥad.* In Ms Oxford 366, the version of the incantation is more extensive: *Ḥad ḥad ḥar ḥar neḥet belaʿ belaʿ neḥet ḥar ḥar ḥad ḥad.* The addition *ḥar ḥar* may convey the choking sounds of one who had a bone stuck in his throat. In both cases the incantation contains many guttural letters.

22. Thus also in the Soncino printed version. Ms Munich 95 and Ms Vatican 130 include no mention of a new house and note only "between the bricks."

There is also a prescription and a story preceding it concerned with sobering up.

> Like that of R. Huna [when he would return from] the house of Rav, and Rav from R. Ḥiyya's house, and R. Ḥiyya from Rabbi's house, when they were drunk, someone would bring oil and salt and rub it into the palms of their hands and the soles of their feet and say: "Just as this oil is becoming clear, [so] let NN's wine become clear."[23] And if not [if one cannot do this of if it does not prove effective], he should bring the plug of a wine vessel, soak it in water, and say: "Just as this plug becomes clear, so let the wine of NN become clear." (TB *Shabbat* 66b)

Besides incantation prescriptions such as these, the rabbis also offered prescriptions for ritual acts of healing that do not include incantations (and are therefore not magical in the definitive, adjurational sense of the word). Their ritual character, however, makes it hard to perceive them as merely folk medicine. So, for instance, the following prescription, also cited in the name of Abaye's foster mother, was meant to heal tertian fever (meaning a fever that rises in 72-hour cycles, that is, malaria):

> One should bring seven thorns from seven palm trees, seven chips from seven beams, seven pegs from seven bridges, seven [heaps of] ashes from seven ovens, seven [mounds of] earth from under seven door-sockets,[24] seven specimens of pitch from seven ships, seven handfuls of cumin, seven hairs from the beard of an old dog, and tie them in the shirt collar [of the sick person's garment] with a white thread. (TB *Shabbat* 67a)

The following prescription, also from the same source, may also belong to this category: "For a daily fever, he should take a silver *zuz*, go to a salt pool, take its weight in salt, and tie it up in the shirt collar with a white thread" (TB *Shabbat* 66b). This is a good example of a borderline case; it

---

23. Ms Oxford 366 does not mention the palms of the hands, and the incantation opening is slightly different.

24. See Rashi ad locum and Jastrow (1903, 983, s.v. סינרא).

is hard to decide whether a certain amount of salt (tied near the neck)[25] is meant to act by itself and heal the body or whether this is perhaps a salt amulet that mediates other powers residing within it by virtue of ritual acts. The demand to tie this bundle with a white thread, mentioned also in the ritual resorting to a prickly bush to get rid of fever (and in a prescription for healing an anal fissure),[26] appears to hint at the second option.

Finally, in the context of magic healing in general and the knowledge on this matter in the name of Abaye's foster mother in particular, her reference to healing and protective knots (qesharim) also deserves mention: "Abaye said, My mother told me: 'Three stop [illness], five cure [it], seven [work] even against witchcraft'" (TB Shabbat 66b).[27] Even though the details of the actual practice in this last source are unclear, they explicitly denote awareness of the dangers of malefic sorcery that, according to the context, seem to be related here to a particularly serious illness.[28]

A similar notion is intimated in the snake's response to the rabbis' puzzlement at the nature of its harm—killing not for the sake of eating: "if the snake bites without a charm."[29] Indeed, the snake hurries to explain that the charm (laḥash) is the divine command "I would not bite unless I was told to do so from heaven." Beyond the clarification,

---

25. The meaning of the Aramaic ba-ḥalala' de-bei ṣavara' is equivocal. On the one hand, similar instructions are mentioned in a prescription for the healing of an anal fissure (TB Avodah Zarah 28b): "Take seven grains of red aloe, wrap it [the bundle of grains] in the shirt collar (ba-ḥalala' de-bei ṣavara'), and tie a white thread on it. Dip it in white naphtha, burn it, and spread [the ashes] on him [the patient]." These instructions attest that the reference is not to the place of tying the bundle to the patient's clothing (near the neck) but to the particular piece of the shirt from which one should prepare the bundle (cf. Rashi ad locum). On the other hand, if this is the intended meaning in the prescription for fever as well, it is not clear what should be done with the bundle. Hence either the prescription in TB Shabbat is missing something or, despite the linguistic similarity between these two cases, it should be understood as referring to the place for tying the bundle to the patient's clothing—the shirt collar.

26. See the previous note for the prescription for healing an anal fissure.

27. On magical knots, see Harari (1997a, 133–34). On the "knots shirt" from the Cave of Letters (in the Judean Desert), see also the "Amulets" subsection in chapter 5. On Abaye's foster mother and her medical-magical knowledge, see Lesses (2001, 362–64).

28. On aggressive Jewish magic, see Harari (1997a).

29. PT Pe'ah 1:1 and parallel versions. See Ecclesiastes 10:11.

however, we see inklings of an approach conveyed in the literal meaning of the verse, whereby snakes are harmful agents in the service of the charmer. This stance is one side of the approach that generated on its other side the idea of "the rabbis' snake" (*ḥivya' de-rabanan*)—a snake sent by the rabbis to harm transgressors who turn to heretics for assistance. The harm inflicted by such a snake is particularly harsh and incurable—"it has no remedy at all."[30] An additional source that is presumably connected is the statement that "whoever behaves modestly in the privy is delivered from three things—from snakes, from scorpions, and from evil spirits. And some say, nor will his dreams disturb him" (TB *Berakhot* 62a). The hypothesis that this passage refers to exposure to injury by harmful magical agents is supported by Ben Azzai's explicit comments there: "Touch yourself before sitting and do not sit and then touch yourself, for anyone who sits and then touches himself, even witchcraft practiced in Aspamia will reach him."

These traditions are part of a more extensive series of testimonies showing the rabbis' profound acknowledgment of the power of harmful sorcery.[31] The most pronounced expression of this view is the many traditions touching on the power of cursing through the invocation of the divine name, part of the more comprehensive rabbinic conception about the performative potential latent in the Ineffable Name.[32] Use of the Ineffable Name was perceived as an extremely serious offense and was absolutely forbidden. Hillel's succinct formulation on this issue is well known: "He who uses the crown (*taga'*)—shall pass away" (M. *Avot* 1:9). Its meaning becomes clear in the parallel version in *Avot de-Rabbi Natan* (version A, 12): "And he that puts the crown to his own use shall utterly perish. How? Since he who makes use of the Ineffable Name has no share in the world to come."[33] Cursing with the Ineffable Name was also

---

30. TB *Shabbat* 110a; TB *Avodah Zarah* 27b; PT *Shevi'it* 9:1.

31. Cf. Blau (1898, 49–54).

32. See Blau (1898, 117–46), Bohak (2008, 376–78), Gruenwald (1994), Trachtenberg (1970, 78–103), and Urbach (1975, 124–34).

33. The use of "the crown of Torah" is ascribed also to R. Tarfon, who broke loose from the sack in which he had been tied. The story is followed by a statement by Rabbah b. Bar Ḥanna: "Whoever makes use of the crown of Torah, is uprooted from the world" (TB *Nedarim* 62a). However, *taga'* is not mentioned here but literally "the crown of

forbidden by the rabbis,[34] but its power never ceased to threaten. Several midrashic traditions link it to Moses's slaying of the Egyptian: "He uttered God's name over him and killed him."[35] In the Palestinian Talmud the use of this curse is attributed to the Second Temple priests "who would kill each other through sorcery" (PT *Yoma* 1:1). The Babylonian Talmud often mentions this curse when referring to the ritual power of the rabbis, of whom it is said, "The curse of a rabbi, even when undeserved, comes to pass."[36]

Other traditions, however, suggest that the power of the Ineffable Name was also available to ordinary people, women, and even Gentiles. R. Yitzhak warned, "You should never consider the curse of an ordinary man a trifling matter" (TB *Bava Kamma* 93a). We are told about Shmuel that "he heard a Persian curse his son with it [the Ineffable Name] and he [the son] died" (PT *Yoma* 3:8). In a parallel version, God complains about the offensive use of his names: "If when I concealed from them the Ineffable Name they slay with a substitute name, how much more so had I given and revealed the Ineffable Name to them!" (*Ecclesiastes Rabbah* 3:11).[37]

Stories describing the literal performance of women's curses in an attempt to preempt their harmful effects attest to the extent of the fear evoked by their power. In one case students turned over the chair of Rabbah, son of Rav Huna, and stood it up again after a woman, who had been harmed by his decision on her case, shouted at him, "May his chair turn over!" In another story students soaked Rava's clothes in water after

---

Torah," and it seems that no ritual-performative meaning should be ascribed to R. Tarfon's deeds. See also the discussion of these sources in Gruenwald (1994, 91–93).

34. M. *Sanhedrin* 7:4, 8; M. *Shevu'ot* 4:13; M. *Yevamoth* 2:5; Tosefta *Makkot* 5:10.

35. *Exodus Rabbah* 1:29, and cf. *Leviticus Rabbah* 32:4 and *Pirke de-Rabbi Eliezer* 48. On these traditions and on Moses's magical powers, see Harari (2005b). The *Midrash on Psalms* (36:8) reads, "What is a war weapon? That is the Ineffable Name. They would go to war and they would not fight, and their enemies would fall [before them]."

36. TB *Berakhot* 56a; TB *Sanhedrin* 90b; TB *Makkot* 11a.

37. For a halakhic dimension of the difference between a curse by a divine attribute and one by the divine name, see M. *Sanhedrin* 7:8 (and parallel versions): "One who curses his father or his mother is not punished unless he curses them by the divine name. If he cursed them by an attribute, R. Meir holds him liable, but the rabbis rule that he is exempt."

another woman, also in her bitterness, called at him, "May your ship sink!" Yet these efforts proved useless, and the curses were ultimately fulfilled as intended.[38]

Finally, the story about the scholar who killed his neighbor by cursing him in an original fashion deserves mention here.

> There was a violent man who tormented a certain scholar. He [the scholar] came to R. Joseph [and told him about it]. Said he [the rabbi]: "Go and curse him." "I am afraid of him," he replied. Said he: "Then go and take [out] an exclusion writ against him." "I am all the more afraid to do that!" [because the exclusion writ, unlike the curse, is public]. Said he [the rabbi]: "Take it [the exclusion writ or the curse] put it into a jar, take it [the jar] to a graveyard, and blow into it a thousand horn blasts in forty days." He did so. The jar burst and the violent man died. (TB *Mo'ed Katan* 17a–b).

Belief in the aggressive power of sorcery was not limited to "women and ordinary people" or to "provincial ignoramuses," as scholars have previously suggested.[39] Its influence is evident in rabbinic discourse in general and in the Halakhah they formulated in particular. Besides the mentions noted, two more issues deserve attention: erotic magic and sorcery used to derail justice. Two traditions hint at the power of erotic magic.[40] The first is that of R. Shimon b. Lakish in a discussion about Nazirite uncleanness, whereby one defense against an accusation of forbidden sexual relations is to claim that "I was constrained to do it because of the spells she cast on me" (PT *Nazir* 8:1). The second tradition is the rabbis' determination that, although a virgin is to marry on Wednesday, the court (which meets on Thursdays) will accept the husband's request to bring charges against her (stating that she is not a virgin) even if he

---

38. TB *Gittin* 35a; TB *Bava Bathra* 153a.

39. See the discussion on the study on magic in the sages literature in the "*Kishuf,* Halakhah, and Aggadah: Magic in Rabbinic Literature" subsection in chapter 2.

40. On Jewish erotic magic, see Harari (2000) and Saar (2008). On erotic magic in the Greco-Roman world, see Faraone (1999), Frankfurter (2001), Gager (1992, 78–115), and Ogden (2002, 227–44).

had married her on Monday, if he claims that the Monday wedding was "due to a constraint." And they explain, "What is meant by 'due to a constraint'? Due to sorcery" (PT *Ketuboth* 1:1).[41] The reference is probably to harmful spells meant to prevent the husband from consummating the union, fear of which forced the couple to deviate from the law and put the marriage forward.[42] In both cases, acknowledging the power of sorcery serves as the basis of the halakhic stance.

The second issue is the use of sorcery to pervert the course of justice. This practice is mentioned in the Tosefta together with a series of negative behaviors that precipitated disasters on the nation of Israel and ultimately destroyed it: "As the whisperers of incantations in judgment multiplied, wrath came upon the world and the *Shekhinah* ceased in Israel" (Tosefta *Sotah* 14:3). Precisely on these grounds, R. Yoḥanan may have held that members of the Sanhedrin also had to be "knowledgeable in sorcery."[43]

We must therefore reject the view that the basis for the rabbis' struggle against sorcery and sorcerers is their conceptual denial of the actual human ability to operate through sorcery because of the tension between this power and God's omnipotence.[44] Statements such as "'There is none other besides Him' (Deuteronomy 4:35)—even in matters of sorcery" (TB *Sanhedrin* 67b) or "R. Natan said, 'The Holy One, blessed be He, said—were all the magicians of the world to gather together and try to change morning into evening, they would not succeed'" (*Tanhuma, Korah* 3) should not be understood as negating the possibility of sorcery but as demarcating its limits in the cosmos, for which only God is responsible.[45] At the same time, sorcery implied human daring against Heaven

---

41. The entire issue is discussed in the context of the rabbis' attempt to shorten as far as possible the time between the couple's first sexual contact and the husband's "virginity claim" to the court. Cf. M. *Ketuboth* 1:1 and the discussion of this mishnah in the Babylonian Talmud.

42. Cf. *Midrash Leqah Tov*, Genesis 16:2.

43. On incantations for perverting the course of justice in Jewish magic literature, see Harari (1998, 202). *Defixiones* from the Greco-Roman world attest to the actual use of this practice. See, for instance, Gager (1992, 116–50).

44. Urbach (1975, 97).

45. This was indeed how the authors of Jewish magical writings understood their activity. Their literature attests to a pragmatic worldview that in most cases prompted the application of magical strategies for the purpose of improving the chances of what

and a forceful intrusion into God's distinct and exclusive domain, which seemingly narrowed God's infinite realm of action. R. Yoḥanan excelled at articulating this perception of sorcery in his statement "Why are they called sorceries (*keshafim*)? Because they deny/diminish (*makhishin*) the heavenly court" (TB *Sanhedrin* 67b),[46] attributing to sorcery the absence of blessing in the world and particularly the desolation of the Jewish people.[47] Nevertheless, in light of the extensive evidence about the ritual power of the rabbis and especially in the context of their struggle against witches and wizards (discussed later), their objections to sorcery do not seem to rest solely on ideological grounds. As I will show, social considerations played a decisive role in shaping the rabbis' hostile discourse in this regard.

Ways of the Amorites

Although we lack an essentialist definition of sorcery as practice in the way the rabbis understood it (and I doubt whether they had any such definition), the category "ways of the Amorites" (*darkei ha-Emori*) that recurs in their writings affords an opening for a partial clarification of activity in this area and for the foundations of the resistance to it. The

---

was also considered possible without them. This action was not presented in magical writings as a negation of the divine court but rather the opposite. As noted, the author of *Ḥarba de-Moshe* actually anchored human magical knowledge and powers in divine omnipotence and in God's explicit support for human control of the angels and of the heavenly sword of holy names. See Harari (1997b, 67–73).

46. The Hebrew root *kḥš* has a dual meaning here: to deny and to diminish (weaken). Both meanings are recorded in the Talmud (Jastrow 1903, 629). In this passage the root apparently serves both meanings. The meaning of "to deny" touches on the spiritual dimension of the belief in sorcery—a denial of divine omnipotence—and the meaning of "to diminish" touches on its practical aspect—its diminution and weakening as a result of human magic.

47. M. *Sotah* 4:5, 9:13; Tosefta *Sotah* 14:3. This approach may also have been the basis of Rabban Yoḥanan b. Zakkai's response to his disciples, who were puzzled by the comparison he drew in a conversation with a Gentile between the ritual of purification with the ashes of the red heifer and the exorcism of an evil spirit. His response— "It is neither the dead that defiles nor the water that purifies, but the decree of the Holy One, blessed be He" (*Pesikta de-Rav Kahana* 4:7)—denies any performative power to the religious rite as such and presents it as the technical implementation of a divine decree.

term *ways of the Amorites* denotes acts that are forbidden because of the biblical prohibition "neither shall you walk in their practices" (Leviticus 18:3), that is, because of the desire to differentiate the people of Israel from the surrounding nations. In Deuteronomy 18:10–14 the prohibition of resembling the Gentile nations is explicitly related to practices of sorcery and divination, which are presented as the typical feature of the surrounding foreign culture.[48] For this feature—resemblance to the Gentiles, particularly in the context of magic and divination—the rabbis reserved the term *ways of the Amorites*.

The ways of the Amorites category is mentioned in the Mishnah as a basis for forbidding acts of magic-apotropaic character, such as carrying a locust egg, a fox's tooth, or a nail from one who has been crucified (M. *Shabbat* 6:10) or the ritual use of an animal placenta (its burial at a crossroads or hanging it from a tree; M. *Hullin* 4:7). The Tosefta makes dual use of this category. On the one hand, it uses it to label forbidden ritual (and other) acts, such as

He who ties a pad onto his thigh and a red thread on his finger . . . he who stops up a window with thorns, and he who ties a piece of iron to the leg of the bed of a woman in childbirth, and he who sets a table before her . . . he who pours out water onto the street and says *ḥada'* . . . he who throws a piece of iron between graves and says *ḥada'* . . . he who puts a staff of wood or iron under his head . . . she who shouts at an oven not to let the bread fall, she who puts chips into the handle of a pot that it should not boil over . . . she who puts eggs and grass into the wall and covers them over the plaster and counts seven and one . . . she who sets out a brood of chicks in a sieve, or puts pieces of iron among a brood of chicks . . . he who says *dagan qardan* . . . he who says *dani dano*. . . . He who says "Healing" . . . these are ways of the Amorites. (Tosefta *Shabbat* 6–7)

On the other hand, the Tosefta uses the category ways of the Amorites to condone acts that seem to be part of it but are not (*Shabbat* 7; *Shevi'it*

48. See Schmidt (2002). Cf. also Leviticus 20:23 and Exodus 23:24. On the Amorites' sorcery, cf. *2 Baruch* 60:1.

1:10). Discussions of the ritual practices that fall within or beyond the definition of ways of the Amorites in tannaitic and amoraic sources,[49] as well as the very choice of the term, denote their identification with Gentiles. This conception fits in well with the trend pointed out by many scholars in recent decades whereby sorcery is the ritual performed by the "other" to achieve power.[50] Labeling ritual practices as ways of the Amorites, then, thereby seemingly suggesting that they are prohibited because they are foreign, reflects a rabbinic attempt to eradicate performative foreign cults in favor of the canonic Jewish worship of the kind they themselves had fashioned, which is also a power tool. At the same time, the rabbis endeavored to put a Jewish garb on and symbolically refashion practices they had apparently been unable to uproot.[51] The trouble is that none of the discussions on the ways of the Amorites offer any systematic model for determining the types of action in this category and use this category only as a label to designate certain acts.[52] Hence, rather than pointing to the defined shared essence of specific practices, the label "ways of the Amorites" attests to the rabbis' hostile attitude toward the ritual power of the "others" and to the rhetorical halakhic means they resorted to in order to delegitimize it.

In this light, a sweeping ruling by Abaye and Rava that excludes from the list of the forbidden anything useful to medicine is particularly remarkable: "Anything that can be used as a remedy is not deemed ways of the Amorite" (TB *Shabbat* 67a). This empirical pragmatic approach, reflected also in the ruling that permits carrying an "expert amulet" on the Sabbath, was not generally accepted. R. Aqiva, for instance, was in principle opposed to the use of incantations for medical purposes and stated that one who recites incantations for an illness and says, "I will

---

49. See PT *Shabbat* 6:10; TB *Shabbat* 67a–b; TB *Sotah* 49b; TB *Bava Kamma* 83a, 91b; TB *Sanhedrin* 52b; TB *Avodah Zarah* 11a; TB *Hullin* 77a–b; and Minor Tractates *Semahot* 8:1. For a discussion of these sources, see Avishur (1979), Bohak (2008, 382–85), Lieberman (1992, 2: 492, 3: 79–105), Seidel (1995), and Veltri (1994; 1997, 93–220).

50. See chapters 1 and 2.

51. See Lieberman (1942, 100–103).

52. Discussions that are more systematic may have existed in the "Amorite chapter" mentioned in TB *Shabbat* 67a, which has not reached us.

put none of these diseases upon you, which I have brought upon Egypt, for I am the Lord that heals you" (Exodus 15:26), has no place in the world to come.[53] R. Joshua b. Levi ruled, "It is forbidden to heal oneself with words of Torah" altogether (TB *Shevu'ot* 15b), whereas R. Yoḥanan restricted the prohibition to cases where the reading of the verses is attached to spitting, "for the Name of Heaven is not to be mentioned in connection with spitting" (TB *Shevu'ot* 15b).[54]

Another kind of limitation to the medical use of incantations was set by R. Ishmael and R. Joshua b. Levi, who chose to have their loved ones die rather than heal them in the name of Jesus. We are told in the Tosefta about R. Ishmael (close to a broad and detailed objection to contact with heretics, which ends with the admonition, "You shall seek neither financial nor medical assistance from them").

> R. Elazar b. Damah was bitten by a snake. Jacob of Kefar Sama came to heal him in the name of Jesus b. Pandera and R. Ishmael did not allow him. He said to him: "You are not allowed [to accept healing from him], Ben Damah." He [R. Elazar] said to him: "I shall bring you proof [that he may] heal me," but he had no time to bring such proof before he died. Said R. Ishmael: "Happy are you Ben Damah for you have left [the world] in peace and without breaking down the hedge erected by the rabbis. For whoever breaks down the hedge erected by the rabbis, calamity befalls him, as it is said, 'whoever breaks through a hedge, a snake shall bite him'" (Ecclesiastes 10:8). (Tosefta *Hullin* 2:22)[55]

About R. Joshua b. Levi, we read:

---

53. M. *Sanhedrin* 10:1. On the use of Exodus 15:26 in amulets and magic prescriptions, see Naveh and Shaked (1993, 23). The Mishnah evidence allows us to date it considerably earlier than the magic sources.

54. The practice of spitting to chase away the evil eye is hinted at in the famous story of R. Meir and the woman who wanted to listen to his teachings (PT *Sotah* 1:4; *Leviticus Rabbah* 9:9).

55. Cf. PT *Avodah Zarah* 2:2. On "Jesus b. Pandera," see Kohut (1926, 2: 118–19, s.v. בן סטדא).

R. Joshua b. Levi . . . his grandson choked. Someone came and whispered his (Jesus b. Pandera's)[56] name and he recovered. [When the man came out] he [R. Joshua b. Levi] said to him: "What did you say over him?" Said he: "Such and such a word." He said: "It would have been better if he had died and not thus [i.e., if he had not been healed in the name of Jesus]." And it was for him [the grandson] so [that he died, since R. Joshua's words were as a] mistake from the mouth of a ruler [that, although it is a mistake, it is carried out]. (PT *Shabbat* 14:4 [=*Avodah Zarah* 2:2])

These stories, even if they express an ideological struggle with Christian culture in general, express above all the rabbis' fears that agents of its ritual power will penetrate Jewish society. The gap between the views conveyed by Abaye and Rava and those of R. Ishmael and R. Joshua b. Levi, beyond their different geographic-historical realities, reflects the gap between the rabbis' tolerance of foreign practices on the one hand and of alien power agents on the other. As I will show, in all that concerns such agents the rabbis adopted a resolutely hostile and uncompromising view.

Rabbis, Women, and Heretic Sorcerers

The rabbis, who are the creators and protagonists of rabbinic literature, are often portrayed in it as agents of ritual power. Unsurprisingly, in their literature it is the rabbis and not others who are the worthy and legitimate agents of this power. The source of this power is attributed to a holy way of life and to constant ritual contact with God, to the point of identification with him through the internalization of his word—the Torah.[57]

The rabbis' supernatural power is manifest in stories about their power to curse and send a snake whose bite is incurable, to cause rain or

---

56. These words were deleted from Ms Leiden in both versions of the story and were returned in the proofreading.

57. On the ritual significance of being a rabbi and on its implications in the context of ritual power, see Blau (1898, 54–61), Garb (2005, 28–46), Gruenwald (1994), and Neusner (1969; 1970).

direct it as they wish,[58] to fill a field with gourds and collect them by means of speech (TB *Sanhedrin* 68a), to fill a valley with golden dinars (*Midrash on Psalms* 92:8; *Exodus Rabbah* 52:3), to control the sea (PT *Sanhedrin* 7:11), to kill a snake through their mere contact with it (TB *Berakhot* 33a), to move a tree, to shift the flow of water by a cubit, to bring down walls and halt their fall (TB *Bava Metsia* 59b), to raise corpses from the earth (PT *Shevi'it* 9:1), to kill with words or with a stare,[59] to revive the dead (TB *Megillah* 7b), to divine and contend with demons, to overcome witches and sorcerers, and so forth. The apex of this trend is in the attribution to the rabbis of the capacity to create. Earlier we encountered R. Joshua's statement about his power to create real ram and deer that can reproduce and the story about the 3-year-old heifer that was created through the rabbis' study of the laws of creation. Note also Rabbah's resolute statement whereby "if the righteous wished, they would create a world" (TB *Sanhedrin* 65b) and the adjoining story about the anthropoid (golem) he himself created.

> Rava created a man and sent him to R. Zera. He [R. Zera] would speak to him but he [the man-golem] would not answer. He [R. Zera] said to him: "You are from the charmers, return to your dust! (TB *Sanhedrin* 65b)

One can hardly imagine a more far-reaching event than the one related here so laconically. In fact, what we encounter here is not only the rabbis' actual powers of creation (even if imperfect) but a kind of inside game the group engages in, hinting at the routine nature of such creations. Rava does not act clandestinely. Quite the contrary, he flaunts his powers, whose quality is intimated in the assonance that opens the story, *Rava bara' gavra'* (Rava created a man), which hints at an incantation

---

58. See the traditions about Ḥoni ha-Me'agel (the circle drawer) in M. *Ta'anit* 3:8, TB *Ta'anit* 23a, and PT *Ta'anit* 3:8. Cf. Josephus's story about Onias, who ended the drought with his prayers (Josephus, *Jewish Antiquities* 14.22). See also the series of stories in the long cycle on bringing about rain in TB *Ta'anit* 23a–25b (with Yassif 2004, 57–59) and the stories in TB *Yoma* 53b and PT *Ta'anit* 3:9. Cf. Harari (2001, 23–24).

59. PT *Shevi'it* 9:1, TB *Berakhot* 58a, TB *Shabbat* 34a, TB *Bava Bathra* 75a, *Pesikta de-Rav Kahana* 18:5, and many more. See also Ulmer (1994, 83–104).

formula.[60] He then boasts about these powers, as it were, by actually sending the golem to his colleague, who, for his part, is not at all impressed by this creation and is not baffled when the human creature standing before him fails to answer. He understands immediately that this is a creation of charmers and seeks to dismiss it with words of his own.[61]

From the standpoint of the current study, it makes no difference whether influence is attained through study, prayer, and divine help or through adjurations and the aid of an angel or a demon. All are ritual means and agents of supernatural power that help human beings in their world. But from an intracultural perspective, that of the rabbis, who viewed themselves as representing God and his word in the world and sought to affirm the social and political authority to which they aspired through such supernatural proofs as well, the difference was vast. Because *magic*, *sorcerer*, and *sorceries* are rhetorical terms that served for the hostile labeling of the "other" and the forbidden, rabbis were from the outset excluded from this realm by definition. Their powers were indeed beyond anything that Jewish sorcerers dared to convey in their writings, as articulated in such statements as "I rule man, who rules me? The righteous" (TB *Mo'ed Katan* 16b), "You decreed below and the Holy One, blessed be He, fulfills your words above" (TB *Ta'anit* 23a), or "The Holy One, blessed be He, annuls His decree on account of the decree of the righteous man" (PT *Ta'anit* 3:12). Nevertheless, the source of these powers was not magic but normative righteousness, implying extreme closeness to God.[62] From here, as a living expression of the sanctified norm of life that they themselves fashioned and sought to impart to their

---

60. *Nomina barbara* such as *abra*, *abra brax*, and *abrasax* appear in incantations in Greek magical papyri. Similar assonances appear to have been the source of the well-known formula *abracadabra*. See Brashear (1995, 3577).

61. On this issue, see also Idel (1990, 27–43) and Schäfer (1995). The Aramaic plural *ḥbryy'* seems to be a pun containing two possible readings: *ḥabaraya'* (charmers, magicians) and *ḥavraya'* (friends, the scholar's community).

62. In this sense, the rabbis followed in Moses's magic-miraculous course no less than in that of his leadership. On this aspect of Moses, see Harari (2005b). Cf. also the explicit tradition about Moses as controlling God: "He [Moses] decrees over the Holy One, blessed be He, and He fulfils, and he raises Him up . . . and makes Him sit down" (*Deuteronomy Rabbah* 2:3).

communities, the rabbis wrestled with other agents of ritual power—sorcerers, in their rhetoric—mainly women and heretics.

The need to grapple with sorcerers was apparently the reason for the dispensation to study sorcery: "You will not learn so as to do, but in order to understand and instruct" (TB *Shabbat* 75a). R. Yohanan held that members of the Sanhedrin should have "knowledge of sorcery."[63] And Rashi explains: "[So as] to put to death sorcerers who rely on their charms to save themselves from the court, and to expose wizards who seduce and incite with their spells, such as Jesus Christ" (Rashi on TB *Sanhedrin* 17a). If Rashi is correct in his explanation here, the issue is clearly not only theoretical knowledge for the sake of identifying opponents who possess ritual power and denouncing them as sorcerers but actual magic powers that would enable members of the Sanhedrin to overcome charms meant to pervert justice. This knowledge, beside the immanent power of their holiness and at times even trickery for its own sake, often helped the rabbis in their struggles against heretics, sorcerers, and witches.

Several sources, particularly the Babylonian Talmud, point to a general approach that links sorcery to women and vice versa. This is a later development of a trend succinctly and clearly conveyed in Hillel's statement in M. *Avot* (2:7), "The more women, the more witchcraft." Linking sorcery to lewdness and both sorcery and lewdness to the destruction of the world (M. *Sotah* 9:13) substantiates sorcery as the spiritual parallel and complement of female physical licentiousness.[64] This trend assumes various expressions, but all share a consistent, deep-rooted approach that even extends to influence over halakhic decisions. The following are several examples. In the *Mekhilta de-Rabbi Shimon b. Yohai*, sorcery is linked to women: "And why are [these deeds] called *keshafim* (sorceries)?

---

63. TB *Sanhedrin* 17a, TB *Menahoth* 65a.

64. The basis for this stance is found in the biblical determination "You shall not suffer a witch to live" (Exodus 22:17), which is phrased in female terms (*mekhashefah*) when discussing a concrete accusation of sorcery. Harlotry and witchcraft were already tied together in biblical discourse. See, for instance, 2 Kings 9:21–22 and Nahum 3:4. As noted, these trends were developed in the Apocrypha. On the women-sorcery-lust linkage in Greco-Roman traditions, see Caro-Baroja (1971, 31–34). On women as witches in rabbinic literature, see Bar-Ilan (1993), Bohak (2008, 393–98), Fishbane (1993), Levinson (2006), Seidel (1992), and Stratton (2007, 143–76).

Because of *nashim* (women). For most sorceries are among women."[65] Other traditions tie women to sorcery. In a discussion on the biblical command "You shall not suffer a witch (*mekhashefah*) to live" (Exodus 22:17), we find "Our Rabbis taught, A witch—this applies to both a man and a woman. If so, why does it say witch? Because it is mostly women who deal in witchcraft" (TB *Sanhedrin* 67a). R. Shimon b. Yohai formulates this idea in more extreme terms: "Even the most pious of women is a sorceress."[66] In a discussion on whether to bless a fragrance of unknown source, R. Yosi says, "Even if a majority [around] are Jews, he does not recite a blessing, because daughters of Israel use incense for witchcraft" (TB *Berakhot* 53a). R. Yohanan stated in the name of R. Shimon b. Yohai, "In recent generations, when the daughters of Israel have indulged in witchcraft," one should no longer touch food found on the way (lest it is a magic bait; TB *Eruvin* 64b). The talmudic version of Ben-Sira's claim (Sirach 42:11) ties sorcery specifically to old women: "A daughter is a vain treasure to her father who, fearful for her, will not sleep at night—as a child lest she be seduced, as a young girl lest she engage in forbidden relations, as a grownup lest she not marry, if she marries lest she bear no children, if she grows old lest she engage in witchcraft."[67] Other general discussions of women as witches or as dabbling in sorcery deepen the suspicion of sorcery in every woman.[68]

Completing the picture are stories of female sorcery in which women function as personae who participate in the concrete and familiar reality. At the same time, however, these personae, almost invariably anonymous, represent any woman and the entire female collective. Such, for instance, are the daughters of R. Nahman, who would stir the pot with their hands by means of sorcery (TB *Gittin* 45a); the matron who tied the boat of R. Hisda and Rabbah bar Rav Huna with incantations because they had refused to take her with them (TB *Shabbat* 81b); the woman who tried to take dust from under R. Hanina's feet in order to hurt him with it through magic (TB *Sanhedrin* 67b); the women who cursed

---

65. *Mekhilta de-Rabbi Shimon bar Yohai, Mishpatim* (1955, 209).

66. PT *Kiddushin* 4:11. Cf. Minor Tractates, *Soferim* 15:7.

67. TB *Sanhedrin* 100b. On the misogynous tendency in the talmudic quotes from Ben-Sira, see Ilan (2000).

68. TB *Pesahim* 110a, 111a; TB *Yoma* 83b. Cf. PT *Yoma* 8:6.

Rabbah and Rabbah bar Rav Huna in anger (on two separate occasions) because they had refused to accede to their wishes (TB *Bava Bathra* 153a; TB *Gittin* 35a); and the woman who sought to harm with sorcery the husband who had divorced her when he came to drink at the shop of her new husband (TB *Pesahim* 110b).

The story about the witch who prevented a Jew in Rome from fathering children (to be discussed later) also fits into this trend, and so does the story about the innkeeper who tried to cast a spell on Yanai and about her friend who broke Yanai's spell.

> Yanai came to an inn. He said to them: "Give me water to drink." They brought him *shatita'* [a kind of porridge]. He saw that her [the innkeeper's] lips were moving.[69] He spilled some of it [the *shatita'*], which turned into scorpions. He said to them: "I have drunk of yours, you too drink of mine." He gave her to drink and she turned into an ass. He rode on her to the market. Her friend came and broke the spell. He was seen riding a woman in the market. (TB *Sanhedrin* 67b)[70]

In practice, almost all talmudic traditions concerned with actual performance of sorcery (*kishuf, keshafim*) ascribe this activity to women. Nevertheless, it seems we must adopt the distinction between the activity of sorcery and the accusation of sorcery and examine these traditions as the expression of a social reality in which an accusation of sorcery carried sociopolitical significance. According to this approach, we need not see the rabbinic stories about the magical power of women as

---

69. The words "he saw that her lips were moving" are missing from the Yemenite manuscript at Yad Harav Herzog but appear (in different versions) in other manuscripts.

70. On the fear of spells at the inn, cf. further TB *Pesahim* 110b and also the following tradition, which shows structural similarities with the Yanai story: "R. Isaac b. Samuel b. Martha chanced upon an inn. Some oil was brought to him in a vessel, he rubbed [himself with the oil] and blisters broke out on his face. He went to the market. A woman saw him. She said: 'I see here the Hamat demon.' She did something [*milta'*, meaning both "something" and "a word"] to him and he was healed" (TB *Sanhedrin* 101a). Here too, the account begins with harmful spells in an inn, in this case an incantation that was recited over the oil in the vessel (this is the context in which the story is cited), and ends with a woman releasing the spell in the market.

expressing a reality in which sorcery was a distinctly female realm of action but rather as another reality, where men in general and rabbis in particular attempted to cope with the threatening power of the female gender by symbolizing it as a supernatural-mystical power and labeling it as illegitimate—magic. The concept of witch (*mekhashefah*), identified in the Babylonian Talmud with femininity in general and potentially with every single woman, rather than denoting women's ritual behavior, reflects anxiety about their power as the "other" in the masculine society pivoting around rabbis and an effort to push this power outside the proper social order.[71]

The most prominent expressions of this anxiety are traditions that identify sorcery with women who are less subject to male control (older women, innkeepers, women in the market,[72] and possibly widows[73]) and traditions that touch on the struggle against organized sorceresses, who

---

71. For further reflections in this direction, see Stratton (2007, 166–76).

72. Besides being public spaces, the market and the inn were associated with harlotry. See Sperber (1998, 15–17). The widespread association of witchcraft and harlotry is thus in the background of the cited stories.

73. The extension to widows has no basis in the Talmud itself but rather in Rashi's gloss on Yoḥani, daughter of Retivi. According to Rashi (on TB *Sotah* 22a), she was a midwife, and she would use sorcery to close the womb of women giving birth and later release the spell under cover of prayer and piety (cf. Kohut 1926, 4: 117–18). The Talmud, however, provides no information about this widow, whose name it indeed mentions derogatorily, and the widespread inclination to ascribe Rashi's commentary to the rabbis is apparently groundless. In any event, this tradition is a revealing illustration of the gender-determined manner adopted by males, as outsiders, when contemplating events during the exclusively female occasion of birth. Though excluded from it, men heard about how events unfolded in the course of deliveries and were full participants in its frequently tragic consequences. The ascription of harmful sorcery to the midwife, whose power, related to exclusive control over knowledge, marginalized males and left them powerless and helpless outside this life-creating event, makes a profound statement concerning anxiety about the power of women in a male society dependent on the "other" gender for its very existence. A close expression of this hostile conception of female power is the attribution of the demonic harm linked to the pain of birth and to the death of mother and child in its course to Lilith, a *female* demon. In both cases male consciousness links the "mysterious" life power pulsating in the female to another mysterious female power, destructive, magic, or demonic. In this fashion it raises the level of existential danger to the very existence of uncontrolled and unrestricted female power.

also remain in the public space unsupervised. The intensity of the anxiety about organized female sorcery underlies the fact that mentions of it are part of stories about overcoming it or of instructions on how to do this. The language of the following passage, which illustrates this feature, illustrates the way in which troubled male thought seeks to contend with a female threat.

> When two women sit at a crossroads, one on one side of the road and one on the other facing each other, they are surely engaged in witchcraft. What is the remedy [for one who wishes to pass]? If there is another road, he should take it. And if there is no other road—if another man is with him, let them hold hands and pass through [in front of the women]. If there is no other man, he should say, "Agrat Azlat Asya Belusia[74] [the names of the demons through whom the women operate?] are killed with arrows." (TB *Pesahim* 111a)[75]

A higher degree of organization (and danger) lurks in the words of Ameimar about the "chief of the sorceresses." The credibility of the antisorcery knowledge and the level of assertiveness implied in its mention are also accordingly greater, because Ameimar learned from the chief of sorceresses herself how to defeat them. And he says so to his audience.

> The chief of the sorceresses told me: "He who meets them, the women sorceresses, should say, 'Hot dung in perforated [or

74. These words appear in different variations in the manuscripts. In some, the name Agrat appears twice instead of Agrat Azlat; Ms Oxford 336 reads "Agrat Agrat bat Maḥalat."

75. This passage is cited between a discussion about the harm of a menstruating woman to the men among whom she is passing ("if it is at the beginning of her menstruation, she will slay one of them, and if it is at the end of her menstruation, she will cause strife between them") and a discussion about the spirit of harlotry evoked in the wake of intercourse after seeing a woman emerge from a ritual immersion. Thereby the dangers of impurity, sorcery, and harlotry borne by women are tied together, enhancing the general threat that femaleness poses to male society, a threat spread through the uncontrolled presence of women in the public, male space. On this issue, see also Seidel (1992).

despicable]⁷⁶ baskets for your mouths, ye witches! *Karaḥ karḥeikhi*, your crumbs be carried [in the wind],⁷⁷ your spices be scattered, the wind carry off the new saffron [plant] that sorceresses hold! As long as God showed his grace to me and to you, I did not come among you; now that I have come among you, may He show his grace to me and to you."⁷⁸ (TB *Pesahim* 110a–b)

The broadest and best known tradition in this context is the story about the struggle of R. Shimon b. Shetaḥ against eighty sorceresses in a cave in Ashkelon that ends with their crucifixion, all on the same day. It begins with the story of a holy man (*ḥasid*) who hears about R. Shimon b. Shetaḥ's vow that, if made patriarch, he will kill off all the witches but then, after being made a patriarch, "he did not kill them; and lo, there are eighty witches in a cave in Ashkelon, destroying the world." The man is sent to warn the patriarch, who acknowledges the critique hurled at him.

Forthwith Shimon b. Shetaḥ stood up on a stormy day and took with him eighty young men. He gave them eighty clean cloaks and they put them in eighty new pots, which they turned over. He said to them: "When I whistle⁷⁹ once, put on your garments. When I whistle a second time, all of you come in at once. And as you come in, each one of you will lift up one of them and hold

---

76. In the original, *ḥari ḥamimi be-diqula' bazuyya'*. This formulation is preferable to *'ari be-diqula'* in Ms Columbia T-893X141, because it appears almost verbatim in a magic bowl from Babylon. See Gordon (1934b, 326–27).

77. *Karaḥ karḥeikhi paraḥ parḥeikhi* in the original and *kar kadrikhi paraḥ parḥiḥi* in Ms Columbia T-893X141. This formulation is close to that found in an adjuration bowl: *karkadikhi parparrikhi*. See Segal (2000, 74, bowl 35A, line 5, and photograph 36). Cf. Sokoloff (2002, 1038–39, s.v. קרח). All these formulations are hard to decipher, and their meaning is uncertain.

78. The meaning of the last two words, *qaraḥanani ve-ḥanankhi*, is unclear, and they are probably miswritten. See Sokoloff (2002, 1038–39, s.v. קרח). My translation attempts to give this text some coherent meaning.

79. In the original, "if I whistle." It seems, however, that these words should be read as I translated them rather than in a conditional sense, as explicit in the *Sanhedrin* version of the story. The meaning of the root *spr* is not clear. It is probably a reference to a whistle or a high-pitched tone made with a whistle or a similar instrument that, according to the context, must be loud enough to be heard outside the cave.

her off the ground, for if you hold a charmer (*mekhashef*) off the ground he is incapable of doing anything." He went and stood at the mouth of the cave and said: "'*Oyim, 'oyim*! Open up for me. I am one of yours."[80] They said to him: "How did you come here on such a day?" He replied: "I walked between the raindrops." They said to him: "And what did you come to do here?" He said: "To learn and to teach; let each one come and do what he knows." And so it was. One said what she said and brought bread [by means of an incantation].[81] One said what she said and brought meat. [Yet another] said what she said and brought cooked food. [And one] said what she said and brought wine. They said to him: "And what can you do?" He said to them: "I can whistle twice and bring to you eighty young men. They will have pleasure with you and give pleasure to you." They said to him: "Yes, we want." He whistled once and the [men outside] put on their clothes. He whistled a second time and they all came in at once. He said: "Let each one of you pick a partner." They loaded them [on their backs], and they went, and they crucified them. (PT *Hagigah* 2:2)[82]

The gist of this story is a description of the struggle between two opposing camps. On one side are men, wisdom, cunning, knowledge, physical power, and on the other are women, licentiousness, sorcery, supernatural power. R. Shimon b. Shetah overcomes the witches by what seems to them (following his equivocal declaration that he had come to learn and to teach) to be complicity in sorcery but is merely male cunning and might defeating the power of female sorcery. His ruse exploits two essential components of female sorcery or, more precisely, its widespread image, which the story exposes: (1) their licentiousness, expressed

---

80. The call '*Oyim, 'oyim* does not appear elsewhere, and its meaning is uncertain. It is probably something like "Ho, ho."

81. In a looser translation, "and bread appeared." On the linguistic formulation "one said what one said," as pointing to the performance of spells, see Sperber (1994, 60–66).

82. This account is in the extended version of the story quoted in the text. For a more concise version, see PT *Sanhedrin* 6:4. On this issue, see Amir (1994), Ilan (2006, 214–41), and Yassif (1999, 156–58). Cf. also Efron (1988).

in their gathering together in a cave, for the purpose of the sorcery that they choose to display before him (bringing food and drink for the celebration), and in their lust for the men that he brings with him to their cave; and (2) the earthy subterranean source of their magical power (obviously the reverse of the celestial source of the rabbis' power and wisdom). Important information is hidden here; the physical detachment of the witches from the ground annuls their power. The struggle against organized female sorcery, removed from (male) culture, enclosed within the space of the earth (with all the erotic implication intimated by this space), and drawing from it its magical-licentious power, demands more than an incantation. For this purpose, what is required is male cooperation, discipline, and force. The physical might of a disciplined unit of men led by a wise patriarch overcomes, as expected and in a promising and consoling fashion, the magical unruly and licentious might of the women in the cave and eliminates it. The sharp ending of the story, horrifying in its single-mindedness—"they loaded them, and they went, and they crucified them"—highlights the military character of the action and also emphasizes the triviality of anything that is beyond the actual ploy of overcoming the power of female sorcery. As opposed to the struggle itself, described colorfully and in great detail, their crucifixion is a trivial matter, a technical act of lifting, carrying, and killing.

An additional important aspect in the stories of the struggle between rabbis and sorcerers is the power advantage of the Jewish holy sage over the foreign sorcerer or witch. Besides the trend to play down foreign sorcery to the level of mere trickery, two struggle stories deserve special note. These stories appear next to one another in the Palestinian Talmud and feature R. Joshua and R. Eliezer, together with Rabban Gamaliel (in one) and R. Aqiva (in the other). In the two stories, which are cited in what follows, the plot traces the struggle between R. Joshua and a foreign sorcerer or witch who has brought harm to Jews (the rabbis themselves or their host). In both stories R. Eliezer turns to R. Joshua and asks him to solve the crisis, in a request whose phrasing attests to recognition of R. Joshua's power and his trust in it.[83] The plots of the two stories are

---

83. Beside the following traditions on the power of R. Joshua, recall his claim about his ability to turn gourds and watermelons into rams and deer who would produce rams and deer (PT *Sanhedrin* 7:11). On R. Eliezer's magic powers and his vast

guided by an implicit principle whereby the rabbi cannot cancel with his own sorcery the malefic witchcraft that has already been cast, and the struggle is taken beyond the specific spell to the unconditional surrender of the "other" sorcerer (woman or heretic).[84]

This principle is not fundamental to the stories of the rabbis' struggle against foreign magic and, in at least two other cases, a different picture is presented. In one, R. Joshua intervenes directly to annul the harmful sorcery that heretics cast on his nephew: "Hanina, the son of R. Joshua's brother, went to Capernaum and the heretics cast a word on him[85] and brought him [to the village] riding an ass on the Sabbath. He went to Joshua his uncle and he [R. Joshua] anointed him with oil and he recovered" (*Ecclesiastes Rabbah* 1:4, on Ecclesiastes 1:8). The other case is that of R. Hisda and Rabbah bar Rav Huna, who refuses to take a certain matron with them in their boat and try to sail without her: "She uttered a word—and bound the boat; they uttered a word—and freed it."[86] We do not exactly know what dispelled the sorcery in the first case. Most likely, R. Joshua said whatever he said over the oil and only then did he anoint his nephew with it. The second case is more explicit: The spell that bound the boat was dismissed by the rabbis' contrary spell. The parallel is highlighted not only by the contents but also by the form: the identical terms that the narrator chooses in the description of both

---

knowledge in this area, see TB *Sanhedrin* 68a. The threat that this power and its agents (even if they are themselves rabbis) posed to the social order that the rabbis wanted to establish is well illustrated in the famous story known as "The Oven of Akhnai" (TB *Bava Metsia* 70a–b). In this story, when the introduction of R. Eliezer's ritual power into the house of study threatens to bring down its walls and with them the entire institution, R. Joshua displays impressive performative abilities and prevents their fall by means of words. The end of the story is that R. Eliezer kills his brother-in-law R. Shimon b. Shetah through a falling-forward (*nefilat 'apayim*) prayer. Thus the ritual power that unites and exalts the rabbinic community when directed outward, splits it and destroys it when it is turned inward. This story has been extensively discussed. See Rubinstein (1999, 34–63, 314n1), which includes an extensive bibliography. See also Alexander (1995b, 414–18).

84. For a detailed examination of these stories, see Levinson (2006). Cf. Hirshman (1988). On the rabbi's struggle with heretics by means of magic, see Bohak (2003b).

85. Literally "did a word to him."

86. TB *Shabbat* 81b (=TB *Hullin* 105b).

parties' actions. Such a linguistic parallel is also prominent in the story about R. Joshua's contest with a heretic in a Tiberias bathhouse. In both cases the parallel is meant to point out that not only are the rabbis well versed in acts of magic and incantation but also that, when they perform them, their power prevails over the magic power of the "other."

One struggle story of R. Joshua takes place in the house of Jews in Rome where he is hosted together with his companions, R. Eliezer and Rabban Gamaliel. The part of the plot that is of interest here opens with a description of a strange and suspicious practice of the hosts, which the rabbis witness: All the food served to them is taken first to a side room. Their questions lead them to the head of the family who has closed himself up in that room. After they are introduced to him as "sages of Israel," he asks of them, "Pray for my son, who has no children." R. Eliezer then turns to R. Joshua as one who understands what is at stake and pleads with him to find out what he can do. R. Joshua does not pray. Instead, he sows flax on the table, which grows immediately. When he tears it off the table, he thereby pulls the hair of the (most probably local) witch, who has thwarted the son's sexual power.[87] His threat to expose her publicly, which would cost her her life according to Roman law,[88] forces her to consent to the demand to annul her action. But because she has thrown her spell into the sea (so as to preclude any possibility of ever canceling it?), she cannot do so until R. Joshua commands the lord of the sea to eject the spell onto land. We do not know what happened technically at that stage. Perhaps the ejection of the spell from the sea and its exposure canceled its power, or perhaps the witch did what she did for this purpose. In any event, at this time, and only at this time, the rabbis pray, and the host's son does indeed father a son.

> When R. Eliezer, R. Joshua, and Rabban Gamaliel went up to Rome . . . they said: "It appears that there are Jews here." They

---

87. Spells for hatred and impotence were widespread in the Greco-Roman world. See, for instance, Ogden (2002, 227–30). Binding spells for love also included, if necessary, formulas for separating the beloved from other partners. See Gager (1992, 78–115).

88. On the Roman legislation against witchcraft, see Kippenberg (1997), Liebeschuetz (1979, 126–39), McMullen (1966, 95–127), and Ritner (1995, 3355–58).

came into a place and were received there gracefully. . . . He [the host] said to them: "Pray for my son, for he has not produced a child." Said R. Eliezer to R. Joshua: "R. Joshua b. Hanania, now see what you [can] do." He [R. Joshua] said to them: "Bring me flax seeds," and they brought him flax seeds. He appeared to have sown the seed on the table; he appeared to have watered it; it appeared to have come up [and grown]; he appeared to tear [and draw] it out until he raised a woman by her tresses. He said to her: "Release what you have done." She said to him: "I will not." He said to her: "If you do not, I shall expose you." She said to him: "I cannot do it, for [the spell] has been cast into the sea." R. Joshua issued a decree to the Prince of the Sea, who ejected it. And they prayed for him and he fathered a son, R. Judah b. Bathera. (PT *Sanhedrin* 7: 11)

The second story takes place in Tiberias and has two parts. The first takes place in the bathhouse and the second outside it.

R. Eliezer, R. Joshua, and R. Aqiva went in to bathe in the bathhouse of Tiberias. A *min* [heretic] saw them. He said what he said and they were caught in the dome [of the bathhouse]. Said R. Eliezer to R. Joshua: "Now Joshua b. Hanina, see what you [can] do." When that *min* went out, R. Joshua said what he said and the doorway held him [the *min*], so that whoever went in would give him a punch and whoever went out would give him a push. He said to them: "Undo what you have done." They said to him: "Release us, and we shall release you." They released one another. Once they came out, R. Joshua said to that *min*: "Is that [all] you know?" Said he [the *min*]: "Let's go down to the sea." When they got down to the sea, that *min* said what he said and the sea split open. He said to them: "Is this not what Moses, your rabbi, did at the sea?" They said to him: "Will you not concede to us that Moses, our rabbi, walked through it?" He said to them: "Yes." They said to him: "[Then] you walk through it." He walked through it. R. Joshua issued a decree to the Prince of the Sea, who swallowed him up. (PT *Sanhedrin* 7:11)

The story opens with a hurtful prank: A heretic wizard arbitrarily provokes the rabbis and imprisons them under the dome of the bathhouse. While they are sitting there, confined to their places, R. Eliezer turns to R. Joshua with the same phrase found in the previous story and asks him, as one who is well aware of his powers, "Now Joshua b. Ḥanina, see what you can do." Here, too, R. Joshua tries to release the spell but adopts a different tactic, intended to force the sorcerer to do so himself. He waits for an appropriate moment, and then, in a perfect parallel to the wizard's act, "said what he said," and relying on a magic incantation, he affixes the heretic to the doorway. In their spells, then, both act in exactly the same way and the results of their actions also appear to be identical, but the rabbis' advantage is obvious—they are imprisoned under the dome without any damage, whereas the heretic, who is caught in the doorway, is hit by every person going in or out. We learn that he cannot release R. Joshua's spell either, and therefore he blinks first and asks to be set free. R. Joshua's tactic, supported by the power of his charms, proves successful, and the parties release one another.

The second part opens with an opposite provocation. This time it is R. Joshua who provokes and belittles the heretic. The heretic falls into the trap and takes the rabbis to the sea to display his power. Like Moses, he splits the sea before them in a rather peerless spectacle and even dares them to walk on the dry land. The rabbis had indeed been waiting for this and, with the help of the Prince of the Sea, who again obeys R. Joshua's order, they get rid of the heretic and, with him, the threatening power of heresy. Incantation, order, and cunning are thus bound together in this story to ensure the destruction of one who had dared and even dangerously succeeded in imitating Moses's power, by those who viewed themselves as the sole legitimate heirs of the master prophet in both knowledge and deed.

DEMONS AND THE EVIL EYE

As is true of sorcery in general, the textual evidence of actual (magical) antidemonic activity concerning demons and the evil eye is now so extensive that rabbinic texts must be examined in its light. This examination reveals an interesting picture concerning rabbinic demonology, particularly concerning the rabbinic use of the demonic theme in their stories.[89] Jewish amulets, bowls, and adjuration formulas from antiquity attest to a conception that identified calamities in general and illnesses in particular with demonic harm. The evil eye is often mentioned in them among the supernatural malefic agents from which sorcery users sought to draw. Demons, then, were part of Jewish cosmology at the end of antiquity—hidden elusive entities, changing form as they wished and wielding mainly vast destructive powers. The attitude toward them and toward the evil eye, as reflected in the magical literature, was unequivocal: to keep them outside the living realm of the one seeking protection from them, to remove them from this realm, or to remove them from a person's body if circumstances indicated that they had already penetrated it and were engaged there in their harmful activity.[90] Rabbinic literature broadens the picture and mainly attests to the didactic and propagandistic use that the rabbis made of it for their own benefit.

The Evil Eye and the Eye of the Evil

Many rabbinic sources mention the evil eye (*'ayin ra'ah*) and the eye of the evil (*'ein ha-ra'*)—close and possibly even synonymous terms but still distinct.[91] The rabbis used the terms in a spectrum of meanings wavering between, on the one hand, feelings of envy, hatred, and a negative social attitude toward another person that attest unfavorably to the general moral personality of the one who has cast the eye,[92] and on the other hand, to the power to harm that other person, which follows from this feeling and rests on the gaze. The second meaning is the important one for the current discussion.

The malefic power of the evil eye is expressed mostly in bodily harm to the victim that could result in death, as noted in both aggadic and halakhic sources. Prominent in this context are midrashim that

---

89. For an excellent summary of the rabbinic sources on this topic, see Strack and Billerbeck (1922). See also Blau (1898), Gafni (2002, 238–53), and Yassif (1999, 144–56).

90. See the examples cited in chapter 5.

91. For discussions on the evil eye in rabbinic literature, see Ulmer (1994). Cf. Blau (1898, 152–56) and A. Cohen (1978, 270–74). On the evil eye in the literature of the ancient East, see Ford (1998; 2000).

92. "Evil eye" (*'ayin ra'ah*) also denotes stinginess (e.g., M. *Terumot* 4:3). "Narrow eye" (*'ayin sarah*) is used in a similar sense, in contrast with the positive "good eye" (*'ayin tovah*) or "beautiful eye" (*'ayin yafah*).

emphasize a biblical character's envy, up to a willingness to cause harm by having the evil eye enter the opponent. It is said about Sarah that her evil eye entered Hagar and caused her to miscarry (*Genesis Rabbah* 45:5). About Joseph's brothers we are told, "They tormented him with an evil eye and he therefore fathered wicked men" (*Genesis Rabbah* 84:10); and Og, king of Bashan, was punished because, when sitting with Pharaoh, he began to cast an evil eye upon Jacob and his sons (*Deuteronomy Rabbah* 1:25). Although these midrashim indicate that the influence of the evil gaze penetrates a person's body and stays in it, rabbinic literature does not explicitly offer an approach that assumes the demonic personification of the human evil gaze, resembling the *ruḥa' maskorita'* (spirit of the gaze) mentioned in the adjuration literature.[93]

A similar matter, recorded in magic literature and found in rabbinic literature as well, is the harm inflicted by the gaze of supernatural evil entities themselves.[94] The formulation "eye of the evil" may have been coined on this basis and can be interpreted not only in a human context but also as the gaze of metaphysical evil, whose name is not mentioned because of the fear of it. Such evil could be the angel of death or a demon, such as the one called Ketev Meriri, regarding whom we are explicitly told,

> Ketev Meriri is covered with scales, hairy all over, and full of eyes. . . . He has one eye set in his heart, and anyone who sees him can never survive, whether it be man or beast. Anyone who sees him drops down dead. (*Numbers Rabbah* 12:3)[95]

As for the angel of death, the significant tradition in the present context is the one stating, "They said about the angel of death that he is all full of eyes" (TB *Avodah Zarah* 20b). Given traditions that assign him harmful involvement in the Sinai epiphany,[96] the angel of death's eye is most probably the one mentioned in the following tradition about the breaking of the tablets of the Law.

---

93. See Naveh and Shaked (1987, A1; 1993, A26). For the meaning of *skr* in magical texts, see Naveh and Shaked (1993, 64–65).

94. See, for instance, Naveh and Shaked (1993, A23).

95. Cf. *Lamentations Rabbah* 1:29 and *Midrash on Psalms* 91:3.

96. See TB *Shabbat* 89a, *Exodus Rabbah* 41:7, and *Tanhuma, Ki Tisa* 13.

R. Joshua of Sikhnin, in the name of R. Levi, said: To what may the matter be compared? To a king who betrothed his daughter in a large ceremony that was ruled by the evil eye. When the king came to give away his daughter in marriage, what did he do? He gave her an amulet and said to her: "Keep this amulet upon you so that the evil eye may have no power over you any longer." The Holy One, blessed be He, did the same when He came to give the Torah to Israel. He arranged it [the betrothal with the people in Sinai] in a large public display, as is written: "And all the people perceived the thunderings" (Exodus 20:15). But this had been only a betrothal, as is written: "Go to the people and sanctify them today and tomorrow" (Exodus 19:10). An evil eye affected them and the tablets of the Law were broken, as it is said: "And [he] broke them at the foot of the mountain" (Exodus 32:19). He [the Holy One, blessed be He] did not do so [the next time and was careful at the marriage]. Once they went and built the Tabernacle, the Holy One, blessed be He, gave them the blessings first so that no evil eye might affect them. Hence, it is written first: "The Lord bless thee, and keep thee" (Numbers 6:24)—from the evil eye. And then, "And it came to pass on the day . . ." (Numbers 7:1). (*Numbers Rabbah* 12:4)

Apparently, this is also the eye from which Abraham delivered his son Isaac after binding him: "'So Abraham returned unto his young men' (Genesis 22:19)—And where was Isaac? R. Jose b. R. Ḥanina said, 'He sent him away in the night, for fear of the eye.'"[97] It is in this context, apparently, that one should also understand the provocative statement "an arrow in the eye of Satan," which is ascribed to several rabbis in the Babylonian Talmud.[98]

---

97. On Satan's involvement in the binding of Isaac, see also TB *Sanhedrin* 89b and *Pesikta Rabbati* 40. Cf. *The Book of Jubilees* 17:15–18:13

98. In the story about Pelimo (TB *Kiddushin* 61a–b), his daily provocation of Satan through the uttering of this expression leads to Satan's counterprovocation. We are told about R. Aḥa b. Jacob, who would say about the *lulav* that "this is an arrow in the eye of Satan," and the rabbis warn against this saying, which could provoke Satan to respond (TB *Sukkah* 38a, TB *Menahoth* 62a). Cf. also TB *Kiddushin* 30a, where this expression is mentioned while equating Satan with the evil inclination.

The harm of the evil eye could be evident in any act or artifact.[99] Hence, "Blessing is only found in matters hidden from the eye," given that then "the eye has no control over it" (TB *Ta'anit* 8b).[100] Most traditions still identify the evil eye with sickness and death, as evident also in amulets and magic bowls.[101] Rav attributed to it ninety-nine out of every hundred deaths.

> "And the Lord will take away from thee all sickness" (Deuteronomy 7:15). Said Rav: "This is the [evil] eye." This is in accordance with his opinion, for Rav went to a cemetery, did what he did. He said: "Ninety-nine [have died] because of an evil eye, and one because of natural causes." (TB *Bava Metsia* 107b)[102]

And although in the Palestinian Talmud rabbis remark, "Rav rules according to his view . . . because Rav lived over there [in Babylonia, a place where] the evil eye [is found]" (PT *Shabbat* 14:3), Palestinian traditions attest that in Palestine too, beliefs in the destructive power of the eye were widespread.

As in the case of demons, the harm caused by the evil eye is described mostly in terms of penetration, possession, and control of a person. The evil eye could affect an individual (e.g., "It happened to R. Aqiva, who was possessed by the evil eye"; PT *Shabbat* 14:3) or many people (e.g., "It happened that twenty-four people appointed by the House of Rabbi gathered at Lydda to intercalate the year, and an evil eye entered them and they all died at the same time"; PT *Sanhedrin* 1:2).[103] Hence the rabbis state, "A person should be on his guard against an evil eye" (TB *Bava Bathra* 118a), and even recommend refraining from awakening it in the first place.[104] According to the story, Abraham and Jacob did indeed act in this spirit to protect their children (*Genesis Rabbah* 56:11, 91:6), and it is

---

99. See, for example, the harm of the evil eye to property (TB *Pesahim* 26a; *Genesis Rabbah* 58:7) and to marriage (*Numbers Rabbah* 12:4).

100. For this reason, the eye has no control over fish (TB *Bava Bathra* 118b).

101. See, for instance, Naveh and Shaked (1993, A19).

102. The text in brackets appears in Ms Florence II I 7–9.

103. See also the tradition about the death of Ḥananiah, Mishael, and Azariah, who were harmed by the evil eye (TB *Sanhedrin* 93a).

104. In this context, see the tradition about R. Zera, who protected himself from "the fire of Gehenna" through 100 fasts and would examine his strength every thirty

also in this spirit that Joshua told the children of Joseph who had boasted about themselves, "Go and hide yourselves in the forests so that no evil eye may have power over you" (TB *Bava Bathra* 118a).

The rabbis' question to R. Yoḥanan, who displayed his beauty to the women coming up from the ritual bathing house, "Is the Master not afraid of the evil eye?"[105] exposes a stance heard also elsewhere, stating it is better to downplay what might evoke envy and hide it, both actually and symbolically. The other side of the desire to prevent envy and the accompanying evil eye is apparent in the recommendation of R. Judah to Rabin b. Rav Naḥman not to buy a field that is close to the city and the accompanying explanation, which relies on Rav's statement: "One is forbidden to stand over the field of one's neighbor at the time its crop is standing [i.e., when its crop is at its height]" (TB *Bava Metsia* 107a).[106] Finally, for one who fears the potential harmful power of one's own eye, the rabbis suggest looking "at the side of his left nostril," thereby preventing the evil power from entering the other person.[107]

All were exposed to the harm of the evil eye, except for the seed of Joseph, who, like their ancestor, were protected from it.[108] Protective measures were therefore vital. The rabbis mention in this context the use of amulets[109] and protective magical actions, such as creating a

---

days by entering a heated oven. "One day the Rabbis cast an eye upon him and his legs were singed" (TB *Bava Metsia* 85a).

105. TB *Berakhot* 20a (=TB *Bava Metsia* 84a). See also TB *Pesahim* 26b.

106. Rashi says on TB *Bava Metsia* 107a, "'One should not buy'—one should not buy a field close to the city, since the eye of people always rules it. 'One is forbidden and so forth'—so that he should not lose it through the evil eye."

107. TB *Berakhot* 55b. In Ms Oxford 366 the instruction is broader: "And if he is afraid of his own eye, he should look at the nubble in his left nostril; and if his eye harms others, he should look at the nubble in his right [nostril]." These dual instructions would appear to refer to two kinds of harm, and because the latter points to harm inflicted on others, the former seemingly refers to self-inflicted harm. This reading, however, seems implausible. I am not aware of traditions indicating that one casting an evil eye can harm oneself through his or her own gaze, and even then, it is hard to understand how looking at oneself could prevent the harm cast by one's own gaze.

108. TB *Bava Bathra* 118a; TB *Berakhot* 20a, 55b; TB *Bava Metsia* 84a.

109. *Numbers Rabbah* 12:4. For an amulet for healing from the evil eye, see Naveh and Shaked (1987, A2). Cf. the eyes mentioned in Naveh and Shaked (1987, A1), which was also written for healing purposes.

CHAPTER 7

circle with one's arms and reciting, "I, NN, am of the seed of Joseph over which the evil eye has no power" (TB *Berakhot* 55b). If one was nevertheless harmed and required healing, the rabbis allowed it even on the Sabbath: "One may recite [an incantation] in case of an [evil] eye or a snake or a scorpion and may remove the eye on the Sabbath, but one may not recite [an incantation] in case of demons" (Tosefta *Shabbat* 7:23).[110] A distinction was thus drawn between an evil eye sickness and a demonic sickness. Apparently, then, at least in circles where this distinction was formulated, the evil eye was not perceived as part of the demonic inventory but rather as an accompaniment to it.

Demons and Evil Spirits

Demons (*shedim*), harmful entities (*maziqim*), and evil spirits (*ruḥot ra'ot*) played an important role in the Jewish cosmology of late antiquity.[111] Yet, contrary to the other supernatural beings included in it—God, the angels, and the dead—their place was on earth beside human beings. Knowledge about them, concentrated mainly in the Babylonian Talmud, was transmitted by the rabbis in three main modes of discourse: general remarks about them, instructions on how to protect oneself from them, and stories about them. The survey presented in this section is organized according to this order.

The rabbis offered several answers to the question of the origin of demons in the world. One answer was that God created them on the eve of the Sabbath at sunset (M. *Avot* 5:6). Another answer is intimated in fragments of tradition that, when put together, state that demons originated from a hybrid mating between Adam and a female demon—"the first Eve" created for Adam before Eve, "the mother of all life," and then abandoned. The more prominent story among these traditions is that in the Babylonian

---

110. This is the version in Ms Erfurt (*Tosefta*, ed. Zuckermandel 119). But cf. also the reading in Ms Vienna (*Tosefta*, ed. Lieberman, 2: 28–29), and see PT *Shabbat* 14:3 and TB *Sanhedrin* 101a.

111. Harmful entities have many names, which at times are generic names denoting subgroups of the broad category of demons. See Strack and Billerbeck (1922). The most prominent demons, such as Asmodeus, Ketev, Lilith, and Agrat, daughter of Maḥalat, are referred to by their individual names. On the various groups of demons in magical sources, see Montgomery (1913, 67–94) and Shaked (2002, 72–80).

Talmud: "In all the years that Adam was under the ban, he begot spirits, and demons, and liliths" (TB *Eruvin* 18b). This tradition could possibly be tied to two Palestinian traditions that mention "the First Eve," who was "full of discharge and blood and separated from him [Adam]" (*Genesis Rabbah* 17:7, 22:7).[112] A third tradition, echoing the one concerning the origin of demons in the Apocrypha, states that all the dead will arise at the resurrection of the dead "except the generation of the Flood. . . . All their souls become spirits and injure the children of Israel." (*Pirke de-R. Eliezer* 33)[113] Yet a fourth tradition sees demons as the last link in a chain of natural metamorphoses: "A male hyena after seven years turns into a bat, a bat after seven years turns into a vampire, a vampire after seven years turns into a prickle, a prickle after seven years turns into a thorn, a thorn after seven years turns into a demon" (TB *Bava Kamma* 16a).[114]

Demons were perceived by rabbis as creatures between a human being and an angel.

> Six things are said concerning demons—three [claim they are] like the ministering angels, and three [claim they are] like human beings. Three like the ministering angels: they have wings like the ministering angels, and they fly from one end of the world to the other like the ministering angels; and they know what will happen like the ministering angels. . . . And three like human beings: they eat and drink like human beings, they propagate like human beings, and they die like human beings. (TB *Hagigah* 16a)[115]

---

112. According to later traditions, this was Lilith. See Krebs (1975) and Yassif (1984, 63–71, 231–34). On the biblical and Mesopotamian background of Lilith, see Hurwitz (1980, 19–66), Krebs (1975), and van der Toorn et al. (1999, 520–21). On Lilith in the demonology of magic bowls, see Fauth (1986) and Lesses (2001, 354–59).

113. See the discussion in the "Demons" subsection in chapter 6.

114. Manuscripts differ from one another regarding the first metamorphoses in the chain.

115. Cf. *Avot de-Rabbi Nathan*, Version A, 37. This source also places evil spirits between trees and beasts: "Seven creatures, one above the other and one above the other. . . . Above the trees He created the evil spirits, for evil spirits go hither and thither and trees do not move from their place. Above the evil spirits He created the beast, for a beast works and eats and evil spirits neither work nor eat."

The rabbis held that there were far more demons than human beings and, were they not hidden from sight, their very appearance would be overpowering.

> Abba Benjamin says: "If the eye were allowed to see them, no creature could confront the demons."[116] Abaye said: "They are more than we are and they surround us like mounds of earth around a pit." R. Huna said: "Every single one among us has a thousand of them on his left and ten thousand on his right." (TB *Berakhot* 6a)

The demons' presence is evident in failures, disaster, sickness, and death, and even in day-to-day reality: "Overcrowding in the *Kallah* assemblies—from them. Fatigue—from them. The wearing out of scholars' clothes—from them. Bruised feet—from them" (TB *Berakhot* 6a).

Although the demons were by nature hidden, they could be seen, but this could be dangerous.

> Whoever wishes to see them, let him bring the afterbirth of a black female cat who is the offspring of a black female cat, the firstborn of a firstborn, let him roast it in fire and grind it to powder and let him fill his eye [with the ashes] and he will see them. Let him put [the remaining ashes] into an iron tube and shut it with an iron seal, lest they [the demons] should steal it [the ashes] from him. And let him close his mouth [while doing this], lest he come to harm. R. Bivi b. Abaye did so, saw [the demons], and came to harm. (TB *Berakhot* 6a)

Their traces could also be tracked down: "Whoever wishes to find out about them should take sifted ashes and spread them around his bed and in the morning he will see [traces in the ashes] resembling a cock's legs" (TB *Berakhot* 6a).

---

116. Rabbinic stories are divided on this issue. R. Bivi b. Abaye, who saw the demons, was indeed harmed (TB *Berakhot* 6a). By contrast, Ḥanina b. Dosa and Abaye, who saw Agrat, daughter of Maḥalat, and Ketev Meriri came out of these meetings unharmed (TB *Pesahim* 111b, 112b).

As for demons' physical appearance, only scattered evidence is available.[117] Their feet resemble a cock's legs. They have no hair (*Tanhuma, Bo* 16); Lilith is winged, and her hair is disheveled.[118] Ketev Meriri's "head is like a calf's, and one horn protrudes from its forehead . . . he is covered with scales, hairy all over, and full of eyes . . . and he has one eye set in his heart" (*Numbers Rabbah* 12:3). Demons can change their appearance and assume the shape of a man, a temptress, or a seven-headed monster.[119] They cast a shadow but have no "shadow of a shadow."[120] Usually, however, demons are hidden, "seeing but unseen,"[121] and they generally appear to one who is alone (then inflicting severe harm) or at most in a pair.[122]

The adjurations in magic bowls indicate that no time or place is immune from these harmful entities, and this is also the view that surfaces in rabbinic literature. As a rule, the night is the time of their domain, but they can also cause harm during the day.[123] There are demons of shade and others, *shabrirei yom* (TB *Gittin* 69a), for whom daylight is their time. Ketev Meriri was said to rule at midday, between the fourth and ninth hour of the day, but other traditions said that there were two kinds of Ketev, one active before noon and one after.[124] Certain days and seasons are particularly perilous. Agrat, daughter of Maḥalat, and her

---

117. On the iconic figures of the demons in Babylonian magic bowls, see Hunter (1998; 2000a, 189–204; 2000b) and Vilozny (2010; 2013).

118. TB *Eruvin* 100b; TB *Niddah* 24b; *Numbers Rabbah* 12:3. Cf. Lesses (2001, 354–59) and Levene (2003c, 116–19).

119. On the demons' ability to change shape, see *Avot de-Rabbi Nathan*, Version A, 37; and TB *Yoma* 75a. Cf. on this issue the evidence from magic bowls in Levene (2007) and Naveh and Shaked (1993, B25). On demons' appearance in the shape of the figures mentioned in the text, see TB *Megillah* 3a (a person), TB *Kiddushin* 29b (a seven-headed monster), and PT *Shabbat* 1:3 (a temptress).

120. TB *Yevamoth* 122a. On the "shadow of a shadow" (*bavu'ah de-bavu'ah*), see Rashi on TB *Avodah Zarah* 48b.

121. *Avot de-Rabbi Nathan*, Version A, 37.

122. TB *Berakhot* 43b. But cf. TB *Pesahim* 111b, where Ketev Meriri appears to Abaye, who was accompanied by Rav Papa and Rav Huna.

123. On nightly demons, see TB *Berakhot* 5a, 6a; TB *Megillah* 3a; TB *Shabbat* 151b; TB *Kiddushin* 29b; TB *Gittin* 69a; and *Numbers Rabbah* 12:3. On daytime demons, see TB *Hullin* 105b, TB *Kiddushin* 29b, TB *Pesahim* 111b, and *Lamentations Rabbah* 1:3.

124. On the first hypothesis, see *Lamentations Rabbah* 1:29, *Numbers Rabbah* 12:3, and *Midrash on Psalms* 91. On the second hypothesis, see TB *Pesahim* 111b.

legions are active on the eve of the Sabbath and on Wednesday evenings (TB *Pesahim* 112b). All of these harmful entities "are certainly common" from the first until the sixteenth of the month of Tamuz (TB *Pesahim* 111b), whereas Ketev Meriri is active from the seventeenth of Tamuz until the ninth of Ab.[125]

Demons are not confined by space either. Some of them fly through the air and strike as an arrow (*Numbers Rabbah* 12:3), whereas others are on the ground. The ground-based demons could be anywhere: in water sources, along byways, on the city's streets and alleyways, on the roof and in rooms of the house, on or under the bed, in food, in drinking water, and even in the crumbs on the floor.[126] Shady places were known to be especially dangerous: the shadow of certain trees, particularly those with many branches or with hard thorns, the shadow of a boat, the shadow of a rooftop, the shadow of a squill smaller than a foot, morning and evening shadows smaller than a foot, and, above all, the shadow of the privy. Some rabbis avoided shadows altogether.[127]

Demons can even be found in the holiest of places and at the holiest of times. According to one tradition, they were present at Mount Sinai at the giving of the Torah. Another tradition suggests that even the house of study was not beyond their influence. A third tradition, however, states that from the moment the Tabernacle was built and the *Shekhinah* dwelt on earth, "the harmful beings were annihilated from the world."[128]

Demons are mentioned in rabbinic literature as large and small, individuals and groups, male and female. They are divided into generic groups named according to their character and the time and place of their activity. Some of them are common, others honorable, and some

---

125. *Numbers Rabbah* 12:3; *Lamentations Rabbah* 1:29; *Midrash on Psalms* 91.

126. In water sources, see TB *Pesahim* 112a; *Leviticus Rabbah* 24:3; *Tanhuma, Keddoshim* 9; and *Midrash on Psalms* 20:7. Along byways, see Minor Tractates *Derekh Eretz, Ha-Yotse* 18. For the other places, see TB *Pesahim* 111b–113a, TB *Berakhot* 6a, and TB *Shabbat* 151b.

127. TB *Pesahim* 111b. Ketev Meriri operated in the narrow margin "between shade and sun" (*Numbers Rabbah* 12:3; *Lamentations Rabbah* 1:29; *Midrash on Psalms* 91:3). The *tulin* (shade spirits) are also mentioned in magical sources. See, for instance, Naveh and Shaked (1987, 270; 1993, 268).

128. On the first and third traditions, see *Numbers Rabbah* 12:3. On the tradition of demons in the house of study, see TB *Kiddushin* 29b.

even ride horses (TB *Pesahim* 112b–113a). Asmodeus is their king, but he is not mentioned as the leader of their activity in the world.[129] Agrat, daughter of Maḥalat, on the other hand, leads a "chariot" of harmful beings[130]—180,000 destructive angels, each one of whom "is allowed to wreak destruction independently" (TB *Pesahim* 112b). Ketev, who is mentioned by name, is perceived as especially dangerous.

According to rabbinic traditions, the harmful entities operate individually or in groups. Often, they initiate attacks without any provocation, simply because that is their nature.[131] Occasionally, they attack in response to some human action: staying alone in demons' domain (beyond the city limits, in a privy, in a shadow) or at the time demons are active (e.g., at night), drinking water in which demons are found, or engaging in various other activities, such as drinking an even number of cups, relieving oneself, placing one's head on the stump of a palm tree, or walking on a stump (TB *Pesahim* 110a–111b). At times, demons wait for the right moment, when people perform acts that expose them to their harm. Then they pounce on their prey.

R. Ishmael b. Elisha said: "Three things were told to me by Suriel, the Officer of the [Divine] Presence: Do not take your shirt from the hand of your attendant when dressing in the morning, and do not let water be poured over your hands by one who has not already had water poured over his hands, and do not return a cup of asparagus brew to anyone save the one who has given it to you because *takaspit*, and some say *'istlagnit* [i.e., leaders][132] of destroying angels lie in wait for a man and say: "When will someone who has done one of these things come near me and be caught." (TB *Berakhot* 51a)

129. TB *Pesahim* 110a; TB *Gittin* 68a.

130. *Numbers Rabbah* 12:3. The word *chariot* (*merkavah*) is widespread in *Hekhalot* and *Merkavah* literature to indicate the world of angels and the celestial entities below the divine throne.

131. TB *Kiddushin* 29b; TB *Hullin* 105b; TB *Shabbat* 151b; TB *Pesahim* 112b.

132. On the possible meaning of these miswritten words, see Krauss (1898, 98). Ms Oxford 366 offers, "*'istaglilit* of destroying angels and some say *'istagsisit* of an evil spirit sits and waits for a man and says . . ." The reference appears to be to a group of harmful agents.

Similar to the detailed accounts found in magic antidemonic literature, rabbinic literature also describes the malicious harm of demons
and evil spirits as entering and staying in a living body, bringing sickness
and death. The exception to this rule is the story in PT *Shabbat* 1:3 about
temptation into sin by an evil spirit, which emphasizes the moral aspect
of demonic injury.[133] Demonic possession may occur in human beings,
animals, and even artifacts, and its destructive consequence could be
contagious. Shmuel, who was one of the leading spokesmen on medical
matters in the Babylonian Talmud, stated that most deaths were caused
by a spirit.[134] He also attributed the behavior typical of a "mad dog" (sick
with rabies, an illness, which, as is known, spreads death through the
dog's bite) to the presence of an evil spirit—"the spirit of restlessness"
(*ruah tezazit*)—in its body.[135] According to the same principle, the rabbis warned against consuming food or drinks placed under the bed
("even when covered with an iron vessel"), against drinking water left
uncovered on Wednesday evening and on the eve of Sabbath, and
against using a knife made from the bark of reeds for fear of infection
with the evil spirit that dwells in them by inhaling it or even by contact
with it.[136]

An attack initiated by demons also resulted in possession that, as
noted, was expressed in a series of illnesses. The spirit Ṣaliḥta', also
known as Palga', was identified with migraine (TB *Gittin* 68b). The
spirit Kaṣarin was identified with asthma and possibly also with epilepsy
attacks (TB *Bekhorot* 44b). Qordiakos, mentioned in the Mishnah as
causing confusion, was later perceived as a demon whose harm was
linked to the drinking of new wine.[137] The harm of the "spirit *tezazit*"

---

133. This type of harm characterizes demons in Qumran literature. They are
described there as inciters and instigators. See Alexander (1997; 1999a).

134. TB *Bava Metsia* 107b. The word *ruah* is presumably used here to mean an evil
spirit (*ruah ra'ah*) rather than its other denotation of "wind."

135. TB *Yoma* 83b; PT *Yoma* 8:5. Cf. also *Genesis Rabbah* 12:9.

136. TB *Pesahim* 112a; PT *Shabbat* 8:6. On the "law of contact" in magic, see the
discussion on Frazer's theory in chapter 1. For a study of the laws of contact and similarity in the context of rabbinic thought, see Bar-Ilan (2002).

137. M. *Gittin* 7:1 (and cf. TB *Gittin* 70b); TB *Gittin* 67b. The Greek origin of the
word—καρδιακός—suggests harm to the heart or the stomach, perhaps as an indication of melancholy. See Krauss (1898, 519) and Preus (1983, 178–79, 320–21).

was connected to a loss of self-control and to wild behavior.[138] *Shabririm* of day and night were identified with blindness (TB *Gittin* 69a).[139] *'Eshata* also may have been perceived not only as a fever spreading through the body but as an evil spirit that inflames it, as found in many amulets (TB *Shabbat* 66b–67a).[140] This may also be the meaning of the *baruqti* (cataract) (TB *Gittin* 69b), as in the "male and female *baruqta*'" mentioned in magic bowls as demons.[141] *Simta'* was a skin disease requiring an adjuration (in the second-person singular) so that it should not multiply (TB *Shabbat* 67a). Also mentioned are Kuda', who is known from other sources as inflicting harm on women in labor (TB *Avodah Zarah* 29a), Shivta', who is apparently perceived as attacking infants and killing them (TB *Yoma* 77b; TB *Hullin* 107b), and the "spirit of Sereda'," who attacks at meals (TB *Hullin* 105b).[142]

The threatening reality of living beside demons generated a series of means of protection. First, the existence of the rabbinic "demonological discourse" contributed to the defense capability against demons, because it exposed them and made them more apprehensible, expected, and intelligible. The clarification of their kinds, names, preferred places, times of action, and the circumstances of the damages they inflicted equipped the participants in this discourse with tools that enabled them to organize their lives, taking the danger into account and minimizing the demons' harm. Beyond this, the rabbis also offered precise instructions concerning the removal of demons.

The gist of the active practices for protection against demons and their exorcism is the use of oral or written performative formulas. Prominent among these are formulas that rely on canonic sources: psalms and the bedtime recital of the Shema prayer. The better known antidemonic psalms are Psalms 3 and 91, known as the Song of Injuries or the Song of Afflictions. Psalm 91 has a long antidemonic history dating back to the Second Temple period.[143] A midrashic tradition holds that it was used by

138. *Pesikta de-Rav Kahana* 10:3, 4:7, and parallel versions. Cf. *Genesis Rabbah* 12:9.

139. See Sokoloff (2002, 1106, s.v. שברירא).

140. See also Naveh and Shaked (1993, 36–37).

141. Naveh and Shaked (1993, B25).

142. See Kohut (1926, 8: 24, s.v. שבתא) and Sokoloff (2002, 555, s.v. כודא).

143. See Nitzan (1986; 1994, 227–72). Cf. Baumgarten (1986) and Ta-Shma (1986).

Moses when he ascended Mount Sinai and that R. Joshua b. Levi recited it for protection.[144] Rabbis also recommend using Psalm 29, which alludes to the seven "voices" mentioned by David, starting with "the voice of the Lord is upon the waters." This psalm should be recited over water before drinking it in the (dangerous) case of a thirsty person who cannot avoid drinking on Wednesday evening or on the eve of the Sabbath, times that, as noted, were especially sensitive to the harm of bad spirits (TB *Pesahim* 112a). On the protection afforded by bedtime recital of the Shema, R. Yitzhak said, "Whoever recites the *Shemaʿ* upon his bed, harmful demons (*mazikin*) keep away from him" (TB *Berakhot* 5a).

Beside the canonic formulas, the rabbis also suggest using anti-demonic incantations. Some were meant for "the demon," meaning general protection from demons, and some for protection against specific demons, such as the demon of the privy or demons identified with illnesses. The following are several examples:

> For *simta* [a skin disease], one should say thus: "Baz Bazya, Mas Masya, Kas Kasya, Sharlai, and Amarlai, these are the angels who were sent from the land of Sodom." And to heal boils and ulcers[145] [he should say]: "Bazakh, Bazikh, Bazbazikh, Masmasikh, Kamon, Kamikh, may your appearance [be confined] to you, your appearance [be confined] to you, your place [be confined] to you, your place [be confined] to you, your seed be [like that] of a *qalut* and [like that] of a mule that is not fruitful and does not propagate; so [you, the boil] may you not be fruitful nor propagate in the body of NN." . . . Against a demon, one should say thus: "You were closed up; closed up were you, cursed, broken, and banned, Ben Tit, Ben Tame, Ben Heimar like Shemgez [or, possibly, in the name of Gez], Merigez, and Istemai." For a demon of the privy one should say thus: "On the scalp of a lion and on the snout of a lioness I found the demon

---

144. See TB *Shevuʾot* 15b, PT *Eruvin* 10:12, *Numbers Rabbah* 12:3, and *Midrash on Psalms* 91:1.

145. According to Ms Oxford 366, Ms Vatican 108, and Ms Munich 95, which read *shihnin ve-kivin*.

Bar Shirika Panda,[146] in a bed of leeks; I knocked him down, and with the jawbone of an ass I hit him." (TB *Shabbat* 67a)[147]

In a discussion on the danger posed by pairs—drinking an even number of glasses was perceived as evoking the harm of demons and the rabbis therefore recommended avoiding this—another protection formula is quoted, followed by testimony about its effectiveness.

R. Papa said, Joseph the demon told me: "For [drinking] two [cups] we kill, for four [cups] we do not kill. For four we cause harm. For two [we harm], whether [drunk] unwittingly or deliberately. For four—[if drunk] deliberately, we do [harm, but if drunk unwittingly] we do not [harm]. And if one forgot [to be precise about the number of cups] and chanced upon [a place of danger], what is his remedy?[148] Let him take his right-hand thumb in his left hand and hold his left-hand [thumb] in his right hand and say: 'You and I are three.' And should he hear a voice [say]: 'You and I are surely four,' let him say [to the demon speaking]: 'You and I are surely five.' And should he hear [the voice] say: 'You and I are surely six,' let him say: 'You and I are surely seven.'" Once, it happened [that the man counted] until a hundred-and-one, and the demon burst. (TB *Pesahim* 110a)

Artifacts are also mentioned as useful in treating harm caused by demons. Above all, amulets deserve particular attention (TB *Pesahim* 111b). In fact, the equating of illness with possession suggests that the entire discussion on healing amulets, in particular amulets prepared by an expert (in which epilepsy is mentioned), refers to an antidemonic practice even

---

146. I have translated in the singular, as required by the continuation of the text and as it appears in Ms Oxford 366 (cf. also Ms Vatican 108 and Ms Munich 95). A formula similar to this one is also found in a Babylonian magic bowl. See Levene (2003a, 40, bowl M101, l. 12). See also Bohak (2006).

147. Slight variations in the language of the incantations appear in the manuscripts. Cf. the incantations for the exorcism of the daytime and nightly blinding *shabririm* in TB *Gittin* 69a.

148. In a previous passage the determination was that drinking pairs of cups was dangerous outside the home—on the way or in the privy—and even in sleep.

if this is not explicitly noted. A seal and a chain with the letters of the Ineffable Name engraved on them are mentioned as means for controlling demons in the story about Solomon and Asmodeus,[149] whereas the story of R. Yosi of Tsitur and the demon of the well points to the belief in the power of iron to exorcise demons and perhaps even to kill them.[150]

Beside these traditions, the rabbis' use of the demon motif in their stories for their own social and didactic purposes also merits attention. In general, rabbinic demonological stories—stories about rabbis in which demons are secondary figures—deviate from the norm reflected in magical sources, the sole concern of which is the absolute separation of human beings and demons, which is attained through human protection rituals. Instead, these stories portray a variety of relationships between demons and human beings, based on an approach that includes the demons in the single ethical system that God established in the world, a system whose spokespersons and representatives are rabbis. Accordingly, demons are subject to the rabbis' legal or charismatic power.[151]

The rabbis' advantage in the protection against demons is evident, above all, in a steady inner immunity that is based on Torah study.

> The Holy One, blessed be He, says: "I shall forge a weapon for all who trade in the truth of the Torah." R. Shimon b. Yoḥai said: "The truth of the Torah is a weapon to its owners." R. Shimon b. Yoḥai said: "The Holy One, blessed be He, gave Israel a weapon at Sinai on which the Ineffable Name was written: 'You shall not be afraid of the terror by night' (Psalms 91:5)—of Agrat, daughter of Maḥalat, and her chariot, nor of any of the demons who hold sway at night." (*Numbers Rabbah* 12:3)

---

149. TB *Gittin* 68a–b. The story is founded on ancient traditions about Solomon's rule over demons. See the discussion on demons and the antidemonic use of seals in chapter 6. For studies on the talmudic story, see Yassif (1999, 87–89). Cf. Levene (2003b).

150. *Leviticus Rabbah* 24:3; *Tanhuma, Keddoshim* 9. The parallel version in *Midrash on Psalms* 20:7 makes no mention of beating with iron tools but only with sticks in order to assist the friendly demon to kill the one causing the harm. The traditions cited first also end with the sight of blood on the water, but the killing of the demon is not mentioned in them explicitly.

151. For a discussion of demonological stories in rabbinic literature, see Yassif (1999, 144–56).

As a result of this merit, the rabbis are exempt from the bedtime recitation of the Shema prayer (which, as noted, keeps the demons away): "R. Joshua b. Levi says: Though a man has recited the *Shema*ʿ in the synagogue, it is a good deed to recite it again upon his bed. . . . R. Naḥman says: If he is a scholar, he need not do so" (TB *Berakhot* 4a–5a).[152]

Further examples of the rabbis' advantage in all that is related to demons appear in various traditions, such as the one about Abaye's faculty to see Ketev Meriri when he approached a group of rabbis and to protect them from him (by placing R. Papa as a human shield between them and the demon), or the one that links knowledge of magic to Torah study and intimates that only a true scholar possesses the knowledge necessary for writing an amulet helpful in exorcising demons.

> A thicket of canes[153] that is near a town has no less than sixty demons. Why should it be noted? To write him [the one who has been harmed in the thicket] an amulet. [As in the case of] a certain town-officer who went and stood by a thicket of canes near the town. Sixty demons entered him and he was in danger. He went to a scholar who did not know that sixty demons had been in the thicket. He [the scholar] wrote him an amulet for one demon. He then heard them [the demons] holding a celebration within him and singing. "The man's turban is like a scholar's, we examined him and found he does not know 'Blessed art Thou'" [i.e., although he looks like a scholar, he lacks the appropriate liturgical-normative knowledge showing that he is indeed one!]. A scholar came who knew that in the thicket are sixty demons and wrote him an amulet for sixty demons. He then heard them [the demons] saying: "Clear away your vessels from here" [leave]. (TB *Pesahim* 111b)

---

152. Abaye's objection, "Even a scholar should recite one verse of supplication," and the connection drawn between the bedtime recital of the Shema and protection from harmful agents indicate that the discussion is focused on the advantage of scholars in protection from demons.

153. In the original, *zirdeta*ʾ. On this denotation of the word, see Sokoloff (2002, 420). Cf. Harari (1997b, 43, secs. 81, 93).

The rabbis' advantage was not confined to protection from demons. Some succeeded in defeating them as well. R. Ḥanina b. Dosa and Abaye are mentioned as having set limits on Agrat, daughter of Maḥalat, and her cohorts concerning the time (Sabbath eve and Wednesday evenings) and place (byways on the edge of inhabited areas) of their demonic activities.[154] Others expressed their power in actual struggles with and even in harm to the demons. One tradition states that the rabbis' prayer helped to heal R. Bivi b. Abaye, who had sought to see them (TB *Berakhot* 6a). Another links the miracle of rescue from a particularly violent demon, which had been staying in Abaye's house of study, to the merit and the prayer sword of R. Aḥa b. Jacob, who had come to study there and had been forced to sleep alone at the house of study.

> R. Jacob, son of R. Aḥa b. Jacob, was sent by his father to Abaye. When he [the son] returned, he [his father] saw that his learning was dull and said: "I am better than you, you remain here and I will go." Abaye heard that he was coming. In Abaye's house of study was a demon and, when a pair would enter, even in the daytime, they would be injured. He [Abaye] told them: "Let no one allow him a place to sleep, perhaps a miracle will happen [through his merits]." He [R. Aḥa] entered and spent the night in that house of study. He [the demon] appeared to him in the guise of a seven-headed dragon, and every time he [R. Aḥa] knelt [in prayer], one of its heads fell off. The next day he told them: "Had not a miracle occurred—you would have endangered me [my life]." (TB *Kiddushin* 29b)[155]

A third tradition reports on the summoning of a demon to trial and on Mar b. R. Ashi's judgment against him, while "domesticating" the demon into the rabbinic normative and discursive framework.

---

154. TB *Pesaḥim* 112b–113a. On this tradition in Babylonian magic bowls, see Shaked (2005a, 10; 2005b) and Shaked et al. (2013). On Ḥanina b. Dosa as a wonder worker, see Vermes (1972; 1973).

155. On the folkloristic elements of the story, see Yassif (1999, 152–54). On its place in the Jewish perception of the "sword of the tongue," see Harari (2005b).

And Abaye said: "Initially, I used to say that one does not sit under a drainpipe because of the waste water, but my Master told me it is because demons are to be found [there]." Some carriers bearing a barrel of wine wanted to rest. They put it down under a drainpipe and it burst. They came to Mar b. R. Ashi, who took out trumpets and banned him [the demon who had caused this]. He [the demon] came before him. Said he [Mar b. R. Ashi]: "Why did you do this?" Said he [the demon]: "What could I do? They put it in my ear." Said he [Mar]: "What were you doing in a public place? You are the one who changed [the agreed division of space between people and demons]; go pay [compensation to the carriers]. Said he [the demon]: "Let the master set a date and I will pay." He set him a date. When it arrived, he [the demon] delayed [and did not come to pay]. When he [the demon] came, he [Mar] said: "Why did you not come on time?" Said he: "We have no right to take away anything that is tied up, sealed, and counted, and can only take something that has been abandoned." (TB *Hullin* 105b)[156]

Finally, the network of relations between rabbis and demons expands to the point of cooperation between them. The traditions about the information transmitted to the rabbis by Yosef Sheda (the demon) and Jonathan Sheda, cited in the talmudic discussion as though they had been words of the rabbis themselves, are a limited expression of this trend (TB *Pesahim* 110a; TB *Yevamoth* 122a). More significant is the story mentioned earlier about the joint struggle of the pious R. Yosi of Tsitur (and the members of his village) and a friendly demon dwelling in the local well against an alien and violent demon who had tried to expel the friendly demon and take over the well. Another step in the same direction is the passing reference to "that demon in the house of R. Papa" that would assist him in various matters, including drawing water from the river (TB *Hullin* 105b).

This trend culminates in the story about a rule that the demon Ben Temalion suggested to R. Shimon bar Yohai: He would enter the body of the emperor's daughter and allow the rabbi to exorcise him, so as to

---

156. On this story, see Yassif (1999, 150–52).

ensure the abolition of draconic measures that had been imposed on the Jews.

> The government once issued a decree that they should not keep the Sabbath or circumcise their children and that they should have intercourse with menstruating women. . . . They said: "Who will go and annul the decrees? Let R. Shimon b. Yoḥai go for he is learned in miracles." . . . Ben Temalion came to meet him. "Do you wish me to come with you?" R. Shimon wept and said: "To my ancestor's handmaid [Hagar], an angel appeared three times, and to me not even once [but this demon instead]? Let the miracle come anyhow!" He [Ben Temalion] preceded him and entered the emperor's daughter. When he arrived there, he said: "Ben Temalion, come out! Ben Temalion, come out!" And since they called him, he came out and left. He [the emperor] said to them: "Ask for whatever you came to ask." They entered the treasure house to take [whatever] they chose. They found that bill [of the decrees], took it, and tore it. (TB *Me'ilah* 17a–b)

This is not historical reality, nor is it a parody of Christian exorcisms,[157] but hagiography—the use of miracle stories in the context of propaganda for the values that the saint represents. Against the technical performance of exorcising demons through incantations and amulets, the rabbis place their own ethical and religious model as an effective means of protection from demons and, moreover, for making use of them. The practice of adjurations is replaced by the normative course of piety and miracle.

A service that the demon performs for his master is the highest degree of surrender on his part. Accordingly, this is the highest degree of human control over the demonic element in the world. Although the perception of Ben Temalion's act as a miracle subjects it to God rather than to humans, it ties the service he performs in the world to those who merit miracles. In reporting this, the rabbis extract the use of demons from the realm of magic, where professional magicians are the expert agents of power,[158] and tie it instead to the religious-moral virtue of

---

157. Bar-Ilan (1995); Yassif (1999, 154–55); Yavetz (1963, 6: 318–20).
158. On the use of demons in magic practice, see Harari (1998, 156–57).

those who find grace in the eyes of God. In this sense, Ben Temalion represents the apex of the complex relationship between rabbis and demons. The inclusion of the demon as a positive element in the system of divine providence is a conclusive sign of the trend that domesticates the demonic into the world of values sustained in the house of study, which characterizes the rabbinic demonological stories.

DIVINATION

Divination refers to a series of practices applied to the attainment of information through means other than standard forms of study. Accordingly, the knowledge that is acquired through divination is not standard but rather esoteric, accessible only through divination methods or agents.[159] Such methods and agents were widespread in antiquity in Mesopotamia and in the eastern Mediterranean as the foundation of a shared (and variegated) culture of divination, which played a significant role in the knowledge-power systems of the local cultures, including Jewish culture.[160] Because of the advantage of the social power attached to knowledge in general and to hidden knowledge in particular, social establishments did not remain indifferent to divination agents. Like agents of occult power, agents of esoteric knowledge were also split between forbidden and allowed, and here too the split was more often based on social ascription than on actual deeds.[161]

---

159. The principal root in Hebrew regarding divination is *nḥš*. The term *naḥash* appears in Numbers 23:23: "Surely there is no divination (*naḥash*) in Jacob nor is there any enchantment (*qesem*) in Israel." On the biblical meaning of *naḥash* as a means for accessing the occult, see Jeffers (1996, 74–78). In rabbinic literature, both *naḥash* and *niḥush* served to denote divination practices. See, for instance, TB *Hullin* 95b, TB *Nedarim* 32a (*naḥash*), and PT *Sanhedrin* 7:4 (*niḥush*). Cf. Ben-Yehuda (1948–1959, 7: 3599–3600, 3613). The change in the meaning of the word *niḥush*—from, in antiquity, a means for attaining hidden knowledge to, in modern Hebrew, an uncertain guess in the absence of any possibility of attaining precise knowledge (Even-Shoshan 1988, 2: 824)—articulates well the change in the attitude of Western modern culture toward the possibility of attaining knowledge through divination.

160. See Harari (2005c, 306–8 and references).

161. On the political contexts of divination in the Roman world, see, for example, McMullen (1966, 128–62).

Underlying divination is a conception stating that everything that occurs in the world (past, present, and future), everywhere (in this world and beyond it), and in every dimension of reality (concrete or spiritual) is available to human consciousness as potential knowledge. In the Hellenistic world divination methods were classified into two main groups: inductive divination, based on signs and signals; and intuitive divination, based on special psychic powers.[162] Rabbinic literature shows evidence of both. The first group includes a series of events that were interpreted as signs, astral signs, and dreams. The second group comprises the divination of those who, by their very nature, were agents of hidden knowledge—rabbis, children, and fools, as well as necromancers (*ba'al 'ov*), those who consult the dead (*doresh 'el ha-metim*), mediums (*yide'oni*), and those seeking guidance from demons and angels.

Even though the rabbis prohibited divination and warned against it—for instance, "Whoever engages in divination, it will eventually come upon him" (PT *Shabbat* 6:10)—they seldom succeeded in restricting it and certainly failed to eradicate it. The words of Ahavah b. R. Zera attest to the prevailing circumstances in this regard: "Whoever does not practice divination is brought within a barrier [i.e., in proximity to God] that even the ministering angels cannot go beyond" (TB *Nedarim* 32a).[163] If such was the reward offered to those who did not practice divination, they must have certainly been exceptional.[164]

Agents

The Bible mentions several practices and agents of divination, including "*qosem qesamim, me'onen,* and *menahesh,* and *mekhashef,* and *hover haver,* and *sho'el 'ov,* and *yide'oni,* and *doresh 'el ha-metim*" (Deuteronomy 18:11).[165]

---

162. This is also the prevalent typology in the scholarly research, though others have also been suggested for divination practices. See, for example, Zuesse (1987). Cf. Harari (2005c, 304–5).

163. Cf. PT *Shabbat* 6:10.

164. For general surveys on divination and the rabbis, see A. Cohen (1978, 274–97), Jöel (1881–1883, 1: 85–105), L. Rabinowitz (1972), and Swartz (2003).

165. The precise translation of these terms is difficult because we hardly know the kind of practice denoted by each of them. Apart from the *mekhashef* (magician), they all relate to practitioners of divination. *Sho'el 'ov, yide'oni,* and *doresh 'el ha-metim* are necromancers.

It rejects these, however, as "abominations of the Gentiles" in favor of the one legitimate pattern for acquiring hidden knowledge: prophecy. The rabbis also adopted this model. They saw in the biblical prophets (Moses in particular) the leading agents of the esoteric knowledge brought down to earth from God. Accordingly, they tied to the last prophets the cessation of divinely inspired prophecy.[166] Nevertheless, they too recognized a broad range of alternative means and agents of knowledge, both for spreading the word of God and for attaining necessary day-to-day information. Most agents (including their means of divination) were rejected by the rabbis as illegitimate for reasons that, as in the case of sorcery, linked together ideological and social considerations. However, all were judged to be effective. Some, such as astrologers, necromancers, and dream interpreters were professionals.[167] Some were laypeople experienced in widespread popular divination practices, most of them forbidden. Yet others—children, fools, and rabbis—were agents of knowledge by their very nature.

Considering rabbis as agents of knowledge is not surprising. As in the case of their supernatural power, their grasp of the occult was also presented as resulting from their greater closeness to God and from the holiness resting on them as an additional benefit of their involvement in the study and practice of Torah.[168] An explicit manifestation of this view appears in the following statements in the context of a discussion on "words of prophecy" (referring to hidden knowledge):

R. Avdimi from Haifa said: "Since the day the Temple was destroyed, prophecy has been taken from the prophets and given to the rabbis." But is not a rabbi [also] a prophet? Rather, say thus: "Although it [prophecy] has been taken from the prophets, from the rabbis it has not been taken." Ameimar said: "A rabbi is

---

166. See Urbach (2002c) and Yeivin (1975).

167. On astrologers and dream interpreters, see the "Astrology" and "Dreams and Their Interpretation" sections in this chapter. On necromancers, see M. *Sanhedrin* 7:7, Tosefta *Sanhedrin* 10:6, TB *Sanhedrin* 65b, TB *Keritoth* 3b, and TB *Berakhot* 59a for *ba'al 'ov*; and M. *Sanhedrin* 7:7, Tosefta *Sanhedrin* 10:6, TB *Sanhedrin* 65a, and PT *Sanhedrin* 7:7 for *yide'oni*.

168. Cf. Urbach (1975, 577–78 and note 20).

even superior to a prophet, as is said: 'And a prophet has a heart of wisdom' (Psalms 90:12). Who is compared to whom? That is to say—the smaller [the prophet] is compared to the greater [the rabbi]." (TB *Bava Bathra* 12a)

Wisdom, which is based on Torah study, is thus an alternative to the prophets' divine inspiration concerning the presentation of God's word as revealed to humanity.[169]

Connected to this matter are the many traditions about the "heavenly voice" (*bat qol*), a weak echo of the explicit divine speech to the prophets that rabbis received and "used."[170] Diverse messages were delivered through it. The heavenly voice served God to reveal the divine view on such matters as Jonathan b. Uzziel's translation of the books of the prophets, the suicide of Hannah, the mother of the seven sons, or the rabbis' study of heavenly mysteries. It also become involved in halakhic controversies,[171] expressed divine sorrow over the destruction of

---

169. Apparently, this is the meaning of "prophecy" (*nevu'ah*) here. Another aspect of it—predicting a hidden reality—is discussed further along in the talmudic passage. In any event, the rabbis' attitude toward prophecy and toward the relationship between prophet and rabbi is far more complex than that suggested by Avdimi and Ameimar. See Urbach (1975, 577–78; 1999; 2002a).

170. TB *Sotah* 48b; PT *Sotah* 9:12; PT *Shabbat* 6:10. The "heavenly voice" (*bat qol*) is discussed here in the limited and widespread context of divine speech that is spontaneously revealed or, in rabbinic language, "comes out." This type of divine revelation also is ascribed in rabbinic literature to a few biblical figures. See Urbach (2002a, 26–27). In a broader context, the term *bat qol* denotes divination through human speech of unknown origin. The reference to the use (*shimush*) of a *bat qol* (i.e., TB *Megillah* 32a) may hint at an active attempt to hear it. In any event, in light of the explicit traditions about the use of a *bat qol* of the latter type—that is, casual human speech or from an unknown source (M. *Yevamot* 16:6; PT *Shabbat* 6:10)—we should perhaps understand all references to the use of a *bat qol* and acting in accordance with it in this context. See Lieberman (1950, 194–99) and Urbach (2002a, 23–24).

171. TB *Bava Metsiah* 59a–b. In this famous story, known as "The Oven of Akhnai," the rabbis explicitly reject the decision of the *bat qol* in their halakhic controversy. The explicit statement "We pay no attention to a *bat qol*" is ascribed to R. Joshua in three more places where the heavenly voice is involved in the dispute between the Shamai and Hillel schools: TB *Berakhot* 52a (=TB *Pesahim* 114a), TB *Yevamoth* 14a, and TB *Hullin* 44a.

the Temple and the exile, brought tidings concerning the nation's future, and announced the rabbis' special holiness and their place in the world to come. In addition, the heavenly voice bothered with earthly matters. Some were national issues, such as proclamations of military defeats or victories and the annulment of evil decrees, and some were personal, relating to matchmaking and property.[172] In any event, the *bat qol* (in the sense discussed here) tends to appear of its own accord, either as a matter of course or as a result of the holiness of the people associated with its message. It is not summoned through a rite or a performative formulation for the sake of a necessary revelation. A *sefiyah* or a *kavanah be-ruah ha-qodesh*, meaning a vision or a discernment inspired by the holy spirit, is slightly different and refers to the rabbis' potential for esoteric knowledge by virtue of their unique holiness.[173] Nor are these in any way related to ritual activity or to any hermeneutical method; unlike the *bat qol*, they originate in the rabbi himself and focus on particular issues for which he "uses" divine inspiration (*Genesis Rabbah* 37:7).

Another means of knowledge available to the rabbis was the revelation of a heavenly being: Elijah or an angel. Rabbis do not summon these agents of knowledge by resorting to some ritual power, and they reveal themselves of their own accord, though in at least one case we hear mention of a ritual initiative that encourages their appearance. After Elijah ceased to reveal himself to R. Joshua b. Levi, "he [R. Joshua] fasted a number of times and he appeared to him" (PT *Terumoth* 8:11).[174] In most stories, Elijah appears in (varying) human forms wherever the

---

172. See the references in R. Margalioth (1957, 27–35) and Urbach (2002a, 23–27).

173. See, for instance, *Tosefta Pesahim* 2:15, PT *Sotah* 1:4, *Avodah Zarah* 1:8, and *Leviticus Rabbah* 9:9, 37:3. A vision by means of the holy spirit is also ascribed to biblical figures. See, for example, Tractate *Kalla Rabbati* 3:15, PT *Horayot* 3:8, PT *Sanhedrin* 6:2, *Genesis Rabbah* 93:12, and *Numbers Rabbah* 19:3.

174. Although the fast, proclaimed to be due to Ulla's delivery to the authorities, did not compel Elijah to reveal himself, it surely paved the way for the revelation. The practice of fasting for the sake of revelation is also mentioned in the Palestinian Talmud in stories about R. Yose and R. Shimon b. Lakish, who wished to see R. Ḥiyya (PT *Kilayim* 9:4 and *Ketuboth* 12:3). On this tradition and its parallels, see Kipperwaser (2005, 214–16) and Schwartzbaum (1993, 33–44).

rabbis are, meeting them along the way or even staying with them as a routine event. Mostly, he guides them in thought and action, as a way of revealing the divine will to them. At times, he reveals to them hidden knowledge concerning events in this world or beyond and various other matters.[175]

Rabbinic traditions about angelic revelations are closely linked to a key idea in the mystical and magic Jewish literature of antiquity. According to this idea, human contact with the angels yields knowledge that is highly valuable in this world. This matter is mentioned in the Babylonian Talmud in the description of Moses's ascent to Heaven to receive the Torah and his preceding struggle with the angels. After he defeats them, the angels give Moses gifts/things/words (*devarim*), meaning names serving to control them.[176] In another version of this tradition, which greatly expands the description of Moses's voyage to the Heavenly Throne, he encounters on his way "an angel, Gallizur, who stands and says: 'This year wheat will thrive and wine will be cheap'" (*Pesikta Rabbati* 20). This source of knowledge is also available to the rabbis. The tradition that ascribes to R. Yoḥanan b. Zakkai the study of the "conversation of the ministering angels"[177] attests to it in general terms. R. Yoḥanan b. Dahabai's statement about the angelic knowledge he possesses concerning the connection between sexual transgressions and birth defects in the children born from them (TB *Nedarim* 20a) and R. Ishmael b. Elisha's statement about the three warnings he received from "Suriel, the angel of the Presence" (TB *Berakhot* 51a) translate this idea into concrete information. Yet, judging by their literature, rabbis seldom relied on angelic knowledge, perhaps in a deliberate reaction to the many traditions on knowledge in general and practices about the adjuration of angels for this purpose in particular, which were popular in contemporary mystical-magic circles.[178]

---

175. See, for example, TB *Shabbat* 33b, TB *Bava Metsiah* 59b, and *Pesikta de-Rav Kahana* 18:5. See also the many assorted traditions in Gross (1993, 1: 63–65) and R. Margalioth (1957, 36–39).

176. TB *Shabbat* 88b–89a. On the meaning of the *devarim* (pl. of *davar*, "something" or "a word") that Moses received from the angels, see Harari (2005b).

177. TB *Sukkah* 28a, TB *Bava Bathra* 134a.

178. See also the angelic endorsement of knowledge founded on inquiry into the mystery of the chariot in TB *Hagigah* 14b.

Some of the rabbis used more defined methods of divination. Shmuel "examined the book" (bibliomancy). R. Yoḥanan divined by relying on verses recited by children.[179] Ḥanina b. Dosa divined through prayer.

> They said about R. Ḥanina b. Dosa that when he used to pray for the sick, he would say: "This one lives and this one dies." They said to him: "How do you know?" He replied: "If my prayer comes out fluently, I know that he is accepted, and if not—I know that he is rejected." (M. *Berakhot* 5:5).

The Talmud adds a story on the matter.

> Once the son of R. Gamaliel fell ill. He sent two scholars to R. Ḥanina b. Dosa to ask him to pray for him. When he [R. Ḥanina] saw them, he ascended to an upper chamber and prayed for him. When he came down, he said to them: "Go, his fever has left him." They said to him: "What, are you a prophet?" He replied: "I am neither a prophet nor the son of a prophet, but I have learned this from experience—if my prayer comes out fluently, I know that he is accepted, but if not—I know that he is rejected." They sat down and made a note of the exact moment [of this event]. And when they came to R. Gamaliel, he said to them: "Astonishing! No less and no more, but that is exactly how it happened! At that very moment his fever left him and he asked for water to drink." (TB *Berakhot* 34b)

Finally, some rabbis used a "sign" (*siman*), which they distinguished both categorically and normatively from divination (I discuss this issue later in the "Practices" subsection).

The two additional groups mentioned in the context of prophecy are fools and children: "R. Yoḥanan said: 'From the day the Temple was destroyed, prophecy has been taken from the prophets and given to fools and children'" (TB *Bava Bathra* 12b). The juxtaposition of this statement to that of R. Avdimi of Haifa on the one hand and to the contiguous stories on the other (one about Mar b. R. Ashi who took

---

179. TB *Hullin* 95b. On these practices, see later discussion.

steps to lead the academy of Mata Meḥasia following the proclamation of a fool in the market and another about R. Ḥisda's daughter who naïvely predicted her dual marriage to Rami b. Ḥama and to Rabbah; TB *Bava Bathra* 12b) indicates that R. Yoḥanan's words should be understood literally.

Children were perceived in the ancient world as particularly effective agents of divination.[180] The Talmud shows that they were used as living books, in a form of oral bibliomancy. Rabbis (and others) would listen to a random verse recited by a child or even ask him, "Tell me your verse" (referring to a scriptural verse that would come to the child's mind), and derive from it an answer to the question that concerned them. The brief story that follows is an instance of divination through verses heard from a child that was not asked and unwittingly mediated the information requested.

R. Yoḥanan and R. Shimon b. Lakish wanted to go see Shmuel. They said: "We shall follow a *bat-qol*." They passed by a house of study. They heard a child's voice: "Now Shmuel died" (1 Samuel 28:3) and noted [the date? to themselves]. And so it was for him [for Shmuel]. (PT *Shabbat* 6:10)

The well-known story about Aḥer (literally, the Other, the byname attached to R. Elisha b. Avuya) makes impressive use of the power attached to the deliberate divination practice of "tell me your verse" (*pesoq li pesuqkha*) through a wordplay on the double meaning of the Hebrew root *psq*: "to tell a verse" and also "to determine" (the truth by means of a verse).

Once Aḥer was riding on a horse on the Sabbath, and R. Meir was walking behind him to learn Torah from him. He [Elisha] said: "Meir, turn back, for I have already measured by the paces of my horse that we have reached the Sabbath limit." Said he [R. Meir]: "You, too, turn back." Said he [Elisha]: "Have I not already told you that I have already heard [that it was said]

180. See Johnston (2001). Cf. Brashear (1995, 3503 and note 511) and Lieberman (1950, 196–98).

behind the curtain,[181] 'Return you backsliding children except for Aḥer?'" He [R. Meir] overwhelmed him and drew him into a schoolhouse. He said to a child [who was there]: "Tell me your verse!" He [the child] said: "There is no peace, says the Lord, for the wicked" (Isaiah 48:22). He took him to another schoolhouse. He said to a child: "Tell me your verse." He said: "For though you wash yourself with lye, and take much soap, yet the stain of your iniquity is before me, says the Lord God" (Jeremiah 2:22). He took him to yet another schoolhouse. He said to a child: "Tell me your verse!" He said: "And you, O ruined one, what will you do? Though you clothe yourself with crimson, though you deck yourself with ornaments of gold, though you enlarge your eyes with paint, in vain shall you make yourself fair . . ." (Jeremiah 4:30). He took him to yet another schoolhouse until he had taken him to thirteen schools. [All the children] told him such things. To the last one he said: "Tell me your verse!" He said: "But to the wicked man (ve-larasha') God said, What have you to do to declare my statutes . . ." (Psalms 50:16). That child was a stutterer, so it sounded as though he had said: "But to Elisha (ve-leElisha') God said." Some say he [Aḥer] had a knife with him, and he cut him up [the child] and sent [the pieces] to the thirteen schools, and some say he said: "Had I a knife in my hand, I would have cut him up." (TB Hagigah 15a–b)[182]

On the divinatory powers of fools, the rabbis say little. These powers may originate in the fools' limited intelligence, which made them fit to serve as channels for occult knowledge. They may have been perceived as possessed, expressing what the demon lodged inside them put in their mouths.[183] Perhaps their dwelling in cemeteries (Tosefta Terumot 1:3) and their contact with the dead added to their

---

181. In Ms Munich 6 (unlike all other manuscripts): "I have already heard through a bat qol."

182. On this practice of divination, see also TB Gittin 68a, TB Hullin 95b, and Esther Rabbah 7:13. See further the story that ascribes its use to Emperor Nero in TB Gittin 56a.

183. Cf., for instance, the possession story in Luke 4:31–37.

wisdom. If the latter hypothesis holds any truth, then fools were human mediators of knowledge originating in supernatural agents: demons and the dead.

According to the Babylonian Talmud, demons too, like the ministering angels, "know what will happen" (TB *Hagigah* 16a), and although their knowledge was limited to what they heard "behind the curtain" (and not in the presence of God), it was still desired and sought after. The study of "the conversation of demons" was attributed to R. Yoḥanan b. Zakkai.[184] If Rashi is correct when stating that the debate on the question of whether "one may ask in matters of demons on the Sabbath" refers to consultations with demons (in his view, to locate lost items), then the Talmud attests to deliberate use of them as agents of knowledge (TB *Sanhedrin* 101a and Rashi ad locum). As noted, information provided by two of them, Yosef Sheda (the demon) and Jonathan Sheda, touching on the harm inflicted by demons and on their appearance, is incorporated into the talmudic discussion as though these had been rabbinic statements (TB *Pesaḥim* 110a).

The dead were also perceived by the rabbis, as well as by the ancient world in general and by the culture of Jewish magic in particular, as mediators of esoteric knowledge.[185] One tradition holds that their souls attained this knowledge when they drifted away from their graves and listened in on conversations behind the curtain.[186] According to another tradition, the dead could be summoned for a period limited to twelve months after their death.

> A certain heretic (*min*) said to R. Abbahu: "You say that the souls of the righteous are hidden under the Throne of Glory. So how did the necromancer raise Samuel?" Said he [R. Abahu]: "There it was within twelve months [of his death. For] it is taught: For a full twelve [months] the body [of the dead] is in existence and his soul ascends and descends. After twelve months,

---

184. TB *Sukkah* 28a; TB *Bava Bathra* 134a.

185. See Harari (2005c, 335–36). On divination through the dead in medieval and early modern Judaism, see Harari (2015).

186. See the story about the pious man who slept in the cemetery later in this discussion.

the body ceases to exist and the soul ascends but no longer descends. (TB *Sabbath* 152b–153a)

Knowledge was acquired from the dead either through their revelation in a dream or by consulting with them, be it in a cemetery or through necromancy. About revelation in a dream, we hear, for instance, the following story:

A man died in the neighborhood of R. Judah and there were none to be comforted. Every day [of the seven days of mourning], R. Judah assembled ten [men] and they would sit in his place. After seven days, he [the dead man] appeared to R. Judah in a dream and said to him: "Your mind be at rest, for you have set my mind at rest." (TB *Shabbat* 152a–b)

In this case the revelation is not the initiative of the living, who apparently does not even expect it, nor does the knowledge delivered by the dead deviate from his relationship with the dreamer.[187]

Not so in the following two stories. In them, the knowledge transmitted by the dead is about themselves (the pain of their own death), but the basis for the revelation of the dead is the active curiosity of the living in their regard. While still alive, the future-dead are invited to reveal themselves after their death in the dream of their friends, a dream where they are asked about the pain of death they had experienced.[188]

R. Se'orim was Rava's brother. He sat by Rava's bedside, and saw that he was about to die. Said he [Rava to his brother]: "Do tell him [the angel of death] he should not hurt me [in my death]." Said he [R. Se'orim]: "Are you not his intimate friend?" Said Rava: "Since my lot has been rendered [meaning I am fated to

---

187. See also, for instance, the revelation of R. Elazar b. Shimon in a dream to explain why a worm had appeared in the ear of his corpse, which had been placed in the attic (TB *Bava Metsiah* 84b).

188. Revelation in a dream is mentioned explicitly in Ms Oxford 366, Ms Munich 140, and Ms Vatican 108. In the rest of the manuscripts, including Ms Munich 95 and Ms Vatican 104, as well as in the printed version, the phrase "in a dream" is absent. In any event, this is probably the drift of the text.

die] he heeds me not [and what I say]." Said he [R. Se'orim]: "Do show yourself to me in a dream [after death]." He showed himself in a dream. He [R. Se'orim] said: "Did you suffer pain?" Said he: "As from the cut of a scalpel." Rava sat before R. Naḥman and saw he was about to die. Said he to Rava: 'Tell him [the angel of death] not to hurt me [in my death]." Said he [Rava]: "Are you not an honored man?" Said he: "Who is honored, who is distinguished, who is strong?" Said he: "Do show yourself to me in a dream." He did show himself in a dream. He said: "Did you suffer pain?" He replied: "As pulling out a hair from milk. And [yet], were the Holy One, blessed be He, to say to me, 'Go [back] to that world [i.e., our world] as you were,' I would not want to, for the dread of him [the angel of death] is great." (TB *Mo'ed Katan* 28a)

In both these stories, the revelation of the dead is achieved through a simple device—a request to the dead from their living friends to reveal themselves after their death. No trace of a planned contact with the dead is found here. We hear briefly of this possibility elsewhere, where a practical step is advised, "Touch his coffin so that you may see him by night,"[189] and perhaps also in the stories about R. Yose and R. Shimon b. Lakish, both of whom fasted for many days in order to see R. Ḥiyya (and failed).[190] These stories indicate that seeing the dead is impossible for one of a lesser spiritual rank and that even the attempt is dangerous: R. Yose "saw R. Ḥiyyah's escorts and his eyes dimmed." In any event, the kind of harm inflicted on R. Yose shows that this was not at all an instance of seeing the dead in a dream. In this case, these stories should be viewed as a preface to traditions about contact with the dead while awake.

Deliberate contact with the dead outside a dream assumed two forms: consulting the dead and raising them through necromancy. The possibility

---

189. Tosefta *Shabbat* 6:7, with Lieberman (1992, 3: 86–87) and H. Weiss (2011, 34–37).

190. PT *Kilayim* 9:4 (=*Ketuboth* 12:3); *Ecclesiastes Rabbah* 9:10. The traditions in the Palestinian Talmud do not mention revelation in a dream, whereas *Ecclesiastes Rabbah* explicitly alludes to it.

SORCERY, DEMONOLOGY, AND DIVINATION

of consulting the dead was seemingly open to all, whereas necromancy required professional mediation. I discuss the methods of necromancy and consultation with the dead in the next subsection on practices. Two stories of notable ideological and social context deserve mention here. One is the story about Onkelos b. Kalonikos (or Kalonymus), the nephew of Titus, who, just before his conversion to Judaism, raised the spirits of Titus, Balaam, and Jesus to learn from them what is said about the people of Israel in heaven, what they think about his intention to convert, and what happened to them after their death.[191]

> Onkelos b. Kolonikos was the son of Titus' sister. He thought of converting to Judaism and used necromancy to raise Titus from the dead. He said to him: "Who is respected in that world?" He [Titus] told him: "Israel." Said he: "Is it worth joining them?" He said: "Their matters [i.e., their commandments] are many and you will not be able to carry them out. Go and attack them, since in that world [meaning our world] you [will become] the head, as it is written, 'Her adversaries have become the head' (Lamentations 1:5). Whoever harasses Israel becomes head." Said he [Onkelos]: "What is your sentence?" He [Titus] said to him: "What he [i.e., Titus himself] decreed for himself—every day they collect him, his ashes, and they pass sentence on him, and they burn him and scatter him [over] the seven seas." He went and raised Balaam through necromancy. He asked him: "Who is respected in that world?" He [Balaam] told him: "Israel." Said he: "Is it worth joining them?" Said he: "You shall not seek their peace nor their prosperity all your days for ever" (Deuteronomy 23:7). Said he: "What is your sentence?" Said he: "A layer of boiling hot semen." He then went and raised Jesus by necromancy. He asked him: "Who is respected in that world?" He replied, "Israel." Said he, "Is it worth joining them?" He replied: "Seek their welfare and seek not their harm [since] whoever touches them touches the apple of His eye." Said he: "What is your sentence?" Said he: "Boiling hot excrement, since whoever

---

191. In this story the manuscript and the printed version are quite different. The version discussed here is from Ms Munich 95.

mocks the rabbis' words is punished with boiling hot excrement." (TB *Gittin* 56b–57a)

The normative knowledge conveyed by the three dead figures about the advantage that Israel enjoys in the world to come and about the harsh punishment of their enemies and the presumable assistance of this information in Onkelos's conversion were the basis for integrating this story into the discourse of the house of study. As a result of this knowledge, we do not hear in its margins any surprise or complaint from the rabbis about the act of necromancy, either directly and explicitly or by questioning the credibility of the information attained through it. This is obviously a good example of the way in which necromantic divination as a legitimate source of knowledge slipped easily into this discourse, if only it helped to support its didactic objectives.

The other story concerns a dispute between R. Kattina and a necromancer about the source of an earthquake that had taken place, though it ultimately shifts from the question of knowledge to the question of the social power associated with it.

> R. Kattina was going along the road. When he reached the door of a necromancer's[192] house, there was a rumbling of the earth. He [R. Kattina] said: "Does the necromancer know what this rumbling is?" He [the necromancer] raised his voice: "Kattina, Kattina, why should I not know? When the Holy One, blessed be He, remembers his children, who are plunged in suffering among the nations of the world, he lets two tears fall into the ocean, and the sound is heard from one end of the world to the other, and that is the rumbling." Said R. Kattina: "The necromancer lies and his words are false. Were it as he says, there should be one rumbling after another" [two rumblings for the two tears]. And yet, it was indeed so, and there was one rumbling after another [!]. But he [R. Kattina] did not admit this,

---

192. In the original, *'ova' ṭamya'*. According to Jastrow (1903, 21, 539), *ṭamya'* is derived from bone and *'ova' ṭamya'* refers to a specific type of necromancer (*ba'al 'ov*), a necromancer of bones. However, Sokoloff (2002, 84, 506) suggests that the denotation of *'ova' ṭamya'* is a necromancer in general.

lest everyone go astray after him [the necromancer]. (TB *Berak-hot* 59a)[193]

Particularly important in this context is the closing remark—though R. Kattina appears to challenge the necromancer's assertions, he actually concedes their accuracy. Such an admittance implies acceptance of the necromancer's authority and of the effectiveness of the practice he implements as a source of credible knowledge. R. Kattina, therefore, blatantly lies for ideological-political—to preclude the necromancer's proven power of divination from becoming a source of appeal to people who may "go astray" after him (instead of following the rabbis and their Torah). The authority and the social power linked to professional divination, which in this case is necromantic, is thus conveyed in this brief remark in all its sharpness and with great candor.

Angels were also perceived as potential supernatural agents of divination. Their revelations to the rabbis were discussed earlier. Here, I refer to one further matter, the mention of "princes of oil and princes of eggs" with whom consultation is allowed, "except that they lie" (TB *Sanhedrin* 101a).[194] If I am correct in hypothesizing that "princes" (*sarim*) are angels (as in the usual denotation of this term in rabbinic literature as well as in *Hekhalot* and *Merkavah* literature) rather than demons (as Rashi claims ad locum), then the Talmud here affords us a narrow glimpse into the magical praxis of consulting them.

Finally, the tradition by which "the conversation of mountains, hills and valleys, the conversation of trees and grass, the conversation of beasts and animals" serve as a source of information for one who knows how to understand it also merits mention.[195] One appropriate instance is the story about R. Ilish, in which "one man who understood the language of birds"

---

193. The version of the story in Ms Oxford 366 differs in several stylistic details from the printed one. Generally, however, both versions are identical.

194. The meaning of the phrase "except that they lie" (*'ela' mipnei she-mekhazvin*) is not clear. Rashi explained: "That is why they refrained from asking them," meaning that one is allowed to ask them, but because they lie, they refrained from doing so. In some of the manuscripts the word *'ela'* ("except") is missing and a different meaning emerges: Because they lie, asking them is permitted. See R. Rabinowitz (1960, *Sanhedrin*, 306n9).

195. Minor Tractates *Soferim* 16:7. Cf. TB *Sukkah* 28a and TB *Bava Bathra* 134a.

interpreted the calls of the raven and the dove as telling him to flee, and so he did (TB *Gittin* 45a).

Practices

The means of divination known to the rabbis and described in their literature are many and varied. Some, such as the "heavenly voice" (*bat-qol*), Elijah's revelation, or a divinely inspired vision, were associated, as noted, with the holiness of the person who received them, and prophecy, as it were, resonated within them. In other words, they constitute a permitted and even desirable form of esoteric knowledge spontaneously revealed to a person (intuitive divination), with which the rabbis were entrusted. Other practices, such as consulting a book, a child, or the dead, were carried out by rabbis or explicitly permitted by them, so that one may assume that no flaw was found in them. Even astral divination, which was associated with foreign professional diviners, was perceived in many traditions as harmless in that it was irrelevant to the people of Israel. By contrast, necromancers (*ba'al 'ov* and *yid'eoni*), who were also professionals, were forbidden and sentenced to stoning.[196] Additional means of divination, almost all of them based on omens, that is, on establishing the meaning of some event as a sign concerning a matter that affects a person who consults them, were prohibited as ways of the Amorites.

Regarding the divination of omens, the rabbis sought to distinguish categorically and normatively between two kinds: divination (*nihush*), which was forbidden, and sign (*siman*), which was permitted. The key text in this regard is a story about Rav, who interpreted an approaching boat as a propitious sign, and his ruling in this connection: "Any divination that is unlike that of Eliezer, Abraham's servant, or Jonathan, the son of Saul, is not divination."[197] The principle underlying this distinction is the relationship between the time of the event and its determination as an omen. Determining a priori that a given event will be interpreted as an omen (as Eliezer and Jonathan did) is divination, whereas determining it as such after the fact is a sign. According to

---

196. M. *Keritoth* 1:1; M. *Sanhedrin* 7:4, 7; Tosefta *Sanhedrin* 10:6.

197. See TB *Hullin* 95b and Rashi on this passage. And see Genesis 24:12–14 and 1 Samuel 14:8–11. Cf. Keller (1985).

this distinction, however, the category of signs does not include the divination of omens by means of a candle, a cock, or shadows, from which R. Ami proposes to know the future concerning life and death matters, commercial success, and the prospects of returning from a journey (TB *Horayot* 12a). Nor does it fit divination through dogs, of which the rabbis taught, "Dogs howl—the Angel of Death has come to town, dogs play—Elijah the prophet has come to town" (TB *Bava Kamma* 60b). In both cases the rabbis attribute prior significance to actual events, as in the forbidden methods labeled ways of the Amorites in rabbinic literature.[198]

Various forms of divination are included in the ways of the Amorites category. The Tosefta mentions reliance on candle sparks, the calls of fowl, a snake falling onto the bed,[199] and divining with a rod. Expanding further, it states:

198. Maimonides later tied together all forms of divination and prohibited them: "It is forbidden to resort to divination like the Gentiles, as it is said, 'You must not practice divination' (Leviticus 19:26). What is divination? Like those who say: 'Since my piece of bread dropped out of my mouth or my staff fell from my hand, I shall not go today to such a place, for if I go, my business will not be successfully accomplished'; [or], 'since a fox has passed me on the right, I shall not today go outside the door of my house, for if I do, a cheat will accost me'; or those who hear a bird twittering and say: 'It will happen thus and not thus'—'it is good to do this and bad to do that'; or those who say: 'Kill this cock because it crowed in the evening'; 'kill this hen because it crowed like a cock'; or if one sets signs for himself and says, 'If a certain thing happens to me, I will follow this course of action; if it does not happen, I will not do so,'—as Eliezer, Abraham's servant did—these and all things similar are forbidden. Whoever does any of these things is punished" (Maimonides, *Code*, Laws of Idolatry 11:4 [Maimonides 1962, 79a], with slight changes).

199. For parallel Babylonian traditions concerning the meaning of a snake falling on the bed, see Avishur (1979, 27–28). The Babylonian Talmud states that a snake appearing in a dream is also a sign: "One who sees a snake in a dream will prosper" (TB *Berakhot* 57a). Römer (1969, 175) points to the special importance of snakes among animals used in divination in Mesopotamia. The linguistic connection in Hebrew between נַחַשׁ (divination) and נָחָשׁ (snake), both pronounced *nahash*, may also hint at the snake's significance in divination. Similarly, the terms *oiônos* and "augur," whose original denotation in Greek and Latin is one who divines through birds, later became in the Greco-Roman world general references to a visionary, a prophet, or a diviner through omens (Halliday 1913, 248–49; Luck 1986, 250).

Who is a diviner? One who says: my staff has fallen from my hand, my bread has dropped from my mouth, so-and-so has called me from behind, a crow has called out to me, a dog has barked at me, a snake has passed me on my right and a fox on my left, and a deer has crossed the path before me, do not start with me for it is the morning, and it is the new moon, and it is the end of the Sabbath. (Tosefta *Shabbat* 7:13)[200]

Additional sources mention divination through a mole, through fowl and fish,[201] and through arrows.[202] To these variations one should also add bibliomancy[203] and divination through verses, both the one mediated by children and the one that takes place by itself, as noted by R. Yoḥanan: "If one rises early and a verse comes to his mouth, this is a small prophecy"

---

200. For a discussion of these divination practices, see Avishur (1979), Lieberman (1992, 3: 79–105); and Veltri (1997, 93–220). To all these, R. Aqiva adds the *'onenim*, who divine suitable times for action (Tosefta *Shabbat* 7:14). Cf. the parallels in *Sifrei Deuteronomy* 171, and TB *Sanhedrin* 65b–66a, and see the discussion on Tosefta *Shabbat* 7:14 in Lieberman (1992, 3: 97–99). R. Yoḥanan b. Zakkai's study of the "cycles" (*tequfot*) may also be related to this issue (TB *Sukkah* 28a; TB *Bava Bathra* 134a). For his part, Blau (1898, 46) ties this matter to astrology.

201. TB *Sanhedrin* 66a. Cf. the version in *Sifra, Kedoshim* 6, which mention stars rather than fish. The mole may have served as a means of divination because of its subterranean life, which was perceived as connecting it to a world beyond revealed reality. In that sense, it indeed resembles a snake. On the mole as a subterranean creature, see TB *Pesahim* 118b, PT *Mo'ed Katan* 1:4, and *Midrash on Psalms* 58:9. See also Ben Yehuda (1948–1959, 3: 1556, s.v. חלד). Fowl divination relied on the interpretation of their flight, their calls, their eating patterns, their location in relation to humans, and so forth. Beside the raven call mentioned earlier, the Tosefta also mentions divination using a cock or a hen (*Shabbat* 6:5). See also Lieberman (1992, 3: 85). The resistance of a Jewish mercenary serving in the Greek army to fowl divination is mentioned by Josephus in *Against Apion* 1.22.200–204. On fowl divination in the Greco-Roman world, see Bouché-Leclercq (1963b, 1: 127–45), Gil (1989), Halliday (1913, 246–71), and Luck (1986, 250–51, and bibliography). Mesopotamian records of fowl divination are rare. See Oppenheim (1977, 219–20) and Erica Reiner (1995, 86–87 and note 358).

202. TB *Gittin* 56a. Cf. Ezekiel 21:26–27. See also Greenberg (1991).

203. TB *Hullin* 95b. Bibliomancy was also widespread in the Greco-Roman world through the Homeric epic and other books. See Alexander (1995a, 233) and Brashear (1995, 3503 and note 511).

(TB *Berakhot* 55b). In all these, visual, audible, and verbal signs serve as a basis for the study of unrevealed knowledge. Additional practices enabled this activity directly through the summoning of supernatural agents of knowledge: the dead, angels, and demons.

Necromancy (*'ov*) and consulting the dead (*derishah 'el ha-metim*), and apparently also the practice of the *yide'oni* mentioned together with them in the Bible[204] and in rabbinic literature, are the common designations for necromantic practices in Jewish sources. The sources are not in full agreement concerning their precise nature. *Ba'al 'ov* and *yide'oni* were apparently professionals who resorted to various methods. Some of the sources note that the *ba'al 'ov* does not speak from his mouth but from "between his joints and arms" or "from his armpit."[205] We read in the Babylonian Talmud that the dead "ascends and sits between his joints [of the necromancer] and speaks" (TB *Sanhedrin* 65b). In this context, a distinction is also suggested between two kinds of necromancers—"those who conjure up . . . [the dead] using a phallus [*ha-ma'aleh bi-zekhuro*] and those who use a skull [*ha-nish'al be-gulgolet*]"—and their effectiveness on the Sabbath.[206] R. Yasa's view in the Palestinian Talmud, stating that the *ba'al 'ov* "burns incense to the demons" (PT *Sanhedrin* 7:7), sheds some light on the ritual context of necromantic praxis or at least on its perception by the rabbis. Other sources mention the *ba'al 'ov* "flapping his arms."[207]

By contrast, *yide'oni* speaks with his mouth. According to Palestinian sources, he does so by placing a bone in it.[208] Targum Pseudo-Jonathan on Leviticus 19:31 translates *yide'oni* as "consulting the *yedo'a* bone." The Babylonian Talmud unites these versions: "A *yide'oni* is one who places a *yedo'a* bone in his mouth and speaks through it" (TB

---

204. Deuteronomy 18:11; Leviticus 19:31; 2 Chronicles 33:6.

205. On speaking between his joints and arms, see Tosefta *Sanhedrin* 10:6. On speaking from his armpit, see M. *Sanhedrin* 7:7, *Sifra, Kedoshim* 11, and PT *Sanhedrin* 7:7.

206. See Tosefta *Sanhedrin* 10:6, M. *Sanhedrin* 7:7, *Sifra, Kedoshim* 11, and PT *Sanhedrin* 7:7. On the practice of conjuring up by means of the phallus, cf. Targum Pseudo-Jonathan on Leviticus 19:31. On the magical use of human skulls, see chapter 5. In any event, as far as I can gather, the magic skulls we know of served for exorcising demons rather than for divination.

207. TB *Sanhedrin* 65a; TB *Keritoth* 3b.

208. M. *Sanhedrin* 7:7; PT *Sanhedrin* 7:7; Tosefta *Sanhedrin* 10:6.

Sanhedrin 65b) The Talmud may perhaps thereby connect the practice of the *yide'oni* with that of automatic speech.

The Tosefta and the Palestinian Talmud mention *derishah 'el ha-metim* as the parallel of the types of necromancy cited in the Babylonian Talmud, at times equating it with the *'ov* practice of raising the dead by means of the phallus or the skull.[209] In the Babylonian Talmud, by contrast, the practice is tied to the location of the dead and is described as one that involves fasting and spending the night between graves: "And the one who consults the dead (*doresh 'el ha-metim*)—this is one who starves himself and goes and spends the night in a cemetery so that an unclean spirit may rest upon him."[210] "One who starves himself" is a derogatory expression meant to distinguish between ritual noneating to attain contact with an unclean spirit in the cemetery and a fast, which is normative noneating for the sake of attaining divine inspiration or a holy revelation. In this context an unclean spirit is the spirit of divination of "one who adheres to impurity."[211] As for its origin and value, this spirit is the antithesis of the divine inspiration (*ruah ha-qodesh*) in which prophets prophesized and through which rabbis gained discernment (*kavanah*) and vision (*sefiyah*). This could be the source for identifying fools as divination agents. Sleeping between graves is one of the signs of a fool (Tosefta *Terumoth* 1:3). At least one source juxtaposes it with the burning of incense to demons, which are also agents of knowledge and dwell in cemeteries (PT *Terumoth* 1:1).

Various stories show that consulting the dead, in the broad sense of seeking their help to attain knowledge, was not perceived as intrinsically negative and forbidden. Three such stories appear in sequence in the context of a discussion on whether the dead know what happens in the world of the living. The narrators also present, quite nonchalantly,

---

209. Tosefta *Sanhedrin* 10:7; PT *Sanhedrin* 7:7. The Palestinian Talmud draws an additional distinction in this context: the hierarchical relationship between the necromancer and the dead he attempts to conjure.

210. TB *Sanhedrin* 65b. Cf. TB *Hagigah* 3b.

211. Cf. *Sifrei on Deuteronomy* 173. Rashi (on *Sanhedrin* 65b) suggests that the entire issue is meant to attain help for magic actions from one of the demons dwelling in the cemetery (most probably relying on the statement in PT *Terumoth* 1:1; cf. also PT *Sanhedrin* 7:7). His interpretation, however, seems to deviate from the explicit literal statement, "so that an unclean spirit may rest upon him."

the issue of the living learning from the dead. The first story deals with a pious man who spends the night in a cemetery and hears a conversation between spirits. He sows his field based on what he has heard and succeeds where all others fail. Consequently, he goes back to sleep there in the following years to profit further from the spirits' conversation.

A pious man once gave a dinar to a poor man on the eve of the New Year in a year of drought and his wife scolded him, so he went and spent the night in the cemetery. There he heard two spirits conversing. One said to its companion: "My friend, come and let us wander about the world and let us hear from behind the curtain what suffering is coming upon the world." Said its companion: "I cannot go because I am buried in a mat of reeds, but you go and whatever you hear, tell me." So the spirit went, wandered about, and returned. Said its companion: "My friend, what have you heard from behind the curtain?" It replied: "I heard that whoever sows after the first rainfall will have his crop smitten by hail." He [the pious man] went and sowed in the second rainfall. Everyone's crop was smitten, his was not. The next year he went and spent the night in the cemetery, and heard the same two spirits in conversation. Said one to its companion: "My friend, come and let us wander about the world and let us hear from behind the curtain what suffering is coming upon the world." Said the other: "Have I not told you that I cannot go because I am buried in a mat of reeds? But you go and whatever you hear, come and tell me." It went and wandered about and returned. Said its companion: "My friend, what have you heard from behind the curtain?" It replied: "I heard that whoever sows after the second rain will have his crop smitten with blight." He [the pious man] went and sowed after the first rain Everyone's crop was blighted, his was not. Said his wife to him: "How is it that last year everyone else's crop was smitten and yours was not, and this year everyone else's crop is blighted and yours is not?" He told her all these things. They said that soon afterwards a quarrel broke out between the wife of that pious man and the mother of that girl. Said she: "Come and I will show you your daughter buried in a mat of reeds." The next year the man again went and spent the night in the cemetery and heard the same spirits conversing. Said one: "My friend, come and let us wander about the world and hear from behind the curtain what suffering is coming upon the world." Said the other: "My friend, let me be, words between us have already been heard among the living." (TB *Berakhot* 18b)

For my purposes, the important issues are obviously the night spent between the graves and the learning from the dead there. The story's testimony in this regard is explicit (though it does not match the view that learning from the dead is limited to twelve months from the time of death), and not only do the rabbis not condemn the man's actions or even show surprise at them, but the entire issue is shown in a positive light—a reward for his act of generosity.

This tradition about the pious man is followed by two more stories with Babylonian rabbis as the protagonists: Ze'iri and Shmuel. In both stories the rabbis require information from the dead, Ze'iri from his innkeeper and Shmuel from his father, concerning the location of money that had been deposited with them. For this purpose, they go to the cemetery and learn from the dead what they need to know.

Ze'iri used to deposit money with his innkeeper. Once, while he was at the house of Rav—she died. He followed her to the court of death [the cemetery]. He said to her, "Where is the money?" She replied: "Go and take it from under the door hinge in such and such a place, and tell mother to send me my comb and my tube of eye-paint with so-and-so, who is coming here [meaning she will die] tomorrow.

Shmuel's father used to hold money meant for orphans in deposit. When he died, Shmuel was not with him [and did not know where the money was]. They would call him, "a son who eats orphans' money." He followed his father to the court of death. He said to them [the dead who were there]: "I am looking for Abba [a first name that also means father]." They said to him: "There are many Abbas here." Said he to them: "I want Abba b. Abba." They replied: "There are also many Abba b. Abba here." He then said to them: "I want Abba b. Abba, the father of Shmuel." . . . Meanwhile his father came. . . . Said he [Shmuel]: "Where is the orphans' money?" He replied: "Go and take it from the millstones." The upper and lower [money found there]—is ours, that in the middle—is the orphans'." He said to him: "Why did you do that?" He replied: "So that if thieves came—they should steal from us (and) if the earth destroyed any, it would destroy ours." (TB *Berakhot* 18b)

Possibly, the tradition that Rav went to the cemetery, "did what he did," and thus found out how the dead had died is also related to this issue, although bringing the dead to talk is not explicitly mentioned.[212]

Finally, note in this context the story about R. Elazar b. R. Shimon, who, because of his fear that the rabbis would not handle his body respectfully after his death, asked his wife to place it in the attic. According to the story, his body laid there "no less than eighteen nor more than twenty-two years" without rotting. During this time, "when two would come before him, they would stand at the door. Each stated his case. A voice [the dead's?] issued from the attic and said: "So-and-so, you are liable; so-and-so, you are innocent" (TB *Bava Metsia* 84b).

These traditions show that the rabbis saw in the cemetery (and in R. Elazar's case, in the place where the body was laid) a legitimate meeting place between the living and the dead. Hence, rather than overruling actual contact with the dead to acquire esoteric knowledge, they rejected the professional mediation offered for this purpose, including its accompanying ritual practices.[213]

Angels and demons, as noted, were also perceived as agents of knowledge that could be summoned and consulted. If Rashi is correct when combining these two sentences into one issue—"It is permitted to consult princes of oil and princes of eggs, except that they lie. One may whisper a charm over oil in a vessel, but one may not whisper a charm over oil in the hand, we therefore anoint with oil that is in the hand and we do not anoint with oil that is in a vessel" (TB *Sanhedrin* 101a)—then

---

212. See TB *Bava Metsia* 107b. Indeed, Blau and Trachtenberg understood the issue in these terms (Blau 1898, 53; Trachtenberg 1970, 222). Rashi, by contrast, explains: "He knew how to whisper on graves and find out about each one how he had died."
213. Cf. Blau (1898, 53).

the second part reveals a practice of divination with oil in a vessel that is associated with spells.[214] Although much is still unknown on this matter, it might be connected to evidence from magic sources, both Hellenistic and Jewish, and explained as divination through the shiny stains of oil or eggs. These sources indicate that this kind of divination was often carried out by children instructed to look at the shiny surface or the liquid and identify in it the image of a god or a demon (and in this case, a prince, that is, an angel), bringing it to speak according to the sorcerer's instructions.[215] Yet the Talmud might be hinting at a different kind of oil divination, such as that recorded, for instance, in *Sefer ha-Razim*.[216] Rashi, however, explained the entire matter as consultation with demons.

214. Rashi on TB *Sanhedrin* 101a writes: "Those who act by means of demons tend to utter a spell (*liḥosh*) on oil that is in a vessel but not on oil that is in the hand, which is not effective. Therefore, one may anoint one's hands with oil that is in the hand and there is no fear lest it has been used for demonic acts, and it carries no demonic risk." By "those who act by means of demons" (*ma'aseh shedim*), Rashi is apparently referring to the ones he had mentioned previously: "There is a demonic act of consulting through oil and it is called the princes of oil (*sarei shemen*), that is, the princes of thumb, and others consult through an eggshell and it is called the princes of eggs." On the other hand, the Talmud may not be talking here about consulting princes of oil but rather about healing through oil that was empowered by spells. See Daiches (1913, 7, 10–11). Anointing with oil accompanied by a spell is also mentioned in the Palestinian Talmud: "Shimon bar Aba in the name of R. Ḥanina: 'He who utters spells (*loḥesh*), puts oil on the head and says the spell, so long as he does not put on the oil by hand or with a vessel.' R. Jacob bar Idi [in the name of] R. Yoḥanan in the name of R. Yanai: 'One may put it on either by hand or by a vessel'" (PT *Shabbat* 14:3; cf. PT *Ma'aser Sheni* 2:1). The medical context of the act is explained in a parallel version: "R. Judah said in the name of R. Ze'ira, 'He who has pain in his ear should put oil on his head and utter the spell (*loḥesh*), so long as he does not put on the oil by hand or with a vessel'" (PT *Shabbat* 6:5). For the formulation of this version, cf. Lieberman (2008, 110). Cf. Blau (1898, 71) and Daiches (1913). Anointing with oil and with salt accompanied by a spell is mentioned in the Babylonian Talmud as a way of sobering up (BT *Shabbat* 66b).

215. For the Hellenistic sources, see Johnston (2001). For the Jewish sources, see Daiches 1913, Dan (1963), and Trachtenberg (1970, 219–22). Cf. the recipe for children looking in the mirror in search of a vision in Schäfer and Shaked (1994–1999, 3: 92–93). On psychological aspects of this practice, see Bilu (1982). For later evidence of divination practices of this type, see Ben Naeh (2000, 99) and Huss (2000, 214).

216. M. Margalioth (1966, 71–72) and Morgan (1983, 29–31).

This practice is not explicitly mentioned in Jewish sources but is apparently alluded to in the discussion on whether "one may consult demons on the Sabbath" (TB *Sanhedrin* 101a, and see Rashi ad locum). In any event, it remains entirely opaque.

DREAMS AND THEIR INTERPRETATION

Many ancient cultures viewed dreams as a source of knowledge that is greater in scope and authority than that acquired while awake. In general, the dream was not considered an inner elaboration of daytime experience but a message transmitted from a metaphysical reality in the special interval between being and nonbeing.[217] The contents of the dream involved two aspects: a message (explicit) and a symbol (enigmatic).[218] Dream divination also involved two aspects: the explanation of signs that appeared in an incidental dream and the invitation of a solution dream (to a predefined question) through ritual means, such as incubation and a dream inquiry. The biblical position on dreams is not consistent and wavers between admiring dreams as divine revelation and dismissing them altogether.[219] The rabbinic approach to dreams and

217. This approach was widespread in antiquity. Extensive research is available on this subject, and a selected list follows. For a comprehensive study on the perception of the dream and on interpretation methods in Mesopotamia, see Oppenheim (1956). See also Cryer (1994, 157–59), Gnuse (1984, 11–55), and Oppenheim (1969b). For dreams in ancient Egypt, see Szpakowska (2003). Cf. Gardiner (1935, 1: 9–23) and Szpakowska (2001; 2010; 2011). For dreams in Mari texts, see Sasson (1986). On the dream in the Greco-Roman world, see Cox Miller (1994). See also Berchman (1998, 116–32), Bouché-Leclercq (1963b, 1: 277–329), Dodds (1959, 102–34), J. S. Hanson (1980), and Luck (1986, 231–39). In this context, the work of Artemidori Daldiani, *Oneirocritica*, deserves special mention. See Artemidori Daldiani (1963) and White (1975). On the parallels between this work and the rabbinic book of dreams, see Alexander (1995a) and Lewy (1893b). On dreams in early Christianity, see Cox Miller (1994, 129–83, 205–53) and J. S. Hanson (1980, 1421–25).

218. For the distinction between message dreams and symbol dreams in the Bible, see Fidler (2005, 1–41, esp. 23–29), Gnuse (1984, 57–118), and Jeffers (1996, 125–39). This distinction is also mentioned by Artemidorus of Daldis (Artemidori Daldiani); see White (1975, 23–24). See also Cox Miller (1994, 77–106).

219. See, for instance, Genesis 20:6 and Numbers 12:7 and, by contrast, Jeremiah 29:8, Zechariah 10:2, and Ecclesiastes 5:6.

their interpretation is not consistent either, and in rabbinic literature we find three trends: (1) accepting the dream as a prophetic message, (2) linking it to the dreamer's psychological reality and negating its significance as a means of divination, and (3) perceiving it as a potential for interpretation that does not expose its hidden meaning but rather determines it.[220]

Extensive evidence supports a view of the dream as a message of truth originating in a metaphysical reality, capable of not only pointing to the future of the dreamer and the subjects of his dream but also actually determining it. Prominent among these testimonies are expressions such as "A dream is one sixtieth part of prophecy" (TB *Berakhot* 57b);[221] Rava's comment "The Holy One, blessed be He, said: Although I hide my face from them, I shall speak to them in a dream" (TB *Hagigah* 5b) and his wish for the revelation of a solution to a halakhic problem in his dream (TB *Menahoth* 67a); the statement that excommunication in a dream can only be annulled by ten halakhic experts (TB *Nedarim* 8a); the view that "when a person sleeps, his soul leaves him and wanders around the world, and these are the dreams that one sees" (*Midrash on Psalms* 11:6); and particularly the ritual practices recommended for turning bad dreams into good omens, which go beyond the stage of a mere idea to actual deeds. Two such practices are mentioned in rabbinic literature: a dream fast (*ta'anit ḥalom*) and reversing a dream (*hatavat ḥalom*). Concerning the dream fast, "Rav said, Fasting is to a [bad] dream as fire to chaff. And R. Ḥisda said, And it [should be done] on that very day. And R. Joseph said, even on the Sabbath" (TB *Shabbat* 11a).[222] Reversing a bad dream requires a more serious effort.[223]

> He should go and sit before three who love him and say to them: "I have seen a good dream." And they should say to him

---

220. On the rabbinic conception of dreams and their interpretation, see Afik (1990), Alexander (1995a), Hasan-Rokem (1996; 1999; 2000, 88–107), Kalmin (1994, 61–80), Kristianpoller (1923), Lewy (1893b), Lieberman (1950, 70–77), R. Margalioth (1957, 3–24), Niehoff (1992), Trachtenberg (1970, 230–48), and H. Weiss (2011).

221. Cf. *Genesis Rabbah* 17:5, 44:17.

222. Cf. TB *Ta'anit* 12b and *Ecclesiastes Rabbah* 5:1 (verse 6).

223. The following translation is from Ms Oxford 366, where instructions differ in several details from the printed version.

seven times: "It is good and it will be good, and the Merciful will make it good. And from Heaven they will decree that it will be good and it will be good and good it will be. And they should recite three [biblical] "turns" [*hafikhot*] three "deliverances" [*pediyot*] and three "peaces" [*shlomiyot*]. (TB *Berakhot* 55b)[224]

People who are not sure whether their dream was good or bad are advised to improve it by performing a ritual.[225]

Let him stand before the priests when they spread out their hands [over the congregation, at the time of the priestly blessing] and say as follows: "Sovereign of the Universe, I am Yours and my dreams are Yours. I have dreamt a dream and I do not know what it is. Be it dreams I have dreamt [about myself] or dreams that my friends have dreamt [about] me,[226] if they are good, strengthen them and encourage them like the dreams of Joseph, and if they require a remedy, heal them, as the waters of Marah [were healed] by Moses, our teacher, and the waters of Jericho by Elisha, and as Miriam of her leprosy, and as Na'aman of his leprosy, and Hezekiah of his sickness. And as You turned the curse of Balaam into a blessing, so turn all my dreams into something good for me." He should direct his intention to conclude [his prayer] together with the priests, [when] the congregation answers, Amen![227] And should he be unable to say all this, he should say: "You who are majestic on high, who abide in might, You are peace and Your name is peace. May it be Your will to bestow peace upon us." (TB *Berakhot* 55b)

---

224. These are the three threesomes of biblical verses (dealing with turns, deliverance, and peace) to be recited: on turns, Psalms 30:12, Jeremiah 31:12, and Deuteronomy 23:6; on deliverance, Psalms 55:19, Isaiah 35:10, and 1 Samuel 14:45; on peace, Isaiah 57:19, 1 Chronicles 12:19, and 1 Samuel 25:6.

225. Here too I cite Ms Oxford 366, where instructions are broader than those in the printed version.

226. The printed version adds here, "or I have dreamt about others."

227. This instruction, which also appears in Ms Paris 671 in a somewhat corrupted version, was omitted from the printed version.

These accounts join a trove of stories dealing with the transmission of a true message in a dream, directly or though dream agents. The agents mentioned include God, angels, and demons as being responsible for dreams in general,[228] whereas a "dream man" ('*ish ha-ḥalom*) or a "master of dreams" (*ba'al ha-ḥalom*), as well as Elijah and the dead, appear in dreams as bearers of particular messages.[229] All of them, with the exception of demons (TB *Berakhot* 55b), transmit a reliable and almost invariably explicit message. They occasionally reveal themselves on their own initiative; at other times, as in the case of the dead, their appearance comes in response to a call from the living (TB *Mo'ed Katan* 28a). The evidence of ritual practices used to bring about their appearance is limited. The Tosefta mentions kissing the dead person's coffin so as to see him in a dream and also upturning the garment and sitting on a broom to receive a dream generally (Tosefta *Shabbat* 6:7)—all categorized as ways of the Amorites.[230] The Babylonian Talmud hints at the Gentile practice of incubation in a pagan temple for this purpose (TB *Avodah Zarah* 55a).

Often, the actual dream is revealed without a personal medium. In this case its contents might be explicit[231] or they may appear in symbolic form. The symbol may be textual, such as a verse "read" to dreamers in their sleep,[232] or visual. Both types of symbols required interpretation to

---

228. TB *Hagigah* 5b; TB *Berakhot* 55b. A distinction is required between expressions touching on the source of the dream and stories about revelation in it. God is revealed to the dreamer in many dream stories involving biblical figures, but I have not found evidence of divine revelations to rabbis in their sleep. Nor are angels mentioned as direct dream agents, contrary to the use of them for revelation within a dream, which is recorded in Jewish magic praxis (Harari 2005c, 341–44; 2011).

229. On the dream man and the master of dreams, see TB *Sanhedrin* 30a; Tosefta *Ma'aser Sheni* 5:9; *Avot de-Rabbi Natan*, version A, 17; and *Midrash Tanna'im on Deuteronomy* 32:30. Cf. the adjuration of "Ragshael the Great, the prince of the dream (*sar shel ḥalom*)," and the mention of the angel Azriel as an emissary of knowledge in the adjuration of the Prince of Dream in Schäfer (1981, secs. 501–7). See also Lesses (1998, 325–36). On Elijah, see *Genesis Rabbah* 83:4 and *Pesikta Rabbati* 22. On the dead, see TB *Shabbat* 152a–b and TB *Mo'ed Katan* 28a.

230. On these practices, see H. Weiss (2011, 34–39).

231. For example, TB *Hagigah* 14b, PT *Hagigah* 2:2, and *Leviticus Rabbah* 3:5.

232. TB *Berakhot* 56a, TB *Sanhedrin* 81b–82a, TB *Hullin* 133a, TB *Sotah* 31a, and many more. Cf. the adjuration of the Prince of Dream: "Come to me on this night . . .

disclose the message hidden in them. But whereas the textual symbol, the biblical verse, rested on rabbinic culture and thus, by its very nature, called for interpreters versed in the Torah, the interpretation of the visual message was part of a broader cross-cultural phenomenon of interpreting dream symbols. A long list of dream symbols and their interpretations is concentrated in a kind of professional lexicon in the Babylonian Talmud (TB *Berakhot* 56b–57b). The items included in it can be split into two main groups. One group includes symbols that could be called dream midrashim—interpretations based on the linkage of the dream symbol to a biblical verse so that the dream can be interpreted favorably. The other group includes interpretations tied to a broader network of linguistic, cultural, and associative contexts. Many of the dream symbols mentioned in the lexicon are universal in character and include animals, plants, beverages, eggs, metals, colors, breaking vessels, snake bites, rising and falling, bloodletting, intercourse with forbidden women, naked exposure, entering a forest or a lake, and relieving oneself. Some are typically Jewish, such as the seven species, biblical kings, biblical books, rabbis, prayer, and donning phylacteries. All these symbols share a consistent tendency toward propitious interpretations. This technical-professional trend presents the reader with a wide range of dream symbols and their interpretations. Other traditions deal with dream interpreters and systematic dream interpretations by rabbis, heretics, and others, often connected to fees, pointing both to methods of dream interpretation and to the rabbis' use of this motif in their literature in the context of disputes with Gentiles.[233]

The significance of a bad dream as a category in the rabbinic dream discourse in general and as statements conveying fears of bad dreams in particular is a further expression of the belief in the mantic value of dreams as signs of future reality.[234] The detailed list of distinctions between good and bad dreams cited in the Babylonian Talmud is a striking

---

and speak with me and give me a sign and a wonder, or a verse to hold on to" (Schäfer 1981, sec. 505).

233. TB *Berakhot* 56a; PT *Ma'aser Sheni* 4:12; *Lamentations Rabbah* 1, 1. See Hasan-Rokem (2000, 88–107) and later discussion.

234. For a detailed discussion of various rabbinic attitudes concerning the validity of dreams, see H. Weiss (2011, 62–91).

example of this trend (TB *Berakhot* 55a–56b). This approach has two practical aspects: (1) a call to refrain from a bad dream in the first place through the study of Torah, supplication prayers, rejoicing in the commandments, and even behaving appropriately when relieving oneself[235] and (2) advice on how to prevent the bad dream's realization, if it has already been dreamt, through such normative means as prayer, charity, repentance, and supplication[236] or through the ritual means mentioned earlier: a dream fast and the reversal of the dream.

Shmuel's unique approach when drawing a distinction between good and bad dreams is worth noting in this context: "When Shmuel had a bad dream, he used to say, 'the dreams tell falsehood' (Zechariah 10:2). When he had a good dream, he used to say, 'Do the dreams tell falsehood? Lo, it is written, 'I speak to him in a dream' (Numbers 12:6)" (TB *Berakhot* 55b).[237] The liberty that Shmuel takes in linking the mantic value of the dream (true or false) to its contents (good or bad) is a limited expression of a trend leading to the control of waking thought over the dream by removing it from its power setting. This trend assumes more radical dimensions in other traditions.

Absolute negation of the dream's mantic value in general and in the context of halakhic decisions in particular is conveyed in various sources by the recurring rule that "dreams are of no effect either way"[238] (*lo' ma'alin ve-lo' moridin*). The other dimension of this trend is the setting of the dream in the dreamer's psychological reality: "A man is shown [in his dream] only his own thoughts" (TB *Berakhot* 55b). Rava, whose (admittedly strange) view is cited contiguously, goes further when he refuses to concede the presence of irrational elements in dreams: "A man is never shown in a dream a palm of gold or an elephant going through the eye of a needle." Accounts about the dreams of the emperor and of

---

235. TB *Berakhot* 14a, 60b, 62a; TB *Shabbat* 30b; TB *Pesahim* 117a.

236. TB *Berakhot* 10b; PT *Sanhedrin* 10:2.

237. Shmuel's statement follows a series of traditions seeking to distinguish good dreams from bad ones regarding their origin, their mantic value, and the moral character of the individual who dreams them.

238. TB *Gittin* 52a; TB *Sanhedrin* 30a; TB *Horayot* 13b; Tosefta *Ma'aser Sheni* 5:9; PT *Ma'aser Sheni* 4:12; *Genesis Rabbah* 68:12. But cf. TB *Menahoth* 67a, where Rava expresses hope of discovering a solution to a halakhic problem in his dream.

King Shapor, whom the rabbis annoyingly accuse of thinking about the dream throughout the day, are the ultimate manifestation of the rabbinic psychologization of the dream—its removal from the "he is shown" category and its exclusive location in the "thoughts of his heart."

> The emperor said to R. Joshua b. R. Ḥananiah:[239] "You [Jews] profess to be very clever. Tell me, what will I see tonight in my dream?" Said he [R. Joshua]: "You will see that the Persians came and captured you and ground by you [i.e., forced you to grind] hard seeds in a grindstone of gold." He [the emperor] thought about it the whole day and saw [this in his dream]. King Shapor said to Samuel: "You [Jews] profess to be very clever. Tell me, what shall I see in my dream?" Said he [Shmuel]: "You will see that the Romans came and captured you and herded by you [forced you to herd] swine with a crook of gold." He [King Shapor] thought [about this] and saw [it in his dream]. (TB Berakhot 56a)[240]

Between "one sixtieth part of prophecy" and "of no effect either way," the rabbis also suggest an approach by which "no dream is without vain matter"; therefore "a dream, though part of it is fulfilled, the whole of it is not fulfilled," or, in another formulation, "neither a good dream is wholly fulfilled nor is a bad dream wholly fulfilled" (TB Berakhot 55a).[241] Shmuel, as noted, also adopts a midway stance between absolute acceptance and absolute rejection of dreams. And so does Rava, who is cited in a contiguous passage and explains the contradiction between "I speak to him in a dream" (Numbers 12:6) and "dreams tell falsehood" (Zechariah 10:2): "In the one case it is through an angel, in the other through a demon" (TB Berakhot 55b). Yet another view ranks the mantic value of dreams according to the dreaming event. As R. Yoḥanan and others

---

239. The original—Ḥanina—is mistaken. On conversations of R. Joshua b. Ḥananiah with the emperor, see, for instance, TB Shabbat 119a, TB Ḥullin 59b, and TB Bekhorot 8b.

240. I cite Ms Oxford 366, which is different from and clearer than the printed version.

241. Cf. also Nedarim 8b.

state, "Three kinds of dream are fulfilled: an early morning dream, a dream another has dreamt [about oneself], and a dream interpreted in a dream. Some say also a recurring dream."[242]

The trend that diverts the source of authority concerning the actual realization of a dream from the dream itself to its interpreter (which according to Shmuel's approach is limited to either true or false) is the basis for the third view on dreams prevalent in rabbinic literature. This approach is epitomized by the saying "All dreams follow the mouth," meaning that dreams are fulfilled according to their interpretation.[243] Its foundation is the biblical verse on the chief butler's report to Pharaoh about Joseph's interpretation of his own dream and that of the chief baker: "And it came to pass, as he interpreted to us, so it was" (Genesis 41:13). This view is remarkably conveyed in the story of R. Banaa.

There were twenty-four interpreters of dreams in Jerusalem. Once I dreamt a dream and I went round to all of them and all gave different interpretations, all of which were fulfilled. (TB *Berakhot* 55b)

This approach, which dismisses the significance of the dream's contents so far as its fulfillment is concerned and turns it merely into a potential for interpretation, entails clear social implications. In stating that "a dream that is not interpreted is like a letter that is not read" (TB *Berakhot* 55b), the rabbis shifted the crux of the interpretive discourse on dreams from the dream's symbols to their interpretation and, by implication, to the interpreters, taking the power of interpretation away from professional dream interpreters specializing in dream symbols and their meaning. Instead, they paved the way for the transfer of the interpreters' life-changing powers to those whom the dreamers would view as appropriate to the task because of their worthy moral character.

The implications of this approach, which involves significant danger, is explicitly evident in two well-known stories on dream interpretation. First is the story about Bar Hedya, to whom Abaye and Rava bring identical dreams for interpretation. They are given, respectively,

242. TB *Berakhot* 55b; *Genesis Rabbah* 89:8.
243. TB *Berakhot* 55b. Cf. PT *Ma'aser Sheni* 4:12 and *Genesis Rabbah* 89:8.

favorable and unfavorable interpretations (in Rava's case to the point of disaster) according to their payment (or nonpayment) for the interpreter's services. The following are several passages from this long story:

Bar Hedya was an interpreter of dreams. To one who gave him a zuz—he [would] give an auspicious interpretation, and to one who did not give him a zuz—he [would] give an inauspicious interpretation. Abaye and Rava saw a dream. Abaye gave him a zuz, and Rava did not give him a zuz. They said to him: "In our dream we saw that they read to us [the verse], 'Your ox shall be slaughtered before your eyes . . .'" ["Your ox shall be slaughtered before your eyes, and you shall not eat of it; your ass shall be violently taken away from before your face, and shall not be restored to you; your sheep shall be given to your enemies and you shall have none to come to the rescue" (Deuteronomy 28:31)]. To Rava, he [Bar Hedya] inauspiciously told: "Your business will be a failure, and you will slaughter an ox and will not eat of it because of the grief in your heart." To Abaye he auspiciously told: "Your business will prosper, and an ox will be slaughtered in your house and you will not enjoy eating it for sheer joy." They said to him: "We saw that we read in the dream, 'You shall beget sons and daughters . . .'" ["You shall beget sons and daughters, but you shall not enjoy them; for they shall go into captivity" (Deuteronomy 28:41)] . . . To Rava he said: "As bad as is written." To Abaye he said: "You will have many sons and daughters, and they will marry strangers and it will seem to you as if they had gone into captivity." They said to him: "We saw in our dream that [a verse] was read to us, 'Your sons and your daughters shall be given to another people'" ["Your sons and your daughters shall be given to another people, and your eyes shall look, and fall with longing for them all the day long and there shall be no might in your hand" (Deuteronomy 28:32)]. To Abaye he said: "You will have many sons and daughters. You will say, to my relatives I will give them, and your wife will say, to my relatives we will give them. Until she forces you [to agree with her] and they will be given to her relatives and it will seem to you as if they had been given to another people." To Rava he said that his wife would die and his sons and daughters would come to be ruled by another woman. . . . Rava went to him alone. He said to him: "I saw [in my dream] that my house collapsed and fell." He [Bar Hedya] said to him: "Your wife will die." He [Rava] said to him: "I saw in my dream two teeth that broke and fell." He said to him that he [would] have two dead sons. . . . Finally, Rava gave him a *zuz*. He said to him: "I saw [in my dream] a new wall that fell down." He said to him: "Buy assets and you will not be sorry." Said he [Rava]: "I saw that they pull down my house and spread it all over the world." He said to him: "Your teachings will spread." He [Rava] said to him: "I saw that Abaye's house collapsed and I was covered in its dust." He [Bar Hedya] said to him: "Abaye will die and you will be offered [the chairmanship of] the yeshiva at Pumbedita." (TB *Berakhot* 56a)[244]

Two explicit statements in the story (not cited here) indicate that events that Bar Hedya had predicted concerning Rava when interpreting his dreams—his wife's death and his imprisonment on charges of stealing from the king's treasure—did come true. The circumstances of Rava's life, which were known to the narrator and to his audience and are present in the background, strengthen this message even further. The story, then, is woven in a way that excels at pointing to the extreme danger lurking in an irresponsible performative interpretation, in a reality where dreams follow the mouth and are fulfilled according to their interpretation. The end, in any event, contrasts the power of the cheating interpreter with that of the worthy rabbi and, obviously, signals the rabbi as having the last word. When Rava discovers in Bar Hedya's book, which he had dropped, that "all dreams follow the mouth," he curses Bar Hedya for having doomed him to such a cruel fate only because he had failed to pay. Rava's curse on him, that he would be delivered to a merciless ruler, is indeed ruthlessly fulfilled (TB *Berakhot* 56a–b).

The other story about dream interpretation also contrasts the power of the worthy rabbi with the power of others, which is granted to them by dint of the approach linking the fulfillment of the dream to its

---

244. The translation follows Ms Oxford 366, which differs in several details from the printed version. For a detailed discussion of this story, see H. Weiss (2011, 92–172).

interpretation. This time, however, the cause of the disaster is not wickedness or greed but rather ignorance and haste.

> A certain woman went to R. Eliezer and said to him: "I saw in a dream that the supporting beam of the house split open." "You will conceive a son," he told her. She went away and so it happened. She saw this [in her dream] a second time. She went to R. Eliezer and told him. And he said: "You will conceive a son," and so it happened. She saw it a third time. She went to him and did not find him. She told his disciples: "I saw in my dream that the supporting beam of the house split open." They told her: "That woman [meaning you] will bury her husband." And so it happened. R. Eliezer heard her voice [as she was] wailing. He said to them [to his disciples]: "What happened? They told him what had occurred. He said to them: "You have killed a man." (*Genesis Rabbah* 89:8)[245]

The story does not point to an evil act but rather to an unintentional mistake on the part of the disciples, who are unaware of the performative power of their words and turn naturally to a logical and symbolic, though devastating, interpretation. They lack R. Eliezer's sensitivity and moral responsibility, which had seemingly led the woman to come to him repeatedly with her distressing dream, a responsibility whose presence or absence determined, as it turned out, the distinction between a new life and death.

When wickedness, charlatanism, and ignorance are juxtaposed to the performative power of dream interpretation that everyone has recourse to, we may do better if we simply refrain from telling our dreams. We may do better if we let a dream remain sealed and unresolved, like an unread letter (TB *Berakhot* 55b), and even if it lingers, oppressive and bothersome, at least the sting of its harmful interpretation is thereby removed. Possibly, this is the basis for rejecting R. Yoḥanan's ruling "One who sees a dream and his soul is distraught should go and have it interpreted in the presence of three" in favor of the saying "He should repair it in the presence of three" (TB *Berakhot* 55b). But should people

---

245. Cf. *Lamentations Rabbah* 1:1 and PT *Ma'aser Sheni* 4:12.

not wish to remain distraught, should they no longer be able to contain the strange, harsh, frightening message they have received during their sleep, what should they do? To whom should they turn?

The clear, real danger inherent in the performative interpretation of dreams immediately reveals the advantage of the potential power that the rabbis sought to reserve for themselves concerning dream interpretation and its fulfillment. The rabbis sought to tame the anarchic, wild element breaking into the sleeper's helpless consciousness and threatening his or her serenity to the point of tearing apart the ordered course of life[246] by resorting to the normative means underlying their spiritual and social world. If "death and life are in the power of the tongue"—any tongue!—then dreamers would do well to choose the one tongue that could interpret their dreams creatively and most auspiciously. Lists of healing dream interpretations that rely on biblical verses denote that this expertise was found in the house of study. This is the proper context for understanding the practice of self-interpretation by means of a "good verse" (i.e., one that conveys a positive message), chosen quickly "before another [bad verse] intervenes," in order to tilt the dream in a positive direction (TB *Berakhot* 56b), and even more so for tracing the rational of the dream midrashim, which offer favorable interpretation of dream symbols, however harsh they may be, by linking them to verses conveying a positive message. For instance:

> If one sees an ass in a dream, he may hope for salvation, for it says: "Behold, the king comes to you: he is just, and victorious, humble, and riding upon an ass" (Zechariah 9:9). . . . If one sees a reed (*qaneh*) in a dream, he may hope for wisdom, for it says: "Get (*qeneh*) wisdom" (Proverbs 4:7). . . . If one dreams that he has intercourse with his mother (*'em*), he may expect to obtain understanding, for it says: "For if (*'im*) you call out for understanding" (Proverbs 2:3). . . . If one dreams that he has intercourse with his sister, he may expect to obtain wisdom, for it says: "Say unto wisdom, you are my sister"

---

246. A suitable example here is stories about the interpretation of bad dreams among R. Aqiva's students, which prevented them from studying until their rabbi interpreted them favorably and dismissed the problem. See *Lamentations Rabbah* 1:1.

(Proverbs 7:4). . . . If one sees wheat in a dream, he will see peace, for it says: "He makes peace in your borders, and fills you with the finest of the wheat" (Psalms 147:14). (TB *Berakhot* 56b–57a)[247]

This method of favorable dream interpretation—any dream!—through biblical verses exposes a hermeneutical potential that everyone desires but only a few are capable of. These few, rabbis who are experts in the Torah and in its accompanying hermeneutical midrashic discourse, are thus the address for the application of this skill to the metaphysical domain of dream interpretation that brings together knowledge and power, up to the sealing of one's fate.

This approach is also at the basis of the polemical use of dream interpretation stories in rabbinic literature. These stories became part of a general trend that excluded alien agents from the realm of supernatural knowledge and power, preserving it as a monopoly for the rabbis themselves. One noteworthy instance is the story about a struggle between a Cuthean (a Samaritan) who pretended to be an interpreter of dreams and always expounded them favorably and R. Ishmael b. R. Yose, who, through the dreams' symbols, consistently exposed embarrassing details about the transgressions of the dreamers and their relatives (*Lamentations Rabbah* 1:1). R. Ishmael's threatening (and obviously superior) power, which in this case was directed against those who dared to turn to "other" dream interpreters, is more concretely evident in an event that closes this section. In this case, R. Ishmael turns to a man whose dreams had already been interpreted favorably by the Cuthean ("You will attain greatness") and offers to interpret them himself for a fee (!) in a way that "you [the dreamer] would not lose out." Despite the direct threat intimated in R. Ishmael's words, the man prefers the Cuthean. R. Ishmael, therefore, interprets his dreams unfavorably and envisages harm to the dreamer (*Lamentations Rabbah* 1:1). The polemical message is sharp and clear: In the

---

247. Although some of the interpretations in this talmudic "dream book" parallel those found in Babylonian or Hellenistic lists, its methodological and hermeneutical uniqueness is remarkable. For discussions of this list of dream symbols and their interpretation, see Alexander (1995b), Lewy (1893b), Lieberman (1950, 70–77), and H. Weiss (2011, 173–234).

power struggle over the fulfillment of dreams, the rabbis' interpretation prevails, and whoever does not turn to them will lose out.[248]

The culmination of this trend is the story of the encounter between a Cuthean who invented a dream to tease "this elder of the Jews," in his mocking formulation, and R. Ishmael who was asked to interpret it.

A Cuthean said: "(Why) should I not go and tease this elder of the Jews?" He went to him [R. Ishmael b. R. Yose] and said to him: "I saw in my dream four cedars and four sycamores, a bunch of reeds, a silo, a cow, and this man [i.e., himself] sits asleep."[249] He [R. Ishmael] said to him: "May you perish! That is no dream! Even so, you should not go away empty-handed. [And he interpreted it for him:] The four cedars—four sides of the bed; the four sycamores—four legs of the bed; the bunch of reeds—the bottom [of the bed]; the silo—a mattress of straw; a cow—a leather cover [spread on the bed]; and that man (who) sits asleep—you, lies on it neither alive nor dead. And thus it happened to him." (PT *Ma'aser Sheni* 4:12)[250]

R. Ishmael's response to the prank is sharp and quick. His interpretation of the "dream" becomes reality, demonstrating to the reader the rabbis' actual power of creation. This power that, so far, had consistently been tied to the dream's supernatural potential, is now completely detached from it and is presented as an immanent quality of the rabbi. The clear border between dream and reality, the foundation of every hermeneutical methodology of dream symbols that had already been quite blurred in the conception that "a dream follows only its interpretation"

---

248. R. Ishmael's interpretations of dreams are cited also in the Palestinian Talmud (*Ma'aser Sheni* 4:12) but without the polemical context of their appearance in *Lamentations Rabbah*. The didactic threatening message is transmitted here as well, but only its culmination—the direct struggle with the Cuthean—is presented in a polemical context.

249. In the original *medarekh*. I follow Jastrow's (1903, 314) suggestion to see it as a corruption of *medamekh* (from the root *dmk*, "to sleep" and also "to die"), which indeed fits R. Ishmael's interpretation of the dream. Cf. also Sokoloff (1990, 156).

250. Cf. *Lamentations Rabbah* 1:1, where R. Ishmael is mentioned by name as the victim of the prank.

(PT *Ma'aser Sheni* 4:12), is completely erased here, given the rabbi's power to control reality and fashion it as he wishes. The taming and domestication of the dream within the walls of the house of study has thus apparently been completed.

ASTROLOGY

Astrology, meaning the belief in the influence of heavenly bodies on events in the world and their study for the purpose of learning about the future, was widespread in the ancient world and was a central divination method in the ancient cultures of Mesopotamia, Egypt, and the Hellenistic world.[251] Jews were also well acquainted with this method. The Bible hints at a belief in astrology but rejects it as alien to Jewish faith.[252] The Apocrypha is ambivalent toward it, rejecting it and acknowledging it at the same time. The origin of astrology is admittedly heavenly, but it is part of the evil knowledge brought down to earth by the rebellious angels. The Jewish Hellenistic authors Artapanus and Pseudo-Eupolemos offer a different approach. Both take pride in Abraham as having imparted this wisdom to the rabbis of Egypt (which was acknowledged as the cradle of astrology). Philo and Josephus use astrological principles in their works to clarify ritual symbols in the Temple service. The practical manifestation of astral divination is recorded in several passages in the Qumran scrolls, and its traces are even discernible in Jewish politics in Palestine in antiquity.[253]

---

251. For a general survey of astrology in antiquity, see Barton (1994). Prominent studies in the extensive research corpus on this subject in the Greco-Roman world include Bouché-Leclercq (1963a), Cramer (1954), Cumont (1960), and Gundel and Gundel (1966). For a limited selection of studies on astrology in Egypt and Mesopotamia, see Oppenheim (1969a), Parker (1978), Rochberg-Halton (1988; 1989), von Beckerath (1975), and von Stuckrad (1996, 19–54).

252. See, for instance, Isaiah 47:13–14 and references to the Chaldeans, who were famous as soothsayers, in Daniel 2:5, 10; 4:4, 7; and 5:7, 11. See also Ness (1990, 162–69), von Stuckrad (1996, 87–105), and Zatelli (1991).

253. The main works on this subject are the *Book of Shem*, the *Epistle to Rehoboam*, the *Testament of Solomon*, *1 Enoch* and *2 Enoch*, *The Book of Jubilees*, and the *Sibylline Oracles*. For a broad review of astrology in these works and in Jewish-Hellenistic and Qumran literature, see Charlesworth (1987), Ness (1990, 169–99), and von Stuckrad

Textual and archaeological sources attest to the place of astral elements in Jewish culture in the period following the destruction of the Temple. Mosaic floors in Palestinian synagogues from the fifth and sixth centuries, decorated with the image of the sun god Helios (or Sol) riding his chariot at the center of the zodiac, attest to the penetration of such motifs into Jewish places of worship.[254] Their mention in sermons and *piyyutim* points to their penetration into the synagogue discourse.[255] Magic texts, among them *Sefer ha-Razim* and later also several works that were found in the Cairo Genizah, show a strong link between astrology and magic. The two main aspects of this link are the use of astrology as a diagnostic basis for determining magic-medical treatment and the magical activation of astral bodies in the performance of a certain task.[256]

The rabbis were also well acquainted with the astrological worldview, with the divination involved in it, *'istagninut* in their terms, and with the professionals who engaged in it: *'istrologin* or Chaldeans.[257] Evidence of

(2000a, 160–222; 2000b). On horoscopes and astrological texts in Qumran, see also Albani (1999), Greenfield and Sokoloff (1995), and Wise (1994, 13–50). On astrology in the interpretation of ritual symbols and in Jewish politics in Palestine in the Hellenistic era, see von Stuckrad (2000a; 2000b).

254. The scholarly literature in this field is quite extensive. See, for instance, Englard (2000), Foerster (1987), Goodenough (1953–1968, 4: 3–62; 8: 167–77, 195–218; 12: 40–48), L. I. Levine (1998, 149–60), Mack (1998), M. Smith (1982), S. Stern (1996), and Urbach (2002b).

255. In sermons, see, for instance, *Pesikta Rabbati* 20, 27. In *piyyutim*, see Yahalom (1999, 20–24).

256. On Jewish astromagic literature, its sources, and development, see Leicht (2006a, chaps. 5–6).

257. Palestinian sources use the Greek term in transcription, *'astrologos* (pl. *'astrologin*) and their variations to denote diviners by means of stars (e.g., PT *Shabbat* 6:10; PT *Avodah Zarah* 2:2; *Genesis Rabbah* 1:4, 87:4; *Exodus Rabbah* 1:18, 21; *Numbers Rabbah* 19:3; and *Ecclesiastes Rabbah* 1:1). In the Babylonian Talmud the term *kalda'ei* (Chaldeans) is widely used to denote soothsayers (e.g., TB *Berakhot* 64a; TB *Shabbat* 119a, 156b; and TB *Pesahim* 113b). The basis for the term is the identification of divination with the Chaldean tribe, who became famous for their divination skills and who are mentioned by this name (*Chaldaioi*) in Greco-Roman literature, particularly in the context of astrological divination but also in the context of wisdom in general and mathematics and sorcery in particular. See Dickie (2001, 110–12). Most probably, the Chaldeans of the Talmud are also astrologers, but this is not stated explicitly. See Sokoloff (2002, 581). The term also occurs in magic bowls. See Naveh and Shaked (1987, B13).

this acquaintance is the many Babylonian and Palestinian traditions that deal with the matter—those that acknowledge astral fate and the divination related to it and those that reject them.[258] The uniqueness of astrology as divination (with implications for sorcery and medicine) follows from the structured and systematic complexity of the astral data that the astrologer is expected to study and interpret. Extensive astronomic and mathematical knowledge was a precondition for a professional concern with astral divination. No wonder, then, that few rabbinic pronouncements attest to genuine astrological knowledge.

Astrology was also, by its very nature, tainted with pagan echoes. The sun, the moon, the planets, and the constellations were all perceived as powerful personified entities or as being governed by such entities. Astral fatalism is, as such, problematic in the rabbinic worldview, which emphasizes moral freedom as the basis of a person's divinely determined fate. This fatalism, however, far exceeds the predestination principle underlying divination methods as a whole, because it is conditioned on faith in the existence and the power of such entities to control reality. Not in vain, therefore, did the rabbis reject consultation with the stars by claiming that it contradicted the injunction "You must be wholehearted with the Lord your God" (Deuteronomy 18:13; TB *Pesahim* 113b). Others linked the rejection to the biblical commandment "You must not divine" (Leviticus 19:26).[259] *'Iṣṭagninut* is widely presented in rabbinic literature as a Gentile wisdom in general and as wisdom of Egyptian sorcerers in particular. In this fashion, it was indeed recognized as a true wisdom (as in the other cultures of the ancient world) but also as an alien and hostile element that should be overpowered and defeated. Biblical heroes such as Moses and Solomon indeed do so in several Midrash stories and so do the people of Israel in general, as will be shown.[260]

---

258. On astrology in rabbinic literature, see Bar-Ilan (2011, 28–60), Leicht (2011), and von Stuckrad (2000b, 431–511). See also Charlesworth (1987, 930–32), Gafni (1990, 165–67), Lieberman (1942, 97–100), Neusner (1969–1970, 4: 330–34), Urbach (1975, 275–78), and Wächter (1969).

259. *Sifra, Kedoshim* 6. Cf. also Ms Munich 95, version of *Sanhedrin* 66a (R.≈Rabinowitz 1960, *Sanhedrin*, 187). The printed version reads "fish" (rather than "stars"), thereby dismissing the link between this tradition and astrology.

260. See, for example, TB *Sanhedrin* 95a, 101b; TB *Sotah* 12b, 13b, 15b; TB *Shabbat* 75a; *Genesis Rabbah* 63:2; *Exodus Rabbah* 1:21; *Pirke de-Rabbi Eliezer* 44; and *Tanhuma*,

Acknowledgment of an astral fate and even acquaintance with astrology as such are recorded in rabbinic literature in explicit sayings and stories. Yet traditions about rabbis studying astrology or astronomy (which in antiquity were mutually related) are rare. One explicit talmudic statement deserves note: "It is one's duty to calculate the cycles and courses of constellations (*tequfot u-mazalot*)" (TB *Shabbat* 75a). The explanation for this instruction removes the pagan aspect from astral calculations: "He who knows how to calculate the cycles and courses of constellations and does not, of him Scripture says: 'But they regard not the work of the Lord, neither consider the operation of his hands' (Isaiah 5:12)."[261]

Additional traditions associate rabbis with astral and even astrological knowledge. Shmuel attests about himself, "I am as familiar with the paths of heaven as with the streets of Nehardea, with the exception of the comet, about which I am ignorant" (TB *Berakhot* 58b). This statement resonates elsewhere.

What is [the meaning of the verse]: "It is not in heaven" (Deuteronomy 30:12)? Shmuel said: "The Torah is not to be found among astrologers whose work is in heaven." They said to Shmuel: "But lo, you are an astrologer and yet you are a great Torah sage!" He said to them: "I would only engage in astrology when I was free from studying the Torah."[262]

---

va-Yakhel 5. Particularly interesting is the story of Moses's struggle against an Amalekite sorcerer who would "set up people" from Amalek on their birthday to protect them in their struggle against the people of Israel, because "a man does not speedily fall on his birthday." Moses, who became aware of the sorcerer's action, "mixed up the stars" and thereby dismissed it altogether (PT *Rosh Hashanah* 3:8).

261. And further on: "And he who knows how to calculate cycles and planetary courses but does not, one may not converse with him" (TB *Shabbat* 75a). Rashi ad locum ties this calculation to divination. The desire to eradicate the pagan element from the astral system is clearly conveyed in the law stating "One who sees the sun at its turning point, the moon in its power, the planets in their orbits, and the constellations in their orderly progress, should say: 'Blessed be He who has wrought the work of creation'" (TB *Berakhot* 59b; cf. *Leviticus Rabbah* 23:8).

262. *Deuteronomy Rabbah* (ed. Lieberman), *Nitsavim* 6. For traditions (and instructions) from Shmuel bearing on astral influence in the world, see TB *Shabbat* 129b and TB *Eruvin* 56a.

Shmuel obviously does not deny his astrological knowledge and his pro-fessional standing as an astrologer, but he absolutely separates it from the Torah, that is, from rabbinic knowledge, and establishes a clear hierar-chy between them.

Beside this general statement, to which one could possibly add R. Yoḥanan b. Zakkai's knowledge of the cycles (*tequfot*),[263] some traditions ascribe to rabbis more concrete forms of astrological knowledge. Accord-ing to one of these traditions, R. Joshua b. Levi linked sickness to the influence of the moon: "Said R. Joshua b. Levi, If a man eats beef with turnips and sleeps in the moon on the nights of the fourteenth and fif-teenth of the month in the cycle of Tamuz, he is liable to *aḥilu* [a kind of sickness]" (TB *Gittin* 70a). Elsewhere, horoscopic knowledge is cited from his notebook in relation to the influence of the day of the week at birth on a person's character. The list is the closest thing to the lists of astral divination that prevailed later in Jewish texts, both as such and as a diag-nostic element in magic treatment. In any event, the discussion that accompanies it shifts the knowledge included in it from the realm of astrology to the world of Torah. This is a crucial example of the Judaiz-ing of astrological elements that gained hold in Jewish culture.[264] The text reads:

> It was recorded in R. Joshua b. Levi's notebook: He who [is born] on the first day of the week . . . will be either completely virtuous or completely wicked. Why? Because light and dark-ness were created on it [on the first day]. He who [is born] on the second day of the week will be bad-tempered. Why? Because the waters were divided on that day. He who is [born] on the third day of the week will be wealthy and unchaste. Why? Because herbs were created on that day.[265] He who [is born] on the fourth day of the week will be wise and erudite. Why? Because the luminaries were suspended thereon. He who [is

---

263. TB *Sukkah* 28a; TB *Bava Bathra* 134a. See also Blau (1898, 46).

264. Cf. Lieberman (1942, 97–100).

265. Rashi explains: "Since it is written 'Let the earth bring forth grass' (Genesis 1:11), meaning it will grow and multiply greatly and hasten to grow and flourish, which is licentiousness."

born] on the fifth day of the week will be charitable. Why? Because fish and birds were created on that day.[266] He who [is born] on the eve of the Sabbath will be a suitor. What [does that mean]? R. Naḥman b. Yitzhak said: "A suitor of good deeds." He who [is born] on the Sabbath—will die on the Sabbath, because the great day of the Sabbath was desecrated on his account. (TB *Sabbath* 156a)

R. Joshua's view was not unanimously accepted. R. Ḥanina held that greater precision is required and that what determines a person's character is not the day of the week at birth but rather the hour of birth and the influence of the dominant sign at the time.

R. Ḥanina said to them: "Go out (and) tell the son of Levi [i.e., R. Joshua b. Levi]—not the sign of the day (*mazal yom*) determines but the sign of the hour (*mazal sha'ah*). One [born] in the sun [meaning under the influence of the sun] will be a bright man. He will eat of his own and drink of his own, and his secrets are open. Should he steal, he will not be successful. One [born] in the planet of Venus [meaning under its influence] will be rich and lewd. Why? Because fire hangs[267] on it [on this planet]. One [born] in Mercury will be erudite and wise, because [this planet, which is the closest to the sun] is the sun's scribe. One [born] in the moon will be a sick man; he will build and destroy, destroy and build, and will not eat his own and drink his own, and his secrets will be hidden. Should he steal—he will succeed. One [born] in Saturn will be a man of idle thoughts, and some say: all (thoughts) about him will be idle. One [born] in Jupiter (*Sedeq*) will be righteous (*sadqan*)." Said R. Naḥman b. Yitzhak: "And righteous in observance. One [born] in Mars will shed blood." Said R. Ashi, "He will engage in bloodletting, or he will be a thief, or a slaughterer, or do circumcisions." (TB *Sabbath* 156a)

---

266. Rashi explains: "because they need not take pains for their food and they eat through the mercy of the Holy One, blessed be He."

267. The original is miswritten. I follow Ms Vatican 108 and Ms Munich 95.

Other rabbis also expressed views on astral questions. There is a tradition in the name of R. Efes, for instance, on the course of stellar orbits in the sky (*Genesis Rabbah* 10:4), and R. Meir and R. Yoshiya stated that eclipses are ominous events.[268] To this general statement, further details were later added on the meaning of unusual appearances of the sun (TB *Sukkah* 29a).

Beside these traditions, which deal with concrete astral knowledge, many others fundamentally acknowledge the stars' influence on the world. Some of the more noteworthy are the following: (1) the statement of R. Simon and others that "there is not a single herb that does not have its own star in the sky that strikes it and tells it, Grow!" (*Genesis Rabbah* 10:6); (2) the statement that ties together planetary influence, sorcery, and healing: "Man is under planetary influence, and it [the amulet] helps him. An animal is not under planetary influence, and it [the amulet] does not help him" (TB *Shabbat* 53b);[269] (3) mentions of the planetary influence that accompanies human beings and influences their fate and even their halakhic thinking;[270] (4) R. Papa's recommendation not to sue a Gentile during the month of Av, whose planetary influence is bad, but rather during the month of Adar, whose planetary influence is strong and positive (TB *Ta'anit* 29b); (5) Shmuel's recommendation not to engage in bloodletting on Tuesdays because of the influence of Mars (TB *Shabbat* 129b); and (6) the comparison "Just as the stars rule from one end of the world to the other, so too Israel" (*Deuteronomy Rabbah* 1:14).

A few midrashim and tales about rabbis are based on an acknowledgment of astral divination and the fatalism attached to it. Thus, for instance, the midrash on Abraham says:

Why did the Holy One, blessed be He, tell him: "So shall your seed be" (Genesis 15:5)? God showed him Isaac's planetary influence (*mazal*) whose name is planet "yonder," as it is said: "Stay here with the ass, and I and the lad will go yonder" (Genesis 22:5), and I see Isaac's *mazal* between the stars. For Abraham

268. Tosefta *Sukkah* 2:6; *Mekhilta de-Rabbi Ishmael, Bo,* 1. But cf. the view on eclipses as resulting from the world's moral eclipse in Tosefta, *Sukkah* 2:5, and TB *Sukkah* 29a.
269. See also TB *Bava Kamma* 2b.
270. TB *Yevamoth* 64b, TB *Shabbat* 146a, TB *Megillah* 3a, and TB *Bava Bathra* 12a.

was an astrologer of the stars. And why did he say to them—"we will prostrate ourselves, and come again to you" (ibid.)? Rather, Abraham prophesied that he and Isaac would return in peace from the altar. (*Midrash Zuta on Song of Songs* 1:1)

R. Yosef's refusal to accept the leadership of the Pumbedita academy because of a prophecy by Chaldeans that he would rule for only two years points to a similar ideological trend. His fear lest he should die two years after the start of his term later proved justified (TB *Berakhot* 64a).

The well-known story about R. Joseph who-honors-the-Sabbaths also attests to the absolute validity of astral fate but does so from a particularly interesting angle.

In the neighborhood of Joseph who-honors-the-Sabbaths was a Gentile who owned much property. The Chaldeans [known as astrologers] told him: "All your assets—Joseph who-honors-the-Sabbaths will consume them." He went and sold all his assets. With the proceeds, he bought a precious stone and set it in his turban. As he was crossing a bridge, the wind blew his hat away and cast it in the water. A fish swallowed it. They [some fishermen] hauled it out [fished it] and brought it [to the market] on the eve of the Sabbath. They [the fishermen] said: "Who buys at this [late] hour?" They [the market people] said to them: "Go and take it to Joseph who-honors-the-Sabbaths, who usually does." They brought it (and) he bought it. He tore it up and found a stone in it. He sold it for thirteen roomfuls[271] of golden dinars. An old man met him and said: "He who lends to the Sabbath, the Sabbath repays him." (TB *Sabbath* 119a)

This story has two protagonists, a Gentile and a Jew, who represent two facets of reality, and proceeds in a direct line from the Gentile to the Jew. Whereas the Gentile loses all his assets to the Jew by virtue of his astral fate, which he cannot escape, Joseph, the Jew, attains property by virtue of an entirely different principle—a reward for his virtuous act in

---

271. For the original *'ilita'*, denoting a large size of some kind, see Jastrow (1903, 1070) and Sokoloff (2002, 855).

observing the Sabbath. The Gentile's perspective, which is the principle of absolute astral fate, collapses in the course of the story and is replaced by the Jew's perspective, which releases his fate from the rule of the stars and founds it on the principle of free choice and of divine reward for a worthy virtuous life.[272]

The story about Joseph who-honors-the-Sabbaths thus gives artistic articulation to the stance explicitly and succinctly conveyed elsewhere through the statement that "Israel has no astral fate" (*'ein mazal le-yisra'el*), implying that the astral fate that rules the world cannot breach the border delimiting the Jewish people and distinguishing them from everyone else.[273] Against this view, two sayings that almost defiantly express explicit and absolute faith in astral fate deserve mention here. R. Ḥanina stated, "*Mazal* (astral fate) determines wisdom, *mazal* determines wealth, and Israel does have *mazal* (*ve-yesh mazal le-yisra'el*)" (TB *Shabbat* 156a). And Rabbah said: "Life, children, and sustenance are not determined by merit, but by astral fate" (TB *Mo'ed Katan* 28a).[274] R. Ḥanina explicitly negates the opposite view, whereby "Israel has no astral fate." Raba strengthens the power of astral fate above the principle of divine reward and punishment resting on human deeds.

The clash between astrological fatalism and the principle of free choice as the basis for human destiny is what moved some rabbis to a solution summed up in the saying "Israel has no astral fate." This view, as noted, does not deny astral influence in the world altogether but only excludes Israel from it. Whereas the Gentiles are subject to the influence of stars and planets (and astral divination is thus valid for them), Israel has its Father in Heaven (the Creator of the stars and planets) and the Torah, with all that this implies—divine omnipotence, free choice, and individual providence.[275] R. Yoḥanan learned that Israel has no *mazal*

---

272. See Frenkel (1981, 16–18).

273. For further traditions dealing with Chaldean prophecies or astral fate, see TB *Sanhedrin* 95a, TB *Ta'anit* 25a, TB *Yevamoth* 21b, and the stories cited later in the discussion.

274. On the place of this statement in Rava's theology and on its Persian context, see Elman (2004, 43–56).

275. A good illustration of the relationship between God and the constellations appears in the following account: "He showed him [God to Abraham] all the planets surrounding the *Shekhinah*. . . . The Holy One, blessed be He, said to him: 'As the

from the scriptural verse "Be not dismayed at the signs of heaven; for the nations are dismayed at them" (Jeremiah 10:2). And he interprets it to mean, "They are dismayed, but not Israel" (TB *Shabbat* 156a).[276] Rav, following earlier traditions, tied this matter to the call to Abraham to go outside and count the stars.

> How do we know that Israel has no *mazal*? As it is said: "And He brought him outside" (Genesis 15:5). . . . [Abraham] said to Him: "Sovereign of the Universe, I have looked at my astrological fate (*iṣṭagninut*) and found that I am not destined to give birth to a son." Said He to him: "Abandon your astrological concern, for Israel has no astral fate." (TB *Shabbat* 156a)[277]

Originally, then, Abraham was himself an astrologer, wise and well acquainted with the deep, all-encompassing, and most powerful of Gentile wisdoms.[278] Not only was he an astrologer but also "great astrological devotion was in his heart" (TB *Yoma* 28b). Several traditions state that he was world famous. According to R. Elazar ha-Modai, he was blessed with the "'*iṣṭagninus* that he possessed . . . such that all would come before him" (Tosefta *Kiddushin* 5:17), and in another version, "All the kings of East and West would seek him frequently" (TB *Bava Bathra* 16b).[279] This description of the nation's patriarch is profoundly significant:

---

constellations surround me and my honor is at the center, so will your children multiply and stand with their flags and my *Shekhinah* is at the center'" (*Deuteronomy Rabbah* [ed. Lieberman], Deuteronomy 16). The wavering between free will and astral fatalism was a concern outside the Jewish world too. On the struggle of the church fathers against astrology on these grounds, see Barton (1994, 64–85). See also Barton (1994, 76n47) for an idea parallel to "Israel has no astral fate," whereby baptism releases Christians from astral fate. On a similar conception in Hellenistic esoteric sects, see Bram (1976). Cf. also with Firmicus Materanus, who stated that the emperor has no astral fate (Barton 1994, 65–66).

276. Cf. TB *Sukkah* 29a.

277. See also TB *Nedarim* 32a.

278. As noted, this was the view of Artapanus and Pseudo-Eupolemos, who pointed to Abraham as the precursor of Egyptian astrology. See Charlesworth (1987, 934).

279. See also, however, Lieberman (1992, 8: 985–86), whose view is that the *'iṣṭagninus* mentioned in the Tosefta does not mean *'iṣṭagninut* (astrology), as in the version of the Babylonian Talmud there, but rather a precious stone.

His being chosen by God and brought outside at the time of the covenant between them (and more precisely, right before they entered this
covenant) delivered from astral fate one who had been not only subject to
it but also a key expert in its mysteries. One body of formative knowledge was therefore replaced with another—fear of the stars with fear of
God—and one authority was replaced with another: "'And He brought
him outside.' . . . The rabbis say: You are a prophet and you are not an
astrologer [anymore]" (*Genesis Rabbah* 44:12).[280]

Not only was Abraham brought outside but, potentially, so was his
entire seed. God's election of Israel implies the possibility of deliverance
from the arbitrariness of astral destiny through the power of the Torah,
the commandments, and good deeds. This principle is well demonstrated
in several stories dealing with the triumph of the merit derived from a
righteous act over fate, even to the extent of deliverance from a death set
in the stars. Here are two examples, cited together in the Babylonian
Talmud.

> And from [what happened] to Shmuel we also [learn]: "Israel
> has no *mazal*." Shmuel and Ablat were sitting and certain people
> were going to a lake. Said Ablat to Shmuel [pointing to one of
> them]: "That man is going but will not return. A snake will bite
> him and he will die." Said Shmuel to him: "If he is a Jew, he will
> go and he will return!" While they were sitting—he [that man]
> went and returned. Ablat stood up and threw off his [the man's]
> knapsack. He found in it a snake cut up and lying in two pieces.
> Shmuel said to him: "What did you do?" Said he: "Every day we
> pool our bread [for a joint meal] and eat. Today, one of us had
> no bread and was ashamed. I said to them [to my friends]: 'I
> will get up and collect' [gather the bread and put all the slices
> together in the common tray]. When I reached him, I pretended

---

280. This is obviously the source for the hierarchical relationship between astrological knowledge and its agents as opposed to "prophetic," normative knowledge and
its agents. See further the midrash about God taking Abraham beyond the heavenly
firmament and the accompanying release from fear of the stars (*Genesis Rabbah*
44:12). Cf. *Numbers Rabbah* 2:12 and *Deuteronomy Rabbah* (ed. Lieberman) 14, and see
further *Genesis Rabbah* 10.

to take from him so that he would not be ashamed." [Shmuel] said to him: "You have done a good deed!" Shmuel went out and taught: "Righteousness delivers from death" (Proverbs 10:2, 11:4)—and not from unnatural death, but from death itself."

And also, from [what happened] to R. Aqiva [we learn]: "Israel has no *mazal*." For R. Aqiva had a daughter. Chaldeans [meaning astrologers] told him: "On the day she goes under the bridal canopy, a snake will bite her and she will die." He worried greatly about this. On that day [the day of her marriage] she took a brooch, stuck it onto the wall. It happened to lodge itself in the eye of a snake. In the morning, when she took it [from the wall], a [dead] snake tagged along. Her father said to her: "What did you do?" She said to him: "A poor man came to our door in the evening, called out from the gate, and everybody was busy with the meal and no one heard him. I took the serving that had been given to me and gave it to him." Said he to her: "You have done a good deed!" R. Aqiva went out and taught: "Righteousness delivers from death"—and not from unnatural death, but from death itself." (TB *Shabbat* 156b)[281]

These episodic stories do not negate the principle of astral fate. Quite the contrary, they confirm it as the default option of human existence, but they give the Jewish people (and only the Jewish people) a way out from its edict through the power of righteousness. This belief obviously implies a danger. If the fate decreed in the stars is indeed the default option, human beings must be ready and constantly aware so as to be saved from it when it is expected to be bitter.

And [from what happened] to R. Naḥman b. Yitzhak [we also learn]: "Israel has no *mazal*." For R. Naḥman b. Yitzhak's mother was told by Chaldeans: "Your son will be a thief." She did not let him go bareheaded. She said to him: "Cover your head so that the fear of heaven may be upon you and ask for mercy [from God]. He [R. Naḥman] did not know why she had said [this] to him. One day he was sitting and studying under a

---

palm tree. The cover fell off his head. He raised his eyes and saw the palm tree. His evil inclination overcame him, he climbed up and bit off a cluster [of dates] with his teeth. (TB *Shabbat* 156b)

This is a disturbing story. Ostensibly, it expands the range of Israel's deliverance from the edict of the stars even further and relies not only on righteousness but on the fear of heaven in general. In this sense, it illustrates well the didactic power of the claim that Israel has no *mazal*. Contributing to this aspect of the claim is the fact that this story does not prophesy an event requiring a one-time cancellation but is instead a prophecy about character.[282] R. Naḥman's mother tries to rescue him from a fate that will accompany him throughout his life and seeks to grant him permanent protection. This turns out to be harder than she thought it would be and indeed proves impossible. The story clearly indicates that fear of God as such, in its spiritual sense, is not sufficient. Not by chance, R. Naḥman is busy studying when the cover falls off his head, and in light of his mother's dual (and to him incomprehensible) instruction, it is definitely possible that he raised up his eyes to ask for mercy as this mishap befell him. Nevertheless, once the actual, concrete artifact providing protection was removed, the powerful intensity of the astral fate again erupted and completely overtook R. Naḥman. What had begun as yet another sure proof of the principle so persuasively illustrated in the previous two stories ends here rather feebly. The sweeping power of astral fate, so it seems, cannot be stamped out but only suspended.

The solution to this fragile condition is found in two additional stories that are cited together in the Palestinian Talmud; they explicitly emphasize the contrast between astral fate and God's rule in the world. The first story, which to some extent parallels that of Shmuel and Ablat, highlights God's position as the supreme arbiter between astral fate and

---

282. This type of prophecy, whose contents are different—"you will be a teacher"—is one that R. Ḥisda had heard from the Chaldeans in his youth (TB *Yevamoth* 21b). Cf. also the tradition in *Deuteronomy Rabbah* (ed. Lieberman): "[This can be compared] to a man to whom a handsome son was born and, upon seeing him, an astrologer says: 'This boy will become a burglar, his father should cast him away.' The father heard this and said: 'Cast away my son?' The astrologer's father heard this and said: 'Whatever my son says to you, listen to him.'"

the rights of the (Jewish) person. The second story proposes a further ideological move: renouncing astral divination altogether and trusting God alone. In both cases evidence that God's power is greater than the power of astral fate is validated even further because it is actually articulated by the astrologers themselves.

> Two disciples of R. Ḥanina were going out to cut wood.[283] An astrologer saw them. [He said]: "These two will go out but not come back." When they went out, an old man met them. He said to them: "Please help me, for I have not eaten in three days." They were carrying one loaf of bread. They cut off half and gave it to him. He ate and prayed for them. He said to them: "May you live out this day, just as you have helped me to live out this day." They went in peace and returned in peace. And there were people in that place who had heard him [the astrologer]. They said to him: "Did you not say—these two will go out and not come back?" They said: "Either he is a liar [or] his astrology lies." Even so, they went and searched and found a snake (cut in half), one half in this knapsack [belonging to one of them], and one half in that knapsack [belonging to the other]. They said: "What good deed did you do today?" And they told their story. He [the astrologer] said: "And what can I do if the God of the Jews is appeased by half a loaf?"
>
> A certain astrologer converted to Judaism. One time he wanted to go out [on a work trip]. He said: "Is now the time to go out [meaning, do the stars show that this is an auspicious time to go out]? Then he retracted and said: "Did I not cleave unto this holy people in order to draw away from such things? I will go out in the name of our Creator." He reached the tax collection station. His donkey beat him and made him fall [and he left him and entered the city.[284] Thus, since the donkey went through the tax collection station on its own, the convert was

---

283. See Sokoloff (1990, 491, s.v. קיס). Jastrow suggests "thorns" (Jastrow 1903, 643).

284. This addition, missing from the manuscript, appears in Hameiri. On this version and the whole episode, see Lieberman (2008, 114–16). See also the parallel version in *Tanḥuma, Shofetim* (Warsaw ed.), 10.

spared having to pay]. What made him fall?—That he considered [checking his fate in the stars]. What saved him?—That he trusted his Creator. (PT *Shabbat* 6:10)[285]

This conceptual direction crystallizes into a principle in another (and later) story whose course resembles the one about two who went out and an astrologer prophesied about them that they would not return. In this version the two astrologers clarify for those about whom their prophecy failed what they did on that day. Their answer, suggesting a normative pattern of God-fearing behavior, extracts from the astrologers an admission about Jewish uniqueness.

> The astrologers looked at them: "Tell us what you did today?" Said they: "We did nothing except what we were taught to do—we recited the *Shema'* [prayer] and we prayed." Said they: "You are Jews! What astrologers say is not fulfilled concerning you because you are Jews." (*Tanhuma, Shofetim* 10)

As far as Jews are concerned, then, divine providence replaces astral fatalism and saves them from it. Nevertheless, the onus of proof that they indeed merit this is on them, and this proof is formulated in terms of the ideology propounded in the house of study. The rabbis do not dissociate themselves from the astrological outlook as such, including its theoretical and practical aspects, but they limit the extent of its influence and exclude from it those privileged to enjoy God's direct providence. Should Israel submit to the "God of the Jews"—in the format determined by the rabbis!—they will succeed in "going outside," like Abraham, to attain liberation from the fear and the power of stars and planets.

CONCLUDING REMARKS

The rabbinic discourse on magic, demonology, and divination points to the significant place of esoteric knowledge and hidden forces in the Jewish cosmology of late antiquity. Belief in the involvement of angels,

---

285. The translation is based on the corrected version according to a Genizah manuscript published in the edition by the Academy of the Hebrew Language.

demons, and planetary forces in worldly events, in the power of human beings to overcome them and even control them for their own benefit, in the power of the human tongue and of rites to direct reality and even to create and destroy life, and in the efficiency of various means of divination for obtaining esoteric knowledge was a considerable part of Jewish cosmology and the day-to-day confrontation with the reality derived from it. Often, this confrontation required turning to human agents of knowledge and power of this kind. The ritual power of these agents—one that their clients believed in, resorted to, and consumed—had a sociopolitical facet as well. Rabbis, who often acknowledged these agents' power, sought to marginalize them by delegitimizing the ritual practices that served them. They did not deny the possibility of attaining knowledge or power through ritual means, but they tried to delimit these means within clear boundaries of forbidden and allowed. Although the prevalent justification for this course was ideological, a special interest can also be glimpsed through this cover. The rabbis sought to label other agents of knowledge and power as illegitimate and to appropriate the legitimate power of holiness for themselves. The rabbinic discourse on the occult, then, exposes facets concerning not only the web of beliefs and deeds in the realm of magic, demonology, and divination in the Jewish society of late antiquity but also, and often mainly, the rabbis' struggle for a hegemony based on their monopoly of esoteric knowledge and power.

Epilogue

If visitors from another world were to look at the laws setting the frame of our lives—the volumes of ordinances and regulations, limitations and prohibitions, directives and permits—they would be sure that this, finally, is paradise. What could be better than a society where everyone is considerate and polite? No deceit, no theft, no usury; no one hurts anyone, no one strikes another, no one kills; no rape, no exploitation, no discrimination, no oppression or humiliation. Everyone is careful not to hurt or harm the other. Or could it be that this is not so?

A map is not territory and the law is not reality, not even the Ten Commandments, or talmudic Halakhah, or the infinite number of rulings that have been derived from it by halakhists and exegetes, and exegetes of exegetes, generation after generation, century after century. The attempt to identify everyday life, reality as is, with the law, the ordinance, the scholarly ruling, or ideological speech, is unrealistic. These are, at best, the spine of social life but not the actual body. Obviously, one should ask where people go when searching for everyday life. Where do they start their search? What segments of everyday life do they look at? The picture changes from one to another. Yet only there, in everyday life and not in the book of laws, does living reality thrive. That is where the various forms of life—through ongoing negotiation and based on partial resemblances—somehow come together into a dense and blurred family picture (lacking any definition except for the ostensive "that") of our existence.

So also concerning "Judaism." First, where does one look for it? Jewish theology has always been formulated by leisured and learned elites, who were sufficiently strong to bequeath to the next generation their ideological and social genes in the shape of new elites, who fixated and enhanced the authority of those preceding them while drawing from it their own. A large gap separated this theology from the everyday life of Jewish masses, whose "true" religiosity this theology purportedly represented. Where, then, should we look for "Judaism"? One could of course say that the people are merely "the masses," at times ignorant, at times weak, at times deceived into the dredges of alien faiths and customs, whereas theology is Judaism as is—pure and refined, as conceived by God, given to and preserved by its faithful. When Jewish religious elites make this claim, they are stating the obvious. They thereby enhance their power and strengthen their position. But we look at this culture from the outside, so why should we favor ideology over reality as an expression of "true" Jewish existence? Why persist in the search for ways to—"nevertheless," "despite," and "even though hard"—adapt the reality of life to the ideology? Why not outline Jewish ideologies—the halakhic, the philosophical, the mythical—as merely segments and, even more significantly, segments of equal value in the general picture of Judaism? Why not be satisfied with their perception as aspects of a changing and diversifying phenomenon teeming with many others, no less essential and true? Why not remove from the various manifestations of Jewish forms of life the additional judgmental category—correct/incorrect, authentic/alien, whole/partial, true/false—and look at all of them as of equal value? The time seems ripe for abandoning the tendency to organize Jewish forms of life on the truth axis we have inherited, naturally and almost unwittingly, from both the religious and learned elites. We are probably ready to forgo the entrenched preference for the Maimonidean version of religiosity over that of those who exalt him, prostrate themselves on his grave, and spread amulets "composed by him."

The main issue is not merely recognizing the existence of diverse forms of Jewish life, which have long been acknowledged, but their equality! What is required is not a nodding acceptance of "margins," even broad ones, but a renunciation of the view that recognizes a center; not a silent or even conscious acquiescence to the presence of wild weeds that have stubbornly struck roots in a soil alien to them, but a contemplation of diversity. And I am not referring merely to "popular," "forgivable," or "inoffensive" practices on the "margins" of theology but to what seems its total reversal.

Faith in the existence of a supernatural power in the world and in the ability of human agents to rule over it and activate it at will has been prevalent in the people of Israel since biblical times and is also prevalent today. Its presence in day-to-day life is well documented in Jewish writings, as an expression of both the power of the writing elites themselves—obviously excluding this power from the category of *kishuf* (magic)—and the danger posed to society (and indeed to the power of these elites) by some "other," either a non-Jew or one who has deviated from the norms of the "proper and true" Judaism that they sought to impose. The voices of members of these circles—"the masses," "the ignorant," "women," "those lacking in faith," "the superstitious"—were not heard in the canonic discourse. Their voices were constantly mediated by the dominating (and at times hostile) voice of some writing establishment, which often used the image it ascribed to them as a mirror image of itself and its ideological ancestors. This was the view that prevailed for generations in the realm of religious, theological-halakhic creativity and the one that persisted among scholars and researchers at the outset of the scientific, modern, and, as it were, objective discourse known as *Wissenschaft des Judentums* (and at times in our time as well). Both these schools, each for its own reasons that are ultimately not so far from one another, took pains to uproot from "Judaism" whatever could be uprooted and to conceal what had struck deep and bitter roots—the establishment by Judaizing it and the modern writers through exclusion and denial.

This situation is now changing radically—not among the writers on the inside, those who create more and more "Jewish texts," but among those seeking to look in from the outside (and indeed, always from some specific outside) at such texts and at the cultural space where they are anchored: objects, symbols, rituals, practices, and belief. In the context discussed in this book, several interrelated elements that draw on one another can perhaps be identified at the root of the change. First, an increasingly growing flow of magic artifacts and texts that have been found and published in recent decades brings to life the existence of adjuration practices among Jews at the time. Their social, geographic, and historical scope is so wide that sweeping the phenomenon under the theological carpet, as scholars sought to do in the past, is no longer possible. Second, a profound change affecting entrenched dichotomous value distinctions such as central/peripheral, high/low, genuine/feigned, worthy/despicable, led to a new and nonapologetic perspective on Jewish practitioners of religion that is different from those perspectives we had been accustomed to seeing as the faithful representatives of Judaism. Finally, the growing concern with spirituality in the Western world has created discourses and goods through which concepts such as energy (positive or negative), spirituality (harmful or healing), and magic (white or black), including their symbolic and objective expressions, are present almost everywhere in our lives. Indirectly, this presence also affects the measure of interest in the historical roots of these phenomena and the social, including the academic, legitimation bestowed on the interest in them.

In the first two chapters of this book I traced the course of the change in the study of early Jewish magic and its place in the context of the perception of magic and religion outside Jewish studies. Chapters 3 and 4 were devoted to methodological questions. I suggested resting the perception of early Jewish magic on a textual basis—an adjuration text—as the foundation of a corpus of Jewish magic texts, and I discussed the performative character of the act of adjuration. These discussions set the methodological ground for the second part of the book, where I presented the available sources for describing Jewish magic culture in late antiquity and the early Islamic period at length. My method, presented in chapter 3, is the organizing principle at their basis. I first considered insider (or primary) sources, those that are adjuration texts in the strong sense of the term: adjurations, artifacts bearing adjurations, recipes for the ritual carrying out of adjurations, and treatises compiling such recipes in broader conceptual frameworks (chapter 5). In the last two chapters (chapters 6 and 7), I presented outsider (or secondary) sources, which are not classic magic texts but works that express or reflect ideas and modes of action found in the first corpus.

The task can now be completed by embarking on a detailed description of early Jewish magic as a cultural system. Such a description must be written, above all, by relying on the textual and material products of this culture, that is, on the performance and instructional writings of practitioners and of parties interested in adjurations. It will be expanded through studies of other sources, wherein the use of adjurations is not the primary concern. With the completion of this task, for which this book laid modest foundations, we will have a general broad picture of Jewish magic culture in late antiquity and the early Islamic period. For now, this culture has been shifted to center stage and its presence and vitality fully exposed as an essential component of Jewish life and faith.

Bibliography

Rabbinic Sources

Avot de-Rabbi Natan, ed. Solomon Shechter, with a prolegomenon by Menahem Kister. New York: JTSA, 1997.

Masakhtot Ketanot [Minor Tractates], *Derekh Erez*, ed. Michael Higger. New York: Moinester, 1935.

Masakhtot Ketanot [Minor Tractates], *Semaḥot*, ed. Michael Higger. New York: Bloch, 1931.

Masakhtot Ketanot [Minor Tractates], *Soferim*, ed. Michael Higger. New York: Debei Rabanan, 1937.

Masakhtot Ketanot [Minor Tractates], *Tefilin*, ed. Michael Higger. New York: Bloch, 1930.

Masekhet Kalah Rabbati. In *Masakhtot Kalah*, ed. Michael Higger, 169–344. New York: Debei Rabanan, 1936.

Mekhilta de-Rabbi Shimon bar Yohai, ed. Jacob N. Epstein and Ezra Z Melamed. Jerusalem: Mekizei Nirdamim, 1955.

Midrash Leqaḥ Tov, ed. Shlomo Buber (Genesis, Exodus) and Aharon M. Padwa (Leviticus, Numbers, Deuteronomy). Jerusalem: Vagshal, 1986.

Midrash Mishlei, ed. Baruch (Burton) L. Visotzky. New York: JTSA, 2002.

Midrash on Psalms, ed. Shlomo Buber. Vilnius: Romm, 1891.

Midrash Rabbah on Deuteronomy, ed. Saul Lieberman. Jerusalem: Wahrman 1974.

Midrash Rabbah on Deuteronomy, ed. members of Machon Hamidrash Hamevoar. Jerusalem: Machon Hamidrash Hamevoar 1993.

Midrash Rabbah on Ecclesiastes, ed. members of Machon Hamidrash Hamevoar. Jerusalem: Machon Hamidrash Hamevoar, 1993.

Midrash Rabbah on Exodus, ed. members of Machon Hamidrash Hamevoar. Jerusalem: Machon Hamidrash Hamevoar, 1993.

Midrash Rabbah on Genesis, ed. Yehuda Theodor and Chanoch Albeck. Jerusalem: Shalem, 1995.

Midrash Rabbah on Lamentation, ed. Shlomo Buber. Vilnius: Romm, 1899.

Midrash Rabbah on Leviticus, ed. Mordechai Margalioth. New York: JTSA, 1993.

Midrash Rabbah on Numbers, ed. members of Machon Hamidrash Hamevoar. Jerusalem: Machon Hamidrash Hamevoar, 1993.

Midrash Tanhuma, ed. Shlomo Buber. Jerusalem: Vagshal, 1990.

Midrash Tannaim on Deuteronomy, ed. David Z. Hoffmann. Jerusalem: Mifalei Sefarim Le-Yitsu, 1984.

Midrash Zuta on Song of Songs, ed. Shlomo Buber. Vilnius: Romm, 1925.

Mishnah, ed. Chanoch Albeck. Jerusalem: Bialik Institute, 1952.

Pesikta de-Rav Kahana, ed. Dov (Bernard) Mandelbaum. New York: JTSA, 1987.

Pesikta Rabbati, ed. Meir Ish-Shalom (Friedman). Tel Aviv: n.p., 1973.

Pirke de-Rabbi Eliezer, ed. Michael Higger. In *Horev* (1944): 82–119, (1946): 94–166, (1948): 185–294.

Sifra, ed. Shakhna Koliditsky. Jerusalem: Sifriyah Toranit, 1992.

Sifre on Deuteronomy, ed. Eliezer A. (Louis) Finkelstein. New York: JTSA, 1969.

Talmud Yerushalmi, ed. Academy of the Hebrew Language. Jerusalem: Academy of the Hebrew Language, 2001.

Tosefta, ed. Saul Lieberman, 5 vols. New York: JTSA, 1955–1988.

Tosefta, ed. Moshe Zuckermandel. Jerusalem: Wahrmann, 1970.

~~~

Afik, Izhak. 1990. "The Rabbinic Perception of the Dream." Ph.D. diss., Bar-Ilan University (Hebrew).

Albani, Matthias. 1999. "Horoscopes in Qumran Scrolls." In Peter W. Flint and James C. Vanderkam (eds.), *The Dead Sea Scrolls After Fifty Years*, 2: 279–330. Leiden: Brill.

Alexander, Philip. 1983. "3 (Hebrew Apocalypse of) Enoch." In James H. Charlesworth (ed.), *The Old Testament Pseudepigrapha*, 1: 223–315. Garden City: Doubleday.

———. 1986. "Incantations and Books of Magic." In Emil Schürer, *The History of the Jewish People in the Age of Jesus Christ (175 B.C.–A.D. 135)*, ed. Géza Vermes, Fergus Millar, Matthew Black, and Martin Goodman, 3(1): 341–79. Edinburgh: T. & T. Clark.

———. 1993. "Response." In Peter Schäfer and Joseph Dan (eds.), *Gershom Scholem's* Major Trends in Jewish Mysticism *50 Years After*, 79–83. Tübingen: Mohr Siebeck.

———. 1995a. "Bavli Berakhot 55a–57b: The Talmudic Dreambook in Context." *Journal of Jewish Studies* 46: 230–48.

———. 1995b. "'A Sixtieth Part of Prophecy': The Problem of Continuing Revelation in Judaism." In Jon Davis, Graham Harvey, and Wilfred G. E. Watson (eds.), *Words Remembered, Texts Renewed: Essays in Honour of John F. A. Sawyer*, 414–33. Sheffield, UK: Academic Press.

———. 1997. "'Wrestling Against Wickedness in High Places': Magic in the Worldview of the Qumran Community." In Stanley E. Porter and Craig A. Evans (eds.), *The Scrolls and the Scriptures: Qumran Fifty Years After*, 318–37. Sheffield, UK: Academic Press.

———. 1999a. "The Demonology of the Dead Sea Scrolls." In Peter W. Flint and James C. Vanderkam (eds.), *The Dead Sea Scrolls After Fifty Years*, 2: 331–53. Leiden: Brill.

———. 1999b. "Jewish Elements in Gnosticism and Magic c. CE 70–c. CE 270." In William Horbury, W. D. Davies, and James Sturdy (eds.), *The Cambridge History of Judaism: The Early Roman Period*, 3: 1052–78. Cambridge, UK: Cambridge University Press.

———. 2003a. "Contextualizing the Demonology of the Testament of Solomon." In Armin Lange, Hermann Lichtenberger, and K. F. Diethard Römheld (eds.), *Die Dämonen: Die Dämonologie der israelitisch-jüdischen und frühchristlichen Literatur im Kontext ihrer Umwelt*, 613–35. Tübingen: Mohr Siebeck.

———. 2003b. "*Sefer Ha-Razim* and the Problem of Black Magic in Early Judaism." In Todd E. Klutz (ed.), *Magic in the Biblical World: From the Rod of Aaron to the Ring of Solomon*, 170–90. London: T. & T. Clark.

———. 2005. "The Talmudic Concept of Conjuring (*Ahizat Einayim*) and the Problem of the Definition of Magic (*Kishuf*)." In Rachel

Elior and Peter Schäfer (eds.), *Creation and Re-Creation in Jewish Thought*, 7–25. Tübingen: Mohr Siebeck.

Alon, Gedalyahu. 1950. "By the Name." *Tarbiz* 21: 30–39 (Hebrew).

al-Qirqisani, Yaʿqub. 1939–1943. *Kitab al-Anwar wal-Maraqib: Code of Karaite Law*, ed. Leon Nemoy. New York: Alexander Kohut Memorial Foundation.

Alston, William P. 1967. "Religion." In *The Encyclopedia of Philosophy*, 7: 140–45. New York: Macmillan.

Amir, Abraham. 1994. "Shimon ben Shetah and the Witches: Three Sources and Three Approaches." *Sinai* 112: 144–61 (Hebrew).

Apuleius of Madaura. 1909. *The Apologia and Florida*, trans. Harold E. Butler. Oxford: Clarendon Press.

———. 1994. *Pro Se de Magia Liber (Apologia)*, ed. Rudolfus Helm. Stuttgart: B. G. Teubner.

Arbel, Vita D. 2003. *Beholders of Divine Secrets: Mysticism and Myth in the Hekhalot and Merkavah Literature*. Albany: SUNY Press.

Arrington, Robert, and Mark Addis (eds.). 2001. *Wittgenstein and Philosophy of Religion*. London: Routledge.

Artemidori Daldiani. 1963. *Onirocriticon Libri V*, ed. Roger A. Pack. Leipzig: Tuenber.

Asad, Talal (ed.). 1973. *Anthropology and the Colonial Encounter*. London: Ithaca.

Audollent, August. 1904. *Defixionum Tabellae, quotquot innotuerunt, tam in Graecis orientis, quam in totius occidentis partibus praeter Atticas in corpore inscriptionum Atticarum editas*. Paris: Albert Fontemoing.

Aune, David E. 1980. "Magic in Early Christianity." In W. Haase (ed.), *Aufstieg und Niedergang der Römischen Welt*, pt. II, 23.2: 1507–57. Berlin: de Gruyter.

Austin, John. 1962. *How to Do Things with Words*. Oxford: Oxford University Press.

Avishur, Yitzhak. 1979. "'Ways of the Amorite': The Canaanite-Babylonian Background and the Literary Structure." In C. Rabin, D. Patterson, B.-Z. Luria, and Y. Avishur (eds.), *Studies in the Bible and the Hebrew Language Offered to Meir Wallenstein on the Occasion of His Seventy-Fifth Birthday*, 17–47. Jerusalem: Kiryat Sefer (Hebrew).

———. 1998. *In Praise of Maimonides: Folktales in Judaeo-Arabic and Hebrew from the Near East and North Africa*. Jerusalem: Magnes (Hebrew).

Baer, Yitzhak F. 1985. *Studies in the History of the Jewish People*. Jerusalem: Historical Society of Israel (Hebrew).

Baillet, Maurice. 1982. *Qumrân Grotte 4:3*. Discoveries in the Judaean Desert 7. Oxford: Clarendon Press.

Baker, Gordon P., and Peter M. S. Hacker. 1983. *Wittgenstein: Meaning and Understanding*. Oxford: Blackwell.

Bamberger, Avigail. 2012. "The Contribution of the Babylonian Incantation Bowls to the Study of the Talmud and Its Time." M.A. thesis, The Hebrew University of Jerusalem (Hebrew).

Baramki, Dimitri C. 1932. "Note on a Cemetery at Karm Al-Shaikh, Jerusalem." *Quarterly of the Department of Antiquities in Palestine* 1:\ 3–9.

Barb, Alphons A. 1963. "The Survival of Magic Arts." In Arnaldo Momigliano (ed.), *The Conflict Between Paganism and Christianity in the Fourth Century*, 100–125. Oxford: Clarendon Press.

Bar-Ilan, Meir. 1988. "Magic Seals on the Body Among Jews in the First Centuries C.E." *Tarbiz* 57: 37–50 (Hebrew).

———. 1993. "Witches in the Bible and in the Talmud." *Approaches to Ancient Judaism*, n.s., 5: 7–32.

———. 1995. "Exorcism by Rabbis: Talmudic Sages and Magic." *Daat* 34: 17–31 (Hebrew).

———. 1999. "Medicine in Eretz Israel During the First Centuries C.E." *Cathedra* 91: 31–78 (Hebrew).

———. 2002. "Between Magic and Religion: Sympathetic Magic in the World of the Sages of the Mishnah and Talmud." *Review of Rabbinic Judaism* 5: 383–99.

———. 2011. *Astrology and Other Sciences Among the Jews of Israel in the Roman-Hellenistic and Byzantine Periods*. Jerusalem: Bialik Institute (Hebrew).

Barkai, Ron. 1987. *Science, Magic, and Mythology in the Middle Ages*. Jerusalem: Van Leer (Hebrew).

Barkay, Gabriel. 1989. "The Priestly Benediction of the Ketef Hinnom Plaques." *Cathedra* 52: 37–76 (Hebrew).

Barkay, Gabriel, Andrew G. Vaughn, Marilyn J. Lundberg, and Bruce Zuckerman. 2004. "The Amulets from Ketef Hinnom: A New Edition and Evaluation." *Bulletin of the American School of Oriental Research* 334: 41–71.

Bar-Kochva, Bezalel. 1996. *Pseudo-Hecataeus, "On the Jews": Legitimizing the Jewish Diaspora*. Berkeley: University of California Press.

Barton, Tamsyn. 1994. *Ancient Astrology*. London: Routledge.

Baumgarten, Joseph M. 1986. "The Qumran Songs Against Demons." *Tarbiz* 55: 442–45 (Hebrew).

———. 1991–1992. "On the Nature of the Seductress in 4Q184." *Revue de Qumran* 15: 133–43.

Bazak, Jacob. 1968a. "Cucumbers and Witchcraft." *Bar-Ilan: Annual of Bar-Ilan University Studies in Judaica and the Humanities* 6: 156–66 (Hebrew).

———. 1968b. "Hover Haver." *Sinai* 62: 167–71 (Hebrew).

———. 1972. *Judaism and Psychical Phenomena: A Study of Extrasensory Perception in Biblical, Talmudic, and Rabbinical Literature in the Light of Contemporary Parapsychological Research*, trans. Simon M. Lehrman. New York: Garret.

Beattie, John. 1964. *Other Cultures: Aims, Methods, and Achievements in Social Anthropology*. London: Cohen & West.

Beidelman, Thomas O. 1974a. *A Bibliography of the Writings of E. E. Evans-Pritchard*. London: Tavistock.

———. 1974b. "Sir Edward Evans-Pritchard (1902–1973): An Appreciation." *Anthropos* 69: 553–67.

———. 1974c. *W. Robertson Smith and the Sociological Study of Religion*. Chicago: University of Chicago Press.

Bellah, Robert N. 1964. "Religious Evolution." *American Sociological Review* 29: 358–74.

Bellusci, Alessia. 2011. "Dream Requests from the Cairo Genizah." M.A. thesis, Tel Aviv University.

Benayahu, Meir. 1972. "R. Yosheph Tirshom's *Sefer Shoshan Yesod Haolam*." In Israel Weinstock (ed.), *Temirin: Texts and Studies in Kabbalah and Hasidism*, 1: 187–269. Jerusalem: Mossad Harav Kook (Hebrew).

Benedict, Ruth. 1933. "Magic." In *The Encyclopedia of the Social Sciences*, 10: 39–44. New York: Macmillan.

———. 1938. "Religion." In Franz Boas (ed.), *General Anthropology*, 627–65. Boston: D. C. Heath.

Ben Naeh, Yaron. 2000. "'A Tried and Tested Spell': Magic Beliefs and Acts Among Ottoman Jews." *Pe'amim* 85: 89–111 (Hebrew).

Benoit, Pierre. 1951. "Fragment d'une prière contre les esprits impurs." *Revue Biblique* 58: 549–65.

Ben-Sasson, Menahem. 1996. *The Emergence of the Local Jewish Community in the Muslim World: Qayrawan, 800–1057.* Jerusalem: Magnes (Hebrew).

Ben Yehuda, Eliezer. 1948–1959. *A Complete Dictionary of Ancient and Modern Hebrew*, 16 vols. Tel Aviv: La'am (Hebrew).

Berchman, Robert M. 1998. "Arcana Mundi: Magic and Divination in the De Somiis of Philo of Alexandria." In Robert M. Berchman (ed.), *Mediators of the Divine: Horizons of Prophecy, Divination, Dreams, and Theurgy in Mediterranean Antiquity*, 115–54. Atlanta: Scholars Press.

Besnard, Philippe. 1938. *The Sociological Domain: The Durkheimians and the Founding of French Sociology.* Cambridge, UK: Cambridge University Press.

Betz, Hans D. 1982. "The Formation of Authoritative Tradition in the Greek Magical Papyri." In Ben F. Meyer and Ed P. Sanders (eds.), *Jewish and Christian Self-Definition*, vol. 3, *Self Definition in the Greco-Roman World*, 161–70. Philadelphia: Fortress Press.

———. 1986. *The Greek Magical Papyri in Translation.* Chicago: University of Chicago Press.

———. 1991. "Magic and Mystery in the Greek Magical Papyri." In Christopher A. Faraone and Dirk Obbink (eds.), *Magika Hiera: Ancient Greek Magic and Religion*, 244–59. New York: Oxford University Press.

Bever, Edward. 2012. "Current Trends in the Application of Cognitive Science to Magic." *Magic, Ritual, and Witchcraft* 7: 3–18.

Bilu, Yoram. 1982. "Pondering the 'Princes of the Oil': A Jewish Method of Divination as Hypnotic Induction." *Megamot* 27: 251–61 (Hebrew).

———. 2003. "*Dybbuk, Aslai, Zar*: The Cultural Distinctiveness and Historical Situatedness of Possession Illnesses in Three Jewish Milieus." In Matt Goldish (ed.), *Spirit Possession in Judaism: Cases and Contexts from the Middle Ages to the Present*, 346–65. Detroit: Wayne State University Press.

Blau, Ludwig. 1898. *Das Altjüdische Zauberwesen.* Budapest.

———. 1904. "Magic." In *Jewish Encyclopedia*, 8: 255–57. New York: Funk & Wagnalls.

Bleich, David J. 1993. "Maimonides on the Distinction Between Science and Pseudoscience." In Fred Rosner and Samuel S. Kottek (eds.), *Moses Maimonides: Physician, Scientist, and Philosopher*, 105–15. Northvale, NJ: J. Aronson.

Bohak, Gideon. 1997. "A Note on the Chnoubis Gem from Tel Dor." *Israel Exploration Journal* 47: 255–56.

———. 1999. "Greek, Coptic, and Jewish Magic in the Cairo Genizah." *Bulletin of the American Society of Papyrologists* 36: 27–44.

———. 2000. "Rabbinic Perspectives on Egyptian Religion." *Archiv für Religionsgeschichte* 2(2): 215–31.

———. 2003a. "Hebrew, Hebrew Everywhere?" In Scott Noegel, Joel Walker, and Brannon Wheeler (eds.), *Prayer, Magic, and the Stars in the Ancient and Late Antique World*, 69–82. University Park: Pennsylvania State University Press.

———. 2003b. "Magical Means for Handling *Minim* in Rabbinic Literature." In Peter J. Tomson and Doris Lambers-Petri (eds.), *The Image of the Judeo-Christians in Ancient Jewish and Christian Literature*, 267–79. Tübingen: Mohr Siebeck.

———. 2004a. "Art and Power in Ancient Magical Gems and Amulets." *Art and Culture Magazine* 12: 4–11.

———. 2004b. "A Jewish Myth in Pagan Magic in Antiquity." In Ithamar Gruenwald and Moshe Idel (eds.), *Myth in Judaism: History, Thought, Literature*, 97–122. Jerusalem: Zalman Shazar Center (Hebrew).

———. 2005. "Reconstructing Jewish Magical Recipe Books from the Cairo Genizah." *Ginzei Qedem* 1: 9*–29*.

———. 2006. "Babylonian Incantation Bowls: Past, Present and Future." Review of *A Corpus of Aramaic Magic Bowls: Incantation Bowls in Jewish Aramaic from Late Antiquity*, by Dan Levene. *Pe'amim* 105–106: 253–65 (Hebrew).

———. 2007. "Ancient Magic: Cross-Cultural Exchanges." *Zemanim* 100: 6–17 (Hebrew).

———. 2008. *Ancient Jewish Magic: A History*. Cambridge, UK: Cambridge University Press.

———. 2009a. "The Jewish Magical Tradition from Late Antique Palestine to the Cairo Genizah." In Hannah M. Cotton, Robert G. Hoyland, Jonathan J. Price, and David J. Wasserstein (eds.), *From*

Hellenism to Islam: Cultural and Linguistic Change in the Roman Near East, 324–42. Cambridge, UK: Cambridge University Press.

———. 2009b. "Prolegomena to the Study of the Jewish Magical Tradition." *Currents of Biblical Research* 8(1): 107–50.

———. 2009c. "Some 'Mass-Produced' Scorpion Amulets from the Cairo Genizah." In Zuleika Rogers, Margaret Daly-Danton, and Fitzpatrick McKinley (eds.), *A Wandering Galilean: Essays in Honour of Seán Freyne*, 36–49. Leiden: Brill.

———. 2010a. "Cracking the Code and Finding the Gold: A Dream Request from the Cairo Genizah." In Juan A. Álvarez-Pedrosa Núñez and Sofia T. Tovar (eds.), *Edición de Textos Mágicos de la Antigüedad y de la Edad Media*, 9–23. Madrid: Consejo Superior de Investigaciones Científicas.

———. 2010b. "Mezuzot with Magical Additions from the Cairo Genizah." *Diné Israel: Studies in Halakhah and Jewish Law* 26–27: 387–403 (Hebrew).

———. 2010c. "Towards a Catalogue of the Magical, Astrological, Divinatory, and Alchemical Fragments from the Cambridge Genizah Collections." In Ben Outhwaite and Siam Bhayro (eds.), *"From a Sacred Source": Genizah Studies in Honour of Professor Stefan C. Reif*, 53–79. Leiden: Brill.

———. 2011a. "The Charaktêres in Ancient and Medieval Jewish Magic." *Acta Classica: universitatis scientiarum Debreceniensis* 47: 25–44.

———. 2011b. "The Magical Rotuli from the Cairo Genizah." In Gideon Bohak, Yuval Harari, and Shaul Shaked (eds.), *Continuity and Innovation in the Magical Tradition*, 321–40. Leiden: Brill.

———. 2012a. "Ancient Jewish Magic." *Oxford Bibliographies in Jewish Studies.* www.oxfordbibliographies.com/view/document/obo-9780199840731/obo-9780199840731-0022.xml?rskey=RdzFlY&result=1&q=Ancient+Jewish+Magic#firstMatch (accessed January 4, 2016).

———. 2012b. "From Qumran to Cairo: The Lives and Times of a Jewish Exorcistic Formula." In Ildiko Csepregi and Charles Burnett (eds.), *Ritual Healing: Magic, Ritual, and Medical Therapy from Antiquity Until the Early Modern Period*, 31–52. Florence: SISMEL edizioni del Galluzzo.

————. 2012c. "Gershom Scholem and Jewish Magic." *Kabbalah* 28: 141–62 (Hebrew).

————. 2012d. "Jewish Exorcism Before and After the Destruction of the Second Temple." In Daniel R. Schwartz and Zeev Weiss (eds.), *Was 70 CE a Watershed in Jewish History? On Jews and Judaism Before and After the Destruction of the Second Temple*, 277–300. Leiden: Brill.

————. 2014a. *A Fifteenth-Century Manuscript of Jewish Magic: MS New York Public Library, Heb 190 (Formerly Sassoon 56)—Introduction, Annotated Edition, and Facsimile*, 2 vols. Los Angeles: Cherub.

————. 2014b. "Hekhalot Genuzim: Reconstructing a New Hekhalot Text from the Cairo Genizah." *Tarbiz* 82: 407–46 (Hebrew).

Bokser, Baruch M. 1985. "Wonder-Working and the Rabbinic Tradition: The Case of Hanina ben Dosa." *Journal for the Study of Judaism* 16: 42–92.

Bolle, Kees W. 1987. "Animism and Animatism." In *The Encyclopedia of Religion*, 1: 296–302. New York: Macmillan.

Bonfil, Robert. 2009. *History and Folklore in a Medieval Jewish Chronicle: The Family Chronicle of Aḥima'az ben Paltiel*. Leiden: Brill.

Bonner, Campbell. 1950. *Studies in Magical Amulets, Chiefly Graeco-Egyptian*. Ann Arbor: University of Michigan Press.

Bouché-Leclercq, Auguste. 1963a. *L'Astrologie Grecque*. Paris: Culture et Civilisation.

————. 1963b. *Histoire de la divination dans l'antiquité*, 4 vols. Brussels: Culture et Civilisation.

Boustan, Ra'anan S. 2005. *From Martyr to Mystic: Rabbinic Martyrology and the Making of Merkavah Mysticism*. Tübingen: Mohr Siebeck.

Boustan, Ra'anan, Martha Himmelfarb, and Peter Schäfer (eds.). 2013. *Hekhalot Literature in Context: Between Byzantium and Babylonia*. Tübingen: Mohr Siebeck.

Bow, Beverly A., and George W. E. Nickelsburg. 1991. "Patriarchy with a Twist: Men and Women in Tobit." In Amy-Jill Levine (ed.), *"Women Like This": New Perspectives on Jewish Women in the Greco-Roman World*, 127–43. Atlanta: Scholars Press.

Bram, Jean R. 1976. "Fate and Freedom: Astrology vs. Mystery Religions." In George McRae (ed.), *Society of Biblical Literature 1976 Seminar Papers*, 326–30. Missoula, MT: Scholars Press.

Brandewie, Ernst. 1983. *Wilhelm Schmidt and the Origin of the Idea of God.* Lanham, MD: University Press of America.

Brandt, Richard B. 1967. "Ethical Relativism." In *The Encyclopedia of Philosophy*, 3: 75–78. New York: Macmillan.

Brashear, William M. 1995. "The Greek Magical Papyri: An Introduction and Survey—Annotated Bibliography (1928–1994)." In W. Haase (ed.), *Aufstieg und Niedergang der Römischen Welt*, pt. II, 18.5: 3380–3684. Berlin: de Gruyter.

Brecher, Gideon. 1850. *Das Transcendentale, Magie und Magische Heilarten im Talmud.* Vienna: Typ. U. Klopf und A. Euric.

Bremmer, Jan N. 2002. "The Birth of the Term 'Magic.'" In Jan N. Bremmer and Jan R. Veenstra (eds.), *The Metamorphosis of Magic: From Late Antiquity to the Early Modern Period*, 1–11. Leuven: Peeters.

Brock, Sebastian. 1989. Review of *Incantations magiques syriaques* by Philippe Gignoux. *Journal of Jewish Studies* 40: 121–24.

Brown, Peter. 1970. "Sorcery, Demons, and the Rise of Christianity from Late Antiquity into the Middle Ages." In Mary Douglas (ed.), *Witchcraft, Confessions, and Accusations*, 17–45. London: Tavistock.

Budge, Ernst A. W. 1934. *From Fetish to God in Ancient Egypt.* Oxford: Oxford University Press.

———. 1991. *Egyptian Magic.* New York: Random House.

Burkert, Walter. 1987. *Ancient Mystery Cults.* Cambridge, MA: Harvard University Press.

———. 1995. *The Orientalizing Revolution: Near Eastern Influence on Greek Culture in the Early Archaic Age*, trans. Margaret E. Pinder and Walter Burkert. Cambridge, MA: Harvard University Press.

Burn, Andrew. 1966. *The World of Hesiod.* New York: B. Blom.

Caro-Baroja, Julio. 1971. *The World of the Witches*, trans. Nigel Glendinning. Chicago: Chicago University Press.

Cazeneuve, Jean. 1972. *Lucien Lévy-Bruhl*, trans. Peter Rivière. Oxford: Blackwell.

Chajes, Jeffrey H. 2003. *Between Worlds: Dybbuks, Exorcists, and Early Modern Judaism.* Philadelphia: University of Pennsylvania Press.

Charlesworth, James H. 1983. *The Old Testament Pseudepigrapha.* Garden City, NY: Doubleday.

————. 1987. "Jewish Interest in Astrology During the Hellenistic and Roman Period." In W. Haase (ed.), *Aufstieg und Niedergang der Römischen Welt*, pt. II, 20.2: 926–50. Berlin: de Gruyter.

Chazon, Esther. 1999. "4QIncantation." In Esther G. Chazon et al. (eds.), *Qumran Cave 4.20: Poetical and Liturgical Texts, Part 2*, 367–78. Discoveries in the Judaean Desert 29. Oxford: Oxford University Press.

Chesterton, Gilbert. 1905. *Heretics*. New York: J. Lane.

Cioffi, Frank. 1998. *Wittgenstein on Freud and Frazer*. Cambridge, UK: Cambridge University Press.

Clack, Brian R. 1999. *Wittgenstein, Frazer, and Religion*. New York: Palgrave.

————. 2001. "Wittgenstein and Magic." In Robert L. Arrington and Mark Addis (eds.), *Wittgenstein and Philosophy of Religion*, 12–28. London: Routledge.

Clifford, James, and George E. Marcus (eds.). 1986. *Writing Culture: The Poetics and Politics of Ethnography*. Berkeley: University of California Press.

Cohen, Abraham. 1978. *Everyman's Talmud*. New York: Schocken.

Cohen, Shaye J. D. 1981. "Epigraphical Rabbis." *Jewish Quarterly Review* 72: 1–17.

Collins, John J. 1978. "Methodological Issues in the Study of 1 Enoch: Reflections on the Articles of P. D. Hanson and G. W. Nickelsburg." In Paul J. Achtemeier (ed.), *Society of Biblical Literature Seminar Papers*, 1: 315–22. Missoula, MT: Scholars Press.

Cowley, Arthur E. 1915. "Notes on Hebrew Papyrus Fragments." *Journal of Egyptian Archaeology* 2: 209–13.

Cox Miller, Patricia. 1994. *Dreams in Late Antiquity: Studies in the Imagination of a Culture*. Princeton, NJ: Princeton University Press.

Cramer, Frederick H. 1954. *Astrology in Roman Law and Politics*. Philadelphia: American Philosophical Society.

Crawford. J. R. 1967. *Witchcraft and Sorcery in Rhodesia*. London: International African Institute.

Crawley, Ernest. 1909. *The Idea of the Soul*. London: A. and C. Black.

Cryer, Frederick H. 1994. *Divination in Ancient Israel and Its Near Eastern Environment*. Sheffield, UK: JSOT Press.

————. 2001. "Magic in Ancient Syria-Palestine and in the Old Testament." In Bengt Ankarloo and Stuart Clark (eds.), *Witchcraft and*

Magic in Europe: Biblical and Pagan Societies, 97–152. Philadelphia: University of Pennsylvania Press.

Cumont, Franz. 1960. *Astrology and Religion Among the Greeks and the Romans*. New York: Dover.

Cunningham, Graham. 1999. *Religion and Magic: Approaches and Theories*. Edinburgh: Edinburgh University Press.

Curbera, Jaime B. 1999. "Maternal Lineage in Greek Magical Texts." In David R. Jordan, Hugo Montgomery, and Einar Thomassen (eds.), *The World of Ancient Magic*, 195–303. Bergen: Norwegian Institute at Athens.

Daiches, Samuel. 1913. *Babylonian Oil Magic in the Talmud and in Later Jewish Literature*. London: Jews' College Publications.

D'Alviella, Goblet C. 1951. "Animism." In *Encyclopedia of Religion and Ethics*, 1: 535–37. New York: C. Scribner's Sons.

Dan, Joseph. 1963. "The Princes of Thumb and Cup." *Tarbiz* 32: 359–69 (Hebrew).

———. 1968. Review of *Sepher ha-Razim*, edited by Mordechai Margalioth. *Tarbiz* 37: 208–14 (Hebrew).

———. 1981. "The Beginnings of Jewish Hagiographic Literature." *Jerusalem Studies in Jewish Folklore* 1: 82–101 (Hebrew).

———. 1986. "Hagiographic Literature: East and West." *Pe'amim* 26: 77–86 (Hebrew).

———. 1987a. "The Entrance to the Sixth Gate." *Jerusalem Studies in Jewish Thought* 6: 197–220 (Hebrew).

———. 1987b. "The Religious Experience of the Merkavah." In Arthur Green (ed.), *Jewish Spirituality*, 1: 289–307. New York: Crossroad.

———. 1992a. "The Beginning of Ancient Jewish Mysticism." *Daat* 29: 5–25 (Hebrew).

———. 1992b. "Theophany of the Prince of the Torah: Narrative, Magic, and Mysticism in *Merkabah* Literature." *Jerusalem Studies in Jewish Folklore* 13–14: 127–57.

———. 1993. *The Ancient Jewish Mysticism*, trans. Shmuel Himmelstein. Tel-Aviv: MOD.

———. 1995. "The Mystical 'Descenders to the Chariot' in Historical Context." *Zion* 60: 179–99 (Hebrew).

———. 1996. "The Concept of the Pleroma in *Hekhalot* Mystical Literature." In Joseph Dan and Rachel Elior (eds.), *Kolot Rabim: Rivkah*

Shatz-Uffenheimer Memorial Volume, 1: 61–140. Jerusalem: Institute of Jewish Studies (Hebrew).

———. 1998. *On Sanctity: Religion, Ethics, and Mysticism in Judaism and Other Religions*. Jerusalem: Magnes (Hebrew).

———. 1998–1999. *Jewish Mysticism*, 4 vols. Northvale, NJ: J. Aronson.

———. 2008–2014. *History of Jewish Mysticism and Esotericism*, 10 vols. Jerusalem: Zalman Shazar Center (Hebrew).

Daniel, Robert W., and Franco Maltomini (eds.). 1990–1992. *Papyrologica Coloniesia*, vol. 16.2, *Supplementum Magicum* I and II. Opladen, Germany: Westdeutscher Verlag.

Dauphin, Claudine. 1993. "A Greco-Egyptian Magical Amulet from Mazzuvah." *Atiqot* 22: 145–47.

———. 1998. *La Palestine byzantine: Peuplement et Population*, 3 vols. Oxford: Archaeopress.

Davie, Grace. 2007. *The Sociology of Religion*. London: Sage.

Davila, James R. 2001. *Descenders to the Chariot: The People Behind the Hekhalot Literature*. Leiden: Brill.

———. 2013. *Hekhalot Literature in Translation: Major Texts of Merkavah Mysticism*. Leiden: Brill.

Davis, Eli, and David A. Frenkel. 1995. *The Hebrew Amulet: Biblical-Medical-General*. Jerusalem: Institute for Jewish Studies (Hebrew).

Davis, Winston. 1987. "Sociology of Religion." In *The Encyclopedia of Religion*, 13: 393–401. New York: Macmillan.

Dean-Otting, Mary. 1984. *Heavenly Journeys: A Study of the Motif in Hellenistic Jewish Literature*. Frankfurt am Main: P. Lang.

Deines, Roland. 2003. "Josephus, Salomo und die von Gott verliehene τέχνη gegen die Dämonen." In Armin Lange, Hermann Lichtenberger, and K. F. Diethard Römheld (eds.), *Die Dämonen: Die Dämonologie der israelitisch-jüdischen und frühchristlichen Literatur im Kontext ihrer Umwelt*, 365–94. Tübingen: Mohr Siebeck.

De Jong, Albert. 1997. *Traditions of the Magi: Zoroastrianism in Greek and Latin Literature*. Leiden: Brill.

Derrida, Jacques. 1977. "Signature Event Context." *Glyph* 1: 172–97.

Dickie, Matthew W. 2001. *Magic and Magicians in the Greco-Roman World*. London: Routledge.

Dieleman, Jacco. 2005. *Priests, Tongues, and Rites: The London-Leiden Magical Manuscripts and Translation in Egyptian Ritual (100–300 CE)*. Leiden: Brill.

Dimant, Devorah. 1974. "'The Fallen Angels' in the Dead Sea Scrolls." Ph.D. diss., The Hebrew University of Jerusalem (Hebrew).

———. 1983. "The Biography of Enoch and the Books of Enoch." *Vetus Testamentum* 33: 14–29.

Dodds, Eric R. 1959. *The Greeks and the Irrational*. Berkeley: University of California Press.

———. 1973. *The Ancient Concept of Progress and Other Essays on Greek Literature and Belief*. Oxford: Clarendon Press.

Douglas, Mary. 1980. *Edward Evans-Pritchard: His Life, Work, Writings, and Ideas*. New York: Viking Press.

———. 2002. *Purity and Danger: An Analysis of Concepts of Pollution and Taboo*. London: Routledge.

———. 2003. *Natural Symbols: Explorations in Cosmology*. London: Routledge.

Duling, Dennis C. 1975. "Solomon, Exorcism, and the Son of David." *Harvard Theological Review* 68: 235–52.

———. 1983. "Testament of Solomon." In James H. Charlesworth (ed.), *The Old Testament Pseudepigrapha*, 1: 935–87. Garden City, NY: Doubleday.

———. 1985. "The Elazar Miracle and Solomon's Magical Wisdom in Flavius Josephus's *Antiquitates Judaicae* 8.42–49." *Harvard Theological Review* 78: 1–25.

Duppont-Sommer, André. 1950–1951. "Deux lamelles d'argent à inscription Hébréo-Araméenne trouvée à Agabeyli (Turki)." *Jahrbuch für Kleinasiatische Forschung* 1: 201–17.

Durkheim, Émile. 1967 [1912]. *The Elementary Forms of the Religious Life*, trans. Joseph W. Swain. New York: Free Press.

Edelstein, Monika D. 2001. "Zar Spirit Possession Among Ethiopian Jews in Israel: Discourses and Performances in Religious Identity." Ph.D. diss., Tulane University.

———. 2002. "Lost Tribes and Coffee Ceremonies: 'Zar' Spirit Possession and the Ethno-Religious Identity of Ethiopian Jews in Israel." *Journal of Refugee Studies* 15: 153–70.

Efron, Joshua. 1988. "The Deed of Simon of Shatah in Ascalon." In Aryeh Kasher (ed.), *Canaan, Philistia, Greece, and Israel: Relations of the Jews in Eretz-Israel with the Hellenistic Cities (332 BCE–70 CE)*, 298–320. Jerusalem: Yad Izhak Ben-Zvi (Hebrew).

Ego, Beate. 2003. "'Denn er liebst sie' (Tob. 6:15 MS. 319): Zur Rolle des Dämons Asmodäus in der Tobit-Erzählung." In Armin Lange, Hermann Lichtenberger, and K. F. Diethard Römheld (eds.), *Die Dämonen: Die Dämonologie der israelitisch-jüdischen und frühchristlichen Literatur im Kontext ihrer Umwelt*, 309–17. Tübingen: Mohr Siebeck.

Eiseley, Loren C. 1958. *Darwin's Century: Evolution and the Men Who Discovered It*. Garden City, NY: Doubleday.

Elgavish, Joseph. 1994. *Shiqmona: On the Seacoast of Mount Carmel*. Tel Aviv: Hakibbuz Hameuchad (Hebrew).

Elior, Rachel. 1987. "The Concept of God in Hekhalot Literature." *Jerusalem Studies in Jewish Thought* 6: 13–64 (Hebrew).

———. 1993. "Mysticism, Magic, and Angelology: The Perception of Angels in *Hekhalot* Literature." *Jewish Studies Quarterly* 1: 3–53.

———. 1997. "From Earthly Temple to Heavenly Shrines: Prayer and Sacred Song in the *Hekhalot* Literature and Its Relation to Temple Traditions." *Jewish Studies Quarterly* 4: 217–67.

———. 1998. "The Various Faces of Freedom: Studies in Jewish Mysticism." *Alpayim* 15: 9–119 (Hebrew).

———. 2004a. *Hekhalot Literature and Merkavah Tradition: Ancient Jewish Mysticism and Its Sources*. Tel Aviv: Yediot Aharonot (Hebrew).

———. 2004b. *The Three Temples: On the Emergence of Jewish Mysticism in Late Antiquity*, trans. David Louvish. Oxford: Littman Library of Jewish Civilization.

Elkayam, Abraham. 1990. "Between Referentialism and Performativism: Two Approaches to the Understanding of the Kabbalistic Symbol." *Daat* 24: 5–40 (Hebrew).

Ellegard, Alvar. 1990. *Darwin and the General Reader: The Reception of Darwin's Theory of Evolution in the British Periodical Press, 1859–1872*. Chicago: University of Chicago Press.

Elliot, Hugh. 1951. "Spencer, Herbert." In *Encyclopedia of Religion and Ethics*, 11: 764–67. New York: C. Scribner's Sons.

Elman, Yaakov. 2004. "Acculturation to Elite Persian Norms and Modes of Thought in the Babylonian Jewish Community of Late Antiquity." In Yaakov Elman, Bezalel Halivni, and Zvi A. Steinfeld (eds.), *Neti'ot Ledavid: Jubilee Volume for David Weiss Halivni*, 31–56. Jerusalem: Orhot.

Emanuel, Simchah. 1995. *Newly Discovered Geonic Responsa*. Jerusalem: Ofeq Institute (Hebrew).

Englard, Yaffa. 2000. "The Eschatological Significance of the Zodiac in the Mosaic Pavements of Ancient Synagogues in Israel." *Cathedra* 98: 33–48 (Hebrew).

Epstein, Jacob N. 1921. "Gloses babylo-araméennes." *Revue des études juives* 73: 27–58.

———. 1922. "Gloses babylo-araméennes." *Revue des études juives* 74: 40–72.

Eshel, Esther. 1999. "Demonology in Palestine During the Second Temple Period." Ph.D. diss., The Hebrew University of Jerusalem (Hebrew).

———. 2003. "Genres of Magical Texts in the Dead Sea Scrolls." In Armin Lange, Hermann Lichtenberger, and K. F. Diethard Römheld (eds.), *Die Dämonen: Die Dämonologie der israelitisch-jüdischen und frühchristlichen Literatur im Kontext ihrer Umwelt*, 395–415. Tübingen: Mohr Siebeck.

Eshel, Esther, Hanan Eshel, and Armin Lange. 2010. "'Hear, O Israel' in Gold: An Ancient Amulet from Halbturn in Austria." *Journal of Ancient Judaism* 1: 43–64.

Eshel, Hanan, and Rivka Leiman. 2010. "Jewish Amulets Written on Metal Scrolls." *Journal of Ancient Judaism* 1: 189–99.

Evans-Pritchard, Edward E. 1929. "The Morphology and Function of Magic: A Comparative Study of Trobriand and Zande Ritual and Spells." *American Anthropologist*, n.s., 31: 619–41. Reprinted in John Middleton (ed.), *Magic, Witchcraft, and Curing*, 1–22 (Garden City, NY: Natural History Press, 1967).

———. 1931. "Sorcery and Native Opinion." *Africa* 4: 22–55.

———. 1933. "The Intellectualist (English) Interpretation of Magic." *Bulletin of the Faculty of Arts (The Egyptian University)* 1: 282–311.

———. 1937. *Witchcraft, Oracles, and Magic Among the Azande*. Oxford: Clarendon Press.

————. 1951. *Social Anthropology*. London: Cohen & West.

————. 1956. *Nuer Religion*. Oxford: Oxford University Press.

————. 1965. *Theories of Primitive Religion*. Oxford: Clarendon Press.

————. 1970. "Lévy-Bruhl's Theory of Primitive Mentality." *Journal of the Anthropological Society of Oxford* 1: 39–60.

————. 1981. *A History of Anthropological Thought*. London: Faber & Faber.

Even-Shoshan, Avraham. 1988. *The New Dictionary*. Jerusalem: Kiryat Sefer (Hebrew).

Fallding, Harold. 1974. *The Sociology of Religion: An Explanation of the Unity and Diversity in Religion*. Toronto: McGraw-Hill Ryerson.

Faraone, Christopher A. 1991. "The Agonistic Context of Early Greek Binding Spells." In Christopher A. Faraone and Dirk Obbink (eds.), *Magika Hiera: Ancient Greek Magic and Religion*, 3–32. New York: Oxford University Press.

————. 1992. *Talismans and Trojan Horses*. New York: Oxford University Press.

————. 1993. "Molten Wax, Spilt Wine, and Mutilated Animals: Sympathetic Magic in Near Eastern and Early Greek Oath Ceremonies." *Journal of Hellenic Studies* 113: 60–80.

————. 1999. *Ancient Greek Love Magic*. Cambridge, MA: Harvard University Press.

————. 2011. "Magic and Medicine in the Roman Imperial Period: Two Case Studies." In Gideon Bohak, Yuval Harari, and Shaul Shaked (eds.), *Continuity and Innovation in the Magical Tradition*, 135–56. Leiden: Brill.

Fauth, Wolfgang. 1986. "Lilits und Astarten in aramäischen, mandäischen und syrischen Zaubertexten." *Die Welt des Orients* 17: 66–94.

Favret-Saada, Jeanne. 1980. *Deadly Words: Witchcraft in the Bocage*, trans. Catherine Cullen. Cambridge, UK: Cambridge University Press.

Feldheim, Louis H. 1971. "Prolegomenon." In Montague R. James, trans., *The Biblical Antiquities of Philo*, ix–clxix. New York: Ktav.

Ferguson, Everett. 1984. *Demonology of the Early Christian World*. New York: E. Mellen.

Ferguson, John. 1989. *Among the Gods*. London: Routledge.

Fidler, Ruth. 2005. *"Dreams Speak Falsely"? Dream Theophanies in the Bible*. Jerusalem: Magnes (Hebrew).

Finnegan, Ruth. 1969. "How to Do Things with Words: Performative Utterances Among the Limba of Sierra Leone." *Man*, n.s., 4: 537–52.

Firth, Raymond W. 1956. *Human Types: An Introduction to Social Anthropology*. London: Thomas Nelson.

———. 1957. *Man and Culture: An Evaluation of the Work of Bronislaw Malinowski*. London: Routledge & Kegan Paul.

———. 1967. *Tikopia Ritual and Belief.* Boston: Beacon Press.

Fishbane, Simcha. 1993. "'Most Women Engage in Sorcery': An Analysis of Sorceresses in the Babylonian Talmud." *Jewish History* 7: 27–42.

Fitzmyer, Joseph A. 1995a. "The Aramaic and Hebrew Fragments of Tobit from Qumran Cave 4." *Catholic Biblical Quarterly* 57: 655–75.

———. 1995b. "Tobit." In Magen Broshi et al. (eds.), *Qumran Cave 4:14: Parabiblical Texts, Part 2*, 1–76. Discoveries in the Judaean Desert 19. Oxford: Clarendon Press.

———. 2004. *The Genesis Apocryphon of Qumran Cave 1 (1Q20)*. Rome: Editrice Pontificio Istituto Biblico.

Flint, Valerie I. J. 1991. *The Rise of Magic in Early Medieval Europe*. Oxford: Clarendon Press.

Flusser, David. 1979. *Jewish Sources in Early Christianity: Studies and Essays*. Tel Aviv: Sifriyat Hapoalim (Hebrew).

Foerster, Gideon. 1987. "The Zodiac in Ancient Synagogues and Its Place in Jewish Thought and Literature." *Eretz Israel* 19: 225–34 (Hebrew).

Ford, James N. 1998. "'Ninety-Nine by the Evil Eye and One from Natural Causes': KTU2 1.96 in Its Near Eastern Context." *Ugarit-Forschungen* 30: 201–78.

———. 2000. "Additions and Corrections to Ninety-Nine by the Evil Eye." *Ugarit-Forschungen* 32: 711–15.

———. 2002. Review of *Catalogue of the Aramaic and Mandaic Incantation Bowls in the British Museum* by J. B. Segal. *Jerusalem Studies in Arabic and Islam* 26: 237–72.

Ford, James N., and Alon Ten-Ami. 2012. "An Incantation Bowl for Rav Mešaršia Son of Qaqay." *Tarbiz* 80: 219–30 (Hebrew).

Fowden, Garth. 1993. *The Egyptian Hermes*. Princeton, NJ: Princeton University Press.

Franco, Fulvio. 1978–1979. "Five Aramaic Incantation Bowls from Tell Baruda (Choche)." *Mesopotamia* 13–14: 233–49.

Frankfurter, David. 1994. "The Magic of Writing and the Writing of Magic: The Power of the Word in Egyptian and Greek Traditions." *Helios* 21: 189–221.

———. 1995. "Narrating Power: The Theory and Practice of the Magical Historiola in Ritual Spells." In Marvin Meyer and Paul Mirecki (eds.), *Ancient Magic and Ritual Power*, 457–476. Leiden: Brill.

———. 2001. "The Perils of Love: Magic and Countermagic in Coptic Egypt." *Journal of the History of Sexuality* 10: 480–500.

———. 2015. "Scorpion/Demon: On the Origin of the Mesopotamian Apotropaic Bowl." *Journal of Near Eastern Studies* 74: 9–18.

Frazer, James G. 1900. *The Golden Bough: A Study in Magic and Religion*, rev. ed. London: Macmillan.

———. 1905. *Lectures on the Early History of the Kingship*. London: Macmillan.

———. 1925. *The Golden Bough: A Study in Magic and Religion*, abridged ed. London: Macmillan.

Frenkel, Jonah. 1981. *Studies in the Spiritual World of the Talmudic Aggadah*. Tel Aviv: Hakibbutz Hameuchad (Hebrew).

Freud, Sigmund. 1985 [1913]. "Totem and Taboo." In *The Origins of Religion: Totem and Taboo, Moses and Monotheism, and Other Works*, trans. James Strachey, 43–224. London: Penguin.

Freudenthal, Gad. 1993. "Maimonides' Stance on Astrology in Context: Cosmology, Physics, Medicine, and Providence." In Fred Rosner and Samuel S. Kottek (eds.), *Moses Maimonides: Physician, Scientist, and Philosopher*, 77–90. Northvale, NJ: J. Aronson.

Gafni, Isaiah. 1990. *The Jews of Babylonia in the Talmudic Era*. Jerusalem: Zalman Shazar Center (Hebrew).

———. 2002. "Babylonian Rabbinic Culture." In David Biale (ed.), *Cultures of the Jews: A New History*, 244–50. New York: Schocken.

Gager, John G. 1972. *Moses in Greco-Roman Paganism*. Nashville: Abingdon Press.

———. 1992. *Curse Tablets and Binding Spells from the Ancient World*. Oxford: Oxford University Press.

———. 1994. "Moses the Magician: Hero of an Ancient Counter-Culture?" *Helios* 21: 179–88.

Garb, Jonathan. 2005. *Manifestations of Power in Jewish Mysticism: From Rabbinic Literature to Safedian Kabbalah*. Jerusalem: Magnes (Hebrew).

Gardiner, Alan H. (ed.). 1935. *Hieratic Papyri in the British Museum: Third Series—Chester Beatty Gift*. London: British Museum.

———. 1951. "Magic, Egyptian." In *Encyclopedia of Religion and Ethics*, 8: 262–69. New York: C. Scribner's Sons.

Gaster, Moses. 1971a [1896]. "The Sword of Moses." In Moses Gaster, *Studies and Texts in Folklore, Magic, Mediaeval Romance, Hebrew Apocrypha, and Samaritan Archaeology*, 1: 288–337; 3: 69–103. London: Maggs.

———. 1971b. "Two Thousand Years of a Charm Against the Child-Stealing Witch." In Moses Gaster, *Studies and Texts in Folklore, Magic, Mediaeval Romance, Hebrew Apocrypha, and Samaritan Archaeology*, 2: 1005–38. London: Maggs.

Gaudant, Mireille, and Jean Gaudant. 1971. *Les théories classiques de l'evolution*. Paris: Dunod.

Geertz, Clifford. 1973. *The Interpretation of Cultures: Selected Essays*. New York: Basic Books.

———. 1988a. *Local Knowledge*. New York: Basic Books.

———. 1988b. *Works and Lives: The Anthropologist as Author*. Stanford, CA: Stanford University Press.

Geller, Markham J. 1985. "An Aramaic Incantation from Oxyrhynchus." *Zeitschrift für Papyrologie und Epigraphik* 58: 96–98.

———. 1991. "Akkadian Medicine in the Babylonian Talmud." In Dan Cohn-Sherbok (ed.), *A Traditional Quest: Essays in Honour of Louis Jacobs*, 102–12. Sheffield, UK: JSOT Press.

———. 1997. "More Magic Spells and Formulae." *Bulletin of the School of Oriental and African Studies* 60: 327–35.

———. 2000. "An Akkadian Vademecum in the Babylonian Talmud." In Samuel Kottek and Manfred Horstmanshoff (eds.), *From Athens to Jerusalem: Medicine in Hellenized Jewish Lore and in Early Christian Literature*, 13–32. Rotterdam: Erasmus.

———. 2010. *Ancient Babylonian Medicine: Theory and Practice*. Malden, MA: Wiley-Blackwell.

Gellman, Jerome I. 1991. "Maimonides' 'Ravings.'" *Review of Metaphysics* 45: 309–28.

Gerth, H. H., and Wright C. Mills (eds. and trans.). 1958. *From Max Weber: Essays in Sociology*. New York: Oxford University Press.

Gibson, McGuire, James A. Armstrong, and Augusta McMahon. 1998. "The City Walls of Nippur and an Islamic Site Beyond: Oriental Institute Excavations, 17th Season, 1987." *Iraq* 60: 11–29.

Gibson, McGuire, J. A. Franke, M. Civil, M. L. Bates, J. Boessneck, K. W. Butzer, T. A. Rathbun, and E. F. Mallin. 1978. *Excavations at Nippur: Twelfth Season.* Chicago: Oriental Institute, University of Chicago.

Gignoux, Philippe. 1987. *Incantations magiques syriaques.* Louvain: E. Peeters.

Gil, Moshe. 1989. "Augures, *Meonenim,* and More." In Zeev Robinson and Hanah Roisman (eds.), *Perlman Book: Studies in Classic Culture,* 74–87. Tel Aviv: Tel Aviv University Press (Hebrew).

Gill, Sam D. 1978. "Prayer as Person: The Performative Force in Navajo Prayer Acts." *History of Religions* 17: 143–57.

Glass, Bentley, Owsei Temkin, and William M. Straus (eds.). 1959. *Forerunners of Darwin, 1745–1859.* Baltimore: Johns Hopkins University Press.

Glick, Thomas F. (ed.). 1975. *The Comparative Reception of Darwinism.* Austin: University of Texas Press.

Gnuse, Robert K. 1984. *The Dream Theophany of Samuel: Its Structure in Relation to Ancient Near Eastern Dreams and Its Theological Significance.* New York: University Press of America.

Goitein, Shlomo D. 1967–1993. *A Mediterranean Society: The Jewish Communities of the Arab World as Portrayed in the Documents of the Cairo Geniza,* 5 vols. Berkeley: University of California Press.

Golb, Norman. 1967. "Aspects of the Historical Background of Jewish Life in Medieval Egypt." In Alexander Altman (ed.), *Jewish Medieval and Renaissance Studies,* 1–18. Cambridge, MA: Harvard University Press.

Goldin, Judah. 1976. "The Magic of Magic and Superstition." In Elisabeth Schüssler Fiorenza (ed.), *Aspects of Religious Propaganda in Judaism and Early Christianity,* 115–47. Notre Dame, IN: University of Notre Dame Press.

Goldish, Natt (ed.). 2003. *Spirit Possession in Judaism: Cases and Contexts from the Middle Ages to the Present.* Detroit: Wayne State University Press.

Golinkin, David. 2002. "The Use of Matronymic in Prayers for the Sick." *These Are the Names* 3: 59–72.

Goode, William J. 1949. "Magic and Religion: A Continuum." *Ethnos* 14: 172–82.

———. 1951. *Religion Among the Primitives*. Glencoe, IL: Free Press.

Goodenough, Erwin R. 1953–1968. *Jewish Symbols in the Greco-Roman Period*, 11 vols. New York: Pantheon.

Gordon, Cyrus H. 1934a. "An Aramaic Exorcism." *Archiv Orientální* 6: 466–74.

———. 1934b. "Aramaic Magical Bowls in the Istanbul and Baghdad Museums." *Archiv Orientální* 6: 319–34.

———. 1951. "Two Magic Bowls in Teheran." *Orientalia* 20: 306–15.

———. 1957. *Adventures in the Nearest East*. London: Phoenix House.

———. 1964. "Incantation Bowls from Knosos and Nippur." *American Journal of Archeology* 68: 194–95.

Gottheil, Richard, and William H. Worrel. 1972. *Fragments from the Cairo Genizah in the Freer Collection*. New York: Macmillan.

Gough, Kathleen. 1968. "New Proposals for Anthropologists." *Current Anthropology* 9: 403–7.

Graf, Fritz. 1991. "Prayer in Magic and Religious Ritual." In Christopher A. Faraone and Dirk Obbink (eds.), *Magika Hiera: Ancient Greek Magic and Religion*, 188–213. New York: Oxford University Press.

———. 1997. *Magic in the Ancient World*, trans. Franklin Philip. Cambridge, MA: Harvard University Press.

Green, William S. 1979. "Palestinian Holy Men: Charismatic Leadership and Rabbinic Tradition." In W. Haase (ed.), *Aufstieg und Niedergang der Römischen Welt*, pt. II, 19.2: 619–47. Berlin: de Gruyter.

Greenberg, Moshe. 1991. "Nebuchadnezzar and the Parting of the Ways: Ezek. 21:26–27." *Scripta Hierosolymitana* 33: 267–71.

Greenfield, Jonas C. 1980. "The Genesis Apocryphon: Observations on Some Words and Phrases." In Gad B. Sarfatti, Pinhas Artzi, Jonas C. Greenfield, and Menahem Kaddari (eds.), *Studies in Hebrew and Semitic Languages, Dedicated to the Memory of Eduard Yechezkel Kutcher*, 32–39. Ramat-Gan: Bar-Ilan University Press.

Greenfield, Jonas C., and Joseph Naveh. 1985. "A Mandaic Lead Amulet with Four Incantations." *Eretz Israel* 18: 97–107 (Hebrew).

Greenfield, Jonas C., and Michael Sokoloff. 1995. "An Astrological Text from Qumran (4Q 318) and Reflections on Some Zodiacal Names." *Revue de Qumran* 16: 507–25.

Greenfield, Jonas C., and Michael E. Stone. 1977. "The Enochic Pentateuch and the Date of the Similitudes." *Harvard Theological Review* 70: 51–65.

Griffith, Francis, and Herbert Thompson. 1974. *The Leiden Papyrus: An Egyptian Magic Book*. New York: Dover.

Grisaru, Nimrod, and Eliezer Witztum. 1995. "The *Zar* Phenomenon Amongst Ethiopian New Immigrants to Israel: Cultural and Clinical Aspects." *Sihot: Dialogue* 9: 209–20 (Hebrew).

Gross, Moshe D. 1993. *The Treasure of Aggadah*. Jerusalem: Mossad Harav Kook (Hebrew).

Gruenwald, Ithamar. 1969. "New Passages from Hekhalot Literature." *Tarbiz* 37: 354–72 (Hebrew).

———. 1980. *Apocalyptic and Merkavah Mysticism*. Leiden: Brill.

———. 1988. *From Apocalypticism to Gnosticism*. Frankfurt am Mein: P. Lang.

———. 1994. "The Letters, the Writing, and the Ineffable Name: Magic, Spirituality, and Mysticism." In Michal Oron and Amos Goldreich (eds.), *Masu'ot: Studies in Kabbalistic Literature and Jewish Philosophy in Memory of Prof. E. Gottlieb*, 75–98. Jerusalem: Bialik Institute (Hebrew).

———. 1996. "The Magic and the Myth: Research and Historical Reality." In Havivah Pedayah (ed.), *Myth in Judaism*, 15–28. Jerusalem: Bialik Institute (Hebrew).

Gudovitz, Shlomo. 1996. "A Burial Cave from the Roman Period in Upper Moza." *Atiqot* 29: 63*–70* (Hebrew).

Gundel, Wilhelm, and Hans G. Gundel. 1966. *Astrologumena: Die astrologische Literatur in der Antike und ihre Geschichte*. Wiesbaden: Steiner.

Gyselen, Rika. 1995. *Sceaux magiques en Iran sassanide*. Studia Iranica 17. Paris: Association pour l'avancement des études iraniennes.

Hachlili, Rachel. 2001. *Menorah, the Ancient Seven-Armed Candelabrum: Origin, Form, and Significance*. Leiden: Brill.

Hadas-Lebel, Mireille. 1979. "Le Paganisme à travers les sources rabbiniques des IIe et IIIe siècles: Contribution à l'étude du syncrétisme dans l'empire romain." In Wolfgang Haase (ed.), *Aufstieg und Niedergang der Römischen Welt*, pt. II, 19.2: 397–485. Berlin: de Gruyter.

Hadassi, Judah. 1836. *Eshkol ha-Kofer*. Eupatoria, Crimea (Hebrew).

Hägg, Thomas. 1993. "Magic Bowls Inscribed with an Apostles-and-Disciples Catalogue from the Christian Settlement of Hambukol (Upper Nubia)." *Orientalia* 62: 376–99.

Halbertal, Moshe. 2000. *Between Torah and Wisdom: Rabbi Menachem ha-Meiri and the Maimonidean Halakhists in Provence*. Jerusalem: Magnes (Hebrew).

Hallett, Garth. 1977. *A Companion to Wittgenstein's "Philosophical Investigations."* Ithaca, NY: Cornell University Press.

Halliday, William R. 1913. *Greek Divination: A Study of Its Methods and Principles*. London: Macmillan.

Halperin, David J. 1980. *The Merkavah in Rabbinic Literature*. New Haven, CT: American Oriental Society.

———. 1988. *The Faces of the Chariot*. Tübingen: Mohr Siebeck.

Hamburger, Anit. 1968. "Gems from Caesarea Maritima." *Atiqot* 8: 1–38.

Hamilton, Gordon J. 1996. "A New Hebrew-Aramaic Incantation Text from Galilee: 'Rebuking the Sea.'" *Journal of Semitic Studies* 41: 215–49.

Hamilton, Victor P. 1971. "Syriac Incantation Bowls." Ph.D. diss., Brandeis University.

Hammond, Dorothy. 1971. "Magic: A Problem in Semantics." *American Anthropologist* 72: 1348–56.

Hanson, John S. 1980. "Dreams and Visions in the Graeco-Roman World and Early Christianity." In W. Haase (ed.), *Aufstieg und Niedergang der Römischen Welt*, pt. II, 23.2: 1395–1427. Berlin: de Gruyter.

Hanson, Paul D. 1977. "Rebellion in Heaven: Azazel and Euhemeristic Heroes in 1 Enoch 6–11." *Journal of Biblical Literature* 96: 195–233.

Haran, Menahem. 1989. "The Priestly Blessing on Silver Plaques: The Significance of the Discovery at Ketef Hinnom." *Cathedra* 52: 77–89 (Hebrew).

Harari, Yuval. 1997a. "'If You Wish to Kill a Person': Harmful Magic and Protection from It in Early Jewish Magic." *Jewish Studies* 37: 111–42 (Hebrew).

———. 1997b. *The Sword of Moses: A New Edition and Study*. Jerusalem: Academon (Hebrew).

————. 1997–1998. "How to Do Things with Words: Philosophical Theory and Magical Deeds." *Jerusalem Studies in Jewish Folklore* 19–20: 365–92 (Hebrew).

————. 1998. "Early Jewish Magic: Methodological and Phenomenological Studies." Ph.D. diss., The Hebrew University of Jerusalem (Hebrew).

————. 2000. "Love Charms in Early Jewish Magic." *Kabbalah* 5: 247–64 (Hebrew).

————. 2001. "Power and Money: Economic Aspects of the Use of Magic by Jews in Ancient Times and the Early Middle Ages." *Pe'amim* 85: 14–42 (Hebrew).

————. 2005a. "Magic Vessels in Late Antiquity and the Islamic World." *Pe'amim* 103: 55–90 (Hebrew).

————. 2005b. "Moses, the Sword, and *The Sword of Moses*: Between Rabbinical and Magical Traditions." *Jewish Studies Quarterly* 12: 293–329.

————. 2005c. "Opening the Heart: Magical Practices for Knowledge, Understanding, and Good Memory in the Judaism of Late Antiquity and Early Middle Ages." In Zeev Gries, Haim Kreisel, and Boaz Huss (eds.), *Shefa Tal: Studies in Jewish Thought and Culture*, 303–47. Beer-Sheva: Ben-Gurion University Press (Hebrew).

————. 2005d. "What Is a Magical Text? Methodological Reflections Aimed at Redefining Early Jewish Magic." In S. Shaked (ed.), *Officina Magica: The Working of Magic*, 91–124. Leiden: Brill.

————. 2006a. "The Sages and the Occult." In Joshua Schwartz, Peter Tomson, and Zeev Safrai (eds.), *The Literature of the Sages: Midrash and Targum, Liturgy, Poetry, Mysticism, Contracts, Inscriptions, Ancient Science, and the Language of Rabbinic Literature*, II(3b): 521–64. Assen: Van Gorcum.

————. 2006b. "The Scroll of Ahima'az and Jewish Magic Culture: A Note on the Ordeal of the Adulteress." *Tarbiz* 75: 185–202 (Hebrew).

————. 2007. "Jewish Magic Plates in the Modern Period: From the Islamic World to Israel." *Pe'amim* 110: 55–84 (Hebrew).

————. 2010. "A Different Spirituality or 'Other' Agents? On the Study of Magic in Rabbinic Literature." In Vita D. Arbel and Andrei A. Orlov (eds.), *With Letters of Light: Studies in the Dead Sea Scrolls, Early*

Jewish Apocalypticism, Magic, and Mysticism, 169–95. Berlin: de Gruyter.

———. 2011. "Metatron and the Treasure of Gold: Notes on a Dream Inquiry Text from the Cairo Genizah." In Gideon Bohak, Yuval Harari, and Shaul Shaked (eds.), *Continuity and Innovation in the Magical Tradition*, 289–319. Leiden: Brill.

———. 2012a. "Jewish Magic: An Annotated Overview." *El Prezente* 5: 13*–85* (Hebrew).

———. 2012b. "*The Sword of Moses (Ḥarba de-Moshe)*: A New Translation and Introduction." *Magic, Ritual, and Witchcraft* 7: 58–98.

———. 2014. "Genizah Fragments of *The Sword of Moses*." *Ginzei Qedem* 10: 29–92 (Hebrew).

———. 2015. "Divination Through the Dead in Jewish Tradition of Magic (Jewish Dream Magic I)." In Eliezer Papo, Haim Weiss, Yuval Harari, and Jacob Ben Tolila (eds.), *Damta le-Tamar: Studies in Honor of Prof. Tamar Alexander*, 1: 167–219. Beer Sheva: Gaon Center for Ladino Culture (Hebrew).

Harding, Gerald L. 1950. "A Roman Family Vault on Gebel Jofeh, 'Amman.'" *Quarterly of the Department of Antiquities in Palestine* 14: 81–94.

Harre, Rom, and Michael Krausz. 1996. *Varieties of Relativism*. Oxford: Blackwell.

Hartland, Edwin. 1914. *Ritual and Belief*. London: Williams & Norgate.

Harviainen, Tapani. 1981. "An Aramaic Incantation Bowl from Borsippa: Another Specimen of Eastern Aramaic 'Koiné.'" *Studia Orientalia* 51(14): 3–28.

———. 1993. "Syncretistic and Confessional Features in Mesopotamian Incantation Bowls." *Studia Orientalia* 70: 29–37.

———. 1995. "Pagan Incantations in Aramaic Magic Bowls." In Markham J. Geller, Jonas C. Greenfield, and Michael P. Weitzman (eds.), *Studia Aramaica: New Sources and New Approaches*, 53–60. Oxford: Oxford University Press.

Hasan-Rokem, Galit. 1996. "'A Dream Amounts to the Sixtieth Part of Prophecy': On Interaction Between Textual Establishment and Popular Context in Dream Interpretations by the Jewish Sages." In

Benjamin Z. Kedar (ed.), *Studies in the History of Popular Culture*, 45–54. Jerusalem: Zalman Shazar Center (Hebrew).

―――. 1999. "Communication with the Dead in Jewish Dream Culture." In David Shulman and Guy Stroumsa (eds.), *Dream Cultures: Explorations in the Comparative History of Dreaming*, 213–32. New York: Oxford University Press.

―――. 2000. *Web of Life: Folklore and Midrash in Rabbinic Literature*, trans. Batya Stein. Stanford, CA: Stanford University Press.

Hayman, Peter. 1989. "Was God a Magician? Sefer Yesira and Jewish Magic." *Journal of Jewish Studies* 40: 225–37.

―――. 2004. *Sefer Yesira: Edition, Translation, and Text-Critical Commentary*. Tübingen: Mohr Siebeck.

Hengel, Martin. 1984. *Rabbinische Legende und frühpharisäische Geschichte: Schimeon b. Schatach und die achtzig Hexen von Askalon*. Heidelberg: C. Winter.

Henniger, Joseph. 1987. "Schmidt, Wilhelm." In *The Encyclopedia of Religion*, 13: 113–15. New York: Macmillan.

Herr, Moshe D. 1979. "Matters of Palestinian Halakhah During the Sixth and Seventh Centuries CE." *Tarbiz* 49: 62–80 (Hebrew).

Herskovits, Melville J. 1938. *Dahomey: An Ancient West African Kingdom*. New York: J. J. Augustin.

―――. 1952. *Man and His Work: The Science of Cultural Anthropology*. New York: Knopf.

Himmelfarb, Gertrude. 1962. *Darwin and the Darwinian Revolution*. New York: Chatto & Windus.

Himmelfarb, Martha. 1993. *Ascent to Heaven in Jewish and Christian Apocalypses*. Oxford: Oxford University Press.

―――. 2006. "Merkavah Mysticism Since Scholem: Rachel Elior's *The Three Temples*." In Peter Schäfer and Elisabeth Müller-Luckner (eds.), *Wege mystischer Gotteserfahrung: Judentum, Christentum und Islam*, 19–36. Munich: R. Oldenbourg.

Hirshman, Menachem [Marc G.]. 1988. "Stories of the Bath-House of Tiberias." In Yizhar Hirschfeld (ed.), *Tiberias: From Its Founding to the Muslim Conquest*, 119–22. Jerusalem: Yad Izhak Ben-Zvi (Hebrew).

Hoffman, Christopher A. 2002. "Fiat Magia." In Paul Mirecki and Marvin Meyer (eds.), *Magic and Ritual in the Ancient World*, 179–94. Leiden: Brill.

Holl, Karl (ed.). 1915. *Ancoratus und Panarion*, vol. 1. Leipzig: J. C. Hinrichs.

Hollis, Martin, and Steven Lukes. 1982. *Rationality and Relativism*. Cambridge, MA: MIT Press.

Horton, Robin. 1960. "A Definition of Religion and Its Uses." *Journal of the Royal Anthropological Institute* 90: 201–226. Reprinted in Horton's *Patterns of Thought in Africa and the West*, 19–49 (Cambridge, UK: Cambridge University Press, 1993).

———. 1967. "African Traditional Thought and Western Science." *Africa* 37: 50–71, 155–187. Reprinted in Horton's *Patterns of Thought in Africa and the West*, 197–258 (Cambridge, UK: Cambridge University Press, 1993).

———. 1968. "Ritual Man in Africa." In Morton H. Fried (ed.), *Readings in Anthropology*, 651–73. New York: Crowell.

———. 1973. "Lévy-Bruhl, Durkheim, and the Scientific Revolution." In Robin Horton and Ruth Finnegan (eds.), *Modes of Thought*, 249–305. London: Faber. Reprinted in Horton's *Patterns of Thought in Africa and the West*, 63–104 (Cambridge, UK: Cambridge University Press, 1993).

Hsu, Francis L. K. 1952. *Religion, Science, and Human Crises: A Study of China in Transition and Its Implications for the West*. London: Routledge & Kegan Paul.

Hubert, Henri, and Marcel Mauss. 1902–1903. "Equisse d'une Théory Générale de la Magie." *L'Année Sociologique* 7: 1–146.

Hull, John M. 1974. *Hellenistic Magic and the Synoptic Tradition*. London: SCM Press.

Hunter, Erica C. D. 1995a. "Aramaic Speaking Communities of Sasanid Mesopotamia." *Aram* 7: 319–35.

———. 1995b. "Combat and Conflict in Incantation Bowls: Studies on Two Aramaic Specimens from Nippur." In Markham J. Geller, Jonas C. Greenfield, and Michael P. Weitzman (eds.), *Studia Aramaica: New Sources and New Approaches*, 61–75. Oxford: Oxford University Press.

———. 1998. "Who Are the Demons? Iconography of Incantation Bowls." *Studi Epirafici e Linguistici sul vicino Oriente antico* 15: 95–115.

———. 2000a. "Technical Tables." In Judah B. Segal, *Catalogue of the Aramaic and Mandaic Incantation Bowls in the British Museum*, 189–204. London: British Museum.

————. 2000b. "The Typology of the Incantation Bowls: Physical Features and Decorative Aspects." In Judah B. Segal, *Catalogue of the Aramaic and Mandaic Incantation Bowls in the British Museum*, 163–88. London: British Museum.

Hurwitz, Siegmund. 1980. *Lilith die erste Eve*. Zurich: Daimon Verlag.

Huss, Boaz. 2000. *Sockets of Fine Gold: The Kabbalah of Rabbi Shim'on Ibn Lavi*. Jerusalem: Magnes and Ben-Zvi Institute (Hebrew).

————. 2007. "The Mystification of the Kabbalah and the Myth of Jewish Mysticism." *Pe'amim* 110: 9–30 (Hebrew).

Idel, Moshe. 1981. "The Concept of the Torah in Heikhalot Literature and Kabbalah." *Jerusalem Studies in Jewish Thought* 1: 23–84 (Hebrew).

————. 1988. *Kabbalah: New Perspectives*. New Haven, CT: Yale University Press.

————. 1990. *Golem: Jewish Magical and Mystical Traditions on the Artificial Anthropoid*. Albany: SUNY Press.

————. 1991. "Perceptions of the Kabbalah in the Second Half of the 18th Century." *Journal of Jewish Thought and Philosophy* 1: 55–114.

————. 1993. "Defining Kabbalah: The Kabbalah of the Divine Names." In Robert A. Herrera (ed.), *Mystics of the Book: Themes, Topics, and Typologies*, 97–122. New York: P. Lang.

————. 1997. "On Judaism, Jewish Mysticism, and Magic." In Peter Schäfer and Hans G. Kippenberg (eds.), *Envisioning Magic*, 195–214. Leiden: Brill.

————. 2004. "Foreword." In Joshua Trachtenberg, *Jewish Magic and Superstition: A Study in Folk Religion*, ix–xxv. Philadelphia: University of Pennsylvania Press.

————. 2006. "The Anonymous Commentary on the Alphabet of Metatron: A Treatise by R. Nehemiah ben Shlomo." *Tarbiz* 76: 255–64 (Hebrew).

Ilan, Tal. 2000. "Ben Sira's Attitude to Women and Its Reception by the Babylonian Talmud." *Jewish Studies* 40: 103–11 (Hebrew).

————. 2006. *Silencing the Queen: The Literary Histories of Shelamzion and Other Jewish Women*. Tübingen: Mohr Siebeck.

Irshai, Oded. 2004. "The Priesthood in Jewish Society in Late Antiquity." In Lee I. Levine (ed.), *Continuity and Renewal: Jews and Judaism in Byzantine-Christian Palestine*, 67–106. Jerusalem: Yad Izhak Ben-Zvi (Hebrew).

Isbell, Charles D. 1975. *Corpus of the Aramaic Incantation Bowls.* Missoula, MT: Scholars Press.

Jacobson, Howard. 1996. *A Commentary on Pseudo-Philo's Liber Antiquitatum Biblicarum.* Leiden: Brill.

Janowitz, Naomi. 1989. *The Poetics of Ascent: Theories of Language in a Rabbinic Ascent Text.* Albany: SUNY Press.

———. 2001. *Magic in the Roman World: Pagans, Jews and Christians.* London: Routledge.

———. 2002. *Icons of Power: Ritual Practices in Late Antiquity.* University Park: Pennsylvania State University Press.

Jastrow, Marcus. 1903. *A Dictionary of the Targumim, the Talmud Babli and Yerushalmi, and the Midrashic Literature.* London: Luzac.

Jeffers, Ann. 1996. *Magic and Divination in Ancient Palestine and Syria.* Leiden: Brill.

Jeruzalmi, Isaac. 1964. "Les coupes magiques araméenes de Mésopotamie." Ph.D. diss., Université Paris–Sorbonne.

Jevones, Frank B. 1896. *An Introduction to the History of Religion.* London: Methuen.

Jöel, David. 1881–1883. *Der Aberglaube und die Stellung des Judenthums zu demselben,* 2 vols. Jahresbericht des Jüdische-theologischen Seminars 1876–1884. Breslau: Koebner.

Johnson, Janet H. 1986. "Introduction to the Demotic Magical Papyri." In Hans D. Betz (ed.), *The Greek Magical Papyri in Translation,* lv–lviii. Chicago: University of Chicago Press.

Johnston, Sarah I. 1999. *Restless Dead: Encounter Between the Living and the Dead in Ancient Greece.* Berkeley: University of California Press.

———. 2001. "Charming Children: The Use of the Child in Ancient Divination." *Arethusa* 34: 97–117.

———. 2002. "Sacrifice in the Greek Magical Papyri." In Paul Mirecki and Marvin Meyer (eds.), *Magic and Ritual in the Ancient World,* 344–58. Leiden: Brill.

Jordan, David. 1985a. "Defixiones from a Well near the Southwest Corner of the Athenian Agora." *Hesperia* 54: 205–55.

———. 1985b. "A Survey of Greek Defixiones not Included in the Special Corpora." *Greek, Roman, and Byzantine Studies* 26: 151–97.

Jordan, Louis H. 1986. *Comparative Religion: Its Genesis and Growth.* Atlanta: Scholars Press.

Josephus Flavius. 1925–1965. *Josephus, with an English Translation*, trans. Henry St. J. Thackeray and Ralph Marcus, 9 vols. Cambridge, MA: Harvard University Press.

Juusola, Hannu. 1999a. *Linguistic Peculiarities in the Aramaic Magic Bowl Texts*. Helsinki: Finnish Oriental Society.

———. 1999b. "Who Wrote the Syriac Incantation Bowls?" *Studia Orientalia* 85: 75–92.

———. 2004. "Notes on the Aramaic Sections of Havdalah de-Rabbi Aqiba." In Hannu Juusola, Juha Laulainen, and Heikki Palva (eds.), *Verbum et Calamus: Semitic and Related Studies in Honour of the Sixtieth Birthday of Professor Tapani Harviainen*, 106–19. Helsinki: Finnish Oriental Society.

Kahn, Geoffrey A. 1986. "The Arabic Fragments in the Cambridge Genizah Collection." *Manuscripts of the Middle East* 1: 54–60.

Kalmin, Richard L. 1994. *Sages, Stories, Authors, and Editors in Rabbinic Babylonia*. Atlanta: Scholars Press.

———. 2004 "Holy Men and Rabbis in Late Antiquity." In Lee I. Levine (ed.), *Continuity and Renewal: Jews and Judaism in Byzantine-Christian Palestine*, 210–32. Jerusalem: Yad Izhak Ben-Zvi (Hebrew).

Kaminsky, Jack. 1967. "Spencer, Herbert." In *The Encyclopedia of Philosophy*, 7: 523–27. New York: Macmillan.

Kaufman, Stephen A. 1973. "A Unique Magic Bowl from Nippur." *Journal of Near Eastern Studies* 32: 170–74.

Kaufmann, Yehezkel. 1955. *The Religion of Israel: From Its Beginnings to the Babylonian Exile*, 4 vols. Jerusalem: Dvir (Hebrew).

———. 1960. *The Religion of Israel*, trans. Moshe Greenberg. Chicago: University of Chicago Press.

Kee, Howard C. 1967–1968. "The Terminology of Mark's Exorcism Stories." *New Testament Studies* 14: 232–46.

Keil, J. 1940. "Ein rätselhafter Amulett." *Wiener Jahreshefte* 32: 79–84.

Keller, Aharon. 1985. "*Niḥush* and *Siman*." *Barkai* 2: 50–58 (Hebrew).

Kellner, Menachem M. 2004. "Maimonides on the 'Normality' of Hebrew." In Jonathan W. Malino (ed.), *Judaism and Modernity: The Religious Philosophy of David Hartman*, 413–44. Aldershot, UK: Ashgate.

Kent, Ronald G. 1911. "The Etymology of Syriac *dastabira*." *Journal of the American Oriental Society* 31: 359–64.

Kilair. 1841. "On Foreign Wisdom in the Talmud." In Isaac M. Jost and Michael Creizenach (eds.), *Zion: Ephemerides Hebraicae* 2: 65–67, 81–83 (Hebrew).

King, John H. 1892. *The Supernatural: Its Origin, Nature, and Evolution.* London: Williams & Norgate.

Kippenberg, Hans G. 1997. "Magic in Roman Civil Discourse: Why Ritual Could Be Illegal." In Peter Schäfer and Hans G. Kippenberg (eds.), *Envisioning Magic,* 137–63. Leiden: Brill.

Kipperwasser, Reuven. 2005. "Midrashim on Kohelet: Studies in Their Redaction and Formation." Ph.D. diss., Bar-Ilan University (Hebrew).

Klein-Franke, Felix. 1971. "Eine Aramäische tabelae devotionis (T. Colon. Inv.nr.6)." *Zeitschrift für Papyrologie und Epigraphik* 7: 47–52.

Kluckhohn, Clyde. 1967. *Navaho Witchcraft.* Boston: Beacon.

Knaani, Jacob. 1960–1989. *Ozar ha-Lashon ha-Ivrit: A New Hebrew Dictionary,* 18 vols. Jerusalem: Masada (Hebrew).

Kohut, Alexander. 1866. *Über die Jüdische Angelologie und Dämonologie in ihrer Abhängigkeit vom Parsismus.* Leipzig: F. A. Brockhaus.

———. 1926. *Aruch Hashalem,* 8 vols. Vienna: Menorah (Hebrew).

Kotansky, Roy. 1991a. "An Inscribed Copper Amulet from Evron." *Atiqot* 20: 81–87.

———. 1991b. "Two Inscribed Jewish Aramaic Amulets from Syria." *Israel Exploration Journal* 41: 267–81.

———. 1994. *Greek Magical Amulets: The Inscribed Gold, Silver, Copper, and Bronze Lamellae,* vol. 1, *Published Texts of Known Provenance.* Papyrologica Coloniensia 22(1). Opladen, Germany: Westdeutscher Verlag.

———. 1995. "Greek Exorcistic Amulets." In Marvin Meyer and Paul Mirecki (eds.), *Ancient Magic and Ritual Power,* 243–77. Leiden: Brill.

———. 1997. "The Chnoubis Gem from Tel Dor." *Israel Exploration Journal* 47: 257–60.

Kotansky, Roy, Joseph Naveh, and Shaul Shaked. 1992. "A Greek-Aramaic Silver Amulet from Egypt in the Ashmolean Museum." *Le Muséon* 105: 5–24.

Krauss, Samuel. 1898. *Griechische und Lateinische Lehnwörter im Talmud, Midrash und Targum.* Berlin: S. Calvary.

Krebs, Walter. 1975. "Lilith: Adams erste Frau." *Zeitschrift für Religions- und Geistesgeschichte* 27: 141–52.

Kreisel, Howard. 1994. "Maimonides' Approach to Astrology." *Proceedings of the Eleventh World Congress for Jewish Studies* 3(2): 25–32 (Hebrew).

Kristianpoller, Alexander. 1923. *Traum und Traumdeutung*. Monumenta Hebraica 4(2.1). Vienna: Harz.

Kropp, Angelicus M. 1930–1931. *Ausgewählte Koptische Zaubertexte*. Brussels: Fondation egyptologique reine Elisabeth.

Kuper, Adam. 1983. *Anthropology and Anthropologists*, rev. ed. London: Routledge & Kegan Paul.

———. 1988. *The Invention of Primitive Society*. London: Routledge.

Kuyt, Annelies. 1995. *The "Descent" to the Chariot: Toward a Description of the Terminology, Place, Function, and Nature of Yeridah in Heikhalot Literature*. Tübingen: Mohr.

Lain-Entralgo, Pedro. 1970. *The Therapy of the World in Classical Antiquity*, trans. and ed. L. J. Rather and John M. Sharp. New Haven, CT: Yale University Press.

Lane-Fox, Robin. 1987. *Pagans and Christians*. New York: Knopf.

Lang, Andrew. 1901. *Magic and Religion*. London: Longmans, Green.

Lange, Armin. 1997. "The Essene Position on Magic and Divination." In Moshe Bernstein, Florentino García Martínez, and John Kampen (eds.), *Legal Texts and Legal Issues: Proceedings of the Second Meeting of the International Organization for Qumran Studies, Cambridge 1995*, 377–435. Leiden: Brill.

Lange, Armin, Hermann Lichtenberger, and K. F. Diethard Römheld (eds.). 2003. *Die Dämonen: Die Dämonologie der israelitisch-jüdischen und frühchristlichen Literatur im Kontext ihrer Umwelt*. Tübingen: Mohr Siebeck.

Langerman, Tzvi Y. 1991. "Maimonides' Repudiation of Astrology." *Maimonidean Studies* 2: 123–58.

Lauterbach, Jacob Z. 1925. "The Ceremony of Breaking a Glass at Weddings." *Hebrew Union College Annual* 2: 351–80. Reprinted in Jacob Z. Lauterbach, *Studies in Jewish Law, Custom, and Folklore*, 1–29 (New York: Ktav, 1970).

———. 1939. "The Belief in the Power of the Word." *Hebrew Union College Annual* 14: 287–302. Reprinted in Jacob Z. Lauterbach, *Studies in Jewish Law, Custom, and Folklore*, 143–58 (New York: Ktav, 1970).

Layard, Austen H. 1853. *Discoveries in the Ruins of Ninveh and Babylon.* New York: Putnam.

Leach, Edmund R. 1966. *Rethinking Anthropology.* London: Athlone Press.

Leicht, Reimund. 2006a. *Astrologumena Judaica.* Tübingen: Mohr Siebeck.

———. 2006b. "*Mashbiʻa Ani ʼAlekha*: Types and Patterns of Ancient Jewish and Christian Exorcism Formulae." *Jewish Studies Quarterly* 13: 319–43.

———. 2011. "The Planets, the Jews, and the Beginnings of 'Jewish Astrology.'" In Gideon Bohak, Yuval Harari, and Shaul Shaked (eds.), *Continuity and Innovation in the Magical Tradition*, 271–88. Leiden: Brill.

Lemberger, Dorit. 2003. "Wittgenstein and Religious Belief: Between 'Theology as Grammar' and 'A Religious Point of View.'" *Iyyun* 52: 399–424 (Hebrew).

Lerner, Ralph. 1968. "Maimonides' Letter on Astrology." *History of Religions* 8: 143–58.

Lesses, Rebecca M. 1995. "The Adjuration of the Prince of the Presence: Performative Utterance in a Jewish Ritual." In Marvin Meyer and Paul Mirecki (eds.), *Ancient Magic and Ritual Power*, 185–206. Leiden: Brill.

———. 1998. *Ritual Practices to Gain Power: Angels, Incantations, and Revelation in Early Jewish Mysticism.* Harrisburg, PA: Trinity Press International.

———. 2001. "Exe(o)rcising Power: Women as Sorceresses, Exorcists, and Demonesses in Babylonian Jewish Society of Late Antiquity." *Journal of the American Academy of Religion* 69: 343–75.

Levene, Dan. 1999. "'. . . and by the Name of Jesus . . .': An Unpublished Magic Bowl in Jewish Aramaic." *Jewish Studies Quarterly* 6: 283–308.

———. 2002. *Curse or Blessing, What's in the Magic Bowls?* Parke Institute Pamphlet 2. Southampton, UK: University of Southampton Publications.

———. 2003a. *A Corpus of Magic Bowls: Incantation Texts in Jewish Aramaic from Late Antiquity.* London: Kegan Paul.

———. 2003b. "'A Happy Thought of the Magicians': The Magical Get." In Robert Deutsch (ed.), *Shlomo: Studies in Epigraphy, Iconography,*

History, and Archaeology in Honor of Shlomo Moussaeiff, 175–84. Tel Aviv: Archaeological Center Publications.

———. 2003c. "Heal O' Israel: A Pair of Duplicate Magic Bowls from the Pergamon Museum in Berlin." *Journal of Jewish Studies* 54: 104–21.

———. 2005. "Jewish Liturgy and Magic Bowls." In Robert Hayward and Brad Embry (eds.), *Studies in Jewish Prayer*, 163–84. Oxford: Oxford University Press.

———. 2006. "Calvariae Magicae: The Berlin, Philadelphia, and Moussaieff Skulls." *Orientalia* 75: 359–79.

———. 2007. "'If You Appear as a Pig': Another Incantation Bowl (Moussaieff 164)." *Journal of Semitic Studies* 52: 59–70.

———. 2011. "'This Is a Qybl' for Overturning Sorceries': Form, Formula Threads in a Web of Transmission." In Gideon Bohak, Yuval Harari, and Shaul Shaked (eds.), *Continuity and Innovation in the Magical Tradition*, 219–44. Leiden: Brill.

———. 2013. *Jewish Aramaic Curse Texts from Late-Antique Mesopotamia*. Leiden: Brill.

Levene, Dan, and Siam Bhayro. 2005–2006. "'Bring to the Gates . . . Upon a Good Smell and Upon Good Fragrances': An Aramaic Incantation Bowl for Success in Business." *Archiv für Orientforschung* 51: 242–46.

Levene, Dan, and Gideon Bohak. 2012. "Divorcing Lilith: From the Babylonian Incantation Bowls to the Cairo Genizah." *Journal of Jewish Studies* 63: 197–217.

Levine, Baruch A. 1970. "The Language of the Magical Bowls." In Jacob Neusner, *A History of the Jews in Babylonia*, 5: 343–73. Leiden: Brill.

Levine, Lee I. 1989. *The Rabbinic Class of Roman Palestine in Late Antiquity*. Jerusalem and New York: Yad Izhak Ben-Zvi and JTSA.

———. 1998. *Judaism and Hellenism in Antiquity: Conflict or Confluence?* Seattle: University of Washington Press.

———. 2000. *The Ancient Synagogue: The First Thousand Years*. New Haven, CT: Yale University Press.

———. 2001. "The History and Significance of the Menorah in Antiquity." *Cathedra* 98: 7–32 (Hebrew).

Levinson, Joshua. 2006. "Enchanting Rabbis: Contest Narratives Between Rabbis and Magicians in Rabbinic Literature of Late Antiquity." *Tarbiz* 75: 295–328 (Hebrew).

Lévi-Strauss, Claude. 1963 [1949]. "The Sorcerer and His Magic." In Claude Lévi-Strauss, *Structural Anthropology*, trans. Claire Jacobson and Brooke Grundfest Schoepf, 167–85. New York: Basic.

Levy, Moritz A. 1855. "Ueber die von Layard aufgefunderen chaldäischen Inschriften auf Topfgefässen: Ein Beitrag zur Hebräischen Paläographie und zur Religionsgeschichte." *Zeitschrift der Deutschen Morgenländischen Gesellschaft* 9: 465–91.

Lévy-Bruhl, Lucien. 1985 [1912]. *How Natives Think*, trans. Lilian A. Clare. Princeton, NJ: Princeton University Press.

Lewis, Spencer. 1905. "Maimonides on Superstition." *Jewish Quarterly Review*, o.s., 17: 475–88.

Lewy, Heinrich. 1893a. "Morgenländischer Aberglaube in der Römichen Kaiserzeit." *Zeitschrift des Vereins für Folkskunde* 3: 23–40, 130–43, 238.

———. 1893b. "Zu dem Traumbuch des Artemidoros." *Rheinisches Museum für Philologie*, n.f., 48: 398–419.

Liddell, Henry G., Robert Scott, and Henry S. Jones. 1948. *A Greek-English Lexicon: A New Edition, Revised and Augmented*. Oxford: Clarendon Press.

Lieberman, Saul. 1942. *Greek in Jewish Palestine: Studies in the Life and Manners of Jewish Palestine in the II–IV centuries C.E.* New York: JTSA.

———. 1950. *Hellenism in Jewish Palestine: Studies in the Literary Transmission, Beliefs, and Manners of Palestine in the I Century B.C.E.–IV Century C.E.* New York: JTSA.

———. 1991. "On Adjurations Among the Jews." In David Rosenthal (ed.), *Studies in Palestinian Talmudic Literature*, 90–96. Jerusalem: Magnes (Hebrew).

———. 1992. *Tosefta Ki-Fshutah: A Comprehensive Commentary on the Toseftah*, 8 vols. Jerusalem: JTSA (Hebrew).

———. 2008. *Hayerushalmi Kiphshuto*. New York: JTSA (Hebrew).

Liebes, Yehuda. 1990. *The Sin of Elisha: The Four Who Entered Paradise and the Nature of Talmudic Mysticism*. Jerusalem: Academon (Hebrew).

———. 2000. *Ars Poetica in Sefer Yetsira*. Tel Aviv: Schocken (Hebrew).

———. 2004. "Introduction: Magic and Kabbalah." In Esther Liebes (ed.), *Devils, Demons, and Souls: Essays on Demonology by Gershom Scholem*, 3–7. Jerusalem: Ben-Zvi Institute (Hebrew).

———. 2005. "Physiognomy in Kabbalah." *Pe'amim* 104: 21–40 (Hebrew).

Liebeschuetz, John H. W. 1979. *Continuity and Change in Roman Religion*. Oxford: Clarendon Press.

Lightstone, Jack N. 1985. "Magicians, Holy Men, and Rabbis: Patterns of the Sacred in Late Antique Judaism." In William S. Green (ed.), *Approaches to Ancient Judaism*, vol. 5, *Studies in Judaism and Its Greco-Roman Context*, 133–48. Atlanta: Scholars Press.

Littleton, Scott C. 1985. "Lucien Lévy-Bruhl and the Concept of Cognitive Relativity." In Lucien Lévy-Bruhl, *How Natives Think*, trans. Lilian A. Clare, v–lviii. Princeton, NJ: Princeton University Press.

Loewenstamm, Samuel E. 1976. "Demons." *Encyclopedia Biblica*, 7: 524–25. Jerusalem: Bialik Institute (Hebrew).

Longrigg, James. 1998. *Greek Medicine: From the Heroic to the Hellenistic Age*. London: Duckworth.

Lowe, Joyce E. 1929. *Magic in Greek and Latin Literature*. Oxford: Blackwell.

Lowie, Robert H. 1924. *Primitive Religion*. New York: Boni & Liveright.

Luck, Georg. 1986. *Arcana Mundi: Magic and the Occult in the Greek and Roman Worlds*. Baltimore: Johns Hopkins University Press.

Macintosh, A. A. 1969. "A Consideration of Hebrew גער." *Vetus Testamentum* 19: 471–79.

Mack, Hananel. 1998. "The Unique Character of the Zippori Synagogue Mosaic and Eretz Israel Midrashim." *Cathedra* 88: 39–56.

Magness, Jodi. 2005. "Heaven on Earth: Helios and the Zodiac Cycle in Ancient Palestinian Synagogues." *Dumbarton Oaks Papers* 59: 1–52.

Maimonides, Moses. 1961. *The Code of Maimonides (Mishne Torah), Book III: The Book of Seasons*, trans. Solomon Gandz and Hyman Klein. New Haven, CT: Yale University Press.

———. 1962. *Mishneh Torah, Book I: The Book of Knowledge; Book II: The Book of Adoration*, ed. and trans. Moses Hyamson. Jerusalem: Kiryah Ne'emanah.

———. 1963. *The Guide of the Perplexed*, trans. Shlomo Pines. Chicago: University of Chicago Press.

———. 1963–1968. *Mishna with Maimonides' Commentary*, 6 vols., trans. and ed. Yosef Qafih. Jerusalem: Mossad Harav Kook (Hebrew).

Malinowski, Bronislaw. 1932. *The Sexual Life of Savages in North-Western Melanesia*. London: Routledge.

―――. 1935. *Coral Gardens and Their Magic: A Study of the Methods of Tilling the Soil and of Agricultural Rites in the Trobriand Islands.* London: Allen & Unwin.

―――. 1948 [1925]. "Magic, Science, and Religion." In Bronislaw Malinowski, *Magic, Science, and Religion and Other Essays*, 1–71. Glencoe, IL: Free Press.

―――. 1964 [1922]. *Argonauts of the Western Pacific: An Account of Native Enterprise and Adventure in the Archipelagoes of Melanesian New Guinea.* London: Routledge & Kegan Paul.

―――. 1966. *A Scientific Theory of Culture and Other Essays.* New York: Oxford University Press.

Mann, Jacob. 1972. *Texts and Studies in Jewish History and Literature.* New York: Ktav.

Manns, Frédéric. 1978. "Gemmes de l'époque greco-romaine provenant de Palestine." *Liber Annuus* 28: 147–70.

Marett, Robert R. 1951. "Magic (Introductory)." In *Encyclopedia of Religion and Ethics*, 8: 245–52. New York: C. Scribner's Sons.

―――. 1979 [1909]. *The Threshold of Religion*, rev. ed. New York: AMS Press.

Margalioth, Mordechai, 1966. *Sepher Ha-Razim: A Newly Discovered Book of Magic from the Talmudic Period.* Jerusalem: Yediot Acharonon (Hebrew).

Margalioth, Reuven. 1957. *Responsa from Heaven by R. Yaakov from Mervege.* Jerusalem: Mossad Harav Kook (Hebrew).

Marmorstein, Arthur. 1923. "Beiträge zur Religionsgeschichte und Volkskunde." *Jahrbuch für Jüdische Volkskunde* 25: 280–319.

Marrassini, Paolo. 1979. "I frammenti aramaici." *Studi Classici e Orientali* 29: 125–30.

Martínez, Florentino G., and Eibert J. C. Tigchelaar. 1998. *The Dead Sea Scrolls Study Edition.* Leiden: Brill.

Martínez, Florentino G., Eibert C. J. Tigchelaar, and Adam S. van der Woude. 1998. *Qumran Cave 11:II (11Q2–18, 11Q20–31).* Discoveries in the Judaean Desert 23. Oxford: Clarendon Press.

Marwick, Max G. 1970. *Witchcraft and Sorcery.* Harmondsworth, UK: Penguin.

―――. 1987. "African Witchcraft." In *The Encyclopedia of Religion*, 15: 423–28. New York: Macmillan.

Marx, Alexander. 1926. "The Correspondence Between the Rabbis of Southern France and Maimonides About Astrology." *Hebrew Union College Annual* 3: 311–58.

Matras, Hagit. 1994. "Forms and Intentions of Contemporary Printed Charm Books." *Proceedings of the Eleventh World Congress of Jewish Studies* 4(2): 29–36 (Hebrew).

———. 1997. "Hebrew Charm Books: Contents and Origins (Based on Books Printed in Europe During the 18th Century)." Ph.D. diss., The Hebrew University of Jerusalem (Hebrew).

———. 2005. "Creation and Re-Creation: A Study in Charm Books." In Rachel Elior and Peter Schäfer (eds.), *Creation and Re-Creation in Jewish Thought: Festschrift in Honor of Joseph Dan on the Occasion of His Seventieth Birthday*, 147*–164*. Tübingen: Mohr Siebeck (Hebrew).

Mauss, Marcel. 1972. *A General Theory of Magic*, trans. Robert Brain. London: Routledge & Kegan Paul.

Mazlish, B. 1967. "Comte, Auguste." In *The Encyclopedia of Philosophy*, 1–2: 173–77. New York: Macmillan.

McCown, Chester C. 1922. *The Testament of Solomon*. Leipzig: J. C. Hinrichs.

McCullogh, William S. 1967. *Jewish and Mandaean Incantation Bowls in the Royal Ontario Museum*. Toronto: University of Toronto Press.

McCullough, C. Thomas, and Beth Glazier-McDonald. 1996. "An Aramaic Bronze Amulet from Sepphoris." *Atiqot* 28: 161–65.

———. 1998. "Welcome to the World of Magic." *Archaeology Odyssey* 1(3): 50–56.

McMullen, Ramsay. 1966. *Enemies of the Roman Order: Treason, Unrest, and Alienation in the Empire*. Cambridge, MA: Harvard University Press.

Meier, John P. 1991–2009. *A Marginal Jew*, 4 vols. New York: Doubleday.

Merchavya, Hen. 1967. "The Book of Mysteries." *Kiryat Sefer* 42: 297–303 (Hebrew).

———. 1972. "Razim, Sefer Ha-." In *Encyclopedia Judaica*, 13: 1594–95. Jerusalem: Keter.

Meyer, Marvin, and Paul Mirecki (eds.). 1995. *Ancient Magic and Ritual Power*. Leiden: Brill.

Meyer, Marvin, and Richard Smith. 1994. *Ancient Christian Magic: Coptic Texts of Ritual Power*. San Francisco: Harper.

Middleton, John (ed.). 1967. *Magic, Witchcraft, and Curing*. Garden City, NY: Natural History Press.

———. 1987. "Theories of Magic." In *The Encyclopedia of Religion*, 9: 82–87. New York: Macmillan.

Middleton, John, and Edward H. Winter (eds.). 1963. *Witchcraft and Sorcery in East Africa*. London: Routledge & Kegan Paul.

Milik, Józef T. 1967. "Une amulette judéo-araméenne." *Biblica* 48: 450–51.

———. 1976. *The Books of Enoch: Aramaic Fragments of Qumran Cave 4*. Oxford: Clarendon Press.

Montgomery, James A. 1911. "Some Early Amulets from Palestine." *Journal of the American Oriental Society* 31: 272–81.

———. 1913. *Aramaic Incantation Texts from Nippur*. Philadelphia: University Museum.

Moore, Carey A. 1996. *Tobit: A New Translation with Introduction and Commentary*. New York: Doubleday.

Morgan, Michael A. 1983. *Sepher Ha-Razim: The Book of the Mysteries*. Chico, CA: Society of Biblical Literature.

Morgenstern, Matthew. 2007a. "The Jewish Babylonian Aramaic Magic Bowl BM 91767 Reconsidered." *Le Muséon* 120: 5–27.

———. 2007b. "On Some Non-Standard Spellings in the Aramaic Magic Bowls and Their Linguistic Significance." *Journal of Semitics Studies* 52: 245–77.

———. 2012. "Mandaic Magic Bowls in the Moussaieff Collection: A Preliminary Survey." In Meir Lubetski and Edith Lubetski (eds.), *New Inscriptions and Seals Relating to the Biblical World*, 157–70. Atlanta: Society of Biblical Literature.

———. 2013. "Linguistic Features of the Texts in This Volume." In Shaul Shaked, James N. Ford, and Siam Bhayro (eds.), *Aramaic Bowl Spells: Jewish Babylonian Aramaic Bowls I*, 39–49. Leiden: Brill.

Moriggi, Marco. 2014. *A Corpus of Syriac Incantation Bowls: Syriac Magical Texts from Late-Antique Mesopotamia*. Leiden: Brill.

Morony, Michael G. 1984. *Iraq After the Muslim Conquest*. Princeton, NJ: Princeton University Press.

———. 2003. "Magic and Society in Late Sassanian Iraq." In Scott Noegel, Joel Walker, and Brannon Wheeler (eds.), *Prayer, Magic, and the Stars in the Ancient and Late Antique World*, 83–107. University Park: Pennsylvania State University Press.

Müller-Kessler, Christa. 1996. "The Story of Bguzan-Lilit, Daughter of Zanay-Lilit." *Journal of the American Oriental Society* 116: 185–95.

———. 1998. "A Mandaic Gold Amulet in the British Museum." *Bulletin of the American Society of Oriental Studies* 311: 83–88.

———. 1999. "Interrelations Between Mandaic Lead Rolls and Incantation Bowls." In Tzvi Abusch and Karl van der Toorn (eds.), *Mesopotamian Magic: Textual, Historical, and Interpretative Perspectives*, 197–210. Groningen: Styx.

———. 2001. "Lilit(s) in der aramäisch-magischen Literatur der Spätantike." *Altorientalische Forschungen* 28: 338–52.

———. 2001–2002. "Die Zauberschalensammlung des British Museum." *Archiv für Orientforschung* 48–49: 115–46.

———. 2005. *Die Zauberschalentexte in der Hilprecht-Sammlung, Jena, und weitere Nippur-Texte anderer Sammlungen*. Wiesbaden: Harrassowitz.

Munday, John T. 1956. *Witchcraft in Central Africa and Europe*. London: United Society for Christian Literature.

Murphy, Frederick J. 1993. *Pseudo-Philo: Rewriting the Bible*. Oxford: Oxford University Press.

Na'aman, Nadav. 2011. "The Silver Amulets from Ketef Hinom Reconsidered." *Cathedra* 140: 7–18 (Hebrew).

Naveh, Joseph. 1985. "'A Good Subduing, There Is None Like It.'" *Tarbiz* 54: 367–82 (Hebrew).

———. 1989. "The Aramaic and Hebrew Inscriptions from Ancient Synagogues." *Eretz Israel* 20: 302–10 (Hebrew).

———. 1992. *On Shred and Papyrus: Aramaic and Hebrew Inscriptions from the Second Temple and Talmudic Periods*. Jerusalem: Magnes (Hebrew).

———. 1996. "On Jewish Books of Magic Recipes in Antiquity." In Isaiah M. Gafni, Aharon Oppenheimer, and Daniel R. Schwartz (eds.), *The Jews in the Hellenistic-Roman World: Studies in Memory of Menahem Stern*, 453–65. Jerusalem: Zalman Shazar Center (Hebrew).

———. 1997a. "Illnesses and Amulets in Antiquity." In Ofra Rimon (ed.), *Illness and Healing in Ancient Times*, 24*–28*. Haifa: University of Haifa (Hebrew).

———. 1997b. "A Syriac Amulet on Leather." *Journal of Semitic Studies* 42: 33–38.

————. 1998. "Fragments of an Aramaic Magic Book from Qumran." *Israel Exploration Journal* 48: 252–61.

————. 2002. "Some New Jewish Palestinian Aramaic Amulets." *Jerusalem Studies in Arabic and Islam* 26: 231–36.

Naveh, Joseph, and Shaul Shaked. 1987. *Amulets and Magic Bowls: Aramaic Incantations of Late Antiquity*. Jerusalem: Magnes.

————. 1993. *Magic Spells and Formulae: Aramaic Incantations of Late Antiquity*. Jerusalem: Magnes.

Needham, Rodney. 1972. *Belief, Language, and Experience*. Chicago: University of Chicago Press.

Nemoy, Leon. 1952. *Karaite Anthology: Excerpts from the Early Literature*. New Haven, CT: Yale University Press.

————. 1954. "Maimonides' Opposition to Occultism." *Harofé Haivri* 27: 102–9 (Hebrew).

————. 1986. "Al-Qirqisani on the Occult Sciences." *Jewish Quarterly Review* 76: 329–67.

Ness, Lester J. 1990. "Astrology and Judaism in Late Antiquity." Ph.D. diss., Miami University.

Neusner, Jacob. 1966–1967. "Rabbi and Magus in Third-Century Sasanian Babylonia." *History of Religions* 6: 169–78.

————. 1969. "The Phenomenon of the Rabbi in Late Antiquity." *Numen* 16: 1–20.

————. 1969–1970. *A History of the Jews in Babylonia*. Leiden: Brill.

————. 1970. "The Phenomenon of the Rabbi in Late Antiquity II: The Ritual of 'Being a Rabbi' in Late Sasanian Babylonia." *Numen* 17: 1–18.

————. 1989. "Science and Magic, Miracle and Magic in Formative Judaism: The System and the Difference." In Jacob Neusner, Ernest S. Frerichs, and Paul V. M. Flesher (eds.), *Religion, Science, and Magic in Concert and in Conflict*, 61–81. New York: Oxford University Press.

Newsom, Carol A. 1980. "The Development of 1 Enoch 6–19: Cosmology and Judgment." *Catholic Biblical Quarterly* 42: 310–29.

Nickelsburg, George W. E. 1977. "Apocalyptic and Myth in 1 Enoch 6–11." *Journal of Biblical Literature* 96: 383–405.

————. 2001. *1 Enoch 1: A Commentary on the Book of 1 Enoch*. Minneapolis: Fortress.

Niehoff, Maren R. 1992. "A Dream Which Is not Interpreted Is Like a Letter Which Is not Read." *Journal of Jewish Studies* 43: 58–84.

Nielsen, Kai. 1967. "Wittgensteinian Fideism." *Philosophy* 42: 191–209.

———. 2001. "Wittgenstein and Wittgensteinians on Religion." In Robert Arrington and Mark Addis (eds.), *Wittgenstein and Philosophy of Religion*, 137–66. London: Routledge.

Niggermeyer, Jens-Heinrich. 1975. *Beschwörungsformeln aus dem "Buch der Geheimnisse" (Sefär Harazim): Zur Topologie der magischen Rede.* Hildesheim, Germany: Olms.

Nilsson, Martin P. 1940. *Greek Popular Religion.* New York: Columbia University Press.

———. 1964. *A History of Greek Religion*, trans. Frederick J. Fielden. New York: Norton Library.

Nitzan, Bilha. 1986. "Hymns from Qumran *'lefaḥed u-levahel'* Evil Ghosts." *Tarbiz* 55: 19–46 (Hebrew).

———. 1994. *Qumran Prayer and Religious Poetry*, trans. Jonathan Chipman. Leiden: Brill.

Nock, Arthur D. 1972. *Essays on Religion and the Ancient World*, 2 vols. Oxford: Clarendon Press.

Norbeck, Edward. 1961. *Religion in Primitive Society.* New York: Harper & Row.

Norris, Christopher. 1982. *Deconstruction: Theory and Practice.* London: Methuen.

O'Dea, Thomas F. 1966. *The Sociology of Religion.* Englewood Cliffs, NJ: Prentice Hall.

Odeberg, Hugo. 1928. *3 Enoch or the Hebrew Book of Enoch.* Cambridge, UK: Cambridge University Press.

Ogden, Daniel. 2002. *Magic, Witchcraft, and Ghosts in the Greek and Roman Worlds: A Source Book.* Oxford: Oxford University Press.

O'Keefe, Daniel L. 1982. *Stolen Lightning: The Social Theory of Magic.* New York: Continuum.

Oppenheim, Leo A. 1956. *The Interpretation of Dreams in the Ancient Near East.* Transactions of the American Philosophical Society, n.s., 46(3). Philadelphia: American Philosophical Society.

———. 1969a. "Divination and Celestial Observation in the Last Assyrian Empire." *Centaurus* 14: 97–135.

————. 1969b. "New Fragments of the Assyrian Dream Book." *Iraq* 31: 153–65.

————. 1977. *Ancient Mesopotamia: Portrait of a Dead Civilization*, rev. ed. Chicago: University of Chicago Press.

Oppenheimer, Aharon. 1977. *The Am Ha-Aretz*. Leiden: Brill.

Otto, Bernd-Christian. 2013. "Towards Historicizing 'Magic' in Antiquity." *Numen* 60: 308–47.

Pagels, Elaine. 1991. "The Social History of Satan, the 'Intimate Enemy': A Preliminary Sketch." *Harvard Theological Review* 84: 105–28.

Parker, Richard A. 1978. "Egyptian Astronomy, Astrology, and Calendrical Reckoning." *Dictionary of Scientific Biography*, 15: 706–27. New York: C. Scribner's Sons.

Patai, Raphael. 1939. "The 'Control of Rain' in Ancient Palestine: A Study in Comparative Religion." *Hebrew Union College Annual* 14: 251–86.

————. 1983. *On Jewish Folklore*. Detroit: Wayne State University Press.

Pels, Peter, and Oscar Salemink (eds.). 1995. *Colonial Ethnographies.* Reading, UK: Harwood Academic.

Penny, Douglas L., and Michael O. Weise. 1994. "By the Power of Beelzebub: An Aramaic Incantation Formula from Qumran (4Q560)." *Journal of Biblical Literature* 113: 627–50.

Pernigotti, Sergio. 1995. "La magia copta: i testi." In W. Haase (ed.), *Aufstieg und Niedergang der Römischen Welt*, pt. II, 18.5: 3685–3730. Berlin: de Gruyter.

Peterson, Erik. 1948. "La Libération d'Adam de l'anagke." *Revue Biblique* 55: 199–214.

————. 1953. "Das Amulet von Acre." *Aegyptus* 33: 172–78.

Pettersson, O. 1957. "Magic-Religion: Some Marginal Notes to an Old Problem." *Ethnos* 22: 109–19.

Philips, Charles R. 1986. "The Sociology of Religious Knowledge in the Roman Empire to A.D. 284." In W. Haase (ed.), *Aufstieg und Niedergang der Römischen Welt*, pt. II, 16.3: 2677–2773. Berlin: de Gruyter.

Philo of Alexandria. 1929–1962. *Philo with an English Translation*, 10 vols., trans. F. H. Colson and G. H. Whitaker. Cambridge, MA: Harvard University Press.

Piaget, Jean. 1997 [1925]. *The Child's Conception of the World*, trans. Joan and Andrew Tomlinson. London: Routledge.

Pinch, Geraldine. 1994. *Magic in Ancient Egypt*. London: British Museum Press.

Pines, Shlomo. 1982. "Wrath and Creatures of Wrath in Pahlavi, Jewish, and New Testament Sources." In Shaul Shaked (ed.), *Irano-Judaica: Studies Relating to Jewish Contacts with Persian Culture Throughout the Ages*, 76–82. Jerusalem: Ben-Zvi Institute.

―――. 1988. "On the Term Ruḥaniyyot and Its Origin and on Judah Halevi's Doctrine." *Tarbiz* 57: 511–34 (Hebrew).

Pognon, Henri B. 1979 [1898]. *Inscriptions mandaïtes des coupes de Khouabir*. Paris: Imprimerie nationale.

Polliack, Meira (ed.). 2003. *Karaite Judaism: A Guide to Its History and Literary Sources*. Leiden: Brill.

Popkin, Richard H. 1987. "Relativism." In *The Encyclopedia of Religion*, 12: 274–75. New York: Macmillan.

Preisendanz, Karl. 1972. "Fluchtafeln (defixion)." In *Reallexikon für Antike und Christentum*, 8: 1–29. Stuttgart: A. Hiersemann.

―――. 1973–1974. *Papyri Graecae Magicae: Die Griechischen Zauberpapyri*, rev. ed. Stuttgart: B. G. Teubner.

Preus, Julius. 1983. *Biblical and Talmudic Medicine*, trans. Fred Rosner. New York: Hebrew Publishing.

Puech, Émile. 1989–1990. "11QpsApa, Un rituel d'exorcismes: Essai de reconstruction." *Revue de Qumran* 14: 377–408.

Rabinowitz, Louis I. 1972. "Divination, in the Talmud." In *Encyclopedia Judaica*, 6: 116–18. Jerusalem: Keter.

Rabinowitz, Raphael N. 1960. *Sefer Dikdukei Sofrim*, 15 vols. New York: Gross & Weiss (Hebrew).

Radcliffe-Brown, Alfred R. 1948. *The Andaman Islanders*. Glencoe, IL: Free Press.

―――. 1958. *Method in Social Anthropology: Selected Essays*. Chicago: University of Chicago Press.

―――. 1965. *Structure and Function in Primitive Society: Essays and Addresses*. New York: Free Press.

Radin, Paul. 1957. *Primitive Religion: Its Nature and Origin*. New York: Dover.

Raffaeli, Samuel. 1920. "A Recently Discovered Samaritan Charm." *Journal of the Palestine Oriental Society* 1: 143–44.

Rahmani, Levi. 1961. "The Maon Synagogue: The Small Finds." *Eretz Israel* 6: 82–85 (Hebrew).

Rapoport, Shlomo J. L. 1852. *Sefer Erech Millin*. Prague (Hebrew).

Ratzaby, Yehuda. 1992. "The Sorcery Motif in Bridegroom Songs." *Tarbiz* 61: 117–25 (Hebrew).

Ravitzky, Aviezer. 2010. "'The Ravings of Amulet Writers': Maimonides and His Disciples on Language, Nature, and Magic." In Ephraim Kanarfogel and Moshe Sokolow (eds.), *Between Rashi and Maimonides: Themes in Medieval Jewish Thought, Literature, and Exegesis*, 93–130. New York: Yeshiva University Press.

Ray, Benjamin. 1973. "Performative Utterances in African Rituals." *History of Religions* 13: 16–35.

Rebiger, Bill. 1999. "Bildung magischer Namen im Sefer Shimmush Tehillim." *Frankfurter Judaistische Beiträge* 26: 7–24.

———. 2003. "Die Magische Verwendung von Psalmen im Judentum." In Erich Zenger (ed.), *Ritual und Poesie: Formen und Orte religiöser Dichtung im Alten Orient, im Judentum und im Christentum*, 265–81. Freiburg: Herder.

———. 2010. *Sefer Shimush Tehillim: Buch vom magischen Gebrauch der Psalmen: Edition, Übersetzung und Komentar*. Tübingen: Mohr-Siebeck.

Rebiger, Bill, and Peter Schäfer. 2009. *Sefer ha-Razim I/II: Das Buch der Geheimnisse I/II*, 2 vols. Tübingen: Mohr-Siebeck.

Reed, Annette Y. 2005. *Fallen Angels and the History of Judaism and Christianity: The Reception of Enochic Literature*. Cambridge, UK: Cambridge University Press.

Reifenberg, Adolf. 1950. *Ancient Hebrew Arts*. New York: Schocken.

Reinach, Salomon. 1905–1923. *Cultes, mythes et religion*, 5 vols. Paris: E. Leroux.

Reiner, Elchanan. 2004. "Joseph the Comes of Tiberias and the Jewish-Christian Dialogue in Fourth Century Galilee." In Lee I. Levine (ed.), *Continuity and Renewal: Jews and Judaism in Byzantine-Christian Palestine*, 355–86. Jerusalem: Yad Izhak Ben-Zvi (Hebrew).

Reiner, Erica. 1995. *Astral Magic in Babylonia*. Philadelphia: American Philosophical Society.

Ritner, Robert K. 1992. "Religion vs. Magic: The Evidence of the Magical Statue Bases." In Ulrich Luft (ed.), *The Intellectual Heritage of Egypt*, 493–501. Studia Aegyptia 14. Budapest: Eoetvoes Lorand University.

———. 1993. *The Mechanics of Ancient Egyptian Magical Practices*. Chicago: Oriental Institute, University of Chicago.

———. 1995. "Egyptian Magical Practice Under the Roman Empire: The Demotic Spells and Their Religious Context." In W. Haase (ed.), *Aufstieg und Niedergang der Römischen Welt*, pt. II, 18.5: 3333–79. Berlin: de Gruyter.

Robertson, Roland. 1970. *The Sociological Interpretation of Religion*. Oxford: Blackwell.

———. 1987. "Functionalism." In *The Encyclopedia of Religion*, 5: 446–50. New York: Macmillan.

Robertson Smith, William. 1972 [1889]. *The Religion of the Semites*. New York: Schocken.

Rochberg-Halton, Francesca. 1988. *Aspects of Babylonian Celestial Divination: The Lunar Eclipse Tablets of Enuma Anu Enlil*. Horn, Austria: F. Berger.

———. 1989. "Babylonian Horoscopes and Their Sources." *Orientalia* 58: 102–44.

Róheim, Géza. 1955. *Magic and Schizophrenia*. New York: International Universities Press.

Rohrbacher-Sticker, Claudia. 1996. "From Sense to Nonsense, from Incantation Prayer to Magical Spell." *Jewish Studies Quarterly* 3: 24–46.

Römer, Willem H. P. 1969. "The Religion of Ancient Mesopotamia." In C. Jouco Bleeker and Geo Widengren (eds.), *Historia Religionum: Handbook for the History of Religions*, 1: 115–94. Leiden: Brill.

Rosenfeld, Ben-Zion. 1999. "R. Simeon b. Yohai: Wonder Worker and Magician Scholar, *Saddik* and *Hasid*." *Revue des études juives* 158: 349–84.

Rosengren, Karl E. 1976. "Malinowski's Magic: The Riddle of the Empty Cell." *Current Anthropology* 17: 667–75.

Rossell, William H. 1953. *A Handbook of Magical Aramaic Texts*. Ringwood, NJ: Shelton College.

Rubenstein, Jeffrey. 1999. *Talmudic Stories: Narrative Art, Composition, and Culture*. Baltimore: Johns Hopkins University Press.

Rubin, Salomon. 1887. *Maʿaseh Taʿatuʿim: History of Superstitions Among All the Peoples with Special Attention to the Jewish People.* Vienna. (Hebrew).

Rundel, Bede. 1990. *Wittgenstein and Contemporary Philosophy of Language.* Oxford: Blackwell.

Saar, Ortal-Paz. 2003. "Superstitions in Israel During the Roman and Early-Byzantine Periods." M.A. thesis, Tel Aviv University (Hebrew).

————. 2007. "Success, Protection, and Grace: Three Fragments of a Personalised Magical Handbook." *Ginzei Qedem* 3: 101*–135*.

————. 2008. "Jewish Love Magic: From Late Antiquity to the Middle Ages." Ph.D. diss., Tel Aviv University (Hebrew).

————. 2013. "'And He Burned His Heart for Her': The Motif of Fire in Love Spells from the Cairo Genizah." *Peʿamim* 133–134: 209–239 (Hebrew).

Safrai, Shmuel. 1965. "Teachings of Pietists in Mishnaic Literature." *Journal of Jewish Studies* 16: 15–33.

————. 1985. "The Pious (Hasidim) and the Men of Deeds." *Zion* 50: 133–54 (Hebrew).

Safran, Bezalel. 1992. "Maimonides' Attitude to Magic and to Related Types of Thinking." In Bezalel Safran and Eliyahu Safran (eds.), *Porat Yosef: Studies Presented to Rabbi Dr. Yosef Safran*, 93–110. Hoboken, NJ: Ktav.

Said, Edward W. 1978. *Orientalism.* New York: Pantheon.

Salmon ben Yeruhim. 1934. *Sefer Milḥamot Adonai*, ed. Israel Davidson. New York: JTSA (Hebrew).

Salzer, Dorothea M. 2010. *Die Magie der Anspielung: Form und Funktion der biblischen Anspielungen in der magischen Texten der Kairoer Geniza.* Tübingen: Mohr Siebeck.

Sarfatti, G. B. 1957. "Pious Men, Men of Deeds, and the Early Prophets." *Tarbiz* 26: 126–53 (Hebrew).

Särkiö, Pekka. 2004. "Salomo und die Dämonen." In Hannu Juusola, Juha Laulainen, and Heikki Palva (eds.), *Verbum et Calamus: Semitic and Related Studies in Honour of the Sixtieth Birthday of Professor Tapani Harviainen*, 305–22. Helsinki: Finnish Oriental Society.

Sartre, Jean-Paul. 1948. *The Emotions: Outline of a Theory*, trans. Bernard Frechtman. New York: Philosophical Library.

Sasson, Jack M. 1986. "Mari Dreams." *Journal of American Oriental Studies* 103: 283–93.

Schaefer, Karl R. 2001. "Eleven Medieval Arabic Block Prints in the Cambridge University Library." *Arabica* 48: 210–39.

Schäfer, Peter. 1981. *Synopse zur Hekhalot-Literatur.* Tübingen: Mohr.

———. 1984. *Geniza-Fragmente zur Hekhalot-Literatur.* Tübingen: Mohr.

———. 1988. *Hekhalot-Studien.* Tübingen: Mohr.

———. 1990. "Jewish Magic Literature in Late Antiquity and Early Middle Ages." *Journal of Jewish Studies* 41: 75–91.

———. 1992. *The Hidden and Manifest God: Some Major Themes in Early Jewish Mysticism.* Albany: SUNY Press.

———. 1993. "Merkavah Mysticism and Magic." In Peter Schäfer and Joseph Dan (eds.), *Gershom Scholem's Major Trends in Jewish Mysticism 50 Years After,* 59–83. Tübingen: Mohr Siebeck.

———. 1995. "The Magic of the Golem: The Early Development of the Golem Legend." *Journal of Jewish Studies* 46: 249–61.

———. 1996. "Jewish Liturgy and Magic." In Hubert Cancik, Hermann Lichtenberger, and Peter Schäfer (eds.), *Geschichte-Tradition-Reflexion: Festschrif für Martin Hengel zum 70. Geburstag,* 1: 541–57. Tübingen: Mohr Siebeck.

———. 1997. "Magic and Religion in Ancient Judaism." In Peter Schäfer and Hans G. Kippenberg (eds.), *Envisioning Magic,* 19–43. Leiden: Brill.

Schäfer, Peter, and Shaul Shaked. 1994–1999. *Magische Texte aus der Kairoer Geniza,* 3 vols. Tübingen: Mohr Siebeck.

Schaff, Philip (ed.). 1978. *A Select Library of the Nicene and Post-Nicene Fathers of the Christian Church.* First Series, vol. 10, *Saint Chrisostomos: Homilies on the Gospel of Saint Matthew.* Grand Rapids, MI: T & T Clark.

Schiffman, Lawrence H., and Michael D. Swartz. 1992. *Hebrew and Aramaic Incantation Texts from the Cairo Genizah.* Sheffield, UK: JSOT Press.

Schmidt, Brian B. 2002. "Canaanite Magic vs. Israelite Religion: Deuteronomy 18 and the Taxonomy of Taboo." In Marvin Meyer and Paul Mirecki (eds.), *Magic and Ritual in the Ancient World,* 242–59. Leiden: Brill.

Schmitt, Rüdiger. 2004. *Magie im Alten Testament*. Münster: Ugarit.

Scholem, Gershom. 1946. *Major Trends in Jewish Mysticism*. New York: Schocken.

———. 1965. *Jewish Gnosticism, Merkabah Mysticism, and Talmudic Tradition*, 2nd ed. New York: JTSA.

———. 1974. *Kabbalah*. Jerusalem: Keter.

———. 1981. "*Havdalah de-Rabbi Aqiba*: A Source of the Jewish Magical Tradition from the Geonic Period." *Tarbiz* 50: 243–81 (Hebrew).

———. 1990. *Origins of the Kaballah*, ed. Zvi Werblowsky. Princeton, NJ: Princeton University Press.

Schüngel-Straumann, Helen. 2000. *Tobit*. Freiburg: Herder.

Schwab, Moïse. 1890. "Les coupes magiques et l'hydromancy dans l'antiquité orientale." *Proceedings of the Society of Biblical Archaeology* 12: 292–342.

———. 1891. "Coupes á inscriptions magiques." *Proceedings of the Society of Biblical Archaeology* 13: 583–95.

———. 1906. "Une amulette judéo-araméenne." *Journal Asiatique*, 2nd ser., 7: 5–17.

Schwabe, Moshe, and Abraham Reifenberg. 1946. "A Greek Jewish Amulet from Syria." *Bulletin of the Jewish Palestine Exploration Society* 12: 68–72 (Hebrew).

Schwartz, Dov. 2004. *Amulets, Properties, and Rationalism in Medieval Jewish Thought*. Ramat-Gan: Bar-Ilan University Press (Hebrew).

———. 2005. *Studies on Astral Magic in Medieval Jewish Thought*, trans. David Louvish and Batya Stein. Leiden: Brill.

Schwartz, Yosef. 1996. "From Negation to Silence: Maimonides' Reception in the Latin West." *Iyyun* 45: 389–406 (Hebrew).

Schwartzbaum, Haim. 1993. *Roots and Landscapes: Studies in Folklore*, ed. Eli Yassif. Beer-Sheva: Ben-Gurion University Press (Hebrew).

Schwartzman, Ori. 2007. *White Doctor, Black Gods: Psychiatric Medicine in the Jungles of Africa*. Tel Aviv: Aryeh Nir (Hebrew).

Searle, John R. 1970. *Speech Acts: An Essay in the Philosophy of Language*. Cambridge, UK: Cambridge University Press.

———. 1974. "What Is a Speech-Act? In John R. Searle, *The Philosophy of Language*, 39–53. London: Oxford University Press.

———. 1985. *Expression and Meaning: Studies in the Theory of Speech Acts*. Cambridge, UK: Cambridge University Press.

Segal, Alan F. 1981. "Hellenistic Magic: Some Questions of Definition." In Roelof van den Broeck and Maarten J. Vermaseren (eds.), *Studies in Gnosticism and Hellenistic Religions*, 349–75. Leiden: Brill.

Segal, Judah B. 2000. *Catalogue of the Aramaic and Mandaic Incantation Bowls in the British Museum*. London: British Museum.

Seidel, Jonathan. 1992. "'Release Us and We Will Release You!' Rabbinic Encounters with Witches and Witchcraft." *Journal of the Association of Graduates in Near Eastern Studies* 3: 45–61.

———. 1995. "Charming Criminals: Classification of Magic in the Babylonian Talmud." In Marvin Meyer and Paul Mirecki (eds.), *Ancient Magic and Ritual Power*, 145–66. Leiden: Brill.

———. 1996. "Studies in Ancient Jewish Magic." Ph.D. diss., University of California, Berkeley.

Septimus, Bernard. 1994. "Maimonides on Language." In Avivah Doron (ed.), *The Culture of Spanish Jewry*, 35–54. Tel Aviv: Levinsky College of Education.

Shachar, Isaiah. 1981. *Jewish Tradition in Art: The Feuchtwanger Collection of Judaica*, trans. Rafi Grafman. Jerusalem: Israel Museum.

Shaked, Shaul. 1983. "On Jewish Magical Literature in Muslim Countries: Notes and Examples." *Pe'amim* 15: 15–28 (Hebrew).

———. 1985. "Bagdāna, King of the Demons, and Other Iranian Terms in Babylonian Aramaic Magic." *Acta Iranica* 25: 511–25.

———. 1994. "Between Judaism and Islam: Some Aspects of Folk Religion." *Pe'amim* 60: 4–19 (Hebrew).

———. 1995. "'Peace Be upon You, Exalted Angels': On Hekhalot, Liturgy, and Incantation Bowls." *Jewish Studies Quarterly* 2: 197–219.

———. 1997. "Popular Religion in Sasanian Babylonia." *Jerusalem Studies in Arabic and Islam* 21: 103–17.

———. 1999a. "Jesus in the Magic Bowls: Apropos Dan Levene's '. . . and by the name of Jesus . . . .'" *Jewish Studies Quarterly* 6: 309–19.

———. 1999b. "The Poetic of Spells: Language and Structure in Aramaic Incantations of Late Antiquity, 1: The Divorce Formula and Its Ramifications." In Tzvi Abusch and Karl van der Toorn (eds.), *Mesopotamian Magic: Textual, Historical, and Interpretative Perspectives*, 173–95. Groningen: Styx.

———. 2000a. "Manichaean Incantation Bowls in Syriac." *Jerusalem Studies in Arabic and Islam* 24: 58–92.

———. 2000b. "Medieval Jewish Magic in Relation to Islam: Theoretical Attitudes and Genres." In Benjamin H. Hary, John L. Hayes, and Fred Astren (eds.), *Judaism and Islam: Boundaries, Communication, and Interaction*, 97–109. Leiden: Brill.

———. 2002. "Jews, Christians, and Pagans in the Aramaic Incantation Bowls of the Sasanian Period." In Andriana Destro and Mauro Pesce (eds.), *Religions and Cultures*, 61–89. Binghamton, NY: Global Publications.

———. 2005a. "Form and Purpose in Aramaic Spells: Some Jewish Themes (The Poetics of Magic Texts). In S. Shaked (ed.), *Officina Magica: The Working of Magic*, 1–30. Leiden: Brill.

———. 2005b. "Incantation Bowls and Amulet Tablets: How to Get Rid of Demons and Harmful Beings." *Qadmoniyot* 129: 2–13 (Hebrew).

———. 2010. "Time Designations and Other Recurrent Themes in Aramaic Incantation Bowls." In Jeffrey Stackert, Barbara Nevling Porter, and David P. Wright (eds.), *Gazing on the Deep: Ancient Near Eastern and Other Studies in Honor of Tzvi Abusch*, 221–34. Bethesda: CDL.

———. 2011. "Transmission and Transformation of Spells: The Case of the Jewish Babylonian Aramaic Bowls." In Gideon Bohak, Yuval Harari, and Shaul Shaked (eds.), *Continuity and Innovation in the Magical Tradition*, 219–34. Leiden: Brill.

Shaked, Shaul, James N. Ford, and Siam Bhayro. 2013. *Aramaic Bowl Spells: Jewish Babylonian Aramaic Bowls*, vol. 1. Leiden: Brill.

Shapiro, Marc B. 2000. "Maimonidean Halakhah and Superstition." *Maimonidean Studies* 4: 61–108.

Sharpe, Eric J. 1975. *Comparative Religion: A History*. London: Duckworth.

———. 1987. "Tylor, E. B." In *The Encyclopedia of Religion*, 15: 107–8. New York: Macmillan.

Shinan, Avigdor. 1983. "Miracles, Wonders, and Magic in the Aramaic Targums of the Pentateuch." In Alexander Rofé and Yair Zakovitch (eds.), *Isaac Leo Seligmann Volume: Essays on the Bible and the Ancient World*, 2: 419–26. Jerusalem: E. Rubinstein (Hebrew).

———. 1992. *The Embroidered Targum: The Aggadah in Targum Pseudo-Jonathan of the Pentateuch*. Jerusalem: Magnes (Hebrew).

Simon, Marcel. 1986. *Verus Israel: A Study of the Relations Between Christians and Jews in the Roman Empire (135–425)*, trans. H. Mckearing. Oxford: Oxford University Press.

Simone, Michel. 2001. *Die Magischen Gemmen im Britischen Museum.* London: British Museum Press.

Sirat, Colette. 1975. *Jewish Philosophical Thought in the Middle Ages.* Jerusalem: Keter.

———. 1985. *Les papyrus en caractères hébraïques.* Paris: CNRS.

Smith, Jonathan Z. 1973. "When the Bough Breaks." *History of Religions* 12: 342–71.

———. 1995. "Trading Places." In Marvin Meyer and Paul Mirecki (eds.), *Ancient Magic and Ritual Power,* 13–27. Leiden: Brill.

Smith, Kirby F. 1951. "Magic, Greek and Roman." In *Encyclopedia of Religion and Ethics,* 8: 269–89. New York: C. Scribner's Sons.

Smith, Morton. 1978. *Jesus the Magician.* San Francisco: Harper & Row.

———. 1981. "Old Testament Motifs in the Iconography of the British Museum's Magical Gems." In Lionel Casson and Martin Price (eds.), *Coins, Culture, and History in the Ancient World: Numismatic and Other Studies in Honor of Bluma L. Trell,* 187–94. Detroit: Wayne State University Press.

———. 1982. "Helios in Palestine." *Eretz Israel* 16: 199*–214*.

———. 1996. "The Jewish Elements in the Magical Papyri." In Morton Smith, *Studies in the Cult of Yahweh,* 2: 242–56. Leiden: Brill.

Sokoloff, Michael. 1990. *A Dictionary of Jewish Palestinian Aramaic.* Ramat-Gan: Bar-Ilan University Press.

———. 2002. *A Dictionary of Jewish Babylonian Aramaic of the Talmudic and Geonic Periods.* Ramat-Gan: Bar-Ilan University Press.

Sørensen, Jesper. 2007. *A Cognitive Theory of Magic.* Lanham, MD: Alta Mira.

Spencer, Herbert. 1893. *The Principles of Sociology.* New York: D. Appleton.

Sperber, Daniel. 1994. *Magic and Folklore in Rabbinic Literature.* Ramat-Gan: Bar-Ilan University Press.

———. 1998. *The City in Roman Palestine.* New York: Oxford University Press.

Spier, Jeffrey. 2007. *Late Antique and Early Christian Gems.* Wiesbaden: Reichert.

Starr, Chester G. 1991. *The Origins of Greek Civilization, 1100–650 B.C.* New York: Norton.

Stein, Dinah. 2005. *Maxims, Magic, Myth: A Folkloristic Perspective of Pirkei de Rabbi Eliezer.* Jerusalem: Magnes (Hebrew).

————. 2009. "Let the 'People' Go: The 'Folk' and Its 'Lore' as Tropes in the Reconstruction of Rabbinic Culture." *Prooftexts* 29: 206–41.

Stern, Ephraim, and Ilan Sharon. 1995. "Tel Dor, 1993: Preliminary Report." *Israel Exploration Journal* 45: 26–36.

Stern, Josef. 2000. "Maimonides on Language and the Science of Language." In Robert S. Cohen and Hillel Levine (eds.), *Maimonides and the Sciences,* 173–226. Dordrecht: Kluwer.

Stern, Sacha. 1996. "Figurative Art and Halakhah in the Mishnaic-Talmudic Period." *Zion* 61: 397–419 (Hebrew).

————. 2005. "Rachel Elior on Ancient Jewish Calendars: A Critique." *Aleph* 5: 287–92.

Stocking, George (ed.). 1992. *Colonial Situations: Essays on the Contextualization of Anthropological Knowledge.* Madison: University of Wisconsin Press.

Stone, Michael E. 1976. "Lists of Revealed Things in the Apocalyptic Literature." In Frank M. Cross, Werner E. Lemke, and Patrick D. Miller (eds.), *Magnalia Dei: The Mighty Acts of God,* 414–52. Garden City, NY: Doubleday.

Strack, Hermann L., and Paul Billerbeck. 1922. "Zur altjüdischen Dämonologie." In *Kommentar zum neuen Testament aus Talmud und Midrasch,* vol. IV, pt. I, 501–35. Munich: Beck.

Stratton, Kimberly B. 2007. *Naming the Witch: Magic, Ideology, and Stereotype in the Ancient World.* New York: Columbia University Press.

Stroumsa, Sarah. 1999. "The Sabians of Haran and the Sabians of Maimonides' Theory of the History of Religions." *Sefunot* 22: 277–95 (Hebrew).

————. 2001, "'Ravings': Maimonides' Concept of Pseudo-Science." *Aleph* 1: 141–63.

Stuckenbruck, Loren T. 2003. "Giant Mythology and Demonology: From the Ancient Near East to the Dead Sea Scrolls." In Armin Lange, Hermann Lichtenberger, and K. F. Diethard Römheld (eds.), *Die Dämonen: Die Dämonologie der israelitisch-jüdischen und frühchristlichen Literatur im Kontext ihrer Umwelt,* 318–38. Tübingen: Mohr Siebeck.

Styers, Randall. 2004. *Making Magic: Religion, Magic, and Science in the Modern World.* Oxford: Oxford University Press.

Subbotsky, Eugene. 2010. *Magic and the Mind: Mechanisms, Functions, and Development of Magical Thinking and Behavior.* New York: Oxford University Press.

Sullivan, Lawrence E. 1986. "Sound and Senses: Toward a Hermeneutic of Performance." *History of Religions* 26: 1–33.

Sviri, Sarah. 2002. "Words of Power and the Power of Words: Mystical Linguistics in the Work of al-Hakim al-Tirmidhi." *Jerusalem Studies in Arabic and Islam* 27: 204–44.

Swanson, Guy E. 1960. *The Birth of the Gods.* Ann Arbor: University of Michigan Press.

Swartz, Michael D. 1990. "Scribal Magic and Its Rhetoric: Formal Patterns in Medieval Hebrew and Aramaic Incantation Texts from the Cairo Genizah." *Harvard Theological Review* 83: 163–80.

———. 1992. *Mystical Prayer in Ancient Judaism.* Tübingen: Mohr-Siebeck.

———. 1994. "Book and Tradition in Hekhalot and Magical Literature." *Journal of Jewish Thought and Philosophy* 3: 197–219.

———. 1995. "Magical Piety in Ancient and Medieval Judaism." In Marvin Meyer and Paul Mirecki (eds.), *Ancient Magic and Ritual Power*, 167–83. Leiden: Brill.

———. 1996. *Scholastic Magic: Ritual and Revelation in Early Jewish Mysticism.* Princeton, NJ: Princeton University Press.

———. 2000. "The Seal of the Merkavah." In Richard Valantasis (ed.), *Religions of Late Antiquity in Practice*, 322–29. Princeton, NJ: Princeton University Press.

———. 2001a. "The Dead Sea Scrolls and Later Jewish Magic and Mysticism." *Dead Sea Discoveries* 8: 182–93.

———. 2001b. "Temple Ritual in Jewish Magic Literature." *Pe'amim* 85: 62–75 (Hebrew).

———. 2002. "Sacrificial Themes in Jewish Magic." In Paul Mirecki and Marvin Meyer (eds.), *Magic and Ritual in the Ancient World*, 302–15. Leiden: Brill.

———. 2003. "Divination and Its Discontents." In Scott Noegel, Joel Walker, and Brannon Wheeler (eds.), *Prayer, Magic, and the Stars in the Ancient and Late Antique World*, 322–29. University Park: Pennsylvania State University Press.

———. 2006a. "The Aesthetics of Blessing and Cursing: Literary and Iconographic Dimensions of Hebrew and Aramaic Blessing and Curse Texts." *Journal of Ancient Near Eastern Religions* 5: 187–211.

———. 2006b. "Jewish Magic in Late Antiquity." In Steven T. Katz (ed.), *The Cambridge History of Judaism*, 4: 699–720. Cambridge, UK: Cambridge University Press.

Szpakowska, Kasia. 2001. "Through the Looking Glass: Dreams and Nightmares in Pharaonic Egypt." In Kelly Bulkeley (ed.), *Dreams: A Reader on the Religious, Cultural, and Psychological Dimensions of Dreaming*, 29–43. New York: Palgrave.

———. 2003. *Behind Closed Eyes: Dreams and Nightmares in Ancient Egypt*. Swansea: Classical Press of Wales.

———. 2010. "Nightmares in Ancient Egypt." In Jean-Marie Husser and Alice Mouton (eds.), *Le cauchemar dans les sociétés antiques*, 21–39. Paris: De Boccard.

———. 2011. "Dream Interpretation in the Ramesside Age." In Mark Collier and Steven Snape (eds.), *Ramesside Studies in Honour of K. A. Kitchen*, 509–17. Bolton: Rutherford.

Tambiah, Stanley J. 1968. "The Magical Power of Words." *Man* 3: 175–208.

———. 1973. "Form and Meaning of Magical Acts: A Point of View." In Robin Horton and Ruth Finnegan (eds.), *Modes of Thought*, 199–229. London: Faber.

———. 1985a. "On Flying Witches and Flying Canoes: The Coding of Male and Female Values." In Stanley J. Tambiah, *Culture, Thought, and Social Action: An Anthropological Perspective*, 287–315. Cambridge, MA: Harvard University Press.

———. 1985b. "A Performative Approach to Ritual." In Stanley J. Tambiah, *Culture, Thought, and Social Action: An Anthropological Perspective*, 123–66. Cambridge, MA: Harvard University Press.

———. 1995. *Magic, Science, Religion, and the Scope of Rationality*. Cambridge, UK: Cambridge University Press.

Ta-Shma, Israel. 1986. "Notes to 'Hymns from Qumran.'" *Tarbiz* 55: 440–42 (Hebrew).

Tax, Sol. 1969. *Evolution After Darwin*, 3 vols. Chicago: University of Chicago Press.

Teitelbaum, I. 1964. "Jewish Magic in the Sasanian Period." Ph.D. diss., Dropsie College.

Temkin, Owsie. 1994. *The Falling Sickness: A History of Epilepsy from the Greeks to the Beginnings of Modern Neurology*, rev. ed. Baltimore: Johns Hopkins University Press.

Ten-Ami, Alon. 2013. "Ashmedai in Babylonian Incantation Bowls." *Pe'amim* 133–134: 185–208 (Hebrew).

Testa, Emmanuel. 1967. *L'Huile de la Foi: L'Onction des malades sur une lamelle du 1er siècle.* Jerusalem: Imprimerie des PP. Franciscains.

Thomas, Keith. 1971. *Religion and the Decline of Magic: Studies in Popular Beliefs in Sixteenth and Seventeenth Century England.* London: Weidenfeld & Nicolson.

Thomas, Nicolas. 1994. *Colonialism's Culture: Anthropology, Travel, and Government.* Princeton, NJ: Princeton University Press.

———. 1996. "Colonialism." In Alan Barnard and Jonathan Spencer (eds.), *Encyclopedia of Social and Cultural Anthropology*, 111–14. London: Routledge.

Thompson, Reginald C. 1908. *Semitic Magic.* London: Luzac.

Thomsen, Marie-Louise. 2001. "Witchcraft and Magic in Ancient Mesopotamia." In Bengt Ankarloo and Stuart Clark (eds.), *Witchcraft and Magic in Europe: Biblical and Pagan Societies*, 1–95. Philadelphia: University of Pennsylvania Press.

Titiev Misha. 1960. "A Fresh Approach to the Problem of Magic and Religion." *Southwestern Journal of Anthropology* 16: 292–98.

Tocci, Franco M. 1984. "Metatron, 'Arcidemonio' e Mytrt (Μιθρας?) nel *Pisra de-R. Hanina ben Dosa*." In L. Lanciotti (ed.), *Incontro di Religioni in Asia tra il III e il X secolo d. C., Atti del Convegno Internazionale*, 79–97. Civiltà Veneziana 39. Florence: Olschki.

———. 1986. "Note e documenti di letteratura religiosa e parareligiosa giudaica." *Annali dell'Instituto Orientale di Napoli* 46: 101–8.

Tomlin, Roger S. O. 1988. *Tabellae Sulis: Roman Inscribed Tablets on Tin and Lead from the Sacred Spring of Bath.* Oxford: Oxford University Committee for Archaeology.

Torijano, Pablo A. 2002. *Solomon, the Esoteric King: From King to Magus, Development of a Tradition.* Leiden: Brill.

Trachtenberg, Joshua. 1970 [1939]. *Jewish Magic and Superstition.* New York: Atheneum.

Trompf, Garry W. 1987. "Spencer, Herbert." In *The Encyclopedia of Religion*, 14: 4–6. New York: Macmillan.

Tsereteli, Konstantin G. 1996. "An Aramaic Amulet from Mtskheta." *Ancient Civilizations from Scythia to Siberia* 3: 218–40.

Twelftree, Graham H. 1993. *Jesus the Exorcist: A Contribution to the Study of the Historical Jesus.* Tübingen: Mohr.

Twersky, Isadore. 1972. *A Maimonides Reader.* New York: Behrman House.

———. 1980. *Introduction to the Code of Maimonides (Mishneh Torah).* New Haven, CT: Yale University Press.

———. 1988–1989. "Halakha and Science: Perspectives on the Epistemology of Maimonides." *Shenaton Ha-Mishpat Ha-Ivri* 14–15: 121–51 (Hebrew).

Tylor, Edward B. 1874. *Primitive Culture: Researches into the Development of Mythology, Philosophy, Religion, Language, Art, and Custom.* New York: Holt.

———. 1964 [1870]. *Researches into the Early History of Mankind.* Chicago: University of Chicago Press.

Ulmer, Rivka. 1994. *The Evil Eye in the Bible and in Rabbinic Literature.* Hoboken, NJ: Ktav.

———. 1996. "The Depiction of Magic in Rabbinic Texts: The Rabbinic and the Greek Concept of Magic." *Journal for the Study of Judaism* 27: 289–303.

Urbach, Ephraim E. 1967. "The Traditions About Merkabah Mysticism in the Tannaitic Period." In Ephraim E. Urbach, R. J. Zwi Werblowsky, and Chaim Wirszubski (eds.), *Studies in Mysticism and Religion Presented to Gershom Scholem on His Seventieth Birthday,* 1–28. Jerusalem: Magnes (Hebrew).

———. 1975. *The Sages: Their Concepts and Beliefs,* trans. Israel Abrahams. Jerusalem: Magnes.

———. 1999. "Prophet and Sage in the Jewish Heritage." In Ephraim E. Urbach, *Collected Writings in Jewish Studies,* 393–403. Jerusalem: Magnes.

———. 2002a. "Halakha and Prophecy." In Ephraim E. Urbach, *The World of the Sages: Collected Essays,* 21–49. Jerusalem: Magnes (Hebrew).

———. 2002b. "The Laws of Idolatry in the Light of Historical and Archaeological Facts in the Third Century." In Ephraim E. Urbach, *The World of the Sages: Collected Essays,* 125–78. Jerusalem: Magnes (Hebrew).

———. 2002c. "When Did Prophecy Cease?" In Ephraim E. Urbach, *The World of the Sages: Collected Essays,* 9–20. Jerusalem: Magnes (Hebrew).

van Binsbergen, Wim, and Frans Wiggermann. 1999. "Magic in History: A Theoretical Perspective and Its Application to Ancient Mesopotamia." In Tzvi Abusch and Karl van der Toorn (eds.), *Mesopotamian Magic: Textual, Historical, and Interpretative Perspectives*, 3–34. Groningen: Styx.

VanderKam, James C. 1989. *The Book of Jubilees*. Louvain: E. Peeters.

———. 2003. "The Demons in the *Book of Jubilees*." In Armin Lange, Hermann Lichtenberger, and K. F. Diethard Römheld (eds.), *Die Dämonen: Die Dämonologie der israelitisch-jüdischen und frühchristlichen Literatur im Kontext ihrer Umwelt*, 339–64. Tübingen: Mohr Siebeck.

van der Toorn, Karl, Bob Becking, and Pieter W. van der Horst (eds.). 1999. *Dictionary of Deities and Demons in the Bible*, rev. ed. Leiden: Brill.

van Gennep, Arnold. 1960 [1909]. *The Rites of Passage*, trans. Monika B. Vizedom and Gabrielle L. Caffee. Chicago: University of Chicago Press.

Vasilios, Iakovos. 2001. "Wittgenstein, Religious Belief, and *On Certainty*." In Robert L. Arrington and Mark Addis (eds.), *Wittgenstein and Philosophy of Religion*, 29–50. London: Routledge.

Veltri, Giuseppe. 1993. "Inyan Sota: Halakhische Voraussetzungen für einen magischen Akt nach einer theoretischen Abhandlung aus der Kairoer Geniza." *Frankfurter Judaistische Beiträge* 20: 23–48.

———. 1994. "Defining Forbidden Foreign Customs: Some Remarks on the Rabbinic Halakhah of Magic." *Proceedings of the Eleventh World Congress of Jewish Studies* 3(1): 25–32.

———. 1996a. "Jewish Traditions in Greek Amulets." *Bulletin of Judaeo-Greek Studies* 18: 33–47.

———. 1996b. "Zur Überlieferung medizinisch-magischer Traditionen: Das *metra*-Motiv in den Papyri Magicae und der Kairoer Genizah." *Henoch* 18: 157–75.

———. 1997. *Magie und Halakha: Ansätze zu einem empirischen Wissenschaftsbegriff im spätantiken und frühmittelalterlichen Judentum*. Tübingen: Mohr Siebeck.

———. 1998. "On the Influence of 'Greek Wisdom': Theoretical and Empirical Sciences in Rabbinic Literature." *Jewish Studies Quarterly* 5: 300–317.

———. 1998–1999. "The 'Other' Physicians: The Amorites of the Rabbis and the Magi of Pliny." *Korot* 13: 37–54.

————. 2002. "The Figure of the Magician in Rabbinical Literature: From Empirical Science to Theology." *Jerusalem Studies in Arabic and Islam* 26: 187–204.

————. 2011. "Steinschneider's Interstitial Explanation of Magic." In Reimund Leicht and Gad Freudenthal (eds.), *Studies on Steinschneider: Moritz Steinschneider and the Emergence of the Science of Judaism in Nineteenth-Century Germany*, 233–46. Leiden: Brill.

Venco Ricciardi, Roberta. 1973–1974. "Trial Trench at Tel Baruda (Choche)." *Mesopotamia* 8–9: 15–20.

Verman, Mark W., and Shulamit H. Adler. 1993. "Path Jumping in the Jewish Magical Tradition." *Jewish Studies Quarterly* 1: 131–48.

Vermes, Géza. 1972. "Hanina ben Dosa: A Controversial Galilean Saint from the First Century of the Christian Era (I)." *Journal of Jewish Studies* 23: 28–50.

————. 1973. "Hanina ben Dosa: A Controversial Galilean Saint from the First Century of the Christian Era (II)." *Journal of Jewish Studies* 24: 51–64.

Versnel, Henk S. 1991a. "Beyond Cursing: The Appeal to Justice in Judicial Prayers." In Christopher A. Faraone and Dirk Obbink (eds.), *Magika Hiera: Ancient Greek Magic and Religion*, 60–106. New York: Oxford University Press.

————. 1991b. "Some Reflections on the Relationship Magic-Religion." *Numen* 38: 177–97.

Vidas, Moulie. 2013. "Hekhalot Literature, the Babylonian Academies, and the *tanna'im*." In Ra'anan Boustan, Martha Himmelfarb, and Peter Schäfer (eds.), *Hekhalot Literature in Context: Between Byzantium and Babylonia*, 141–76. Tübingen: Mohr Siebeck.

Vilozny, Naama. 2010. "Figure and Image in Magic and Popular Art: Between Babylonia and Palestine, During the Roman and Byzantine Periods." Ph.D. diss., The Hebrew University of Jerusalem (Hebrew).

————. 2011. "Bound You Should Be Forever: Binding Imagery of Jewish Incantation Bowls from Babylonia." *El Presente: Studies in Sephardic Culture* 5: 185*–202* (Hebrew).

————. 2013. "The Art of the Aramaic Incantation Bowls." In Shaul Shaked, James N. Ford, and Siam Bhayro (eds.), *Aramaic Bowl Spells: Jewish Babylonian Aramaic Bowls I*, 29–37. Leiden: Brill.

Vincent, Louis-Hugues. 1908. "Amulette Judéo-araméenne." *Revue Biblique*, n.s., 5: 382–94.

von Beckerath, Jiirgen. 1975. "Astronomie und Astrologie." In *Lexikon der Ägyptologie*, 1: 511–14. Wiesbaden: O. Harrassowitz.

von Stuckrad, Kocku. 1996. *Frömmigkeit und Wissenschaft: Astrologie in Tanach, Qumran und frührabbinischer Literatur.* Frankfurt am Main: Peter Lang.

———. 2000a. "Jewish and Christian Astrology in Late Antiquity: A New Approach." *Numen* 47: 1–40.

———. 2000b. *Das Ringen um die Astrologie: Jüdische und Christlische Beiträge zum antiken Zeitverständnis.* Berlin: de Gruyter.

Vyse, Stuart A. 1997. *Believing in Magic: The Psychology of Superstition.* New York: Oxford University Press.

Wächter, Ludwig. 1969. "Astrologie und Schicksalsglaube im rabbinischen Judentum." *Kairos* 11: 181–200.

Walker, Deward E. 1970. *Systems of North American Witchcraft and Sorcery.* Anthropological Monograph 1. Moscow: University of Idaho.

Wallace, Anthony F. C. 1966. *Religion: An Anthropological View.* New York: Random House.

Wandrey, Irina. 2003. "Fever and Malaria 'for Real' or as a Magical-Literary Topos?" In Klaus Herrmann, Margarete Schlüter, and Giuseppe Veltri (eds.), *Jewish Studies Between the Disciplines*, 257–66. Leiden: Brill.

———. 2004. *"Das Buch des Gewandes" und "Das Buch des Aufrechten."* Tübingen: Mohr Siebeck.

Warner, William L. 1958. *A Black Civilization: A Social Study of an Australian Tribe*, rev. ed. New York: Harper.

Wasserstrom, Steven M. 1991. "The Unwritten Chapter: Notes Towards a Social and Religious History of Genizah Magic." *Pe'amim* 85: 43–61.

———. 1992. "The Magical Texts in the Cairo Genizah." In Joshua Blau and Stefan C. Reif (eds.), *Genizah Research After Ninety Years: The Case of Judaeo-Arabic*, 160–66. Cambridge, UK: Cambridge University Press.

Wax, Rosalie, and Murray Wax. 1961–1962. "The Magical World View." *Journal for the Scientific Study of Religion* 1: 179–88.

———. 1963. "The Notion of Magic." *Current Anthropology* 4: 495–503.

Webb, Clement C. J. 1916. *Group Theories of Religion and the Individual.* London: Allen & Unwin.

Weber, Max. 1965 [1922]. *The Sociology of Religion*, trans. Ephraim Fischoff. London: Methuen.

Webster, Hutton. 1948. *Magic: A Sociological Study.* Stanford, CA: Stanford University Press.

Weinroth, Avraham. 1996. *Spiritualism and Judaism.* Tel Aviv: MOD (Hebrew).

Weinstock, Israel. 1982. "Alpha-Beta of Metatron and Its Meaning." In Israel Weinstock (ed.), *Temirin, Texts, and Studies in Kabbalah and Hasidism*, 2: 51–76. Jerusalem: Mossad Harav Kook (Hebrew).

Weiss, Haim. 2011. *"All Dreams Follow the Mouth?" A Literary and Cultural Reading in the Talmudic "Dream Tractate."* Beer-Sheva: Heksherim Institute (Hebrew).

Weiss, Zeev. 2005. *The Sepphoris Synagogue: Deciphering an Ancient Message Through Its Archaeological and Socio-Historical Context.* Jerusalem: Israel Exploration Society.

Wesselius, Jan W. 1991. "New Syriac Magical Texts." *Bibliotheca Orientalis* 48: 705–16.

White, Robert J. 1975. *The Interpretation of Dreams:* Oneirocritica, *by Artemidorus.* Park Ridge, NJ: Noyes Press.

Whiting, Beatrice B. 1950. *Paiute Sorcery.* New York: Viking Fund.

Winch, Peter. 1964. "Understanding a Primitive Society." *American Philosophical Quarterly* 1: 307–24.

Winkelman, Michael G. 1982. "Magic: A Theoretical Reassessment." *Current Anthropology* 23: 37–44.

———. 1983. "The Anthropology of Magic and Parapsychology." *Parapsychology Review* 14: 13–19.

———. 1992. *Shamans, Priests, and Witches: A Cross-Cultural Study of Magico-Religious Practitioners.* Tucson: Arizona State University.

Winkler, Hans A. 1930. *Siegel und Charaktere in der Muhammedanischen Zauberei.* Berlin: de Gruyter.

Wise, Michael O. 1994. *Thunder in Gemini, and Other Essays on the History, Language, and Literature of Second Temple Palestine.* Sheffield, UK: JSOT Press.

Wittgenstein, Ludwig. 1953. *Philosophical Investigations*, trans. Gertrude E. M. Anscombe. Oxford: Blackwell.

————. 1993. "Remarks on Frazer's *Golden Bough*." In James C. Klagge and Alfred Nordmann (eds.), *Philosophical Occasions, 1912–1951*, 118–55. Indianapolis: Hackett.

Wolfson, Elliot R. 2001. "Phantasmagoria: The Image of the Image in Jewish Magic from Late Antiquity to the Early Middle Ages." *Review of Rabbinic Judaism* 4: 78–120.

Worsley, Peter. 1968. *The Trumpet Shall Sound: A Study of "Cargo" Cults in Melanesia*, rev. ed. London: MacGibbon & Kee.

Wundt, Wilhelm M. 1916 [1906]. *Elements of Folk Psychology*, trans. Edward Schaub. London: Allen & Unwin.

Wünsch, Richard. 1897. *Appendix continens defixionum tabellas in Attica regionse repertas: Inscriptions Graecae II/III—Corpus Inscriptionum Atticarum*. Berlin: G. Reime.

Yadin, Yigael. 1962. *The Scroll of the War of the Sons of Light Against the Sons of Darkness.*, trans. Batya Rubin and Chaim Rubin. Oxford: Oxford University Press.

————. 1963. *The Finds from the Bar Kokhba Period in the Cave of Letters*. Jerusalem: Israel Exploration Society.

————. 1971. *Bar-Kokhba: The Rediscovery of the Legendary Hero of the Second Jewish Revolt Against Rome*. Jerusalem: Weidenfeld & Nicolson.

Yahalom, Joseph. 1999. *Poetry and Society in Jewish Galilee in Late Antiquity*. Tel Aviv: Hakibbutz Hameuchad (Hebrew).

Yamauchi, Edwin. 1967. *Mandaic Incantation Texts*. New Haven, CT: American Oriental Society.

————. 1986. "Magic or Miracles: Diseases, Demons, and Exorcism." In David Wenham and Craig Blomberg (eds.), *Gospel Perspectives*, vol. 6, *The Miracles of Jesus*, 89–183. Sheffield, UK: JSOT Press.

Yardeni, Ada. 1991. "Remarks on the Priestly Blessing on Two Ancient Amulets from Jerusalem." *Vetus Testamentum* 41: 176–85.

Yassif, Eli. 1984. *The Tales of Ben Sira in the Middle Ages*. Jerusalem: Magnes (Hebrew).

————. 1999. *The Hebrew Folktale: History, Genre, Meaning*, trans. Jacqueline S. Teitelbaum. Bloomington: Indiana University Press.

————. 2004. *The Hebrew Collection of Tales in the Middle Ages*. Tel Aviv: Hakibbutz Hameuchad (Hebrew).

Yavetz, Zeev. 1963. *History of the People of Israel*. Tel Aviv: Am Olam (Hebrew).

Yeivin, Shmuel. 1975. "The End of Prophecy." *Ha'umah* 13: 70–79 (Hebrew).

Yellinek, Adolph. 1938. *Bet ha-Midrash*. Jerusalem: Bamberger & Wohrmann.

Yinger, Milton J. 1971. *The Scientific Study of Religion*. London: Macmillan.

Zatelli, Ida. 1991. "Astrology and the Worship of Stars in the Bible." *Zeitschrift für die Alttestamentliche Wissenschaft* 103: 86–99.

Zegwaard, Gerard A. 1968. "Headhunting Practices of the Asmat of Netherlands New Guinea." In Andrew P. Vayda (ed.), *Peoples and Cultures of the Pacific: An Anthropological Reader*, 421–50. Garden City, NY: Natural History Press.

Zuesse, Evan M. 1987. "Divination." In *The Encyclopedia of Religion*, 4: 375–82. New York: Macmillan.

Index of Sources

General Index

Amidah prayer (cont.)
blessing, 267; *Teshuvah* blessing, 267; treatises on systematic use of liturgical blessings, 265, 266–67
Amorites, ways of the (*darkei ha-Emori*), 2, 84, 102–4, 331, 344, 348, 358, 422–23, 434
amulets, 216–30; adjuration texts in, 174, 218–19; from Cairo Genizah, 150, 171, 213n15, 223, 225–26, 227, 229–30; comparison of amulet and bowl texts by same person, 194n51; defined, 216–17; demons, protection against, 401–2; excavated, 227–29; expert amulets, 218n24, 225n49, 337, 348–49, 357, 370, 401–2; harm, meant to cause, 223–24; healing amulets, 220–21; intended clients, 219–20, 224–26, 228–29; Jewish magical literature from, 141, 145, 148, 209; magic bowls compared, 243; Maimonides on, 345–49; matronymic denotation of client in, 219; multilingual, 211n8, 228; parallels with magic recipes, 211–16; placement of, 219; preparation of, 226–27; purposes of, 219–26; *qame'a*, etymology of, 217–18; in rabbinic literature, 357–58; rolled, 218, 220, 222, 224, 228, 230, 233, 241n94, *Pl. 6*; roots, amulets of, 216n22, 306n30, 349n145, 357; subjugation amulets, 221–23; survival of, 227; in synagogues, 148. *See also specific texts* in Index of Sources
Andaman Islanders, Radcliffe-Brown's study of, 50–51
Angel of Darkness, 297
angel of death, 388, 417–18, 423
angels: adjuration of, 88n39; in *Book of Watchers*, 298–99, 313–14; *charac-*
têres (magic signs) as script of, 260n139; divination, as agents of, 412, 421, 429–30; dreams and, 434; *Hekhalot* and *Merkavah* literature, relationship between angels and humans in, 114, 323n76, 352; hierarchy of, 280, 285–86; intermediacy of, viewed as defining characteristic of Jewish magic, 127; Moses, dispute with, 236, 286–87, 324–25, 412; as princes, 421; in Second Temple period literature, 296–99; *Sefer ha-Razim* list of harmful acts performed with help of, 190–92
animals: divination through, 421–22, 423–24; magic bowls, animal bones found in, 234–35n78
animism, 17–19, 26
Année sociologique circle (of Durkheim), 32, 38
anthropological field studies on religion and magic, 7–8, 45–67; Andaman Islanders, Radcliffe-Brown's study of, 50–51; essentialist distinctions versus continuity, 63–67; rabbinic literature, application of anthropological insights to, 96–97; on rationality, 49n89, 52–56, 60–63; on social contexts of witchcraft, 57–60; sociological approach and, 39, 44; speech act theory applied to magic speech, 180–86; Trobriand Islanders, Malinowski's research on, 16n3, 45–50, 55–56n103. *See also* Evans-Pritchard, Edward
Apion of Alexandria, 306n30
Apocrypha and Pseudepigrapha: gender and magic in, 99; heavenly world, hierarchy of, 280; on

Haltburn golden leaf amulet, 229n65
Hamilton, Victor, 136n160
Ha-Minim blessing, 267
Hammond, Dorothy, 65, 122n124
R. Ḥanina, 355, 376, 389, 430n214,
    450, 453, 458
R. Ḥanina b. Dosa, 140, 146, 236,
    270–72, 394n116, 404, 413
Harari, Yuval, 152–53
Ḥarba de-Moshe (The Sword of
    Moses), 284–90; on *Amidah* prayer
    and blessings, 267n157; compared
    to other treatises, 286, 288;
    contents and organization, 285–89;
    dating, 289; divine omnipotence,
    human magical knowledge
    anchored in, 368n45; Greek
    elements in, 211n8; *Hekhalot* and
    Merkavah literature, historical
    studies of, 119, 133n151; literary
    framework, as treatise with,
    264n150, 275, 284–90; magic
    recipes from, 258, 258–59nn136–137,
    260, 288–89, *Pl. 21;* Moses receiv-
    ing magic mysteries from angels
    in, 200n59; multiple languages in,
    289; performative language and
    speech act theory, 190, 192, 195,
    200; rabbinic literature, historical
    studies of, 88n39; response of Rav
    Hai Gaon to sages of Kairouan
    on, 336; as type of Jewish magical
    treatise, 140–41, 146n192, 153, 255
harlotry and witchcraft, relationship
    between, 314, 354–55, 375n64,
    378n72
ha-Satan/Satan, 296, 389
Hasidism, 107
Havdalah de-Rabbi Aqiva: Hekhalot
    and *Merkavah* literature, historical
    studies of, 119, 133n141; magic

bowls, Aramaic dialect of,
    270n165; performative language in,
    190, 191–92, 195; performative
    nucleus, as Jewish magical treatise
    with, 270–71; purpose of, 271n166;
    as type of Jewish magical treatise,
    145–46, 255
Havdalah prayer, 191–92
healing: amulets, 220–21; *Ḥarba
    de-Moshe* magic recipes for, 288;
    Havdalah de-Rabbi Aqiva, healing
    incantation from, 191–92; Jesus, in
    name of, 371–72; legitimate versus
    illegitimate, in rabbinic literature,
    108–9; magic bowls, 243–46; in
    nonmagic Jewish literature, 207–8;
    rabbinic literature, beneficial
    magical prescriptions in, 357–64;
    skulls, magic, 252
Hekhalot and *Merkavah* literature, 11,
    113–32, 316–30; adjurations and
    performative language in, 118–19,
    122–23, 124–28, 131, 148, 174, 187–88,
    189, 193; angels and humans in,
    114, 323n76, 352; Bohak on, 129–31;
    from Cairo Genizah, 114n101, 128,
    329; cosmological order in, 280;
    Davila on, 128–29; defined, 114,
    316; demons, chariots used by,
    397n130; Elior on, 117–18; existen-
    tial gap experience, efforts to
    bridge, 108; *Havdalah de-Rabbi
    Aqiva* compared, 146; historical
    study of, 9, 68, 113–14; holy names
    in, 116, 117; Idel and Gruenwald
    on, 116; Karaites on, 331–32;
    liturgical blessings, treatises on
    use of, 266n155; magic bowls and,
    137, 140, 241; Moses, ascent of,
    324–25; on mysteries and their
    revelation, 278n180; performative

psalms, treatises on systematic use of, 265–66

Pseudepigrapha. *See* Apocrypha and Pseudepigrapha

Pseudo-Eupolemos, 445, 454n278

psychological research and study of magic, 7, 24–28

psychological view of dreams, 432, 436–38

Pygmies, 19n11

qameʿa (amulet), etymology of, 217–18. *See also* amulets

qefiṣat ha-derekh ("shortening of the way"), 108n92

qibla' incantation bowls, 242–43

al-Qirqisani, Yaʿqub: on gems used for easing birth pains, 233–34n76; *Kitab al-anwâr wal-marâqib (The Book of Lights and Watchtowers)*, 2n2, 3n4, 151–52, 332–34; on Rabbanites' belief in purity, 268n159

Qordiakos, 398

quasi-ostensive and ostensive definitions of magic, 159–60n2

al-Qumisi, Daniel, 268n159, 273, 283, 330

Qumran Scrolls: astrology in, 445; on demons and evil spirits, 297, 398n137; *gʿr* root in, 220n32; magic passages from, 210n3; magic recipes from, 256–57, 281–82n190; on mysteries and their revelation, 278n180. *See also specific scrolls, in* Index of Sources

Rabbah, 373, 377, 414, 453

Rabbah b. Bar Ḥanna, 364n33

Rabbah b. Rav Huna, 365–66, 376, 377, 383

Rabbi (as title). *See* Rav or Rabbi

rabbinic literature, 11, 81–113, 353–460; adjuration texts in, 174; anthropological insights, application of, 96–97; on astrology, 445–59 (*See also* astrology and astral-magic tradition); beneficial magical prescriptions in, 356–64; Blau's *Das Altjüdische Zaubervesen*, 81–82; Bohak's study of, 110–12; defining magic, problem of, 2–3; on demons and evil spirits, 82–83, 102, 386–87, 392–407 (*See also* demons); descriptive approach to magic in, 96n59; on divination, 407–31 (*See also* divination); on dreams and their interpretation, 431–45 (*See also* dreams and their interpretation); Efron, Weinroth, and Liebes on, 90–93, 109; evil eye in, 386–92; gender and magic in, 88, 97–101, 375–82; hidden knowledge, rabbis as agents of, 409–13; historical study of, 81; Lieberman and Urbach, studies of, 84–90, 108; literary-folkloristic approach, 102; magic bowls and, 137, 140; Maimonides ignoring magic elements in, 342n123; Neusner on, 93–96; power of rabbis over magic combined with rejection of magic, 208; as secondary or outsider source, 207–8; *Sefer Shem ben Noah* (The Book of Shem Son of Noah), 331, 445n253; sociological approach to, 96–105; on sorcery, 354–86 (*See also* sorcery); systematic studies of Mishnah and Babylonian Talmud, 81–82; Trachtenberg's *Jewish Magic and Superstition*, 83–84; unification/separation/linking of magic and

CPSIA information can be obtained
at www.ICGtesting.com
Printed in the USA
JSHW040555211222
35144JS00002B/10